A History of the Canadian Peoples

Fifth Edition

A History of the Canadian Peoples

J.M. Bumsted and Michael C. Bumsted

OXFORD

UNIVERSITY PRESS

OXFORD
UNIVERSITY PRESS

Oxford University Press is a department of the University of Oxford.
It furthers the University's objective of excellence in research, scholarship,
and education by publishing worldwide. Oxford is a registered trade-mark of
Oxford University Press in the UK and in certain other countries.

Published in Canada by
Oxford University Press
8 Sampson Mews, Suite 204,
Don Mills, Ontario M3C 0H5 Canada

www.oupcanada.com

First Edition published in 1998
Second Edition published in 2003
Third Edition published in 2007
Fourth Edition published in 2011

Library and Archives Canada Cataloguing in Publication

Bumsted, J. M., 1938-, author
A history of the Canadian peoples / J.M. Bumsted,
Michael C. Bumsted. – Fifth edition.

Includes bibliographical references and index.
ISBN 978-0-19-901491-0 (paperback)

1. Canada–History–Textbooks. 2. Canada–Biography–
Textbooks. I. Bumsted, Michael C., author II. Title.

FC164.B862 2016   971   C2015-906397-3

Background map image: © iStock/duncan1890; Biography box image: © iStock/duncan1890;
Backrounder box image: © iStock/Nic_Taylor; Document box image: © iStock/Linda Steward;
Histiography box image: © iStock/duncan1890; Material Culture box image: © iStock/juliedeshaies;
Contemporary Views box image: © iStock/Pillon

Oxford University Press is committed to our environment.
Wherever possible, our books are printed on paper which comes from
responsible sources.

Printed and bound in the United States of America

1 2 3 4 — 19 18 17 16

Table of Contents

List of Maps

Preface

From the Publisher

Oxford University Press is delighted to present the fifth edition of *A History of the Canadian Peoples* by J.M. Bumsted and Michael C. Bumsted. For nearly two decades, the textbook has offered students of Canadian history a rich and nuanced picture of Canada from pre-contact times to the present, through a balanced selection of historical perspectives and primary-source documents brought together into an articulate overarching narrative. The new edition has been thoroughly revised and updated with the addition of new pedagogical features; new full-colour images and corresponding captions; expanded coverage of Aboriginal peoples, women, and children; greater emphasis of the pre-Confederation period; and up-to-date treatment of the twenty-first-century events that have shaped the cultural and political landscape of this country.

Outstanding Features of the Fifth Edition

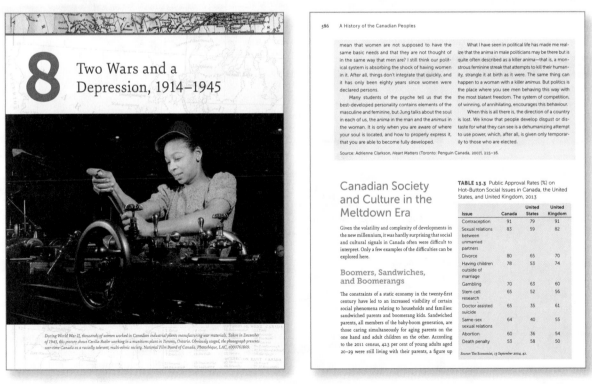

- **Balanced, accessible coverage.** The wide-ranging stories of Canada's social, political, cultural, economic, and military past are carefully integrated into a well-structured, compelling narrative, prefaced by a unique essay on the importance of studying history today.

- **NEW! Material Culture boxes.** A newly created set of boxes, highlighting the relationship between people and their things, explores items of historical significance and how they impact the story of Canada's past.
- **Biographical portraits.** A wealth of boxes profile the women and men, both famous and lesser known, who played a role in the story of Canada's past.

CANADA Material Culture

Timber Ships

Interior of a lumber ship in Quebec, 1872. While politicians and settlers in central Canada concerned themselves with territorial expansion during the mid-nineteenth century, those living in the Atlantic region were constrained to the older transatlantic way of life, of which shipping was integral. © McCord Museum.

The holds of timber ships like that pictured here carried thousands of immigrants to Canada on their voyage (usually 10 to 12weeks in duration) from the British Isles in the nineteenth century. Although the British government continually passed legislation improving provisioning of food and water and controlling numbers, it never really altered the primitiveness of the space itself. At first glance, the timber trade seemed a perfect fit for developing colonies. Timbering removed a major impediment to agricultural settlement: trees. From the standpoint of the incoming settler trees were the enemy, for fields could not be plowed and seeded until the trees were gone. The need for removal was so urgent that settlers would often burn forests in vast fires if no other way existed to clear them. Fortunately, entrepreneurs could often be found to cut the timber and ship the wood to market in the mother country. In the eighteenth century, the principal demand in Britain was for timber for shipbuilding, especially the tall pines that would be turned into the masts for sailing ships. By the nineteenth century, the British demand changed from tall

timber to square (the trees were tri
from their rounded shape to a squa
(the square timber cut into planks at
thick). During the first half of the ni
Britain encouraged the shipment
and deals from British America by th
duties levied on wood originating e
ing the Baltic region. The vessels c
frequently were unable to find a re
solving the problem by converting
decks to accommodate human
practice provided inexpensive—if
passage for many immigrants, es
driven from their homes by famin
ideal arrangement, removing unw
returning much wanted populatio
den drawbacks, however. One was
extremely wasteful. Much of the tre
on the forest floor to rot. The tim
merely removed and never replac
large tracts of land were systemat
cover with no thought of sustaina
the mentality of those cutting the
sheer exploitation, totally lacking i
reinvestment in the country they
for the human return cargo, condi
ber ships encouraged disease an
unpleasant at best.

As with many forms of materi
ships provided a dual purpose for
ber that the country supplied was
to the British Empire, as well as
ships that transported people in th
ply were part of a larger commodi

Biography

Nellie Letitia McClung

Nellie McClung. CP PHOTO.

Born in Chatsworth, Ontario, Nellie McClung (née Mooney) (1873–1951) moved with her family to Manitoba in 1880. After attending normal school in Winnipeg, she taught in rural Manitoba for many years. She was active in temperance work and in suffrage agitation. In 1896 she married Robert Wesley McClung, a druggist, who promised, Nellie later reported, that "I would not have to lay aside my ambitions if I married him." Her emergence to prominence began when she entered an American short story competition in 1902 and was encouraged by an American publisher to expand the story into the novel that became *Sowing Seeds in Danny*, a lighthearted look at village life on the prairies published in 1908. The book sold over 100,000 copies, was in its seventeenth edition at the time her death, and brought her both fame and fortune.

She and her husband moved to Winnipeg with their four children in 1911, where she helped organize the Political Equality League in 1912. Frustrated with the difficulty of arousing male politicians to suffrage reform, after some humiliating experiences she turned herself into a first-rate platform speaker. In 1914 she organized the Mock Parliament of Women, in which women played all the political roles. McClung herself was Manitoba Premier Rodmond Roblin, one of the major opponents of women's right to vote. McClung and her associates, supporting the Liberal Party, were unable to defeat Roblin's government in the 1914 election, but it soon fell under the weight of a construction scandal. The Liberal government of Tobias Crawford soon made Manitoba the first province in Canada to grant women the right to vote.

Meanwhile, the McClungs had moved to Edmonton, where Nellie again led the fight for female suffrage. She was also a strong supporter of the war effort and the Red Cross. In 1921 she was elected to the Alberta legislature, where she championed a host of radical measures of the time, ranging from mothers' allowances and dower rights for women to sterilization of the mentally unfit. She was defeated in 1926 when her temperance stance became unpopular. Nellie subsequently helped in the successful fight for Canadian woman senators. The McClungs moved to Victoria in 1933. In her west coast years, she became a CBC governor (1936–42), a delegate to the League of Nations (1938), and an advocate of divorce reform.

Throughout her life she was an active Methodist and subsequently a member of the United Church, and was prominent at the national and international levels in her church work. Apart from her first novel, none of her subsequent fiction has withstood the test of time very well. McClung did better with her autobiographical memoirs, all of which were highly regarded and reprinted. Like many early feminists, she was clearly a figure of her own time. She supported the Great War with almost bloodthirsty enthusiasm and was an active advocate of eugenics.

Document

Radio Programming, 1939

Wednesday 2 August

Network Highlights

CBC

7:00	Songs of the World
7:30	Percy Faith's Music
8:00	Sunset Symphony
8:30	Nature Talk
9:15	Sunset Symphony
10:00	Everyman Theatre

NBC—BLUE

7:30	Idea Mart
8:00	Kay Kyser's Quiz
8:30	Fred Waring Orch.
10:30	Lights Out

CBS

9:00	Amos 'n' Andy
9:30	Paul Whiteman orch.

Station Programs

5:00	The Lone Ranger, sketch—CKY
5:00	Dinner Concert—CBC-CJRC, CBK
5:00	Fred Waring Orch.—KFYR
5:30	Crackerjacks, songs—CBC-CJRC, CBK
5:30	Jimmy Allen, sketch—CKY
5:45	Howie Wing, sketch—CJRC
5:45	Waltz Time—CKY
5:45	Canadian Outdoor Days, Ozark Ripley—CBC-CBK . . .
7:00	Songs of the World, mixed choir, Montreal—CBC-CKY
7:00	Reports—CJRC
7:00	Horse and Buggy Days, songs of the 90s—KFYR
7:00	Percy Faith's Alt, soloists,
7:30	Modern Mu
7:30	Idea Mart—
8:00	Interview fr CKY, CBK
8:00	Reports, Bla
8:00	Kay Kyser's KFY until 9.
8:15	Teller of Cu
8:30	Dan McMu CKY, CBK
8:30	Five Esquire
8:45	Lieder Recit
9:00	Canadian P
9:00	Reports; Pia
9:00	Amos 'n' A KMOX, KBL
9:00	Fred Waring
9:15	Summer Sy ducting fro CBC-CKY, CB
9:30	Milt North
9:30	Tommy Dor
9:30	Horace Heid
9:30	Paul Whiten KMOX, KSL
9:45	Reports—CJ

Source: *Winnipeg Tribune*, 2 August 1939, 2.

Historiography

Studying Canada's Military Effort in World War I

Roger Sarty, Wilfrid Laurier University

Personal favourites, among many short, introductory accounts, are D.J. Goodspeed, *The Road Past Vimy: The Canadian Corps 1914–1918* (Toronto, 1969) and Terry Copp, Matt Symes, and Nick Lachance, *Canadian Battlefields 1915–1918* (Waterloo, Ont., 2011).

Books about Canada's role began to appear during the conflict[1] and continued to pour forth in the following decades. These included memoirs, popular works, and regimental histories. Many are still very useful. The regimental histories, for example, present detailed accounts of operations and sketches of personalities available nowhere else.[2] Among the most distinguished memoirs are those of the wartime leader, Prime Minister Robert Borden, assembled by his nephew, who drew heavily on Borden's papers.[3]

The project initiated by the Department of National Defence for an eight-volume official history, however, produced only the first volume and a supporting volume of documents. These appeared in 1938 and cover the initial year of the war. Immensely detailed, they are still an essential resource.[4] A full official account of Canadian participation in land warfare—nearly 500,000 Canadian troops served overseas—appeared in a single volume in 1962.[5] Colonel G.W.L. Nicholson, a senior member of the professional Army Historical Section, and the noted academic C.P. Stacey led the team that was organized during and after World War II to work on this history. They drew on the vast archives organized by the original historical section and the book is still the best starting place.

Nicholson produced two other thoroughly referenced, foundational volumes. *The Fighting Newfoundlander: A History of The Royal Newfoundland Regiment* (St John's: Government of Newfoundland, 1964) is the first comprehensive account of the extraordinary sacrifice by this British Dominion, separate from Canada, that did not join Confederation until 1949. Nicholson's *The Gunners of Canada: The History of the Royal Regiment of Canadian Artillery, vol.1, 1534–1919* (Toronto and Montreal, 1967) details the organization and operations of the immensely powerful artillery arm of the Canadian Corps, which was a key element in its formidable striking power.

Canada's large contribution to the air war—the provision of some 20,000 personnel to the British flying services—was the least well recorded part of the military effort. This was belatedly corrected when the Army Historical Section became the tri-service Directorate of History in 1965 and focused on aviation history. S.F. Wise, *Canadian Airmen in the First World War*, The Official History of the Royal Canadian Air Force, vol. 1 ([Toronto], 1980)is still a foremost authority on not just the Canadian role, but on aviation more generally during World War I.

At the leading edge of scholarly work that started in the 1960s with the opening of government archives was Robert Craig Brown's biography, *Robert Laird Borden: A Biography*, 2 vols (Toronto, 1975–80). Another benchmark in superbly researched biography is Michael Bliss's volume on Sir Joseph Flavelle,[6] who headed munitions production in Canada from 1916 to 1918. This is the fullest published account of Canada's industrial effort. Strong in its research on both the home front and the overseas effort is Ronald G. Haycock's life of Sir Sam Hughes, Minister of Militia and Defence from 1911 until 1916, when Prime Minister Borden finally lost patience with Hughes's erratic, scandal-prone administration.[7] General Sir Arthur Currie, the militia officer who succeeded brilliantly on the battlefield and commanded the Canadian Corps in 1917–18, has had three major biographies written about him, all well worth consulting.[8]

Robert Craig Brown joined Ramsay Cook to produce a survey of signal importance, *Canada 1896–1921:*

- **Primary-source material.** A vast selection of excerpted historical documents—from maps and journal entries to white papers and Royal Commission reports—gives students the chance to work with the raw materials of Canadian history.
- **NEW! Historiographical essays.** Written by a selection of historians from across the country and the authors, new end-of-chapter historiographical essays help students conceptualize how historians "do" history, highlight ongoing research, and reveal the value of studying history.

- **Chapter-opening timelines.** Each chapter begins with a timeline of the events and themes that marked the historical period covered, providing a framework for the discussion and an excellent revision tool for students.

- **End-of-chapter learning tools.** Study questions challenge students to engage critically with what they have read in the chapter, while short annotated bibliographies provide reliable starting points for further study.

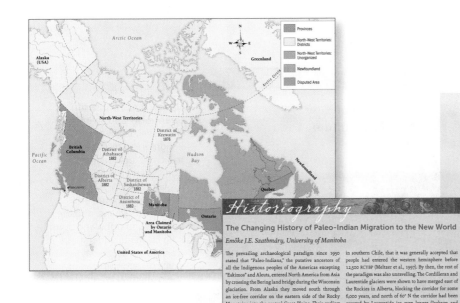

- **Outstanding art program.** A dynamic array of over 200 full-colour maps, photos, paintings, and figures helps to bring history to life.

- **Expanded coverage of the pre-Confederation period.** New material on the pre-Confederation period, including an analysis of life in New France and an exploration of the American interior, helps to round out students' understanding of Canada's past.

- **Extensive coverage of women, children, and Aboriginal peoples throughout the history of Canada.** New insights into these groups, the roles they played, the contributions they made, and the challenges they faced provide a rich, balanced account of Canada's past.

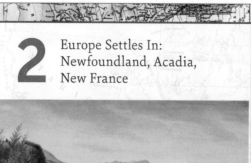

2 Europe Settles In: Newfoundland, Acadia, New France

The village of Château-Richer (on the north shore of the St Lawrence northeast of Quebec City), 1787, watercolour. Included in this pastoral scene are whitewashed stone farmhouses, wooden barns, and eel traps in the river. © LAC, Canada, 6275.

Irish emigrants awaiting departure on the quay at Cork, as depicted in the Illustrated London News, *10 May 1851. How would you interpret this scene? What is the artist trying to depict? LAC, C-3904.*

BACKGROUNDER

The Famous Five and the "Persons" Case

In 1916, feminist activist and author Emily Murphy (1868–1933), who wrote under the name "Janey Canuck," was appointed a police magistrate in Alberta, thus becoming the first female judge in the British Empire. Her appointment was challenged on the grounds that only males were persons as stated in the British North America Act of 1867. A year later the Alberta Supreme Court found that women were persons in a ruling that applied only within the province. Murphy was subsequently ruled ineligible by Prime Minister Robert Borden to be appointed to the Canadian Senate, and in 1927 she gathered a consortium of four other Alberta women to sign a petition to the Supreme Court of Canada, which asked the question: "Does the word 'persons' in section 24 of the British North America Act, 1867, include female persons?" Murphy's four collaborators were: Irene Parlby (1868–1965), a former president of the United Farm Women of Alberta and an Alberta cabinet minister in 1921; Nellie McClung (1873–1951), author, female suffrage advocate, and Alberta MLA (1921); Louise McKinney (1868–1931), the first woman elected to a legislature in the British Empire in 1917 and a temperance supporter; and Henrietta Edwards (1849–1931), a founding member of the Victorian Order of Nurses and a leading member of the National Council of Women.

The Supreme Court brought down its decision on 24 April 1928. The Court's answer to the question was that women were not persons, because at the time of the drafting of the BNA Act, women could not vote or ho[...]. [...] pointed out, the Act [...] out. The five women [...] Judicial Committee [...] which declared on [...] were indeed persons [...] senators. The Privy C[...] sion of women from a [...] more barbarous than [...] would ask why the [...] females, the obvious [...] This decision was no[...] rights, but also beca[...] ple that the BNA Ac[...] growth and expansion [...] Constitution thus req[...] that was different fro[...] utes. This principle re[...] ent of modern Cana[...] Minister Mackenzie K[...] a few months later [...] (1885–1962) to the Se[...]

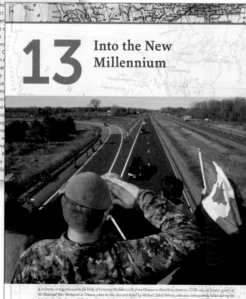

13 Into the New Millennium

A military cortege transports the body of Corporal Nathan Cirillo from Ottawa to Hamilton, Ontario. Cirillo was an honour guard at the National War Memorial in Ottawa when he was shot and killed by Michael Zehaf-Bibeau, who was subsequently killed during his failed raid on Parliament Hill's Centre Block. Cirillo's death, along with the murder of Warrant Officer Patrice Vincent in a parking lot days earlier, outraged many Canadians, and both attacks were identified as terrorism by the Prime Minister. The Canadian Press/Patrick Doyle.

- **Updated coverage of twentieth- and twenty-first-century events.** Enlightening discussions of topics including international conflict and the role of Canada's military; the Arctic; health, health care, and elderly Canadians; and the Internet and popular culture help students understand Canada's present-day political, economic, and socio-cultural identities.

Supplements

Instructors and students alike will benefit from the rich suite of ancillary materials available on the textbook's companion website: **www.oupcanada.com/Bumsted5e**.

For the Instructor

- An *Instructor's Manual* features chapter summaries, suggestions for lectures and further readings, discussion questions, and annotated lists of key figures, places, terms, research topics, and recommended resources.
- A *Test Generator* provides a comprehensive selection of multiple-choice, true–false, short-answer, and essay questions.
- *PowerPoint® slides*, fully updated to reflect the content of this edition, summarize key points from the text and provide a framework for course lectures.
- An *Online Image Bank* provides instructors with access to all photos, maps, and tables found in the text so that these materials may be incorporated into lectures and discussions.

For the Student

- A *Student Study Guide* offers a variety of useful learning tools, including chapter summaries, learning objectives, self-grading quizzes, recommended print and online resources, study and research tips, sample exams, and interviews with historians.
- An *Online Primary-Source Library* features over 60 canonical and lesser-known primary sources from both pre- and post-Confederation history. Each source is accompanied by an introduction offering students a contextual and social perspective that will enrich their study of Canadian history.
- *Visual History Online* is a dynamic resource comprising captioned images grouped into units that correspond to each chapter of the textbook. Images are accompanied by provocative questions that encourage students to consider the importance of visual history and stimulate discussion.

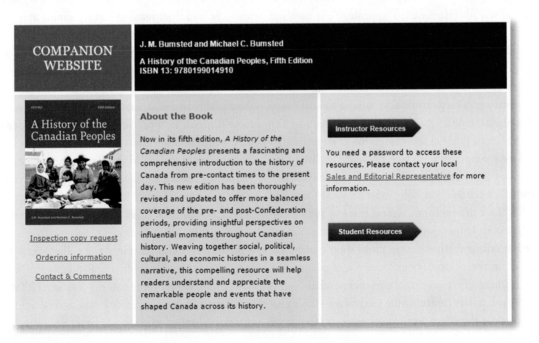

COMPANION WEBSITE

J. M. Bumsted and Michael C. Bumsted

A History of the Canadian Peoples, Fifth Edition
ISBN 13: 9780199014910

A History of the Canadian Peoples

Inspection copy request

Ordering information

Contact & Comments

About the Book

Now in its fifth edition, *A History of the Canadian Peoples* presents a fascinating and comprehensive introduction to the history of Canada from pre-contact times to the present day. This new edition has been thoroughly revised and updated to offer more balanced coverage of the pre- and post-Confederation periods, providing insightful perspectives on influential moments throughout Canadian history. Weaving together social, political, cultural, and economic histories in a seamless narrative, this compelling resource will help readers understand and appreciate the remarkable people and events that have shaped Canada across its history.

Instructor Resources

You need a password to access these resources. Please contact your local Sales and Editorial Representative for more information.

Student Resources

Introduction

Understanding History

Every experienced historian has at some point encountered someone from a totally different background who assumes that "anyone can do history." In the sense that anyone can research, write, and even publish historical work without specialized training, that assumption is correct. History is one of those fields—creative writing is another—where the standards of achievement can be flexible and intuitive, and where much of the methodology is based on plain common sense. History's accessibility to almost all of us, not simply as readers but as actual researchers, is one of its great charms and greater merits. And many people do engage in historical research without calling it by that name. Everyone who tries to trace her ancestry through the labyrinth of historical records (often called "genealogy") is involved in a form of historical research. Everyone who tries to research the background to a business project as part of a report on its present status, or to explain how a sports team achieved a championship season, is in a sense "doing history." Every criminal trial (and almost every civil one) is at some level a historical reconstruction. The historical mode is one of the most common ways through which we attempt to understand the world we live in.

To say that nearly all of us engage in some form of historical reconstruction, often unconsciously, is not to say that there are no fundamental rules to such activity. Most of us know instinctively that witnesses can be biased or mistaken, that human motivation is complex, and that in the chronological sequence of events—the establishment of which many non-professional historians regard as the centre of the enterprise—the cause must precede the effect. But history is not a laboratory science. Even the simplest rules of evidence and argument can be difficult to apply in specific situations, particularly if the researcher is operating intuitively. Understanding what causes these difficulties is important, and becoming sensitive to the problems of history is one of the chief benefits of formal historical study.

A good many Canadians (probably nearly as many as commonly read fiction or poetry) read history, for recreation and for information. Unfortunately, general readers often approach historical writing in much the same way they approach fiction, judging a work's value by its success in telling "a good story." But of course storytelling is only one of numerous ways in which history can be written. Although, as with fiction, there is great pleasure to be had from reading history simply at the level of entertainment, to remain at that level would be to miss much of the best modern historical writing. It is possible without training or formal critical tools to recognize that a Harlequin romance offers a far less complex view of the world than a Margaret Atwood novel; it is somewhat more difficult to appreciate a parallel difference in history. Readers who expect writers of fiction to have distinctive voices and world views still often assume that all historians participate equally in the effort to recover the truth of the past through application of some unspecified "scientific" method: if history is about truth, then all historical writing must be more or less equally true, at least if the historian has "the facts" right. The ordinary reader is frequently unable to distinguish between "facts" and "truth," failing to appreciate on one level that factual accuracy is in itself a complex issue and on another level that it has limited value as a critical test.

In addition, many readers fail to distinguish between history as everything that has happened before the present moment (also commonly known as "the past") and history as the record (usually written) of the unfolding of some event(s) in that past. Yet that past can never be recovered, for reasons I shall discuss. All we can do is attempt to recreate and analyze discrete parts of that past, refracted through the historian's prism. Only this history can be studied and investigated. As a further confusion, history can mean not only the historian's account of the past, but the systematic study of the past as a discipline or a craft. The study of either the work of individual historians or the discipline itself is often known as historiography. Just as filmmakers make a surprising number of movies about the process of making movies, so historians devote more of their energy to examining the making of history than they do to any other single project.

The processes of both reading and researching history can obviously be greatly enhanced by some understanding of the problems that engage historians as they pursue their craft. Before we turn to some of those problems, however, it might be well to consider the question of the value of history.

The Value of History

Once upon a time, especially in the nineteenth and earlier twentieth centuries, most people did not question the value of historical study or wonder how it was relevant to their lives. They did not doubt the value of the liberal arts or the humanities, much less debate the benefits of studying languages like Greek or Latin. There are really two separate but related issues inherent in the "value of history" question. One is whether or not historical study has a sufficient grip on truth and meaning in our modern world to have any value at all, intrinsic or extrinsic. Ultimately, this question involves us in high philosophy and theory, but it also has a particular Canadian edge. The other question is whether or not historical work has a sufficiently attractive vocational payoff to justify its study at the university. Perhaps we should turn to the latter question first, since it is easier to answer and may be of more interest to the beginning historian.

For many centuries, the opportunity to attend a university was available only to those of outstanding intellectual abilities or privileged socio-economic standing. In a world that did not question the importance of religion, the original purpose of universities was to educate clerics. The university gradually became the centre of humanistic scholarship and enterprise generally, but so long as society valued education for its own sake—chiefly because it was something available only to the privileged few—its specific vocational role was quite insignificant. Universities turned out educated and "cultured" men (not women until well into the nineteenth century) into a world that took it for granted that such people were important to the society. Specific occupational training was not part of the university's function, and preparation even for such elevated professions as law and medicine was done outside its doors. Yet gradually the notion of vocational training did enter the cloistered world of the university, particularly in North America, and by 1940 it was possible to prepare for nearly any occupation through specialized studies at a university, although such opportunities were still limited to members of the elites. Despite the new vocational bent of the university, occupational studies were largely confined to the post-graduate level; most undergraduate students at universities (as opposed to acknowledged vocational centres such as teachers' training colleges) still expected An Education rather than A Vocation.

The great change in the nature of the university really came after 1945, when the idea took hold that all Canadians were entitled to attend university and the number of university places was greatly expanded. A dynamic relationship has existed between the democratization of the university and the introduction of the idea that there should be some demonstrable economic value to a university degree. Thus specific occupational training now starts at the undergraduate rather than the graduate level. Today at many universities it is likely that the majority of students are enrolled in such programs, and even those who are not in such programs themselves commonly expect a university education to provide some kind of occupational entrée or advantage. In the new occupational sweepstakes, a field like history is of less obvious relevance than one like management or accounting or pharmacy or computing. Some historians would prefer to ignore the question of occupational relevance altogether, but the days of a simple liberal arts education for most university students are probably gone forever. History may not ever compete with accounting or pharmacy or medical school as preparation for employment, but it is still superb preparation for many professional programs (assuming that they do not insist on specialization from day one). And one can do more in the workforce with a history specialization than most students might at first think.

There are numerous history-related occupations besides teaching. They include work in archives, libraries, and museums, as well as in government service. "Heritage" in itself is a major industry in Canada. Other occupations, such as law, journalism, and some branches of the civil service (the diplomatic corps, for example), have traditionally recruited heavily among history graduates, but any job requiring the ability to gather and analyze evidence and then communicate the findings is ideally suited to someone with a background in history. One individual with a graduate degree in history, Mike Smith, has become the general manager of several National Hockey League teams. What students have to do is learn to translate their historical training into the jargon of the contemporary job market. "Researching term essays in history," for example, can be translated into "using documentary resources to abstract and analyze complex information." (At one recent "interview" for a summer job with a government department, the student applicant was simply asked to summarize a complex document quickly and accurately.) To the extent that history is a discipline that teaches students both to think and to communicate, it should improve their qualifications for almost any job.

Beyond developing essential skills in research, analysis, and communication, what are the uses of history? Certainly few historians today believe—if they ever did—in the use of historical "laws" of human conduct for predictive purposes. Most historians who have employed historical laws, such as Arnold Toynbee in *A Study in History*, Oswald Spengler in *The Decline of the West*, or Karl Marx in *Capital*, have done so on such an abstract level that it is difficult to translate those laws into specific terms. Toynbee's notion that civilizations pass through recognizable stages paralleling the human

life cycle is attractive, but it does not tell us when our civilization will die. Employing the insights of Karl Marx, no reader could have concluded that the "dictatorship of the proletariat" would come first in Russia, or that it would eventually lead not to a classless society but to the collapse of the Soviet Union. No discipline has worked harder than economics to achieve scientific status, but the whole world has come to appreciate that economists constantly disagree on even the most general level of prediction and analysis.

Yet if history cannot predict, it can help us to understand the difficulty of prediction. In the same way it can help us to recognize the recurrent and ongoing nature of many of society's problems. By and large, historians were far more sanguine about the outcome of the 1992 referendum on the Charlottetown constitutional accord than were the scaremongers on either side of the debate or many of the journalists covering the "crisis." Indeed, those with an understanding of Canadian history, constitutional and otherwise, were bound to find the very concept of a "crisis" suspect, just as they would any other popular journalistic concept, such as "conspiracy." The historical record tells us that there have been crises and conspiracies, but equally that these terms have so often been used without justification that they have lost any real meaning.

History provides us not only with a social context but with a personal one as well. The genealogical search for "roots" has become important for many Canadians seeking to trace their family backgrounds and to understand the circumstances that drove their ancestors across the ocean, or the ways their ancestors' lives changed as a result of the newcomers' arrival. Nor is the question of personal identity merely an individual matter. It is no accident that as minority groups in Canada work to develop themselves as collectivities, they need to establish and assert their historical experience. Over the past 30 years some Canadians have lost interest in the historical mode, adopting what we might call the "irrelevance of history" position. But this has not been the case with collective "minorities" such as women, Native peoples, blacks, and ethnic minorities. For these groups, establishing their rightful place in Canadian history has been an absolutely primary function. That these groups' interpretations of their histories have often run counter to the traditional versions of Canadian history does not render them any less consequential—or less historical.

The Elusive Fact

More than 50 years ago a television series called *Dragnet* became famous for a catchphrase used by one of its characters, a police detective named Sergeant Joe Friday. When questioning witnesses, Friday always repeated the same request, delivered in an emotionless monotone: "All I want is the facts, just give me the facts." The monotone was intended to indicate Friday's objectivity and to extract from his witness a response devoid of personal bias and colouration. Of course he seldom got "just the facts"—which from our perspective is exactly the point. Somehow, just as the popular mind in the 1950s associated Joe Friday with facts, so it has more recently come to think of historians as dealing in the same coin. The equation of facts and history has doubtless been assisted by the traditional way of teaching history in the schools, by marching out one name, date, event after another for students to commit to memory and regurgitate at the appropriate time in the course of an examination. Of course, historians do rely on facts as their basic building blocks; but they do not think of them the way Sergeant Friday did, nor do they use them the way common opinion believes they do.

The *Canadian Oxford Dictionary* offers several meanings for "fact." The most familiar is probably number 1: "a thing that is known to have occurred, to exist, or to be true," although number 4—"truth, reality"—is also very common. Facts, as *Dragnet* suggested, are true things, unsullied by any process of interpretation or conclusion. Such things may exist, but they are much harder to come by than one might expect, for several reasons. One problem is the language in which "facts" must be stated. Another is the context in which they become significant.

Over the last century we have become increasingly aware that language is not a neutral instrument, but one that carries with it a heavy freight of cultural experience and usage. "John Cabot discovered Newfoundland in 1497" may seem a straightforward statement of fact, but at least half of the words in it conjure up a whole host of meanings. One of those words is "discovered."

The implication is that what Cabot found was previously unknown—but of course an Aboriginal population had been living in the area for millennia. Even qualifying "discovered" by saying that Cabot "was the first European to discover Newfoundland" doesn't help much, since we now know that the Vikings had settled at L'Anse aux Meadows in the eleventh century, and even they may not have been the first Europeans to cross the Atlantic. "Discovery" is a complex concept. The term "Newfoundland" is equally problematic, since in modern geographic terms Cabot was not at all precise about his movements, and the land he sighted may not have been part of the island that we know as Newfoundland today. Indeed, Cabot called the land he saw "the New-Founde Land," and it was only later that the label was applied to the island. Moreover, Cabot's sightings were not confirmed by anything other than vague self-declarations. To top matters off, there are questions about the identity of John Cabot himself, who started in Italy as Giovanni (or Zuan) Caboto and became John Cabot Montecalunya, a resident of Valencia, in the early 1490s, before he called himself John Cabot of Bristol. Almost all but the most simplistic statements are subject to the same difficulties. Philosophers have spent thousands of years trying to formulate "true" statements, with very little success, and historians are unlikely to do much better. Almost any "factual" statement worth making has to be expressed in a language heavily weighted with values and contexts. Language is only one of the challenges in the quest for the fact.

Even if facts could be expressed in a neutral language, such as numbers, we would still need to decide which facts are important. At any given moment there exists a virtual infinity of pieces of information that could be isolated and stated. Most "historical facts" are simply labels of events and dates, names and movements, which by themselves do not tell us very much. They are not statements in which anything is asserted, and therefore they have no standing as facts. Only when their significance is implicitly or explicitly understood do they acquire any utility or susceptibility to truth. "The Battle of Vimy Ridge" is not a fact since it does not assert anything capable of being either true or false. "The Battle of Vimy Ridge in 1917 was won by the Canadian army" is an assertion the validity of which can be assessed. Whether it is false or true (and hence "a fact") is another matter entirely. The validity of the statement requires a detailed account of the battle in the context of the war.

One of the chief benefits of modern historical study is that it promotes a healthy skepticism about the neutrality and ultimate truth of the notorious fact. Taken by itself, in isolation, the fact has little meaning. It is only when facts are arranged into some larger picture—some sort of interpretive account—that they acquire significance. Those interpretive pictures themselves are subject to change over time. Anyone today who reads a Canadian history textbook written 30 years ago will be struck by the almost complete absence of any reference to women as important historical figures. Yet 30 years ago the majority of readers—even female readers—took that absence for granted. The absence of women does not mean that women were not present. It simply means that historians of that generation did not regard their activities as worthy of attention. The historian can uncover whole constellations of new facts simply by asking a new question of the historical record, as happened when some scholars asked: "What about the women?" History is not the study of something eternally fixed, of something that can be "discovered," but rather the continual dynamic re-investigation and re-evaluation of the past.

If historians can recover new facts, however, they are still limited to those facts that have been recorded in some way. The records need not be in written form; sometimes they take the form of oral history, sometimes of artifacts. Whatever form the evidence takes, it has to have been preserved. Preservation may be deliberate or serendipitous, but in either case certain biases may be observed. If we think about our own personal history, we realize that not every part of it has been recorded, let alone recorded with equal care; and much of the individual record that does exist has been preserved not through personal choice but to serve bureaucratic purposes. Not every society keeps public records, however, and even in the record-keeping societies, not everyone produces an equal quantity of evidence. Only a relative handful of historical actors, for example, have left behind their own written accounts. Personal evidence tends to be limited to those involved in self-consciously important activity, as defined by any particular society. Such recorders usually represent that society's elite, and what they record represents what the elites think needs recording. We know far more about taxation in the Middle Ages than we do about sexual behaviour, for example. Whatever their limitations, it is with the records that historians must start. They are the primary sources for historical investigation, as distinguished from secondary sources (usually other historians' research gleanings and interpretations). In working with primary sources, historians face two problems: the first one of authenticity, the second one of credibility.

For understandable reasons, historians have to be certain that the records they study are genuine. Historians thus prefer to work with original documents, the so-called "manuscript" sources (although not all manuscripts are necessarily handwritten). The republication of such material often raises questions of accuracy, which become even more problematic when the documents have been translated from one language to another. Even the most scrupulous of editors may subtly alter the meaning of a document through changes in punctuation or spelling, and until our own time the editors of historical documents often intervened in other ways as well. A famous editor of Shakespeare named Thomas Bowdler expurgated material that he considered to be in bad taste (his name is now commemorated in the verb "to bowdlerize"). Other editors silently rewrote texts to what they regarded as the advantage of their authors. Even the appearance of authenticity is no guarantee; many skilful forgeries have been designed to pass close inspection. The famous Shroud of Turin (supposedly showing the imprint of the body of Christ) is not necessarily a deliberate forgery, but recent scientific investigation has found that it could not be authentically associated with the crucifixion. As for the supposedly fifteenth-century "Vinland Map," discovered in the 1960s, it still has not been satisfactorily authenticated, and many scholars think it is a fake.

Even if we are dealing with an "authentic" document, there are still many potential problems to face before we can use it as evidence. Many documents cannot be precisely dated or attributed to a specific author. But these questions must be addressed before the historian—acting all the parts in a court of law except that of witness—can determine the document's credibility.

Was the author in a position to be authoritative? Are there reasons, obvious or subtle, for suspecting bias of some kind? Bias may appear in many forms. Authors may seek to justify themselves; they may place their interpretation of events in a context resulting from their place in society or from their ideological assumptions; they may report hearsay; they may adjust their accounts for literary reasons or simply to tell "a good story." Evidence is best if it can be corroborated by more than one source; but supporting evidence is not always available, particularly for specific details. Like the "facts" derived from them, the documents themselves are seldom unassailable as sources. Historians work with probabilities rather than certainties, and the more evidence is available, the more likely it is that there will be complications. In any event, students of history need to be both skeptical and critical of what they read, whether documentary evidence itself or interpretations of such material.

The Conventions of History

Historians have developed a series of conventions for dealing with their raw data. Historical information presented in its unexplicated form—as a series of unrelated facts—is not history as historians understand it, and insufficient attention to interpretation and context is one of the most common faults of beginning historians. Traditionally, the chief mode for historians has been narrative, the recounting of past events in the sequence in which they occurred. Like all aspects of historical work, narrative requires selection—cutting into the seamless web of the past to isolate a particular sequence of events involving a limited number of characters. Narrative deals with the passage of time, and—since it is axiomatic that cause and effect must be in the right sequence—chronology is critical to historical understanding. Many great historians of the past concentrated almost exclusively on narrative, appropriately embellished with description and context; an example is Francis Parkman, who wrote extensively on the early conflict of the French and British in North America. But most modern historians would agree with Arthur

Marwick (1970: 144) that "the historian must achieve a balance between narrative and analysis, between a chronological approach and an approach by topic, and, it should be added, a balance between both of these, and, as necessary, passages of pure *description* 'setting the scene,' providing routine but essential information, conveying the texture of life in any particular age and environment." Some historians have even dropped narrative entirely, although the sequence of events remains implicitly crucial to their work.

Despite the common use of the term "causation" in historical writing, particularly among beginners, philosophers of history have long emphasized that historians really do not deal much in the sort of cause-and-effect relationships usually associated with scientific work. The past is too complex to isolate factors in this way. Instead, historians talk about "explanation," which is not quite the same as scientific causation. Explanation requires the inclusion of enough context and relevant factors to make it clear that the events in question were neither totally predetermined nor utterly capricious. As E.H. Carr (1964: 103–4) has observed:

> . . . no sane historian pretends to do anything so fantastic as to embrace "the whole of experience"; he cannot embrace more than a minute fraction of the facts even of his chosen sector or aspect of history. The world of the historian, like the world of the scientist, is not a photographic copy of the real world, but rather a working model which enables him more or less effectively to understand it and to master it. The historian distils from the experience of the past, or from so much of the experience of the past as is accessible to him, that part which he recognizes as amenable to rational explanation and interpretation, and from it draws conclusions.

In their efforts at narrative and/or explanation, historians also use many other conventions. Among them, let us focus on periodization. The division of the past into historical "periods" serves purposes beyond the organization of a teaching curriculum. By focusing attention on units of time, periodization serves to narrow and limit the range of material to be considered and helps to provide a structure for what would otherwise be a meaningless jumble of events and dates. The choice of beginning and end dates for larger historical sequences is hardly arbitrary, but it is still a matter of interpretation. Take, for example, the standard decision to divide Canadian history at 1867, the year of Confederation. This fundamental periodization reflects the assumption not only that political and constitutional development shaped everything else, but also that the creation of a national state called the Dominion of Canada was the critical point in that development. However, it makes little sense for many other themes in Canadian history. Historians of Canada continually debate the question of relevant periods. The authors of the first survey of the history of women in Canada, for example, were forced to find a new way of periodizing their account, since the standard political and constitutional periodization reflected a chronology that was mainly masculine in emphasis.

New Interpretations

Like all academic disciplines, history is constantly reinterpreting its subject matter. Some of the pressure for reinterpretation is a simple matter of growth: within the past quarter-century, the number of academic positions for historians in Canada has more than quadrupled, with the result that more individuals are now researching and writing within the field. At the same time, technological advances (in computers and photocopiers, for example) and the advent of the relatively inexpensive airline ticket have made it possible for historians to examine and process documentary materials in ways and quantities that would have been unthinkable at the beginning of the 1960s. Other pressures for revision, of course, come from changes in the social context, which is continually raising new questions for historians to explore and causing shifts in the climate of opinion.

In history, revisionist movements usually arise out of new developments in three (often related) areas: subject matter, conceptual frameworks, and methodologies. A new development in any one of these areas may be enough on its own to provoke significant revision. When

two or three come together (as is often the case), they can completely alter our understanding of the past.

Addressing new subject matter involves asking new questions about hitherto neglected aspects of the past. In Canadian history, with its traditional focus on the political and constitutional ways in which a national state was created, the opportunities for new questions have been quite substantial. Out of a variety of new subjects, we can perhaps offer three examples: women, Aboriginal peoples, and ethnic groups. While each of these subjects would today be regarded as central to any contemporary understanding of Canadian history, they were virtually neglected until recent years. As we have seen, lack of attention to women in the past did not reflect lack of information but lack of interest on the part of historians. With the simple act of focusing attention on women, a new field of study was opened. In the case of Aboriginal peoples, the subject had not been entirely neglected, but it had virtually always been approached from the perspective of the developing national state. Thus many of the new questions raised today are aimed at understanding the First Nations' perspectives. As for ethnic groups, research has tended to involve scholars from a variety of disciplines, such as sociology and geography, and has been encouraged by the availability of grant money from governmental agencies at both the federal and provincial levels. Ethnic studies have proved to be politically popular within Canada.

New areas of study often suggest—if not require— new conceptual contexts. In general, all three of the new areas noted above fall under the rubric of "social history." As early as 1924, an article on "The Teaching of Canadian History" advocated the study of the "actual life of the Canadian people" in "their efforts to secure a livelihood and then to provide for the higher demands of mind and spirit" (McArthur, 1924: 207). Until recent years, however, much of the research in the social history area concentrated on the upper echelons of society in Canada, the so-called "elites." Broadening the social base to include individuals outside the ranks of those whose lives were normally documented (women, Aboriginal people, racial and ethnic minorities, ordinary working folk) involved a substantial reconceptualization of the nature of Canada's past.

Studying those "inarticulate" groups often required new methodologies as well. Perhaps the most important methodological innovation was quantification: generating new data sets by processing existing information not previously practicable for historical purposes out of data such as name-by-name census returns. At its worst, quantification could be little more than mindless number-crunching, but at its best it enabled historians to open up whole categories of hitherto unusable documentation. The information collected by the Dominion Bureau of the Census or the various provincial departments of Vital Statistics has provided much new insight into the way ordinary Canadians have lived (and loved) in the past. Computers have made it easier for historians to process large amounts of aggregate information—although the axiom "Garbage In, Garbage Out" continues to apply. The complex processes of collecting and analyzing new categories of data have been contentious, and beginning historians should understand that the apparently simple act of producing a new set of information involves many steps and many disagreements. "Hard" numbers and percentages are no more sacrosanct than information that appears "softer." Moreover, quantified data still require interpretation and are subject to all the standard rules that apply to historical explanation.

Although explicit controversies do arise within the field of Canadian history, they are probably less common than controversies among historians of other nations, notably the United States and Great Britain. To some extent the profession has avoided confrontations by allowing each practitioner his or her own area of specialization (or "turf"). This has made good sense because the number of questions not yet adequately explored in the history of Canada is considerable. Whatever the reasons for the muting of controversy, disagreements in Canadian historiography have had less to do with specific points and interpretations within a single tradition than with first principles and underlying assumptions. Thus Canadian historians tend to disagree only at the mega-level, as in the recent debate over Canadian "national history," which was really a debate among scholars with different sets of assumptions about the role of narrative in the past. Those on the moving frontier of scholarship are in some ways far less

embattled than those still working in older traditions, since they can simply add their "new" interpretations on to the old ones.

But at the same time, the interpretation and practice of history, in Canada as elsewhere, is constantly changing, presenting new issues and questions. As noted above, research over the past half-century has been greatly altered by a variety of technological developments, including the photocopier, the computer, and most recently, the Internet. This last tool, which few fully understand in all its complexity, can alter research processes and provides access to vast amounts of mostly unsorted information, and while it raises new possibilities for acquiring documentation and exchanging information it also opens a Pandora's box of new questions. Its users must develop new ways of authenticating what is credible in essentially unsupervised and uncontrolled material. We must figure out how to protect intellectual property in a world where a mere click of a mouse can copy and transfer thousands of pages of material from one file to another, and the resulting risks of plagiarism are enormous. New techniques for documenting the past will have to be developed so that we can be assured that what we are reading online is not simply another "urban myth." Contemporary teachers and students of history are thus faced with many new challenges.

The search for a credible past has been recently influenced not simply by the emergence of a totally unsupervised database, but, on the other hand, by new efforts on the part of public bodies to shape what we accept as "truth." Over the years, most historical arguments and interpretations have always been judged in the free marketplace of opinion by one's historical peers, and there has seldom been a "final judgment." The philosophical problems involved when complex historical questions are actually adjudicated by the judicial process are many. In court cases, increasingly employed in Canada in Aboriginal land claims disputes, the judge listens to a variety of expert testimony and pronounces a verdict that appears to rely on and thus to validate one or more particular historical interpretations or methodological approaches. Does this court approval mean that the judge's verdict takes on the character of the truth? Is it susceptible to revision? Has anything actually been validated? Apart from court pronouncements are others of an official nature. The Canadian government has recently (November 2009) issued a revised guide for new citizens that undertakes to summarize Canadian history in 10 pages. That history is now formally allowed to include the abuse of Aboriginal peoples and the mistreatment of several ethnic communities, although few details are given. Whether it has managed to be sufficiently vague so as not to introduce a new level of misconceptions is another matter entirely.

Simply because history is a cumulative subject, students should not think that the latest books and journal articles are necessarily better by virtue of their dates of publication. Many older works of historical scholarship can still be regarded as the best treatments of their topics. This is particularly true in traditional areas of study that have not attracted much attention from modern scholars, such as the military history of the War of 1812. Earlier generations were fond of publishing editions of documents, which, if well-transcribed, translated, and edited, are just as valuable today as they were a century ago. The complete (and most commonly used) edition of the *Jesuit Relations* in English was published between 1896 and 1901 (and, as times do change, that entire 73-volume collection is now available online in facsimile from Creighton University, a Jesuit institution in Omaha, Nebraska). On some topics our only sources are earlier documents; for example, Richard Hakluyt's sixteenth-century accounts are still essential for any study of English overseas voyages.

By now it should be clear that both the writing and the reading of history are extremely complicated enterprises. Whole books with titles like *Understanding History* or *The Nature of History* have been devoted to introducing students to the complexities of the craft, and in the space of a few pages it is impossible to explore all the potential dimensions. In any case, readers of this book should understand that every work of history involves a series of decisions to hold various contradictions in dynamic tension. Among the most important issues held in tension in this book are the following.

1. *Interpretive complexity versus authority.* Virtually every sentence in this work (or any other work of history) could be hedged in with conflicting evidence and interpretation. The result would almost certainly be incomprehensible. I have chosen to favour readability over total academic accuracy. This is not to say that I do not recognize the issues of interpretive complexity. Rather, I have consciously addressed them in two ways: by introducing questions of interpretation into the text on a regular basis, and by including essays on historiography—"How History Has Changed'—at the end of each chapter.

2. *Individual biography versus groups and forces.* One problem that all historians face (or ought to face) is how to make the material interesting to readers. As any newspaper editor will tell you, readers like their stories to have people in them. This work uses the experiences of individual people to represent and suggest the complex groups and forces that lie behind them. I do not subscribe to the Great Person theory of history, but I do believe in personalizing history as much as possible.

3. *Overarching master narrative versus the complex voices of social and cultural history.* Whether or not Canadian history has a single narrative is a hotly debated issue today, sometimes posed in the form of the question "Is there a national history?" The single narrative is also related to the problem of authority, although the two are not the same. A coherent and connected single narrative could be based on the concept of the development of the nation, or on viewing events from the perspective of that nation, or on something quite different. The point is that any such narrative line represents an abstraction. Critics of the abstract, single narrative approach associate it with the imposition of a hegemonic "master principle" that in turn is often taken to represent the sequence of events preferred by the "men in suits" or the "ruling class" or the "politicians in Ottawa." Many groups are commonly left outside such a master narrative: workers, racial and cultural minorities, women, inhabitants of marginalized regions, inhabitants of alienated regions (e.g., Quebec for much of the twentieth century). Over the past 30 years, Canadian historians have concentrated on recovering the voices of these groups. But if those voices were all we heard, telling their own stories in their own tongues, the resulting cacophony would be unintelligible; and to establish chronology and

meaningful periodization, we need a structure that will provide some common reference points. Hence a master narrative of some kind is still essential.

The master narrative around which this book is structured, into which all the other stories are woven, is a highly abstract one that may be labelled "a history of Canada." I hope this discussion will help readers to understand the chapters that follow.

J.M. Bumsted

1 The Beginnings

Although there was not a written alphabet in North America before European "discovery," a record of the history and culture of the First Peoples was preserved in oral traditions and material culture, and it was permanently imprinted on the landscape, engraved on rock surfaces all across the continent. The engravings shown here—from the "Teaching Rocks" in Nephton, Ontario—are a relatively modern example, dating from between 900 AD and 1100 AD, although there are others that are millennia older.

Timeline | *Major Events in the Early History of the First Nations*

12,000 BCE (Before Common Era)

Mammal retaining stone weapon killed in New Mexico.

11,000 BCE

Glacial retreat escalates with warming trend.

10,000 BCE

Continued warming alters physical environment as ice retreats.

9000 BCE

Fluted Point people spread across North America.

7000 BCE

Maritime Archaic culture develops the harpoon.

5500 BCE

Maritime Archaic culture develops burial mounds. Notched projectile points appear in British Columbia.

3000 BCE

Forest reaches its northernmost extension.

2000 BCE

Paleo-Eskimos and other Archaics begin displacing Maritime Archaics on eastern seaboard and in Arctic regions.

1000 BCE

Ceramic pottery appears in Great Lakes area and spreads east.

500 BCE

Dorset people appear in Arctic Canada. Climate deteriorates.

500 CE (Common Era)

Maize cultivation begins in southern Ontario. Climate improves.

600

Beothuk culture replaces the Dorset Eskimos in Newfoundland.

1000

Norse settle briefly in eastern North America.

1150

Dorset culture is replaced by Thule culture among Inuit.

1350

Squash and bean cultivation appears in southern Ontario.

1497

First recorded European arrival in North America since Norse.

1634

Beginning of the destruction of Huronia.

Timeline | *Major Events in the Early European History in Northern North America*

982–5 CE
Eric the Red explores Greenland.

***c*. 1000**
L'Anse aux Meadows is established by the Norse.

1497
John Cabot reaches Newfoundland.

1500
Gaspar Corté-Real lands at Tierra Verde (Newfoundland).

1501
Gaspar Corté-Real brings the first Aboriginals to Europe.

1534
Jacques Cartier erects cross at Gaspé Harbour.

1576
First voyage of Martin Frobisher to Baffin Island.

1585
John Davis enters Davis Strait.

1605
Port-Royal established.

1608
Champlain builds habitation at Quebec.

1610
First English settlers arrive in Newfoundland.

1615
Étienne Brûlé investigates New York and Pennsylvania.

1616
Robert Bylot sails through Davis Strait.

1618
Champlain proposes major French colony on St Lawrence.

1628
Scottish settlement expedition arrives in Maritime region.

Once upon a history, Canada began with the arrival of the European "discoverers" at the end of the fifteenth century. These events, at best, now mark only the moment at which the inhabited land and its people enter the European historical record, not the beginning of their history. Thousands of years of human development preceded the appearance of the Europeans. The First Nations of North America also have their history. The work of countless modern specialists, chiefly linguistic scholars and archaeologists, has only begun to uncover the barest outlines of the pre-European period. The record of human settlement in Canada clearly does not begin with the Europeans.

The First Arrivals

Unlike other continents on planet Earth, North America did not produce indigenous archaic human forms going back thousands of generations. No evidence suggests that any of the many ancestors of *Homo sapiens* developed on this continent. There were no Old Stone Age people as in Africa, Asia, or Europe. Instead, the first humanlike inhabitant of North America was *Homo sapiens*, who probably arrived in the New World during the last Great Ice Age—which ended 10,000 years ago—and did so via Beringia, the now submerged land bridge stretching between what is now Siberia and Alaska. "Land bridge" is a bit of a misnomer for Beringia, estimated to be twice the size of modern Manitoba, and current evidence suggests that humans were living in there in a sort of refugium from the Ice Age, and according to the Beringia standstill model, were first isolated in the territory, then migrated into the western hemisphere 15,000 years ago.

Until recently, the 30,000 years or more of the human occupation of the North American continent before the arrival of the Europeans usually were labelled "prehistoric." That term has fallen out of common usage, however, because it produces so many misconceptions. No written record of North American development may have existed before the Europeans, but to assume that "history" begins only with writing is misleading. Plenty of earlier records of human activity exist, including oral traditions of the First Nations. From them a fascinating picture of the early history of what is now Canada can be reconstructed. That picture is hardly a static one. Instead, it displays constant movement, adaptation, and change. These early people did not attempt to modify their environment so much as adapt to it. That environment, in turn, was continually shifting, perhaps not over a single season but over several generations.

One of the chief factors influencing the early inhabitants of North America was climate. Until very recently—as the history of the planet goes—most of what is now Canada was covered with glacial ice, which began retreating about 10,000 years ago. Several ice-free corridors ran from Alaska south, through which the first immigrants from Asia probably travelled by land into the warmer regions of the continent, while others, it seems, took a coastal route and entered the southwestern part of the continent by sea. By the time of Christ, around 2,000 years ago, most of Canada had acquired the natural environment recognizable to us today. The land had also acquired permanent inhabitants.

Much of what we know about these people comes to us in the form of physical artifacts, but increasing genetic evidence has recently led to a number of new conclusions. Where there was once some debate over whether these first humans had come from Asia or from Europe, in the forms of the Clovis and Solutrean hypotheses respectively, the Asian ancestry of North America seems assured. Most notably, the genome sequence of 12,500-year-old Anzick-1, the infant skeleton found in Montana, shows indisputable links to Asia and to contemporary Native Americans. Found in association with over a hundred stone and bone Clovis tools, Anzick-1 is clearly a part of the Clovis culture, and this connection allows scholars to re-examine previous evidence in a clearer context.

Because of the limited nature of the evidence, the early history of humankind in Canada is often described in terms of surviving tools and weapons, especially projectile points. Archaeologists can infer much from tool-making technology and its geographical spread across the continent. Using various dating techniques, including laboratory testing of organic substances to determine what remains of a radioactive isotope called carbon-14, it has been possible to provide some overall sense of chronological development. The Clovis tool type, which is associated with tools made from bifacial percussion flaking and the distinctive fluted spear point, is found throughout the Americas. They were mega-faunal hunters of mammoth and other large game, who lived in small units, although not in total isolation from neighbours. Evidence also survives of trade and the exchange of goods.

Clovis, eventually, was replaced by the Folsom culture and a different style of projectile point. Folsom evidence, which dates back to 9000 BCE, suggests that new technology, possibly the atlatl, allowed these big-game hunters to kill more effectively the bison of the Lake Agassiz region—a vast glacial lake that covered much of present-day Manitoba and parts of northwestern Ontario, central Saskatchewan, and northern Minnesota and North Dakota.

As the ice melted and the continental ice sheet receded northward, hunters who made fluted points spread more widely across the continent and into what is now Canada. These people have come to be known by archaeologists as the Plano People and had their own distinctive projectile-point technology. They flourished from 8000 to 6000 BCE. By 4000 BCE a number of regional offshoots of the Plano People had developed. Over the next 3,000 years these cultures stabilized to some extent, although there was still substantial physical movement. On the western Plains, a culture organized around communal bison-hunting emerged, perhaps as early as 3000 BCE. The High Arctic was occupied by Paleo-Eskimos, who gradually moved to the south into the Barren Lands west of Hudson Bay. The northeastern seaboard was occupied between 2000 and 1000 BCE. On the west coast, a semi-sedentary lifestyle based on the salmon had developed by 2000 BCE.

From 1000 BCE to 500 CE, substantial cultural changes occurred across North America. Once we stop trying to compare these developments with what was going on in Europe and see them instead in their own terms, we can appreciate how substantial the technological innovations of this period were. The bow and arrow spread rapidly, for example, profoundly altering hunting techniques. In the same years, pottery-making moved from the Yukon to eastern districts. The introduction of the pot changed food preparation substantially, but pottery also provides evidence of rapidly changing aesthetic sensibilities, as ornamentation was added to design.

Archaeologists have shifted their classification systems from the projectile point to the pot to characterize peoples of this era. Another new development was the rapid expansion from the south of new funeral practices, chiefly burial in large mounds. This change, of course, helped provide a new self-consciously created richness of physical evidence.

The First Nations Population around 1500

Although on the eve of European intrusion all Aboriginal peoples lived in a reciprocal relationship with nature, not all experienced the same relationship. Much depended on the resources of the region in which they lived and the precise combination of survival skills they possessed. Most of the many groups were hunters and gatherers, organized into mobile bands that followed the seasons and the cycles of game. On the coasts, fishing was the principal means of collecting a food supply.

BACKGROUNDER

Kennewick Man

In 1996 two young men found a human skull in the Columbia River near Kennewick, Washington. Over the next month, other parts of the skeleton were found by archaeologist James C. Chatters. Within the skeleton's right hipbone was embedded a projectile point, possibly of great antiquity. Forensic examination disclosed that the nearly complete skeleton, which included a full set of teeth, was of a male between 40 and 55 years, of tall but slender build. He had suffered numerous injuries over his lifetime, including a basalt spear tip lodged in his hip. Radiocarbon dating of a bone fragment indicated that this man had lived about 7,500 years before the birth of Christ. The skull lacked Mongoloid characteristics and displayed many signs associated with modern Caucasoids, as a forensic reconstruction illustrates. The skeleton was caught up for some years in a legal dispute between modern American Indian tribes and scientists, which tended to obscure the purely scientific significance of the find. Having now been analyzed, skeletal evidence connects Kennewick man to the Ainu, the ancient Asian culture. Nitrogen and oxygen isotope analysis suggests that Kennewick man lived coastally, and not in the Columbia River Valley where he was found, although the care taken in his interment suggests that he was buried by other humans.

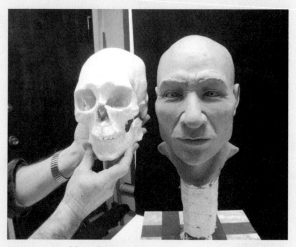

Tri-City Herald/André Ranieri

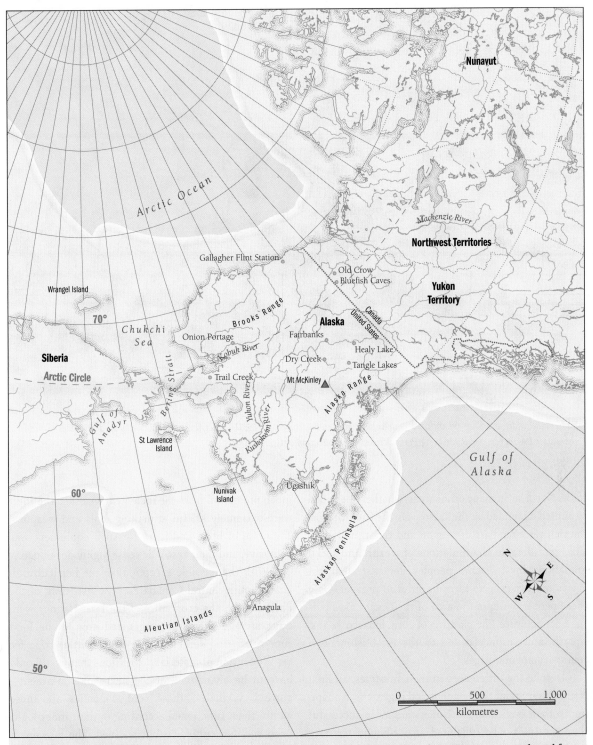

Beringia: the "land bridge" at its greatest extent. Shaded area was above sea level approximately 20,000 years ago. Adapted from Brian M. Fagan, The Great Journey: The Peopling of Ancient North America *(London: Thames and Hudson, 1987), 100*

Sadlermiut man paddling an inflated walrus-skin boat, watercolour, c. 1830, artist unknown. Library and Archives Canada (hereafter LAC), Acc. No. R9266-30, Peter Winkworth Collection of Canadiana.

In the North, as in many other areas, whether one fished or hunted depended on the season. On the Pacific Slope, the rich resource base of salmon and cedar made possible considerable accumulations of wealth and social gradation. These Pacific peoples demonstrated that it was not essential to farm in order to prosper. Only those people living in the area of the Great Lakes pursued horticulture. The planting of corn, tobacco, beans, squash, and sunflowers led to the establishment of semi-permanent villages.

Despite the differences in their lifestyles, all First Nations were remarkably adept and ingenious at adapting to their environment. None were more successful than the Inuit, who inhabited an ice-bound territory in the North. At sea they used the speedy kayak and on land the dogsled. They lived in domed snow-huts (igloos) in winter and in skin tents in summer. Caribou hides served as the basic clothing material and provided

much protection from the inclement weather. The Inuit were extremely skilful at making tools and weapons. Their use of bone and ivory for such equipment was extensive, and their aesthetic sense highly developed.

With the possible exceptions of the horticulturalists of south-central Canada and the fisherfolk of the Pacific Slope, the economies of the First Nations were quite simple. They were organized around the food supply, offering semi-nomadic people little scope for the acquisition of material possessions that would only have to be abandoned at the next—and imminent—move. Nevertheless, these were economies, and those within them functioned according to their inner logic. Food was not cultivated but pursued. The movement of fish and game had certain rhythms, but was potentially capricious. When food was available, the population was galvanized into action, gathering as much as possible and consuming it almost immediately. When food ran out, energetic questing for new sources did not necessarily begin at once. The people knew the general patterns of the wildlife and vegetation they sought, and hurry often did little good. It was, for example, useless to hunt for berries in February. Such economies put little premium on the disciplined pursuit of goals, or on the deferral of expectations.

The First Peoples: A Regional Introduction

The number of First Nations peoples living in Canada on the eve of European intrusion has become the subject of debate. One point seems clear. The Aboriginal population, lacking immunities to a variety of European diseases, was quickly decimated by epidemics, which spread across the land, often in advance of the actual appearance of a European human carrier. The size of the population observed by the first European arrivals may have already been modified by disease brought by the earliest fishermen, who may well have preceded the recorded explorers. The Indigenous pre-contact population of Canada was probably substantially larger than the most generous estimates of first-contact observers. Another general point that needs emphasizing is that great diversity existed among the Aboriginal inhabitants living in what is now Canada at the time Europeans arrived. As the map on page 29 indicates, 12 major language groups existed in this vast territory.

In the Atlantic region, the earliest traces of a human presence have been found near Cobequid Bay, Nova Scotia, where the remains of a Paleo-Indian site have been dated to roughly 8600 BCE. Hard archaeological evidence can be hard to find in this region because coastal settlements may have been washed away by rising sea levels. The first traces of habitation on Newfoundland can be dated to approximately 5,000 years ago, arrivals from Labrador. Two successive waves of settlement are thought to have disappeared around 800 CE. By this time a new people had settled on the island. Their origins obscure, they would come to be known as the Beothuk. Their language was probably Algonquian, and they relied on the fruits of the sea for

much of the year, following the caribou inland in the depths of winter. In the modern Maritime provinces and on the Gaspé Peninsula, by 1500 Mi'kmaq speakers of Eastern Algonqian had taken hold. The region was not well suited to agriculture, and the Mi'kmaq were primarily hunters and fishermen who employed an extensive river system to travel between interior and coast, summering on marine life and hunting in the winter. Two other groups of Algonquian speakers— the Wuastukwiuk (Maliseet) around the Saint John River basin and the Passamaquoddy around the Bay of Fundy—resided to the west of the Mi'kmaq. Both peoples were principally hunters.

To the north of the Maritime region was a vast expanse of Precambrian Shield stretching to the north of the St Lawrence River between modern Labrador and the James Bay drainage basin. In a region fairly inhospitable to agriculture lived the Innu (Montagnais-Naskapi), Algonquian speakers who ranged widely in small hunting bands in search of moose and caribou. Further west lived several groups called by Europeans "Algonquins," and to their west—north of the Great Lakes as far as the prairies—resided the Ojibwa or Chippewa. Traditionally hunters, the inhabitants adapted to warmer temperatures by seeking a variety of game animals, supplemented by such plant foods as berries and wild rice. They continued to travel in small hunting bands.

South of the Ojibwa, in more temperate and fertile woodlands around the Lower Great Lakes, resided several peoples belonging to the Iroquian language family. The Huron lived south of Georgian Bay in what is today Simcoe County, Ontario. The Petun were found to their west, the Attiwandaronk (Neutrals) along the north shore of Lake Erie, and the Five Nations Iroquois (Mohawk, Oneida, Onondaga, Cayuga, and Seneca) south of the lakes in modern New York State. Beginning about 1,500 years ago, these peoples picked up a practice coming northward from the south in the Mississippi Valley. They began to grow corn. The results were dramatic. Domesticated plants produced a much more stable food supply than hunting, and made possible for a substantial population to exist in a small area. People here would still hunt and fish, but they no longer travelled long distances looking for food, and they could settle in one place more or less permanently. The

Iroquoians began to establish villages made up of long-houses: large communal homes typically housing five to ten nuclear families each. A large village might contain as many as 100 longhouses and some 3,000 people.

In the slash-and-burn agriculture practised by the Iroquoians, the land was cleared for fields by cutting the trees and burning off the ground cover; seeds (first corn, then beans, squash, sunflowers, and tobacco) were planted in holes made with a digging stick; then earth was hoed up around the plants in mounds—up to 6,000 per hectare in fields as extensive as 25 hectares in area. Once the men had cleared the land, the women and children did the planting, cultivating, and harvesting. The soil was a sandy loam, easy to work but easily exhausted. After several years of steady production, the entire community would move to another site with fresh soil. Land was treated as a unit of production. It did not confer status or wealth, and unused land was held in common. But families possessed their own farm plots, as large as they could reasonably cultivate. Unlike hunting and gathering people, these horticulturalists were able to accumulate possessions, including food supplies for the winter, and to that extent agricultural produce did represent a form of wealth. Hoarding was discouraged, however, and goods were shared through games of chance and ceremonies such a gift-giving. Artifacts discovered hundreds of kilometres from their presumed points of origin demonstrate the development of complex trading patterns among these early Eastern Woodland peoples.

In the vast expanse between the Great Lakes and the Rocky Mountains, large mammals remained the centre of human economies. When the mammoth, the earliest prey, became extinct it was replaced by species more familiar to our own time, including the Plains buffalo (or bison). With the arrival of the horse—an introduction into southwestern North America by the Spaniards in the sixteenth century, which gradually moved north over the next 200 years—the Plains people would develop one of the world's great equestrian cultures, but until then they hunted on foot, often stampeding the animals over cliffs or herding them into gullies or "pounds" where they could be dispatched with spears or stone hammers. Head-Smashed-In Buffalo Jump in present-day Alberta (today a UNESCO World Heritage Site) was used by four cultures in succession over more than 5,000 years. Because they needed to follow the herds as they grazed for forage, the Plains cultures did not establish permanent habitations. Instead, they developed the portable hide tipi, using dogs as pack animals. Changes in spear and arrow points indicate that the Plains cultures were influenced by developments to their south. Burial practices also suggest southern influences and graves containing goods from distant regions, such as shells and copper, indicate elaborate trade networks. Although horticulture was practised at times in several areas of the prairies, recurring droughts made hunting and gathering a more reliable survival strategy.

Not all of the region between the Great Lakes and Rockies was prairie, however. Between the Shield and the southern Plains was a zone of heavy forest alternating with open clearings covered with tall grasses. This parkland, as it came to be called, extended west from the Red River to the north branch of the Saskatchewan River and ultimately into the Peace River country. The lives of people in this region had more in common with those of the eastern hunters than of the buffalo hunters to the south. The two largest groups in the western interior were the Assiniboine and the Cree; the former were based mainly in the buffalo country and the latter mainly in the woodlands. Linguistically, both peoples belonged to the Algonquian family, as did their western neighbours the Blackfoot. The Gros Ventre and the Sarcee—who, with the Blackfoot, inhabited what is now Alberta—spoke Athapaskan languages.

On the Pacific slope, rivers and coastal waters, set in a temperate climate and teeming with fish and marine animals, made possible a more varied economy than was possible for the bison-centred cultures east of the Rockies. One fish and one tree became central to the cultures of the Northwest Coast: the salmon—fresh, smoked, dried—provided a year-round food supply, while the towering cedar of the coastal rain forest furnished material for everything from large houses and sea-going dugout canoes to totem poles, ceremonial masks, and baskets and clothing woven from bark and roots. In this rich environment with the gentlest climate of any in the northern part of the continent, there was little need to pursue a migratory food supply. Relatively large populations were able to settle in one place. Over time they developed highly complex social systems with sharp class divisions based on kinship and wealth, both material and immaterial (such as rights to cultural property, including dances, songs, or rituals). People such as the Haida, Nun-chah-nulth, Kwakwaka'wakw, and Tsimshian also owned slaves, often prisoners of war taken in raids on less powerful peoples such as the Salish of southern Vancouver Island. A strong aesthetic sensibility expressed itself in all aspects of these cultures, and the linguistic diversity of the region—of the 12 Aboriginal language families in Canada, half are found only in present-day British Columbia—suggests that it has been occupied for a very long time.

The peoples of the Interior Plateau were heavily influenced by the coastal societies, with clan-based social organization and hierarchical divisions between chiefs, nobles, commoners, and slaves. In their economies, however, groups such as the Interior Salish, Kootenay, Chilcotin, and Okanagan were more closely akin to the hunting and gathering societies of eastern Canada. Semi-migratory, dependent on hunting and fishing, most of these peoples spoke Athapaskan languages.

North of the fifty-sixth parallel, in the basins of the Mackenzie and Yukon rivers, lived several other Athapaskan-speaking woodlands people. The lives of the Chipewyan, Dogrib, and Gwich'in were centred on a constant search for game: moose, caribou, bear, beaver, and smaller mammals. Historically, the direction of these groups was southward, away from the Barrens—that vast, bleak area stretching from northern Manitoba to the shore of Coronation Gulf (an arm of the Arctic Ocean). In the west they had gradually extended into the Interior of British Columbia, but to the southeast they had found their way blocked by other groups. Their lives were hard and insecure: the sparse, difficult terrain could not support a dense population, and their social organization was that of the small hunting band.

Finally, the earliest human occupants of the High Arctic and Subarctic coasts, known to us as Paleo-Eskimos, had been land-based hunters of caribou and muskoxen. As the climate became more moderate and the sea level stabilized, producing a more reliable food supply based on marine mammals, they expanded eastward from Alaska beginning about 2000 BCE, eventually reaching as far as northern Greenland. The Paleo-Eskimos were succeeded by the Dorset culture and the Dorset by the Thule, the direct ancestors of the modern Inuit. Survival in the intractable environment of the Far North demanded extreme ingenuity. Without trees for building, the Inuit used the materials at hand, which varied from place to place but were largely derived from the animals they hunted for food: caribou, seal, and whale. Boats were made from animal skins stretched over driftwood or whalebone frames; sled-runners began as animal bones; tools and weapons (including the toggling harpoon) came from bone and ivory. Dwellings were constructed either of snow blocks (igloos) or rocks, sod, and skins. For transportation, on water these people used both the small, speedy kayak and the large flat-bottomed umiak; for land travel they employed the dogsled. Most of their clothing came from caribou skins, which provided a warmth unknown in the skins of other animals. As in other societies reliant on the hunt, political organization was simple, based on the extended family.

The First Arrivals from Europe

As every Canadian schoolchild knows, Norsemen made the first documented European visitations to North America. Contemporary evidence of these visits is found in the great Icelandic epic sagas, confirmed in our own time by archaeological excavations near L'Anse aux Meadows on the northern tip of Newfoundland. The sagas describe the landings to the west of Greenland made by Leif Ericsson and his brother Thorvald. They also relate Thorfinn Karlsefni's colonization attempt at a place Leif had called Vinland, an attempt that was thwarted by hostile residents labelled in the sagas as "Skraelings." It is tempting to equate Vinland with the archaeological discoveries, although there is no real evidence for doing so.

Later Greenlanders may have timbered on Baffin Island. They may also have intermarried with the Inuit. Attempts have been made to attribute the Thule culture of the Inuit to such relationships. But Greenland gradually lost contact with Europe, and the Icelandic settlement there died away in the fifteenth century. The Norse activities became part of the murky geographical knowledge of the late Middle Ages.

In our own time the uncovering of a world map executed in the mid-fifteenth century, showing a realistic Greenland and westward islands, including inscriptions referring to Vinland, created much speculation about Europe's geographical knowledge before Columbus. This Vinland map has never been definitively authenticated, and many experts have regarded it with skepticism. The current scholarly view, however, has turned back to a positive evaluation of the map.

Like the Vinland map, none of the various candidates for North American landfalls before Columbus—except for the Norse in Newfoundland—can be indisputably documented. In the fifteenth century, Portuguese and possibly English fishermen may have discovered the rich fishing grounds off the Grand Banks. An occasional vessel may even have made a landfall. The fishermen did not publicize their knowledge, although many scholars insist that awareness of lands in the western Atlantic was probably in common circulation in maritime circles by the end of the fifteenth century.

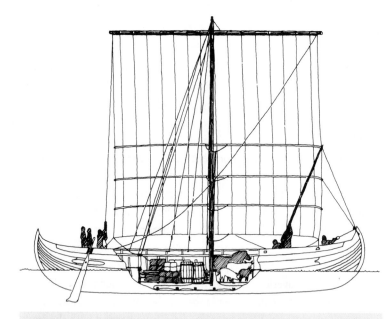

Sketch of an ocean-going Viking vessel of the eleventh century. In the 1950s archaeologists began excavating a collection of five Viking ships sunk between 1070 and 1090 to create a blockade across a narrow channel at Skuldelev, Denmark. One of these ships was a double-decked cargo carrier with higher sides (called a "knarr") of the sort the Norse would have sailed in the open Atlantic. It had extra trusses and a sheltered cargo space below deck for people and animals. Source: The Viking Ship Museum, Denmark. Illustration: Morten Gøthche.

Europe around 1500

The arrival of Europeans in the Americas at the end of the fifteenth century was a collaborative effort by mariners and contemporary scholars of many nations, behind which were profound changes in economies and polities. The ambition to visit new lands was fuelled by the surge of intellectual confidence and the explosion of knowledge associated with the Renaissance. By the end of the fifteenth century, geographers—led by Paolo dal Pozzo Toscanelli, an Italian cosmographer in Portuguese service—were convinced that Europe and Asia were closer than the ancients had conjectured. The schemes of Christopher Columbus were influenced both by Toscanelli and by Portuguese notions of oceanic islands. Geographical speculation and ship design pointed towards transatlantic voyages. Some time in the twelfth century, the Germans developed the cog, a single-masted ship decked over and fitted with rudder and tiller. In the early fifteenth century the cog's hull was lengthened and the vessel was given two additional masts, becoming the carvel (or caravel). Early explorers found smaller ships more manoeuvrable than larger ones and came to prefer them on their voyages. Rigging also improved, particularly with the addition of the square sail to the earlier lateen (triangular) variety.

The art of navigation showed development parallel to ship design, a gradual result of trial and error by countless mariners. The greatest advance was in written sailing directions based on taking latitudes in relation to Polaris (the North Star) and the sun. Longitudes still were based largely on guesswork, mainly on a mariner's estimates of his vessel's speed. In addition to the compass, seamen used quadrants and astrolabes to determine latitude, and were familiar with the need to transfer their data on latitude and longitude onto charts ruled for these variables. *Routiers*—coastal pilot charts of European waters—were

Karlsefni and the Skraelings

The Norse sagas began as manuscripts of the history of the Icelandic Norsemen collected in the thirteenth century. The following selection is from a manuscript called in English "Eirik the Red's Saga," which is a reworking of original material in agreement with well-established rules of the saga tradition. Despite its title, "Eirik the Red's Saga" is much more interested in the Icelanders Gudrid and Karlsefni than in the family of Eirik the Red.

Karlsefni sailed south along the land with Snorri and Bjarni and the rest of their company. They journeyed a long time till they reached a river which flowed down from the land into a lake and so on to the sea. There were such extensive bars off the mouth of the estuary that they were unable to get into the river except at full flood. Karlsefni and his men sailed into the estuary, and called the place Hop, Landlock Bay. There they found self-sown fields of wheat where the ground was low-lying, and vines wherever it was hilly. Every brook there was full of fish. They dug trenches at the meeting point of land and high water, and when the tide went out there were halibut in the trenches. There were vast numbers of animals of every kind in the forest. They were there for a fortnight enjoying themselves and saw nothing and nobody. They had their cattle with them.

Then early one morning when they looked about them they saw nine skin-boats, on board which staves were being swung which sounded just like flails threshing—and their motion was sunwise.

"What can this mean?" asked Karlsefni.

"Perhaps it is a token of peace," replied Snorri. "So let us take a white shield and hold it out towards them."

They did so, and those others rowed towards them, showing their astonishment, then came ashore. They were small, ill-favoured men, and had ugly hair on their heads. They had big eyes and were broad in the cheeks. For a while they remained there, astonished, and afterwards rowed off south past the headlands.

Karlsefni and his men built themselves dwellings up above the lake; some of their houses stood near the mainland, and some near the lake. They now spent the winter there. No snow fell, and their entire stock found its food grazing in the open. But once spring came in they chanced early one morning to see how a multitude of skin-boats came rowing from the south round the headland, so many that the bay appeared sown with coals, and even so staves were being swung on every boat. Karlsefni and his men raised their shields, and they began trading together. Above all these people wanted to buy red cloth in return for which they had furs to offer and grey pelts. They also wanted to buy swords and spears, but this Karlsefni and Snorri would not allow. They had dark unblemished skins to exchange for the cloth, and were taking a span's length of cloth for a skin, and this they tied round their heads. So it continued for a while, then when the cloth began to run short they cut it up so that it was no broader than a fingerbreadth, but the Skraelings gave just as much for it, or more.

The next thing was that the bull belonging to Karlsefni and his mates ran out of the forest bellowing loudly. The Skraelings were terrified by this, raced to their boats and rowed south past the headland, and for three weeks running there was neither sight nor sound of them. But at the end of that period they saw a great multitude of Skraeling boats coming up from the south like a streaming torrent. This time all the staves were being swung anti-sunwise, and the Skraelings were all yelling aloud, so they took red shields and held them out against them. They clashed together and fought. There was a heavy shower of missiles, for the Skraelings had war-slings too. Karlsefni and Snorri could see the

Continued...

Skraelings hoisting up on poles a huge ball-shaped object, more or less the size of a sheep's paunch, and blue-black in colour, which they sent flying inland over Karlsefni's troop, and it made a hideous noise when it came down. Great fear now struck into Karlsefni and all his following, so that there was no other thought in their heads than to run away up along the river to some steep rocks, and there put up a strong resistance.

Source: Gwyn Jones, *The Norse Atlantic Saga: Being the Norse Voyages of Discovery and Settlement to Iceland, Greenland, America* (London: Oxford University Press, 1964), 181–3. Reprinted by permission of the publisher.

readily available, but none of the early explorers who reached North America had the faintest idea of the hazards he was risking. The most remarkable feature of the first known voyages was the infrequency with which mariners ran into serious problems with rocks, shoals, and tides. Such master mariners had an instinctive "feel" for the sea. They were able to read and deduce much from its colour and surface patterns.

Though the early explorers had their blind spots, they were without exception skilled sailors, suitably cautious in uncharted waters, which may explain many glaring failures to uncover rivers and bays obvious on any modern map. Once ashore, however, the first Europeans to reach North America threw caution to the winds, particularly in collecting rumours of rich mineral deposits or routes to Asia. Neither they nor their sponsors were at all interested in the scientific accumulation of knowledge. What they sought was wealth, equivalent to the riches the Spaniards were already taking out of their territories to the south. While other motives—such as national advantage and missionary fervour directed against the resident inhabitants—also entered the picture, the easy and rapid exploitation of the resources of the New World long remained the principal attraction.

The assumption of sovereignty by European states in the early period of exploration consisted chiefly of the performance of various symbolic acts or ceremonies of possession. Such ceremonies were intimately bound up with the culture and language of a particular nation, so that no two nations meant quite the same thing by their actions. The Portuguese, for example, thought that mere discovery was sufficient to establish legitimate dominion, and the word "discovery" in Portuguese carried that nuanced meaning, while other nations had quite different concepts of what produced a legitimate right to rule. For the English, settlement in the form of "first building

and habitation" was one important test, as was "replenishing and subduing" a land that had previously existed in common and was seemingly undeveloped (Seed, 1995: 9, 31). Every European nation had its own understanding of the meaning of "possession." But in any case, no Aboriginal peoples could comprehend the European concept either of ultimate political authority embodied in a state or of the private ownership of land. In North America, land was used rather than possessed, and one of the continuing gulfs between the First Nations and the Europeans—lasting from first arrival until the present—was over the meaning of the transfer of territory from the Aboriginals to the newcomers, often in formal treaties.

Among those European powers who explored in North America, the French were the most likely to take into account the feelings of the Indigenous peoples they encountered. Indeed, the French—whose monarchical political customs at home relied heavily on the use of ritual and ceremony—often incorporated the consent of the Aboriginal people into their ceremonies as a central component. The early French explorers assumed that physical gestures and body language could be universally understood, and made sure that the Aboriginal people either gave appropriate signs of agreement, or better still, actually participated in the ceremonies of possession. Thus, the French explorers did not simply raise objects of possession like crosses and pillars, but sought to communicate something of their meaning to the Native witnesses and interpreted Native responses as evidence of acceptance or even enthusiasm of the French ceremonialism.

French accounts of ceremonies usually include detailed descriptions of the bodily movements and sounds of the Indigenous observers, which were taken to mean formal consent. For the English, on the other hand, cultural symbols of land possession usually involved signs of successful occupation, such as housing, fencing, and cultivation of the land. Such actions had their own justification. Since the local inhabitants in most places obviously did not exhibit such signs of permanent occupation, they were not regarded as having proper jurisdiction over the country in which they resided (Seed, 1995: 41–68).

BACKGROUNDER

L'Anse aux Meadows

In 1961 the Norwegian explorer Helge Ingstad announced that he had found Norse buildings in northern Newfoundland. Many were skeptical, but in excavations executed between 1961 and 1968 by Ingstad and his wife Anne (and continued by Parks Canada in the 1970s), eight ruined buildings were uncovered in a grassy cove overlooking the Strait of Belle Isle. Seven of the buildings are grouped into three complexes located on a north–south axis. Each complex includes a hall of several rooms and a smaller one-room hut. Each of the huts may represent housing for a different vessel. Radiocarbon dating indicates an occupation between 980 and 1020. The buildings are substantial, with sod walls and permanent roofs. They were obviously constructed to be lived in year-round by up to 100 people. Each hall had a workshop: the southernmost one a smithy, the middle one a carpentry shop, and the northern one a boat-building lean-to. This was not a typical Norse arrangement, for there were no signs of livestock or domestic animals. The settlement was apparently not intended for farming, but probably as a base for further exploration of the region. The short duration of the season of navigation in these northern waters demanded that the Norse winter over in Vinland in order to scout out the region. The settlement was abandoned fairly swiftly in an orderly manner, leaving behind little equipment and no burial site. Archaeologists speculate that the site was the headquarters of Leif Ericsson himself, for the population here represented as much as 10 per cent of the Greenland Norse colony, mainly comprising workmen. Apparently this location (and the region surrounding it) was not sufficiently attractive to produce a permanent colony, both because of the climate and because of the unfriendly local inhabitants. But it co-ordinates well with what is known of the Norse experience in Vinland as reported in the Vinland sagas.

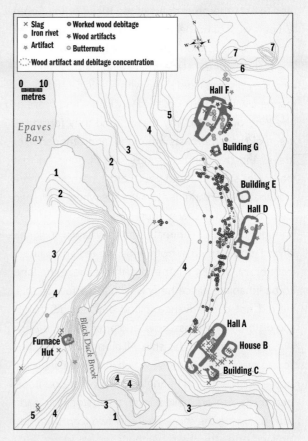

Source: William Fitzhugh and Elisabeth I. Ward, eds., *Vikings: The North Atlantic Saga* (Washington and London: Smithsonian Institution Press, 2000).

John Cabot Reaches Land across the Atlantic, 1497

Over the winter of 1497–8, the English merchant John Day wrote a letter to "El Gran Almirante" (probably Christopher Columbus), giving him an account of a recent voyage by John Cabot. This account provides some of our best evidence for Cabot's landfall.

From the said copy [of "the land which has been found," which is no longer extant] your Lordship will learn what you wish to know, for in it are named the capes of the mainland and the islands, and thus you will see where land was first sighted, since most of them was discovered after turning back. Thus your Lordship will know that the cape nearest to Ireland is 1800 miles west of Dursey Head which is in Ireland, and the southernmost part of the Island of the Seven Cities is west of Bordeaux River, and your Lordship will know that he [Cabot] landed at only one spot of the mainland, near the place where land was first sighted, and they disembarked there with a crucifix and raised banners with the arms of the Holy Father and those of the King of England, my master; and they found tall trees of the kind masts are made, and other smaller trees, and the country is very rich in grass. In that particular spot, as I told your Lordship, they found a trail that went inland, they saw a site where a fire had been made, they saw manure of animals which they thought to be farm animals, and they saw a stick half a yard long pierced at both ends, carved and painted with brazil, and by such things they believe the land to be inhabited. Since he was with just a few people, he did not dare advance inland beyond the shooting distance of a cross-bow, and after taking in fresh water he returned to his ship. All along the coast they found many fish like those which in Iceland are dried in the open and sold in England and other countries, and these fish are called in English "stockfish"; and thus following the shore they saw two forms running on land one after the other, but they could not tell if they were human beings or animals; and it seemed to them that there were fields where they thought might

also be villages, and they saw a forest whose foliage looked beautiful. They left England toward the end of May, and must have been on the way 35 days before sighting land; the wind was east-north-east and the sea calm going and coming back, except for one day when he ran into a storm two or three days before finding land; and going so far out, his compass needle failed to point north and marked two rhumbs below. They spent about one month discovering the coast and from the above mentioned cape of the mainland which is nearest to Ireland, they returned to the coast of Europe in fifteen days. They had the wind behind them, and he reached Brittany because the sailors confused him, saying that he was heading too far north. From there he came to Bristol, and he went to see the King to report to him all the above mentioned; and the King granted him an annual pension of twenty pounds sterling to sustain himself until the time comes when more will be known of this business, since with God's help it is hoped to push through plans for exploring the said land more thoroughly next year with ten or twelve vessels—because in his voyage he had only one ship of fifty "tonnes" and twenty men and food for seven or eight months—and they want to carry out this new project. It is considered certain that the cape of the said land was found and discovered in the past by the men from Bristol who found "Brasil" as your Lordship well knows. It was called the Island of Brasil, and it is assumed and believed to be the mainland that the men from Bristol found. Since your Lordship wants information relating to the first voyage, here is what happened: he went with one ship, his crew confused him, he was short of supplies and ran into bad weather, and he decided to turn back.

Source: J.A. Williamson, ed., *The Cabot Voyages and British Discoveries under Henry VII* (Cambridge: Hakluyt Society of the University Press, 1962), 211–14. (The Hakluyt Society was established in 1846 for the purpose of printing rare or unpublished Voyages and Travels. For further information please see their website at www.Hakluyt.com.)

The European Entry into North America

John Cabot went briefly ashore at the "newfoundland." Of Italian origin, he had convinced Henry VII of England to finance one small ship of 50 tons and a crew of 18 to sail west and find a short route to Asia. Cabot was lost at sea on a second voyage, and his mantle fell to a number of Portuguese mariners, some in English service, who produced a more clearly defined understanding of Newfoundland. Most of the sixteenth-century place names in Newfoundland were Portuguese rather than English. Portugal actually attempted to settle a colony on the Newfoundland coast under the leadership of Juan Fagundes, who had earlier sailed as far as the Gulf of St Lawrence. Fagundes ended up on Cape Breton Island, where his little settlement was apparently destroyed by the local residents, who "killed all those who came there." Nevertheless, by 1536 Newfoundland was sufficiently familiar, if exotic, to Europeans that a tourist voyage to the island was organized. London merchant Richard Hore (fl. 1507–40) signed 120 passengers, "whereof thirty were gentlemen." When provisions ran short on the Newfoundland coast, some participants allegedly resorted to eating their compatriots. Those surviving were understandably relieved to get back to England.

In 1523 the French entered the picture through the activities of Italian master mariner Giovanni da Verrazzano (c. 1485–c. 1528). Of high birth, Verrazzano persuaded Francis I to sponsor a voyage of exploration. He made three voyages in all, opening a French trade with Brazil and convincing himself that what he was investigating was not Asia but a totally new continent. Verrazzano was succeeded by Jacques Cartier (1491–1557), who had allegedly been to Brazil and Newfoundland. In 1534 Francis I ordered him to uncover new lands, "where it is said that a great quantity of gold, and other precious things, are to be found." Little concern was given to the conversion of Aboriginal peoples in Cartier's efforts. He, too, made three voyages: the first to make a great "discovery," a second to locate some mineral resource there that would attract investors and the royal court, and a final large-scale effort that failed to produce any profit.

On his first voyage in 1534 Cartier explored the Gulf of St Lawrence. His second voyage in 1535 took him upriver as far as Mont Royal. He visited several First Nation villages and wintered at one of them, Stadacona. Here he heard about the fabulous kingdom of the Saguenay, somewhere farther west. A third voyage was actually headed by a great nobleman, the Sieur de Roberval (c. 1500–60). It was a disaster, finding little wealth to exploit and accomplishing nothing. The gold and diamonds Cartier brought back turned out to be iron pyrites and quartz. "False as Canadian diamonds" became a common French expression of the time. Despite the lack of accomplishment, a French claim to the St Lawrence region had been established, and the French ultimately would return there.

The next major adventurer to what is now Canada was the Englishman Martin Frobisher (1539?–94), who spent several years searching for the Northwest Passage and great wealth in the Arctic region. Frobisher was a leading English "sea dog"—part pirate and part merchant. In 1576 he raised the funds for an expedition to sail west to Asia through northern waters. He did not find the passageway, but did bring back mineral samples from Baffin Island. These were pronounced to be gold-bearing, leading to a second expedition in 1577, which brought back 200 tons of ore. About the first of October in 1578, a third fleet returned to England from the land called "Meta Incognita." Its principal cargo consisted of 1,350 tons of rocks, collected with great effort and at considerable expense on Baffin Island. Accounts of the return appeared in print before the experts had a chance to examine the cargo. Everyone was demanding to be paid. The owner of one vessel wrote desperately to the government for money to pay his crew, noting, "Chrystmas beynge so nere, every man cryythe out for

Jacques Cartier Meets with Aboriginal People, 1534

In the summer of 1534, the French mariner Jacques Cartier cruised along the northern coast and St Lawrence region of North America. His original journal or log of this expedition does not survive, but a printed version appeared in Italian in 1565. Various versions of the journal were collated and translated by Henry Percival Biggar and published in 1924.

On Thursday the eighth of the said month [of July] as the wind was favourable for getting under way with our ships, we fitted up our long-boats to go and explore this [Chaleur] bay; and we ran up it that day about twenty-five leagues. The next day, at daybreak, we had fine weather and sailed on until about ten o'clock in the morning, at which hour we caught sight of the head of the bay, whereat we were grieved and displeased. At the head of this bay, beyond the low shore, were several high mountains. And seeing there was no passage, we proceeded to turn back. While making our way along the shore, we caught sight of the Indians on the side of a lagoon and low beach, who were making many fires that smoked. We rowed over to the spot, and finding there was an entrance from the sea into the lagoon, we placed our long-boats on one side of the entrance. The savages came over in one of their canoes and brought us some strips of cooked seal, which they placed on bits of wood and then withdrew, making signs to us that they were making us a present of them. We sent two men on shore with hatchets, knives, beads, and other wares, at which the Indians showed great pleasure. And at once they came over in a crowd in their canoes to the side where we were, bringing furs and whatever else they possessed, in order to obtain some of our wares. They numbered, both men, women, and children, more than 300 persons. Some of their women, who did not come over, danced and sang, standing in the water up to their knees. The other women, who had come over to the side where we were, advanced freely towards us and rubbed our arms with their hands. Then they joined their hands together and raised them to heaven, exhibiting many signs of joy. And so much at ease did the savages feel in our presence, that at length we bartered with them, hand to hand, for everything they possessed, so that nothing was left to them but their naked bodies; for they offered us everything they owned, which was, all told, of little value. We perceived that they are people who would be easy to convert, who go from place to place maintaining themselves and catching fish in the fishing-season for food. Their country is more temperate than Spain and the finest it is possible to see, and as level as the surface of a pond. There is not the smallest lot of ground bare of wood, and even on sandy soil, but is full of wild wheat, that has an ear like barley and the grain like oats, as well as of pease, as thick as if they had been sown and hoed; of white and red currant-bushes, of strawberries, of raspberries, of white and red roses and of other plants of a strong, pleasant odour. Likewise there are many fine meadows with useful herbs, and a pond where there are many salmon. I am more than ever of opinion that these people would be easy to convert to our holy faith.

Source: H.P. Biggar, ed., *The Voyages of Jacques Cartier: Published from the originals with translations, notes and appendices* (Ottawa: F. Acland, 1924), 54–7.

mony" (Stefansson, 1938). No money was forthcoming and for five years the sponsors of the expedition tried without success to find evidence of value in the cargo. The rock proved to be nothing more than sandstone flecked with mica. The business degenerated into an unseemly exchange of recriminations and accusations among the investors, and the rock was used eventually in Elizabethan road construction.

The frontispiece to The Voyages of Jacques Cartier, *edited by H.P. Biggar. This portrait of Cartier—if such it is—is imaginary, since we do not have a likeness. Thomas Fisher Rare Book Library, University of Toronto.*

of the great voyages of discovery had been completed by the end of the sixteenth century, even though much of the North American continent remained to be mapped and charted. They occurred against a complex European backdrop of dynastic manoeuvring, the rise of the modern nation-state, the religious disputes of the Protestant Reformation and Catholic Counter-Reformation, and the growth of capitalistic enterprise fuelled by the infusion of new wealth in the form of gold and silver bullion from the Indies. In the sixteenth century Henry VII and Elizabeth I of England joined Francis I of France as important patrons of master mariners who set sail for the West hoping to obtain wealth and national advantage from the voyages they sponsored. The dissolution of an earlier alliance between Spain and England in the wake of the latter nation's becoming Protestant, as well as the complex relationships between the ruling houses of the two countries, encouraged Elizabeth to turn her "sea dogs" (like Frobisher) loose upon the Spanish empire. English exploration was inextricably bound up with "singeing the Spanish beard" and with political hostility to Spain heightened by religious grievances. English adventurers often combined the roles of explorer, pirate, and even colonizer. The French had entered the American sweepstakes in the hopes of competing with the Spaniards and Portuguese. After Cartier's pioneering (and unsuccessful) voyages of 1534, 1535–6, and 1541–2, France was preoccupied with its internal dynastic struggles more than with overseas adventuring. The French government did not show much interest in North America until the end of the century, by which time France's Henry IV had stabilized the monarchy.

In both France and England, overseas investment by an emerging mercantile class took over gradually from the earlier efforts of intrepid mariners backed by the Crown. Cartier's third voyage marked for France the transition from public to private enterprise, and the 1576 voyage of Martin Frobisher in search of the Northwest Passage to the East demonstrated the new importance of mercantile investment to the English.

By the end of the sixteenth century Europe had established that there were no wealthy Aboriginal civilizations to be conquered on the eastern seaboard, nor any readily apparent sources of rich mineral wealth to be exploited. When it was clear that what the

Frobisher's quest for the Northwest Passage in Arctic waters inspired a series of explorers, mainly Englishmen backed by English capital, over the next 50 years. The best-known of these adventurers was Henry Hudson (d. 1611), who sailed under both English and Dutch auspices. On his last voyage in 1610 he entered Hudson Bay and navigated its eastern coastal waters southward to James Bay before his crew mutinied against him and cast him adrift on a small boat, never to be seen again. Most

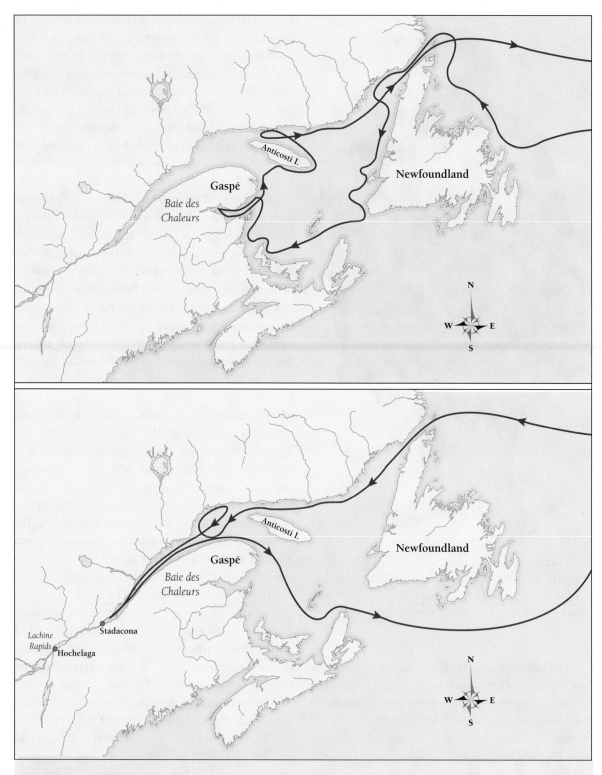

Top: Cartier's first voyage, 1534.
Bottom: Cartier's second voyage, 1535–6.

Three Baffin Island Inuit—a man, a woman, and her child—who were taken prisoner by Frobisher on his expedition to the Arctic in 1577. All three died a month or so after arriving in England. British Museum Images.

continent had in abundance were fish and furs, a more complex pattern of exploitation had to be developed that required the year-round presence of settlers. Both France and England shifted their energies from maritime thrusts to colonization.

The Impact of Disease on the Aboriginal Peoples

However rapidly European artifacts and animals (such as the horse) may have spread ahead of the newcomers, what dispersed across the continent with even greater rapidity was disease. North America in the sixteenth century was relatively isolated in a geographical sense. A host of

Map of the North Pole, 1595, by Gerardus Mercator. LAC, NMC-016097.

Henry Hudson

Like many another early European explorer, Hudson has left no paper trail beyond the events of the years at the high point of his reputation. We do not know where he was born or when, except that he was apparently an Englishman. In 1607 he was employed by the Muscovy Company (an English company trading with Russia) to seek a Northeast Passage to China across the North Pole, and he followed this voyage up with another in 1608, which sailed to the Russian Arctic but found nothing. This employment has been taken to mean that, whatever his background, he was regarded as highly competent. The Dutch East India Company hired him in 1609 to continue searching for the Northeast Passage in his ship *Half Moon*. His crew mutinied near Norway, and he changed his course as a result, crossing the Atlantic to search instead for the Northwest Passage and sailing up the Hudson River, which still bears his name.

Hudson subsequently was hired by a consortium of English merchants to search for a route to Asia through North America. His ship *Discovery* was manned by a number of experienced seamen, including Robert Bylot, who had earlier sailed with William Baffin. The crew was quite quarrelsome, and the voyage was replete with open conflict and at least one mutiny in which the mutineers backed down only at the last minute. As was the case with the notorious Captain Bligh less than two centuries later, Hudson was a better mariner than a manager of men. He took reprisals against the mutineers. For reasons unknown, he exhibited blatant and continual favouritism to one young man, who eventually turned against him in consort with several others. Hudson refused to pause to replenish provisions at Digges Island, apparently expecting to be in China very shortly. On 23 June 1611, shortly after beginning the voyage back from a winter on Hudson Bay and desperately short of food, the conspirators, led by the former favourite, cast Hudson, his son, and seven other men into a small shallop and cut it adrift. They persuaded Robert Bylot (if his story is to be believed) to pilot the ship back to England. Nothing more is known of the passengers on the shallop, but Bylot brought the *Discovery* back to England after a desperate battle with the Inuit at Digges Island in which several mutineers were killed. Most of what we know about the post-mutiny adventures of the *Discovery* comes to us via a narrative by one of the participants, the curiously named Abacuk Pricket. Bylot was pardoned by a court and went on to a distinguished Arctic career; the other mutineers were eventually tried on a charge of murder and acquitted. Hudson's widow, Katherine, impoverished by her husband's disappearance, had to fight hard to receive compensation from the East India Company, which called her "that troublesome and impatient woman." Finally, it allowed her to trade in India on her own account. She returned in 1622 with considerable wealth. Considering the discontent aboard the *Discovery*, Hudson's accomplishment in navigating through Hudson Strait and hundreds of miles into Hudson Bay was outstanding, although his leadership skills left much to be desired.

communicable diseases common to the "known world" of international trade and commerce either did not exist or were not so virulent on the North American continent, and the population had less immunity to them. Measles, smallpox, typhus, typhoid, mumps, and venereal disease—the last perhaps first contracted by Europeans in the Caribbean region—were as much European introductions as the gun and the horse. Although these diseases spread unusually quickly among an Aboriginal population that had little immunity to them, we must not think that communicable disease was totally unknown in early North America or that the pre-contact population lived in an Edenic state of robust health. In any case, trade and war, including the Aboriginal custom of replenishing population losses by adopting captive women and children, spread new and virulent diseases far beyond points of actual European contact. In fairness to the newcomers, they simply did not understand that their sexual promiscuity with First Nations women, or their taking Aboriginals back to Europe as prize specimens or informants, would be devastating to the Native populations. Europeans themselves had become callous about epidemic disease; it was part of life, and they did not understand the concepts of contagion and immunity. They had no reason to view the Aboriginal propensity for dying in captivity as something resulting from European intervention. For their part, the Aboriginals did not understand that crowding around a sick person

A confrontation between Inuit and English sailors, 1577. The artist, John White, was a member of Martin Frobisher's second expedition in search of a Northwest Passage. British Museum Images.

to offer affection only spread disease, or that sitting in a sweat lodge and then plunging into cold water was not an effective remedy for a disease like smallpox.

As James Axtell points out, the Aboriginal peoples used three techniques to respond to the demographic disaster. The first, the employment of warfare to replenish the population through captivity and adoption, was of mixed success, particularly when extended to the Europeans. While the process worked well in some ways, it also helped to spread disease, and it certainly increased the hostility of European settlers to the First Nations. The second strategy was intermarriage, which ignored colour bars and many of the social assumptions of European society. The third strategy was to move after depopulation, often joining with other tribes and peoples. The attraction of the Catholic reserves around

Montreal and Quebec after the 1640s was in large part a result of the population devastations of the preceding period throughout the Northeast region of the continent.

The introduction of new diseases renders all attempts to estimate the size of the Indigenous population at the time of first contact on the eastern seaboard highly problematic. Estimates for the population of North America north of the Rio Grande River at the beginning of the sixteenth century range as high as 18 million and beyond (Dickason, 2002: 9). We have already noted that the Indigenous pre-contact population of Canada was substantially larger than the most generous estimates of all the first-contact observers, most of whom spoke of great numbers but were not very specific. The east coast population had probably been seriously reduced by epidemic disease during the

Biography

Henri Membertou

Membertou claimed to have been a grown man when he met Jacques Cartier, which would mean that he had been born in the early years of the sixteenth century. Regardless of his exact birth date, Membertou was a venerable age when the French appeared at Port-Royal in 1605. He was the leader of a small band of Mi'kmaq whose hunting and fishing territory included Port-Royal. The opportunities afforded his band by the arrival of the Europeans were the envy of other Aboriginal leaders, and Membertou was a firm friend of the newcomers. He certainly looked like a leader. Father Biard described him as being taller and larger-limbed than his colleagues, and he apparently sported a beard. Much of what has been written about Membertou by the early chroniclers falls properly into the category of legend, but it was true that he was the first Aboriginal to be baptized in New France, as opposed to being carried to France and baptized there. The ceremony was performed by the newly arrived priest, Jessé Fléchéon, on 24 June 1610. All of Membertou's immediate family were baptized as well, without any proper preparation

because the missionary could not speak the Algonquian language and the Aboriginals could not speak enough French. Membertou was given the European name of the king, Henri. After his baptism Membertou appeared eager to become a proper Christian. He wanted the missionaries to learn Algonquian so that he could be properly educated. However, by 1611 he had contracted dysentery, one of the many infectious diseases brought by the Europeans, and by September of that year he was clearly very ill. He insisted on being buried among his ancestors, which annoyed the missionaries, but they gave him extreme unction anyway, and at the end he apparently requested burial among the French. He died on 18 September 1611. The closing year of his life illustrates a pattern often repeated among the Indigenous people who were "Christianized" by the first European missionaries. Unable to understand properly the precepts of Christianity, they could hardly have been said to be converted, and they often died shortly after baptism, succumbing to contagious diseases probably introduced by the missionaries themselves.

CANADA **Material Culture**

Astrolabe

The astrolabe, a device about six inches in diameter, was one of the tools that had allowed European navigators to determine their locations and keep their headings. They were critical for the dangerous Atlantic crossing, as well as to accurately create the maps that would allow them to return. The disk, or mater, was designed to hold a plate, called tympans, which, when used correctly, allowed the user to move the rete, or pointer, and determine coordinates. Most mariners' astrolabes would have only featured half of a scale in the upper half. This one, known as the "Champlain astrolabe" or the "Cobden astrolabe" (after the small community in eastern Ontario where it was found), already archaic in design by 1600, is divided into all four quadrants. Also unique is the ring (restored) shown here at the top of the device. Jose Galveia/Shutterstock.

Astrolabes were essential not just to the navigation of Europeans to and from "the New World," but also in their ability to map the spaces they were moving through when they arrived there. A simple, if multi-purpose tool, astrolabes allow their users to plot the moon, the Sun, and the stars, determine time if the latitude is known, and most importantly, determine latitude if time is known.

Very few seventeenth-century astrolabes still exist, making the "Cobden astrolabe," shown here, an object of note regardless of its origins. However, having been discovered in 1867, near to where Champlain was believed to have lost his own such device in 1613, the connection to Champlain has led to this particular astrolabe having a much more interesting "object biography."

Discovered at Green Lake, Ontario, by 14-year-old Edward Lee while clearing dead pine trees with his father, the astrolabe was found alongside two silver cups and a series of nesting copper pans, which the family sold to a peddler and melted down for scrap, respectively. There was also a rusted chain with a weight that Lee left behind. The astrolabe, thought to be a sort of compass, was bought by the steamboat captain Charles Overman for $10.

As Champlain became more prominent in the 1870s, so too did the astrolabe, and the connection between the two was made. Historians looking at Champlain's cartography connected some errors in the Green Lake region with a story of Champlain losing his own device in 1613, and as the device changed hands it became known as the "Champlain astrolabe." It was even included, albeit held upside down, in the 1915 statue of Champlain erected at Nepean Point in Ottawa. By 1942, it was donated to the New York Historical Society, which eventually sold the compass to the current owner, the Canadian Museum of Civilization. While the museum does not ascribe the astrolabe to Champlain, displaying it only as an astrolabe, it does draw the possible Champlain connection in the panels around it.

Regardless of its original owner, the connection to Champlain has given this astrolabe a much more interesting object biography, in the same way that

Continued...

Heinrich Schliemann's connection of his discoveries in Mycenae to Agamemnon and the Trojan War raised the profile of those objects as well. Despite its rarity, one of fewer than a hundred such artifacts discovered, the survival of the "Champlain astrolabe" to the present is very much attributed to the Champlain connection. And Green Lake has since been renamed Astrolabe Lake.

The construction of the narrative surrounding prominent historical figures and then linking them to artifacts was a common part of history and archaeology in the nineteenth century, which was focused on the prominent men of the time. In a 2004 *Beaver* article, Douglas Hunter argues the Jesuit angle, pointing out that when taken in context with the other objects discovered with it, this particular style of astrolabe with its four-quadrant scale would have been better suited to determining topographical features, and that such devices were used in mission construction by contemporary Jesuits.

Whether it was in fact Champlain's, or more likely, given the style of astrolabe and the other artifacts found with it, the instrument of a Jesuit missionary also lost in the same area, the original purpose of the astrolabe would have remained the same: the mapping and surveying of the North American interior. While an anonymous owner made the history of the object less interesting to nineteenth-century historians, modern scholars, particularly those who focus on the day-to-day lives of people, can garner a lot of information about the Europeans and their actions in the region from the discovery and examination of such objects.

sixteenth century, and demographic disaster preceded the Europeans right across the country. At the same time, this inadvertent introduction of the early pandemics should not be allowed to dominate the story of North America in the immediate pre-contact and early contact periods. In the first place, there was no "Golden Age" in pre-European America in which contagious disease did not exist at all. In the second, infectious antigens were not the sole cause of the ultimate reduction (in size and power) of the Aboriginal population. Europeans took deliberate actions apart from epidemics that led to significant reductions in Indigenous populations.

European Contact and the Development of Cultural Conflict

The intrusion of Europeans greatly altered the dynamics of First Nations development, while providing us with a somewhat misleading version of the nature of the population at the moment of contact and beyond. Recorded history was, after all, monopolized by those who had written languages and could make records. In the centuries following European arrival, virtually everything written about the Indigenous population of Canada was produced from the European perspective. That perspective, moreover, tended to involve considerable misunderstanding of First Nations culture and behaviour.

Whatever technological glitter Europe had (the extent of its actual superiority is debatable), it would prove relatively useless in the wilderness of the New World. For several centuries, Europeans in Canada who were successful in surviving adopted First Nations technology. European inventions may have helped give the intruders a sense of superiority, as did their emerging capitalist economic order, their new political organization into nation-states, and especially their Christian system of values and beliefs. These pronounced differences between Europeans and the Indigenous population prevented the visitors from fully comprehending the people they encountered. The Europeans quite unconsciously, often quite subtly, judged First Nations by their own standards.

At the same time, the process of early communication between Europeans and the Aboriginal peoples was a much more difficult business than we might think, or than the contemporary documents would suggest. Europeans and Aboriginals spoke different languages—a good many of them. In Europe, most countries lacked a single national language that was understood in every part of the country. Dialects had both regional and class origins. The great European sea captains, many of whom had connections at the royal court, were likely to have a different pronunciation and vocabulary than the common sailors, although technically both groups spoke the same language. The First Nations spoke several hundred different local languages in a myriad of dialects. Fifty different languages were spoken in what is now Canada, although most of these fell into a few language families. In what is now eastern Canada, the three principal language families were Algonquian, Iroquoian, and Siouan.

But the differences in language between two tribes speaking an Algonquian tongue might be as great as the differences between Spanish and Portuguese. Moreover, local patois would vary from place to place. The Aboriginal tongues were often difficult for Europeans to pronounce, and there were at the outset no dictionaries.

The niceties of grammar and the nuances of language frustrated both Natives and newcomers for centuries. Some Aboriginals who were educated in missionary schools learned to speak and understand European languages very well, and a few Europeans who grew up among the Aboriginals (sometimes willingly, often as

Document

Father Biard on the Mi'kmaq, 1616

In 1616 the Jesuit missionary Pierre Biard (c. 1567–1622), who had been at Port-Royal since 1611, wrote a "Relation," which was published in France, describing his experiences with the Aboriginals of the region. It was subsequently translated and republished by Reuben Gold Thwaites.

They are astonished and often complain that, since the French mingle with and carry on trade with them, they are dying fast and the population is thinning out. For they assert that, before this association and intercourse, all their countries were very populous and they tell how one by one the different coasts, according as they have begun to traffic with us, have been more reduced by disease; adding, that why the Armouchiquois do not diminish in population is because they are not at all careless. Thereupon they often puzzle their brains, and sometimes think that the French poison them, which is not true; at other times that they give poisons to the wicked and vicious of their nation to help them vent their spite upon some one. This last supposition is not without foundation; for we have seen them have some arsenic and sublimate which they say they bought from certain French Surgeons, in order to kill whomsoever they wished, and boasted that they had already experimented upon a captive, who (they said) died the day

after taking it. Others complain that the merchandise is often counterfeited and adulterated, and that peas, beans, bread, and other things that are spoiled are sold them; and that it is that which corrupts the body and gives rise to the dysentery and other diseases which always attack them in Autumn. This theory is likewise not offered without citing instances, for which they have often been upon the point of breaking with us, and making war upon us. Indeed there would be need of providing against these detestable murders by some suitable remedy if one could be found.

Nevertheless the principal cause of all these deaths and diseases is not what they say it is, but it is something to their shame; in the Summer time, when our ships come, they never stop gorging themselves excessively during weeks with various kinds of food not suitable to the inactivity of their lives; they get drunk, not only on wine but on brandy; so it is no wonder that they are obliged to endure some gripes of the stomach in the following Autumn. . . .

Continued...

These are their storehouses. Who is to take care of them when they go away? For, if they stay, their stores would soon be consumed; so they go somewhere else until the time of famine. Such are the only guards they leave. For in truth this is not a nation of thieves. Would to God that the Christians who go among them would not set them a bad example in this respect. But as it is now, if a certain Savage is suspected of having stolen anything he will immediately throw this fine defense in your teeth, We are not thieves, like you.

Source: Reuben Gold Thwaites, ed., *The Jesuit Relations and Allied Documents: Travels and Explanations 1610–1791*, 73 vols (Cleveland, 1896–1901), III, 105–9.

captives) became equally adept at the Native tongues. But most people came to communicate in new "pidgin" languages composed by reducing speech to its simplest elements and amalgamating parts of both European and Aboriginal languages. Pidgin languages were capable of sophistication as time went on, and they eliminated the potentially inflammatory business of preferring one people's language over another. One very venerable pidgin language was spoken on the coasts of the Gulf of St Lawrence, where Basque fishermen had traded with local Natives from the early sixteenth century. "Since their languages were completely different," wrote one observer in 1710, "they created a form of lingua franca composed of Basque and two different languages of the Indians, by means of which they could understand each other very well" (Bakker, 1989: 259). Marc Lescarbot in the early seventeenth century recorded that the Mi'kmaq spoke to the French in a simplified version of their language mixed with "much Basque." In the later fur trade in the interior of the continent, pidgin tongues were a complex amalgam of French, Gaelic, English, Cree, and Assiniboine.

Not surprisingly, as relations between Europeans and Aboriginal peoples became more formalized, the need for skilled official interpreters acquired a new urgency. An interpreter who was trusted by both sides in complex negotiations to translate accurately the meaning and nuances of language was a rare commodity and highly prized. As late as 1873, when Treaty No. 6 was being negotiated between the Canadian government and the Saskatchewan Cree, the question of interpreters remained a critical issue. The government had brought two interpreters of its own, and argued it was unnecessary to add another brought by the Cree. The Cree chief answered, "Very good. You keep your interpreters and we will keep ours. We will pay our own man and I already see that it will be well for us to do so" (Christensen, 2000: 229).

The First Nations economies did not produce political institutions on a European scale. Semi-sedentary people had no need for political organizations larger than the band, which was based on the consolidation of a few family units. Even where horticulture was developed, with its large semi-permanent villages, political structure was not complex by European standards. "Chiefs" were not kings. They may not even have been "head men" in any European sense. Such a concept of rulership was in most places introduced and imposed on the Indigenous population by the newcomers. As is now well known, the Aboriginal notion of property, especially involving land, was beyond the comprehension of the European. While some First Nations groups could conceive of territory as "belonging" to them, the concept was one of usage rather than of ownership. The Indigenous people erroneously identified as kings were quite happy to "sell" to the European newcomers land that neither they nor their people owned, at least as Europeans understood ownership.

Lacking much inclination to create hierarchical political organizations, the First Nations practised war according to different rules than those employed in Europe, where institutions of church and state went to war for "reasons of state." Aboriginal wars were mainly raids by a few warriors, conducted partly because success in battle was an important test of manhood. They were often used to capture women and children to replace those lost within the band. Individual prowess in battle was valued, while long-term military strategy and objectives were not. First Nations had their own military agendas, and were notoriously fickle allies from the European perspective. Only

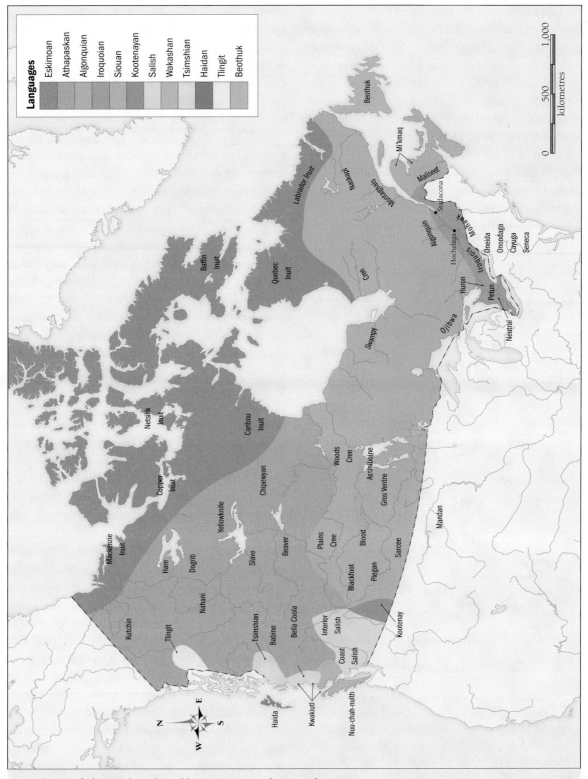

Distribution of Aboriginal peoples and language areas in the sixteenth century.

the Iroquois—who in the seventeenth century may have developed a militarily viable form of political organization partly based on European models—were able to compete with the newcomers and withstand their military power.

Nowhere was the gulf between First Nations and newcomers more apparent than in the spiritual realm. Aboriginal religious beliefs were complex, although not readily apparent to the outside observer. They were part of an intricate religio-magical world that the First Nations inhabited and shared with the flora and fauna. Given the hunting orientation of most groups, it is hardly surprising that animals were endowed with spiritual significance. The very act of food consump-

"Homme acadien": a Mi'kmaq hunter, hand-coloured etching, c. 1788–96, from original by Jacques Grasset de Saint-Sauveur, published in Tableaux des principaux peuples de l'Europe, de l'Asie, de l'Afrique, de l'Amérique et les découvertes des Capitaines Cook, La Pérouse, etc. *(Paris et Bordeaux, 1796–8). LAC, (R9266-3486) Peter Winkworth Collection of Canadiana.*

tion often acquired deep religious meaning, becoming a form of worship of the spirit world through everyday activity. Many peoples had legends about the origins of the world, and some may have believed in a single Creator. The mixture of authentic Aboriginal lore with European thought and missionary teaching has coloured First Nations legends and tales over the last 350 years. It has made it difficult—perhaps impossible—to separate one from the other. Formal religious ceremonies were not readily apparent to the visitors, except for the activities of the shamans, who claimed supernatural powers and engaged in several kinds of folk medicine ranging from herbal treatment to exorcism. Shamans were no more priests than other leaders were kings, but Europeans tended to consider their activities to be at the core of First Nations religion. The newcomers found it impossible to grasp that inanimate objects in nature could be considered to be alive and have their own powers, or that rituals connected with the ordinary round of daily life could have deep spiritual significance. That First Nations religion had no buildings, no clerical hierarchy, and no institutional presence thoroughly disoriented the Europeans.

Tolerance for alternative spiritual values and belief systems was hardly one of Europe's strong suits in the Age of Discovery. The period of European arrival in North America coincided with the Protestant Reformation and the Catholic Counter-Reformation. Christianity was undergoing profound alteration, with traditional Catholicism subjected to reform from both within and without. Protestants and Catholics alike were quite capable of fierce persecution of any deviation from official belief and practice. Both could agree that what was being encountered in Canada was pagan supernaturalism that needed to be uprooted as quickly as possible and replaced with a "true faith." That Europeans could not agree on the truth among themselves perplexed some First Nations people, such as the Iroquois, who were exposed to competing French, English, and Dutch missionaries.

The European intruders could not grasp the notion that Christianity was embedded in an intricately developed European value system, or that Indigenous religious beliefs and practices were integral to First Nations existence. Views of the world and of one's place

Document

Where the First People Came From:
A Cree Legend from the West Coast of James Bay

So then, I shall tell another legend. I'll tell a story, the legend about ourselves, the people, as we are called. Also I shall tell the legend about where we came from and why we came . . . , why we who are living now came to inhabit this land.

Now then, first I shall begin.

The other land was above, it is said. It was like this land which we dwell in, except that the life seems different; also it is different on account of its being cold and mild [here]. So then, this land where we are invariably tends to be cold.

So that is the land above which is talked about from which there came two people, one woman and one man, . . . they dwelt in that land which was above. But it was certainly known that this world where we live was there.

Now then at one time someone spoke to them, while they were in that land of theirs where they were brought up. He said to them, "Do you want to go see yonder land which is below?"

The very one about which they were spoken to is this one where we dwell.

"Yes," they said, "we will go there."

"The land," they were told, "is different, appears different from this one where we dwell in, which you dwell in now during your lifetime. But you will find it different there, should you go to see that land. It is cold yonder. And sometimes it is hot.

"It fluctuates considerably. If you wish to go there, however, you must go see the spider at the end of this land where you are. That is where he lives."

The spider, as he is called, that is the one who is the net-maker, who never exhausts his twine,—so they went to see him, who is called the spider.

Then he asked them, "Where do you want to go? Do you want to go and see yonder land, the other one which is below?"

"Yes," they said.

"Very well," said the spider. "I shall make a line so that I may lower you."

So then, he made a line up to,—working it around up to, up to the top.

"Not yet, not yet even half done," he said.

Then he spoke to them, telling them, better for him to let them down even before he finished it the length it should be.

Then he told them, "That land which you want to go and see is cold and sometimes mild. But there will certainly be someone there who will teach you, where you will find a living once you have reached it. He, he will tell you every thing so you will get along well."

So he made a place for them to sit as he lowered them, the man and the woman.

They got in together, into that thing which looked like a bag.

Then he instructed them what to do during their trip. "Only one must look," he said to them. "But one must not look until you have made contact with the earth. You may both look then."

So, meanwhile they went along, one looked. At last he caught sight of the land.

The one told the other, "Now the land is in sight."

The one told the other, "Now the rivers are in sight."

They had been told however, that "if one, . . . if they both look together, before they come to the land, they will go into the great eagle-nest and they will never be able to get out and climb down from there."

That's where they will be. That's what they were told.

Continued...

Then the one told the other, "Now the lakes are in sight. Now the grass."

Then they both looked before they arrived, as they were right at the top of the trees. Then they went sideways for a short while, then they went into the great eagle-nest. That's where they went in, having violated their instructions. . . .

Then the bear arrived.

So he said to them, . . . and they said to him, "Come and help us."

The bear didn't listen for long; but then he started to get up on his hind legs to go and see them. Also another one, the wolverine as he is called. They made one trip each as they brought them down.

But the bear was followed by those people.

That was the very thing which had been said to them, "You will have someone there who will teach you to survive."

This bear, he taught them everything about how to keep alive there.

It was there that these people began to multiply from one couple, the persons who had come from another land. They lived giving birth to their children generation after generation. That is us right up until today. That is why we are in this country.

And by-and-by the White People began to arrive as they began to reach us people, who live in this country.

That is as much as I shall tell.

Source: C. Douglas Ellis, ed. and trans., *Cree Legends and Narratives from the West Coast of James Bay* (Winnipeg: University of Manitoba Press, 1995), 3–7.

in it were as integral to life for Aboriginals as they were for Europeans, and the way in which First Nations related spiritually to their environment was a critical part of their culture. Europe could not convert First Nations to Christianity without undermining the very basis of their existence. Naturally, the First Nations resisted.

While commenting on the freedom that children were allowed, European observers of every First Nations group in northern North America from coast to coast also wrote that women were badly exploited. European society at the time could hardly be called liberal in its treatment of women. What the newcomers saw as exploitation reflected their inability to comprehend the divisions of labour within a warrior society. Men hunted and fought, while women were responsible for just about everything else. Interestingly enough, when European women were captured by raiding parties and integrated into Aboriginal life, many chose to remain with their captors instead of accepting repatriation back into colonial society. Those captives who were brought home and who wrote about their experiences emphasized that the Aboriginals had a strong sense of love and community and offered—as one set of repatriates acknowledged—"The most perfect freedom,

the ease of living, [and] the absence of those cares and corroding solicitudes which so often prevail with us" (Axtell, 2001: 213).

Almost from the outset, European newcomers to Canada had two contradictory responses to the peoples they were contacting and describing. On the one hand, much of what they saw in First Nations life, particularly beyond mere superficial observation, struck them as admirable. The First Nations exhibited none of the negative features of capitalistic society. On the other hand, there was the equally powerful image of the First Nations as brutal savages and barbarians, particularly in the context of war. This dichotomy of response was particularly keen among the missionaries, who kept trying to "civilize" the First Nations by converting them to Christianity and forcibly educating them in European ways. Mère Marie de l'Incarnation, the head of the Ursuline School for girls at Quebec, wrote of her charges in 1668 that there was "docility and intelligence in these girls, but when we are least expecting it, they clamber over our wall and go off to run with their kinsmen in the woods, finding more to please them there than in all the amenities of our French houses" (Marshall, 1967: 341).

In the eighteenth century, an idealized and romanticized view of Aboriginal society was used by many European philosophers as a literary convention and fictional device for criticizing contemporary European society. As Peter Moogk has pointed out, conditions of press censorship, particularly in France, made it advisable to use fictitious foreigners, including Amerindians, to express negative opinions about church and state (Moogk, 2000: 48–9). The first such character probably was Baron de Lahontan's "Huron" named Adario, who in 1703 observed that the Ten Commandments were routinely ignored in France, while the Aboriginals practised innocence, love, and tranquility of mind. Lahontan's books went through numerous editions and led to the Enlightenment notion of the *bon sauvage* advanced by Voltaire and Rousseau. The First Nations

Historic Sites

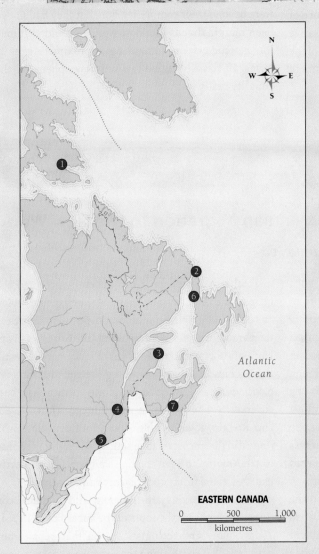

1. **Frobisher National Historic Site:** On Kodlunarn Island in Frobisher Bay (close to Iqaluit). This tiny island has the remains of Martin Frobisher's habitation and the smelting plant he operated between 1576 and 1578.
2. **L'Anse aux Meadows National Historic Park:** At the northern tip of Newfoundland; contains the remains of seven buildings, cook pits, and a smithy.
3. **Gaspé, Quebec:** The site of a 30-foot granite cross commemorating the cross erected by Jacques Cartier in 1534.
4. **Cartier-Brébeuf National Historic Park:** Facing the St Charles River, where Cartier wintered his three ships in 1535–6.
5. **McGill University (Montreal):** A plaque marks the site of the village of Hochelaga.
6. **Port au Choix (Newfoundland) National Historic Park:** Burial sites of the "red paint people" who inhabited the region about 5,000 years ago.
7. **Port-Royal National Historic Site:** Reconstruction of the "habitation" and other buildings of the first French colony established on the banks of the Annapolis River by Champlain in 1605.

EASTERN CANADA

0   500   1,000
kilometres

Atlantic Ocean

possessed none of the worst traits of European capitalistic society, such as covetousness and rapaciousness; and they revered freedom, while eschewing private property. What relationship the "noble savage" bore to the realities of existence in North America is another matter entirely.

Europeans would blunder on for centuries in their attempts to come to terms with the Indigenous peoples of North America. The First Nations would prove tenacious in maintaining their own identity and culture in the face of much effort to Europeanize them, but they lacked the physical power to prevent either constant encroachment on their territory, or the continual undermining of the basic physical and spiritual substance of their way of life. The cultural contact between Native and newcomer truly was a tragedy. Reconciliation of the two cultures proved quite impossible, and the failure of reconciliation resounds still today.

Conclusion

By the mid-1620s the first period of European intrusion into what is now Canada had been completed. Exploration of the new continent's eastern seaboard was done, and Europe could construct a fairly decent map of its coastline. What lay beyond was beginning to be investigated. Europe was on the verge of deciding that major transplantations of people were going to be necessary if this new northern land were to be exploited. As for the Indigenous population, they had been buffeted by epidemic disease, the causes of which were beyond their comprehension, but they had not yet been marginalized. The First Nations could still meet the newcomers on something approximating equal terms. In retrospect, we can see how ephemeral this equality really was.

Historiography

The Changing History of Paleo-Indian Migration to the New World

Emőke J.E. Szathmáry, University of Manitoba

The prevailing archaeological paradigm since 1950 stated that "Paleo-Indians," the putative ancestors of all the Indigenous peoples of the Americas excepting "Eskimos" and Aleuts, entered North America from Asia by crossing the Bering land bridge during the Wisconsin glaciation. From Alaska they moved south through an ice-free corridor on the eastern side of the Rocky Mountains into the central Great Plains. Their earliest cultural remains, called "Clovis," date to 11,500–11,000 radiocarbon years ago (RCYBP). Clovis sites exist across the United States, indicating that the ancestors spread rapidly once they were clear of glaciers.

Challenges to this paradigm accumulated after the 1970s. Though several sites in the Americas appear to be pre-Clovis in age, it was only in 1997, after eminent archaeologists had examined remains at Monte Verde

in southern Chile, that it was generally accepted that people had entered the western hemisphere before 12,500 RCYBP (Meltzer et al., 1997). By then, the rest of the paradigm was also unravelling. The Cordilleran and Laurentide glaciers were shown to have merged east of the Rockies in Alberta, blocking the corridor for some 6,000 years, and north of 60° N the corridor had been covered by Laurentide ice even longer (Jackson and Duk-Rodkin, 1996). With the corridor impassable, what route did the ancestors take south? When did they enter North America to have reached southern Chile so early? Did they come from other places than Asia?

These questions are not new, and evidence continues to show that the roots of the ancestors lie in Asia. Today, many archaeologists reason that people must have travelled south along the northwest coast of North

America. Un-glaciated areas occurred on Haida Gwaii, for example, and plant as well as animal remains have been found in such refugia. However, movement down the Pacific coast would have been very difficult during the last glacial maximum, between 28,000–12,000 RCYBP. Such travel would have been more likely as the glaciers began to retreat. Unfortunately, the rising sea levels that accompanied de-glaciation have also submerged ancient shorelines, leaving no evidence of early journeys southward by foot or by boat. The few sites without dating controversies, for example, On Your Knees Cave on Prince of Wales Island in southeastern Alaska, are dated around 9,800 RCYBP.

Changing ideas about the likely route south have been accompanied by changes in our understanding of Beringia, which was originally conceptualized as the lands now submerged under the Bering Sea, Bering Strait, and the Chukchi Sea. With demonstration that the lands adjacent to these areas were also un-glaciated, the boundaries of Beringia expanded west and to the east. Today, Beringia is regarded as extending from the Verkhoyansk Mountains of Siberia to the Mackenzie River basin of Yukon. This vast plain sustained a mosaic of plant types, with steppe-tundra and shrub tundra in specific regions, and some tree species in local areas (Hoffecker et al., 2014). The vegetation supported large and small mammals, and these supported human life. The Yana Rhinoceros Horn site at 71° N is reliably dated at 28,000 RCYBP in Western Beringia, but the 23,500 RCYBP age of modified mammoth bones used as tools at Bluefish Caves, Yukon, in Eastern Beringia continues to be doubted by many archaeologists (Morlan, 2003). Several sites are dated between these extremes in Alaska, falling between 13,000–11,000 RCYBP.

Also changing is the view that Beringia was just a "bridge" to be crossed in the ancestors' trek south. Theories of temporally sequential migratory waves into the Americas as suggested by Greenberg et al. (1986), for example, have focused on crossing from Asia to America. An alternate scenario considers that Beringia could have been an ice-bounded home to hunting bands that occupied it for several millennia during the last glacial maximum. In this regard, genetic studies of living peoples have been persuasive. The five haplogroups of mitochondrial DNA (mtDNA) that are diagnostic of Native American ancestry have yielded mutations over time, as has the Y chromosome (NRY). Estimates of the ages of these new variants, which are distributed widely in the Americas, overlap: 16,600–11,200 years ago for mtDNA (Tamm et al., 2007), and 15,000–12,000 years ago for NRY (Zegura et al., 2004). The time depths suggest that these markers arose in a population isolated on Beringia, after which the ancestors dispersed into the Americas. These findings reinforce earlier conclusions based on classical genetic markers, especially regarding the ancestry of Eskimos and Na-Dene. Populations south of the glaciers, as pre-Clovis sites indicate, would differentiate genetically as would their cognates in Beringia, yielding differences among their descendants (Szathmary, 1996; Bonatto and Salzano, 1997), while retaining their American (i.e., Beringian) genetic identity.

The future will tell if such deductions are correct. A recent study of nuclear DNA, for example, supported the notion of three migratory waves into the Americas at different times (Reich et al., 2012). Assuming the adequacy of samples and their analyses, the apparent conflict in colonization scenarios may just be a consequence of focusing on different aspects of a migratory process. In the meantime, we must await direct archaeological evidence that could tell us when, where, and how the ancestors moved south from Beringia.

References

Bonatto, Sandro L., and Francisco M. Salzano. 1997. "A Single and Early Migration for the Peopling of the Americas Supported by Mitochondrial DNA Sequence Data." *Proceedings of the National Academy of Sciences* 94: 1866–71.

Hoffecker, John F., Scott A. Elias, and Dennis H. O'Rourke. 2014. "Out of Beringia?" *Science* 343: 979–80.

Jackson, Lionel E., Jr, and Alejandra Duk-Rodkin. 1996. "Quaternary Geology of the Ice-free Corridor: Glacial Controls on the Peopling of the New World." In Takeru Akazawa and Emőke J.E. Szathmáry, eds,

Continued...

Prehistoric Mongoloid Dispersals, 214–27. Oxford: Oxford University Press.

Meltzer, David J., et al. 1997. "On the Pleistocene Antiquity of Monte Verde, Southern Chile." *American Antiquity* 62: 659–63.

Morlan, Richard E. 2003. "Current Perspectives on the Pleistocene Archaeology of Eastern Beringia." *Quaternary Research* 60: 123–32.

Reich, David, et al. 2012. "Reconstructing Native American Population History." *Nature* 488:370–4.

Szathmáry, Emőke J.E.1996. "Ancient Migrations from Asia to North America." In Takeru Akazawa and Emőke J.E. Szathmáry, eds, *Prehistoric Mongoloid Dispersals*, 149–64. Oxford: Oxford University Press.

Tamm, Erika, et al. 2007. "Beringian Standstill and Spread of Native American Founders." *PloS ONE* 2, 9: e829. doi:10.1371/journal.pone.0000829.

Zegura, Stephen L., Tatiana M. Karafet, Lev. A. Zhivitovsky, and Michael F. Hammer. 2004. "High-resolution SNPs and Microsatellite Haplotypes Point to a Single, Recent Entry of Native American Y Chromosomes into the Americas." *Molecular Biology and Evolution* 21:64–75.

Short Bibliography

Axtell, James. *Natives and Newcomers: The Cultural Origins of North America*. New York, 2001. A series of penetrating essays by North America's leading historian of cultural contact.

Bailey, A.G. *The Conflict of European and Eastern Algonkin Cultures, 1534–1700: A Study in Civilization*, 2nd edn. Toronto, 1969. First produced as a doctoral dissertation in 1934, this pioneering study is one of the classics of the field, still as relevant as ever.

Benton, Lauren. *A Search for Sovereignty: Law and Geography in European Empires, 1400–1900*. Cambridge, 2010. This work, which looks at European empires in terms of geography and law, discusses how the two merge and deviate to create debates in both the colonies and their motherlands.

Dickason, Olive Patricia. *Canada's First Nations: A History of Founding Peoples from Earliest Times*, 3rd edn. Toronto, 2002. Easily the best general survey of the history of the First Nations, current and full of detail. A revised and updated abridged edition—*A Concise History of Canada's First Nations*—was first published in 2006 and a third edition, co-authored by William Newbigging, appeared in 2015.

A fourth edition of Dickason's original work, with David T. McNab, came out in 2009 with updates to that year and a new concluding chapter.

Fagan, Brian. *The Great Journey: The Peopling of Ancient America*. New York, 1987. A bit dated, but still the best account of the prevailing scholarly interpretations of the subject.

Fitzhugh, William, and Elizabeth Ward. *Vikings: The North American Saga*. Washington and London, 2000. A splendidly illustrated and authoritative account of the Norse in America.

Harris, R. Cole, ed. *Historical Atlas of Canada*, vol. 1. Toronto, 1987. This is one of the great collaborative works of scholarship in Canada, presenting a visual and cartographic record of the period to 1800.

Hoffeker, John F., and Scott A. Elias. *Human Ecology of Beringia*. New York, 2007. This book addresses the debates surrounding the environment and archaeology of Beringia, and presents an interpretation of how people lived and moved through that now submerged territory.

Hunter, Douglas. *Half-Moon: Henry Hudson and the Voyage that Redrew the Map of the New World*.

New York, Berlin, London, 2009. A new look at one of the most elusive figures of early European exploration.

Jaenen, Cornelius. *Friend and Foe: Aspects of French–Amerindian Culture Contact in the Sixteenth and Seventeenth Centuries*. Toronto, 1976. An early classic, still the best single work on the early contact between the French and the First Nations.

Nuffield, Edward. *The Discovery of Canada*. Vancouver, 1996. A recent survey.

Paul, Daniel. *We Were Not the Savages: A Micmac Perspective on the Collision of European and Aboriginal Civilization*. Halifax, 1993. Probably the first analysis of early cultural contact in Canada written by a First Nations scholar from a First Nations perspective.

Reid, John. *Acadia, Maine, and New Scotland: Marginal Colonies in the Seventeenth Century*. Toronto, 1981.

A stimulating comparative approach to the early settlement of the Maritimes.

Seed, Patricia. *Ceremonies of Possession in Europe's Conquest of the New World, 1492–1640*. Cambridge, 1995. More important than its title suggests, this book distinguishes the various national approaches to conquest taken by the major European nations.

Trigger, Bruce. *Natives and Newcomers: Canada's "Heroic Age" Reconsidered*. Montreal and Kingston, 1986. A revisionist account of early Canadian culture contact by Canada's leading expert.

Trudel, Marcel. *The Beginnings of New France 1524–1663*. Toronto, 1975. Still the authoritative account of the early years of New France, written by a scholar who spent his lifetime working on the period.

Wright, J.V. *A History of the Native People of Canada*, 3 vols. Ottawa, 1995–2000. An encyclopedic survey of Canada's ancient history.

Study Questions

1. Give three examples of ways in which the First Nations lived in a "reciprocal relationship with nature."

2. What realities did the various First Nations cultures share in common?

3. Explain the basic cultural, religious, and political factors behind the European misinterpretation of the First Nations.

4. Comment on the account from Cartier's *Voyages*, "Jacques Cartier Meets with Aboriginal Peoples, 1534." Did Cartier make any assumptions about the Aboriginal peoples that would lead to cultural conflicts later? Explain.

5. What can we learn about cultural conflict from Karlsefni's encounter with the Skraelings? What was the principal cause of the conflict between the Norse and the Skraelings?

6. On what grounds could you defend the European intrusion into North America? Identify three grounds and explain each of them.

Visit the companion website for *A History of the Canadian Peoples*, fifth edition for further resources.

www.oupcanada.com/Bumsted5e

2

Europe Settles In:
Newfoundland, Acadia,
New France

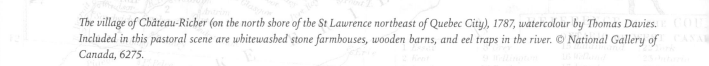

The village of Château-Richer (on the north shore of the St Lawrence northeast of Quebec City), 1787, watercolour by Thomas Davies. Included in this pastoral scene are whitewashed stone farmhouses, wooden barns, and eel traps in the river. © National Gallery of Canada, 6275.

Timeline

1598 Marquis de la Roche de Mesgouez establishes colony on Sable Island.

1605 Settlement established by Pierre Du Gua De Monts moves to Port-Royal.

1607 Port-Royal abandoned.

1611 First French priests arrive in Acadia.

1627 Cardinal Richelieu establishes the Company of One Hundred Associates.

1628 The Kirke brothers capture Quebec.

1632 Treaty of St-Germain-en-Laye restores Canada and Acadia to France.

1633 Champlain returns to the St Lawrence.

1634 The Jesuits set up permanent missions in Huronia.

1635 Champlain dies.

1639 The Jesuits establish Ste-Marie-aux-Hurons.

1640 The Iroquois begin attacking the Huron.

1642 Montreal is established.

1645 Company of One Hundred Associates surrenders its monopoly to local interests. Madame La Tour surrenders Fort La Tour.

1647 Canada adopts government by central council. First horse arrives.

1649 Iroquois destroy St-Louis and St-Ignace. Martyrdom of Jean de Brébeuf and Gabriel Lalemant.

1654 English capture Acadia.

1659 Bishop Laval arrives in Canada.

1660 First pipe organ brought to Canada.

1663 Earthquake strikes Canada. French royal government takes over New France and institutes the Coutume de Paris.

1664 Carignan-Salières Regiment arrives in New France. Jean Talon arrives as first intendant.

1665 First contingent of *filles de roi* arrives. Shipment of 12 horses arrives.

1666 First census in New France.

1667 Peace treaty with Iroquois.

1668 Petit Sèminaire founded.

1685 "Code Noir" defines slavery.

1701 Great Peace with Iroquois.

1703 Counseil Sovereign reorganized.

1711 Edict of Marly. British invasion of Quebec fails.

1719 Colony gets Admiralty Court.

1733 Iron forges at St Maurice established.

1740 Duplessis case confirms Aboriginal slavery.

1759 Battle of Plains of Abraham.

The First European Communities

When generations of painful experience taught Europeans that there was no quick road to wealth by exploiting the Indigenous peoples or the resource base of North America, hopes turned to transplanting Europeans who could take advantage of fish and furs. This shift occurred at the beginning of the seventeenth century. A variety of motives jostled in the minds of the early promoters of settlement, few of whom ever planned to set foot on North American soil. National advantage, religion, humanitarianism, greed, personal ambition, and sheer fantasy were present in various combinations. European monarchs and their supporters were flattered by the "enlarging of Dominions." Missions to the First Nations and the possibilities of refuge from religious persecution at home excited the pious. Many a promoter saw colonization as a way to rid Europe of unwanted paupers and petty criminals. Investors were tempted with talk of titles and large land grants. In the pursuit of great profits, common sense was easily lost. Although large-scale colonization activities were begun by the English in Virginia in 1607, the first ventures undertaken in the northern latitudes typically were more modest. They consisted mainly of trading posts and fishing settlements.

English familiarity with Newfoundland led London merchants to attempt colonization there beginning in 1610. The London and Bristol Company for the Colonization of Newfoundland (usually known as the Newfoundland Company) was organized by 48 subscribers who invested £25 each. The plan was that permanent settlers employed by the company would quickly dominate the fishery over those who came in the spring and went home in the autumn. Europe was desperately short of a protein food for the poor, and dried cod found a ready market, especially in Catholic countries. The first settlement of the company was established by John Guy (d. 1629), who led 40 colonists from Bristol to Cupid's Cove on Conception Bay in July 1610, only months after the company was granted the entire island. The venture was funded by sale of stock. The company did not appreciate how difficult local agriculture would be, given the soil and the climate, or how unlikely it was in the vast expanses of the New World that settlers could be kept permanently as landless employees labouring solely for the profit of their masters.

The Newfoundland Company's fishing settlements prospered no more than did those of courtiers like George Calvert, First Baron Baltimore (1579/80–1632), who began a plantation at Avalon in 1623. Calvert discovered to his surprise, as he wrote his monarch in 1629, that "from the middest of October, to the middest of May there is a sadd face of wynter upon all this land, both sea and land so frozen for the great part of the tyme that they are not penetrable, no plant or vegetable thing appearing out of the earth untill it be about the beginning of May nor fish in the sea besides the ayre so intolerable cold, as it is hardly to be endured" (Cell, 1982: 295–6). Not long after penning this complaint, he left for Virginia. In 1632 Calvert was granted the land north of the Potomac River that would become Maryland.

The French were marginally more successful than the English at establishing colonies in the northern regions, both in Acadia (the region vaguely bounded by the St Lawrence to the north, the Atlantic Ocean to the east and south, and the St Croix River to the west) and in Canada (the St Lawrence Valley). An early effort by the Marquis de La Roche de Mesgouez (c. 1540–1606) on Sable Island failed dismally, with rebellious settlers murdering their local leaders over the winter of 1602–3. The island was subsequently evacuated. A similar result occurred at a settlement at the mouth of the Saguenay River. In May 1604 Pierre Du Gua de Monts (1558?–1628) arrived on the Nova Scotia coast with a young draftsman named Samuel de Champlain (c. 1570–1635). The two men were searching for a suitable site to establish a settlement, a condition of de Monts's grant of a trading monopoly in the region. They tried first on an island in the St Croix River. In 1605 the settlement was moved to Port-Royal in the Annapolis Basin, where de Monts built a habitation, a supposed replica of which still exists today as a historic site. In 1606 the Paris lawyer Marc Lescarbot (c. 1570–1642) joined the colony and wrote a narrative of its development, published in 1609 as *Histoire de la Nouvelle France*. In this work Lescarbot noted the foundation of L'Ordre de Bon Temps in 1607, a sort of dining club with extemporaneous entertainment. He also described the masque he wrote for it (the first stage play composed and performed in North America). The colonists were obliged to leave in 1607 when de Monts was forced to relinquish his monopoly, but a French presence would continue in Acadia from the first establishment of Port-Royal, usually in the form of a handful of individuals trading with the First Nations.

As for Samuel de Champlain, he headed up the St Lawrence in 1608 to found a new trading post for de Monts at Stadacona. Another habitation was erected, this one including three buildings of two storeys—connected by a gallery around the outside, "which proved very convenient," wrote Champlain—surrounded by a moat and palisades. Champlain provided a careful drawing of this habitation in his *Voyages*. He was forced to put down a conspiracy and face a devastating attack of scurvy in the first year. The post survived, however, and Champlain gradually allied himself with the local First Nations, who supplied him with furs and drew the French into war against the Iroquois. Champlain had little alternative to an alliance against the Iroquois, and they became mortal enemies of the French.

Only about 50 Frenchmen resided on the St Lawrence by 1615. Among the early settlers, only Louis

Champlain's drawing of the habitation at Port-Royal, built in 1605 on the north shore of the Annapolis Basin. The parts of the complex are identified in an accompanying key. For example, building A was the artisans' quarters, and B was a platform for cannon. Champlain's own quarters were in building D. LAC, C-7033.

Hébert (1595?–1627), who came to Quebec in 1617 after service as a surgeon at Port-Royal, showed an interest in cultivating the land. But Hébert was most useful for his medical and apothecary skills; the trading company actually attempted to discourage him from agriculture. Not until 1618—when Champlain outlined a grand scheme for the colonization of New France in reports to the King and the French Chamber of Commerce—did anything approaching the plans of the Newfoundland Company enter the French vision. Earlier French activities, including those of Champlain himself, had been underfinanced by a succession of individual entrepreneurs and small syndicates. Trading posts, rather than settlement colonies, were the goal.

Until 1618, Champlain had served as an agent for others rather than as a colonial promoter in his own right. In that year, however, he combined arguments for major investment with a scheme designed to appeal to the imperial pretensions of the Crown. New France and the St Lawrence not only held the possibility of a short route to Asia but could produce "a great and permanent trade" in such items as fish, timber, whale oil, and furs. The annual income was projected at 5,400,000 livres, virtually none of it coming from agriculture and less than 10 per cent coming from furs. Champlain requested that priests, 300 families of four people each, and 300 soldiers be sent to his base on the St Lawrence. Amazingly enough, the French response was enthusiastic, and Louis XIII instructed the syndicate employing Champlain to expedite his plans. The partners and Champlain, however, were unable to agree upon terms or to make any progress in establishing the colony. Not until 1627, when Cardinal Richelieu assumed supervision of New France and established the Company of One Hundred Associates, did Champlain's grandiose schemes receive substantial backing.

Document

The Order of Good Cheer

It would be tedious to attempt to particularise all that was done among us during the winter [of 1606–7] . . . . But I shall relate how, in order to keep our table joyous and well-provided, an Order was established at the board of the said M. de Poutrincourt, which was called the Order of Good Cheer, originally proposed by Champlain. To this Order each man of the said table was appointed Chief Steward in his turn, which came round once a fortnight. Now this person had the duty of taking care that we were all well and honourably provided for. This was so well carried out that, though the epicures of Paris often tell us that we had no Rue aux Ours [meat-market district] over there, as a rule we made as good cheer as we could have in this same Rue aux Ours and at less cost. For there was no one who, two days before his turn came, failed to go hunting or fishing, and to bring back some delicacy in addition to our ordinary fare. So well was this carried out that never at breakfast did we lack some savoury meat of flesh or fish, and still less at our midday or evening meals; for that was our chief banquet, at which the ruler of the feast or chief butler, whom the savages called Atoctegic, having had everything prepared by the cook, marched in, napkin on shoulder, wand of office in hand, and around his neck the collar of the Order, carrying each a dish. The same was repeated at dessert, though not always with so much pomp. And at night, before giving thanks to God, he handed over to his successor in the charge the collar of the order, with a cup of wine, and they drank to each other.

Source: Marc Lescarbot, *The History of New France*, trans. W.L. Grant, intro. H.P. Biggar (Toronto: Champlain Society, 1911), II, 342–3.

Newfoundland

Newfoundland represented the British presence in the Atlantic region before the establishment of Nova Scotia in 1713. Neither John Guy's settlement of Newfoundland in 1610 nor a series of successors sponsored by the Newfoundland Company and private promoters were spectacularly successful. But by the 1660s several communities of permanent settlers totalling 1,500 had taken hold along the rocky coast of the "English Shore." The society of these settlements was considerably more elaborate than historians once assumed, consisting of servants, planter employers, and a planter gentry of literate merchants. Incomes from fishing were reasonably good, and the local communities were no less stable than comparable ones in New England. The elite was dominated by the Kirke family, which was active in the Canadian trade (and buccaneering in the 1620s) and in the Newfoundland sack trade of the 1630s and 1640s, later becoming original investors in the Hudson's Bay Company. In 1675 the widow of Sir David Kirke and her son operated 10 fishing boats, and the Kirke family had 17 boats, employing 81 crew members. Indeed, on the English Shore of Newfoundland, as in many other early communities of North America, widows found opportunities for autonomy in business enterprises that they would not have enjoyed at home. Although Newfoundland had been one of the earliest sites in the New World for English colonization, the focus had quickly shifted south to New England, where the English by 1650 had developed a number of successful colonies with a total population in excess of 100,000. The "newfound" land continued to provide enormous wealth to the British Empire in the form of fish, however, while remaining an unorganized jurisdiction and a marginal area of English settlement.

In the seventeenth century, almost all the year-round residents were of English origin, chiefly from the West Country counties of Cornwall, Devon, and Dorset. As late as 1732, 90 per cent of the permanent population remained English, but most of the eighteenth-century additions came from southern Ireland through the increasing links between Newfoundland and the Irish ports of Waterford and Cork. One census of wintering inhabitants in 1753 showed 2,668 Irish and 1,916 English. The Irish were being pushed out of Ireland by famine and unemployment, and were attracted to Newfoundland by the cheap fare for the voyage combined with work prospects. By 1750 Newfoundland had become a conduit by which Irish Catholics made their way to North America, and it remained so until 1815. Not all who jumped ship on the island remained in residence there.

Parallel to the increase of permanent population in Newfoundland came a shift in fishing practice. After 1714 the English summer visitors abandoned the inshore fishery and turned instead to fishing directly from the offshore banks. By 1750 the inshore fishery was controlled by local residents, but by this time there were already signs of depletion of the inshore fish stocks. The result was not conservation but diversification, with many Newfoundlanders moving into the seal fishery.

The French Maritime Region to 1667

In the Atlantic region, overtones of European imperial rivalries could be detected in the complex conflicts of the seventeenth century, although local factors were equally important. Much of the confusing history of Acadia after 1624 is wrapped up in the activities of the La Tour family, which illustrate the fluid and violent nature of the period. In 1629, when Quebec was captured by the Kirkes, a tiny trading post on Cape Sable (at the southwestern tip of present-day Nova Scotia) was all that was left of the French presence in North America. It was headed by Charles de Saint-Étienne de La Tour (1598–1666). His father, Claude de La Tour (c. 1570–after 1636), had already returned to France to plead for assistance, but on the return voyage was captured and taken to England, where he quickly made himself at home. Accepted at court, he married one of the Queen's ladies-in-waiting. (The English Queen Henrietta was a French princess and surrounded by women from France.) Claude also accepted Nova Scotia baronetcies for himself and his son from Sir William Alexander, a Scottish courtier, who had been granted Nova Scotia in 1621 by James VI of Scotland (who also was James I of England).

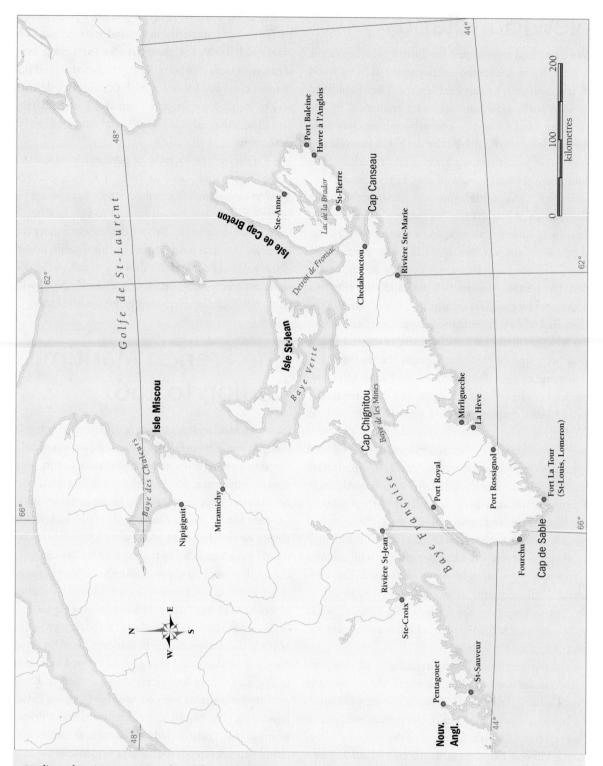

Acadia and environs to 1670. Adapted from A.H. Clark, Acadia: The Geography of Early Nova Scotia to 1760 *(Madison: University of Wisconsin Press, 1968), 76.*

Sir David Kirke

Sir David Kirke, c. 1597–1654. Courtesy of the Centre for Newfoundland Studies Archives (MF231–411), St John's. Image modified by Wendy Churchill, 1999.

Sir David Kirke (*c.* 1597–1654) was one of the notorious Kirke brothers who captured Quebec in 1629. This incident is probably the only one for which most Canadians remember him—if they remember at all. But there was more to his complex North American career than one buccaneering expedition. Kirke was the son of an English merchant who worked out of the French port of Dieppe, and David was apparently born in the French town. In 1627 Kirke's father was one of a consortium of English merchants who financed an expedition, led by David, to drive the French from Canada. David commanded a fleet of three vessels and was accompanied by several of his brothers; hence the common reference to the "Kirke brothers" seizing Quebec. He apparently sailed with a fleet carrying Scottish settlers to Nova Scotia. In 1627 Champlain refused to surrender and Kirke did not press the issue. In the Gulf of St Lawrence, however, his ships met and defeated a French fleet, and Kirke returned to Europe with considerable booty.

The French in Paris protested because they regarded the Kirkes as French citizens. Kirke was rewarded by the British with the exclusive right to trade and settle in Canada, to which Sir William Alexander objected, however. Kirke and Alexander nevertheless negotiated a compromise to establish an Anglo-Scots colony at Tadoussac. The fleet sent out for this purpose (six ships, three pinnaces) also carried Claude de La Tour back to Nova Scotia. Kirke learned from a French deserter of the parlous state of the French garrison in Quebec, and this time Champlain surrendered. The Kirkes not only evacuated the colony but seized all the furs stored in Quebec. They subsequently attempted to work the fur trade with the assistance of a number of bushlopers, including Étienne Brûlé. Quebec was returned to the French by the Treaty of Saint-Germain-en-Laye in 1632, but Kirke was knighted a year later for his services to the Crown.

His North American activities had made Kirke aware of Newfoundland, and in 1637 he was part of a consortium (the Company of Adventurers to Newfoundland) that was made proprietor of that island. In 1639 he became first governor of Newfoundland and moved into Lord Baltimore's house at Ferryland. The four Kirke brothers were made English citizens at about the same time. Sir David began to recolonize Newfoundland, particularly Ferryland, and he attempted to control summer visiting along the island's coasts. He became one of the principal leaders of the Planters on the island, although his political actions always were controversial. In 1651 he was called home and charged with withholding taxes. Throughout the early 1650s he was under a cloud until his death in 1654, although his family continued to live in Newfoundland as merchants. Kirke's heirs, led by Lady Kirke, fought a number of legal battles for compensation (partly for the return of Quebec) after his death. Kirke was a good example of the extremely fluid legal situation among explorers and adventurers in northern North America in the first half of the seventeenth century.

Returning with his bride to Acadia in May 1630 as part of a Scots-English expedition, Claude stopped at Cape Sable to persuade his son to join him. Charles replied that "he would rather have died than consent to such baseness as to betray his King" (MacBeath, 1966: 593). Declaring his son an enemy, Claude led an unsuccessful attack on the fort at Cape Sable and retreated to Port-Royal, only to discover that the English planned to abandon it. He was forced to throw himself on his son's mercy and confess to his wife that he could not return to Europe. Acadia, like Canada, was returned to France by the English with the Treaty of Saint-Germain-en-Laye in 1632. The English monarch Charles I needed French financial subsidies as he attempted to govern without meeting Parliament, a policy that led to the English Civil War.

In Acadia, Charles de La Tour continued to lead an embattled life, coming into conflict with others who claimed royal authority in the region. In 1645 he was defeated by his chief rival, Charles de Menou d'Aulnay (c. 1604–50) and sought refuge in Canada. D'Aulnay controlled Acadia until his death in 1650.

Charles de La Tour returned to France after d'Aulnay's death to demand an inquiry into his case. He was completely vindicated and again received into royal favour. Returning to Port-Royal with a few new

Biography

Françoise-Marie Jacquelin La Tour

According to her husband's chief enemy, Françoise-Marie Jacquelin La Tour (1602–45) was the daughter of a barber who became a Paris actress, but little is known of her background and it is at least as likely that she was a member of a family of lesser nobility in France. In 1640 she received a proposal of marriage in absentia from Charles de La Tour, who claimed the governorship of Acadia in competition with Charles de Menou d'Aulnay, and sailed to Port-Royal to join him. Whether the two had met earlier in France is not clear. After a marriage ceremony was performed at Port-Royal, the couple repaired to La Tour's trading post near Saint John. There Françoise-Marie gave birth to a son. In August 1642 d'Aulnay returned to Acadia with an official order that La Tour appear before the King to answer charges of treason. La Tour decided to send his wife, Françoise-Marie, to represent him at the royal court, suggesting that she had some connections there. She successfully argued her husband's case in 1642, then returned to Acadia in a French warship, carrying supplies for La Tour.

In 1644 she went again to France, but this time was unable to protect her husband's interests against d'Aulnay's charges. Escaping to England with borrowed money, Madame La Tour chartered an English ship to carry her and supplies back to her husband. Off Cape Sable the ship was detained and searched by d'Aulnay, but Madame La Tour hid in the hold. Arriving in Boston, she successfully sued the ship's captain for unwarranted delay, using the money to hire ships to reinforce La Tour at Fort La Tour.

Early in 1645, with her husband again off in Boston seeking fresh assistance, Madame La Tour commanded the defence of Fort La Tour against an attack by d'Aulnay. Her 45 defenders held out for four days against an invading force of 200, but she eventually surrendered on the understanding that d'Aulnay would "give quarter to all." The victor, however, went back on his word. All the captives except one man, who served as the executioner, were hanged. Madame La Tour, who was forced to witness the executions with a rope around her own neck, died scant weeks later.

She was probably the first European woman to have made her home in what is now New Brunswick, but as her experiences demonstrated, early life in the region was dangerous and complicated for both men and women.

settlers in 1653, he successfully courted d'Aulnay's widow. Pursued by creditors, he was forced in 1654 to surrender his garrison of 70 at Fort La Tour to an invading English expedition of 500 men. La Tour was taken to England, where Oliver Cromwell (by now head of the English state) refused to restore his Acadian property but did agree to recognize the long-dormant baronetcy of Nova Scotia (negotiated earlier by Claude) if Charles would accept English allegiance and pay his English debts. Twenty-five years after denying his father and asserting his loyalty to the French Crown, Charles de La Tour accepted Cromwell's terms. He eventually sold his rights in Acadia to English partners and retired to Cape Sable with his wife and family.

For more than 40 years La Tour and his family had kept French interests alive in Acadia, but he was at best a trader and not a colonizer. The few settlers he brought to the New World were only incidental to his economic and military activities. Unlike Champlain in Canada, La Tour had no vision of a settled agricultural presence in Acadia, perhaps because he had to contend with the spillover from complex European rivalries. After his surrender to the English in 1654, the scattered few hundred Acadian residents were left to their own defences until formal French occupation was restored in 1667. While the period of English control from 1654 to 1667 left little internal mark on the region, it did isolate Acadia from the French court's rethinking of its American empire in the early 1660s. Acadia was not initially part of the Crown's decision in 1663 to take a more active interest in its American colonies. As a result, its subsequent status was never properly clarified, leading to an administrative weakness that encouraged its population to have an autonomous outlook and encouraged France (in 1713) under pressure to surrender large parts of the region to the English.

Acadia after 1670

Between 1660 and 1713 Acadians expanded both their population and the extent of territory cultivated. A good deal of data was collected in censuses, although most of these censuses were incomplete. A census in 1671 listed 47 families made up of 400 people, nearly all in the Port-Royal area of the Annapolis Basin. Although it was even-

tually named the capital of the colony in 1700, and was frequently raided by New Englanders, Port-Royal was by no means the whole of the colony. By 1710 the population had grown to more than 1,500, mostly through natural increase, and had planted settlements along the Minas Basin, Cobequid, and Chignecto Bay.

Most of Acadia's people came from a relatively small area of southwestern France. The seigneurial system controlled less of daily life in Acadia than it did in the rest of New France, so the colony expanded in what would become a typical form: settlers moving to new land as resource limits were reached in older communities. Younger members of families moved to new communities, which featured dykes that controlled the inundation of lowland areas by the high tides of the Bay of Fundy. Marsh was drained for farming. Farms were small but prosperous, the main crops being wheat and peas. Fruit, especially apples, was common, as one visitor claimed that farms were "as well planted with Apple [sic] trees as they would have been in Normandy" (Diereville 1933: 95). Even without dyking, the tidal marshlands provided large quantities of hay and grazing. This was used to feed livestock, especially cattle, which was the chief product of the region. Illegal bartering (especially of meat) with New Englanders, their sometimes enemies, was the method by which Acadians obtained most of their imported goods, particularly tools and hardware.

On the outskirts of the tidal settlements, particularly the Cap de Sable district, were small fishing communities, perched upon the coast. In addition to fishing, inhabitants of these communities supported themselves by hunting, trading furs, and occasional timbering. Raiding and privateering also occurred from bases in these communities, which provided most of the access to the farming settlements. Acadia had few roads and little in terms of overland transportation. Movement was by canoe and small boats called *shallops*.

Government sat fairly lightly upon this population. The French never really asserted tight administrative control over the region, although at least eight authorized royal governors were appointed to the region between 1670 and 1710. The Church took a similarly detached view of the colony and operated solely through missionaries who provided some contact with Canada.

BACKGROUNDER

Plaisance (Placentia)

One of the least well-known North American colonies of Europe was Placentia or Plaisance, established in the early 1660s by the French on the western side of the Avalon Peninsula of Newfoundland on the Bay of Plaisance (Placentia Bay). The middle years of the seventeenth century were a particularly confusing period on the northern Atlantic coast. The English Commonwealth under Oliver Cromwell had expanded its naval resources in the region and had taken over most of Acadia. As a result, French access to the Atlantic region was being challenged, especially on the beaches of Newfoundland, where the English fishing fleet required increasingly large expanses of beach to dry its catch. The fishery remained an important imperial factor for all European nations, since mercantilism cherished it both as a training ground for a merchant marine and as a source of protein for hungry citizens. The French decided that a fortified post on the Newfoundland coast would be the best way to demonstrate their claims to the Newfoundland fishery and to protect their subjects in it. A very young Thalour Du Perron was sent ashore at the site about 100 kilometres south of St. John's in October 1662 with a few soldiers and a supply of food. He was murdered over the following winter by a drunken party of his men; the culprits were eventually brought to justice in Quebec. France spent over 10,000 livres a year before 1670 maintaining the tiny colony, but was unsuccessful in establishing much of an agricultural base; a summering population of 256 was fed by only 30 domestic animals and almost no cultivated ground. Basque merchant vessels visiting the colony charged what the traffic would bear, since they were virtually the only source of supplies and labour until the inhabitants managed to develop a trade with other French traders and eventually with vessels from Boston. A deep chasm between the settlers and the visitors soon emerged, which lingered throughout the colony's existence. The soldiers of the garrison were quartered in the homes of the inhabitants and disarmed lest they become unruly, which rendered them virtually useless in times of crisis. The settlement was constantly beset with instability, and easily succumbed in 1690 to a small English party. Restored to France, it survived another two decades, serving as the base for French naval raiders in Newfoundland, until it was turned over to the English in 1713.

The control of Placentia, seen in this 1786 drawing, shuffled between the English and French for over 50 years until the English gained permanent control of the colony in 1713. Sketch by James S. Meres, "The Log Book of His Majesty's Ship Pegasus." LAC, C-002525.

Culturally and politically, the Acadians remained isolated from French Canada. The family (*clan*) and the local community were the important units for a closely knit peasant society. Acadia had developed an inherent sense of autonomy when—in the chess game of eighteenth-century imperial warfare—France was obliged under the Treaty of Utrecht (1713) to surrender territory in North America. Acadia was one of the pawns given up to the British that year. The *anciennes limites* of Acadia mentioned in the treaty were not defined, and the French subsequently insisted that they had surrendered only peninsular Nova Scotia, informally retaining northern Maine and New Brunswick, and formally retaining Île Royale (Cape Breton) and Île St-Jean (Prince Edward Island). As for the population of the ceded territory, which the British called Nova Scotia to emphasize Britain's historic claims there, the inhabitants were given one year to remove to French territory or to remain as subjects of their new masters.

Canada Fights for Survival

In 1627 Cardinal Richelieu, Louis XIII's "grey eminence," assumed supervision of New France and established the Company of One Hundred Associates. However, Richelieu's company, unlike the English Newfoundland Company, was organized from the top of the government rather than from grassroots interest in the profits of colonization. It was to be capitalized at 300,000 livres, each participant contributing 3,000, and profits were not to be distributed initially. Of the 107 members listed in May 1629, only 26 were merchants and businessmen, mainly from Paris. The remainder were courtiers and state officials. The company's initial venture—at a cost of 164,270 livres—was to send to Quebec in 1628 four ships containing 400 people and carrying "all necessary commodities & quantities of workmen & families coming to inhabit & clear the land and to build & prepare the necessary lodging" (quoted in Trudel, 1973: 118). Unfortunately, England and France had gone to war in 1627, and in July 1628 the company's ships were captured off Gaspé by an Anglo-Scottish armed

expedition led by the brothers Kirke. Thus began a military struggle between France and Britain for control of North America lasting more than a century.

In July 1629 David Kirke sent his brothers Lewis and Thomas at the head of an Anglo-Scottish armed expedition that forced Champlain's little outpost on the St Lawrence to surrender. Later that same year, an attempt by the Company of One Hundred Associates to reoccupy Quebec failed dismally. The colony was restored to France in 1632 under the Treaty of Saint-Germain-en-Laye. One of the first French arrivals that year was Father Paul Le Jeune (1591–1664), recently appointed superior-general of the Jesuit missions in Canada. The Jesuits were to be the principal missionary order in the colony. Le Jeune soon began sending the first of his annual reports, the famous *Jesuit Relations*, which were forwarded to the provincial father of the Society of Jesus in Paris to explain and promote in the mother country the missionaries' efforts. They combine a wealth of detail about life in New France, the First Nations, Iroquois warfare, the Huron missions, exploration and travel, as well as accounts of various miracles. Champlain returned to Quebec in May 1633 after a four-year exile, tired but optimistic. He would die at Quebec on Christmas Day 1635, his vision of a prosperous colony still beyond his grasp. At the time there were but 150 settlers along the St Lawrence.

Over the next few decades, the forces along the St Lawrence that met in bitter rivalry were less French and British and more Catholic evangelical energy on the one hand and resistance from the Indigenous population on the other. The prize was control of the fur trade. Conflict along the Atlantic seaboard had more traditional European overtones, while in Canada the long rivalry between the Iroquois and the Algonquian trading allies of the French created much fear and havoc, with disastrous consequences for the Huron people caught in the middle.

The Huron had access to a seemingly inexhaustible supply of furs from the northwest, and the French were determined to keep the flow moving to Montreal and Quebec. The Huron had outnumbered the Iroquois, but in the 1630s their numbers were greatly reduced by diseases chiefly contracted from the French missionaries who lived among them. In 1634, the year the Jesuits set up permanent missions in Huronia, the Huron suffered an epidemic of measles. In 1639 the Jesuits oversaw the building of an elaborate fortified headquarters, Ste-Marie-aux-Hurons, on the Wye River. It eventually comprised 20 buildings, including a residence for priests, a church, a hospital, outbuildings for farming, and residences for lay workers and Huron converts, as well as a canal with three locks.

The Iroquois—supplied by the Dutch with firearms, which the French were reluctant to give to their First Nations allies—were equally determined to control the flow of furs. They ambushed the Huron fur fleets on the Ottawa River, and between 1640 and 1645 they blockaded the river, while also from 1643 onward attacking the settlements on the St Lawrence. Under the force of the assault, the Company of One Hundred Associates virtually withdrew from New France in 1645, giving its fur-trading monopoly to the Communauté des Habitants, an organization of Canadian merchants, which agreed to continue to pay for the administration of the colony. While the devolution of the fur trade to local interests was probably a positive short-term move for the colony, the new company felt the effects of Iroquois hostility, which limited the fur trade for an entire decade. It also meant that the fur traders Radisson and Grosseilliers were badly treated when they returned from the west with a large stock of furs in 1660.

The Iroquois soon turned their full attention to Huronia. In July 1648 Senecas destroyed the mission of St-Joseph and killed 700 Huron. In March 1649 a party of 1,200 Iroquois destroyed St-Louis and St-Ignace, where the priests Jean de Brébeuf (1593–1649) and Gabriel Lalemant (1610–49) were tortured to death. The weakened Huron surrendered, fled, or were killed. Before the Iroquois could reach Ste-Marie, the Jesuits there "applied the torch to the work of our own hands" and fled with some 300 families to Christian Island in Georgian Bay. Most died of starvation or malnutrition.

BACKGROUNDER

Champlain's New France

In 1603 Pierre Du Gua de Monts (1558?–1628) was granted a trading monopoly in northeastern North America in return for an obligation to settle 60 colonists each year and to establish missions among the Aboriginals. Among the first settlers he recruited was a young draftsman, Samuel de Champlain (c. 1570–1635), who had been to Tadoussac in 1603 and would serve as geographer and cartographer for de Monts's expedition. Champlain continued a commitment to explore and colonize the New World that would end only with his death (on Christmas Day, 1635). Unlike his English contemporaries, William Bradford at Plymouth Plantation and John Winthrop at Boston, Champlain had not been able to lead a prospering colony through the problems of internal growth and the establishment of permanent institutions. Instead, much of his career was spent dealing with the preliminaries of settlement, in the interests of which he sailed to France nine times to further his plans for colonization or to resist attempts to negate them.

As a successful geographer and intrepid explorer who was equal to the most arduous demands of wilderness life, and who was capable in complex dealings with Native peoples, Champlain also left a literary legacy. The three volumes of his *Voyages* (published in Paris in 1613, 1619, and 1632) provide much of what we know about New France during this period. Champlain's map of New France (facing page) appeared in the last volume of his *Voyages*. It includes the territories he explored, which are rendered quite accurately, along with inevitably inaccurate renderings of regions for which he had only second-hand information.

The next year the missionaries returned to Quebec with a few hundred Huron, the pathetic remnant of a once-powerful nation.

The Huron were early victims of European ethnocentrism. As for the missionaries themselves, only the Jesuits' profound faith and misguided intentions—to educate the First Nations in French ways and induct them into a completely alien form of religion—kept them on their indomitable rounds of travel and life under extremely harsh and tense conditions. Many of the Huron turned against the missionaries, blaming their problems with disease and with the Iroquois on the Christian interlopers. Indeed, in exposing the Huron to disease and weakening their culture by introducing alien spiritual elements, the missionaries may have inadvertently contributed to the destruction of Huronia.

If the missionaries had only limited success with the First Nations, their influence on the early European population of Canada was far more positive. The missionary enterprise in Canada had two basic wings, often only loosely connected: that of the Jesuits and that of the lay missionaries.

The Society of Jesus was founded by Ignatius Loyola in 1540 as a militant (and militarily organized) order devoted largely to missionary activity around the world. The Jesuits travelled around the globe, especially in the period 1550–1650, preaching and teaching among indigenous people ranging from the Aztecs to the Japanese. They developed a reputation for being able to adapt Christianity to the customs of the local people, and they were probably less rigid than most missionaries in their views of what had to happen for true conversion to take place. Members of the order actually looked forward to martyrdom, although they were not supposed to go out of their way to seek it. As soldiers of Christ, they believed that conversion of pagans occurred only through bloodshed. The Jesuits were obviously highly disciplined and committed; to the usual vows of poverty, chastity, and obedience, they added one of loyalty to the Pope. Despite the suspicions

Champlain's map of New France, 1632. LAC, NMC-15661.

Father le Jeune on the Conversion of the "Savages," 1634

This selection by Father Paul le Jeune (1591–1664), the founding editor of the *Jesuit Relations*, offers some insight into the thinking of the fathers regarding their mission in the early 1630s.

The great show of power made at first by the Portuguese in the East and West Indies inspired profound admiration in the minds of the Indians, so that these people embraced, without any contradiction, the belief of those whom they admired. Now the following is, it seems to me, the way in which to acquire an ascendency over our Savages.

First, to check the progress of those who overthrow Religion, and to make ourselves feared by the Iroquois, who have killed some of our men, as every one knows, and who recently massacred two hundred Hurons, and took more than one hundred prisoners. This is, in my opinion, the only door through which we can escape the contempt into which the negligence of those who have hitherto held the trade of this country has thrown us, through their avarice.

The second means of commending ourselves to the Savages would be to send a number of capable men to clear and cultivate the land, who, joining themselves with others who know the language, would work for the Savages, on condition that they would settle down, and put their hands to the work, living in houses that would be built for their use. . . . I may be mistaken but if I can draw any conclusion from the things I see, it seems to me that not much ought to be hoped from the Savages as long as they are wanderers; you will instruct them today, tomorrow hunger snatches your hearers away, forcing them to go and seek their food in the rivers and woods. Last year I stammered out the Catechism to a goodly number of children; as soon as the ships departed, my birds flew away. . . .To try and follow them, as many Religious would be needed as there are cabins, and still we would not attain our object; for they are so occupied in seeking their livelihood in these woods, that they have not the time, so to speak, to save themselves. . . .

The third means of making ourselves welcome to these people, would be to erect here a seminary for little boys, and in time one for girls, under the direction of some brave mistress, whom zeal for the glory of God and a desire for the salvation of these people, will bring over here, with a few Companions animated by the same courage. May it please his divine Majesty to inspire some to so noble an enterprise, and to divest them of any fear that the weakness of their sex might induce in them at the thought of crossing so many seas and of living among Barbarians.

Source: Reuben Gold Thwaites, ed., *The Jesuit Relations and Allied Documents: Travels and Explorations of the Jesuit Missionaries in New France 1610–1791* (New York, 1959), vol. VI, 145–53.

of the Crown, they were given a monopoly of religious service in Canada in 1632. The Jesuits tended to be more involved with missionary outreach than with the European population.

The lay missions were organized as part of the French Counter-Reformation, and were led by lay people who discovered they had enormous depths of piety that they were anxious to share with others, including the First Nations in North America. When the widow Marie-Madeleine de Chauvigny de la Peltrie (1603–71) recovered from a serious illness in 1635, she made a vow to establish a school for Native girls in New France. She

Contemporary Views

Marie de l'Incarnation on Her Charges

Marie de l'Incarnation, oil portrait attributed to Abbé Hugues Pommier (1637–86). Archives des Ursulines de Quebec.

It is a singular consolation to us to deprive ourselves of all that is most necessary in order to win souls to Jesus Christ, and we would prefer to lack everything rather than leave our girls in the unbearable filth they bring from their cabins. When they are given to us they are naked as worms and must be washed from head to foot because of the grease their parents rub all over their bodies, and whatever diligence we use and however often their linen and clothing is changed, we cannot rid them for a long time of the vermin caused by the abundance of grease. A Sister employs part of each day at this. It is an office that everyone eagerly covets. . . . But after all it is a very special providence of this great God that we are able to have girls after the great number of them that died last year. This malady, which is smallpox, being universal among the Savages, it spread to our seminary, which in a very few days resembled a hospital. All our girls suffered this malady three times and four of them died from it. . . . The Savages that are not Christians hold the delusion that it is baptism, instruction, and dwelling among the French that was the cause of this mortality, which made us believe we would not be given any more girls and that those we had would be taken from us. God's providence provided so benevolent against this that the Savages themselves begged us to take their daughters, so that if we had food and clothing we would be able to admit a very great number, though we are exceedingly pressed for buildings.

Source: Joyce Marshall, ed., *Word from New France: The Selected Letters of Marie de l'Incarnation* (Toronto: Oxford University Press, 1967), 75–6.

persuaded Marie de l'Incarnation to join her, put much of her fortune in trust for the foundation, and even financed a vessel and some immigrants to accompany her. Once in New France, she founded the Ursuline convent in Quebec. Another noblewoman sponsored three nursing sisters of the order of Augustinian Hospitalières on the same ship as the Ursulines. They founded a hospital at Sillery to care for dozens of Aboriginals, most of whom were Montagnais, Algonquin, and Abenaki, with only a few Huron. The Société Notre-Dame de Montréal organized a missionary effort in 1639 that led to the establishment of Montreal in 1642. This work was financed by donations from wealthy lay people. Thirty-four of the 46 members were lay people, and 12 were women. For much of the mid-seventeenth century, Canada would be largely dominated by the energy of its leading women missionaries—Marie de l'Incarnation, Jeanne Mance (founder of the Hôtel-Dieu hospital), and

Marguerite Bourgeoys (founder of the Congrégation de Notre-Dame)—aided by money supplied by lay patrons in France. The missionaries, particularly the women, were always objects of suspicion by the French, both lay and ecclesiastical. They were accused of "Jansenism," a Protestant heresy. The fear was that their excess of piety and inner spiritual experiences would lead them to operate independently of the authorities, and there is some evidence that many of these people were indeed loose cannons in the wilderness, particularly before the colony had a proper hierarchical structure. They were only brought under control after the arrival in 1659 of Bishop Laval, who had been consecrated the vicar apostolic for Quebec.

In 1647 Canada adopted government by a central council, with elected representatives of the districts of Quebec, Trois-Rivières, and Montreal employed for consultative purposes. Such a government was both responsive to the wishes of the inhabitants and autonomous of the mother country, but the arrangement was more a result of emergency conditions than a genuine reform. With the Huron destroyed, the Iroquois turned the full brunt of their fury on the French at Montreal. François Dollier de Casson (1928: 155) observed that "not a month of this summer [1651] passed without our roll of slain being marked in red at the hands of the Iroquois." The attacks subsided over the course of the decade, but the menace never entirely disappeared.

"Mort héroïque de quelques pères de la Compagnie de Jésus dans la Nouvelle France," lithograph by Et. David, 1844. LAC, C-4462. This rendering tells us much about how the French by the nineteenth century interpreted these events. There is no evidence to support this particular view of the deaths of the missionaries. What purpose do you think the artist intended by the depiction of the boiling pot?

Biography

Jeanne Mance

Born in Champagne, France, Jeanne Mance (1606–73) was one of a number of female missionaries to Canada whose spiritual and physical energy sustained the colony through the middle years of the seventeenth century, when the Iroquois threat was at its height. Her family was of the bureaucratic middle class, and she was educated with the Ursulines. She gained experience nursing in the hospitals of the Thirty Years War, and in 1640 she learned of the great missionary endeavour in Canada, in which both men and women, including many Ursulines, were engaged. The hagiographic accounts of her life, which are virtually our only sources, all emphasize her obedience and subordination to her confessors. Travelling to Paris, she met with and impressed Father Charles Lalemant, who was in charge of the Canadian missions, telling him of her great hopes to join in the cause. Thanks to a Parisian lady, she was introduced to the Queen, Anne of Austria, and also to Angélique Faure, one of the leaders of charitable enterprise in the city. Faure asked Jeanne to go to Canada to establish a hospital, providing a substantial sum of money for the purpose.

Prior to setting sail for Canada, she met an associate of Paul de Chomedey de Maisonneuve, who persuaded her to become associated with the Société Notre-Dame de Montréal. Her patron approved her plan for the establishment of a hospital in Montreal, at the western frontier of the colony, and the Hotel-Dieu was founded, in her home, soon after Montreal was established in 1642. The hospital was later transferred to Rue Saint-Paul. In 1650 Mance loaned money to Maisonneuve to recruit soldiers to defend the frontier, and she subsequently recruited three nursing sisters to assist her with the hospital. In 1657 she fell on the ice and fractured her arm and wrist, recovering its use only through a miraculous relic. Her last years were troubled. According to her modern biographer, she "encountered the inability of authorities whom she revered to understand her deeds of deliverance in earlier days" (DCB, I, 487). She died in 1673 after a long illness.

The period of the Iroquois wars was a difficult one for the French fur traders, and many headed northwestward to avoid the enemy. Among these adventurers were Pierre Radisson (c. 1640–1710) and his brother-in-law Médard Chouart Des Groseilliers (c. 1618–96?). Radisson was born in France, but had been captured by Mohawks in 1651. Adopted by a prominent family, he was forced to learn Aboriginal ways in order to survive. In 1659 the brothers-in-law took a journey to Lake Superior that excited their interest in exploring the fur-producing region that they knew extended as far north as Hudson Bay. They returned to Montreal in 1660 with a vast haul of beaver skins, which was seen as the colony's salvation. The two fur traders were not well received, however; their furs were confiscated and both men were prosecuted for trading without official permission. Not surprisingly, they wound up in Boston in 1664, where the English were quite enthusiastic about the Hudson Bay fur trade. Eventually the pair would head for London, where their enthusiastic reports about conditions at the Bay led in 1670 to the establishment by the English of the Hudson's Bay Company, which would contend with the French for control of the region until the French conceded it to the English in 1713.

By the early 1660s the tensions within the colony on the St Lawrence seemed to be manifesting in strange forms. A general state of panic was produced by an incident of alleged witchcraft, and in the midst of carnival season in February 1663 the colony was struck by a serious earthquake. Mère Marie de l'Incarnation noted, "we were all so frightened we believed it was the eve of Judgement, since all the portents were

François de Laval

Portrait of François de Laval, first bishop of New France, from 1674 to 1688. Bishop of Canada (oil on canvas), French School (17th century) / Société des missions-étrangères, Paris, France / Giraudon / Bridgeman Images.

Born at Montigny-sur Abre, his father a member of a younger branch of the distinguished Montmorency family and his mother descended from Rouen legal nobility, François de Laval (1623–1708) was marked from childhood for the Church. He studied for some years at the Jesuit College at La Fléche, then at Paris. His studies were briefly interrupted by a family crisis, but he was ordained as a subdeacon in 1646 and as priest in 1647. As archdeacon of Évreux from 1648, he proved indefatigable in his work, and he seemed destined for missionary work in Indochina.

Before the politics of such an appointment could be negotiated, however, Laval found himself the Jesuit candidate for the post of bishop of New France, an appointment in the giving of the archbishop of Rouen. Again caught up in ecclesiastical politics, Laval ultimately was appointed a vicar apostolic rather than a bishop, and thus subject to the papacy rather than to the archbishop of Rouen. He sailed for his new post in April 1659. His first task was to get his authority recognized. This proved easier than expected, thanks to a letter from Louis XIV to the governor, which ordered Laval's authority recognized everywhere. His next job was to organize the Church in New France, which before his arrival had been a decentralized missionary operation. In 1662 he sailed to France to consult with Louis XIV, returning to Canada with increased powers, an ordinance founding the seminary of Quebec, and an edict creating a Conseil Souverain.

Gradually the Church in Louis XIV's royal province of Canada took shape under his direction, and he was named the first bishop of Quebec in 1674. Laval organized a parochial system, which increased from five parishes in 1659 to 35 in 1688, with 102 clergy. He encouraged missionary activity, especially by the Jesuits, and he took the lead in opposing the liquor trade with the Aboriginals, a battle that he and the missionaries lost eventually. Laval became notorious for his constant disagreements with the governors of the colony over a variety of matters, both moral and political.

In 1684 he sailed for France to resign his bishopric, but after having his resignation accepted, he attempted to remain on the job for fear his successor would undo much of his work. Abbé Saint-Vallier was consecrated bishop early in 1688, and Laval returned to Canada as "Monseigneur l'Ancien," beloved of his people but mainly retired from the fray at his seminary. He permitted his successor to reform the seminary without raising any opposition, and in later years he occasionally performed episcopal functions in the absence of Saint-Vallier, who was away from Canada from 1700 to 1713. Laval died in 1708 from a chilblain on his heel that became infected.

to be seen" (Marshall, 1967: 288–9). About this time the French Crown formally withdrew trading privileges and landownership from the Company of One Hundred Associates and made New France a Crown colony. Given the anxieties and problems of the colony, most of its inhabitants were probably happy to trade autonomy for French financial and military assistance. From the date of the royal takeover, the civil code of Canada became the Coutume de Paris, the code of civil law compiled for the royal region of France. The Coutume was subsequently extended to other French colonies in the New World. It was divided into 16 sections governing family, inheritance, property, and debt. Its provisions tended to be the more responsive to royal authority than those of other regions.

Royal control was not immediately in evidence, but in June 1665 four companies of the Carignan-Salières Regiment arrived to quell the Iroquois. This unit had its origins in Piedmont, where two regiments were merged into one in 1659 in order to avoid disbandment. Returned to 700 men, it was ordered to North America in 1664 and strengthened to 1,000 troops by adding other French companies, some of which may have fought in the Austro-Turkish war of 1663–4. Additional companies were transferred from Martinique to bring the force to full strength. The regiment was brought to New France in seven ships. Despite early campaigns of limited success, the regiment altered the balance of military power and brought the Iroquois to sue for peace in 1667, a peace that would hold for 20 years. Many men of the regiment stayed on in the colony, tempted by offers of land in the Richelieu Valley and other incentives. The regiment departed Canada in 1668, and thanks to the relative peace, virtually no regular French troops were stationed there until 1684.

In September of 1665 an intendant (or chief administrative officer)—Jean Talon (1626–94)—arrived to revitalize the colony. One of the royal government's first aims was to increase the population, and the *filles du roi* (orphan girls raised at the King's expense) were sent over for that purpose. These "King's Daughters" would become a contingent of about 800 young women brought to New France between 1665 and 1673 by Louis XIV, who paid for their passage and provided them with a trousseau and a dowry (the dowry was not always paid

Marguerite Bourgeoys, "Le Vrai Portrait," painted the day after her death in January 1700 by Pierre Le Ber. This work was not discovered until the mid-twentieth century, when x-rays of a work believed to be an authentic likeness revealed the "true portrait" under several layers of paint. Musée Marguerite-Bourgeoys, Montreal.

in cash). The women were mainly between the ages of 15 and 25, and were required to be of high moral standards and considerable physical fitness. Unfortunately, they were recruited chiefly in the cities and were often not well equipped for an agricultural existence on the frontier. Almost half came from the Paris region, and they helped establish the French spoken in the capital as the language of Canada. Normandy (16 per cent) and western France (13 per cent) provided the bulk of the remaining contingent. Between 770 and 850 young women have been identified. Most did remain in New France, although about 300 did not. Many did marry, often to soldiers in the Carignan-Salières Regiment. Mère Marie reported that 100 girls had arrived in 1665, and more would come later. How long the French Crown would continue such support was uncertain, but it certainly rejuvenated the colony. The government had begun making a concerted effort to deal with the Iroquois menace and to reform both the administrative and economic structure of New France. It would shortly attempt to establish a foothold in Newfoundland and later regain control over Acadia. Although success would hold within it the seeds of destruction, the French in 1665 were on the eve of almost a century of expansion and dominance in North America.

One of Intendant Talon's first tasks, undertaken personally, was to conduct a census of the population of the colony. Governments of the time employed the census as a means of asserting their authority. Talon did not count Aboriginal people or those in religious orders, but he found 3,215 inhabitants clustered in three settlements: Quebec (547), Trois-Rivières (455), and Montreal (625). Only one-third of the population was or had been married, and 842 were between 21 and 30 years of ages. Those enumerated represented a broad range of occupations and professions, making clear that a substantial population base existed for the King to improve with positive policies.

Canada, 1663–1760

That part of New France along the St Lawrence known as "Canada" mixed French origins and the North American environment in a way that defied easy characterization. The French background provided institutions, a terminology with which to express them, and a set of assumptions about how society ought to be organized and operated. The French government assumed an ordered and hierarchical society in which the various social orders stayed in their places and duly subordinated themselves to the good of the whole, as defined by the Crown. As a complication, the French Crown was not satisfied simply to replicate the familiar institutions of the Old World in North America, but sought to reform and modernize them by stripping them of centuries of European tradition that had decentralized power and limited royal authority. At the same time, the environment, including the Indigenous population, provided a set of daily realities that subtly subverted European institutions and assumptions, modifying and altering—while never

totally negating—efforts to imitate the mother country. The result was a society that refracted the metropolis in France through the dual prisms of royal reform and North American experience. The external observer was struck at first by the presence of familiar European patterns and terminology, while beneath the surface different social designs constantly were evolving.

The royal takeover of 1663 put French administrative policy for the colonies and its execution in the hands of two men, the governor, Jean-Baptiste Colbert, and the intendant, Jean Talon. Colbert was Louis XIV's chief bureaucrat, a highly experienced civil servant. His major tasks both at home and abroad were to strengthen royal government and expand the French economy. As Minister of Marine, he served as the seventeenth-century equivalent of colonial secretary, in addition to a myriad of other responsibilities. To implement policy in America, Colbert decided to establish the position of intendant, a royal official who, in France, had been designated to cut through the accretion of centuries of devolution of royal power and to act decisively on behalf of the state. Beginning with Talon's appointment as intendant in 1665, the colony's administration was greatly reorganized and centralized. The governor, though the titular head, was responsible for military affairs, external relations, and the colony's connections with the Church (including education). Subsequently, the governor invariably would be a member of the French aristocracy and an experienced military man, while routine administration devolved to the intendant, a career civil servant whose social origins were in the middle class. Classic confrontations between intendants and governors would ensue, particularly during the regime of Louis Buade de Frontenac (1620–98, governor 1672–82 and 1689–98). But the royal regime consistently backed the intendant.

Colbert and Talon not only managed to put the colony on its feet, but established its administrative and institutional structure for the entire century of French royal control. Their task was no easy one. Political institutions had to be established that were simultaneously responsive to the royal will and satisfactory to the populace. External threats had to be confronted. Population growth had to be stimulated. Some kind of economic viability had to be developed that would not endanger the mother country. Out this complex of factors would emerge a society and culture of enormous tenacity, possessing many resources for regeneration and change.

Canada was ruled by the Sovereign Council, made up mainly of the colony's elite and presided over by the intendant. No regularly elected political body represented the inhabitants. Instead, informal means were used in the colony to express public opinion, including the public protest (or "riot"), which was a typical feature of life in both Europe and America at the time. Most Canadian riots were over food shortages, to which the government usually responded favourably. The Church was a major component of the government. Its main political task was to help establish, within the ranks of its communicants, due subordination to spiritual and secular authority. During the French regime the Church often found this job beyond its capabilities, partly because it was chronically understaffed. In 1759, for example, there were only 73 parish priests among 200 clergymen, hardly enough to provide religious services for everyone in the colony, especially outside the towns. The colony contained 114 parishes, many of which obviously did not have a resident *curé*. In the symbiotic relationship between Church and state, moreover, the state dominated. It appointed bishops, granted seigneuries, and provided most of the revenue for religion. At the same time, the subordinate role of the Church did not mean that Canada was irreligious or secular, or that Catholicism did not permeate the lives of most of its inhabitants. Canada had been born in deep Catholic piety, and Catholic orthodoxy remained the norm.

The Church was also charged with responsibility for education and social services, and, as we shall see later, would find itself the chief instrument for the creation of high culture in the colony as well. The first institution of higher learning in North America—a college at Quebec—was opened by the Jesuits a year before Harvard in Massachusetts, and for their part, the Sulpicians founded *petite écoles*, primary schools that provided basic religious instruction. By 1760 the colony was training most of its own priests. The Frères Hospitalières de Saint-Joseph de la Croix (an order founded in Canada) began an orphanage in 1694 and later a hostel for men. The Récollets also ran schools, especially among First Nations children. The Ursulines provided education for the daughters of the colony's

leaders, while the Sisters of the Congregation of Notre-Dame, organized by Marguerite Bourgeoys, opened schools across the colony. From the beginning, nuns founded and operated the hospitals of Canada. Despite the best efforts of the Church, literacy in Canada, particularly in the rural regions, was very low—perhaps as few as 10 per cent of the population could read or write. On the other hand, there was no enormous gender gap regarding literacy as there was in most parts of Europe, including the mother country.

Because Canada was so often in a state of siege, the role of the military was crucial. France was prepared to spend money on the military that it would not have allowed for civilian matters. The soldiers' pay was an important source of money for the Canadian economy, and the army was the best local customer for Canadian merchants. Regular soldiers served as a source of labour and as potential additions to the civilian population, which they were encouraged to join at the expiration of their enlistments. Regular troops were supplemented by the inhabitants after 1669, when the entire adult male population of the colony between the ages of 16 and 60 was required to serve in the militia, locally commanded by *capitaines de milice* chosen democratically from the ranks of the inhabitants. After 1684 the militia was employed in every war. For much of the period of the French regime, regular troops were members of the Troupes de la Marine. They were not highly regarded by the military command, either in the mother country or in the colony, which was one of the reasons why so much reliance was placed on the militia, who until the last years of the regime were held to be superior to the regulars. Much of this militia service was in collaboration with the First Nations in the form of raiding parties, designed to keep the English colonies off balance and to prevent them from using their superior numbers to invade the St Lawrence. The high point of militia-style success came at the end of the seventeenth century, when the exploits of Pierre Le Moyne d'Iberville in the Hudson Bay area and in New York made the Canadian militia much feared by the English.

Because of the nature of guerrilla warfare, soldiers in Canada were not heavily drilled until the end of the period, when warfare became more Europeanized and the militia proved less useful. Foreign observers

Pierre Le Moyne d'Iberville

Pierre Le Moyne d'Iberville (1661–1707) was a younger son of Charles Le Moyne de Longueuilet de Châteauguay and Catherine Thierry. His father was the son of a Dieppe innkeeper who spent his early years in Canada in the Huron country and had settled at Ville-Marie. Renowned as an Indian fighter, Charles Le Moyne led the settlers in several campaigns against the Iroquois, and in later years often served as an interpreter and negotiator with the Five Nations. He was rewarded with several major land grants, and in 1668 was elevated to the nobility. On his death in 1685 Charles not only held many thousands acres of land, but left a personal fortune valued at 125,000 livres, much of it apparently made in the fur trade. He was one of the shareholders in the Compagnie du Nord that had succeeded the Compagnie de la Baie d'Hudson in 1682. Charles's success had been a perfect illustration of how immigration to North American could lead to extraordinary upward mobility. He and his wife had 14 children, 12 of them male. Most of the sons emulated their father in both military activity and heroism. Pierre was usually accompanied by one or more of his brothers in his military campaigns.

Born in Montreal, Pierre began his career in his father's service. Somewhere in his early life he acquired experience at sea. On the eve of his first campaign after his father's death, he was found guilty by the Sovereign Council of seducing a young woman and fathering an illegitimate child (he was made responsible for this child until she was 15). Such charges of sexual excess would continue to plague him throughout his life, although they could be viewed as merely the private side of his public career. Iberville flourished at the margins of Europe's American empires in an age when governments did not make tidy distinctions between public and private sectors, thus encouraging military adventurism by private entrepreneurs if it could be viewed within a larger imperial context. He was, in effect, a buccaneer or *filibustier* rather than a professional soldier in the conventional sense of the term.

Iberville's first independent campaign in James Bay was typical. The expedition—set under way in 1686 while England and France were attempting to resolve their American differences short of war—utilized the Ottawa River and connected waterways to travel to the north, a perilous journey that took 85 days. At Moose Fort (Moose Factory), Iberville singlehandedly gained entrance to the enclosure, but once inside the palisade the post's 17 Englishmen closed the gate; while his companions worked to force the gate open again, Iberville distracted the Englishmen with his bravado. The fort eventually surrendered. A reputation for intrepid heroism was born, and he was put in command of this and two other James Bay posts captured by the French: Forts Rupert and Albany (renamed Saint-Jacques and Sainte-Anne by their captors). In 1687–8 he was in France, returning to James Bay in command of a French vessel. On the Albany River in 1688 he added to his reputation for bravery one of total ruthlessness towards the enemy. When two armed English ships blockaded his own fur-laden vessel in the river in September, and all three ships became immobilized in the ice for the winter, Iberville's arbitrary conduct led to the deaths of many of the Englishmen, most from scurvy. Arriving back in Quebec triumphantly in late 1689 with booty and furs, Iberville was sent off as second-in-command of a French and First Nations expedition raiding English settlements in New York. One of the results was the destruction of Corlaer (now Schenectady) in February 1690.

Sailing with three vessels to Hudson Bay in July 1690, Iberville was driven off York Fort in late August, and in 1692 his naval squadron, complete with French frigates—unable to sail to the Bay before winter ice—was ordered to harass the English coastal colonies. He returned to the Bay in 1694, this time under a buccaneering agreement with the French Crown, and captured York Fort (renamed Fort Bourbon), again with charges of excess ruthlessness in violation of the terms of surrender. After another successful raiding venture to the coast of

Newfoundland in 1696–7 (where 36 small outports were destroyed), Iberville's ship, *Pélican*, became separated from its companions on its way to the Bay. Reaching the Nelson River in early September, he turned to find three sails on the horizon. Thinking the remainder of his fleet had joined him, he sailed out to join them. Unfortunately, the ships were English. Iberville was forced to fight a naval battle with three English warships, sinking one, capturing another, while a third fled the scene. France ended up with York Fort. Finally joined by his fleet, he forced York Factory to surrender as well. This triumph over the European nation that regarded itself as master of the sea was the crowning glory of Iberville's career, and the last of his Hudson Bay exploits. He moved south to the Mississippi River and then to the West Indies for the remainder of his life. Whether Iberville was a great commander or not is worthy of debate, as he was never tested on either a large stage or against a worthy opponent.

were always impressed with the martial spirit of the Canadians, however. One British officer in the eighteenth century commented, "Our men were nothing but a set of farmers and planters, used only to the axe and hoe. Theirs are not only well trained and disciplined, but they are used to arms from their infancy among the Indians, and are reckoned equal, if not superior in that part of the world to veteran groups." For many Canadian elite families, as in France, military service in an officer class was preferable to entrance into commerce and industry. By the eighteenth century, the Canadian elite provided most of the officers for the Troupes de la Marine and even expected commissions to be reserved for the sons of serving officers.

One of Canada's major disadvantages in its constant wars against the English was the small size of its population. After 1660 French Canada matched the English colonies by doubling in population every 25 years, but it could never keep pace numerically. In 1715 the population of New France was 20,000, while that of the English colonies was 434,000. By 1754 the gap had widened, with 70,000 in New France and 1,485,000 in the American colonies to the south. After 1672 few French immigrants arrived in the colony, either publicly sponsored or privately motivated. The reasons for the lack of immigration have been much debated among scholars. One constellation of reasons revolves around the unfavourable publicity that Canada—despite or perhaps because of the *Jesuit Relations*—continually received in France. The colony had a reputation for a harsh climate and an absence of amenities, which did not dispose the French

to emigrate. Another set of reasons involved conditions in France itself. Both the absence of agrarian dislocation

Jean Talon, intendant of New France. This portrait is a nineteenth-century copy, attributed to Théophile Hamel, of a seventeenth-century painting by Frère Luc. Authentic likenesses are in short supply for the early periods of Canadian history, and most portraits, like this one, are later renderings which may—or may not—have been based on earlier originals. LAC, 1952-10-1.

and the insatiable demands of the French military for manpower prevented the development of a discontented and displaced population available for colonial migration on a massive scale. At the same time, the traditional juxtaposition of the French and British colonial experiences is in many ways misleading. In relation to the colonies of most European nations in America—those of the Dutch Republic, Sweden, and Scotland, for example—New France was successful. The British colonies were unusual in their numbers and dynamism. Unfortunately for the French, the British did not have a mere handful of colonies in America, but a large number on the mainland and more in the Caribbean, which were both economically vibrant and located on the exposed flanks of New France and Louisiana. In the imperial rivalries that inevitably ensued, the French were at a substantial disadvantage.

At the time of the royal takeover in 1663, both Colbert and Talon had attempted to diversify the economy. They were especially concerned about the colony's heavy dependence on the fur trade. Colbert even saw the fur trade as a menace. "It is to be feared," he wrote, "that by means of this trade, the habitants will remain idle a good part of the year, whereas if they were not allowed to engage in it they would be obliged to apply themselves to cultivating their land" (quoted in Eccles, 1983: 104). What the French authorities wanted was an agricultural surplus and the exploitation of timber resources, which would enable the colony to supply the French West Indies with goods currently being obtained from the English. But the economy was slow to diversify. Part of the problem was that the fur trade kept expanding, contributing to a circular effect. The successful French quest for furs not only deflected attention from other enterprises but brought Canada into conflict with the English to the south. The ensuing struggle made it virtually impossible to limit the fur traders, since they were the ideal shock troops for engaging the enemy.

The numbers involved in the fur trade (the voyageurs and *engagés*) grew in number from 200 at the end of the seventeenth century to nearly 1,000 by the mid-eighteenth century. The work was both physically and emotionally demanding, and most men were worn out before they reached the age of 40. Perhaps as many as one-quarter of able-bodied Canadian males were involved in the fur

trade at some point in their lives, usually in their younger years before they settled down with wives and families in more sedentary occupations along the St Lawrence. Many left Aboriginal wives and mixed-blood families behind in the forest when they retired to their first families. A few rose to be specialists in the trade, some remaining in the West throughout their lives. A few became *marchands équipeurs* (outfitters), organizing the parties and providing the credit for the voyageurs. Unlike the colony's transatlantic merchants, the fur trade merchants were almost exclusively Canadian-born.

A complex commercial and small-scale artisanal life did develop in New France. A small merchant class supported itself, particularly at the transatlantic level. Overseas trade was complicated and dangerous, and most merchants operated through family and clan connections. Marriage alliances established new branches of family firms in distant ports, and after the deaths of their husbands, women frequently took over the local enterprises. The trading economy over which the merchants presided required peace and stability to perform at its best. Only the years after Utrecht (1713) to the late 1730s provided decent conditions, free from the ravages of the British navy and privateers. The economy also suffered from a chronic shortage of a medium of exchange, which led the colony to produce its own paper money by using decks of playing cards inscribed in various denominations and signed by the intendant. Officially the cards were promissory notes, but they and the military *ordonnances* that circulated as legal tender after 1735 were inflationary. A constant demand existed for the local productions of skilled artisans, particularly those master craftsmen who worked for the Church, providing the furniture, ornaments, and decorations for the many religious buildings in the colony. Artisans also made many things that would have been too bulky and expensive to import, such as furniture. Two major attempts to industrialize New France were made, both in the 1730s. One was an ironworks near Trois-Rivières (the "forges du St-Maurice"), the other a shipyard at Quebec. Both required large amounts of state subsidy to survive, but both demonstrated that Canadian workmen could be mobilized for industrial activity and could manufacture serviceable goods on a large scale. The St-Maurice facility employed as many as 500 workers, and was the

"Montreal from the West." Although agriculture was still the primary form of economic activity in the seventeenth century, a commercial and artisan life emerged in urban centres, such as Montreal, seen in the distance in this painting by Philip John Bainbrigge. LAC, 1983-47-87.

most modern iron manufacturer in North America, producing mainly iron ware, although experiments were made with cannon as well.

Despite the growth of trade and industry, agriculture was always the dominant form of economic activity along the St Lawrence, functioning around the seigneurial system brought to the valley in 1627 and governed after 1663 by the Coutume de Paris. Seigneurialism in New France probably worked less to order society than to provide a means of settlement. The state made property concessions to landlords, who were supposed to find settlers to serve as tenants. Seventy seigneuries were granted before 1663 and over 150 by 1740. Roughly one-quarter of the land granted was in the hands of the Church. Although the *censitaire* (tenant) owed various rents and feudal dues to his seigneur, these amounted to

very little so long as there was more land than settlers. After the Edict of Marly in 1711, the seigneur could no longer withhold land from settlement in anticipation of price increases if there were settlers demanding it. Since they did not own the means of production, the *censitaires* seldom treated agriculture as a long-term business enterprise. The seigneurial system did not tie settlers to the soil and did not encourage large-scale, staple-crop farming so much as family farms on small holdings. The system was not really feudal, since military obligation in the colony was not tied to land occupation or tenure. Not until the end of the French regime was there sufficient pressure on the land to benefit the seigneur economically. He did acquire social status, however, and by the mid-eighteenth century the typical seigneur was an absentee landlord who lived in town and was involved

Intendant Raudot on the Card Money, 1706

Beginning in 1685, New France dealt with its shortage of metallic coins by issuing decks of cards signed by the intendant and inscribed in various denominations. In 1706 Jacques Raudot, who was intendant of New France from 1705 to 1711, wrote a memorandum justifying the practice. It offers a little lesson in mercantilist monetary policy.

Memorandum on the Cards of Canada, Quebec, September 30, 1706

The cards which are issued in Canada serve as money just as coin does in France.

The Kingdom of France derives a certain utility from these cards, since, by this means, the King is not obliged to send funds in coined money for the expenditures which he has the goodness to incur. If it were necessary to send this, it would withdraw from the Kingdom annually 100,000 écus. Consequently this currency leaving the country would render money scarcer. It is true one would not appreciate this disadvantage during the abundance of money, nevertheless it is certain that it would effect a diminution. Moreover, France, by this device, not sending coined money, runs no risk as to it either from the sea or from enemies.

If coined money were sent to Canada, it would afterwards leave the country by two avenues, one part would return to France, the other would go to New England to purchase certain merchandise, which may be had cheaper there than from France. The part of this money returning to France would run the risks of the sea and enemies. The vessels may be taken or lost, and consequently the money they carry is lost to France, and there can be no greater injury to the Kingdom than the loss of its money.

The other part of this money being carried to New England for the purchase of merchandize, results in a considerable injury to France in the loss of its coinage and the advantage which it would produce among her enemies. . . .

Furthermore, there is no fear that money may be carried to New England, which would be very difficult

in a variety of economic and political activities. A seigneury became part of a diversified portfolio of investment for those of the elite, within whose ranks little specialization of function had yet occurred.

By the mid-eighteenth century, Swedish visitor Peter Kalm could describe the heartland of French Canada along the St Lawrence as "a village beginning at Montreal and ending at Quebec, which is a distance of more than one hundred and eight miles, for the farmhouses are never above five arpents [293 metres] and sometimes but three apart, a few places excepted" (Benson, 1937, II: 416–17). Each farmhouse, usually of three or four rooms built of stone and timber, stood alone. Rural architecture in Canada was quite differ-

ent from urban building. Although houses were often made of stone, to protect against the harsh weather they were typically covered with a form of stucco that whitened over time, providing a distinctive colouring to the structures. A larger number of houses were constructed of wood, most commonly with heavy timber frames and infilled with rubble stone. Inside the houses were usually to be found two rooms, one of which was used as a kitchen and living area, and the other as a communal bedroom. Closets were unknown, and most families had a large wooden armoire, many of which still survive. Although stoves began to be seen in the eighteenth century, most houses were heated by the same fireplaces used for cooking. Soups and stews made

to prevent if there were any in the colony, there being as in France persons who to gain something would risk much.

It is even a matter of policy for kings to attach the prosperity of their subjects to their own persons, in order to render the former more submissive and to take care that all the means which the colonies may have in money are always in the kingdom on which they are dependent. Canada, having nothing but cards, which are secured only on the word of the King, and seeing no other resource except in the good faith of the sovereign, will be still more submissive to him and still more attached to France for the reason that all the supply it can have in money depends on it. Hence, it appears to me that one cannot do better than to permit the continuation of the card money in Canada.

There may arise great abuses regarding these cards; they may be counterfeited in the country; this, however, can be prevented by a close attention, the easier bestowed as the resources of every person are known. Counterfeits may also be sent from France and so exactly imitated that one cannot distinguish the true from the false. That is almost impossible to do here, there not being clever people enough of that type. But even if there were some counterfeits they could not remain long without being recognised. To prevent this abuse one has only to change the dies, and shape of the cards every year after the departure of the vessels for France.

It is true that the colony of Canada will suffer somewhat by these cards, it being quite certain that it will buy French merchandise cheaper if it pays for them in coined money and not in cards, for which the merchants receive only bills of exchange which for the most part are not met at maturity. But it is proper that the colony of Canada suffer for the sake of the kingdom from which it receives its benefits, and it is only fair that this kingdom should run no risk of losing its money by the possible loss of its vessels bound for it. . . .

RAUDOT

Source: Adam Shortt, ed., *Documents Relating to Canadian Currency, Exchange and Finance during the French Period* (Ottawa: F.A. Acland, 1925), vol. 1, 157–9.

from the abundance of fresh game available in the colony were the typical fare. The colonists spent much time preparing for winter. Food could be preserved in a variety of ways: by pickling, by drying, by smoking, by burying it deep in a root cellar, or by freezing it. The aromas of cooking, wood smoke, and human bodies was powerful, especially during the long winter when being outside was difficult at best. The inhabitants required special social skills to manage the close living quarters. A few tiny villages formed, usually around churches.

Three towns punctuated the continuous village: Quebec towards the eastern end, Trois-Rivières in the middle, and Montreal towards the west. Quebec and Montreal contained impressive and concentrated public and private buildings, often built of stone, but by our standards both towns were quite small in population and area. On their peripheries, the dominant landscape pattern of the separate but contiguous farmstead resumed. Narrow lots ran back for long distances from the river, and while there were new rows (*rangs*) of lots available behind the riverfront ones, population was slow to move inland. Thus French Canada replicated neither the French medieval village, whence many of its rural settlers had come, nor the English colonial tendency towards isolated farmsteads in the middle of large holdings separated from one another by considerable distances. Instead, the limited population in Canada sought to cover as much landed territory as possible.

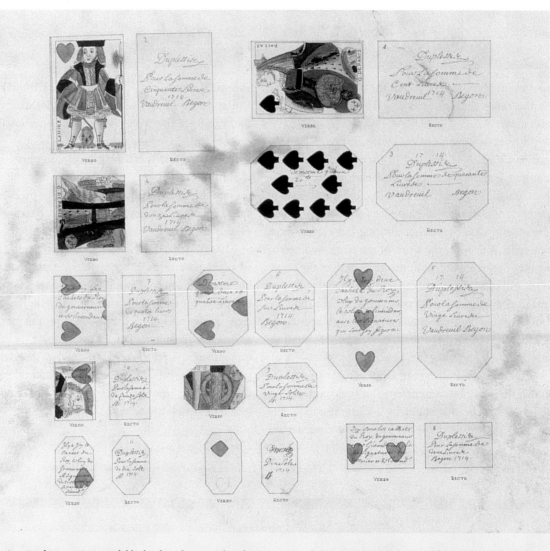

"Playing Card Money," pen with black ink with watercolour by Henri Beau (1863–1949): reproduction of examples of the playing card money used in New France. Beau, an employee of the Public Archives of Canada, was employed in the Paris office specifically to copy views, portraits, etc., and to carry out iconographic research. As with all reproductions, there are likely some discrepancies between these drawings and the real cards. LAC, C-17059.

Although Montreal and Quebec were not large, they did give Canada an urban life and a proportionately larger urban population than that of most North American colonies. These towns were the centres of government, of the direction of economic activity, and of the Church and its social services, such as health care and education. They inevitably included a heavy concentration of the upper classes of French Canada, and had an impressive polite society. While there were, doubtless, gradations of wealth and status, French North America was fundamentally divided into two orders: those with and those without access to government largesse and patronage. The law was available to all, but only some could expect public and military appointments, government contracts, and seigneurial grants. Upward mobility was a possibility, but most observers agreed that the typical Canadian worked no harder than was necessary, spent a disproportionate amount of time pursuing his own pleasures and interests

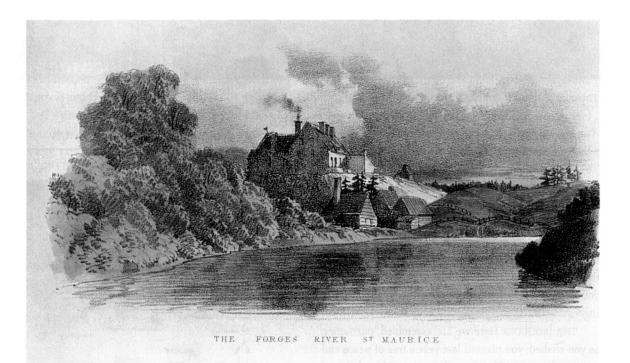

THE FORGES RIVER S⸞ MAURICE

The iron forges on the St-Maurice, by Joseph Bouchette from his book The British Dominion in North America *(London, 1832).* LAC, C-4356.

(which included racing horses and disappearing into the bush), was far more prosperous than his European counterpart, and enjoyed a good deal more liberty.

In 1701 a major international event took place in Montreal. Hosted by "Onontio" (the Aboriginal name for the governor general of New France), this conference involved 1,300 delegates from 39 Aboriginal nations stretched across the interior of North America. The gathering was designed to conclude a peace treaty among all the people of the *pays d'en haut*, but especially the Iroquois, who had been fighting with the French for nearly a century. A number of factors contributed to making this event possible, but the chief ones were the European peace of Ryswick in 1697 and the sudden steep decline in the number of Iroquois warriors, from 2,550 to 1,250, a product of epidemics, missionary success, and the depredations of constant warfare. According to the Onandaga chief Sadekarnaktie in 1694, "the grease is melted from our flesh and drops on our neighbours, who are grown fat and live at ease while we become lean." The Great Peace was ratified at a general assembly on 4 August 1701 in a huge arena 41 metres long and 21 metres wide in present-day Old Montreal, where more than 3,000 people gathered to listen to speeches and witness the signing of the document. This agreement meant the virtual end of Aboriginal involvement in the imperial wars of Europe for many years to come.

Slavery was never prohibited in Canada, but it never flourished because there were no large plantations to employ a slave workforce. What slaves existed were mainly domestic servants. Not all were blacks, although 540 blacks have been identified in Canada during the French regime. Aboriginal prisoners (*panis*) sold to the French were also kept in bondage. The colonial New Englander John Gyles was technically a slave when he was transferred from his Aboriginal captor to a French merchant on the Saint John River at the beginning of the eighteenth century. The image of plantation slavery in the American South or in the Caribbean bears no relationship to the slave situation in French America, still prevailed. Both the decoration of churches and the few examples of early wooden house furnishings that survive reveal a strong aesthetic sense. The churches preferred the baroque style of the French seventeenth and eighteenth centuries, while the everyday furniture featured simple, elegant, and functional designs.

All the artists in the seventeenth century whose names are known were clerics trained in France. Perhaps the finest was Claude François (*dit* Frère Luc, 1614–83), a Récollet father who had studied in Rome and come to Canada in 1670. He spent 15 months in the colony, leaving behind a number of works that influenced his colleagues in their artistic endeavours. Canadian work was often less polished than that done in Europe, but was often the better for it. Pierre le Ber (*c.* 1669–1707) was the son of a wealthy Montreal merchant family who left a large inventory of painting supplies at his death; he has latterly become known as the painter of a portrait of Marguerite Bourgeoys generally regarded as a major work in Canadian art. Non-clerics like le Ber also participated in another important part of artistic expression in New France; the votive painting. These works were contributed to a church or chapel by thankful colonists in fulfillment of a vow, often after a miraculous salvation at sea. Many were dedicated to Ste Anne, the patron saint of sailors. Most tell a story of an event for which the donor was especially grateful. Such paintings were displayed where they could be seen by worshippers entering or leaving a church (see illustration). Many votive paintings were executed by anonymous untrained artists. The best-known painter of early votives is Paul Mallepart de Grandmaison du

Beaucour (*c.* 1700–56), a former soldier who worked mainly in the Quebec City region.

Many of the most impressive buildings in Canada were forts and ecclesiastical structures, including churches, schools and seminaries, and hospitals located in the major cities but also in the rural parishes. Construction of such buildings provided employment for many workers and artisans. Most scholars distinguish three periods: the first runs to 1663, the second to 1700, and the third to 1763. Most building in all three periods was done in stone, with urban structures heavily influenced by contemporary French models and the rural ones mainly simplifications of those in the cities. Considerable similarities exist in many of the designs of the second and third periods, as the bishops sought to maintain some sense of control and order over the production.

Conclusion

A number of societies slowly emerged from roots planted by Europeans beginning in the early seventeenth century. Of these, the largest and most successful was the one begun by Samuel de Champlain along the St Lawrence River. Nevertheless, Canada remained a colony with a relatively small population, a distant province of France. Most institutions were strongly influenced by French origins and by the relatively small population. Left to its own devices, such a society held much promise. But its involvement in war, first against the First Nations and then against the English, much influenced its development, often in unfortunate ways.

Historiography

The Jesuit Missionaries and the *Jesuit Relations*

The French Crown's assumption of sovereignty over large chunks of territory in northeastern North America—most notably the St Lawrence Valley—opened a fertile field for the missionary zeal of the Counter-Reformation.

Several French missionary orders jostled for dominance, but the Jesuits eventually emerged triumphant. Founded in 1534 by a Spanish soldier, the Jesuits were unswervingly loyal to the papacy. They were an order devoted to education and to conversion of the non-Christian peoples being encountered by Europe throughout the world. They first arrived in Canada in 1611, but became particularly important after 1632, thanks to the publication in Europe of the *Jesuit Relations*, a series of 72 sets of self-advertising narratives first published before 1672 and intended to describe the new country and its peoples within a highly literate framework of missionary self-sacrifice and martyrdom. They worked mainly with the Huron because they were a sedentary people.

The *Jesuit Relations* set the template for centuries of accounts of encounters between missionaries and First Peoples in Canada, assuming that the latter were uncouth "savages" who desperately needed to be brought into the European/Christian fold for their own good. (A counter-narrative created by eighteenth-century *philosophes* turned the story upside down by portraying the Aboriginal inhabitants of North America as "noble savages" whose innocence of European decadence and corruption made them superior beings. It flourished briefly among the literati but never penetrated very deeply into the overall portrayal of the encounter). Although he was personally no missionary zealot, Father Pierre Charlevoix (1682–1761), in his extensive eighteenth-century writings on North America, generally accepted and perpetuated the missionary's version of the encounter of the two civilizations, passing it on to French Canada after the Conquest. Quebec-based writers seized on the more evocative passages of the *Jesuit Relations*, such as the martyrdom of Jean de Brébeuf or the miracles experienced by Catherine Tekakwitha, in their search for a native literary tradition.

On the whole, historians of the nineteenth and early twentieth centuries continued to accept the *Jesuit Relations* at face value, lionizing the missionaries as heroes and martyrs. Indeed, the most influential of these historians, the American Francis Parkman (1823–93), compared the French respect for the Aboriginal, best exemplified by the Jesuits, with the contempt of the Spanish and the English. He saw the First Peoples as barriers to the progress of European civilization across North America, and his full-length study of the Jesuits had as its central narrative the hostility to Western civilization of the Aboriginal people, both Huron and Iroquois, in the face of the courageous efforts of the missionaries to convert them to Christianity. A further strengthening of the interpretation of the missions through the eyes of the *Jesuit Relations* came about through their translation into English and publication in their entirety, a project carried out by the American scholar Reuben Gold Thwaites (1853–1913) between 1896 and 1901.

Since 1945, revision of the traditional view of Jesuit missions has focused on three main fronts. (1) Scholars have sought to correct the narrative lines fostered by Francis Parkman. The main figures here have been the Canadian historian William J. Eccles and the American scholar Francis Jennings, both of whom have labelled Parkman a "liar" and a racist for his negative treatment of the First Peoples. (2) An emphasis on viewing the Aboriginal presence on its own terms and not through a European lens employed by the *Relations* started in earnest in the 1960s with the discovery that there was more to Canadian history than politics and warfare. This process produced a succession of major studies of the early Aboriginal populations in Canada and was dominated by anthropologists and economic historians who had only a secondary interest in missionaries. The seminal work was probably Arthur J. Ray's *The Indians in the Fur Trade* (1974). (3) More recently, scholars have placed the Jesuit effort in an international context, comparing the North American missions with those elsewhere in the world, especially in Asia. Takao Abe's *The Jesuit Mission to New France: A New Interpretation in the Light of the Earlier Jesuit Experience in Japan* (2011) exemplifies this international approach.

Short Bibliography

Blackburn, Carole. *The Jesuit Missions and Colonialism in North America, 1632–1650*. Montreal and Kingston, 2000. A study of the missionary activities of the Jesuits with the Huron, placed in a contemporary perspective of colonialism.

Brazeau, Brian. *Writing a New France, 1604–1632: Empire and Early Modern French Identity*. Farnham, UK, 2009. A recent re-examination of the early years of New France.

Cell, Gillian. *English Enterprise in Newfoundland, 1577–1660*. Toronto, 1969. Still the standard account of early settlement and its mercantile connections in Newfoundland.

Choquette, Leslie. *Frenchmen into Peasants: Modernity and Tradition in the Peopling of French Canada*. Cambridge, Mass., 1997. A study of the French settlement of Canada.

Dechêne, Louise. *Habitants and Merchants in Seventeenth-Century Montreal*. Montreal and Kingston, 1992. An award-winning study of the development of early Montreal.

———. *Le people, l'État et la guerre au Canada sous le régime français*. Montreal, 2008. The product of a life's work of study by Quebec's leading social historian.

Delâge, Denys. *Bitter Feast: Amerindians and Europeans in Northeastern North America 1600–1664*, trans. Jane Brierly. Vancouver, 1993. An analysis of the early relationships between First Nations and European intruders.

Douville, Raymond, and Jacques Casanova. *Daily Life in Early Canada*. London, 1968. Still the best study on the subject.

Eccles, W.J. *France in America*. Markham, Ont., 1990. The best overview of the French Empire in North America.

Harris, R.C. *The Seigneurial System in Early Canada: A Geographical Study*. Madison, Wis., 1966. The classic revisionist text on the subject, not yet superseded.

Havard, Gilles. *The Great Peace of Montreal of 1701: French–Native Diplomacy in the Seventeenth Century*. Montreal and Kingston, 2001. A fascinating account of a little-known episode.

Landry, Yves, *Orphelines en France pioneères au Canada: les filles du roi au xviie siècle*. Montreal, 1993. A thorough study of the first large contingent of female colonists.

Moogk, Peter. *La Nouvelle France: The Making of New France—A Cultural History*. East Lansing, Mich., 2000. A fascinating analysis made from the standpoint of culture and cultural studies.

Simpson, Patricia. *Marguerite Bourgeoys and Montreal, 1640–1665*. Montreal and Kingston, 1997. A sympathetic account of one of the leading female figures of seventeenth-century Canada.

Trudel, Marcel. *Introduction to New France*. Toronto, 1968. A textbook summary of New France by its leading modern historian.

Verney, Jack. *The Good Regiment*. Montreal and Kingston, 1991. A thorough study of the Carignan-Salières troops.

Study Questions

1. Reread the excerpt from Father Le Jeune's *Relation*. Identify and explain the three techniques he recommends for converting the Aboriginal people. By what means did the missionaries hope to sell themselves to the Huron?

2. Why were the female missionaries such "loose cannons" in early Canada?

3. Do Marie de l'Incarnation's comments in any way help explain why—as she admitted to her son—so few of her young charges became "civilized"? How would you characterize these comments?

4. What were the advantages and disadvantages of card money?

5. In the matter of its economic development, did Canada owe more to its European origins or to its North American location? Explain.

6. How does Intendant Raudot justify the use of card money? Are his economics sound?

7. What factors limited slavery in Canada?

8. Write a paragraph about the drowned bodies on the river. What can you deduce from this formal account?

Visit the companion website for *A History of the Canadian Peoples*, fifth edition for further resources.

www.oupcanada.com/Bumsted5e

3

Struggling for a Continent, 1627–1763

The fortress (centre background) at Louisbourg exchanged hands multiple times before finally being captured in 1758 by the British, led by General James Wolfe. Painting by Pierre Canot (1762). LAC, 1990-587-3.

Timeline

1667 English return Acadia to France.

1670 Hudson's Bay Company is granted a charter by Charles II.

1682 Louisiana named by La Salle.

1689 War of the League of Augsburg begins.

1690 Port-Royal captured by the English. Quebec is unsuccessfully invaded.

1697 Treaty of Ryswick ends War of the League of Augsburg.

1699 Iberville establishes Fort Biloxi.

1702 War of the Spanish Succession begins.

1703 Kaskaskia established.

1712 Crozat given trading monopoly in Louisiana.

1713 By the Treaty of Utrecht, which ends the War of the Spanish Succession, France surrenders Nova Scotia, Newfoundland, and Hudson Bay claims to Great Britain.

1715 Fort Michilimackinac established.

1717 Illinois Country annexed to Louisiana.

1718 Civil government decreed for Upper Louisiana.

1719 John Law establishes Mississippi Company.

1720 Establishment of Louisbourg. "Mississippi Bubble" collapses.

1724 Code Noir extended to Louisiana.

1731 Louisiana reverts to French Crown.

1744 War of the Austrian Succession begins.

1745 Louisbourg is captured by joint Anglo-American military force.

1748 Treaty of Aix-la-Chapelle ends the War of the Austrian Succession.

1749 Halifax established. Parliamentary inquiry critical of HBC.

1755 General Braddock is defeated on the Monongahela River. Acadians are expelled from Nova Scotia.

1756 Seven Years War officially begins.

1758 Louisbourg taken by force under General James Wolfe. Acadians are rounded up and again expelled from the Maritime region. Nova Scotia's first elected assembly meets. Nova Scotia's government advertises for settlers in New England.

1759 Battle of Quebec.

1760 Final French surrender.

1763 Treaty of Paris transfers New France and Acadia to Great Britain. King George III of England issues the Proclamation of 1763.

The nineteenth-century American historian Francis Parkman wrote of a "Half Century of Conflict," but in truth the imperial struggle between England and France was much more protracted. The struggle would transcend a straightforward European rivalry, increasingly involving as it did both the population of the colonies and the First Nations of the continent—each fighting with individual agendas—as well as other parts of the world as far away as India. The warfare began in the 1620s, when privateers from Newfoundland first invaded and sacked Champlain's Quebec. It continued into the 1650s when Oliver Cromwell's navy was active in the Atlantic region. The French colonies of North America felt the effects of this contest far more than did their British counterparts to the south. The much smaller population in New France was more often in the front lines of the fighting, which frequently occurred on French territory. Between 1627 and the final military defeat of New France more than 130 years later, the French experienced only one extended period (from 1713 to the early 1740s) when they were not constantly at war or under severe military pressure, either from Aboriginal peoples or from the British. The pervasiveness of the international rivalry came equally to affect British colonists and British policy in the northern region. At its greatest extent, "New France" consisted of a number of colonies and regions, including a fishing base in Newfoundland (Plaisance), Acadia (before 1713 all of the Maritimes; after 1713 Île-Royale [Cape Breton] and Île St-Jean [PEI]), Canada, the *pays d'en haut* or frontier country in the West, and both Upper and Lower Louisiana. Beyond this formal empire was a further region of French fur-trading that stretched from south of Hudson Bay to the Rocky Mountains. Canada was the most important part of New France, but not of the French Empire in the New World, for sugar islands were preferred to Voltaire's notorious "arpents of snow." Table 3.1, which shows the amount of correspondence from France's Bureau of Colonies for 1713, indicates the extent to which New France was only one of several items in the French overseas portfolio.

The Beginnings of Overland Exploration

The geographical shakedown of European colonization activity in the late sixteenth and early seventeenth centuries determined that the French would take the lead in exploring the northern interior of the continent, and their activities would extend far beyond the boundaries of what is now Canada. While the English, Scots, Dutch,

TABLE 3.1 Volume of Correspondence of the Bureau of Colonies, 1713

Destination	No. of Folios	Per cent	No. of Letters	Per cent
Îles français de l'Amérique*	225	37.1	440	57.9
New France (Canada)	118	19.5	126	16.6
Louisiana	10	1.7	15	2.0
St Domingue	114	18.8	73	9.6
Martinique and the Îles du Vent	122	20.1	81	10.7
Cayenne	10	1.7	21	2.8
Indes Orientales	7	1.2	4	0.5
Totals	606	100	760	100

Correspondence pertaining to the Marine's shipping to colonial ports.

Source: Kenneth J. Banks, Chasing Empire across the Sea: Communications and the State in the French Atlantic, 1713–1736 *(Montreal and Kingston: McGill-Queen's University Press, 2002), 51, Table 2.1. In addition, a single letter was written to the "Indes d'Espagne" (presumably the Spanish Main), but not included in the microfilmed set analyzed at the National Archives of Canada in Ottawa.*

and Swedes established settlements along the eastern seaboard, the French founded their settlements on the St Lawrence River, in the interior of the continent. Providing access to the Great Lakes and to most of the major river systems of North America, this river would confer enormous power and influence on the nation that controlled it. The St Lawrence focused the French need for new sources of furs to supply the major export commodity of New France. The river's access to the interior ensured that most of the great feats of inland exploration would be executed by the French. The ability of young Frenchmen to adapt themselves to the ways of the First Nations was also critical.

Champlain himself was active in moving inland to investigate territory previously unknown to Europe, but he was not a typical figure. The first major French overland explorer, in many ways quintessential, was Étienne Brûlé (c. 1592–1633), who lived with the Huron near Georgian Bay, Lake Huron, in 1612, and may have been the first European to sight Lakes Superior and Erie. A shadowy, elusive figure, Brûlé, like many early explorers, left no written accounts of his life or adventures. It is likely that he had volunteered in 1610 to live with the First Nations and learn their language. He was probably the young man to whom Champlain referred in 1611 as "my French boy who came dressed like an Indian" (DCB, 1966: I, 131). In 1615 Brûlé accompanied a party of Huron braves into the territory of the Susquehanna to the south of the Iroquois, in what is now southwestern New York State. He took advantage of the opportunity to investigate the neighbouring regions, perhaps reaching Chesapeake Bay and certainly tramping around modern Pennsylvania. Brûlé subsequently journeyed to the north shore of Georgian Bay, and then in the early 1620s along the St Mary's River to Lake Superior. Like many Europeans who "went native," Brûlé was respected by his compatriots as an interpreter, although they were intensely suspicious of his new persona. In Brûlé's case, his moral character and behaviour were criticized by Champlain even before his final "treachery" in 1629 when he entered the employment of the Kirke brothers after they successfully captured the tiny French colony at Quebec. By pursuing his own agenda rather than observing the abstract national loyalties dear to European hearts and

values, he established what would become a familiar pattern among Europeans coming to terms with North America. By 1633 Brûlé was dead, reportedly killed and eaten by the Huron.

Over the course of the seventeenth century, the interpreters, as represented by Brûlé, would be transformed into the coureurs de bois—the "runners of the woods" or "bushlopers," as the English often called them. These men would be responsible for most of the constantly broadening geographical knowledge of the North American continent. Their desire was less to improve cartography than to exploit new sources of wealth, particularly furs, and above all to enjoy an adventurous life in the woods. Whether or not these wilderness bravoes became completely assimilated into First Nations life and culture (some did), they all learned skills from the Aboriginals that made them crucial figures in the economy of New France. Marine skills like sighting latitude or reading the surface of the water were replaced by the ability to live off the land, to paddle a canoe for long distances with few breaks, to hunt animals for food, and of course to communicate successfully with a local First Nations population, not merely at the level of language but at one of genuine empathy. These inland explorers travelled in exposed parties and had no defensive structure such as a ship to protect them from attack. They lived by their wits and had to be constantly adaptable. They made splendid guerrilla warriors when Europe moved into warfare for control of the continent.

When the Iroquois were temporarily cowed by the Carignan-Salières Regiment at the end of the 1660s, the southern Great Lakes were opened to both the coureurs de bois and the Jesuits. For the fur traders, wrote Nicholas Perrot—one of their number—"it was a Peril." By the early 1670s the First Nations had provided enough information that the French were able to construct a fairly accurate map of the region, but they still did not know the ultimate destination of the great river that ran south from the lakes. Early in 1672 Louis Jolliet was chosen by Intendant Talon to answer this question, and he headed west with orders for Father Jacques Marquette to join his expedition "to seek . . . new nations that are unknown to us, to teach them to know our great God." The two men set out in May 1673 from

Michilimackinac, asking directions of local Aboriginal peoples as they proceeded. When they finally found themselves unable to communicate with the locals—somewhere around the present boundary of Arkansas and Louisiana—the Frenchmen decided they had seen enough. Having ascertained that the river they were following flowed into the Gulf of Mexico, which they thought was close by (in fact, it was still some 1,100 kilometres away), they turned back.

The follow-up to this expedition was led by René-Robert Cavelier de La Salle, a scapegrace son of a wealthy Rouen family who, although without much wilderness experience, had received an authorization from Louis XIV in 1677 to explore the American interior. Finally reaching the mouth of the great river early in 1682,

La Salle took possession of the country in a splendid ceremony on 9 April of that year. According to its chronicler, "the whole party, under arms, chanted the *Te Deum*, the *Exaudiat*, the *Domine salvum fac Regem*; and then, after a salute of firearms and cries of *Vive le Roi* . . . and with a loud voice in French" made his proclamation, to which the whole assembly responded with shouts of "Vive le roi!" and salutes of firearms. La Salle went on to establish a French colony in Louisiana, but he was murdered by a colleague with a personal grudge against him. Although his contemporaries saw him as a man who mixed "great defects and great virtues," nineteenth-century historians in both the United States and Canada turned him into the quintessential western explorer. His overblown reputation has been much demolished in recent years.

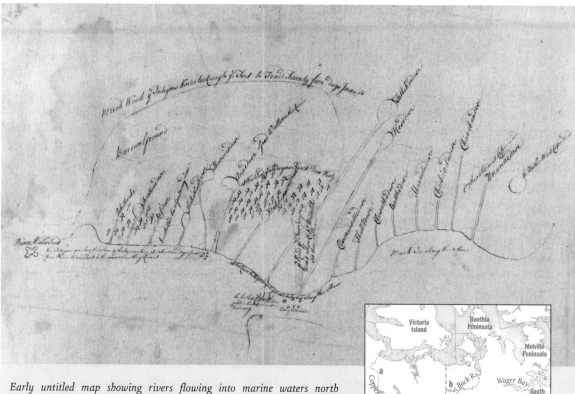

Early untitled map showing rivers flowing into marine waters north of Churchill Fort; drawn c. 1716–17 either by Chipewyan informants themselves or from their reports by James Knight of the HBC. Inset is a modern map of the same territory (based on June Helm, "Matonabbee's Map," Arctic Anthropology 26, 2 [1989]). River A is the Coppermine; B is the Back; C is probably the Thelon; and D is the Thlewiaze. Hudson's Bay Company Archives, Archives of Manitoba, G.1/19.

As Canadian schoolchildren are only too painfully aware, there were a good many overland explorers in the seventeenth and eighteenth centuries, some of whom have had automobiles and hotel chains named after them. While most Canadians could, if pressed, name one or two of these explorers, it is very doubtful whether they could offer the name of a single comparable First Nations explorer. Does this mean that the First Nations did not do any travelling in North America? Of course not. The Native geographical knowledge of the continent—much of which predated the arrival of the Europeans, who relied very heavily on it—has been ignored by most writers on exploration. The First Nations became part of the fuzzy background rather than the sharply focused foreground. Historians of exploration have long known of the great assistance provided by the First Nations in the "discoveries" of the Europeans. The Aboriginals provided much geographical information—even maps—and typically served as guides, interpreters, and canoe paddlers.

The *Pays d'en Haut*

The constant quest for furs also drove Canada inexorably westward into the *pays d'en haut*, where some sort of satisfactory relationship had to be worked out with the First Nations. The upper country was the territory upriver from Montreal, beginning beyond Huronia and stretching through the Great Lakes and then south to Louisiana. This territory was claimed by the French by right of exploration and usage. It was originally an important fur-trading region, inhabited almost exclusively by Aboriginals who were mainly Algonquian speakers. Many of the traditional Native groups of the region had been joined by those fleeing westward from the Iroquois in the seventeenth century. These refugees re-established themselves in the country between the Ohio River and the Great Lakes and extending to the west of Lake Michigan. This area had been reduced in population by the Iroquois. The expansion of the fur trade could continue only as far as the western country of the Sioux, another military people. The French had come to serve as the glue that held the First Nations communities together, and especially after the Great Peace

of 1701, relationships between the Native peoples and the French were carefully orchestrated. Casual liaisons between fur traders and Native women were regularized into formal marriages, accepted by the missionaries although opposed by the authorities in Canada as leading to licentious and independent mixed-blood children who might disrupt the trade. Central to the working relationship of alliances was the exchange of gifts. The authorities in France sought to minimize the expense of gift-giving, but for the First Nations gifts had a great symbolic value beyond the material cost of the goods involved. Gradually after 1700 a number of permanent communities began to develop in the Illinois Country, and in 1717 the French government annexed Illinois to Louisiana under the Coutume de Paris. A year later, a civil government for the region was established by decree from Paris.

Lower Louisiana

Louisiana was named in 1682 in honour of Louis XIV by the French explorer La Salle. Its territory at its greatest extent incorporated much of the drainage basin of the Mississippi River, running north–south from the Great Lakes to the Gulf of Mexico and east–west from the Appalachian Mountains to the Rockies. There were two main areas of settlement: the Illinois Country (Haute Louisiana) and Lower Louisiana, centred on Biloxi, New Orleans, and Mobile. Canadian history tends to lose sight of these colonies, because they ceased to remain within the Canadian ambit, but before 1763 they were definitely a part of New France and cannot be ignored.

Lower Louisiana was first settled in 1699 by Pierre le Moyne d'Iberville, who established a trading settlement at Fort Biloxi. Two years later another settlement was founded on the west side of the Mobile River, later moving to the river's mouth at Mobile. In 1712 the French financier and tax-farmer Antoine Crozat (1655–1738) was given a 15-year trading monopoly in the region, in return for which he was responsible for the territory's settlement (although not its government). Crozat spent his money searching for mineral wealth, bowing out of the picture without any real accomplishments except the establishment of a few colonists. The territory then got into the hands of the Scottish economist John Law, who consolidated the region's trade into the Mississippi Company, thus creating a speculative empire that rose to great heights and fell equally rapidly in 1720. This occurred at the same time as Britain's "South Sea Bubble," brought on when the management of the over-invested South Sea Company sold their shares in the company, which triggered a rush by many smaller investors to sell and caused the bubble to burst. Between 1719 and 1720 Law sent a large contingent of settlers to the territory, and after the collapse of the "Mississippi Bubble" these colonists began importing African slaves to serve as a labour force on their plantations. In 1724 the Code Noir was extended to Louisiana, which reverted to the Crown in 1731. The colony fashioned a successful plantation economy amid much infighting among a number of religious and imperial factions. Lower Louisiana was a drain on the French treasury, costing up to 800,000 livres a year, but along with Upper Louisiana it succeeded in encircling the English colonies, holding them along the eastern seaboard for the first half of the eighteenth century.

Upper Louisiana

Upper Louisiana consisted of two sorts of communities. Some grew up around forts, the largest of which was Fort Michilimackinac, where a permanent population of several hundred became much larger in the summer. Located on the southern shore of the Straits of Mackinac, connecting Lakes Huron and Michigan, it was founded by the French in 1715 along the key fur trade route into the interior. Most communities were fur-trade towns catering mainly to local Aboriginal populations. One such community was Kaskaskia, a town in what is now the state of Illinois, adjacent to the rich bottom land of the Mississippi Valley. A handful of French traders and their wives settled there at a Jesuit mission established in 1703. French and Native residents planted together in the fields, and the crops were abundant. The village of Kaskaskia developed its own local government, with most business conducted in assemblies held in front of the church after mass. Much the same system grew up in Acadia, with which

the Illinois Country could be usefully be compared, although no study has yet been attempted.

The village itself consisted of a central church surrounded by roughly 80 houses in the Canadian style but with the addition of a "galerie" (porch) extending around several sides of the house. Most of the houses had three rooms and a stone fireplace. By 1752 a regional census counted livestock, including more than 600 cattle and around 500 horses. Over 130 arpents of land were under cultivation, and most households had at least one slave. The male householders practised a variety of trades, including toolmakers, joiners, carpenters, masons, gunsmiths, blacksmiths, and even a wig-maker. The community also served as a base for transient voyageurs who traded in the interior. The 1752 census showed a total population for the communities of Kaskaskia, Fort de Chartres, St Philippe, Port du Rocher, Cahokia, and Ste Genevieve of approximately 1,000 Europeans, more than 500 blacks, and several hundred Native people, not counting the 300 soldiers in garrison at several locations.

Beyond the Formal Empires: Hudson Bay and the Prairies

On 2 May 1670, as a result of negotiations with Pierre Radisson and his brother-in-law, Groseilliers, a group of English merchants who had sent two ships to Hudson Bay in 1668 founded, by royal charter, a formal trading company, The Governor and Company of Adventurers of England Trading into Hudson Bay, usually called the Hudson's Bay Company, which received title to the entire drainage basin of Hudson Bay—some 40 per cent of modern Canada. From this date to 1713, the French and the British had vied for supremacy in the region, but the French had relinquished their claims in the Treaty of Utrecht.

Although the English had been trading furs from 1670, they had showed little interest in moving much beyond their posts at the edge of the Bay. By the first third of the eighteenth century, the pattern of trade between the Bay posts and their Aboriginal trappers had settled into its own routine with its own customs and traditions. The fur-trading system that the Hudson's Bay Company developed at the bottom of the Bay was highly institutionalized and ritualized. Ritualization reflected the Aboriginal desire for ceremony as part of a gift-giving and gift-exchange arrangement that carried on practices probably begun long before the Europeans had arrived. The complex trading ceremony began when the Aboriginal trading parties arrived at the trading post, led by their trading captain. Whether trading captains had existed before the arrival of the Europeans is not clear. The position probably reflected the new demands of the fur trade. At the height of the system's prominence, in the mid-eighteenth century, many captains would be given red military coats (the "captain's outfit") as a mark of their status. They also got other gifts, most of which would be subsequently distributed among their followers. The trading captain had little real power among his fellows, but he knew how to speak ceremonially with the European traders and how the system worked so that his people would not be totally out-traded.

The ritual began with the smoking of the peace pipe or calumet before the beginning of trade. The captain would "harangue" the traders, emphasizing how hard his people had worked, how far they had come, how much they loved the English, how much they wanted to be treated fairly. One such speech was recorded by James Isham in 1743:

> You told me last year to bring many Indians; you See I have not lyd; here is a great many young men Come with me; use them Kindly! use them Kindly, I say! give them good goods; give them good goods, I say! we Lived hard Last winter and in want, the powder being short measure and bad, I say! tell your Servants to fill the measure and not to put their fingers within the Brim; take pity of us; take pity of us, I say! we Come a Long way to See you; the French sends for us but we will not hear; we Love the English . . . . (Rich, 1949)

The captain would then make a gift of furs to the factor based on a levy against his people. The HBC factor would respond by stating how much the English loved the Aboriginals, how generous they would be, and how necessary it was for the Aboriginal people to trade only with them. The factor would then return the captain's gift, usually in the form of brandy and tobacco. Tobacco was one commodity in which the English had the advantage over the French, because of their access to the Brazilian tobacco—"of the Sweetest Smell and of a Small Role about the size of a man's little finger" that was "moist and hard twisted"—preferred by the Aboriginal traders. Both of these commodities could be and usually were adulterated. Then, with the captain looking on from inside the warehouse, the trade would be conducted with each individual Native trader through a "hole-in-the-wall" or open window. Native wants were fairly limited given the semi-nomadic way of life of the bands. After the trading was completed, the captain would distribute the gifts he had received to his fellows, and a feast would be held. Then the Aboriginal people would go away for another year. Increasing competition from the French to the south after the 1730s led to political attacks on the Hudson's Bay Company for its lack of activity, and a parliamentary inquiry in 1749 was highly critical of the "sleep by the Frozen Sea." But little changed until after the end of the French wars.

Beginning in 1716 the French resumed their quest for the "Western Sea," a search overland for an equivalent to the Northwest Passage. This Western Sea was also known as the Pacific and the Southern Sea, and was believed by some to be connected to Hudson Bay by the Strait of Anian, an imagined extension of the Northwest Passage. After 1731 the French in Canada began a policy of occupying the fur region of the North-West by the establishment of a line of "forts"—more like primitive trading posts—northwest of Lake Superior. Many of these forts were established by various members of the La Vérendrye family, headed by Pierre Gaultier de Varennes, Sieur de la Vérendrye (1685–1749). Pierre had been born in Trois-Rivières, the son of a lieutenant in the Carignan-Salières Regiment brought to Canada in 1666 who had received a seigneury in the new country. Pierre had fought in the French army at the Battle of Malplaquet in 1709 and was seriously wounded. He then retired to his seigneury on the Île aux Vaches. But like most Canadians, he dabbled in the fur trade. In 1728 la Vérendrye sent the government in Canada a memoir describing the information he had gathered from Aboriginal informants about the Sea of the West, and included a map. He concluded by proposing to establish a trading post on the shores of Lake Winnipeg as a base for further western exploration. The French government consulted Father Charlevoix, who was quite skeptical of the value to exploration of such a post, which "might degenerate into a mere business of fur trading" (Charlevoix, 1866: vol. 4).

The Minister of Marine decided to focus directly on the search for the Western Sea rather than on the expansion of the fur trade, but it was, of course, nearly impossible to explore the region without becoming involved in trade. The government at Versailles did not provide enough money to finance fully an expedition, and La Vérendrye found the remaining money by trading in furs. Whether La Vérendrye was serious about exploration or merely used it as a cloak for his trading is not clear, but in any event, over the next few years he and his family established a number of trading posts (the "Posts of the West") on the lakes and rivers of what is now Manitoba and in adjoining Ontario. In 1734 the first prairie post, Fort Maurepas, was built. The precise location of most of these forts is unknown. The only one of these posts of which we know the exact location

CANADA   Material Culture

The Beaver Skin

The heart of the fur trade was the beaver. Stretched on racks into spherical or ovoid shapes, beaver skins would be left to dry in the sun. While an adult beaver provided 20 to 30 kilograms of fatty meat, bones, claws, and teeth that could be used as food, tools, and as decorative objects—as well as the salicin-rich castoreum sac—the fur provided the greatest trade value to the First Nations and European trappers who pursued them. Parchment beaver was the most basic unit of that material, and is a suitable starting point for any discussion of the trade. Also known as *castor sec* (dry beaver), when stretched, the pelts would typically range from 50 to 70 centimetres in diameter and contain between 12,000 and 23,000 hairs per square centimetre (Coles, 2006: 54). The density of the double-layered hairs with long overcoat and soft undercoat meant that these furs were both warm and waterproof. As such, they were used by many First Nations groups as a clothing material, typically worn with the fur inside, rubbing against the skin of the wearer, keeping the wearer dry and insulating him or her against the cold. Andrew Graham, writing while chief factor of York Factory in 1771–2, described a typical First Nations (probably Cree) man's outfit as follows:

> The dress of the men consists of a close jacket of moose or deerskins finely dressed. . . . Over this in winter they wear another made of deer, or beaver skins, with the hair on, but the sleeves are not joined to the body. . . . Over this is thrown a blanket or garment made of deer, otter or beaver skins; it is only tied over the shoulders and hands loose, being in the day part of the clothing, and at night covers them while they sleep . . . in very cold weather they use mittens made of beaver skins. . . . a piece of beaver or hare skin, or cloth, is put under the chin and reaches to the back of the head where it is tied; this is only used in winter to preserve those parts from freezing. (Williams, 1969: 145–6)

Graham goes on to detail what Cree women wore, stating that "the outer garments are the same in both [sexes]" (Williams, 1969: 149). Over extended was Fort Saint-Charles, built in what is now the North West Angle inlet on American territory southeast of Lake of the Woods. At least one source claims that Fort Maurepas was near the outlet of the Winnipeg River. By 1735 these posts were providing half of the total value of furs for the colony of Canada.

La Vérendrye had been forced by the government of Canada after 1736 to devote his full time to discovery. In 1738 he established a fort commonly known as Fort La Reine, probably at what is now Portage la Prairie, and ostentatiously headed west with an exploration party that ended up meeting with the Mandans somewhere on the Missouri River. He would subsequently dispatch

some of his sons to pursue further exploration between the Missouri and the Cheyenne River, but these forays, while providing much new geographical information about the western prairies, brought no news or sighting of the Western Sea. La Vérendrye insisted that he had been assiduous in the search for the Western Sea, claiming that he had been prevented only by a series of unfortunate accidents from achieving his goal. But clearly he financed his operations by trading extensively in furs, and, equally clearly, he was generous in his gifts to the Aboriginal people with whom he traded. Whatever his ultimate purpose, he had succeeded in winning for France the friendship of the Aboriginal peoples of the region.

CANADA

periods of use, the outer garments would gradually lose their long guard hairs to friction and absorb increasing amounts of the sweat of their owners. Consequently, these would be replaced, presumably because the long hairs were worn away and the coat itself stank. These used coats were known in the trade as *castor gras* (greasy beaver), coat beaver, or made beaver: a pelt with most if not all of its guard hairs gone and a hide soft from being soaked in human sweat. Almost all types of fur were welcomed at the trading post, because, as Susan Sleeper-Smith (2009: xxv) points out, "Furs were highly transportable, required no capital investment in either people or land, and possessed a global receptivity both as a raw material and a finished good." But the used garments, classed by the Europeans as beaver robes, were the most welcome at the posts. The lack of guard hairs and the pliability of the hide made it easier for the undercoat to be removed. It was the undercoat that was coveted by the felters of Europe, and this market, and the desire for hats made of such material, motivated the pursuit of beaver. Regardless of the material used, beaver was such an important part of that process that the hats themselves were referred to as beavers, or *castors*.

With this demand in mind, beaver came to play such an important role in the fur trade that made beaver, referred to as MB, became the standard of exchange for the Hudson's Bay Company, functionally the currency of the posts.

As a result, the object biography of even the meanest beaver skin was very complex. From the back of the living creature it moved from clothing material, to currency, to trade good, and back to clothing material.

Beaver skins played an important role in the expansion of Europeans into the West. In turn, they also played an important role in European material culture. © Ken Gillespie Photography/ First Light/Corbis

Acadia and Nova Scotia

Acadia, an ill-defined geographical region that included more than peninsular Nova Scotia, had been contested ground between the British and the French since the early days of European settlement. Returned to France in 1670, Acadia and especially the village of Port-Royal often were attacked by New Englanders. Port-Royal, which was considered by its British neighbours to be "a Nest of Privateers & a Dunkirk to New England" (Dummer 1825 [1709]) was captured in 1690 by an expedition of seven vessels and a "foot regiment" of 450 New Englanders, but it was returned to France by the Treaty of Ryswick in 1697. New England failed to take Port-Royal in 1707 with a much larger force. When the remaining members of the 1,000-man, 23-transport-ship force returned to Connecticut, they were met by a number of jeering women. According to the Governor of the colony, John Winthrop, the women presented the men with "a great wooden sword, and said wthall 'Fie, for Shame. pull off those iron spits wch hang by yor sides, for wooden ones is all the fashion now'" (Winthrop 1889 [1707]) after which the women encouraged those who lived along the road to pour their chamber pots on the returning soldiers. Though they were successful in a later attempt in 1710, the humiliation of the 1707 defeat remained in the collective memory of New Englanders.

Nobody except the French wanted the Acadians removed, so they were tacitly allowed to remain in Nova Scotia on sufferance. Questions such as their land, language, and religious rights, as well as their political and military obligations to the new rulers, were unresolved. The government of Nova Scotia dealt with the Acadians on an ad hoc basis, accepting their insistence on political neutrality and failing to exercise much authority within the Acadian community. The Acadians were neither the first nor the last group to translate unofficial tolerance born of irresolution into enshrined "rights." The dealings of the Nova Scotian authorities with the Acadians on the question of loyalty before 1740 were never authorized in London, but they led the Acadians to believe that they had an understanding. Unfortunately for the French population of Nova Scotia, their loyalties were tested constantly by the French, who had begun after 1720 to construct a fortress at Louisbourg on the southeastern coast of Île-Royale.

The British capture of Louisbourg in 1745 and its return in 1748 had several important effects in Nova Scotia. One was to encourage the British to counter Louisbourg with some military settling of their own. Another was to turn the attention of the local authorities to the Acadians. The Nova Scotia Council in 1745 declared of the Acadians that "if they are not absolutely to be regarded as utter Enemies to His Majesty's Government they cannot be accounted less than unprofitable Inhabitants for their conditional Oath of Allegiance will not entitle them to the Confidence and Privileges of Natural British Subjects" (Library and Archives Canada, 1745: A27). British settlement and Acadian removal were commonly coupled in the minds of British officials on both sides of the Atlantic. With the founding of Halifax, a sequence of events was set in motion that would result in the forcible expulsion of 6,000 Acadian residents from the colony.

The decision of the British government to use the public purse to populate a British colony—the first time Britain had done so in America and at a cost of more than £600,000 between 1749 and 1764—marked a new British interest in the Atlantic region. In 1749 Britain recruited some 2,500 people, including soldiers and sailors recently disbanded and some London artisans, and shipped them to Nova Scotia. They arrived to find huts, tents, and primitive conditions. The new governor, Lord Edward Cornwallis (1713–76), complained that most of the new arrivals were "poor idle worthless vagabonds" (quoted in Bell, 1990: 344n). The British government soon sought a new source of more reliable settlers, turning to "foreign Protestants" from Switzerland, France, and Germany. It employed as recruiting agent the young Scotsman John Dick (d. 1804), who was empowered by the Board of Trade over the winter of 1749–50 to recruit up to 1,500 "foreign Protestants," who would receive land, a year's subsistence, arms, and tools, but not free transportation. Dick protested that free passage would be the main inducement, but he managed to fill the order. There were again complaints about the recruits, who were labelled "in general old miserable wretches" (Bell, 1990: 344n). In the end Dick sent over 2,700 Germans and Swiss, many

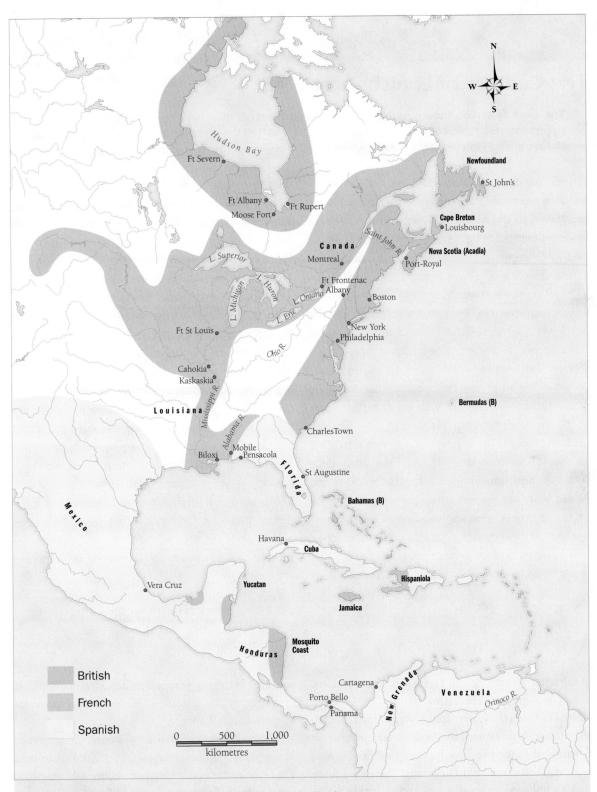

European possessions in North America after the peace of Utrecht (1713).

Contemporary Views

The Capture of Louisbourg, 1745

The capture of Louisbourg by New England militiamen in 1745 was one of the great military success stories of the colonial wars. The following is part of the explanation for the capitulation of the supposedly impregnable fortress given by an anonymous resident of the town.

. . . on the 15th [of June 1745] a squadron of six warships from London reached the English. These, together with the frigates, cruised about in view of the town without firing a single shot. We have, however, since learned that if we had delayed capitulating, all the vessels would have brought their broadsides to bear upon us and we should have had to undergo a most vigorous fire. Their arrangements were not unknown. . . . The siege of Louisbourg . . . notwithstanding our fortifications, would not have lasted so long had we been attacked by an enemy better versed in the art of war. No complaint can be made of the settlers, who served with the same precision as did the troops themselves, and had to bear the greatest fatigues. The regular soldiers were distrusted so that it was necessary to charge the inhabitants with the most dangerous duties. Children, ten and twelve years old, carried arms, and were to be seen on the ramparts, exposing themselves with a courage beyond their years. Our loss scarcely reached one hundred and thirty men, and it is certain that that of the English was more than two thousand. Yet their force was so great that for them this loss was inconsiderable. They had, at disembarking, as many as from eight to nine thousand men. We should have done more injury if we had been able to make sorties. I have told the causes which prevented our doing this. The bombs and bullets of the enemy caused frightful desolation in our poor town; most of our houses were demolished, and we were obliged to remove the floor from the general magazine to expose it to the weather in the King's garden; we feared that it might be burned by the enemy, as most of the bombs fell upon this magazine. More than three thousand five hundred must have been fired against us. I do not know exactly how much flour remained to us still, but I know that there was a large quantity, and there were other provisions in proportion. These, however, could not take the place of the munitions of war, which were absolutely exhausted. We had no more bombs, and if we had had any they would have been perfectly useless, for our mortars had cracked, after some shots had been fired. All misfortunes were ours at once.

Source: G.M. Wrong, ed., *Louisbourg in 1745: The Anonymous Lettre d'un Habitant de Louisbourg* (New York, 1897), 64–8.

of the latter actually French Huguenots from Lorraine. These immigrants were mainly farmers and skilled labourers. Uncertainty over land titles confined them to shantytown Halifax until the Nova Scotia government determined to remove them to a site 50 miles (80 km) west of Halifax, renamed Lunenburg. There they resettled, an unhappy crowd that was "inconceivably turbulent, I might have said mutinous," according to the officer in charge of the relocation, Major Charles Lawrence (*c.* 1709–60) (Bell, 1990: 435).

The settlement of Halifax was only one of a series of new pressures brought upon the province's Acadians. The French were reinforcing Louisbourg and constructing new forts (Fort Beauséjour and Fort Gaspéreau) on

BACKGROUNDER

Louisbourg

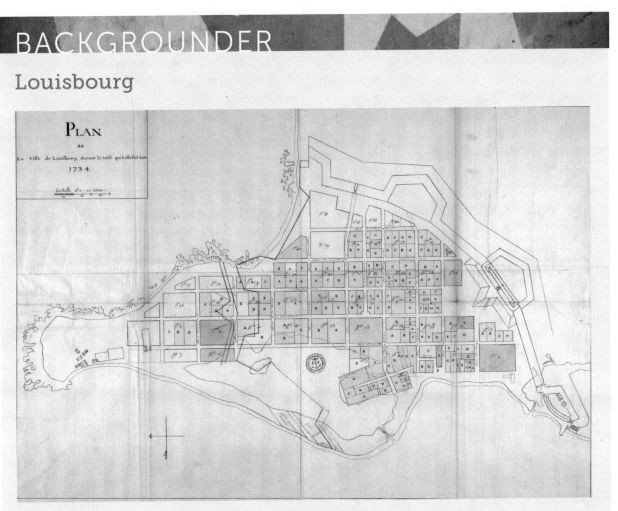

Louisbourg in 1734.
Source: A.J.B. Johnston, *Control and Order in French Colonial Louisbourg, 1713–1758* (East Lansing: Michigan State University Press, 2001), xlii. Direction des Archives de France/Centre des Archives d'Outre-Mer.

After 1713 the French had turned their attention to Île-Royale, and particularly to building a large fortress at Louisbourg on the southeastern coast. In 1716 Louisbourg contained about 600 people, mainly fishermen brought there from Plaisance in Newfoundland, which had been evacuated. After 1720 it grew rapidly as the French government fortified the town, garrisoned it, and employed it as the military and economic nerve centre of the Atlantic region. By 1734 the townsite—four east–west streets on about 100 acres—was surrounded by walls on three sides, with impressive gates. The fortifications—poorly located and poorly built—were never completed. Inside the walls were the huge and stately King's Bastion and barracks (the largest building in New France), and numerous stone dwellings and other structures. In the 1740s the Louisbourg population was made up of 600 soldiers (increased to 3,500 in the 1750s) and some 2,000 administrators, clerks, innkeepers, artisans, fishermen, and families.

We know a substantial amount about Louisbourg, much more than about Acadia, partly because

Continued...

as a fortress it generated a considerable volume of records and partly because its reconstruction as a National Historic Site has produced a minor industry of subsidized historical research. Its complex urban society—consisting of people who came from various parts of France as well as from New France (see Table 3.2)—was heavily subsidized by the Crown and included a wide variety of tradesmen and a substantial servant-keeping class, headed by 20 merchants. Always a major fishing port, serving as the centre of the French fishery after the surrender of Plaisance in 1713, Louisbourg in its prime was also an important naval station harbouring French warships as well as fishing vessels. Since its hinterland was completely undeveloped, supplies had to be imported from afar: from Canada, France, Acadia, and New England. The Yankees even supplied much of the building material for its fortifications, which cost 5 million livres.

By the time open warfare was resumed between Great Britain and France on 27 April 1744, Louisbourg had become a major military and commercial entrepôt in northern North America. The fortress was attacked in 1745 by a joint Anglo–American force under the command of Sir William Pepperell and Sir Peter Warren. Weakened by bad garrison morale that led to mutiny earlier in the winter of 1744–5, the fortress surrendered after only token resistance, leaving the victors to squabble over credit for the success. The fortress was returned to France in 1748 at the Treaty of Aix-la-Chapelle in exchange for Madras in India, but despite considerable reinforcement of fortifications and garrison in the 1750s, it fell quickly to the British again in 1758.

TABLE 3.2 Origins of the Habitants of Louisbourg

	1724		1726		1734	
	No.	%	No.	%	No.	%
New France	18	16.8	25	16.3	31	21.2
Normandy/Brittany	16	15.0	31	20.3	28	19.2
Southwest France	12	11.2	18	11.8	16	11.0
West France	29	27.1	36	23.5	24	16.4
Île de France	10	9.4	14	9.2	11	7.5
France (elsewhere)	21	19.6	25	16.3	27	18.5
Foreign	1	0.9	4	2.6	9	6.2
Total	107	100	153	100	146	100

Source: Adapted from A.J.B. Johnston, Control and Order in French Colonial Louisbourg, 1713–1758 (East Lansing: Michigan State University Press, 2001), xlii.

the disputed Chignecto Peninsula. The French also began encouraging the Acadians in Nova Scotia to remove to French territory, especially the previously neglected Île St-Jean, which grew to more than 2,000 residents by 1752. The bulk of Nova Scotia's Acadians remained where they were, but after the renewal of undeclared war in North America in 1754, the government of the colony decided to settle the question. In July 1755 the Executive Council of Nova Scotia summoned Acadian deputies into a meeting room in Halifax and informed them that conditional fealty was impossible. The Acadians must immediately take the oath of

The Porte Dauphine, the entrance to the reconstructed Louisbourg, with the clock tower of the King's Bastion and barracks in the distance. © Parks Canada / Fortress of Louisbourg National Historic Site.

allegiance in its common form. The Acadian representatives temporized overnight. When they were told that if they refused to take an unconditional oath, "effectual Measures" would be taken "to remove all such Recusants out of the Province," some offered to concede (Akins, 1869: 259–60). The council then refused to administer the oath, however, saying "that as there was no reason to hope their proposed Compliance proceeded from an honest Mind, and could be esteemed only the Effect of Compulsion and Force, they could not now be indulged with such Permission" (Akins, 1869: 259–60). A classic confrontation between the civic inflexibility of the state and a collective minority demanding special treatment was in the closing stages of resolution. The council decided not only to expel the Acadians but to distribute them to several British colonies in the south.

More than 6,000 Acadians were summarily rounded up in the late summer and early autumn of 1755 by the British military and transported by ship to the south. There was little resistance, although many escaped to the woods and headed for French territory or to the uninhabited north. The Acadians were not received with great enthusiasm in the British colonies, which had not been warned to expect them, and many eventually returned to the province. The British government never commented on the action of the Nova Scotia government, which it had never authorized, except to note that the colony had regarded it as "indispensably necessary for the Security and protection of the Province" (quoted in Brebner, 1927: 230). As for those who did escape to the French, after the British forced the surrender of Louisbourg in July 1758 another expulsion began. A further 6,000 Acadians, including 3,500 on Île St-Jean, were summarily rounded up by the British military and sent back to France. A storm at sea destroyed many of the vessels carrying the Acadians, and perhaps as many as half of them drowned. The British never succeeded in eliminating the French presence from the region, however. Many Acadians escaped into the bush, others returned from their exile. What the expulsion did accomplish was to remove the Acadians from their traditional lands and force them to the unsettled margins of the Maritime colonies.

The founding of Halifax also had a substantial impact on the 1,000 Mi'kmaq remaining in the colony. The Mi'kmaq had attempted to pursue their own best interests during the years of warfare between the French and the English. They understood that British concepts of landownership and settlement were disastrous to them. As a result they declared war against the British in 1749 and were met with a policy of extermination ordered by Lord Cornwallis. A final peace treaty with the Mi'kmaq in 1761 did not deal with land rights. No longer a military threat, the Aboriginal people would soon cease to be regarded as important in the colony.

In the wake of the final conquest of Louisbourg, the Nova Scotia government in October 1758 sent out advertisements to New England, offering to those who would settle in the colony free land, free transportation to it, and initial assistance in the form of food and tools. A few days before these advertisements were published, a legislative assembly—the first widely elected governing body in what is now Canada—met in Halifax. Nova

Scotia was now a full-fledged British colony, the four-teenth mainland colony in Britain's North American empire. This point had been reached with brutal measures that were characteristic of the age.

The First Three Anglo–French Wars

Although sporadic warfare had occurred in North America since the earliest settlements, a protracted struggle for the continent between the European imperial powers—in which the First Nations were important players—began only in 1689. North American hostilities had their own dynamic, although they were always associated with the larger international rivalries of the mother countries. There were four wars. The first three were the War of the League of Augsburg (1689–97), settled by the Treaty of Ryswick; the War of the Spanish Succession (1702–13), settled by the Treaty of Utrecht; and the War of the Austrian Succession (1744–8), settled by the Treaty of Aix-la-Chapelle. The North American aspects of these first three wars shared a good deal in common. The North American fighting in these conflicts was conducted mainly by the colonists themselves employing their own military methods. Occasionally, the mother country would undertake a brief initiative, usually disastrous. Much of the fighting occurred in the backcountry and along the frontier. Such conflict involved the First Nations, who joined the battles for reasons of their own.

The strategy of the French was to send out raiding parties on land and sea to keep the British colonies disunited and off balance. The French hoped that the British would not be able to utilize their superior manpower, resources, and command of the sea (the British controlled the Atlantic for all but brief periods throughout these wars) to invade and capture French territory. The British unsuccessfully—and disastrously—attempted to invade the St Lawrence in the first two wars. In the War of the League of Augsburg (also known as King William's War), an expedition under Sir William Phips in 1690 captured Port-Royal, and Phips followed this up

later that year with an attempted invasion of Quebec. Thirty-two vessels brought 2,300 English colonist volunteers—ill-trained and ill-equipped—up the St Lawrence. As the flotilla reached Quebec, smallpox struck and the ice closed in. Hundreds of Canadian farmers swarmed to the fortress from the countryside, and with the militia at his back, Governor Frontenac responded to a demand for surrender with the rejoinder, "I have no reply to make to your general other than from the mouths of my cannon and muskets." The invaders were quickly sent packing. In the War of the Spanish Succession (Queen Anne's War), a large force of New England militiamen were turned back in 1707 from Port-Royal. They were greeted on their return to Boston with the contents of chamber pots. A much larger English invading army, partly marching overland along Lake Champlain and partly transported in 14 ships of the line and 31 transports, was again turned back at Quebec. This war saw the most notorious of colonial raids, on Deerfield, Massachusetts, which led to the capture of Eunice Williams, the seven-year-old daughter of the village's Puritan minister. She was adopted by her Native captors, and later stubbornly refused to return to her people. She married a Mohawk, and although she visited her family several times over the years, she died in Caughnawaga, Quebec, in 1785, the best known of a number of European captives who preferred to remain with the First Peoples.

This war ended with the Treaty of Utrecht of 1713, in which France surrendered much North American territory. It renounced all claims to Newfoundland except for a few fishing rights and the islands of St Pierre and Miquelon, which were returned to France as a refuge for exiled Acadians. At the same time, most of Acadia and all claims to the Hudson Bay territory were granted to the British. In addition, France agreed to Clause XV: "The Subjects of France inhabiting Canada shall hereafter give no Hindrance or Molestation to the Five Nations or Cantons of Indians subject to the Dominion of Great Britain nor to the other natives of America who are Friends to the same."

In the War of the Austrian Succession, New England troops and British naval forces captured Louisbourg in 1745, leading to the dispatch of a major French fleet to North America in 1746. The fleet met bad weather and experienced epidemic disease, limping back to France without ever engaging the enemy. France hoped to make sufficient military gains around the world so that any territory lost in North America would be returned in the peace treaty. This strategy was not always successful. In 1713 it was forced to give up Acadia and its claims to Newfoundland, although in 1697 and 1748 it surrendered nothing of substance in North America. Neither mother country considered the North American theatre anything but a sideshow most of the time until the 1750s, when the British, after settling Nova Scotia at government expense, decided to take the New World seriously.

BACKGROUNDER

The French Naval Expedition of 1746

After years of relative military inaction, based on a defensive strategy for North America, the French government in late 1745 stirred itself finally to respond to the British seizure of the fortified fortress of Louisbourg in late June of 1745. The task of restoring French supremacy fell to the navy, a military arm that had been long neglected and underfunded, with an over-age officer corps, too few ships, and inadequate armaments. Command was given to Jean-Baptiste-Louis-Frédéric de la Rochfoucauld de Roye, duc d'Enville, a man without naval experience and only limited military background, but with the best of family connections. The government, under the direction of the comte de Maurepas, assembled in the early months of 1746 a massive expedition of more than 15 warships (in bad shape and ill-equipped), 45 troop carriers and support vessels, and almost 11,000 soldiers and sailors. Maurepas managed to put this force together despite grave financial shortages and a number of other problems, including a shortage of available seamen. The fleet departed in late June, choosing a safer southern route to America that added thousands of miles to the voyage, which was undertaken with considerable sickness (probably a combination of typhus and typhoid fever) and shortage of provisions (caused chiefly by unfit supplies), and complicated by the appearance of a great storm off the American coast.

Crippled, the expedition sailed into the harbour at Chibouctou, but without most of its warships, which remained lost for days. The commandant, who had been ill for months, promptly died. His replacement, Constantine-Louis, commandeur d'Estourmel, was ill and unprepared for command. On 30 September he told fellow officers, "There is too much to be done. For me all is lost. We shall not succeed." Soon after, he attempted suicide, apparently by falling on his sword, was unsuccessful, and resigned his command to the Marquis de la Jonquière, a capable man who soon realized the extent of the disaster that had befallen the expedition. A statement of the state of the force dated 13 October recorded that of 7,004 seamen and infantry, 603 were dead, 1,478 unfit, and 782 convalescent (for a total of 2,861, or 40 per cent of the force out of action). English estimates were even higher. An attack on Annapolis Royal was withdrawn and the fleet limped back to France. The disaster had little immediate result; it was partially balanced by victories in the Low Countries in 1747, which made it possible for the peace treaty of Aix-la-Chapelle in 1748 to restore matters to their pre-war status. But in 1749 the British made a major settlement in Chibouctou, while the French returned to their defensive thinking.

Source: J.S. Pritchard, Anatomy of a Naval Disaster: The 1746 French Expedition to North America (Montreal and Kingston: McGill-Queen's University Press, 1998).

The Seven Years War

Officially, the Seven Years War began in 1756 in Europe, although the North American contestants had been engaged in open conflict for several years. In 1754, a desperate struggle between the British and the French for the allegiance of the Aboriginal peoples in the Ohio Valley and for sovereignty over the region came to a head. The French had tried to assert their claim in 1749 by sending a military expedition, led by Pierre-Joseph Céleron de Blainville (1693–1759), which planted lead tablets all along the Ohio and Allegheny rivers stating the French claims to the region. The French in 1752 and 1753 built military posts in the area. In the latter year the British sent George Washington with a small party to deliver a letter to the French commandant at one of the French posts, Fort Le Boeuf, claiming the Ohio Valley and requesting the French to leave. They refused. In turn, the British governor of Virginia was authorized to use force to expel the French. He sent Washington back a year later with a force of 159 men, backed by a party of Aboriginals, to establish a fort on the Ohio. On the way, the expedition confronted a small French party of 30 men commanded by Joseph Coulon de Villiers de Jumonville (1718–54), who were travelling east to see whether Washington had entered what the French regarded as their territory. If he had, he was to be ordered formally to withdraw. Jumonville's party was specifically ordered not to provoke trouble; he was on a diplomatic mission, not a military one.

On 28 May 1754, Washington and some of his men entered the French camp, which was not well guarded. In the course of the ensuing melee, Jumonville (who had been wounded) was dispatched in traditional Aboriginal fashion with a tomahawk by one of the warriors. "You are not yet dead, my father," Tanacharison said to the wounded Frenchman in the ritual language of the time, and so he killed him (White, 1991: 241). Washington subsequently did his best to deny that Jumonville had been murdered, arguing that the French had hostile intentions—putting in jeopardy his reputation for never telling a lie. The incident led the French to send out a much larger force from Fort Duquesne, which in early July forced the Virginians to surrender. This surrender

An Acadian Account of the Removal of 1755

Many of the Acadian exiles ended up in the colony of Pennsylvania, which in 1758 collected a number of their narratives, including the following.

A Relation of the Misfortunes of the French Neutrals, as laid before the Assembly of the Province of Pennsylvania, by John Baptiste Galerm, one of the said People.

. . . Almost numberless are the Instances which might be given of the Abuses and Losses we have undergone from the French Indians, on Account of our steady Adhearance to our Oath of Fidelity: and yet notwithstanding our strict Observance thereof, we have not been able to prevent the grievous Calamity which is now come upon us, which we apprehend to be in a great Measure owing to the unhappy Situation and Conduct of some of our People settled at Chignecto, at the bottom of the Bay of Fundi, where the French, about four Years ago, erected a Fort; those of our People who were settled near it, after having had many of their Settlements burnt by the French; being too far from Halifax and Annapolis Royal to expect sufficient Assistance from the English, were obliged, as we believe, more through Compulsion and Fear than Inclination, to join with and assist the French. . . . As these People's Conduct had given just Umbrage to the Government in turn led the British to dispatch two regiments under General Edward Braddock to America, and they were devastated at the Monongahela River in the early summer of 1755. News of this defeat—war still not having formally been declared—contributed to the British decision in Nova Scotia to expel the neutral Acadians from their province. Thus did the imperial struggle in the west impact the maritime region, demonstrating that however marginal these regions were, their domestic development was affected by larger events.

In the beginning, the French seemed to be doing well. They had destroyed General Braddock's army of British regulars in 1755. On this occasion, the French tactics of ambush and guerrilla warfare easily triumphed over professional soldiers. A year later, under General Montcalm, they took 1,700 prisoners at the surrender of the three forts associated with Fort Oswego (on the southern shore of Lake Ontario, known to the French as Fort Chouaguen). Hit-and-run raiders kept the American backcountry in a constant uproar along the Ohio frontier. General Montcalm and other French officers were not happy with the brutality of these military actions. Given their naval weaknesses, however, the French needed to keep the British off balance to prevent a buildup of forces that would lead to an invasion.

In 1757 the French concentrated on New York as the major battlefield. Montcalm won several more notable victories, putting the French in control of the lake route into Canada. But the British continued to pour men and supplies into North America. A year later, the British managed to force the surrender of the garrison at Fort Frontenac on the north shore of Lake Ontario. A sideshow in the Ohio region saw the British capture Fort Duquesne on the Ohio River. The British further increased the number of troops at their disposal, employing their naval superiority to besiege successfully the exposed French fortress at Louisbourg in 1758. The French garrison held out just long enough to prevent the enemy from continuing on to an invasion of Quebec that same year, but the French were pulling back militarily. The situation in New France was becoming desperate. The government was unable to get reinforcements of men or fresh supplies, especially of arms and munitions, because the British controlled the sea. Moreover, the

LE CANADIEN.

and created Suspicions, to the Prejudice of our whole Community, we were summoned to appear before the Governor and Council at Halifax, where we were required to take the Oath of Allegiance without any Exception, which we could not comply with because, as that Government is at present situate, we apprehend that we should have been obliged to take up Arms; but we are still willing to take the Oath of Fidelity, and to give the strongest Assurance of continuing peaceable and faithful to his Britannic Majesty, with that Exception, But this, in the present Situation of Affairs, not being satisfactory, we were made Prisoners, and our Estates, both real and personal, forfeited for the King's Use; and Vessels being provided, we were some time after sent off, with most of our Families, and dispersed amongst the English Colonies. The Hurry and Confusion in which we were embarked was an aggravating Circumstance attending our Misfortunes; for thereby many, who had lived in Affluence, found themselves deprived of every Necessary, and many Families were separated, Parents from Children, and Children from Parents.

—*John Baptiste Galerm*

Source: "Relation of the French Neutrals, 1758," Pennsylvania Archives, 1758, First series, vol. 3, as reprinted in N.E.S. Griffiths, *The Acadian Deportation: Deliberate Perfidy or Cruel Necessity?* (Toronto: Copp Clark, 1969), 151.

Letter from Charles Lawrence regarding the expulsion of the Acadians, 11 August 1755. LAC, MG53, No. 71 2-4.

colony was in terrible shape financially, with runaway inflation. The civilian government and the military leadership were at constant loggerheads, and morale was very low.

At the beginning of 1759, the situation was very grave for New France. After more than a century and a half of successful struggle against the environment, First Nations enemies, French neglect, and British hostility, the Canadians had their backs to the wall. The Acadians had been forcibly removed from Nova Scotia and Louisbourg had been captured. A series of powerful British armies, backed by a wealthy government determined to win, was gathering for the invasion of the St Lawrence. The locus of power was about to shift, to the detriment of the French in North America.

The Conquest and Its Aftermath

The series of abortive and aborted British attempts (in 1690, 1711, and 1746) to seize Quebec, the administrative capital of New France, did not prevent another major expedition under General James Wolfe (1727–59) from trying again. The largest and best-equipped military force that North America had ever known assembled at Louisbourg over the winter of 1758–9, while the frozen ice of the St Lawrence isolated the French. The British force consisted of 8,600 troops, most of them regulars, and 13,500 sailors aboard 119 vessels, including 22 ships of the line and five frigates. This great armada required

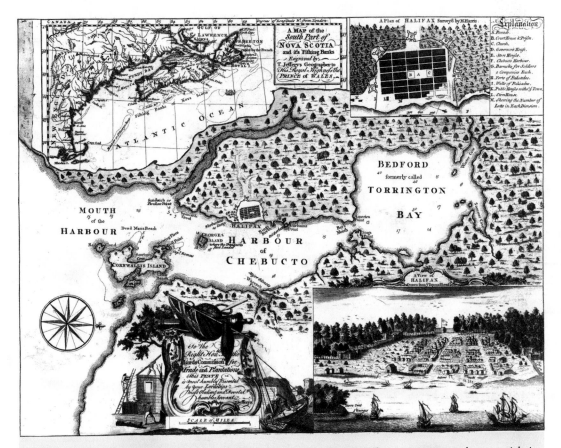

"A Map of the South Part of Nova Scotia and its Fishing Banks," by Thomas Jefferys, 1750. Inset at the upper right is "A Plan of the new town of Halifax Surveyed by M. Harris"; at the lower right, "A View of Halifax drawn from ye top masthead." LAC, NMC 1012.

six days simply to clear Louisbourg harbour in early June 1759. On 27 June, Wolfe landed his army on the Île d'Orléans without serious French opposition. There followed over two months of skirmishing, as Wolfe attempted to land his army closer to the French forces, and the French commander-in-chief, the Marquis de Montcalm (1712–59), sought to prevent such a move. Meanwhile, Wolfe and the British admiral, Sir Charles Saunders (1713?–75), were constantly at loggerheads, and Montcalm found evidence that his forces, mainly French-Canadian militiamen, would not stand up to offensive action.

Wolfe tried a number of plans, all without success. He was becoming desperate. As the end of summer approached, there was less time for the massive British fleet to remain in the St Lawrence, and its commanders were pressing for a final confrontation. Finally, after partially recovering from a fever, Wolfe made a final effort. His troops found a path up the cliffs to the plain above at the Anse au Foulon, and managed to pass the French sentries unmolested. The British drew their battle lines covering the plain above the cliffs. Inexplicably, Montcalm decided to attack the British army without waiting for reinforcements. The French ranks broke first, both Wolfe and Montcalm were mortally wounded, and the British possessed Quebec. The war was not ended, for the bulk of the French army escaped and would fight on valiantly for another year. The Battle of Quebec (or the Battle of the Plains of Abraham) was probably the first military engagement in North America that was fought almost entirely on European rather than on North American terms. A fully professional army, disciplined and on the

A map by Thomas Jefferys showing the British claims to Acadia. Library of Congress, Prints and Photographs Division, 705008.

day well led, defeated a partly untrained one. Backed by a government at home with regular troops and naval support, the British finally breached the defensive position that the French had enjoyed for over a century.

British reinforcements and supplies arrived first on the St Lawrence in 1760, and a traditional three-pronged attack on Montreal—anchored by a large army led by General Jeffrey Amherst (1717–97) from New York—forced the surrender of that town, the final French stronghold, in early September. The 55 articles of capitulation would govern the British occupation of Canada until the governments in Europe finally settled

matters with the Treaty of Paris in 1763. Until Europe made a final determination, Britain dealt with the colony with a fairly light hand. Canada was governed by military administrators who spoke French and accepted it as the "language of the country." A few of the French-Canadian elite departed for France, while a number of new suppliers (mainly American colonials tied to British and American trading patterns) made their inevitable appearance.

Peace negotiations in 1761 proved unsuccessful, not because the French had balked at sacrificing North American territory, but because war minister William

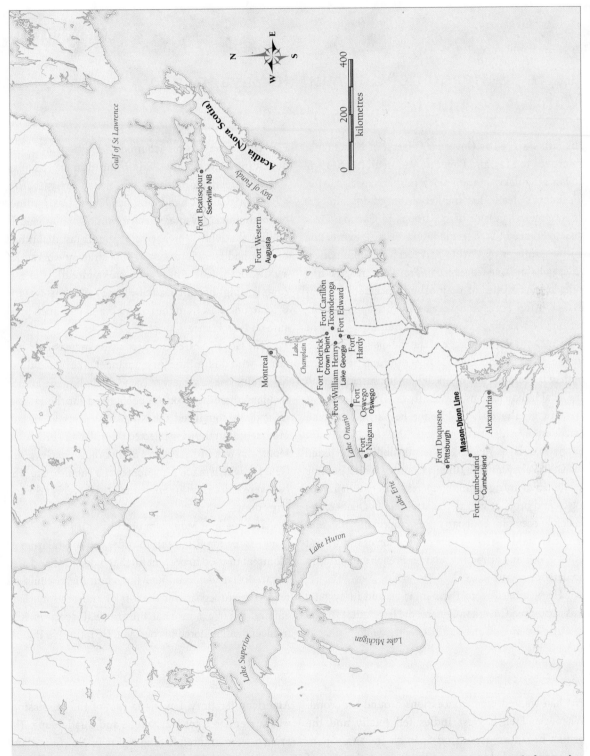

The war in 1755. Adapted from Seymour Schwartz, The French and Indian War 1754–1763: The Imperial Struggle for North America (New York: Simon & Schuster, 1994), 37.

Pierre de Rigaud de Vaudreuil de Cavagnial, Marquis de Vaudreuil

His father served as Governor General of New France from 1703 to 1725, and Pierre de Vaudreuil (1698–1778) advanced quickly in the French military service. After his father's death, his mother arranged for him the appointment as major of the troops in Canada. On a visit to France in 1728 he made a favourable impression on the Minister of Marine and received a promotion. In 1733 he became Governor of Trois-Rivières, the first rung on the ladder of political advancement in New France. After successful service in this appointment, in 1742 he was made Governor of Louisiana, where he was quick to take advantage of the independent authority the distance from Quebec gave him, and he boasted both of his reforms and of his diplomatic successes with the local Indian nations, especially the Choctaws.

In 1746, already in middle age, he married a woman considerably older than himself. The two had a very happy marriage. Vaudreuil's responsibilities included the Ohio Valley and the Illinois Country, which became a hotbed of intrigue and imperial contention in the 1750s and brought him to the attention of Quebec. His major success in Louisiana was improving the economic situation, stressing the production of indigo and other goods and attracting a larger French expenditure on defence.

He was recalled to Paris in 1753, and in 1755 he was appointed Governor General of New France. While in Paris he missed the conflict in the Ohio Valley at Fort Duquesne, but he acquired the responsibility for defending New France against the British. His plan was to defend his territory tenaciously by gathering all authority in his hands and employing interior lines of communication to advantage, while simultaneously hoping that the British would remain as disunified as they had been in the past. This strategy worked for awhile, but it took a heavy toll on Vaudreuil, who was complaining about ill health by late 1756. In this war the British took over from the colonials and put much pressure on New France.

The Governor General became on increasingly bad terms with his military commander, the Marquis of Montcalm, over a variety of issues, including the French regulars' disrespect for the people and for the militia. In 1758 he convinced the King's ministers to replace Montcalm, but the King rejected the order and promoted Montcalm to a military rank higher than the Governor General, which made him Montcalm's subordinate. The two were still disputing while the British were at the colony's door.

The death of Montcalm on the battleground made it necessary for Vaudreuil to order the capitulation of Montreal in 1760 to prevent further bloodshed and also ensured that Vaudreuil and Intendant Bigot would be made the scapegoats for the loss of France's American empire. After a long trial the tribunal declared him innocent and restored his pension. He retired in Paris.

Pitt had wanted more concessions around the world. When the French West Indies fell totally and the British began an assault on Spanish Havana—Spain had earlier foolishly entered the war on the side of France—the French and Spanish had their backs to the wall. The French offered to sacrifice more continental American territory. Louisiana east of the Mississippi was surrendered for Martinique and Guadeloupe. The French were granted fishing rights in Newfoundland and the tiny islands of St Pierre and Miquelon in exchange for the surrender of all other claims to territory in the northern part of the American continent.

Brave Wolfe

The Americans celebrated the victory of Quebec in broadside poetry (often intended to be sung) that was sold in single printed sheets on the streets of Boston. Here is one of those broadsides. This song went through so many variations that it is probably America's first best-seller.

Then forth went this brave youth
And crossed the ocean,
To free America
Was his intention.
He landed at Quebec
With all his party,
The city to attack,
both brave and hearty.

Brave Wolfe drew up his men
In line so pretty,
On the Plains of Abraham
Before the city.
The French came marching down
Arrayed to meet them,
In double numbers 'round
Resolved to beat them.

Montcalm and this brave youth
Together walkéd;
Between two armies they
Like brothers talkéd,

Till each one took his post
And did retire.
'Twas then these numerous hosts
Commenced their fire.

The drums did loudly beat,
With colours flying,
The purple gore did stream,
And men lay dying.
Then shot from off his horse
Fell that brave hero.
We'll long lament his loss
That day in sorrow.

He raiséd up his head
Where the guns did rattle,
And to his aide he said,
"How goes the battle?"
"Quebec is all our own,
They can't prevent it."
He said without a groan,
"I die contented."

Source: Edith Fowke and Alan Mills, eds, *Canada's Story in Song* (Toronto: W.J. Gage, 1965), 49.

The Spanish proved no problem after the fall of Havana. In a complicated arrangement, Britain returned Havana and Puerto Rico and kept Spain's Florida, while France compensated Spain for its losses by ceding to it the western half of Louisiana and the port of New Orleans.

The final arrangement was "sold" to the British public by emphasizing the great gains made in North America. Having stressed the security won for the American colonies as a result of the war—at monumental expense to the British people in manpower and money—the government needed an American policy. The addition to the British Empire in North America of a sizable number of French-speaking Roman Catholics, as well as complete responsibility for the First Nations everywhere east of the Mississippi River, meant that regular troops

The British Landing at the Foot of the Plains of Abraham, 12 September 1759

Rear-Admiral Charles Holmes was in charge of the British landing of troops at the foot of the cliffs of the Plains of Abraham. In this letter, dated 18 September 1759, he describes the outcome of the landing:

In this manner, the General had his Army on the Enemies Shore, within two miles of the Town, before his arrival was well known at their Head Quarters: For Mr. Montcalm had taken all our latter Motions for so many Feints, & thought our grand Aim was still below Quebec & pointed towards Beauport; And he was confirmed in this, by the several well laid Feints & Motions of Mr. Saunders, who laid Buoys in the Night, close in shore, towards Beauport, . . . Montcalm was surprised; but lost not a moment to repair his Misfortune—he marched his Troops with the greatest Expedition from Montmorency & Beauport, to the Heights nearest the Citadel & adjacent to those already possessed by our Troops: But he was deceived to the last; for he could not believe it possible that we had so suddenly thrown over so large a Body of Forces; & the inequalities of the Ground, covered numbers of our Men, & kept him from forming a just opinion of their Strength: He resolved therefore to attack them before they were reinforced, or had got up any Cannon. From eight to near Ten, he was busy assembling & drawing up his Army. It consisted of about 9000 Men, among whom were five Battalions of Regulars. Our Army consisted of 4600 Regulars. About Ten, he marched in order of Battle & attacked us on the Plains of Abraham. His Disposition was excellent, his Army advanced in very good order. Wolfe was entirely prepared; & overjoyed at the unexpected Resolution of the Enemy. They fired twice before he made any return. Then commenced the Battle, which hardly lasted a quarter of an Hour. Lascelles's Regiment was the first that broke in upon them, with fixed Bayonets, and the Highlanders flanked them at the same time: The Body opposed to them was instantly turned & routed; & their whole Army gave way and fled to the Town: the rest was Pursuite & Carnage; in which the Highlanders broad Swords did great Execution. Gen'r Wolfe fell early in the action, & only lived long enough to know that his Troops were victorious: On learning of which he said—"Since I have conquered I dye satisfied."

Source: Special Collections, University of Waterloo Library.

would have to be stationed in North America. This also meant that the Americans would have to contribute at least a token amount for their support. Over the winter of 1762–3 the British government debated imposing a tax on the colonies to support the army, but it paused to seek more information before proceeding.

Its first effort at creating a policy was the Proclamation of 1763. Like most British policy for its northern possessions produced over the next few years, the Proclamation of 1763 was not directly intended to effect fundamental changes for Britain's older seaboard colonies. Four new governments were created out of the American acquisitions, including Quebec, which was limited to its St Lawrence settlements. This truncated province was to be governed by British law and, as soon as possible, an elected assembly. The Island of Saint John and Cape Breton were attached to Nova Scotia. Land grants were to be readily available to retired officers and disbanded servicemen. In the West, beyond the river systems of the Atlantic coast, no land grants were to be made. This territory was to be reserved for the First Nations, and any trading in it was to be regulated by the imperial government.

The British subjected Quebec to a devastating artillery bombardment in 1759, as can be seen in this painting by one of the British officers, Richard Short. In the days before cameras, many officers and travellers created first-hand illustrations, often in watercolours, as the only way to provide visual evidence of the events in which they had been involved. Indeed, a skilled artist was a highly valued member of any military contingent. "A View of the Bishop's House with the Ruins as They Appear in Going down the Hill from the Upper to Lower Town," by Richard Short from a drawing made at the siege in 1759, LAC, 1989-283-11.

At the same time, neither the Proclamation of 1763 nor any other British document ever laid out a fully articulated policy for what is now Canada, although the outlines of such a policy were perfectly plain. The British did not wish to populate their northernmost possessions in America with settlers sent directly from the mother country. Great Britain was just beginning a major economic change usually called the Industrial Revolution, and it wanted to retain its own population, both as a labour force and for military purposes. It was, however, prepared to make land grants to disbanded professional soldiers, who would not represent any great economic loss to the mother country. It was also willing to accept "foreign Protestants" as new settlers, although it clearly hoped that people already living in North America would make up the majority of the fresh

arrivals. As a result of their experience in Nova Scotia, the British had learned two lessons for dealing with its newly acquired territory. First, the state could not afford to subsidize a large movement of people to a new colony (as it had in the case of Halifax and Nova Scotia). Second, the best way to deal with an alien population was to outnumber it; forcible removal, as of the Acadians, was neither humane nor effective.

The Proclamation had ramifications beyond the territory ceded by the French. It was preceded by the beginning of a major Aboriginal uprising in the interior, known as Pontiac's Rebellion. Both the declaration of limits for American westward expansion and the need to finance Britain's new military responsibilities would enrage the American colonials. They began a series of provocative responses to Britain that would escalate

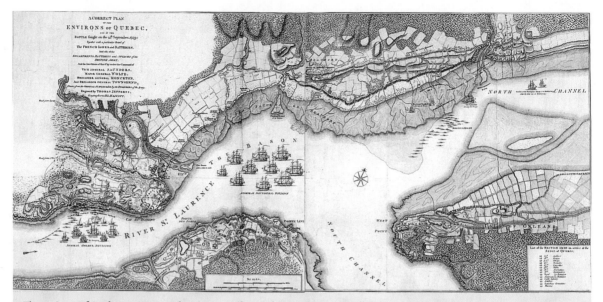

The environs of Quebec, a 1760 map by Thomas Jefferys, who was then geographer to George III, illustrates the Quebec campaign in 1759. Wolfe set up camp on the Île d'Orléans (lower right); tried and failed to land at Montmorency, on the north shore (above the North Channel), in July; moved his fleet upriver past Quebec in September; and landed at l'Anse au Foulon (extreme left) to wage the brief battles on the Plains of Abraham (above). LAC, C-128079.

Preparatory drawing for the engraved print "The Death of Wolfe" by James Barry, watercolour, c. 1763. LAC, Peter Winkworth Collection of Canadiana, R9266-335.

into an organized colonial rebellion or "revolution." It soon became apparent that policy for the new territories could not be executed by Great Britain in isolation.

Conclusion

Before 1763, the French Empire in North America sprawled in a great arc from the Atlantic coast to the Mississippi River and then southward to Louisiana. Although not all sections were equally developed, all posed a threat to the English (British after 1707) colonies to their south, and all were caught up in the constant imperial warfare after 1690. These wars would finally end with the French expulsion from most of North America. This expulsion, in turn, led to some dramatic changes in France itself, some of which would come back to impact other elements of North America. In the course of the conflict, resident populations like the Acadians and the First Nations often became victims of the ongoing struggles, sometimes because of their allegiances, but sometimes simply because of circumstance. For some, the displacement was permanent, and the changes irreversible.

Historiography

Understanding the Colonial Wars

The North American colonial wars, which began in the 1680s and continued sporadically until the 1760s, were of sufficient duration and complexity to sustain a number of competing storylines developed over the years. Perhaps the oldest (and also the most misleading) is concluded by the descriptor "the French and Indian War," in which the first three wars in the conflict have been known in the English colonies/states since the seventeenth century by the names of the British monarchs under which they were fought (King William's War, Queen Anne's War, King George's War), with only the last (and greatest war) named after the two principal opponents of the Americans instead of the term "the Seven Years War" commonly used in Europe.

The concentration on the American aspects of the conflict has long been paramount among American historians, including the greatest of them, Francis Parkman, very much a typical nineteenth-century American in his approach. Parkman greatly downplayed the contributions of the First Nations to the military efforts of both the British and the French in the conflict, especially by focusing his account on the showdown event of the war—the Battle of the Plains of Abraham—which was the first time that a battle was actually fought in this war in European terms and without Aboriginal allies playing an important role. He further skewed his account by treating the confrontation at the Plains of Abraham as a struggle between the two generals, Montcalm and Wolfe, employing a standard (for the time) "great man" approach to the subject, which greatly enhanced its literary potential. Indeed, Parkman's instinct was always to go for the dramatic whenever possible. To some extent, American accounts of the French and Indian wars still suffer from a surfeit of Francis Parkman. If Americans still see the last war against the French as a splendid victory, the conflict looks quite different from the perspective of those who lost this war and their descendants. The losers found themselves, against their wills, trans-ferred from French to British sovereignty. The transfer was accompanied by threats to their language, religion, and culture—indeed, to their very identity—although in the end the losses were less severe than had been anticipated. The Canadian perspective, as seen in Guy Frégault's *La Guerre de la Conquête* (2009), shows that the French were holding their own until the early 1760s, when the British really brought a heavy manpower advantage to bear. Somewhat to the surprise of Spain, which entered the Caribbean aspect of this war very late in the game, Spanish territorial losses were very heavy: Florida and Spanish claims east of the Mississippi River.

Several of the most interesting storylines actually extend beyond the Treaty of Paris, which ended this war in 1763. One of the more intriguing was propounded by Lawrence H. Gipson (1880–1971), whose 15-volume "The British Empire before the American Revolution," published between 1936 and 1970, was generally regarded throughout the twentieth century as the most important scholarly statement made on the subject, although it was heavily laden with British imperial history and had little interest in the international situation beyond London. Gipson suggested in an influential article in 1950 ("The American Revolution as an Aftermath of the Great War for the Empire," *Political Science Quarterly*) that the ultimate real importance of the colonial wars was in setting the stage for the American War of Independence. He saw British policy towards the colonies after the war as a constantly escalating series of clumsy actions, each of which made matters worse. Some of those actions, although not of the same ultimate consequence, involved the British effort after the war to create a new Aboriginal policy that would satisfy the aspirations of the First Nations, notably through the Proclamation of 1763.

In the twenty-first century, there has been a general consensus on seeing the colonial wars in the broader context of international imperial rivalries. William

Continued...

Nestor, in *The First Global War: Britain, France and the Fate of North America, 1756–1775* (2000), and William Fowler, in *Empires at War: The French and Indian War and the Struggle for North America, 1754–1763* (2006), exemplify this broader view of the colonial conflicts. On the whole, the recent studies take a more balanced approach to the conflict, although most of them continue to see it chiefly in North American terms.

Short Bibliography

Banks, Kenneth. *Chasing Empire across the Sea: Communications and the State in the French Atlantic, 1713–1763*. Montreal and Kingston, 2002. A fascinating study of the eighteenth-century French Empire in the New World.

Eccles, W.J. *France in America*. Markham, Ont., 1990. The best overview of the French Empire in North America.

Faragher, John Mack. *A Great and Noble Scheme: The Tragic Story of the Expulsion of the French Acadians from Their American Homeland*. New York, 2005. A recent synthesis by an American scholar.

Griffiths, Naomi. *The Contexts of Acadian History, 1587–1781*. Montreal, 1992. A series of fascinating essays by the leading specialist on early Acadia.

Handcock, Gordon. *"So Longe As There Comes Noe Women": Origins of English Settlement in Newfoundland*. St John's, 1989. The story of early English settlement in Newfoundland.

Head, C. Grant. *Eighteenth-Century Newfoundland: A Geographer's Perspective*. Toronto, 1976. An interesting example of what the historical geographer contributes to Canadian historical analysis.

Johnstone, A.J.B. *Control and Order in French Colonial Louisbourg*. East Lansing, Mich., 2001. A study of the administration of Louisbourg.

MacDonald, M.A. *Fortune and La Tour: The Civil War in Acadia*. Toronto, 1983. A well-written account of the La Tour family and its vicissitudes.

MacLeod, D. Peter. *Northern Armageddon: The Battle of the Plains of Abraham*. Vancouver/Toronto, 2008. The latest attempt to explain this key battle.

Moore, Christopher. *Louisbourg Portrait: Life in an Eighteenth-Century Garrison Town*. Toronto, 1982. An award-winning book based on early court records, demonstrating how much fascinating material can be teased out of such sources.

Nicholls, Andrew D. *A Fleeting Empire: Early Stuart Britain and the Merchant Adventurers to Canada*. Montreal and Kingston, 2010. The early history of the Maritime region cast into an imperial context.

Pritchard, J.S. *Anatomy of a Naval Disaster: The 1746 French Expedition to North America*. Montreal and Kingston, 1998. A wonderful account of the French navy in a time of crisis, demonstrating how difficult it was to co-ordinate military activities in the eighteenth century.

Steele, Ian. *Guerillas and Grenadiers: The Struggle for Canada, 1689–1760*. Toronto, 1969. A useful short history of the Canadian wars, emphasizing the roles of both the regular and irregular forces.

White, Richard. *The Middle Ground: Indians, Empire and Republics in the Great Lakes Region 1650–1815*. Cambridge, 1991. A revisionist work that takes the First Nations seriously in strategic and cultural terms.

Study Questions

1. Is the anonymous habitant in the description of the 1745 siege of Louisbourg a neutral observer?

2. Why was the Acadian expulsion such a tragedy? Could it have been prevented?

3. Briefly explain why the Maritime region was a scene of such violence in the seventeenth century.

4. In the matter of its economic development, did Canada owe more to its European origins or to its North American location? Explain.

5. What were the three chief differences between the earlier colonial wars and the Seven Years War?

6. Does the first-person account of the Battle of the Plains of Abraham surprise you in any way?

7. How did the Proclamation of 1763 respond to the problems of the British in North America at the time? Why did it fail to avert the American Revolution?

Visit the companion website for *A History of the Canadian Peoples*, fifth edition for further resources.

www.oupcanada.com/Bumsted5e

4

Becoming and Remaining British, 1759–1815

The Battle of Quebec of 1759, also known as the Battle of the Plains of Abraham, was a pivotal event in the Seven Years War. The battle left much of the town destroyed and lives uprooted, although this scene emphasizes that life carries on among the ruins. "View of the Bishop's house with the ruins as they appear in going up the Hill from the Lower, to the Upper Town," by Richard Short. © McCord Museum. Compare this view with that by the same artist of the same location, but going down the hill, on p. 105.

Timeline

1769 Publication of *Emily Montague*.

1773 The Island of Saint John calls its first assembly.

1774 Parliament passes the Quebec Act. It also passes Palliser's Act to regulate the Newfoundland fishery.

1775 The Americans invade Canada.

1776 An American party invades Nova Scotia.

1778 Peter Pond reaches the rich Athabasca country. James Cook arrives at Nootka Sound.

1781 The British surrender at Yorktown. A smallpox epidemic decimates the First Nations around Hudson Bay.

1782 The first Loyalist fleet departs for Nova Scotia. Shelburne founded.

1783 Treaty of Paris ends the War of the American Revolution by recognizing American independence.

1784 British North America is reorganized. New Brunswick is separated from Nova Scotia and given a separate government. Cape Breton gets a government but no assembly.

1786 Guy Carleton (now Lord Dorchester) is appointed Governor General of British North America.

1787 Charles Inglis, the first Anglican bishop in North America, arrives at Halifax.

1788 King's College is established by the Nova Scotia Assembly (it actually opens in 1790 in Windsor).

1789 The British and Spanish spar at Nootka Sound.

1791 Upper and Lower Canada are separated by the British Parliament's passage of the Constitutional Act of 1791.

1792 First legislature in Upper Canada is convened at Newark (Niagara-on-the Lake). Captain George Vancouver begins his survey of the BC coast.

1793 Alexander Mackenzie of the North West Company reaches the Pacific Ocean via an overland route from Montreal.

1800 King's College (now the University of New Brunswick) is founded at Fredericton.

1806 *Le Canadien*, the first French-language newspaper, is published in Quebec.

1808 Simon Fraser reaches the Pacific via the Fraser River.

1809 First steam vessel (the *Accommodation*) begins service between Montreal and Quebec.

1811 Hudson's Bay Company makes a land grant of 116,000 square miles (300,429 km²) to Lord Selkirk.

1812 Americans declare war on Great Britain and invade Canada. The first settlers arrive at Red River.

1813 York (Toronto) is sacked by the Americans. Laura Secord treks through enemy territory to warn the British of the American attack.

1814 Treaty of Ghent inconclusively ends the War of 1812.

The British established a foothold in Canada with their victory at the Battle of Quebec in 1759. They consolidated their position in 1760, and kept the conquest at the peace treaty in 1763. The theory was that eliminating the French would stabilize North America. It did not work out that way. Within a few years of the conquest, the American colonists had begun an armed rebellion and attempted unsuccessful invasions of Quebec and Nova Scotia. The British reorganized their North American empire after the Americans left it, taking advantage of the thousands of exiles and refugees, called Loyalists, the war had produced. Within a generation, in 1812, the Americans declared war on Great Britain and attempted another round of invasions of Canada, but they were beaten back by British regulars and colonial militia, albeit with considerable difficulty. The period from 1759 to 1815 was, thus, one of great turmoil and change. British North America would settle down only after 1815.

From the Proclamation to the Rebellion

In Nova Scotia, a third contingent of subsidized settlers was added to the first group at Halifax and to the "foreign Protestants." The New England "Planters" came to the province between 1759 and 1762. Governor Charles Lawrence took advantage of a substantial annual parliamentary grant for Nova Scotia to recruit over 8,000 Yankees. He provided them with land, transportation, and subsidies until the financial tap was turned off in 1762. The New Englanders came mainly from land-hungry areas of Rhode Island, Connecticut, and southeastern Massachusetts. They saw migration to Nova Scotia as a particularly attractive alternative to moving to northern areas of New England because it was financed by the government. The migrants tended to move in kinship groups, often as entire communities. Most were farmers, although others were fishermen seeking improved access to superior fishing grounds. The farmers settled on Acadian land in the Minas Basin region at the top of the Annapolis Valley, while the fishermen moved to south-shore outports they named Yarmouth and Barrington after their New England counterparts.

The Planters had been promised not only cheap land but liberty of conscience and a government "like those of neighbouring colonies," a guarantee they took to mean that they could replicate the participatory local democracy of their former homes. They soon found that Nova Scotia had no intention of permitting strong local government. Political disillusionment was added to disappointment over the climate and the absence of markets. Perhaps half the newcomers left within a few years of the termination of subsidies, complaining of "Nova Scarcity." While Yankee farmers dealt in small parcels of land, the elite office-holding classes (both within and without the colony) acquired large grants of wilderness land—3 million acres (1,214,100 ha) in the last few days before the Stamp Act became effective in 1765. The Stamp Act put a tax—in the form of an embossed stamp—on all paper used in legal transactions; having to buy stamped paper would greatly increase the cost of obtaining the grants. Only a handful of these speculators became active in either settlement ventures or commercial development.

By 1767, when a detailed census of Nova Scotia was taken, the colony was well populated, with 11,072 people in Nova Scotia proper, another 707 in Cape Breton, 1,196 in the northern section (now New Brunswick), and 519 on the Island of Saint John. The census also demonstrated that a heterogeneous population was already in place, consisting of 11,228 Protestants and 2,246 Catholics, and several ethnic groups (see Table 4.1). In addition, the returns showed 95 "Negroes" and a scattering of "Indians" (apparently no serious attempt was made to count them). Within a few years, substantial numbers of Scots would come to the region from the Lowlands but especially the Highlands, adding Gaelic to the English, German, French, and Mi'kmaq already freely spoken throughout the region.

Land speculation also dominated the development of the Island of Saint John. The entire land surface of the island was distributed to absentee owners (mainly British office-holders and military men) by lottery in 1767. These proprietors were supposed to settle the land in return for their grants, but most would merely hold it in the hopes that it would become more valuable. The British allowed the proprietors on the Island of Saint John, which was initially attached to Nova Scotia, to petition for a separate government in 1769, on the understanding that it would not cost the mother country a penny.

TABLE 4.1 Population of Nova Scotia in 1767 by Ethnicity

Place	English	Irish	Scottish	Americans	Germans	Acadians
Nova Scotia	686	1,831	143	5,799	1,862	650
Cape Breton	70	169	6	170	21	271
North (NB)	25	53	17	874	60	147
Saint John	130	112	7	70	3	197
Totals	912	2,165	173	6,913	1,936	1,265

Document

The Lords of Trade and Policy for the West

In the late spring of 1763, the British government turned its attention to what it should do with the new territories ceded to Britain by the Treaty of Paris. It was easily agreed that most of the territories could be included in old colonies or established in new ones, but one exception was "that large Tract of Country bounded by the Mississippi and the Limits of the Hudson Bay Company on the one hand and on the other by the Limits of Canada, East and West Florida and His Majesty's ancient Colonies." The Lords of Trade—the equivalent of a colonial office at the time—offered a different policy for this territory in a report of 5 August 1763. This report led directly to the Proclamation of 1763.

To the King's Most Excellent Majesty . . .

We have taken this important Subject into our most serious Consideration and do most humbly concur in Your Majesty's Opinion, of the propriety of putting this Country under a particular Government, by a Commission under Your Great Seal, with a most precise Description of its Boundaries, in Order to ascertain the actual possession of its Property, and with such Powers as may be necessary, as well to maintain and secure the free Exercise of the Indian Trade, which it is proposed all Your Majesty's Subjects shall enjoy within it, under proper Regulations, as to prevent its becoming a Refuge to Criminals and Fugitives.—But at the same time, we beg Leave to submit to your Majesty, the following Objections which have occurred to us, against the annexing this Country to any particular Government, especially to that of Canada.

1st We are apprehensive that, should this Country be annexed to the Government of Canada, a Colour might be taken on some future Occasion, for supposing that Your Majesty's Title to it, had taken its Rise, singly from the Cessions made by France, in the late Treaty, whereas Your Majesty's Title to the Lakes and

Continued...

circumjacent Territory as well as to the Sovereignty over the Indian Tribes, particularly of the six Nations, rests on a more solid and even a more equitable Foundation; and perhaps nothing is more necessary than that just Impressions on this Subject should be carefully preserved to the Minds of the Indians, whose Ideas might be blended and confounded if they should be brought to consider themselves as under the Government of Canada—

2d We are apprehensive as the whole of this Country would become subject to the Laws of a particular Government or Province, it would give that Province such superior Advantage in respect to the whole of the Indian Trade, which Your Majesty in Your Justice and Wisdom has determined to leave as open as possible to all Your Subjects, as might controul and obstruct it to the Prejudice of Your other Colonies—

3d If this great Country should be annexed to the Government of Canada, we are apprehensive, that the Powers of such Government could not be carried properly into execution, either in respect to the Indians or British Traders, unless by means of the Garrisons at the different Posts and Forts in that Country, which must contain the greatest Part of Your Majesty's American Forces and consequently the Governor of Canada would become virtually Commander in Chief or constant and

inextricable Disputes would arise, between him, and the commanding Officers of Your Majesty's Troops—. . . .

We would further submit, whether the issuing such Commission and Instructions may not be delayed; till by the receipt of such Information, which your Majesty has been graciously pleased to direct, We are enabled to make a full and particular Report on that very important subject.—. . . In the mean time, We humbly propose that a Proclamation be immediately issued by Your Majesty as well on Account of the late Complaint of the Indians, and the actual Disturbances in Consequence, as of Your Majesty's fixed Determination to permit no grant of Lands nor any settlements to be made within certain fixed Bounds, under pretence of Purchase or any other Pretext whatever, leaving all that Territory within it free for the hunting Grounds of those Indian Nations Subjects of Your Majesty, and for the free trade of all your Subjects, to prohibit strictly all infringements or Settlements to be made on such Grounds, and at the same time to declare Your Majesty's Intentions to encourage all such Persons who shall be inclined to commence New Settlements from Your old Colonies, together with all foreign Protestants, coming by themselves or with such Undertakers, in Your new Colonies of East and West Florida or your old Colony of Nova Scotia . . . .

Source: Adam Shortt and Arthur G. Doughty, eds, *Documents Relating to the Constitutional History of Canada 1759–1791* (Ottawa: King's Printer, 1907), 110–12.

In Quebec, a number of military officers (and sometimes their men) took advantage of the British offer of land grants. The anticipated stampede of American settlers to Quebec did not occur, however. The Americans were put off partly by the presence of thousands of francophone Roman Catholics and the absence of familiar institutions such as representative government and universal freehold tenure. In a classic vicious circle, the laws, government, and culture of Quebec could not very well be reconstructed until large numbers of anglophones arrived, and this immigration was not likely to happen until change had occurred. Moreover, Americans did not move north into any of the British colonies after 1763. Most of the newcomers were British,

mainly Scots, who began leaving their homes in the mid-1760s. The Scottish influx had only begun to gain momentum when it was closed down by the warfare of the American rebellion.

Everywhere in the northernmost colonies in these years, freehold land tenure and the concept of the yeoman farmer fought an uphill battle. The seigneurial system still controlled land in Quebec, the Island of Saint John had been distributed to proprietors who were expected to settle as tenant farmers did in Europe, and much of Nova Scotia was held by large landholders. In the absence of aggressive government settlement activity, those who acquired grants of land in North America in order to settle them were committed to replicating a European pattern of landholding, with aristocratic landlords and peasant tenants.

The administration of the new province of Quebec was greatly complicated not only by the small number of anglophones but by the emerging political turmoil to the south. The colonial authorities in Quebec began by introducing some British elements into the system, but ended by confirming many French ones. English criminal law was put into effect, but the French civil law was largely retained. The British in London agreed that British laws against Catholics did not extend to Quebec. Grand-Vicar Jean-Olivier Briand (1715–94) was chosen by his Canadian colleagues to head the Church in Quebec, and was consecrated bishop near Paris on 16 March 1766. Officially he would be only "superintendant" of the Quebec Church, but in practice he was accepted as its bishop and the collecting of tithes was officially supported. There could be no elected assembly until there were more Protestants. The process of confirmation of the institutions of the Old Regime gained a real boost from Governor Guy Carleton (1724–1808). An Anglo-Irishman, Carleton was a firm believer in a landed aristocracy, the subordination of a tenant class, and a close connection between church and state. He came to see that, with adjustments to circumstance, his overall vision for society was quite compatible with that of the Old Regime of New France. As the Americans to the south became increasingly restive and turbulent, Carleton became less eager for reform and more interested in pacification. Inevitably he turned to the handiest instruments at his disposal.

Frances Brooke's The History of Emily Montague

Frances Moore Brooke (1724–89) was an English writer who accompanied her chaplain husband to Quebec in 1763 and remained in the province for a number of years. One contemporary described her as "very short and fat, and squints, but has the art of showing agreeable ugliness." In 1769 she published in London an epistolary novel entitled *The History of Emily Montague*. This letter was written in the voice of her leading female character, Arabella Fermor, who the author used to describe social behaviour and customs in the province.

The corn here is very good, though not equal to ours; the harvest not half so gay as in England, and for this reason, that the lazy creatures leave the greatest part of their land uncultivated, only sowing as much corn of different sorts as will serve themselves; and being too proud and too idle to work for hire, every family gets in its own harvest, which prevents all that jovial spirit which we find when the reapers work together in large parties.

Idleness is the reigning passion here, from the peasant to his lord; the gentlemen never either ride on horseback or walk, but are driven about like women, for they never drive themselves, lolling at their ease in a calache:

the peasants, I mean the masters of families, are pretty near as useless as their lords.

You will scarce believe me, when I tell you, that I have seen, at the farm next us, two children, a very beautiful boy and girl, of about eleven years old, assisted by their grandmother, reaping a field of oats, whilst the lazy father, a strong fellow of thirty two, lay on the grass, smoking his pipe, about twenty yards from them: the old people and children work here; those in the age of strength and health only take their pleasure.

A propos to smoaking, 'tis common to see here boys of three years old, sitting at their doors, smoaking their

Continued...

pipes, as grave and composed as little old Chinese men on a chimney.

You ask me after our fruits: we have, as I am told, an immensity of cranberries all the year; when the snow melts away in spring, they are said to be found under it as fresh and as good as in autumn: strawberries and raspberries grow wild in profusion; you cannot walk a step in the fields without treading on the former: great plenty of currants, plumbs, apples, and pears; a few cherries and grapes, but not in much perfection: excellent musk melons, and water melons in abundance, but not so good in proportion as the musk. Not a peach, nor any thing of the kind; this I am however convinced is less the fault of the climate than of the people, who are too indolent to take pains for any thing more than is absolutely necessary to their existence. They might have any fruit here but gooseberries, for which the summer is too hot; there are bushes in the woods, and some have been brought from England, but the fruit falls off before it is ripe. The wild fruits here, especially those of the bramble kind, are in much greater variety and perfection than in England.

When I speak of the natural productions of the country, I should not forget that hemp and hops grow every where in the woods; I should imagine the former might be cultivated here with great success, if the people could be persuaded to cultivate any thing.

A little corn of every kind, a little hay, a little tobacco, half a dozen apple trees, a few onions and cabbages, make the whole of a Canadian plantation. There is scarce a flower, except those in the woods, where there is a variety of the most beautiful shrubs I ever saw; the wild cherry, of which the woods are full, is equally charming in flower and in fruit; and, in my opinion, at least equals the arbutus.

They sow their wheat in spring, never manure the ground, and plough it in the slightest manner; can it then be wondered at that it is inferior to ours? They fancy the frost would destroy it if sown in autumn; but this is all prejudice, as experience has shewn. I myself saw a field of wheat this year at the governor's farm, which was manured and sown in autumn, as fine as I ever saw in England.

I should tell you, they are so indolent as never to manure their lands, or even their gardens; and that, till the English came, all the manure of Quebec was thrown into the river.

You will judge how naturally rich the soil must be, to produce good crops without manure, and without ever lying fallow, and almost without ploughing; yet our political writers in England never speak of Canada without the epithet of *barren*. They tell me this extreme fertility is owing to the snow, which lies five or six months on the ground. Provisions are dear, which is owing to the prodigious number of horses kept here; every family having a carriage, even the poorest peasant; and every son of that peasant keeping a horse for his little excursions of pleasure, besides those necessary for the business of the farm. The war also destroyed the breed of cattle, which I am told however begins to encrease; they have even so far improved in corn, as to export some this year to Italy and Spain.

Sources: *The History of Emily Montague* (1769), letter 22; *Dictionary of Canadian Biography*, IV, 553–6.

Instinctively grasping the need for collaborators to rule an "alien" population, Carleton recognized the clergy and the seigneurs as natural leaders who could be won over if their rights and privileges were protected. In the process some of the damage to the economy resulting from the geographical dismemberment of Quebec in 1763 could be undone. The result was the Quebec Act of 1774. Most of the ancient boundaries of Quebec were restored to the colony. His Majesty's subjects in Quebec "professing the Religion of the Church of Rome" were granted free exercise of their religion and exempted from the traditional oaths of supremacy (a new one was supplied). The Catholic clergy were allowed "their accustomed Dues and Rights, with respect to such Persons only as shall profess the said Religion." Provision was made for the support of a Protestant clergy. All matters relating to property and civil rights were to be decided by the traditional laws of Canada. This clause, in effect, preserved the seigneurial system. English criminal law was continued, and the province was to be governed by

"Part of the Town and Harbour of Halifax in Nova Scotia, looking down Prince Street to the Opposite Shore," one of six prints of drawings of Halifax made by Richard Short in 1759. LAC, C-4294.

a newly structured legislative council; there was no provision for an elected assembly.

Parliamentary critics of the administration that introduced this measure complained of its "sowing the seeds of despotism in Canada." The Americans assumed a direct connection between it and their own situation, including the Quebec Act as one of the "Intolerable Acts" passed by the British Parliament at this time to punish the Americans for the Boston Tea Party. The legislation was certainly influenced by the need to pacify Quebec, but it was not intended to aggravate the Americans. If the Act was supposed to secure the loyalty of the Canadians, however, the strategy was not entirely successful.

Implementing British policy in the old *pays d'en haut* was, if anything, even more difficult than coming to terms with the old and new subjects of Quebec. Part of the problem was that the British army, which

was responsible for administering this region, did not really appreciate the extent to which the French and the Aboriginals had become connected with one another by trade and by marriage. One soldier commented of the French residents of the region—the British called them the "Interior French"—that "they have been in these upper Countrys for these twelve, twenty, or thirty years, [and] have adopted the very principles and ideas of Indians, and differ little from them only a little in colour." The return of British persons who had been taken prisoner by the Aboriginals would not be easy, since many had become thoroughly integrated into their adoptive tribes. The British did not trust these people, who often took Aboriginal names, and thus did not treat them with the same kindness that the people of Canada received. The British army had expected to be able to employ the sort of imperialistic policies that it thought proper to use with "heathen savages." The army did not

Governor Guy Carleton, painted in 1923 by Mabel B. Messer "from a copy that hung in Rideau Hall"; original artist unknown. LAC, 1997-8-1.

understand the system by which the fur-trading country had long been governed. General Jeffrey Amherst, who was responsible for the West in the early 1760s, saw the region in the simple terms of British conquest and Native subjects. He sought to eliminate the whole mediation process that had governed the "middle ground" under the French, including the gift-giving relationship. "Purchasing the good behaviour, either of Indians or any others is what I do not understand," he wrote. "When men of what race soever behave ill, they must be punished but not bribed." As British fur trader George Croghan observed, "The British and French Colonies since the first Settling America . . . have adopted the Indian Customs and manners by indulging them in Treaties and renewing friendships making them large Presents which I fear won't be so easey to break them of as the General may imagine."

Further complicating matters for the British conquerors was the emergence of an insurgency among the Aboriginal population of the Great Lakes region. This began in the prophetic teachings of Native leaders like Neolin, but soon became a general war against the British when they tried to fill the policy vacuum between the conquest of Canada and its actual cession in 1763. Amherst had no compunctions about suggesting in response that the Aboriginal people be given blankets infected with smallpox. But the uprising quickly burnt itself out. The ostensible leader, the Ottawa chief Pontiac, was unable to unite the many factions, and Amherst's successor, Thomas Gage, decided to try to mend some fences. Gage also determined to take advantage of Pontiac, and offered to treat him as if he really were an Aboriginal leader. In 1765 Pontiac accepted George III as his father and formally made peace. He would die in 1769 in the streets of the French village of Cahokia, clubbed from behind. Some Aboriginal leaders fought on, including Charlot Kaské, a Shawnee leader whose father was German and whose wife was a British captive adopted by the Shawnees since childhood. Kaské insisted that the British would strip his people of their land:

> The English come there and say that the land is theirs and that the French have sold it to them. You know well our fathers have always told us that the land was ours, that we were free there, that the French came to settle there only to protect us and defend us as a good father protects and defends his children.

Despite the Proclamation of 1763, the British army administrators on the spot were prepared to tolerate European settlement in the region, and the Algonquians knew it. The British administration also attempted to resurrect the old alliance of the region between the Europeans and Aboriginals, with the British in place of the French. This policy was limited by the failure of London to provide the money for presents. But its adoption meant that the British began to discourage their fur traders from moving into the lower Great Lakes. Instead, the British used forts to distribute trade goods to the Interior French, who continued to dominate the trade. British traders would have far more success in the Northwest, where trading networks had not yet been established.

The First American Civil War

In early April 1775 British troops, attempting to raid clandestine colonial arms depots in Massachusetts, were fired upon by the Americans. A long-festering imperial political crisis turned into a shooting war. From the vantage point of the American leadership, they were involved in a "revolution" to secure their rights against the arbitrary authority of the British Crown. From the vantage point of the British government, the Americans were engaged in a "rebellion" against duly constituted authority. Whatever its label, for many of the inhabitants in British North America the event meant involvement in an extended civil war in which brother fought brother, friend opposed friend, and many were eventually pushed into exile. Indeed, the proportion of exiles from the new United States (relative to population) exceeded that from France after 1789, from Russia after 1917, and from Cuba after 1955. Instead of seeing the people of the northernmost colonies as impotent victims of the American Revolution taking place to the south, it makes far more sense to view them as participants (although often at a distance) in a great civil war that affected the whole transatlantic region of Britain's vast empire.

The Americans moved quickly in 1775 to organize an alternative government and raise an army, under the command of George Washington of Virginia. While that force was still in embryo, the Second Continental Congress authorized an invasion of Quebec as a move to give "the coup de grace to the hellish junto" governing Great Britain. Washington was somewhat more enthusiastic about this plan than he was about subsequent proposals to invade Nova Scotia. One army was ordered to proceed to Quebec by way of Lake Champlain and the Richelieu River. Another was authorized to travel across northern Maine and along the Chaudière River to the St Lawrence.

The sudden turn of events found the government of Quebec in a state of shock and confusion. Governor Carleton, only recently returned from London with the Quebec Act in his dispatch case, complained he had insufficient military force to withstand an invasion. A public *mandement* from Bishop Briand, ordering the population to ignore American propaganda under threat of denial of the sacraments, had little effect. The seigneurs appointed to raise a militia found it difficult to do so. Carleton's alliance with Quebec's traditional leaders proved useless, largely because he misunderstood the dynamics of the Old Regime. The Church never had much influence on habitant behaviour, and the seigneurs never had much to do with the militia. The British merchants of Quebec had never been cultivated by Carleton and proved singularly unco-operative. Not even the First Nations leapt into action on Britain's behalf; most of the Iroquois would remain neutral until they were forced to side with the British later in the war.

Fortunately for the British, the Americans were neither as well-organized nor as lucky as Wolfe's expedition had been in 1758–9, and the Québécois were not as enthusiastic about "liberation from tyranny" as the invaders had hoped. General Richard Montgomery (1736–75), struggling to bring an invading army up the Lake Champlain route, wrote that "the privates are all generals" and that those from different colonies did not get along together (quoted in Hatch, 1970: 60). Benedict Arnold (1741–1801), bringing his army across what is now Maine under horrendous late autumn conditions, lost nearly half his troops in the process. On 11 November, Montgomery and his troops arrived near Montreal and pressed on to Quebec, although his soldiers were constantly deserting. At the same time, the habitants were hardly rushing to enlist in the American army. In Quebec, Colonel Allan Maclean (1725–84), who had earlier organized two battalions of disbanded Highland soldiers, had stiffened resistance. Montgomery joined Arnold at Pointe-aux-Trembles on 3 December. He quickly determined that he lacked the force and the supplies to besiege Quebec. He decided, instead, to storm the town. The assault on 31 December was a desperate move by the Americans, who were suffering from smallpox as well as problems of logistics and morale.

The garrison held. The result, wrote one British officer, was "A glorious day for us, as compleat a little victory as ever was gained." General Montgomery's frozen body was found not far from the barricade against which he had led the charge. He subsequently was buried with military honours, with Guy Carleton, who had known him from earlier campaigns, as chief mourner. General Arnold took a ball through the left leg at the first battery, and over 300 Americans were taken prisoner. The American forces, now under Arnold's command, remained in military occupation of more than 50 parishes over the winter of 1775–6. Their desperate seizure of foodstuffs, sometimes paid for with worthless Continental currency, according to one American, cost the occupying army "the affections of the people in general." A commission from the Continental Congress, headed by Benjamin Franklin, pronounced from Montreal, "Till the arrival of money, it seems improper to propose the Federal union of this Province with the others." In May 1776 British reinforcements arrived at Quebec, and by mid-June the Americans had completely retreated, never to return. Quebec became an important centre for the British army, later serving as the staging point for a counter-invasion of the United States (equally unsuccessful) in 1778, led by General John Burgoyne.

The Americans had desperately wanted Quebec. George Washington wrote to Benedict Arnold early in 1776: "To whomsoever it belongs, in their favour, probably will the balance turn. If it is ours, success, I think, will most certainly crown our virtuous struggles; if it is theirs, the contest, at least, will be doubtful, hazardous and bloody." The Rebel leaders did not feel the same way about Nova Scotia, partly because of its protection by the British navy, partly because there was not enough visible evidence of enthusiastic residents ready to support an invading army. Some American sympathizers, including Jonathan Eddy (1726/7–1804) and John Allan (1747–1805), recruited a private army in Machias and Maugerville, consisting of 80 men, who marched overland from the Saint John River towards the British outpost at Fort Cumberland in late October and early November 1776. This "invasion" was joined by a few residents from the area, but was quickly suppressed by British reinforcements, leaving those Nova Scotians who had supported the Americans either abjectly explaining away their actions or quickly departing for American lines, leaving behind their wives and families to be sworn at and "often kicked when met in the street." Civil wars were truly nasty ones.

The affair at Fort Cumberland was more typical of this war than was the earlier invasion of Quebec. Away from the armies, the opposing parties—rebel and Loyalist—fought vicious little battles with one another for control of the uncommitted local population, often paying back old scores along the way. On the high seas, legalized pirates (called privateers) captured unarmed ships and attacked unprotected settlements along the coasts. Between 1775 and 1781 the privateers literally brought commerce to a halt in the Atlantic region, causing a number of food shortages, particularly in Newfoundland and the Island of Saint John. Both these colonies went for long periods without the arrival of a single vessel from overseas. On the borders between Loyalist and Rebel territory, guerrilla raiders (often including Native allies) attacked farms and villages. Since most of the population of the northernmost provinces lived on the coast or near an American border, everyone lived in constant fear of attack.

Given the insecurity of the times, it is hardly surprising that the radical preacher Henry Alline (1748–84) had considerable success in the Maritime region in introducing a movement of Christian pietism and rejuvenation often called The Great Awakening. Alline rejected secular affairs in favour of the self-government of the godly, emphasizing that Christ had commanded his followers "to salute no man by the way" (quoted in Bumsted, 1971: 93). He travelled the countryside, composing and singing hymns, regarding music as a way to attract and to hold an audience and as a useful vehicle on the road to salvation. At his death he left a legacy of evangelism and revivalism among his followers, who were called New Lights. In a period of confusion, Alline offered an alternative path to public involvement.

Not all residents of the northernmost colonies who did make a conscious choice selected the British side. One who did not was Moses Hazen (1733–1803), a native of Massachusetts, who had settled in the Richelieu Valley of Quebec after the Conquest. After a period of fence-sitting in 1775, Hazen committed himself to the United States and was appointed by the Continental Congress to command a regiment he was to raise in Canada. Hazen successfully recruited several hundred habitants, many of whom retreated with him from Canada in June 1776 and stayed together as a unit throughout most of the war. His men (and the Nova Scotia refugees) ultimately were compensated by the American Congress with land and financial assistance.

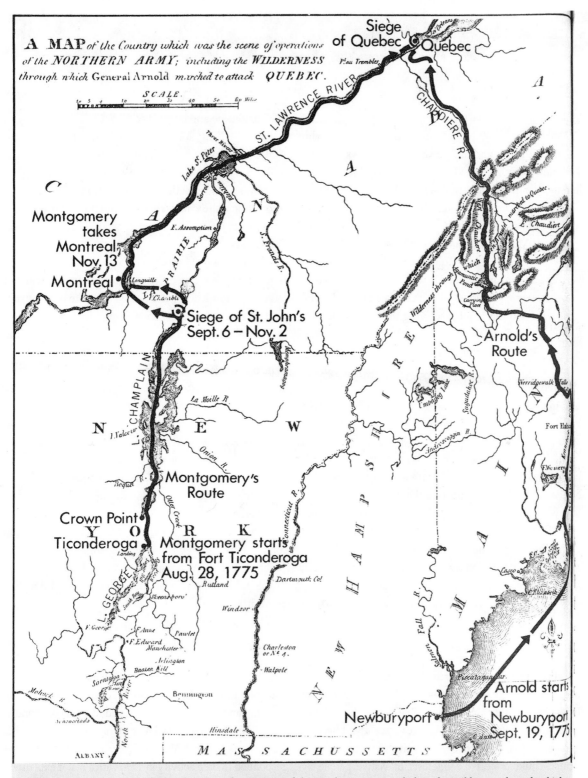

"A Map of the Country which was the scene of operations of the Northern Army; including the Wilderness through which General Arnold marched to attack Quebec." Metropolitan Toronto Reference Library.

Molly (Mary) Brant

Molly Brant (Konwatsi'tsiaiénni, 1736?–96) was born to a Mohawk couple living in Canajoharie, New York, who were completely undistinguished in Mohawk society. We know very little of Molly Brant's early life. In 1753 her mother married a Mohawk sachem named Brant Canagaraduncka, a friend of Sir William Johnson, who brought her children Molly and Joseph into the upper reaches of Mohawk society.

Within a few years, Molly was Sir William's housekeeper and his chatelaine. He was by this time one of the richest men in New York, made a baronet by the King a few months before receiving the appointment as Colonel of the Six Nations and Superintendent of Indian Affairs for the colony in 1756. Johnson found it advantageous to have a Mohawk "wife," who soon became a clan mother as well as a competent household manager and mother of Johnson's youngest children. In 1763 Sir William and his family moved into a grand new house at Johnson Hall. From the beginning he held councils with the Aboriginals at or in his house, including a large peace gathering in 1768 attended by thousands of Native peoples. The result was the peace treaty of Fort Stanwix, soon sundered by the American Revolution. Sir William died in 1774 shortly after another peace gathering at which he had exhausted himself.

Molly was no longer in charge of Johnson Hall, although she was left considerable property and was by now the head of the Iroquois clan matrons. She returned to Canajoharie and began a store. When rebellion began against the King, Molly remained loyal to the Crown. While most of the Johnson clan retreated from the Mohawk Valley in late 1775, Molly remained. Among the Mohawks she counselled loyalty, and she collected what information she could on Patriot plans, even warning her brother Joseph of a colonial army that was met and defeated at Oriskany.

From the beginning, she was suspected by the rebels, and she escaped Canajoharie only minutes ahead of arrest. After leaving her home she spoke publicly at a council meeting at Onondaga, opposing peace with the rebels and declaring the need for friendship with the King of England. She was soon pressed to come to Fort Niagara to help manage her people, and arrived there in late 1777. Gradually her interferences disturbed her hosts, and they encouraged her to move to Montreal. She subsequently went to a large Six Nations settlement at Carleton Island, NY, where she was credited with inducing "uncommon good behaviour" on the part of her people.

She moved in 1783 to Kingston, Upper Canada, and remained there for the remainder of her life, worshipping at the local Anglican Church. In 1787 she contemptuously refused an American offer of compensation for her expropriated lands if she would return to the Mohawk Valley. Although her brother Joseph got most of the publicity, Molly Brant was equally and deeply a committed Loyalist.

Like many other North Americans, most Native people attempted to remain out of the conflict. For the Iroquois, neutrality proved impossible. One of the Mohawk leaders, Joseph Brant (Thayendanegea, 1742–1807), became persuaded that only continued active alliance with the British could protect the interests of Native people by preserving their land from the encroachment of European settlement. Brant and his sister Molly (head of the Iroquois clan matrons) were unable to convince the Iroquois councils, but he recruited a force of about 300 Aboriginal warriors and 100 Loyalist settlers, which was active in scouting and raiding operations, and in 1778 collaborated with Butler's Rangers (a Loyalist regiment) in guerrilla raids in the Mohawk Valley of New York. The Americans responded to such activity in 1779 with a major expedition into the land of the Iroquois, laying waste to the country. The Iroquois, including Brant, were forced to retreat to Fort Niagara, where they became supplicants for British aid.

Contemporary Views

An American Privateering Raid

Simeon Perkins (1734/5–1812) was born in Norwich, Connecticut, and migrated to Liverpool, Nova Scotia, in 1762. When the American Rebellion began, Perkins remained loyal to the Crown. As lieutenant-colonel of the Queen's County militia, he was responsible for the defence of Liverpool.

Thursday, April 9th, [1778]—Pleasant [*sic*] day. Wind N.W. Capt. Hopkins, and Capt. Gorham, Capt. Dean, B. Harrington, are about going to Halifax. Some of them get to the mouth of the Harbour and discover a privateer sloop at anchor back of the Island. . . . She continues at anchor till towards night she came into the Harbour, and the wind being small, rowed up into Herring Cove and sent a boat almost up to the Bar. I went on the Point to hail them but she tacked about and returned on board the sloop. Seeing a sloop full of men come into the Harbour it was truly alarming in our defenceless condition. . . . I had some men under arms, and kept a sentry on the Point, relieved every half hour. Soon after Mr Collins return I found that the sentry, Robert Bramham, was deserted. Had left his musket, and taken a skiff from shore, and no doubt remained but he was gone on board the privateer. This put us in some Consternation, as this Bramham . . . had heard all our Council. The sloop soon got under way, and stood athwart the Harbour, and finally went out of sight. I then ordered a guard of one sergeant and four privates[,] dismissed the remainder of the People, and went home. In less than two hours I was informed that the Privateer was coming in again. I immediately alarmed the People from one end of the street to the other, and mustered about 15 under arms. The sloop came in with Drum and fife going, and whuzzaing, etc. They anchored a little above the Bar, and sent a boat on board Mr Gorham's schooner, and Mr Hopkins schr. I gave orders not to speak to them or fire upon, except they offered to come on shore to rob the stores, etc. If they made any such attempt to engage them. They searched the two schrs. mentioned, and returned on board the Privateer, and hove up their anchor, and went out after daylight. They had boarded a sloop in Herring Cove, Benjamin Harrington, master, and demanded a hhd. of Rum, which was landed as she was coming in, but finally took up with 40 gallons, which Harrington produced. . . .

It is now Fryday morning, April 10th,—The Privateer is gone out. Wind S.E. All is quiet. A small schr., Prince Doan, Master, arrives from Barrington. The Privateer put a man on board her in the night, but released her this morning. I am mutch fatigued, and sleep a sound nap. In the afternoon I hear the Privateer is gone into Portmatoon.

Source: Harold A. Innis, ed., *The Diary of Simeon Perkins, 1766–1780*, vol. 1 (Toronto: Champlain Society, 1948), 139–41.

Farther west in the fur-trading country, Native peoples were better able to ignore the war. The western fur trade was relatively unaffected by the American Revolution. The western movement of the Montreal-based fur trade, now dominated by English-speaking traders, continued unabated. By the time of Lexington and Concord, they were pressing up the Saskatchewan River into the basin of the Churchill River. In 1778 Peter Pond (1740–1807?) broke through into the richest fur trade country of the continent: the Athabasca region. The competition, the "Pedlars from Quebec," as one Hudson's Bay Company man contemptuously labelled them, galvanized the English company into more aggressive action. It moved inland from its posts on the Bay to open up ones on the Saskatchewan. Trading competition was always a mixed blessing to the Native peoples. It gave them a choice and lower prices, but because the Native consumer had a relatively inelastic

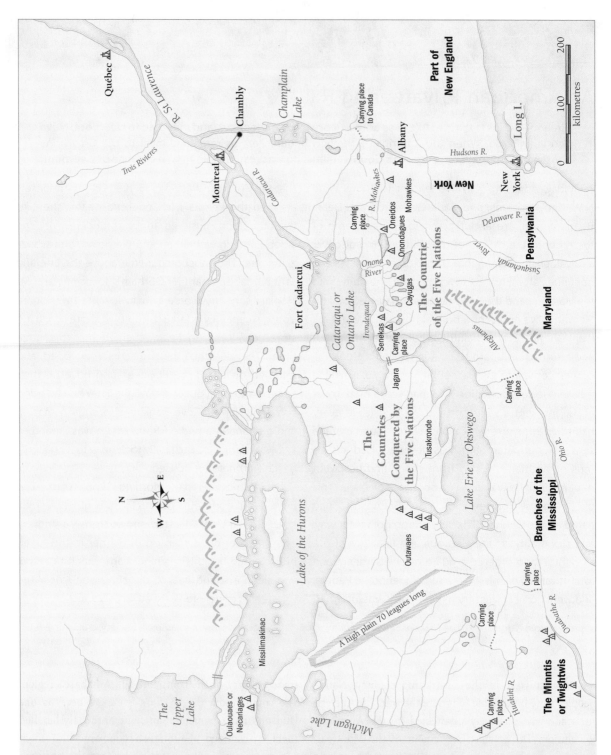

"The country of the Five Nations," based on the frontispiece to vol. 2 of The History of the Five Indian Nations of Canada *(New York, 1902) by Cadwallader Colden (1688–1766), surveyor-general (1720) and lieutenant-governor (1761) of colonial New York.*

need for trade goods, competition also increased the amount of non-material and non-essential consumer goods on offer, particularly tobacco and alcohol, which was a negative feature.

Any official British attempts to limit settler intrusions in the Ohio country were ended by the American assumption of independence. For the duration of the war, the First Nations once again found an opportunity to manoeuvre between conflicting powers, although for the most part the war was a painful experience for them. The Americans sought to keep the Aboriginals neutral, while the British wanted their active military assistance. In the West, small roving bands of settlers fought with the Aboriginals. The Treaty of Paris in 1783 totally ignored the First Nations. Their lands in the West were transferred to the United States, and no provision was made for their protection. Although the British would prove reluctant to evacuate their posts in the West, holding most of them until Jay's Treaty in 1794, the Aboriginals were now at the mercy of punitive American military expeditions and advancing settlement. Many of the more militant First Nations leaders (such as Tecumseh) would support the British in the War of 1812, finding little joy in the eventual military stalemate.

Outside of the trans-Appalachian West, the British assumed after 1763 that in most eastern places the First Nations were a declining people who needed to be integrated into the European population as quickly as possible. Those Aboriginals who insisted on maintaining their old ways were quickly shoved to the margins of society and, at least in Newfoundland, driven to extinction. The situation was different in Upper Canada and in the vast northwestern regions of the continent. The core of British policy in this region since 1763 had consisted of maintaining an orderly frontier. In theory this involved a legal procedure for the orderly purchase of lands, the reservation to the Aboriginals of sufficient land on which to make a living, and, in Upper Canada, the full application of legal rights under the law wherever possible. This approach was taken partly to distinguish Canada symbolically from the United States. It involved the application of the common law to everybody, including the Aboriginals, both because the common law was a bulwark of Tory ideology and because it provided a framework for good government.

The law-centred approach was meant to avoid unnecessary violence and warfare and to re-educate Aboriginal people into the new order. It worked better in theory than in practice. The law-centred approach assumed that the First Nations did not become a part of society until they were thoroughly integrated into Europe's hierarchies and authority structures.

"Portrait of Joseph Brant," c. 1807, by William Berczy, oil on canvas. This portrait was painted after Brant's death in November 1807, perhaps as a tribute, but Berczy had painted him from life at least once. In 1799 he wrote of Brant: "he is near 6 feet high in stance, of a stout and durable texture able to undergo all the inconvenience of the hardships connected with the difficulties to carry on war through immense woods and wildernesses—His intellectual qualities compared with the phisical construction of his bodily frame—he professes in an eminent degree a sound and profound judgement. He bears patiently and with great attention before he replies and answers in general in a precise and laconic stile. But as soon as it is the question of some topic of great moment, especially relative to the interest of his nation he speaks with a peculiar dignity—his speech is exalted energy and endowed with all the charm of complete Retorick." Photo © National Gallery of Canada, 5777.

The revolutionary period did see one curious development in Hudson Bay. A great French fleet had been beaten by the British off Jamaica in 1781, and three of the dispersed vessels ended up in the Bay, where they did significant damage to Hudson's Bay Company posts before returning to France. Far more serious than the French depredations, however, was the appearance in this region in 1781 and 1782 of a major epidemic of smallpox among the Native peoples, who lacked European immunities and suffered heavy mortalities.

On the Pacific coast, the American Revolution was even more remote than on Hudson Bay. From the European perspective, the major event was the appearance in March 1778 of Captain James Cook (1728–79) in Resolution Cove, Nootka Sound, off the western coast of Vancouver Island. Cook was on another quest for the Northwest Passage, spurred by new information that suggested one might exist. In Nootka Sound, he and his crews observed the Nuu-chah-nulth people. The visitors were much impressed with their trading acumen and especially their principal trading commodity: the sleek, thick fur pelt of the sea otter. Cook was killed on the return voyage through the Pacific to England. An impressive account of the voyage in 1784 included descriptions of the sea otter pelts. Soon there was a rush to cash in on their obvious value, for they offered something to trade in the otherwise difficult Chinese market.

While James Cook's crews were still on the high seas returning to England, the British lost the war of the American Revolution. Whether they could ever have won it remains an open question. Military suppression

Biography

Tecumseh

Tecumseh (the name means "shooting star") was born around 1768 in present-day Ohio. He first distinguished himself at the Battle of Falling Timbers in 1794, and subsequently helped translate the prophetic teachings of his brother Tenskwatawa ("the Prophet") into a movement devoted to holding onto First Nations land. As he told one American "Indian agent" in Ohio, "The Great Spirit above has appointed this place for us, on which to light our fires, and here we will remain. As to boundaries, the Great Spirit above knows no boundaries, nor will his red people acknowledge any."

Although the Americans blamed this resistance on the British, it is clear that the Natives had their own agenda. Tecumseh and his brother were active after 1808 in an effort to unite all the First Nations under one banner, but both "the Prophet" and the movement lost credibility when they failed to halt the Americans and were badly beaten in battle by Governor William Henry Harrison at Vincennes late in 1811. When Tecumseh returned to his village from the Vincennes defeat, he found it devastated, and although he rebuilt, he was obviously determined to join the British in an effort of resistance against the Americans.

He led a war party into Upper Canada in June of 1812. At the head of 600 Native warriors, Tecumseh helped cut General William Hull's supply lines and eagerly supported Isaac Brock's aggressive scheme to attack Detroit. Brock would later comment that he never met "a more sagacious or a more gallant Warrior" than Tecumseh. In 1813, Tecumseh was at the head of an even larger party of Aboriginal fighters that helped attack Fort Meigs. He stepped in to prevent his warriors from completing a slaughter of prisoners at this point and became known as a humane leader. Later in 1813, at the Battle of Moraviantown, Tecumseh was killed. His body disappeared. The man himself quickly passed into myth and legend, one of the most popular figures of nineteenth-century Canadian verse and story, most of which attempted erroneously to make him out to be a Canadian patriot rather than a First Nations leader.

of movements of national liberation has never been a very successful strategy. The Americans managed to hold on, assisted by considerable British military stupidity and inefficiency, and they found allies in Europe. France joined the war in 1778. Unable to defeat the Americans with regular troops, the British turned increasingly to provincial Loyalist units to do the actual fighting, thus further enhancing the civil war aspect of the conflict. On the New York and Carolina frontiers, Loyalists and Rebels fought fierce battles in which no quarter was asked or given.

With the help of the French navy, the Americans finally succeeded in 1781 in trapping a large contingent of the British army under Lord Cornwallis in Virginia. The surrender of Cornwallis was really the end of the line for the British. The ministry could no longer pretend that victory was just around the corner. It surrendered, allowing its critics to negotiate the peace. The final agreement worked out with the Americans, signed on 30 November 1782, gave the Rebels most of what they wanted. It recognized the independence of the United States, allowed the new nation fishing rights in the Atlantic, and gave to it the entire Ohio Valley. Equally important, the British negotiators failed to insist on any real security for either their Aboriginal allies or the Loyalists.

Accommodating the Loyalists

From the beginning of the revolutionary conflict, some colonials had supported the British. As the war continued, many more were pressured by events into choosing sides and ended up with Great Britain. The struggle had been a bitter one, and officers of the provincial Loyalist regiments insisted that they be included in any Loyalist resettlement scheme, since "The personal animosities that arose from civil dissension have been so heightened by the Blood that has been shed in the Contest, that the Parties can never be reconciled" (quoted in Wright, 1955: 41–2). The British authorities in New York, where most of the Loyalists had gathered, accepted this argument. They were allowed to join

"A Man of Nootka Sound," drawing by John Webber, c. 1778. The artist was a member of Captain James Cook's expedition of 1778 to the west coast of North America. The expedition was motivated partly by increased European activity in the region, but mainly by a renewed interest in a short route to Asia. Cook arrived in Resolution Cove, Nootka Sound, off the west coast of Vancouver Island in March 1778 and spent more than a month there, devoting much of his time and that of his crew to studying the Aboriginal people he encountered there. Webber's drawings were subsequently published with Cook's journal in 1784. LAC, 1991-265-232, C-013415.

the contingents of Loyalists that departed by ship for Nova Scotia in 1782 and 1783. Other Loyalist regiments already in Quebec joined British regulars in settling there at the close of the hostilities. The British were prepared to make extensive grants of land to these new arrivals and to support them with supplies while they remade their lives. Perhaps 40,000 people received land grants and assistance as Loyalists, with about 30,000 settling in Nova Scotia (part of which would become the province of New Brunswick in 1784), 750 on the Island of

Charles Inglis

Charles Inglis, by Robert Field. Oil on canvas, 1810, 43 in. x 35 in. (1092 mm x 889 mm). Given by the sitter's grandson, Thomas Cochran Inglis, 1895. © National Portrait Gallery, London.

Charles Inglis (1734–1816) was born in Ireland, where his father was a clergyman who died while his son was still young, forcing Charles to seek his fortune in the American colonies. He taught school for some years in Pennsylvania before returning to England in 1758 to take holy orders. He then returned to the New World as a missionary for the Society for the Propagation of the Gospel (SPG), serving for six years in a Delaware parish before becoming curate at Trinity Church in New York City. This position put Inglis in the centre of Anglicanism in North America, and he submerged himself in several fashionable Anglican causes, including the quest for a colonial bishopric and missionary work among the Iroquois. Inglis believed that the British problem with the rambunctious colonies was a product of too much liberty and too little insistence on proper social order, a typical position for Anglican clergymen to take in the years before the outbreak of rebellion. After the American Revolution turned to armed conflict, he took advantage of the British occupation of New York City to become a leading Tory/Loyalist pamphleteer; one of his pamphlets, *The True Interest of America Impartially Stated*, answered Thomas Paine's *Common Sense*.

In New York he developed a reputation as an ambitious clergyman, which turned to notoriety after he sailed to England in 1783 to campaign for promotion. He managed to catch the eye of Lord Dorchester (Guy Carleton), who selected him to become the first bishop of Nova Scotia (and the first Church of England bishop in North America). Inglis was not very popular initially with his clergy, partly because of a deficient classical education and partly because of his strident politicizing during the war. The arrival of Governor John Wentworth in 1791 improved his situation, although he still found much opposition from Loyalist clergymen. Inglis adopted a policy of not maintaining close supervision of his clergy, especially those distant from Halifax (or Windsor after he moved there in 1798). He got the bulk of his funding from the British government and the SPG, using the money to build church structures and a college at Windsor, the first institution of higher learning in what would become Canada. He spent his later years as a gentleman farmer who allowed his son to manage the diocese after 1802. Inglis left a legacy of relative harmony within his church and decent relations with other denominations, both achieved by lack of provocative action, although whether these achievements represented positive policy on his part is another matter.

Sources: R.V. Harris, *Charles Inglis, Missionary, Loyalist, Bishop* (Toronto: General Board of Religious Education, 1937); Judith Fingard, *The Anglican Design in Loyalist Nova Scotia, 1783–1816* (London: The Church Historical Society, 1972).

Saint John, 1,000 on Cape Breton, and the remainder in Quebec—mainly in what would become Upper Canada.

The Loyalists were quite a disparate group of newcomers. Of the total of 40,000, well over 3,000 were blacks who settled in Nova Scotia, and almost 2,000 were Aboriginals who settled in Upper Canada. Over half of the 40,000 were civilian refugees and their families; those remaining were officers and men either from former Loyalist regiments or from British regiments disbanded in America. A large proportion of both groups were neither American nor English in origin. Quite apart from the blacks and the Aboriginals, a substantial number of the new settlers came from Scotland, Ireland, or various German principalities. Anglican clergyman Jacob Bailey (1731–1808) characterized his new neighbours in the Annapolis Valley of Nova Scotia as "a collection of all nations, kindreds, complexions and tongues assembled from every quarter of the globe and till lately equally strangers to me and each other" (quoted in Bumsted, 1986: 34).

Some unknown number of the Loyalist settlers were women. Most of the records of the Loyalists list only the males, who got land grants, served in the military, and received stores. But of the 3,225 individuals who presented claims to the British government for compensation of losses during the war, 468 (or about 14 per cent) were women. Only a small percentage of these women had worked outside the home, and most of them obviously were most familiar with their immediate households. Many other women and their families accompanied their husbands into their new surroundings. The loss of homes and cherished contents was probably more traumatic for Loyalist women than were property losses for men. Certainly the gradual recreation of stability was much more difficult. Men could re-establish friendships and relationships in meeting places outside the home, but women usually could not. Women—who were often not consulted about the decision to support the King or to emigrate—had sacrificed a great deal for a principle. They had every reason to be bitter about their fate.

From the first days of the war, the British military authorities in America had attempted to enlist some of the half-million slaves to fight against their masters, chiefly by promising them their freedom. Thousands of blacks found their way to British lines by whatever means possible, drawn by promises only the British could possibly honour. Loyal blacks usually were evacuated when the British withdrew from an American district. Most of them ended up in New York with the other Loyalists and the British army. More than 3,000 were transported to Nova Scotia. Although they were free, they were not treated well. Only 1,155 of the black Loyalists in the province actually received land grants, which averaged less than 11 acres (4.5 ha) per grant. Blacks became part of the mobile population of the region, taking up whatever employment was available. They suffered many disabilities. In Nova Scotia they were not entitled to trial by jury. In New Brunswick they were not allowed to vote. Freed blacks were treated more harshly in the courts than European people convicted of the same or similar crimes. An unknown number of blacks, who were brought to British North America as slaves by Loyalist masters, continued in that status until the early years of the nineteenth century, when local courts ruled slavery out of existence in the colonies by extending English laws. Not surprisingly, in 1791 nearly half of the Nova Scotia black Loyalists would accept with alacrity a chance to immigrate to the African colony of Sierra Leone.

Throughout the war the British had played on the First Nations' fear that the Americans intended to settle in large numbers on their ancestral lands, which had never been recognized as belonging to them. Some Natives had joined the British, and all were punished for this choice by both sides. The Iroquois were driven from their lands in the state of New York. The First Nations were abandoned by the British in the rush for extrication from an unpopular and expensive war. Britain transferred sovereignty over land south of the Great Lakes and as far west as the Mississippi River to the Americans, totally ignoring the fact that most of that land was claimed by its Aboriginal allies, who would insist they had never surrendered it to the Americans. The Native refugees were given a grant of land along the Grand River in what would become Upper Canada. Here a 1785 census showed 1,843 Native residents, including more than 400 Mohawks.

Few of the Loyalists stayed where they were settled initially. The town of Port Roseway (or Shelburne),

The "Book of Negroes"

In 1781 a regular weekly meeting was held at a New York tavern between representatives of the American and British governments. At issue were the fates of more than 3,000 black residents of the city of New York, most of whom had escaped from slavery by crossing British lines, encouraged to do so by the British military. The British negotiators of the preliminary peace agreement were so anxious to end the war that they agreed to the American demand to return these fugitives to their slave masters, but General Guy Carleton (the commander of New York) refused to consent. Instead, he agreed to keep a record of all blacks being removed and to allow the Americans to dispute individual names. Brigadier General Samuel Birch, whom Carleton placed in charge of evacuation from New York, was instrumental in creating and maintaining this documentation of black Loyalists. In the end, only 14 cases were disputed as Carleton and Birch's "Book of Negroes" was being prepared. The personal information included for those being listed varied. The entry for Billy Williams offers one example:

> 35, healthy stout man, (Richard Browne [former master]). Formerly lived with Mr. Moore of Reedy Island, Caroline, from whence he came with the 71st Regiment about 3 years ago.

Those who were included thought that they were now proper Loyalists, which would prove to be not quite the case. Two copies were made of the list, one for each side. The British original is in the Carleton Papers in the Public Record Office, London, and the American original is in the National Archives in Washington. Copies of the originals exist in the Public Archives of Nova Scotia and the Public Archives of Canada.

As an artifact, the "Book of Negroes" is a complicated part of material culture. In some ways it is an object of resistance, having been constructed by Samuel Birch to prevent the American slave owners from reclaiming those they thought of as their property. The same freemen would name their settlement in Shelburne County, Nova Scotia, in his honour: Birchtown. That said, it also is a symbol of oppression. The need for its construction and the legal disputes that occurred as a result were made possible by the inequality of slavery. It is also, as a historical document, one of the best resources on the daily lives of black Americans. The professions, the ages, the names, and the former masters of these people were recorded and provide insight into the way that free and "escaped" people made their way in the British colonies, including Boston King (discussed below), formerly a slave from South Carolina who made his way to New York, then Nova Scotia, and eventually became a missionary in Africa.

on the southwest coast of the Nova Scotia peninsula, became notorious as a place where almost all of the 10,000 people who had been transported there left within 10 years. The decade of the 1780s saw continual Loyalist relocation, sometimes within the colony of original settlement, sometimes in another colony of greater promise, and often eventually back to the United States after subsidies ran out and the initial American hostility had died down. Much of the land initially granted to the Loyalists had only limited agricultural potential, and everywhere homes had to be hewn out of a wilderness. The Loyalist settlement did reassert the principle of freehold tenure in all the colonies. The most stable newcomers were members of the office-holding elite, who tended to cluster in the provincial capitals.

"Encampment of the Loyalists at Johnston, a New Settlement on the banks of the St Lawrence River in Canada," watercolour by James Peachey, 6 June 1784. An officer in the 60th Regiment, Peachey was deputy surveyor-general at the time, surveying lots for disbanded troops and Loyalist refugees. "Johnston" was the future Cornwall, Ontario. LAC, 1989-218-1.

If the Loyalists were a restless population physically, they were a discontented and highly vocal one politically. Only a small fraction would receive formal compensation for property lost in the United States. All felt that they had suffered for their allegiance to the Crown, and that this made them deserving of both land and government assistance. Since many of the Loyalists were former American colonials, they were accustomed to certain levels of political participation. They also shared many political assumptions with their former neighbours. Loyalists may have supported George III, but they expected to be admitted to full participation in the political process for which they had fought. Quebec Loyalists thus complained bitterly about the absence of a representative assembly in the province. Nova Scotia and Island of Saint John Loyalists were unhappy about the domination of government by earlier inhabitants. Furthermore, Loyalists were divided among themselves, with the chief divisions being between the old elite, who sought to re-establish themselves as the natural leaders of society, and the more articulate among the rank and file, who sought a more democratic and open future. The coming of the Loyalists finally provided the cadre of articulate anglophone settlers that the British had hoped for in 1763. The new settlers not only spoke English, but did so with an American accent.

Patrick Campbell, on the Grand River in Upper Canada in 1792, was answered by a man "in a twang peculiar to the New Englanders": "I viow niew you may depen I's just a-comin." When asked how far, the response was, "I viow niew I guess I do' no,—I guess niew I do' no—I sear niew I guess it is three miles" (Campbell, 1837: 157). In most respects—except for loyalty to George III—the Loyalists were thoroughly Americanized.

Reinventing British North America

The loss of the American colonies, combined with pressure from the Loyalist leadership, gradually produced a political reorganization of British North America. It is at least arguable that since the Americans were the ones who had separated, what remained of British America carried on the imperial continuity in the New World. Stage one came in 1784, after the Treaty of Paris of 1783, when a governor-generalship was established to administer Britain's remaining North American colonies. Sir Guy Carleton, now Lord Dorchester, was the first appointee to this post in 1786. Britain also created two new provinces in 1784. New Brunswick was hived off from Nova Scotia

Biography

Boston King

Boston King (1760–1802) was born a slave on a plantation near Charleston, South Carolina, King's parents were household servants rather than field hands, and he was apprenticed at age 16 to a carpenter, who beat him mercilessly but provided him with a skill useful to him throughout his life. His master adhered to the rebel side when the American Revolution broke out, and in 1780 King took advantage of the British occupation of Charleston and the offer to grant blacks their freedom if they joined the royal standard. Once free in the town, he found ways of making himself useful, although he was constantly in danger of risking re-enslavement, partly through the actions of unsympathetic loyalists.

King managed to get to New York City in 1782, but found himself again in danger when the preliminary peace treaty—in article 7—called for the return of all American property, including slaves, to its owners. He was saved when Guy Carleton, commander of the British forces in New York, refused to accept that slaves were part of the property provision in article 7 and enrolled him in the "Book of Negroes" instead. King and his wife Violet were carried on a ship to Port Roseway (i.e., Shelburne), Nova Scotia, where they were settled with other blacks in a separate community called Birchtown, which by early 1784 had a population of over 1,500 blacks located on small garden lots. A religious revival in Birchtown, led by Methodist evangelists, broke out in 1783, and both King and his wife were converted. "All my doubts and fears vanished away," he later wrote. "I saw, by faith, heaven opened to my view." King became an itinerant evangelist and continued working as a carpenter. He eventually left Birchtown because of the poverty of the settlement—the blacks had not been allocated enough land for successful farming—ending up preaching in a black settlement near Halifax.

In 1791 he joined other black Nova Scotians in supporting John Clarkson's Sierra Leone Company, which planned a black settlement in Africa. In January 1792 he and Violet left Nova Scotia for Sierra Leone. She died soon after arriving in Africa. After serving as a missionary and teacher in the colony, King left for England in 1794 to acquire further education. While in England he wrote his memoirs, and later returned to Africa where he maintained his missionary endeavours until his death. Better educated and prepared for life as a freeman, King's account of his experiences represents one of the few available windows into the world of early blacks in Nova Scotia.

Source: "Memoirs of the life of Boston King, a black preacher, written by himself during his residence at Kingswood School," originally published in *Methodist Magazine* (London), 21 (1798): 105–10, 157–61, 209–13, 261–5.

and given a set of political officials chosen from the "needy" Loyalist elite. The capital, Fredericton, was laid out in 1785, the year the first governor, Thomas Carleton (brother of Guy), arrived. Cape Breton was given a separate government, administered by a lieutenant-governor and a council without an assembly—until it was reunited with Nova Scotia in 1820. No changes were made in the government of Newfoundland, which still was being administered by officials resident in St John's during only the summer months; there was yet no assembly. A court system was operating on the island, however. Nor were alterations made immediately in Quebec, although Dorchester arrived in 1786 with a new chief justice in the person of William Smith (1728–93) of New York. Smith's political views were distinctly Anglo-American. He was known to have little sympathy for the Old Regime. We will use the term "British America" to distinguish the new version of the British colonies in America from the old "British North America."

In 1787 a former Loyalist pamphleteer, the Reverend Charles Inglis (1734–1816), arrived in Halifax as the first North American bishop of the Church of

England. Although most Loyalists were not Anglicans, the British government wished to establish a close connection between church and state. Initially, the new bishop was responsible for Quebec. Inglis worked uphill for years to bring Anglicanism to a level worthy of state support. The Loyalists pressed hard for institutions of higher learning in the colonies. William Smith of Quebec advocated a secular university for his province, Inglis helped establish King's College in Windsor, Nova Scotia, and Benedict Arnold (who lived in Saint John as an unpopular Loyalist refugee from 1786–91) spearheaded a movement for a university in New Brunswick, which did not take root at that time.

In the western part of Quebec, demands for British institutions, particularly an assembly, produced the second stage of political reorganization: the Constitutional Act of 1791. This parliamentary legislation split Quebec into Upper and Lower Canada, giving the former a lieutenant-governor—the first one was John Graves Simcoe (1752–1806)—both an executive and a legislative council, and an assembly. In theory, Upper Canada's lieutenant-governor would be responsible to the governor of Quebec, and all the chief officials in the various colonies to the Governor General, but Britain's efforts to create an administrative hierarchy were not very effective. Each colony of British America continued to turn directly to the British government as the source of real authority.

Despite self-denying legislation by Parliament in 1777 that no direct taxes would be collected in British America without the consent of the governed in a legislative assembly, and however much eighteenth-century British statesmen remained committed to the principle of colonial assemblies, Great Britain was reluctant to universalize these institutions.

French Canada obtained an assembly in 1791 less because Britain felt it was entitled to one than because the Loyalist settlers up-country insisted on having one, and symmetry between Upper and Lower Canada needed to be maintained. For the British, assemblies implied that colonies had come to full maturity, including the control of decent revenue. Cape Breton, because of its small size and remote location, would have to grow into an assembly, which it never did. As for Newfoundland, Britain still hesitated to grant it full

"Part of the Town of Shelburne in Nova Scotia, with the Barracks Opposite," pencil drawing by William Booth (1746–1828), 1789. Booth was a surveyor who laid out much of the town of Shelburne. A competent artist, he depicted much of the early development of the town, especially the section reserved for blacks. LAC 1990-289-1.

colonial status, partly because of its large population of Roman Catholics. The Loyalist period, however, saw the achievement of full political privileges for Roman Catholics in most of British America, both through local legislative initiative and parliamentary fiat (for Quebec). Only on the Island of Saint John (which in 1786 passed laws permitting Catholics to own land but not to vote) and in New Brunswick until 1810 were Catholics still disenfranchised politically. In 1791 the British Parliament passed the Constitutional Act of 1791, which separated Quebec into Upper and Lower Canada and gave each a legislative assembly.

A less publicized development than the introduction of assemblies and the expansion of voting franchises was the elaboration of the legal system of the various colonies. This system was based chiefly on English law and English models except in Quebec, where English criminal law was joined to most aspects of French civil law. The establishment of colonial courts and assemblies meant that new English statute law extended to British America only where specifically authorized, but the colonial legal system took over earlier English statute law and the whole body of the common law, including its patriarchal treatment of women. The introduction of the law was necessary both to good government and especially to business, which would have been lost without the adjudication of the complex system of credit

A Loyalist Woman in New Brunswick

As the text of this letter suggests, Polly Dibblee (1747–1826) was a member of the Jarvis family of Stamford, Connecticut. She moved with her husband to New Brunswick during the Loyalist migration from New York. The new life was often hardest on Loyalist women.

17 November 1787
Polly Dibblee to William Jarvis
Kingston, New Brunswick

Dear Billy

I have received your two Letters and the Trunk, and I feel the good Effects of the Clothes you sent me and my Children, and I value them to be worth more than I should have valued a thousand Pounds sterling in the year 1774. Alas, my Brother, that Providence should permit so many Evils to fall on me and my Fatherless Children—I know the sensibility of your Heart—therefore will not exaggerate in my story, lest I should contribute towards your Infelicity on my account—Since I wrote you, I have been twice burnt out, and left destitute of Food and Raiment; and in this dreary Country I know not where to find Relief—for Poverty has expelled Friendship and charity from the human Heart, and planted in its stead the Law of self-preservation—which scarcely can preserve alive the rustic Hero in this frozen Climate and barren Wilderness—

You say "that you have received accounts of the great sufferings of the Loyalists for want of Provisions, and I hope that you and your Children have not had the fate to live on Potatoes alone"—I assure you, my dear Billy, that many have been the Days since my arrival in this inhospitable Country, that I should have thought myself and Family truly happy could we have "had Potatoes alone"—but this mighty Boon was denied us!—I could have borne these Burdens of Loyalty with Fortitude had not my poor Children in doleful accents cried, Mama, why don't you help me and give me Bread?

O gracious God, that I should live to see such times under the Protection of a British Government for whose sake we have Done and suffered every thing but that of Dying—

May you never Experience such heart piercing troubles as I have and still labour under—You may Depend on it that the Sufferings of the poor Loyalists are beyond all possible Description—The old Egyptians who required Brick without giving straw were more Merciful than to turn the Israelites into a thick Wood to gain Subsistence from an uncultivated Wilderness—Nay, the British Government allowed to the first Inhabitants of Halifax, Provisions for seven years, and have denied them to the Loyalists after two years—which proves to me that the British Rulers value Loyal Subjects less than the Refuse of the Gaols of England and America in former Days—Inhumane Treatment I suffered under the Power of American Mobs and Rebels for that Loyalty, which is now thought handsomely compensated for, by neglect and starvation—I dare not let my Friends at Stamford know of my Calamitous Situation lest it should bring down the grey Hairs of my Mother to the Grave; and besides they could not relieve me without distressing themselves should I apply—as they have been ruined by the Rebels during the War—therefore I have no other Ground to hope, but, on your Goodness and Bounty—

I wish every possible happiness may attend you, and your amiable Wife, and Child—and my Children have sense enough to know they have an Uncle Billy, and beg he will always remember them as they deserve.

I have only to add—that by your Brother Dibblee's Death—my Miseries were rendered Compleat in this World but as God is just and Merciful my prospects in a future World are substantial and pleasing—I will therefore endeavour to live on hopes till I hear again from you— I remain in possession of a graceful Heart,

Dear Billy,

Your affectionate Sister,

Polly Dibblee

Source: Letter from Polly Dibblee to William Jarvis, 17 November 1787, Kingston, [NB], National Archives, London, document no. 13_41, Audit Office, series 13, bundle 41.

employed in commerce. While the law in British America would develop its own characteristics over time, it was always closely linked to its English origins. Here was the origin of what Lord Macaulay would later describe for England as a system where "the authority of law and security of property were found to be compatible with a liberty of discussion and individual action."

The Loyalist migration had ended by 1786, when compensatory land grants and provisioning ceased virtually everywhere in British America. In one decade the loyal provinces of British America had received a substantial contingent of American settlers, well-subsidized by the British government, that they had not previously been able to attract.

So-called "late Loyalists" continued to come to Upper and Lower Canada, drawn by offers of land. The Atlantic region has not since then experienced a substantial American influx. For all colonies of British America, immigration and settlement would have crucial importance, but the post-Loyalist wave would have to be managed under quite different circumstances.

Immigration and Settlement, 1790–1815

Between 1790 and 1815 immigration to British America came from two major sources: the British Isles (mainly the Scottish Highlands and Ireland) and the United States (mainly upstate New York, Pennsylvania, and New England). The British newcomers settled everywhere, while the Americans were almost entirely confined to the Canadas. Most of the Scots were drawn to the Maritime region, where they had already established beachheads of settlement, but some went to Lower Canada and eastern Upper Canada to join Scottish communities there. The major movement from Britain occurred in a brief interlude of European peace between 1801 and 1803, chiefly to the northeast shore of Nova Scotia, to Cape Breton, and to Prince Edward Island (which the Island of Saint John became in 1799). Prosperity in Newfoundland and New Brunswick during the period 1812–15 drew many Irish to these colonies, more of whom were Protestant than Catholic because they came from northern Ireland.

Some of the American arrivals were pacifist Quakers and Mennonites encouraged by offers of exemption from military service in Upper Canada, but they soon were joined by a large influx of settlers who took up readily available land from government or private entrepreneurs. Lieutenant-Governor John Simcoe encouraged such grants. Some of these newcomers were fleeing American policies they disliked, including the new Constitution of 1789 and the severe repression of Pennsylvania whisky distillers in the 1790s, but most simply were part of the North American moving frontier. Until 1798 the Upper Canadian government treated these arrivals as Loyalists. Between 1791 and 1812 the English-speaking population of Lower Canada (mainly American) tripled from 10,000 to 30,000 and represented 10 per cent of the province's population. The Americans were located mainly in the Ottawa Valley and the Eastern Townships. In Upper Canada, by the time of the War of 1812, Americans made up as much as 80 per cent of a population estimated by one contemporary at 136,000. As tensions grew between Britain and the United States after 1807, the British began to be worried by the predominance of Americans in Upper Canada. In both Canadas, Americans tended to recreate their own local culture and institutions rather than to insist on political and legal reform of provincial political systems they regarded as oligarchical and repressive.

Another distinctive population emerged from obscurity in the Maritime region in this period. Despite the best efforts of the British to eliminate the Acadians in the 1750s, the campaign had not been completely effective. We do not understand very well the process by which the Acadians regrouped in the region, since most of the movement occurred outside record-keeping and beyond the reach of central authority, which may well be the point. After the Treaty of Paris of 1763, British policy permitted Acadian resettlement, provided that oaths of allegiance were taken and that the population moved to designated places in small numbers. Acadians gradually returned to the Maritime region to farm and fish, usually in remote districts far from existing settlement and often on marginal land. The governments of the region made no attempt to assist or accept them, but they were tolerated and left to create their own institutions. Those institutions were dominated, as they always had been, by the nuclear family and kinship ties, and to a much lesser extent by the Church. The scattered Acadians had great difficulty in obtaining priests, especially French-speaking ones, from the Quebec Church, which claimed it had few priests to spare for missionary service. As a result, the Acadians became accustomed to a religion dominated by laymen and supplemented by the arrival of occasional missionaries. Many of the regulations of the Church, including those on marriage, were not enforced, and parochial organizations were slow to develop. Despite the problems, by 1803 a religious census showed nearly 4,000 Acadians in Nova Scotia, nearly 4,000 in New Brunswick, and nearly 700 in Prince Edward Island.

It was certainly the case that government and politics everywhere in British America were, to say the least, cozy. The governments of the various provinces were dominated by a small cadre of well-paid officials appointed chiefly in England, in collaboration with local elites represented on the councils. While serious political conflict between the elected assemblies and the provincial oligarchies that governed British America was almost inevitable, it was slow to develop. The oligarchy associated the aspirations of the assemblies with the worst aspects of levelling republicanism—after 1789 the French Revolution succeeded the American as the chief example. Criticism of government was immediately rejected and critics were silenced by any means necessary, including violence.

In most provinces, early political opposition was sporadic and usually conducted within the ranks of the elite according to well-defined rules. Many of the early opponents of government—men like James Glenie (1750–1817) in New Brunswick, William Cottnam Tonge (1764–1832) in Nova Scotia, Robert Thorpe (1764–1836) in Upper Canada, and William Carson (1770–1843) in Newfoundland—were outspoken political gadflies who received very little consistent support from their colleagues. Only in Prince Edward Island and Lower Canada did anything resembling political parties develop before the War of 1812.

Lower Canada started its separate legislative existence with politics divided along class lines. The "French Party" consisted chiefly of Canadian seigneurs, supported by the clergy and a few English officials. They wanted all of the French civil law restored and retained. The bulk of the French-Canadian population was not yet integrated into the political system. The opposition, mainly English merchants, wanted the introduction of English commercial law, radical constitutional changes, and the right of habeas corpus. Over the next few years, the ideas and controversies of the French Revolution gradually made their way to Canada, often assisted by deliberate propaganda and subversion from France via the United States. In 1796–7, the French government actually developed a plan for the invasion of Canada from Vermont, although it had little public support.

The English official elite in Lower Canada overreacted to the French threat, exaggerating the colony's importance to France and the disloyalty (or potential disloyalty) of the Canadian people. The elite acted as though the colony was constantly faced with insurrection, and then engaged in repressive tactics. In 1794, the assembly, opposed by only a few Canadian members, passed an Alien Act that suspended habeas corpus not only in cases of treason but also in cases of sedition. The legislation was used to conduct a witch hunt and to jail many persons without recourse to bail.

As the French-Canadian population became more experienced at electoral politics—and their experience

"Part of York the Capital of Upper Canada on the Bay of Toronto in Lake Ontario," 1804, by Elizabeth F. Hale. Looking east along Palace (now Front) Street, this view shows Cooper's Tavern (at left, facing what is now Jarvis Street) and the houses of Duncan Cameron (a merchant), William Warren Baldwin, and William Allan. In the distance are the government buildings and blockhouse (with flag). LAC, 1970-188-2092 W.H. Coverdale Collection of Canadiana.

grew rapidly—they inevitably reacted to the suspicions and repressive tactics of the official elite. By 1796, the Canadians had won a majority of seats in the assembly. Official Lower Canada saw this election as a victory for treason and the revolt of the Canadian lower orders. The new ethnic division was quickly made more permanent by the authorities' insistence on viewing the French Canadians as determined to turn the colony over to the French "sans-culottes." The ethnic division also ended any possibility of reform of the government created by the Constitutional Act of 1791. The Canadians continued to favour reform, while the former anglophone reformers now allied themselves with the English officials to form the "English Party," which was devoted to preservation of the status quo. The French-Canadian reformers received little support from the Catholic Church, either. Virtually the only emigrants from France to Lower Canada during this period were clergymen, refugees

from the anticlericalism of the Revolution who hardly were likely to preach revolution to their flocks.

By the end of the eighteenth century the ethnic division was probably irreparable, and it only became more entrenched in the years before the War of 1812. The English party in the assembly and the "Château Clique," the anglophone oligarchy that ran the government, continued to fear an imminent French invasion, one that would be warmly supported by the Canadians. Such fears were encouraged by the deterioration of relations between the United States and Great Britain and by the increased pressure of the "Parti Canadien" (as it came to be called) for a constitutional change that the English elite was certain represented the start of rebellion. Partisanship reached a new height during the 1810 elections, in which Governor Lieutenant-General Sir James Henry Craig seized newspaper printing presses and jailed both printers and leaders of the Parti Canadien,

Electoral Behaviour in French Canada

The following notice, by a French-Canadian candidate in the first election for an assembly in Lower Canada, illustrates both the rapidity with which the French Canadians adapted to the new constitution and the ways in which elections were fought in the province. Michel Amable Berthelot Dartigny (1738–1815) became a lawyer in 1771 and a judge in 1791. He was a major property speculator in the town of Quebec. Finally elected to the assembly in 1798, he was an early supporter of the Canadian Party.

TO THOSE ELECTORS OF THE COUNTY OF QUEBEC

Who have voted, and those who were prevented from voting in my favour the 25th, 26th, 27th June last:

The more obstacles you have surmounted, you have shown the greater wisdom and firmness, in a country where liberty is but just dawning; for the general good and at the same time of esteem for myself, in thinking me worthy of being a representative, penetrated like yourselves with patriotism and gratitude for so distinguished a degree of your confidence, I entreat you to accept my sincere thanks and to be persuaded that I will neglect nothing for the accomplishment of your wishes and to obtain the justice due to us.

I cannot help observing on the silence kept by the *Quebec Gazette*, with respect to the extraordinary circumstances of the Upper and Lower town of the County of Quebec, particularly on the abstract and mysterious turn that the *Quebec Gazette* of Thursday last has given to what passed at Charlebourg during the election for the County of Quebec, doubtless the author of that paragraph is one of those who heretofore have so much fatigued themselves to write, print, and vaguely cry against the laws of this country, against the Honourable profession of Advocate, and who have employed such low means as those known to the public, but who have found no advantage in publishing the true facts arising from the Constitution; I shall not, however, undertake to establish them in this paper, the election for the County of Quebec being intended to be a subject for examination and I hope of just censure in the House of Assembly.

I confine myself at present to inform the public of the state of the poll.

Salaberry, Esq...............515
Lynd, Esq....................462
Berthelot, Advocate..........436

It is evident that I find myself the lowest by 26 votes, but the public cannot be ignorant how many are to be deducted from the other two candidates of persons who are neither proprietors nor naturalized. I might depend on this point alone or contest the election altogether. By the means contained in my protest signified by two Notaries when the poll was unexpectedly closed, 62 Voters more on the spot presented themselves in my favor and formally protested even in the building where the election was held, from which they were chased by some gentlemen who demolished it by force, but they continued their protest and finished it in the neighbourhood.

I hope that the country and the truth will not fail to direct resources, and that no personal influence will deprive my fellow countrymen of the advantages of our Constitution, which is in itself so good that the elections have made known the good subjects in this country, as well as the intentions and cabals of some others who have preached up union and non-distinction of birth, while they would secretly favourize a certain class of men who alone are neither able to effect the welfare or the peace of this colony.

—*Berthelot Dartigny*

thus making himself a symbol of British tyranny. The French Canadians had quickly adopted the tactics of a popular party in a British-style legislature. But they had been forced to do more. They had also turned their popular party into one committed to the preservation of French-Canadian values and even the perpetuation of French-Canadian nationalism.

The period before 1815 also saw the beginnings of the settlement of the West. In 1811 the Earl of Selkirk (1772–1820) received from the Hudson's Bay Company a grant of 116,000 square miles (300,417 km²) covering parts of present-day Manitoba, North Dakota, and Minnesota. In return for this grant Selkirk was to supply the HBC with employees to aid in its bitter struggle with the North West Company for control of the western fur trade. Selkirk hoped to be able to keep the colony he intended to establish at the forks of the Red and Assiniboine rivers separate from the fur

Thomas Douglas, Earl of Selkirk. This painting was based supposedly on a portrait by the Scottish artist Henry Raeburn. The location of the original is unknown. LAC, C-1346.

trade rivalry, but this would prove impossible. Miles Macdonell (*c.* 1767–1828) was named the first governor of Assiniboia, as the territory was called in June 1811. On 26 July he and the first contingent of colonists left for Hudson Bay, arriving two months later at York Factory. After wintering on the Nelson River until the breakup of ice (at the end of June), they did not arrive at the junction of the Red and Assiniboine rivers until 30 August 1812. The colony soon ran afoul of the North West Company, which used the Red River region as the source of pemmican for provisioning its traders on the vast inland canoe routes it had established.

The War of 1812

After some years of worsening relations, the Americans declared war on Great Britain on 18 June 1812. There were several factors behind the war. One was Britain's high-handedness in searching American ships on the high seas during the Napoleonic blockade, removing British subjects aboard them, and recruiting them into her navy. Another was the British failure to abandon the Ohio Valley, where military posts continued to monitor the fur trade. Most of all, the Americans coveted Canada and they proceeded again to invade in 1812 and in 1813. Invading armies successively were thrust back through the major entry points: the Detroit–Windsor corridor, the Niagara Peninsula, and Lake Champlain. A relatively small number of British regulars, assisted by colonial militia and Native peoples, held the province against American armies, which were neither well-trained nor well-led. A number of Canadian heroes emerged from the war, their reputations to be further mythologized after it was over: General Isaac Brock, Tecumseh, and Laura Secord.

The appearance of invading American armies posed a crisis of allegiance for many of the American settlers in Upper Canada. Most remained silently on their farms, although some supported their countrymen and retreated across the border with them. A handful of Americans were arrested and tried for treason at Ancaster in 1814, but the Canadian authorities generally did a good job of avoiding unnecessary witch hunts. Civilian damage was heavy (Table 4.2).

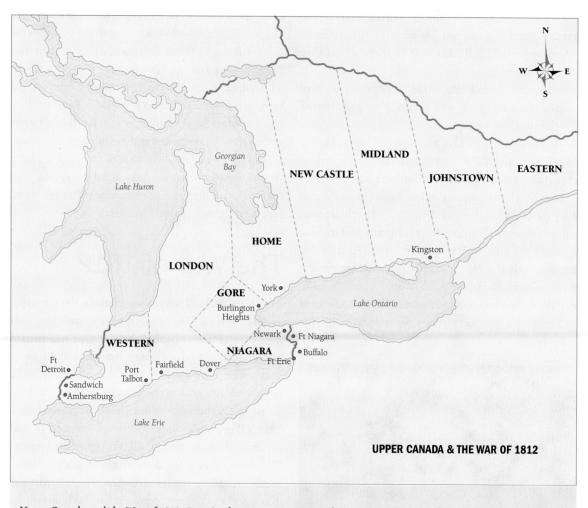

Upper Canada and the War of 1812. Drawing by Cy Morris. Map 1, from George Sheppard, Plunder, Profit and Paroles: A Social History of the War of 1812 in Upper Canada *(Montreal and Kingston: McGill-Queen's University Press, 1994).*

The loyalty question would not emerge as an open political issue until after the war was over. Well-led British regulars were assisted by militiamen from both the Canadas and by a number of Aboriginal allies. The Upper Canadians came out of the war convinced that their militia had won the war single-handed, although most militia died of disease and fewer than 30 died in battle (*Niagara Spectator*, 11 Dec. 1817). When the ministry of Alexander Mackenzie decided in 1875 to grant pensions for War of 1812 veterans, it expected only a few hundred to come forward. Instead, almost 2,000 veterans claimed service.

The "militia myth" contributed to the emergence of an Upper Canadian identity through the middle years of the nineteenth century.

The naval war was fought on several fronts. The first and best-known one was on the Great Lakes, especially Lake Ontario, where both sides built substantial navies from scratch and fought to a standstill from 1812 to 1814. The Atlantic Ocean front consisted of a handful of legendary set battles between individual American and British naval vessels—which the Americans typically won—and a considerable quantity of prize-taking, both by the British navy and by privateers on both sides

TABLE 4.2 Claims for War of 1812 Damages by District, Upper Canada

	Claims Submitted	Percentage of Total	Estimated Damages (£)
Western	415	20.2	65,196
London	296	14.4	50,797
Niagara	678	33.0	182,169
Gore	310	15.1	44,243
Home	80	3.9	12,379
Newcastle	13	0.6	2,633
Midland	21	1.0	6,938
Johnston	63	3.1	6,007
Eastern	167	8.1	12,065
Other*	12	0.6	18,301
Total	2,055	100	400,728

There were 12 claims for damages outside the province.

Source: George Sheppard, Plunder, Profit and Paroles: A Social History of the War of 1812 in Upper Canada *(Montreal and Kingston: McGill-Queen's University Press, 1994), 14, 123, from LAC, RG 19, E5 (a), Board of Claims.*

CANADA Material Culture

Uniform of the De Meuron Regiment

The De Meurons were originally Swiss mercenaries in the service of the Empire. Unlike British regulars, they had a uniform that emphasized their international nature. Zentralbibliothek Zürich, Department of Prints and Drawings/Photo Archive

A military unit of mercenary soldiers initially recruited by Comte Charles de Meuron in 1781 to serve the Dutch East India Company's colonies, especially the Cape of Good Hope, the De Meuron Regiment was soon sent from Capetown to Ceylon, where it helped expel the British from Cuddalore. Returned to Capetown, the regiment did garrison duty until being sent back to Ceylon, where two of its companies were imprisoned by the British in 1795. When the Dutch could not pay their troops, the regiment entered British service. When full service was finally arranged in 1798, the unit consisted of two battalions of five infantry companies each, which were dispatched to India until 1806, and Malta until 1809, under Sir Arthur Wellesley's command in the region. In 1813 the unit added new recruits and as a regiment comprised mostly of Swiss

Continued...

and Germans was sent from Malta to Upper Canada in October 1813. In North America they saw garrison duty and did rearguard duty at the Battle of Plattsburgh (the last battle of the War of 1812 prior to the Treaty of Ghent) in September 1814. The regiment was disbanded by the British in 1816, and a number of men from it and from de Watteville's Swiss Regiment—5 officers, 80 men, and 20 de Wattevilles, still wearing uniforms—were available to be recruited by the Earl of Selkirk as a private army. Under Selkirk's leadership and commanded by their former officers, these soldiers helped capture Fort William in 1816 and recapture Fort Douglas (at Red River) from the Métis in January 1817. They were arguably the deciding factor in the ultimate victory of the Hudson's Bay Company over the North West Company in the fur trade struggle for control of the West. Subsequently brought by Selkirk to Red River as settlers, many of the de Meurons married Swiss and German women imported to the settlement by Selkirk's estate in 1821. Residing on the banks of the Red River, they were flooded out by the Great Flood of 1826 and removed with their families to Fort Snelling, near St Paul, Minnesota.

The uniform of the regiment, redcoats, blue cuffs, and brushed felt hats with plumes, was particularly distinctive, as were the company buttons with their interlocking DM. The use of the blue, to distinguish the Des Meurons from British regulars, was intentional, but that they also ended up wearing the same red uniforms is not to be overlooked. That these uniforms were still used by the regiment after it was disbanded also evokes their connections to the Empire as a whole.

As a result, the uniforms are an element of material culture that shows the international flavour of the British Empire and the growing multicultural nature of the soldiers fighting both in Canada and abroad. The blue cuffs, which associated the regiment with Switzerland, allowed the soldiers to reference their own heritage, in a way similar to the Highland regiments' use of tartan. That said, the redcoats identified them as members of the British army and as a part of the larger Empire.

When looking at the materials the uniforms are made of, the international elements of the Empire become even clearer. The felt that their hats were made of probably had its origins in Canadian fur, while the cotton likely came from India, as did the plumes. Although manufactured in British factories, the materials used to clothe the symbols of British authority in the colonies came from the colonies themselves.

(Table 4.3). The British probably won the war of the prizes. Business-like privateers from Atlantic Canada made a substantial economic contribution to their communities and helped keep the economies of Nova Scotia and New Brunswick humming during the conflict (Kert, 1997).

Before the war had ended, York (Toronto) was burned, the American capital at Washington was sacked in retaliation, and Fort Michilimackinac (on western Lake Huron) was captured and held by Canadian voyageurs. The final struggle for naval control of the Great Lakes took place in 1814; the Americans appeared to be winning. The last battle of the war, at New Orleans on 8 January 1815, was actually fought after a peace of stalemate had been signed at Ghent on 24 December 1814.

Slow communications of the time kept the combatants from knowing that hostilities had ceased.

The Americans treated the War of 1812 as a second War of Independence, a necessary struggle to complete the process of separation from the mother country. National survival was taken as victory—although the United States was had been the aggressor through much of the conflict—perhaps not least because of Andrew Jackson's decisive victory over the attacking British fleet at New Orleans. From the British perspective, the war had been little more than a sideshow to the major struggle, which was fought against Napoleon in Europe. As for British America, in the lower provinces (as the Maritime region was coming to be called) the War of 1812 mainly represented an opportunity to serve as a conduit for

TABLE 4.3 Privateering in the Atlantic Region

Privateer Type	Number	% of Total	Prizes	% of Prizes
Schooner	26	55	182	81
Sloop	6	13	21	9
Brigantine/brig	6	13	18	8
Ship	2	4	0	0
Others*	4	11	5	2
Unknown	3	4	2	

*Includes jebacco boats, cutters, and a lugger.

Source: Faye Margaret Kert, Prize and Prejudice: Privateering and Naval Prize in Atlantic Canada in the War of 1812 was originally published as Research in Maritime History No. 11 (St John's, NL, 1997), and excerpts are reprinted here with the kind permission of the International Maritime Economic History Association.

"The Battle of Queenston. October 18th, 1813 [sic]," by Major James B. Dennis, coloured lithograph, c. 1866, after the original print published in 1836 by J.W. Laird & Co. in London. The Battle of Queenston Heights actually took place on 13 October 1812. LAC, R13133-387.

Laura Secord to the Prince of Wales, 1860

Laura Secord (1775–1868) was born in Great Barrington, Massachusetts. Her father moved to Upper Canada in 1795 to obtain land, and she married a Loyalist. In 1813 she overheard some American soldiers discussing a planned attack on a British installation, and walked 30 miles through enemy territory to warn the British. Later in life she began to petition the government for a pension based on her loyal service, but nothing happened until 1860 when the Prince of Wales responded to a petition (reprinted below) by granting her 100 pounds for her loyalty. Her tale subsequently became part of Canadian mythology. The candy manufacturer has no connection except commercial exploitation of her name, Laura Secord.

This postage stamp, issued by Canada Post in 2013 to commemorate the 200th anniversary of Laura Secord's walk to warn the British of an attack, illustrates how she has become entrenched into Upper Canadian mythology. © Canada Post Corporation 2013. Reproduced with permission.

Having the privilege accorded me this day of presenting myself before your Royal Highness I beg to assure you that I do so with the greatest gratification to my feelings. I am confident your Royal Highness will pardon the liberty I have taken when your Royal Highness is informed of the circumstances which have led me to do so.

I shall commence at the battle of Queenston, where I was at the time the cannon balls were flying around me in every direction. I left the place during the engagement. After the battle I returned to Queenston, and then found that my husband had been wounded; my house plundered and property destroyed. It was while the Americans had possession of the frontier, that I learned the plans of the American commander, and determined to put the British troops under Fitzgibbon in possession of them, and if possible, to save the British troops from capture, or, perhaps, total destruction. In doing so I found I should have great difficulty in getting through the American guards, which were out ten miles in the country. Determined to persevere, however, I left early in the morning, walked nineteen miles in the month of June, over a rough and difficult part of the country, when I came to a field belonging to a Mr Decamp [DeCew], in the neighbourhood of the Beaver Dam. By this time daylight had left me. Here I found all the Indians encamped; by moonlight the scene was terrifying, and to those accustomed to such scenes, might be considered grand. Upon advancing to the Indians they all rose, and, with some yells, said "Woman," which made me tremble. I cannot express the awful feeling it gave me; but I did not lose my presence of mind. I was determined to persevere. I went up to one of the chiefs, made him understand that I had great news for Capt. Fitzgibbon, and that he must let me pass to his camp, or that he and his party would be all taken. The chief at first objected to let me pass, but finally consented, after some hesitation, to go with me and accompany me to Fitzgibbon's station, which was at the Beaver Dam, where I had an interview with him. I then told him what I had come for, and what I had heard—that the Americans intended to make an attack upon the troops under his command, and would, from their superior numbers, capture them all. Benefiting by this information Capt. Fitzgibbon formed his plan accordingly, and captured about five hundred American infantry, about fifty mounted dragoons, and a fieldpiece or two was taken from the enemy. I returned home next day, exhausted and fatigued. I am now advanced in years, and when I look back I wonder how I could have gone through so much fatigue, with the fortitude to accomplish it.

I am now a very old woman—a widow many years. A few short years even if I should so long live will see me no more upon this earth. I feel that it will be gratifying to my family and a pleasure to myself that your Royal Parent the Queen should know that the services which I performed were truly loyal and that no gain or hope of reward influenced me in doing what I did.

I request that your Royal Highness will be pleased to convey to your Royal Parent Her Majesty the Queen the name of one who in the hour of trial and danger—as well as my departed husband who fought and bled on Queenston Heights in the ever memorable battle of 13th Oct. 1812—stood ever ready and willing to defend this Country against every invasion come what might.

Source: Laura Secord's Memorial to the Prince of Wales, 1860, LAC, RG 7, G23, 1.

illicit trade between Britain and the United States; the region was never actively involved in the military struggle. Only in the Canadas did the War of 1812 have any great impact. In Lower Canada, the support the French Canadians gave the British demonstrated their loyalty. In Upper Canada, the war provided a demarcation point between the loyal and the disloyal, the latter composed almost entirely of Americans. During and after the fighting, the Canadian oligarchies (especially in Upper Canada) were able to appropriate Loyalism as their monopoly and use it against their American opponents. The great struggle between British and American allegiance was played out internally in Upper Canada between 1812 and 1815, and the British won. After 1815 the overt American influence on Upper Canada—and the prevalence of American culture—would gradually decline.

Despite the return to the status quo antebellum, the War of 1812 had considerable impact upon British America in several areas. One was in the domestic politics of Upper Canada. To earlier notions of loyalty to the British Crown inherited from the period of the American Revolution was added a new ideological stream. The Upper Canadian Tory elite became convinced that the province had been in great danger, as much from the internal menace of American residents as from the external one of American troops. That elite carried over into the post-war period their beliefs in the necessity of the simultaneous suppression of political opposition and the maintenance of social harmony, by force if necessary. These twin beliefs served as the basis for Upper Canadian Toryism for several generations (Mills, 1988).

Another important effect of the War of 1812 was upon the Aboriginal people, many of whom had supported the British. It was never quite clear how a British victory would contribute to the cause of Aboriginal unity or the dream of a First Nations state, but it was certainly plain that the maintenance of the status quo was—from the Aboriginal perspective—a victory for the American expansionists. The United States had used the war to solidify its control of the "Middle Ground" in the Ohio Valley and to push the Aboriginals farther towards the margins. One of the articles of the Treaty of Ghent stipulated that both the United States and Great Britain would endeavour not only to end hostilities with the Native peoples, but "forthwith to restore to such tribes or nations respectively all possessions, right and privileges which they may have enjoyed or been entitled to in one thousand eight hundred and eleven, previous to such hostilities" (quoted in Allen, 1992: 169). This clause remained a dead letter. As it became clear that the British sought détente with the Americans in the wake of the war, many of the tribes near the border sullenly came to terms with the American government after the Treaty of Ghent, while others retreated farther west to continue a resistance they understood full well was doomed.

In the North-West, a little war between the Hudson's Bay Company and the North West Company ran its own course, occasionally touching on the larger Anglo–American conflict. In 1813, for example, Lord Selkirk very nearly succeeded in persuading the British government to finance the recruiting, equipping, and transporting to the Red River of a Highland regiment that he would command. The purpose of the unit was to protect the West from an American takeover. The scheme won ministerial approval, but was vetoed at the last moment by the commander-in-chief, the Duke of York, not because it would have crushed the North West Company but because it involved Highlanders. In 1816 Selkirk recruited as soldier/settlers a number of disbanded troops from several Swiss regiments that had fought for the British in North America, leading them to the Red River. As in the War of 1812, the western fur trade war was fought to an expensive draw. The two rival companies would settle matters by merging in 1821, shortly after Selkirk's death.

Conclusion

By a diplomatic convention in 1818, Great Britain and the United States would agree to declare the Great Lakes an unarmed zone and the forty-ninth parallel to be the Anglo–American border from the Lake of the Woods to the Rocky Mountains. British policy after the war would consistently be to seek entente rather than trouble with the Americans, so in a sense the Americans had won. The final defeat of Napoleon at Waterloo in 1815, rather than the Treaty of Ghent, marked the major watershed for Britain and her North American colonies, however. After 1815 the shift from an overheated war economy to a peacetime one in the British Isles produced substantial unemployment. Even after the post-war depression had ended, a new round of industrialization and agricultural rationalization left many without work in their traditional occupations and places of residence. The result was a new era of emigration and immigration. Between 1815 and 1860 more than a million Britons would leave their homes and come to British America. In the process they would help bring the colonies into maturity.

Historiography

Studying the Loyalists

Elizabeth Vibert, University of Victoria

In a 1784 petition to the governor of the Colony of Nova Scotia, new settlers Thomas Peters and Murphy Steel made very explicit their identities as Loyalists to the British Crown. They had served Britain in its long war against American rebels, the men explained, and came north with other Loyalists on the expectation that they would be granted land, provisions, and other necessities to start anew:

> We first Inlisted in the year one Thousand Seven Hundred & seventy six & was promised

> when we was swore . . . [that] when [the war] was over we was to be at our own Liberty to do & provide for our selves . . . We would be verrey much obliged to your Excellency if you would be so good as to grant the Articles allowed by Government to us[,] the same as the rest of the Disbanded Soldiers of his Majestys Army.[1]

Peters and Steel viewed themselves as Loyalist soldiers like any others, and equally deserving of a helping hand from the British government. The problem for these men was that the colonial government did not view them as equal to other Loyalists. Peters and Steel were free people of African descent, more than 3,000 of whom were among the 35,000 refugees of the American Revolutionary War who made their way to Nova Scotia and the new colony of New Brunswick at war's end. Their racialized status as formerly enslaved people, their class status as people who had lost no substantial property in the war, and their gender status—black men in the era of slavery were often imagined as lazy or unreliable, black women as sexually available—constrained their options in British North America. As a government official dealing with Loyalist compensation claims in Britain put it at the time, black Loyalists had already gained their freedom: they "ought to be satisfied."[2]

Much Loyalist scholarship in recent years attends closely to the experiences, agency, and self-fashioning of previously ignored categories of Loyalist immigrants. Beginning in the 1970s a substantial body of scholarship developed around the black Loyalists, men and women who had fled slavery and joined the British war effort as soldiers, cooks, servants, and in other roles.[3] One aim of this scholarship has been to highlight the social and racial diversity of the Loyalist influx: these were not simply upper-class pro-British Tories, but ordinary people seeking a new start after the Revolutionary War. Another aim has been to tell the story of the racial discrimination that was stitched into the fabric of these settler colonies. Not only were Indigenous people marginalized and swept aside by settlement; people of African descent were systematically disadvantaged as well. Important as it is to understand the processes of colonial dispossession and marginalization that shape Canadian history, a danger is that such narratives can turn historical actors who lived complex and meaningful lives into passive victims.

Recent approaches include the work of historian Amani Whitfield, who seeks to recover the identities of the perhaps 1,200 still-enslaved people of African heritage who were brought north as the "property" of Loyalist masters in the wake of the revolution. Whitfield is especially interested in these people's efforts to free themselves from enslavement. Historian Cassandra Pybus uses peti-

tions and other productions of free black people to tell the stories of their peripatetic lives around the globe. A recent treatment of Loyalist history by historian Maya Jasanoff makes clear that mobility and migration were common features of many Loyalist lives following the Revolutionary War.[4] Peters and Steel were highly mobile: Peters travelled to London with a petition on behalf of fellow Loyalists unable to "do & provide for [them] selves," and the two were among nearly 1,200 people of African descent who left Nova Scotia in disgust in 1792, taking a chance on yet another new life in West Africa.

The stories that predominate in Loyalist studies today are a fair distance from those told by earlier generations of scholars. In the late nineteenth century, historian Henry Coyne described Loyalist settlers in British North America as "the very cream" of the former American colonies, an image that persisted.[5] Well into the twentieth century, scholars focused on Loyalists of elite status, emphasizing their commitment to all things British and their disdain for America. Those founding scholars of the Loyalist tradition were in search of what has been called a "usable past"—history deliberately infused with political lessons for the present.[6] Might the same be said of more recent approaches to Loyalist history?

Notes

1. NSARM, RG 1, vol. 359, folio 65, petition from Thomas Peters and Murphy Still [sic] to Governor Parr, 24 Aug. 1784.
2. National Archives (UK), Audit Office Papers, Series 12, vol. 99, folio 356.
3. A key work is James W. St G. Walker, *The Black Loyalists: The Search for a Promised Land in Nova Scotia and Sierra Leone* (Halifax and New York, 1976).
4. Harvey Amani Whitfield, "The Struggle over Slavery in the Maritime Colonies," *Acadiensis* 41, 2 (2012): 17–44; Cassandra Pybus, *Epic Journeys of Freedom: Runaway Slaves of the American Revolution and Their Global Quest for Liberty* (Boston, 2006); Maya Jasanoff, *Liberty's Exiles: American Loyalists in the Revolutionary World* (New York, 2011).

Continued...

5. J.H. Coyne, "Memorial to the United Empire Loyalists" (1898), cited in L.F.S. Upton, *The United Empire Loyalists: Men and Myths* (Toronto, 1997), 138.

6. On the Loyalist tradition and mythology, see especially Norman Knowles, *Inventing the Loyalists: The Ontario Loyalist Tradition and the Creation of a Usable Past* (Toronto, 1997).

Short Bibliography

Boyd, Robert T. *The Coming of the Spirit of Pestilence: Introduced Infectious Diseases and Population Decline among Northwest Coast Indians, 1774–1874.* Vancouver and Seattle, 1999. A pioneering study.

Brown, Wallace, and Hereward Senior. *Victorious in Defeat: The Loyalists in Canada.* Toronto, 1984. Somewhat dated, but still the best survey of the Loyalists.

Bumsted, J.M. *The Peoples' Clearance: Highland Emigration to British North America 1770–1815.* Edinburgh and Winnipeg, 1982. A revisionist work that argues the early Scots came to British North America of their own volition.

Clarke, Ernest. *The Siege of Fort Cumberland: An Episode in the American Revolution.* Montreal and Kingston, 1996. A study emphasizing that remaining loyal in revolutionary Nova Scotia was no easy matter.

Dowd, Gregory. *A Spirited Resistance: The North American Indian Struggle for Unity 1745–1815.* Baltimore and London, 1992. A book focusing on the conflicts in the Ohio country from the First Nations perspective.

Greenwood, F. Murray. *Legacies of Fear: Law and Politics in the Era of the French Revolution.* Toronto, 1993. A work making the point that British officialdom and its anglophone allies in Lower Canada helped create the province's ethnic division through their paranoid politics.

Greer, Allan. *Peasant, Lord and Merchant: Rural Society in Three Quebec Parishes 1740–1840.* Toronto, 1985. A detailed localized study of rural French Canada.

Kert, Faye Margaret. *Prize and Prejudice: Privateering and Naval Prize in Atlantic Canada in the War of 1812.* St John's, 1997. A thorough account of the importance of privateering in the War of 1812.

Kimber, Stephen. *Loyalists and Layabouts: The Rapid Rise and Faster Fall of Shelburne, Nova Scotia.* Toronto, 2008. A new look at the biggest failure in Loyalist resettlement.

Knowles, Norman. *Inventing the Loyalists: The Ontario Loyalist Experience and the Creation of Usable Pasts.* Toronto, 1997. A postmodern work more interested in Loyalist mythology than in Loyalist actuality.

Lawson, Philip. *The Imperial Challenge: Quebec and Britain in the Age of the American Revolution.* Montreal and Kingston, 1989. A well-researched study of Quebec in the British Empire.

Neatby, Hilda. *Quebec: The Revolutionary Age 1760–91.* Toronto, 1966. Old, but still the standard study.

Potter-MacKinnon, Janice. *While the Women Only Wept: Loyalist Refugee Women.* Montreal and Kingston, 1993. A pioneer work focusing on Loyalist women in Canada.

Sheppard, George. *Plunder, Profit and Paroles: A Social History of the War of 1812 in Upper Canada.* Montreal and Kingston, 1994. A revisionist study concentrating on the internal struggle in Upper Canada during the War of 1812.

Taylor, Alan. *The Civil War of 1812: American Citizens, British Subjects, Irish Rebels, & Indian Allies.* New York, 2012. The most recent survey of the War of 1812, by an American scholar attempting to be even-handed.

Walker, James St G. *The Black Loyalists: The Search for a Promised Land in Nova Scotia and Sierra Leone,* 1778–1870. Halifax and New York, 1976. The pioneering study of the black Loyalists and their fate.

Study Questions

1. What was the political effect of the American invasions of Canada in 1775–6?

2. Who were the Loyalists?

3. Were the Loyalists the "founders" of English-speaking Canada? Explain your answer.

4. What does the biography of Boston King tell us about the black Loyalists?

5. Identify three reasons to explain why the War of 1812 was so crucial to British North America.

6. Why is a "fair" account of the War of 1812 so difficult to achieve?

7. Why is Laura Secord a heroine?

8. Define the term "oligarchy." Explain how this concept operated in British North America, especially in Lower Canada, during this period.

Visit the companion website for *A History of the Canadian Peoples*, fifth edition for further resources.

 **www.oupcanada.com/Bumsted5e**

As a small capitalist, the typical primary producer—whether boat owner, farmer, or timberer—identified with the commercial system rather than with his labour force, thus impeding the development of any working-class consciousness or the formation of an articulated class structure. Merchants had to be successful entrepreneurs, but found it difficult to move beyond their immediate commercial horizons. They were prepared to invest in processing raw materials within their own sphere of interest, but not outside it. The result was a highly exploitative and unadventurous economy, with a fluid and fuzzy social structure. It was an economy that could celebrate the values of an independent yeomanry at the same time that it took advantage of a labour force not composed of those yeomen.

The Staple Resources

The fishery was the oldest and most rewarding of British America's resource commodities. It had been successfully exploited since the early years of the sixteenth century. Traditionally associated with Newfoundland, it continued to dominate that colony's economic picture throughout the nineteenth century. By the end of the War of 1812, the actual production of fish was almost entirely in the hands of Newfoundland residents. Although after 1815 the market for Newfoundland cod remained stagnant for decades, the fishing economy experienced considerable change. Smaller buyers of fish in the outports were squeezed out by the larger merchants of Water Street in St John's. The fishery expanded into Labrador, and sealing became far more important, representing over one-third of the value of fishery exports by 1831. Newfoundland was unable to gain ground in the lucrative Caribbean trade. Nova Scotia merchants now had their own local suppliers of fish and were able to carry more diversified cargoes to the West Indies. The Lower Canadian fishery of the Gaspé region was the object of the agricultural interests' disdain. While the industry was not a particularly buoyant one after 1815, it did employ a considerable workforce. It produced a significant export trade, and it required a large number of sailing vessels both large and small. These characteristics contributed both to the shipbuilding industry and to the carrying-trade capacity of British America.

The fur trade was the other traditional resource industry. By the nineteenth century, the fur trade's economic value was very small in comparison with that of other resources. In a non-economic sense, however, the fur trade was of enormous importance. It provided the means by which Great Britain retained its claim to sovereignty over much of the northern half of the continent. It also supplied the administration of the British relationship with the Indigenous peoples of that region. With the merger of the two great rivals in 1821, the fur trade stabilized under the aegis of the Hudson's Bay Company. The Pacific coast became increasingly important to the HBC. It deliberately over-trapped in the Far West since it assumed that it would eventually lose out to the Americans. Indeed, the company was able to hold its own against fur competitors, but not against the constant stream of American settlers into the Willamette Valley in the Oregon Territory. The fur trade had a remarkable influence in the West, chiefly because furs were its only export commodity. The entire region was organized politically and economically around the trade.

The old staples of fish and fur were replaced by timber and grain in primary economic importance in the nineteenth century. Both these commodities benefited from imperial preference, which gave them considerable advantage in the large and lucrative British market during their start-up years. Not until the 1840s did Britain begin seriously to eliminate the differential duty scales that the Corn Laws and the Timber Laws had created during the Napoleonic Wars. Every hint of change in imperial regulations brought a chorus of fears of economic disaster from the colonial mercantile community. While colonials may have been chained economically to the mother country, they revelled in the chains and were loath to break them.

Every province of British America except Newfoundland quickly became involved in the timber trade after Napoleon closed the Baltic (the traditional source of British supply) in 1807. Even tiny Prince Edward Island enjoyed a considerable boom from cutting down its trees, most of which were relatively accessible to open water. Primary-growth forest was cut as quickly as possible with no thought for either conservation or oversupplying the market, although the finest white pine forest in North America, in Norfolk County, Upper Canada, was ruthlessly chopped down for potash and firewood. In no province was the industry more important than in New Brunswick. Its dependence on timber as an export commodity had become almost complete by the mid-1820s.

The needs of the industry controlled every aspect of the province's life. Settlement was closely connected to the opening of new timber territory. It was no accident that the few timber princes who controlled the licences to cut on Crown land were also the leading politicians of the province. Under the large entrepreneurs worked a variety of local businessmen—storekeepers, brokers, and sawmill operators—who actually organized and dealt with the hundreds of small parties that wintered in the woods. Provisioning the timberers was a lucrative business. The industry preferred to do as much processing of the timber on the spot as possible, moving inexorably in that direction. As early as 1837 the sawmills of Samuel Cunard, on the Miramichi River in northeastern New Brunswick, were capable of cutting 42,471 feet (12,945 metres) of boards per day, "the produce of 320 logs and 50 workmen" (quoted in Wynn, 1980). Much timber also was processed into wooden sailing ships.

Contemporary Views

Sealing in Newfoundland

Joseph Jukes was an Englishman employed on a geological survey of Newfoundland in 1839. In a book about his experiences published in 1842, he recorded the following from his diary.

March 12th: Again foggy, with a southeast wind. As we stood on deck this morning before breakfast, we heard a cry down to leeward, like the cry of a gull, which some of the men said it was. It became, however, so loud and continued, that both Stuwitz and I doubted its being the cry of any bird, and one of the men took a gaff and went to look. We watched him for some distance with our glasses as he proceeded slowly through the fog till he suddenly began to run, and then struck at something, and presently returned dragging a young seal alive over the ice, and brought it on deck. It was of a dirty white colour, with short close fur, large expressive eyes, and it paddled and walloped about the deck fierce and bawling. A Newfoundland dog called Nestor, belonging to the captain, approached it, but it snapped at his nose and bit him, though its teeth were just beginning to appear. After taking it down below to show the captain and demand the usual quart of rum for the first man who caught a seal, one of the men knocked it on its head and skinned it. Stuwitz then cut off its "flippers" or paws and its head, and after breakfast we took it into the "after-hatch" or steerage where he drew and dissected it. In the middle of the day we heard from some of the men who had been out on the ice, that a vessel a few miles ahead of us had already 2,500 seals on board, so we pushed on through the ice, and shortly came into a lake of water. On the borders of this many young seals were lying and two or three punts were hoisted out to despatch and collect them. I shot one through the head that was scuffling off a pan of ice, but the crew begged me to desist, as they said the balls might glance from the ice and injure some of the men who were about. Having picked up the few which were immediately about us, we hoisted in our punts again, as there were several vessels near us, and more coming up, and bore away farther north through an open pool of water. In passing through a thin skirt of ice, one of the men hooked up a young seal with his gaff. Its cries were precisely like those of a young child in the extremity of agony and distress, something between shrieks and convulsive sobbings. . . . We soon afterwards passed through some loose ice on which the young seals were scattered, and nearly all hands were overboard slaying, skinning and hauling. We then got into another lake of water and sent our five punts. The crews of these joined those already on the ice, and dragging either the whole seals or their "pelts" to the edge of the water, collected them in the punts, and when one of these was full brought them on board.

Source: J.B. Jukes, *Excursions in and about Newfoundland*, 2 vols (London, 1842), as reprinted in Peter Neary and Patrick O'Flaherty, eds, *By Great Waters: A Newfoundland and Labrador Anthology* (Toronto: University of Toronto Press, 1974), 82–3.

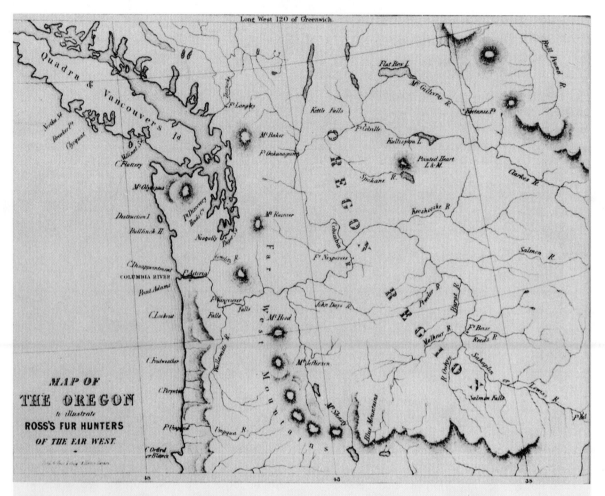

The Oregon Territory. One of the best accounts of the Oregon Territory was written by the fur trader Alexander Ross after he retired to Red River with his Okanagan wife and their children. Fur-Hunters of the Far West *was first published in 1853. This map is from the 1855 edition. Metropolitan Toronto Reference Library.*

Before 1840 the export market for Upper Canadian timber was somewhat limited by transportation difficulties, but after that date the United States took all the timber Upper Canada could produce. The Ottawa Valley was a region of 8,000 square miles, most not arable but initially covered with primary-growth forest. It was timbered by professional crews who fostered a rough and violent society. The first serious ethnic conflicts in British America occurred in the "Shiner's Wars" of the 1830s, as Irish timberers fought with French Canadians and others for dominance of the forests. Much of the forest in Upper Canada and elsewhere was timbered in advance of the arrival of settlement, with little except minimal license fees as the only charge for the cutting.

In the extensive agricultural lands of the St Lawrence Valley and Upper Canada, wheat quickly became the dominant crop. It met a growing demand abroad and it transported well as either grain or flour. Wheat quickly turned farmers into agricultural specialists, who exploited their soil much as did the timberers the forest. Lower Canada's wheat yields on rapidly exhausted soil often cropped for decades were frequently inadequate for home consumption. While Upper Canada was able to transform its wheat profits from great surpluses into non-agricultural investment, by the 1850s it, too, had exhausted its best soils and was looking westward. Most farmers also produced for their own consumption, of course, and some (such as those on Prince Edward Island) produced livestock and potatoes for export or supplied a local market with produce. Even Maritime farmers grew more wheat than was good for them, however.

The Mercantile System

The resource economy worked only because of its capacity to deal with the international market. The merchant capitalist looked after transportation and marketing in a world of totally unsophisticated credit and banking. Merchants operated at all levels of volume and capital investment. Some placed goods in a number of vessels and invested small amounts in other ships and voyages, as had been done in the colonies since the earliest days. The growing extent of the resource trade demanded entrepreneurs with more capital, however. Whether the merchant's business was large or small, international mercantile activity in the first half of the nineteenth century was extremely dangerous. Financial disaster lurked everywhere. Ships could be lost at sea, markets could be miscalculated, debtors could be unable to pay. Communications were incredibly slow. Because of the difficulties in finding trustworthy partners and agents abroad, the extensive family network was still the international basis of much mercantile activity. Few of the large merchant princes of this period avoided at least one bankruptcy, and fewer still left fortunes to their heirs. The sailing ship, filled with outgoing cargoes of resource commodities and incoming ones of manufactured goods and new immigrants, remained the backbone of British America's economic system in this period.

Some manufacturing activity did exist in British America. It involved relatively small establishments that engaged in two kinds of production. One was by artisans producing for local markets goods and services that either could not be imported profitably or could not be imported at all. Every town had its saddler, every village its blacksmith. The second type of production involved the processing of resource commodities. Grain was distilled into whisky, brewed into beer, and milled into flour. Wood from land being cleared by farmers was burned into potash, and timber was cut at sawmills into deals (planks). Among many specialized manufacturing enterprises, shipyards that transformed timber into sailing vessels were the most extensive. The small shipyard was to be found wherever there was timber and open water; the commerce of the Great Lakes required as many sailing vessels as the transatlantic trade.

Shipbuilding was the ideal colonial processing industry. It relied primarily on a rich natural resource—timber—that British America had in abundance. It did not require excessive capital outlay for physical plant or materials, and its end product provided its own transportation to market. On the other hand, even during its heyday it was not an industry with either a future or a capacity to generate industrial development. As early as 1840 wood and sail were being overtaken by iron and steam. These technologies required an entirely different form of industrial organization than a handful of craftsmen employing hand tools, carefully assembling a wooden ship on the edge of open water. Neither the technology nor the industrial organization flowed logically out of the nature of colonial shipbuilding, which became instead the symbol of the mercantile resource economy's limitations.

Providing the infrastructure for trade and commerce was a gradual development. Banks were slow to expand because most colonials were suspicious of institutions that could, in effect, manufacture money. The Bank of Montreal was founded in 1817 and the Bank of Canada was chartered in 1821, opening at York in 1822. Early banks did not co-operate and their services were limited. An expanding internal economic system required roads, bridges, and canals to connect the population with their markets and sources of supply. Most people wanted such facilities, but they did not want to pay for them out of taxes. Much road-building was done by labour levies on the local population. After the American success with the Erie Canal, canal-building became the craze in the Canadas. The early Canadian canals—the Lachine Canal, the Welland Canal, the Rideau Canal, and the Chambly Canal—either opened water access into Lake Ontario

These two photos from the New Brunswick lumber camps obviously postdate 1840 and the invention of the camera, but there is no reason to think that conditions in the timber trade changed much over the course of the nineteenth century. Top: a cookhouse; bottom: men with peaveys on a log-jam. From Adam Shortt and A.G. Doughty, eds, Canada and Its Provinces (Edinburgh, 1914), vol. 14. Metropolitan Toronto Reference Library.

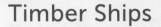

Timber Ships

Interior of a lumber ship in Quebec, 1872. While politicians and settlers in central Canada concerned themselves with territorial expansion during the mid-nineteenth century, those living in the Atlantic region were constrained to the older transatlantic way of life, of which shipping was integral. © McCord Museum.

The holds of timber ships like that pictured here carried thousands of immigrants to Canada on their voyage (usually 10 to 12 weeks in duration) from the British Isles in the nineteenth century. Although the British government continually passed legislation improving provisioning of food and water and controlling numbers, it never really altered the primitiveness of the space itself. At first glance, the timber trade seemed a perfect fit for developing colonies. Timbering removed a major impediment to agricultural settlement: trees. From the standpoint of the incoming settler trees were the enemy, for fields could not be plowed and seeded until the trees were gone. The need for removal was so urgent that settlers would often burn forests in vast fires if no other way existed to clear them. Fortunately, entrepreneurs could often be found to cut the timber and ship the wood to market in the mother country. In the eighteenth century,

the principal demand in Britain was for timber for shipbuilding, especially the tall pines that would be turned into the masts for sailing ships. By the nineteenth century, the British demand changed from tall timber to square (the trees were trimmed with an axe from their rounded shape to a square one) and deals (the square timber cut into planks at least three inches thick). During the first half of the nineteenth century, Britain encouraged the shipment of square timber and deals from British America by the judicious use of duties levied on wood originating elsewhere, including the Baltic region. The vessels carrying the wood frequently were unable to find a return cargo, often solving the problem by converting the space below decks to accommodate human passengers. This practice provided inexpensive—if uncomfortable—passage for many immigrants, especially the Irish, driven from their homes by famine. This seemingly ideal arrangement, removing unwanted wood and returning much wanted population had some hidden drawbacks, however. One was that the trade was extremely wasteful. Much of the tree was left behind on the forest floor to rot. The timberers, moreover, merely removed and never replaced trees, so that large tracts of land were systematically denuded of cover with no thought of sustainability. Worse still, the mentality of those cutting the trees was one of sheer exploitation, totally lacking in any concern for reinvestment in the country they were looting. As for the human return cargo, conditions on the timber ships encouraged disease and were singularly unpleasant at best.

As with many forms of material culture, timber ships provided a dual purpose for Canada. The timber that the country supplied was a critical resource to the British Empire, as well as beyond, and the ships that transported people in that exchange simply were part of a larger commodity chain that saw

Continued...

timber spread far and wide. The influx of immigrants who were essential to the development of Canada made the return journey in poor conditions in the holds that nevertheless were spaces of opportunity. The timber ships were the vehicles of that opportunity.

Source: A.R.M. Lower, *Great Britain's Woodyard: British America and the Timber Trade, 1763–1867* (Montreal and Kingston: McGill-Queen's University Press, 1973).

or improved the St Lawrence River system. Their thrust was to enable the economy to shift from a transatlantic focus to an internal one. This process really took hold with the introduction of the railroads in the 1850s.

Trade and commerce were the basis of urban growth, although the major cities of the British colonies in North America were centres of political activity as well as of commerce. It was easier to flourish, however, without being a capital (e.g., Montreal or Hamilton) than without trade (e.g., Fredericton). No city dominated more than its immediate region and none was very large. Nonetheless, most urban centres in British America were growing rapidly. York in 1795 contained 12 cottages. By the time it was incorporated and renamed Toronto in 1834 it had over 1,000 houses, 100 shops, and a population of 9,252. The cities were small in area as well as in population, many being collections of tightly packed buildings radiating from a port facility. Such a city had little concept of zoning and not many amenities, although by the 1830s matters were improving. Toronto was fairly typical for 1830 in lacking sidewalks, drains, sewers, water supply, and street lighting, all of which became developments of the 1830s and 1840s. Policing consisted at best of a few ward constables and a night watch. For most urban centres in British America, 1840 marked the break between remaining an eighteenth-century town and becoming a nineteenth-century city.

Shipbuilding at Dorchester, New Brunswick, 1875. The technology of shipbuilding remained fairly constant throughout the nineteenth century. Over the years, Dorchester's river silted up, and the community is now landlocked. Alexander Henderson, LAC, C-010103.

"View in King Street [Toronto], Looking East," hand-coloured lithograph, 1835, by Thomas Young. The buildings on the left (north) are the jail, the courthouse, and St James Church at Church Street. King Street is on the extreme right of the lithograph. LAC, 1970-188-1507, W.H. Coverdale Collection of Canadiana.

Immigration

After 1815 circumstances combined to alter patterns of immigration, especially from the British Isles. Resistance to emigration from both the British government and the British ruling classes was quickly broken down by unemployment and a new round of industrialization and agricultural rationalization. Pressures increased on Britain's relief system for the poor, and among those who governed the nation common wisdom again was that Britain was overpopulated. The burgeoning North American timber trade provided the shipping capacity for the transatlantic movement of immigrants at low cost. Immigrants came to British America chiefly to obtain access to land, something that was becoming increasingly difficult to obtain in the British Isles. Many Britons had an extremely idealized picture of

the wilderness. The essayist Thomas Carlyle wrote in 1839 of the vastness of North America, "nine-tenths of it yet vacant or tenanted by nomads, . . . still crying, Come and till me, come and reap me!" Despite the best efforts of a number of writers of immigration manuals, many newcomers failed to appreciate the need for capital or the difficulties involved in clearing much of this vacant land of trees and brush. In 1846, in her book *The Backwoods of Canada*, Catharine Parr Traill included "some official information" "to render this work of more practical value to persons desiring to emigrate."

What we know about the numbers departing the British Isles suggests that Scottish emigration remained relatively steady throughout the period at 10–15 per cent of the total flow. A far higher proportion of Highlanders than Lowlanders departed in these years. Irish emigration was more variable, ranging annually from 30 to 70 per cent of the total numbers. Irish movement to North America before the 1840s was dominated by Protestants from Northern Ireland. Only in the mid-1840s did the Irish emigrants begin to include huge numbers of Catholic southerners. As a result, the whole nature of Irish emigration to British America was quite different from Irish emigration to the United States. British America received far more Irish emigrants in the early period than did the United States. The Irish flow to what is now Canada included far more Protestants and Orangists than did that to the United States, where the emigrants were almost exclusively Catholics from the south. Not all newcomers to British America came from the British Isles. A relative handful, for example, of Sephardic Jews arrived individually or in family groups from Europe after 1763 to form the first continuing synagogue in Montreal, founded in 1768.

The national and regional complexity of the population in the British Isles at this time produces several interesting questions and problems. It is tempting to assume from a twenty-first-century perspective, for example, that the British emigrants were a relatively homogeneous anglophone group of people. Nothing could be further from the truth. Each of the historic nations of Britain continued in the nineteenth century to preserve its own culture and history. The immigrants presented homogeneity neither of language nor of religion. Many of the Irish, especially in the south, spoke the Irish tongue. Almost all Scots from north of the Highland fault spoke Gaelic as a first language, while those in the Lowlands spoke a Scottish variant of English. Dialects and linguistic variants were extensive in England and Wales, also. In the latter place, there was a north–south division whereby the northerners were more likely to speak Welsh than English. At the same time, the nineteenth century saw a considerable growth of a common "Britishness" that to various extents overcame regional distinctions. On the other hand, acceptance of the concepts of Great Britain and Britishness was quite variable. Many of the southern Irish, for example, would not have agreed that they were British or that they were willing subjects of the British Crown.

Another difference between immigration to the United States and to British America occurred in the nature of the vessels employed in the transatlantic passage. This had certain ramifications for the sorts of emigrants who departed for each of the countries. Those going to the United States tended to travel in large vessels specifically designed to carry passengers, while those going to British America usually travelled in smaller vessels designed for the timber trade. These smaller ships carried passengers on the return voyage in makeshift accommodations instead of sailing in ballast. The port of Quebec was the principal entry for immigrants into the Canadas because sailing vessels could collect a load of timber there for the voyage to Britain. One result of the sort of passage provided was that the passage to British America cost significantly less than that to the United States. When this difference in cost is combined with the much shorter duration of the passage from the British Isles to the eastern seaports of British America (which meant that fewer provisions were required for the journey), it seems likely that far more immigrants to British America sailed on extremely limited budgets and without much capital in reserve than was typically the case for those who went to the United States. It is hard to generalize, because the rates for passengers varied substantially from time to time. One Belfast advertisement from 1820 put the charge for a family of husband, wife, and six children to the United States at 80 guineas, for example, and the cost for the same family to New Brunswick at 24 guineas. Either way, such rates meant that only those with considerable capital—or who were willing to acquire considerable debt—could afford to sail at all. Many of those arriving in British American ports without capital may have intended to move on to the United States when they had acquired the means, but how many actually managed to do so is another matter entirely. Large numbers of those arriving with little or no capital were already in debt to friends or relatives at home. They had borrowed the price of steerage passage and were bound to repay the debt out of their first earnings.

Costs and geography also meant that British America rather than the United States throughout the period received the vast bulk of the emigrants from the Highlands of Scotland. Many of these Highlanders arrived virtually destitute in British America and could not afford to continue on to the United States. Sufficient numbers of Gaelic-speakers from Highland Scotland

An Immigrant Letter Home

Letters from immigrants are always a problem to interpret. Most of those surviving sound very positive, but would you send a letter to your kinfolk if you were not succeeding in the new country?

Ann Thomas, Waterloo Township, Upper Canada, to Her Father. 15 October 1832.

MY DEAR FATHER, I write these few lines to you, hoping to find you in good health, as, thank God, it leaves us at present. We had a very long voyage over. We were 9 weeks on the seas. We landed the 7th of June. We were tossed about very much indeed. The rest of May we all thought of being lost, the births all fell down, from one end of the ship to the other. And I was not well after that till I was confined, and that was the 3rd of June. I got about again quite as soon as I could expect. It is a fine boy, and goes on well. I am happy to tell you, that America is quite as good as we expected to find it. Edmund has had plenty of work, ever since we have been here. We have no reason to repent leaving England at present, and I hope we never shall. He has earned 3s.9d. a day, and his board, and sometimes not so much. Give my love and Sarah's [her sister] to my brothers and sisters. Sarah is about 30 miles from me, in service, and is doing very well. Give Edmond's love to his father and mother, and all. Thomas and James are about 100 miles. They are all well, and send their love to all. If Thomas and William should come out next spring, it is Sarah and my wish for you to come with them, as I think we should [be able] to help support you here. The worst of it will be getting over. Edmond's brother has got 100 acres of land each. We might have 100 acres if we liked to go where it is, but we don't like to leave the place where we are, at present. The cholera has been very bad indeed in this country but thank God not one of us has had it. Henry Smart's wife is dead, and both his children. She was confined the same night that I was. Please to thank Mr. Greetham for his kindness to us, and I hope he will do the same for you, if you should come. We have had a very fine summer, but hotter than in England, and they say the winter is much colder. But there is one great comfort here: we have as much wood as we like to burn. If you should come, you had better send us a letter on, when you get to York, for us to meet you. Please to answer this, on the first opportunity, as I should very much like to hear from you. I have no more to say, at present. I remain your affectionate daughter. ANN THOMAS

Source: Wendy Cameron, Sheila Haines, Mary McDougall Maude, eds, *English Immigrant Voices: Labourers' Letters from Upper Canada in the 1830s* (Montreal and Kingston: McGill-Queen's University Press, 2000), 68–9.

arrived in various parts of British America (notably parts of Upper Canada, the eastern townships of Lower Canada, Cape Breton Island, and Prince Edward Island) to make the language an important medium of communication in these areas. This simply did not happen in the United States, where newcomers were strongly encouraged to assimilate immediately to the dominant society.

Four patterns of organized emigration and settlement developed after 1815. The first pattern involved government assistance, which was often a combination of British official recruitment of emigrants and settlement, with public aid, on land made available by the several colonial governments. Such schemes, frequently involving either soldiers disbanded after the wars or excess Irish population, continued sporadically until 1830. What the various schemes best demonstrated was that the financial cost of establishing British emigrants in British America was high and the chances of successful transplantation were low. Even those who argued that the existing operations were unnecessarily profligate estimated £60 subsidy for a family of five. In the

Irish emigrants awaiting departure on the quay at Cork, as depicted in the Illustrated London News, *10 May 1851. How would you interpret this scene? What is the artist trying to depict? LAC, C-3904.*

late 1820s the British government rejected a proposal for a major government resettlement scheme to be financed by local authorities as an alternative to poor relief. It was brought forward by the parliamentary undersecretary at the Colonial Office, Robert John Wilmot-Horton. Thereafter, government policy abandoned public assistance for emigration.

The other three patterns were not mutually exclusive. Some emigrants could even combine all three. The second pattern emphasized settlement on the land. It involved private proprietors of land, usually large land companies. These occasionally offered financial assistance, but most frequently they made land on affordable terms available to emigrants who had managed to make their way to North America. This process was intended to appeal to emigrants with some financial resources. There were three large land companies: the Canada Company, the British American Land Company (in the Eastern Townships of Quebec), and

the New Brunswick and Nova Scotia Land Company. In 1826 the Canada Company had purchased most of the Crown reserves and half of the clergy reserves of Upper Canada, thus providing revenue for the colony. It settled large numbers of emigrants on its lands.

A third pattern emphasized transport to North America but not settlement on the land. Private emigrant contractors would offer passage to North America in sailing vessels. The ships involved were usually in the timber trade, temporarily converted to provide accommodation on the outward passage. The contractor provided low rates of passage but as few services as possible. His passengers were frequently deposited at seaports in British America and left to their own devices. The lucky ones managed to make their way to some destination where they could find employment.

The vast majority of emigrants, whatever their transport and settlement arrangements, fitted into the fourth pattern. They had arranged their own passage,

Advice for Immigrants

Numbers of books and pamphlets were published between 1800 and 1860 devoted exclusively to offering advice for immigrants. Most of the advice was useful, although few authors went into details on how difficult the passage and transition would be.

There is nothing of more importance to Emigrants on arrival at Quebec, than correct information on the leading points, connected with their future pursuits. Many have suffered much by a want of caution, and by listening to the opinions of interested designing characters, who frequently offer their advice unsolicited, and who are met generally about wharves and landing places frequented by strangers. To guard Emigrants from falling into such errors—they should immediately on arrival at Quebec, proceed to the Office of the Chief Agent for Emigrants, in Sault-au-Matelot street, Lower Town, where every information requisite for their future guidance in either getting settlement on lands, or obtaining employment in Upper or Lower Canada, will be obtained (gratis.)

The following directions are of importance to the Emigrant arriving in Canada, and are addressed to him in the simplest language:

Previous to disembarkation arrange your baggage in a small compass, the fewer packages the better, but have them well secured—old dirty clothing, large boxes, and other useless articles, are not worth the carriage. If you have any provisions left, such as oatmeal, potatoes, &c. You can sell them at Quebec at a profit, and avoid the expense of transport, and you can purchase baker's bread, butter, tea, sugar, and other necessaries more suited for your journey. All sorts of provisions, may be bought cheaper, and generally of a better quality, in Montreal and Upper Canada, than at Quebec. Dress yourself in light clean clothing. Females frequently bring on sickness by being too warmly clothed. Cut your hair short, and wash daily and thoroughly. Avoid drinking ardent spirits of any kind, and when heated do not drink cold water. Eat moderately of light food. Avoid night dews. By attending to the preceding directions sickness will be prevented, with other serious inconveniences. When every thing is ready for disembarkation, and, if the ship is lying at anchor in the river—take care in passing from the ship to the boat; avoid all haste, and see that your baggage is in the same conveyance with yourself, or left under the charge of some friend, with your name on it. If the ship hauls to the wharf to disembark, do not be in a hurry, but await the proper time of tide when the ship's deck will be on a line with the quay or wharf. Passengers are entitled by law to the privilege of remaining on board ship 48 hours after arrival; and it is unlawful for the Captain to deprive his Passengers of any of their usual accommodations for cooking or otherwise: you may therefore avoid the expense of lodgings, and make all your arrangements for prosecuting your journey, previous to disembarkation. Should sickness overtake you, proceed immediately, or be removed to the Emigrant Hospital, in St. John's Suburbs, where you will be well taken care of, and provided with every thing needful until restored to health. Medicine and medical advice can also be had at the Dispensary attached to the Quebec Charitable Emigrant Society. This Society will grant relief to all destitute Emigrants. In Montreal there is a similar institution for the relief of Emigrants. It is particularly recommended to Emigrants not to loiter their valuable time at the port of landing; but to proceed to obtain settlement or employment. Many have regretted when too late that they did not pursue this course, and take advantage of the frequent opportunities that presented themselves for settlement in convenient situatious [*sic*] in Upper or Lower Canada, instead of squandering their means and valuable time to looking after an imaginary Paradise in the aguish swamps of Illinois and

Continued...

Missouri, or other distant regions of the Western States. There is no portion of the American continent more congenial to the constitution or habits of Emigrants from the United Kingdom, or that offer a wider field, or surer reward for industry and good conduct, than the fertile districts of Upper Canada or Lower Canada. Many Emigrants will din employment in the city of Quebec and its vicinity, as also in and about Montreal. Single men in particular are advised to embrace the offer; but Emigrants with large families had better proceed without delay, to Upper Canada, as hereafter directed—or, to situations in Lower Canada, particularly the Eastern Townships—and if they have sons and daughters grown up, they will find a sure demand for their services. Artificers, and Mechanics of all denominations, and farming Labourers, if sober and industrious, may be sure of doing well. Blacksmiths, particularly those acquainted with steam engine work, also good Millwrights, Masons and Sawyers, by machinery, are much wanted in the Canadas.

Source: *Information Published by His Majesty's Chief Agent for the Superintendence of Settlers and Emigrants in Upper and Lower Canada. For the Use of Emigrants* (Quebec, 1832).

frequently coming to British America without fixed plans or destination. Sometimes they intended to join relatives or friends who had preceded them. If they had capital, they found land. It was generally estimated that at least £100 (beyond the cost of passage) was required to establish a farm on wilderness land, and even more was required to purchase one already improved. Those who could not afford this expense joined the ranks of the labouring class or, in the case of unattached females, went into domestic service. Most immigrants apparently understood that their important baggage was cash money, good health, and family connections. The transatlantic passage in sailing ships lasted from six to eight weeks, and was long and arduous even for those who could afford cabin accommodation. For those in steerage (the vast majority), the discomfort and health hazards were high. After 1825 the British government abandoned attempts to regulate the traffic in any serious way.

Aside from the assisted settlement schemes, public policy was never really mobilized to settle British America. The major shift in policy after the mid-1820s, apart from the termination of assisted settlement, was the abandonment of the practice of giving colonial land away; now a "sufficient price" was to be charged, to ensure a revenue for colonial improvement, and to guarantee that those acquiring land had some capital. In the end, settlement was achieved out of the trials and tribulations of the many who tried their luck, not always successfully. Apart from their physical energy, the immigrants were also a great source of wealth for the colonies they entered. If every immigrant brought on average only £10, between 1815 and 1845 that amount would have injected £10 million into the local economies.

The Resource Society

The resource society of the early nineteenth century was dominated by two overlapping elites. One governed; the other controlled international commerce. In most colonies their separate identities were easily confused when they battled politically, employing imported rhetoric that suggested deeper divisions than actually existed. By far the majority of the population was composed of the non-elite: small shopkeepers, artisans, minor civil servants; owners of small industries such as gristmills, tanneries, soap factories, and breweries; and resource workers and farmers. In the British sense of distinguishing between those who held land and those who did not, an important distinction in Europe, few "landholders" in British America possessed anything but land that was in the process of becoming farms. Undeveloped land had little value. Most landowners were forced to hold multiple employments, often working side by side with the landless. Women in this society acquired the status of their husbands. Those without spouses had some autonomy, but were severely limited in any upward mobility. Finally, the Indigenous peoples lived completely outside the social

"The Emigrant's Welcome to Canada," c. 1820. In this satirical cartoon, what kind of reception for emigrants is the cartoonist trying to convey to his audience? LAC, R9266-3510, Peter Winkworth Collection of Canadiana.

structure, although the missionaries constantly tried to bring them into it.

The governing elite included the leading appointed colonial officials of government, military officers, church leaders, and the merchants who lived in the capital city. The first three enjoyed the enormous advantage of a substantial guaranteed annual salary, usually paid in London in pounds sterling. This income, the access to credit, and the style of living it encouraged all enabled colonial officials to emulate the British values of the landed gentry. Their houses reflected their aspirations. The magnificent house of John Strachan (1778–1867) on Front Street in Toronto was popularly known as "The Palace" even before he became bishop of Toronto in 1839. In 1819, the year after it was built, his brother visiting from Scotland is alleged to have commented, "I hope it's a' come by honestly, John" (quoted in Arthur, 1986: 44). Not surprisingly, colonial officials believed

in the balance of interests and order, the maintenance of which John Beverley Robinson (1791–1863) once described as "the foundation of good government in the social state" (quoted in Brode, 1984: 175). Such men were well-educated and very able. They governed British America with an extremely limited vision, usually without soiling themselves in sordid graft and corruption.

The most successful merchants (and a few professional men) shared the lifestyle of the major colonial office-holders, usually without their status. What really limited the social positions of the merchants was the impermanence of their incomes, which could be greatly affected by conditions in the market. The British associated status with land because an income from landed estates was rightly regarded as far more permanent and inheritable than income from trade or industry. British America was never able to generate a landed aristocracy. The colonial official's income was only for life, although

This scene is a somewhat romanticized, but probably fairly accurate, depiction of the early days of settlement almost anywhere in British America, with the tree stumps representing logs used to build the cabin. The cabin itself is built with cog joints; the hewn logs (as opposed to unhewn or round logs, a more primitive and less permanent form of cabin construction) have notches cut into them to allow them to interlock and improve structural integrity; chinking, consisting of such materials as mud, straw, moss, and stone, fills in the spaces between the hewn logs. Choosing a site like this one, with easy access to the materials required to build such a cabin, was typical, although there were other factors to consider. "A First Settlement," by W.H. Bartlett, engraved by J.C. Bentley, from N.P. Willis, Canadian Scenery *(London, 1842), vol. 2. LAC, C-2401.*

a few offices were passed on from father to son. The typical seigneur in Lower Canada did not have enough income to cut much of a figure. The trouble with land in North America was its sheer availability. An Upper Canadian backwoods farm consisted of a larger acreage than many an English landed estate. Most land was held for speculation rather than status. Lacking an aristocracy based on land, British America instead began developing a social structure based on wealth and conspicuous consumption. Money might be temporary, but it could be made visible. British America also held in high regard education, professional training, and the life of the mind. The concentrations of leading profes-

sional men in the larger towns were admitted to the ranks of elite society, though in a subordinate position.

While the governing elite and their merchant partners lived mainly in the political capitals that were also the great commercial centres of British America, a sprinkling of others in the hinterlands also assumed the functions of leadership. Such regional leaders included local merchants and professional men, prominent farmers, and retired half-pay officers. These were the men who were elected to the provincial houses of assembly from the countryside, where they inevitably came to contend with the governing elites for political control of the province. Regional prominence was recognized by election to the assembly and appointment to local civic office. Thus, these also were the men who served as local justices of the peace. They tended to be the militia officers as well. Before 1840 most would have described themselves as farmers, although they usually engaged in a variety of occupations, hoping to succeed and survive. One of the most striking features of the lives of most British Americans was their lack of occupational specialization. Over the course of a lifetime most colonials would hold many different jobs, both in succession and simultaneously.

Coming to terms with the remainder of society in British America is more complicated than dealing with the elite. Despite the vaunted availability of land, not everyone represented that British (and American) ideal: a land-holding yeoman farmer. In some places (Newfoundland, Prince Edward Island, and Lower Canada), freehold land was not easily available. Moreover, the land that was worth holding was not wilderness but an improved market farm. Cultivating land carved out of primary-growth forest was a tedious and laborious process. Such "improvement" was hampered by the difficulties of finding a market for surplus agricultural products. Farmers inevitably embraced crops such as wheat, which could be transported into a regular market system. Improvement was further hampered by the availability of alternative employment in fishing, timbering, shipbuilding, and construction—which could sustain a farming family before it was plugged into the market—but would also slow down the land-clearing process essential to agrarian success.

At the bottom of colonial society were the poor. They fell into three categories: permanent, immigrant, and casual; and into two major groups: those who had relations or friends to look after them and those who did not. While British America was spoken of on both sides of the Atlantic as a "land of opportunity" and a "good poor man's country", it was absolutely essential to be healthy or to have kinfolk prepared to help with one's welfare. Those who through disability, incompetence, or misfortune (such as young orphans) could not look after themselves and had no one to do it for them became the objects of charity or lived permanently in squalor. Recent immigrants who arrived in port without capital resources joined the ranks of the poor wherever

they disembarked. Unable to move onto the land, these newcomers merged into the third category, the casually employed. Because of the seasonal nature of most Canadian employment, winter saw the largest number of unemployed. Winter was also the worst time to be poor, for food costs increased and the need to keep warm in a Canadian winter was inescapable. Malnutrition and inadequate clothing, combined with inadequate heating, provided a recipe for the spread of illness and contagious disease. The poor were "relieved" chiefly to prevent their turning "by despair to commit depredations" (quoted in Fingard, 1988: 197). Contemporary society tended to identify poverty with the city and personal failure. It saw poverty as a moral rather than as an economic problem.

Between the poor and the prosperous fell a variety of occupational and social groups that defy ordering by almost any scheme. An examination of the Newfoundland fishing-boat owner suggests some of the difficulties. A property owner and an employer, the boat owner was probably landless except for a small house lot for which he held no deed. He was usually deeply in debt to the merchant who bought his fish and supplied him with essentials. Forced to contract debt, the fisher soon found himself in slavish servitude. The fishery's truck system also operated in the timber districts and the fur trade. In another guise it also worked in farming communities, where families accumulated large debts to local storekeepers who supplied goods that could not be made at home. Moreover, huge portions of British America consisted of uneconomic farms that were kept operating on a subsistence level, often by women and children, while the male landholder was off elsewhere working for wages. As with the elites, houses told the tale. Settlers hoped to progress from log hut (or shanty) to log house to permanent dwelling built of stone or brick or finished lumber in accordance with their prosperity. In 1831 Upper Canada had 36,000 dwellings, of which 75 per cent were constructed of logs and fewer than 1,000 built of brick and stone.

Colonial society also included a number of categories of people who were quite outside the social structure as it was then understood. One such group was women. The law in British America was quite different for men and for women. Women were citizens only in that they were inhabitants of British America whose civil rights had yet to be ultimately decided. They were for the most part "non-legal entities". A variety of disabilities operated against women. They could not be legislators, or lawyers, judges, magistrates, or members of juries that decided the fate of many women in both civil and criminal actions. Politically disenfranchised—several provinces even passed legislation in this period specifically depriving widows of the vote—women were especially disadvantaged by marriage. As the English jurist Sir William Blackstone put it, "In law husband and wife are one person and the husband is that person." All real property passed into the hands of the husband, who was entitled to control his spouse. Women were expected to produce many children in an age when maternal mortality ran very high. Despite the drawbacks, most women preferred marriage to the alternatives.

At least among the elite and the very prosperous, a process began of converting the home into the central social unit for cultural transmission and the pursuit of happiness. As British American society became more settled, and somewhat more urbanized, within the ranks of the middle and upper classes emerged a clear separation of work life and home life, and women withdrew into the privacy of the home. This growth of the concept of domesticity began in the ranks of the elite but gradually made its way into the middle class. It was connected with increasing prosperity and the construction of larger houses, which in turn encouraged new notions of social space. It became possible to conceive of reserving different rooms for different functions (and different people), to distinguish "public" rooms from "private" rooms, and to introduce ideas of privacy as well. Instead of spending his life almost entirely in public spaces, the husband and father now came "home" from work to renew himself. Women were placed on a pedestal as keepers of culture and as civilizing influences.

For most women in British America, struggle with the pioneering conditions of carving farms out of the wilderness was the principal reality of life. An absence of labour-saving devices—except the domestic servant, for those who could afford one—meant that most work associated with the home involved heavy physical drudgery and long hours. Women were not only responsible for food preparation, but for much food production—gardening and berry-picking, churning butter and making cheese, keeping chickens for eggs and meat—and for most of its preservation. In addition, women made soap and candles; they washed clothes; they tended the fires under the maple syrup vats. While conditions could become less primitive over time, there was never any appreciable reduction in the amount of a woman's labour required to keep the family going. She was also responsible for bearing and raising children. In a society in which infant mortality was high and labour outside the family hard to come by, a considerable incentive existed for the production of large families. Women were also expected to help their men in work in the male sphere when required. In the resource society of British America in the first half of the nineteenth century, men were away from home often and for long periods. In their absence, their wives had to run households and farms, as well as to manage businesses. Although women's work was drudgery never done, they were never properly rewarded. Domestic duties were not regarded as a labour to be remunerated, and women's contributions to the success of the family estate were rarely taken into account in inheritance strategies. The typical pattern was for sons (usually eldest sons) to inherit the property, while the caring patriarch specified, at best, that the heir was responsible for the maintenance of his mother. Daughters counted for very little in this pattern of inheritance.

Other groups almost completely marginalized by colonial society included Indigenous peoples and blacks. In much of the eastern region of British America, settlement had eliminated hunting grounds, and there was no place for the Indigenous peoples to go. They were offered the choice of provisions of land in unsurveyed local reserves or general integration into the farming community. Unlike the blacks, the First Nations had no desire to assimilate into British American society. They wanted to remain apart and continue to practice their traditional way of life, at least in so far as that traditional way remained possible. After 1790 living conditions for Aboriginal peoples in eastern British America deteriorated, in direct relation to the initial date of contact. The British government operated on the assumption that the native population was declining, and needed to be integrated into European society as quickly as possible. The year 1836 saw several major and contradictory

Clearing a Farm

The following appeared in Walter Johnstone, *A Series of Letters, Descriptive of Prince Edward Island, in the Gulph of St. Laurence, Addressed to the Rev. John Wightman, Minister of Kirkmahoe, Dumfries-shire* (Dumfries: J. Swan, 1822). Johnstone had travelled extensively on the Island as a missionary.

I may begin by observing, that the country is one entire forest of wood; all the exceptions to the truth of this literally are not much more, even including the present clearances, than the dark spots upon the moon's face, as they appear to the naked eye, compared with the brighter parts thereof. . . .

New settlers (who should always be here as early in the spring as possible) begin to cut down the wood where they intend to erect their first house. As the trees are cut the branches are to be lopped off, and the trunks cut into lengths of 12 or 14 feet. This operation they call junking them; if they are not junked before fire is applied, they are much worse to junk afterwards. Thus, when the space intended to be cleared is cut down, junked, and all lying in a promiscuous manner over the whole surface, fire is applied to it in as dry and windy a day as can be selected, and if the fire runs well, the greater part of the small branches will be consumed, but the trunks will only be scorched. These are next rolled together and made up in piles, lying flat upon the ground; then the remaining small branches are gathered up and thrown upon the heavier wood, to help it to kindle for burning a second time. The stronger part of the family then go on to make up more piles, while the weaker part set fire to those which are thus prepared. In this way they proceed till the whole of what was cut down is gone over; then when the piles go out they are kindled again, and those that continue to burn are thrust closer together, till all is consumed. I must say this is a piece of work of the most dirty and disagreeable nature, and when the wood is heavy, as tiresome as any I have seen in America.

I have often passed by the settlers when engaged in this employment, and what with smoke, sweat, and the dust of the burnt wood, their faces were little fairer than those of the negroes in the West Indies, while their clothes were much the same as if they had been dragged up a sooty chimney. After the wood is all burnt, the stumps are left standing about two feet high, scorched black with the first burning, like so many flocks, of a blacksmith's anvil. The people then begin planting their potatoes, which is done in the following manner;—with their hoes they scratch or rake a little of the [earth] to one side, about eight inches square, and after raking a little of the ashes lying upon the surface into this groove, they place four cuttings of seed potatoes in it in square form, and then cover them up with earth till it resembles a small mole-hill, and still repeating the same operation they go on putting all their seed into the ground by four at a time, and when the space cleared is all planted it looks as if it were all covered with small mole-hills. And this is the only labour bestowed upon the potatoes till they are ready for raising. But when the time for planting arrives, man, wife, children, and all that can handle a hoe, must work, as the season is short; and if the crop is not got in to a sufficient extent, want may stare them in the face, when a supply will be difficult to procure, and when there will be nothing in their pocket to pay for it.—This work of planting with the hoe is very laborious, for there are always a great number of small roots spread over the surface, which they have to cut to pieces with their hoes, otherwise they could not plant it at all. . . .

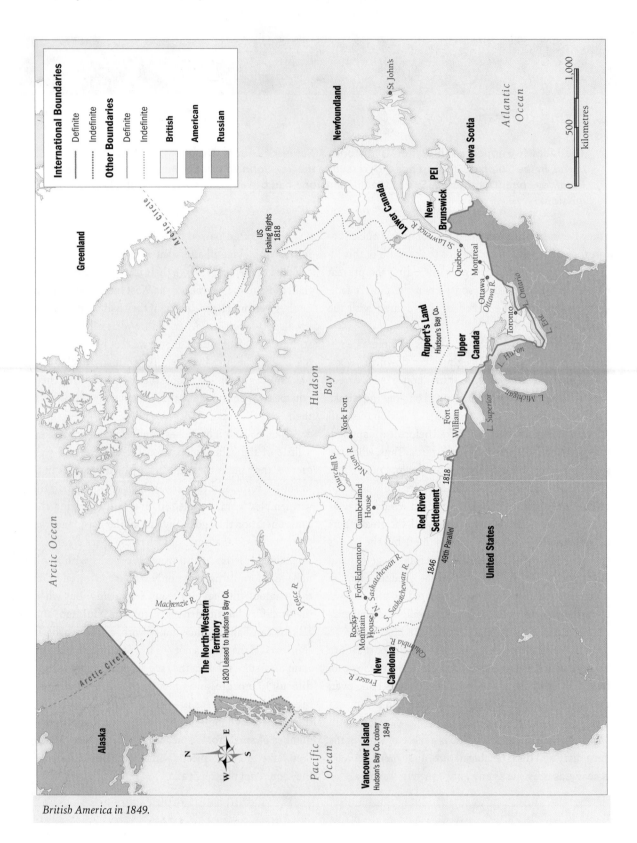

British America in 1849.

Biography

Angélique Pilotte

Angélique Pilotte was born c. 1797 near Michilimackinac to Aboriginal parents. In 1815 she engaged as a servant and accompanied her mistress to France, returning in 1817 to Drummond Island (now Michigan), where she again became a "waiting woman." She went with her mistress to Chippewa, Upper Canada, where in early August the body of a dead baby was discovered in a shallow grave. Pilotte confessed that she was the mother and was subsequently put on trial for infanticide under a 1624 English statute, although there is little evidence that she had admitted to killing the child.

Pilotte had spent most of her life in Ojibwa society and does not appear to have understood much English or most of the legal niceties connected with the charge against her in the Niagara court. Several of the witnesses, including her mistress, thought that she was mentally challenged, although the problem may have been one of language, combined with racial prejudice, rather than mental acuity. In any event, she had admitted to concealing a pregnancy, to bearing a live child, and to burying it when it subsequently died—which were the key points in the law against infanticide. A jury quickly found her guilty but recommended mercy. Nonetheless, the judge—who over the years insisted that Aboriginals should be brought under English justice—sentenced her to be hanged, with the body subsequently given over for dissection.

Pilotte's lawyer, Bartholomew Beardsley, encouraged her to petition for mercy, partly on the grounds of substantial communications problems; Pilotte insisted that she had been misunderstood and misinterpreted. But Beardsley also emphasized that Pilotte was a victim of cultural misunderstanding. In Ojibwa society, the girl had acted perfectly appropriately in the way she had given birth. Pilotte knew only "the customs and maxims of her own nation," which included "the invariable custom of Indian women to retire and bring forth their children alone, and in secret." The jury backed her plea for a pardon. One juror wrote to the local newspaper that the jury had recommended mercy because "she was a savage and had no knowledge of the usages of the Christians." A number of prominent citizens of Niagara, many of whom were involved in trade with Aboriginals, also supported her petition, as did Robert Gourlay (the Scots-born opponent of the Upper Canadian government at the time).

The appeal went to Upper Canada's chief executive, colonial administrator Samuel Smith, who sent it to London for a final decision. Pilotte waited in prison while the appeal crossed the Atlantic. The British authorities altered her sentence to one year's imprisonment. She had already served most of that time, and she was apparently released to return to her people. The Pilotte case could be read in a number of ways. It could be seen as an illustration of the harshness of the laws against women, as an example of the way in which minorities were treated (for the successful appeal was not common practice), or as an instance of the ultimate triumph of British justice.

developments in First Nations policy. In that year the first serious British attempt at co-ordinating policy came with a parliamentary inquiry that covered the entire empire. Canada featured prominently in this investigation, with a litany of abuses exposed from one colony to the next. The government of Nova Scotia refused to provide any information whatsoever. In its 1,000-page report, the committee concluded that First Nations policy should remain under British control. It also recommended against making treaties with local Aboriginals, on the grounds that the treaty process was so heavily weighted in favour of government that it could never produce a satisfactory result. This recommendation was never implemented, and treaty-making was instead transferred from imperial authorities to colonial governments in ensuing years. Together, an unjust treaty process and a tendency toward corrupt administration would leave First Nations people increasingly impoverished and restless.

Symptomatic of the problem were developments in Upper Canada in 1836, when Lieutenant-Governor Sir Francis Bond Head decided that attempts at assimilation were a mistake. Instead, he argued that the "greatest kindness we can perform towards these Intelligent, simpleminded people is to remove and fortify them as much as possible from all Communication with the Whites" (Dickason, 2002: 211). Head subsequently engineered the cession of 3 million acres of land by the Ojibwa in return for a promise that Manitoulin Island and its adjacent islands would be protected as Aboriginal territory. The Ojibwa knew full well that the deal was a bad one, but reasoned that if they did not agree they might lose everything. For all the First Nations, the reverberations of extensive settlement could be felt at long distances from the actual European presence, and settlement was inexorably coming to the west as well as to the east.

Thousands of blacks flocked to Upper Canada between 1820 and 1860. Some were slaves seeking freedom, for it was well known in the United States that slavery was illegal in British America. By and large, the Upper Canadian authorities protected slaves who made their way into the province. After 1830, an increasing level of organization moved fugitive blacks from the United States. One key development was that of the "Underground Railroad." This was, of course, not a railroad at all, but a complex network of organizations, people—black and white, male and female—and safe houses through which black fugitives were smuggled northward and eventually across the border. Fugitive slaves were joined by thousands of freed northern blacks seeking a better life in British America. Many of the freed blacks were active in abolitionist activities and in the Underground Railroad. Harriet Tubman (1820–1913, known as "Moses") made a number of trips into slave territory from her home in St Catharines, rescuing as many as 300 slaves over the course of her career. Unfortunately, all blacks faced prejudice and social disadvantage in their new land. They were granted civil liberty but were never really made to feel at home. The Reverend Thomas Kinnard, a Toronto-based abolitionist and former slave, wrote in 1863, "If

freedom is established in the United States, there will be one great black streak, reaching from here to the uttermost parts of the South" (quoted in Prince, 2009: 217). As he predicted, many blacks returned to the United States after the Emancipation Proclamation of 1863.

Religion and Education

The privileged elites were supported by the clergy of the established church, the Church of England, as well as by the Church of Scotland and the Roman Catholic Church. All these churches taught the doctrine of subordination to rightful authority. Those not associated with these churches found the pretensions of the ecclesiastical establishment, particularly in maintaining such traditional monopolies as marriage rites and education, constant irritants that could be associated with the oligarchic constitutional system. Dissenters chafed under arrangements that granted "liberty of conscience" to all Christians while denying them full powers to act in such matters as the solemnization of marriage. The Church of England fought an unsuccessful rearguard action to maintain its pretense to monopoly.

In Lower Canada, the Catholic Church solidified its position within the political structure, especially under Bishop Joseph-Octave Plessis (1763–1825, bishop and archbishop, 1806–25), who was appointed to the province's legislative council in 1817. Plessis presided over the devolution of the Church in British America. In 1819 Rome elevated him to an archbishopric at the same time that it created new dioceses in Upper Canada and Prince Edward Island, both headed by Highland Scots. Plessis was not himself an ultramontanist. He did not believe that the Church, although the guardian of moral law, must be heeded in all matters relating to politics. But he did attempt, with some success, to strengthen the structure of his Church by educating more clergy, by obtaining government recognition of its legal position (especially in Lower Canada), and by reforming its far-flung governance. His successors were more sympathetic to the pretensions of Rome than Plessis had been.

Biography

Thomas Chandler Haliburton

Thomas Chandler Haliburton (1796–1865) was the first of a long line of internationally known best-selling authors and humorists from what is now Canada. Born in Windsor, Nova Scotia, and a product of King's College, he later practised law in Annapolis Royal. In 1826 he was elected the Tory MHA for Annapolis Royal. In the legislature he became known as a loose cannon, and consequently he was appointed in 1829 as a judge in the Inferior Court of Common Pleas in order to remove a disturbing element from the House of Assembly. In 1841 he was appointed to the Supreme Court of the province, serving industriously but without great distinction until his retirement in 1856. Taking advantage of his literary success, he then moved to England, where in 1859 he was elected to the House of Commons. A convivial man, he was most comfortable consorting with equals in the tavern or in his own home. Despite the demands of his public life, Haliburton produced a considerable quantity of written work, much of it in the form of history and compendiums of humorous writing. Like many authors in the nineteenth century, he was not very solicitous of the intellectual property of others, a characteristic that helps explain his volume of output.

His literary success, however, rests upon his creation of Sam Slick, a Yankee travelling clock salesman whose observations—in Yankee dialect—on society, politics, and human nature made Haliburton a best-selling writer in Britain, British America (although not Nova Scotia), and the United States. Much of Haliburton's writing commented on the Americans, whom he saw as excessively chauvinistic, boasting, and opportunistic, as well as industrious and adaptable. He combined the literary tradition of the moral essay of the eighteenth century with the nineteenth century's dramatic tradition of humorous dialogue, particularly a stage Americanism rooted in excess, bombast, and vulgarity combined with an inventive and basically uneducated or common vocabulary. He was most successful in his observations about his home province, while his comments on England and America tended to be superficial and facile, distorted by his dislike for liberalism and radicalism. Sam Slick was a major creation, although not Haliburton's only attractive character. Not surprisingly, he was not well admired in his home province, partly because of his social attitudes and partly because of the success of his satire. The most accessible of Haliburton's writings for modern readers are probably *The Clockmaker, or The Sayings and Doings of Samuel Slick of Slickville* (Halifax, 1836), and *The Old Judge, or, Life in a Colony* (2 vols, London, 1849).

Dissenters in every colony not only chafed at the conservative social vision of the established churches and their support of hierarchy and privilege but also objected to the view of God they promulgated. The most numerous dissenters were Methodists and their itinerant preachers, although the Baptists also had a considerable following. Most dissenters were evangelicals who believed that God had to be experienced emotionally and spiritually rather than comprehended rationally. This awareness was "awakened" at revivals and at the Methodist "camp meetings" that were so common in Upper Canada. The evangelicals were not only passionate but also populist in their attitude. For many in the establishment, passionate populism was viewed as tantamount to revolution. Education was another area of conflict between establishment privileges and the needs of an expanding population. The Church of England attempted to insist that it alone was entitled to the revenue from Crown lands set aside for the support of a Protestant clergy. It also tried to maintain close control over the institutions of higher education—universities, colleges, and academies—on the grounds that such education had to involve moral as well as technical knowledge. Only a relative handful of students had places at these institutions. For the authorities, education was seen as necessary for social order. For the common folk, it represented a means of mobility and liberation. Systems of education brought to the colonies after 1815 were based on teaching the older children, who in turn passed their lessons by rote to the younger. Only towards the end of the period was there much demand for broadly based public education. The curricula of such schools as existed were extremely eclectic. Despite the absence of regular schooling in most provinces, the population was surprisingly literate. Immigrants brought with them their educational experiences in England, Ireland, Scotland, or America. These experiences often were coloured by a substantial class bias as well as by ethnic and denominational ones.

Colonial Culture

Before 1840 the schools were not yet the bearers of the cultural aspirations of the resource society of British America. While a common stereotype identifies this period as one of extremely limited and primitive cultural and artistic production—particularly by European or American standards—such a view reflects a particular set of assumptions about culture. Locally based high culture was understandably rare. Foreign models were usually employed. There was, however, a substantial folk culture, which included a well-established oral tradition, in the form of tales and songs, handed down from generation to generation and from group to group. There was also a tradition of craftsmanship. The simple pine furniture of clean, uncluttered, functional lines produced by hundreds of anonymous craftsmen during the colonial period found little favour in succeeding generations, which regarded heavy ornamentation and the use of highly polished wood veneers as exemplary. But today we recognize that the aesthetic values of those anonymous furniture-makers were on a level with their high craftsmanship.

Most high culture was produced by people who made their living in some other way, and who often regarded their artistic activity as diversion or by-product rather than conscious art or professional activity. The majority of the producers of elite culture—like

most of the elite of this period—were born abroad. Of the 538 people given entries in Volume VII of the *Dictionary of Canadian Biography*, covering those who died between 1835 and 1850, fewer than 200 were born in the colonies, and most of these were born in Lower Canada. Young people educated in British America were usually trained by those who were educated abroad, usually with emphasis on slavish reproduction of both form and content. Some respectable work was done within these constraints.

In literature, John Richardson (1796–1852) produced one unusual novel, *Wacousta, or, The Prophecy*, published anonymously in London and Edinburgh in 1832. Thomas McCulloch (1776–1843) had literary success with short sketches, *The Letters of Mephibosheth Stepsure*, originally published in a newspaper and not collected in book form until 1960. Thomas Chandler Haliburton (1796–1865) wrote 21 sketches about Sam Slick in 1835–6, which became *The Clockmaker; or The Sayings and Doings of Samuel Slick of Slickville*. Haliburton went on to become an international best-selling writer. Both McCulloch and Haliburton produced their best work for a local colonial audience. When they wrote for international markets, they were less imaginative and inventive.

Another interesting development of this period was the emergence of middle-class female authors, often recent immigrants, who portrayed the colonial scene in their works. The first novel by a native British American—*St Ursula's Convent; or, The Nun in Canada*, published in Kingston in 1824—was written by Julia Catherine Hart (1796–1867), née Julia Beckwith, of Fredericton, New Brunswick. Nearly 150 subscribers paid 9s 4d for copies of the two-volume work. Hart published several other novels, all of which were characterized by unrealistic, often fantastic, plots and settings. In *St Ursula's Convent* she tapped a rich vein of Protestant suspicion of what Catholics "got up to" in convents, although her tale was more of melodrama than of immorality.

The Strickland sisters—Catharine Parr Traill (1802–99) and Susanna Moodie (1803–85)—were more polished writers, and each sister wrote a work based on her experiences as an immigrant in Canada that is now a classic (Gray, 1999).

Foreign models of high culture were generally employed in the early nineteenth century, such as social dances, common in England and France. However, they took place in a very different context and garb. Château St Louis was the seat of the governor of Lower Canada, and where the elite of Quebec would meet. Looking at similar images from Europe, how does this compare? "Dance in the Château St. Louis," by George Heriot, 1801. LAC, 1989-472-1.

Traill's *The Backwoods of Canada* (London, 1836) is made of 18 letters home to family and friends in Suffolk. It is a sensitive early account of the pioneer experience. Never complaining, she leaves readers with an overall impression of cheerful adaptation to the rigours of life in a previously unsettled area of Upper Canada, where she willingly made do with whatever was at hand. Upper Canada itself, however, is portrayed as a land "with no historical associations, no legendary tales of those that came before," and the impenetrable forest all around her is "desolate," "interminable," "a maze." It simultaneously isolates and liberates the author. Susanna Moodie's *Roughing It in the Bush: or, Forest Life in Canada* (1852) is the best known of a number of works by Moodie that offer trenchant (and often discouraging) descriptions of the pioneering experience. Moodie was particularly good at the satirical description of the customs of the average immigrant, customs such as the "bee" and the "charivari."

Another successful writer was Anna Brownell Jameson (1794–1860). More willing to flout the gender rules of her society than most females, Jameson was a frequently published author in 1825 when she married the lawyer Robert Jameson. She did not initially accompany her husband to Dominica or to Upper Canada when he received judicial appointments in the colonies, but joined him temporarily in 1836 as she attempted to negotiate a legal separation. While in Canada she travelled extensively, and the result of her journeys was the book *Winter Tales and Summer Rambles in Canada*

Mephibosheth Stepsure Explains a Nova Scotia Cycle of Failure

Thomas McCulloch (1776–1843) was a Scots-born Presbyterian minister and educator who spent the bulk of a long career in Pictou, Nova Scotia. Here his observations of the frailties of his neighbours led to a series of satirical letters published in a Halifax newspaper in 1821.

My neighbour Gosling is completely an every-day character. His exact likeness may be found at any time, in any part of the Province. About thirty years ago, his father David left him very well to do; and Solomon, who at that time was a brisk young man, had the prospect, by using a little industry, of living as comfortably as any in the town. Soon after the death of old David, he was married and a likelier couple were not often to be seen. But unluckily for them both, when Solomon went to Halifax in the winter, Polly went along with him to sell her turkeys and see the fashions; and from that day the Goslings had never a day to do well. Solomon was never very fond of hard work. At the same time he could not be accused of idleness. He was always a very good neighbour; and at every burial or barn raising, Solomon was set down as one who would be sure to be here. By these means he gradually contracted the habit of running about; which left his own premises in an unpromising plight. Polly, too, by seeing the fashions, had learnt to be genteel; and for the sake of a little show, both lessened the thrift of the family and added to the outlay; so that, between one thing and another, Solomon began to be hampered, and had more calls than comforters. . . . Though Goose Hill farm, from want of industry, had not been productive, it was still a property of considerable value: and it occurred to Solomon, that, converted into goods, it would yield more prompt and lucrative returns than by any mode of agriculture. Full of the idea, accordingly, my neighbour went to town; and, by mortgaging his property to Caliboogus, the West India merchant, he returned with a general assortment of merchandise, suited to the wants of the town. When I say a general assortment, it is necessary to be a little more explicit. It did not contain any of those articles

(1838). Jameson deliberately set out to relate her adventures from both a personal and a feminist point of view. As she records under the date of 13 March 1837, "In these days when society is becoming every day more artificial and complex, and marriage, as the gentlemen assure us, more and more expensive, hazardous and inexpedient, women *must* find means to fill up the void of existence" (quoted in Gerry, 1990–1: 37). Most women from the elite classes did not attempt to publish their literary efforts, but instead composed lengthy and fascinating letters to friends and family or kept diaries that remained in family papers and have only in recent years been read and published.

In the non-literary arts, the official culture of British America was derivative and unadventurous. Painters inevitably emphasized European styles and techniques, which were sometimes acquired from working with established masters, and the market had little interest in anything else. Within this tradition a few fine painters emerged, such as William Berczy (1744–1813), Louis Dulongpré, and Joseph Légaré (1796–1855). In architecture, Late Georgian style predominated. It was not only what architects and craftsmen knew, it symbolized British authority and epitomized British standards.

Rather more interesting developments were occurring in the vernacular culture of the common people,

which are employed in subduing the forest, or in cultivating the soil. These he knew were not very saleable. . . . When a merchant lays in his goods he naturally consults the taste of his customers, Solomon's, accordingly, consisted chiefly of West India produce, gin, brandy, tobacco, and a few chests of tea. For the youngsters, he had provided an assortment of superfine broad cloths and fancy muslins, ready-made boots, whips, spurs and a great variety of gumflowers and other articles which come under the general denomination of notions. In addition to all these, and what Solomon considered as not the least valuable part of his stock, he had bought from Pendulum & Co. a whole box of old watches elegantly ornamented with lacquered brass chains and glass seals; little inferior in appearance to gold and Cairngorms. When all these things were arranged, they had a very pretty appearance. For a number of weeks, little was talked of but Mr. Gosling's Store; for such he had now become by becoming a merchant. . . . Mr. Gosling, too, had in reality considerably improved his circumstances. The greater part of my neighbours being already in debt to old Ledger and other traders about; and considering that if they took their money to these, it would only go to their credit, carried it to Mr. Gosling's Store; so that by these means he was soon able to clear off a number of his encumbrances, and to carry to market as much as cash as established his credit. Among traders punctuality of payment begets confidence in the seller; and the credit which this afford to the purchaser, is generally followed by an enlargement of orders. My neighbour returned with a much greater supply; and here his reverses commenced. Credit could not be refused to good customers who had brought their money to the store. Those, also who formerly showed their good will by bringing their cash, proved their present cordiality by taking large credits. But when the time for returning to the market for supplies arrived, Mr. Gosling had nothing to take thither but his books. These, it is true, had an imposing appearance. They contained debts to a large amount. . . . But when his accounts were made out, many young men who owed him large sums, had gone to Passamaquoddy.

Source: Thomas McCulloch, *The Stepsure Letters* (Toronto: McClelland and Stewart, 1960), 11–13.

which tended to be oral rather than written, traditional rather than imitative, and often connected either with artisan conventions or with religious energy. For all inhabitants of British America, singing religious hymns and secular songs was an important part of their lives. People sang as they worked in the fields, the voyageurs sang as they paddled their canoes, and fishermen sang as they pulled up their nets. Most of what was sung was inherited from Europe, although both music and lyrics were frequently altered by time and new circumstances. Many pioneers sprang from ethnic backgrounds in which the bard, a combination of poet and songster, represented important folk memory. Gaelic-speaking bards from the Highlands of Scotland not only carried on the tradition in British America but extended it. A rich heritage of crafting in wood produced not only furniture and useful ornamentation (such as the weather vane), but the sailing ship, a monument to the skills of carpenters and builders. Popular culture suggested some of the rich possibilities for creative adaptation. By 1840, for example, Scottish settlers familiar with the sport of curling had not only imported the game into a climate ideally suited for it but had made great strides forward in its popularization and regularization. So successful was the game that around 1840 the world's first indoor curling facility was constructed in Montreal.

The Politics of the Elite

Like the culture, the politics of the resource society were in flux. By 1820 the governments of the various provinces of British America were becoming well ensconced in power. The pattern was a fairly standard one, even for Newfoundland, which still did not have representative government and would not acquire it until 1832. Each colonial government was headed by a governor (or lieutenant-governor). Appointed in England, he was often a military man. No mere figureheads, governors of this period had considerable power and autonomy. The governor administered the province in association with the principal office-holders—also imperial appointments, although sometimes colonials were appointed—who, with the prominent merchants, comprised his council or councils. The resultant oligarchies were given various derisive labels. In Upper Canada there was the "Family Compact," in Lower Canada the "Château Clique," in Nova Scotia the "System," and in Prince Edward Island "the Cabal." As administrations, these groups were not necessarily unenlightened Tories. They believed in the need to increase the prosperity of their colonies and usually attempted to mediate among the conflicting interests that emerged, provided they remained orderly. Most of the oligarchies favoured government intervention in the economy, particularly through the creation of new infrastructure such as banks, roads, and canals. Not all members of the official factions in English-speaking colonies belonged to the Church of England, and not all members of the government in Lower Canada

"The Woolsey Family," William Berczy, 1809, oil on canvas. If the sitters in this portrait look oddly detached from one another, the reason is that the artist drew each one separately. Once all the figures had been transferred to the canvas, he painted in the background around them. National Gallery of Canada, Ottawa, 5875. © National Gallery of Canada, 5875.

Petition in Support of Reform, Upper Canada, 1818

This petition was orchestrated by Robert Gourlay. Although he is not named explicitly, Gourlay, who was twice acquitted of sedition earlier in August 1818 (once in Kingston and once in Brockville), was behind these public objections to the "Act to Prevent Certain Meetings," which Maitland, the new lieutenant-governor, had proposed to suppress meetings seen as seditious.

To His Excellency Major General Sir Peregrine Maitland HCB Lieutenant Governor of Upper Canada.

The petition of the undersigned inhabitants of the Township of [named as Ernestown, Hallowell, Cramahe and Percy in each separate copy.]

Humbly Sheweth.

That the undersigned inhabitants of the township of [named] have perused with deep regret that part of your Excellency's speech to the Parliament of Upper Canada wherein it is said "You will, I doubt, not feel a just indignation at the attempts which have been made to excite discontent and to organized sedition" and it is with shame as well as with regret, they have perceived that the Commons House of Assembly have not only confirmed these sentiments but descended to launch out wanton and invidious reflections against an innocent individual.

The undersigned believe that your Excellency has been grossly deceived as to the discontent which exists in Upper Canada, and very ill informed as to any attempt to organize sedition, but they are sorry to think that the reply of the Commons can Plead no such excuse.

The undersigned do not deny that discontent exists; but they speak with a determination which is unalterable in saying that there has been much cause for discontent. As to sedition, the very idea is groundless: yet if it did exist that Courts of Law are open for its prosecution. They have seen an individual prosecuted, nay persecuted, by the present ministry under the plea of promoting sedition and libelling the government: but twice has this individual been honorably acquitted, and far are they from thinking that any new Statute is necessary to circumscribe the liberty of the subject. The organization which has been formed in this Province is such, as, when properly considered, must excite admiration. It manifests a spirit of order and peace. It proves that the People of Upper Canada are advanced in the progress of civilization and above the mobbish habits of European nations. It shews they possess the most valuable knowledge how to redeem their political affairs when sunk in the slough of confusion and pressed down by the weight of installed power.

The undersigned wish to see no other organization save that of the regularly constituted authorities, if these would perform their duty: but they have witnessed their present parliamentary Representatives the third time in session without even the appearance of beneficial result. Twice did these representatives propose an enquiry into the State of the Province:—twice where they ignominiously dismissed in the midst of weighty considerations; and twice have they returned only to display grovelling sentiments and temporizing acts. The late organization of the people never had but one object—that of enquiry and the appointment of a commission to go home to England with a petition to the Throne that the same may be effectual. The accomplishment of this object constitutes the most earnest desire of the undersigned: and if this object is not speedily attained through the manly endeavors of the Present Parliament they most fervently pray that Your Excellency will dissolve it, and issue writs for the assembly of men who may represent more faithfully the wishes, and more ably perform the business, of their constituents.

Source: Civil Secretary's Correspondence, Upper Canada Sundries, 1766–1841, LAC, RG5 A1.

were Anglos. Under pressure from the Colonial Office, they surrendered the revenues in dispute between the assemblies and themselves, particularly those from the sale and lease of Crown lands. The popularly elected assembly, which comprised one part of the legislative system that also included the council (or in some provinces, a separate legislative council), had a very limited role in the process of government. In 1820 the assemblies did not yet have control of the revenue or finances of the provinces, much less any real involvement in their administration, although they gained control over more revenue in the 1830s.

Under this constitutional arrangement, political conflict could take a number of forms. One involved disagreement between the governor and the oligarchy that comprised the provincial administration. This could come about either because the governor was expected to implement unpopular instructions from the mother country, or because he sought to limit the self-perpetuating power of the oligarchs. More frequently after 1820, the conflict involved a fierce struggle between the administration and the leaders of an assembly eager to expand its prerogatives and authority. A new generation of political leaders emerged who were willing to invoke popular support on behalf of their attacks on the prevailing governments. Reform was no more monolithic than the oligarchies. It broke into several main camps with much overlap among them. One group of reformers represented the radicals, the other consisted of various factions with more moderate voices who extolled the glories of the English Constitution and its supposed entrenchment of British rights and liberties. Moderate

"Curling on the lake near Halifax," c. 1867, from Lt Henry Buckton Laurence, Sketches of Canadian Sports and Pastimes (London, 1870). How many other winter sports and pastimes besides curling are depicted in this illustration? LAC, 1970-188-2074, W.H. Coverdale Collection of Canadiana.

William Lyon Mackenzie, 1834, by an unknown artist; lithograph published in Canadiana Military Events, III, 337. LAC, 1958-046, Volume III.

reformers did not wish to eliminate the imperial connection, but instead wanted to employ it to obtain a colonial constitution that more closely resembled what they thought was that of the mother country. Many of the members of the evangelical sects so critical of the Church of England were former Americans, and they would play a prominent role in the rebellions of 1837 and 1838. Four reformers stand out in this period: William Lyon Mackenzie (1795–1861) of Upper Canada, Louis-Joseph Papineau (1786–1871) of Lower Canada, Joseph Howe (1804–73) of Nova Scotia, and William Cooper (1786–1867) of Prince Edward Island. None of these men actually overturned the political system, but each did make some inroads against it, anticipating in a variety of ways a gradual democratization of politics in British America.

All four reformers (and others) sounded radical in their rhetoric. All believed in the importance of the "independent cultivator of the soil," displaying profound hostility to commerce, the merchant classes, and expensive economic development by the public sector

(quoted in Halpenny, 1976: 156). Equality of conditions and opportunity was what mattered. William Cooper sought this equality through "escheat," a process by which the large landholders of Prince Edward Island would be stripped of their ill-gotten holdings and the land redistributed to those who actually tilled the soil. In the 1830s both Papineau and Mackenzie turned to the American ideas of Jacksonian democracy when they found themselves unable either to persuade the British government of the inadequacy of existing constitutional arrangements or to alter the system by political activity. These reformers wanted to overturn the corrupt oligarchies that ran their respective provinces and replace them with administrations that would be responsible to the province as represented in the elected Houses of Assembly. They could also agree, as a result of their agrarian and anti-commercial assumptions, that public "improvements" paid for by the public purse or sponsored by the government (such as canals and banks) represented an unnecessary financial burden on the taxpayer, being in effect "class legislation." As Mackenzie argued, the "true source of a country's wealth" was "labour usefully and prudently applied" (quoted in Fairley, 1960: 217). For Papineau in Lower Canada, an active economic state was being dominated not only by a mercantile class but by a British mercantile class, which promoted capitalism.

It is in the context of the struggle between commercial capitalism and agrarian idealism that we must understand both the Tory commitment to public involvement in economic activity and the reform opposition. These political reformers had no conception that economic development could be directed by government on behalf of the people, any more than they had a general conception of any positive role for the state in ensuring the social well-being of its citizenry. They were instead typical nineteenth-century liberal democrats who sought to reduce (rather than to increase) the influence of government on the lives of the population, as well as to limit the temptation of special privilege. As Mackenzie put it in a broadside entitled "Independence" in late November 1837, "We contend, that in all laws made, or to be made, every person shall be bound alike—neither should any tenure, estate, charter, degree, birth or place, confer any exemption from the ordinary

John Galt

John Galt (1779–1839) was born into a Scottish ship captain's family. He grew up in ill health, and spent much time with the old women who lived with his grandmother. Despite his sickness, he was tall and imposing in appearance. He clerked in a counting house before heading to London, like many another Scot intending to make his fortune. This he did initially as a broker, but his firm soon went bust due to a correspondent's financial failure. The study of law at Lincoln's Inn led to a breakdown in health, and Galt began travelling in 1809 in order to recover. When he returned to London in 1811 he began to make his living by his pen, which he had been employing for years in various literary endeavours. Books based on his travels, self-published, brought him a decent living. Much of his work was published under pen names or anonymously. By his own account he became a professional writer in 1820, when he began writing novels. *Annals of the Parish* in 1821 was his first great success, written in a fictionalized autobiographical voice. His most successful work appeared between 1820 and 1822, although he continued with three historical novels modelled on Walter Scott's successes.

In the early 1820s Galt again became a businessman, becoming involved with the Canada Company, a private firm that eventually would acquire the scattered Crown and Clergy Reserves of Upper Canada for 3s.6d. per acre and offer them for sale. Galt became a resident of Upper Canada in December 1826. Charged with running the company's business in the colony, Galt founded towns in Guelph and Goderich to serve as a basis for settlement. He seemed unable to stay out of trouble with either the political elite or the government (virtually the same people) in the colony, or the company's directors in London. A terrible bookkeeper, he overspent on various schemes of development, most of which were quite ingenious but were very expensive. He returned to England in 1829 to be imprisoned for failure to pay the school fees of his sons. In prison he returned to writing, and used his Canadian experiences as the basis for a series of novels (*Laurie Todd*; *Bogle Corbett*) that returned him to solvency. Galt's contribution to the success of the Canada Company was long under-appreciated, as were his contributions as a novelist. Perhaps his most important achievement was his recognition of the new vocabulary of North America.

course of legal proceedings and responsibilities whereunto others are subjected" (quoted in Fairley, 1960: 223).

Reform and Rebellion

Unrest had been building in the Canadas for a number of years before it first broke out in violent defiance of the government in 1837. Several strands of discontent can be identified. Some of them were common to both provinces, while others were distinctive to only one. In both provinces the uprisings were more than brief affairs occurring in the capital cities and led by the political elite. One of the major strands experienced in common was a sense of challenge to the established oligarchic order in the spirit of liberal democracy and in the name of "the people." Another common strand was a nascent sense of national liberation from the tutelage of the British Empire. A third less abstract strand was rural discontent, caused by clumsy agricultural and land policies of the colonial governments, and enhanced by a series of bad harvests. Structural rural discontent was shared in common by the two Canadas, but its causes were quite different, although both revolved around the land in an era in which large amounts of waste and unsettled land were rapidly disappearing. Upper Canadian rural unhappiness was caused mainly by the inability of the government to distribute sufficient land to settlers at a reasonable price; Lower Canadian dissatisfaction was connected to the carryover from the French regime of the seigneurial system, the various tithes and financial obligations of which had not been so much of a burden before population pressures set in. In addition, Lower Canada's restlessness had an ethnocultural edge, as French Canadians complained of being treated as inferiors by the province's anglos and by the imperial authorities that supported them.

While it is tempting to treat the outbursts in the two provinces as a common event, from a legal perspective they were quite different, which carried over into the way in which rebels and traitors were dealt with by the courts. A complicating feature, moreover, was the subsequent armed return to British America of rebels who had earlier fled the country, now accompanied by American and Irish associates whose presence meant armed invasion. In any event, we are not dealing with a single set of trials but with a number of sets of trials spread over two provinces. There is little pattern to the package of trials, except that government orchestration and even manipulation was endemic. Not all judges took the same view of high treason. Some tended to interpret it narrowly, while others were quite expansionist in the latitude they allowed for judicial interpretation.

Upper Canada

The government of Upper Canada responded to the Yonge Street insurrection led by William Lyon Mackenzie with a special assizes in Toronto in March 1838, where 133 prisoners were indicted with high treason; another 30 escaped. Most of the defendants were people from the Toronto district. The government employed special legislation, a Pardoning Act (1 Vic. c.10), which allowed it to extend a conditional pardon to those involved in the "late treasonable insurrection" who had been misled and seduced into their actions. By petitioning for pardon under this Act, the individual had obviously admitted his involvement in the uprising. Most prisoners thus escaped trial and punishment. Those who were American citizens were banished. The petitioning business was a brilliant stroke that enabled the government to be lenient without seeming to be soft. Twelve cases actually were tried, resulting in seven convictions.

A number of those tried had petitioned for pardons under the Pardoning Act, including Samuel Lount and Peter Matthews, who as supposed ringleaders were deliberately tried to set an example to others. The subsequent executions of these two men were carried out publicly in the sight of the other prisoners. Most of the other cases brought to trial were of small fry who had not petitioned for clemency. In one case the jury found the defendant, tavern-keeper John Montgomery, guilty, but recommended mercy. Montgomery had his sentence commuted to transportation for life, went to the United States to establish a boarding house, which was a home for exiled Canadian patriots, and was pardoned in 1843. Many years later the Ontario legislature awarded him $3,000 for the loss of his tavern. Recent study of these trials by Romney and Wright (2002: 74) concludes that Chief Justice John Beverley Robinson not only exhibited prejudice against some of the defendants, but actually falsified his trial notes in several cases to help produce a conviction. They also note that contemporary charges of jury-packing were probably accurate. Several defendants were acquitted after long deliberations by the jury; these men had been defended by lawyers who argued that their clients had used violent words but denied having acted upon them.

Separate "revolts" in western Upper Canada led to trials at London and Hamilton in the spring of 1838. The defendants here were much less likely to petition under the Pardoning Act. In Hamilton, 27 men were tried, with 10 found guilty. The British Colonial Secretary, Lord Glenelg, had written to Upper Canada that "great circumspection will . . . be requisite in carrying into effect any capital sentences," and a review by the Executive Council of the Hamilton cases led to the decision that the guilty there should be spared because only treason and not other crimes were involved. In London, 15 men were tried for high treason, with nine acquitted. Much debatable evidence was presented, but none were executed.

An incursion from the United States into Canada by a number of exiled Canadians, led by an American, occurred at Short Hills, on the escarpment behind St Catharines in June of 1838. Some of the 50 men who were captured and subsequently tried at Niagara were dealt with under the "Lawless Aggressions" Act passed in January 1838, which permitted foreigners captured with traitorous subjects to be tried for felony by court martial, punishable by death. The lieutenant-governor of Upper Canada wanted the ringleaders of this raid dealt with harshly, and recommended at least four executions. A number of Americans were tried and convicted. In the case of James Morreau—one of the leaders of the raid—defence counsel objected to the "lawless aggression" legislation (already before the Colonial Office for review) as unconstitutional, and, indeed, the British law officers would advise against its proclamation before the execution of the defendant. This was the only execution in these trials. Thirteen Canadians were also tried, with most convicted. Pressure from both the Americans and the British was exerted against more executions, and the 15 men convicted were sentenced to transportation to British penal colonies (such as Australia) rather than being sentenced to banishment, which meant exile from British-controlled territory. Historians have disagreed as to whether this treatment substantiates the charge that the Canadian authorities were severe in the 1837–8 crisis, or followed severity with leniency. The proceedings at Hamilton, London, and Niagara demonstrated no consistent violations of procedure, but inconsistency was the norm, and there was considerable bias in some of the cases.

As Short Hills illustrated, by 1838 Upper Canada was not dealing with simple rebellion but with invasion, usually by Americans with the assistance of Canadians who had been banished from the province. The British government wanted these offenders dealt with under court-martial proceedings, which was done at Kingston and London in late November 1838 and early January 1839. The charge was lawless aggression rather than high treason. In 138 of 140 cases tried in Kingston, at least 10 of which were of British subjects, the result was conviction, and in 43 of 44 cases tried in London, at least nine of which were of British subjects, the result was conviction. Courts martial obviously produced a much higher success rate of conviction, partly because of the limited availability of counsel and partly because the prosecut-

ing judge advocate also acted as adviser on points of law. All but three of the 181 convicted were sentenced to death (the exceptions were adolescents), with the court or judge advocate then recommending lesser treatment in some cases. Of the 181, 17 were executed, 78 were transported, and 83 were pardoned on condition they left the province. The procedure deprived a number of British subjects of rights they would have had in regular treason trials, a point made by a young John A. Macdonald before the Kingston court without much success. Historian Barry Wright insists that while in most of these cases the evidence was "clear and damning," at the same time outcomes might have been different if regular trial procedure had been employed.

Lower Canada

Although martial law went out of favour in Great Britain in the nineteenth century as a legal procedure for dealing with popular insurrection—chiefly on the grounds that martial law could be introduced only where the very fabric of law and order had disintegrated—it became increasingly popular for dealing with colonial movements of resistance to British authority. As Jean-Marie Fecteau points out, one of the implications of this tendency was to distinguish legally the resisting colonials from other British subjects. Martial law was proclaimed by Governor Gosford in Lower Canada on 5 December 1837, without the approval of the assembly, after the peasant resistance at Saint Charles had been ended and before the battle at Saint-Eustache on 14 December. Gosford's successor, Sir John Colborne, continued the policy until the end of April 1838. By the time Lord Durham arrived on 27 May 1838, the uprisings had been well and truly quashed, but 140 prisoners still had to be dealt with. Durham dealt with them by a process of "enlightened despotism," resolving the fate of the leading insurrectionaries without trial by exiling them to Bermuda. He then amnestied the remaining individuals accused or suspected of high treason, thus producing much objection in Britain to arbitrary behaviour and the disallowance of the Bermuda action. Durham justified his decisions by pointing to subsequent acquittals by French-Canadian juries of men involved in the rebellion.

Jean-Olivier Chénier

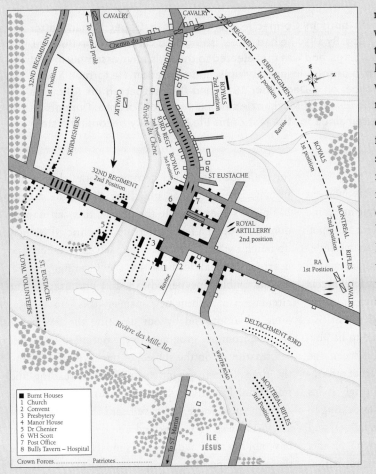

The Battle of St Eustache, 14 December 1837. Based on a sketch drawn by HB Parry and engraved by A. Bourne, 1839, PAC, NMC H3 340 St. Eustache, 1837.

Born probably in Montreal into a family of farmers, Jean-Olivier Chénier (1806–37) trained as a doctor and was licensed to practise in 1828, setting up his practice in Saint-Benoit. Chénier was soon active in politics and a supporter of the Patriotes, although he did not run for public office until October 1837, when he became one of 22 justices of the peace elected at Sainte-Scholastique. Nevertheless, he was one of those for whom the authorities obtained arrest warrants in November of 1837, and he was in effective command of the revolutionary forces in Ste-Eustache, persisting in resistance despite counsels of the hopelessness from many quarters. His badly outnumbered forces met a substantial party of British regulars and local volunteers backed by artillery in the village on 14 December 1837. Under no illusions about the seriousness of the situation, he told those among his men who complained they had no guns: "Don't worry; some will get killed and you can take their arms." As the British forces surrounded the village and cut off retreat, he refused to give up. "Do as you wish," he told those who wanted to surrender, "but as for me, I shall fight and if I am killed, I shall kill some others before dying." He ultimately barricaded himself with a few others in the church buildings. When the church was set on fire, Chénier was killed trying to escape by jumping out of a window. The British insisted on doing an autopsy on his body, leading years later to a considerable controversy over whether his body had been deliberately mutilated. Chénier was one of the few Patriote leaders who stood his ground against the authorities, and his death subsequently would become the subject of much mythology and verbal excess.

Sources: Based on: Dictionary of Canadian Biography; *Elinor Kyte Senior*, Redcoats and Patriotes: The Rebellions in Lower Canada, *1837–38* (Ottawa: Canadian War Museum, 1985), 124–30.

Charles Duncombe to Robert David Burford

Charles Duncombe (1792–1867) was born in Connecticut and came to Upper Canada after graduation from medical school in 1819. By 1830 he had a flourishing medical practice in Burford, Upper Canada, and extensive landholdings, and was first elected to the legislative assembly in that year. In the legislature he led reform in prisons, insane asylums, and education. He formed a rural uprising near Brantford, Upper Canada, on 8 December 1837, and then dispersed his followers on 13 December upon hearing of the defeat of Mackenzie's rebels north of Toronto. Duncombe fled to the United States, where he remained for the rest of his life, eventually becoming a state politician in California.

24 October 1837

Your favor of the 17th instant has this moment come to hand, in which you say that the time has come when reformers ought to be on the alert in forming political unions and in organizing for our common safety;

I heartily concur with you that it is high time for the reformers to be up and doing. When Sir Francis Head declares that the British Government never intended any such absurdity as giving us the British Constitution, (of course we are to continue to be governed by the Oligarchy of Toronto,) And when the doors of the Colonial Office are closed against reformers (or republicans as Sir Francis Head tauntingly styles us;) because we are guilty of the crime of appealing to His Majestys Government with our Complaints, and when we see [the] Province under the dynasty of a foreign Governor and an Orange Oligarchy, retrograding in one year as much as it had advanced in five, the only interest our oppressors have in the Province being the plunder they can amass and take away with them; I think any one not willfully blind, not interested in the continuation of the abuses, must see, that while this baneful domination continues we have not the slightest chance for prosperity and that if we will be well governed we must govern ourselves; Our oppressors have shown us more clearly than ever before, that their great object is to make the rich richer and the poor poorer,

for if the people should become wealthy they would become intelligent and unwilling slaves; my maxim has always been educate the people, this can now be done only upon a few matters upon politics[;] we may do much by "the assembling our selves together" and hearing political lectures, by the forming political unions, publishing periodicals and encouraging the circulation of reform news-papers—this can be best done by union and by our devoting the few pence we save from our grog bills to the purchase of correct information upon the subject of our own affairs—and the time formerly spent in drinking to reading and reflection; I shall be most happy to meet with you any time next week (as I have heard that there is to be a reform meeting in Oakland one day next week but have not heard what day)—and I must (God willing) be there; . . . I hope when you appoint the time you will let me know as the time has come when we are to decide whether we will be bondsmen or slaves—the reformers of Westminister [*sic*] have done nobly; your name I see among the immortal patriots who feel the oppressor's iron rod; thank God we are strong in the justice of our cause, and although we may suffer for a time, we shall assuredly in the end prevail; "A nation never can rebel" those only are rebels who resist the will of the people; from them (the people) emenates all legitimate, constitutional government.

Source: Colin Read and Ronald Stagg, eds, *The Rebellion of 1837 in Upper Canada: A Collection of Documents* (Toronto: Champlain Society, 1985), 88–9. Reprinted by permission of the publisher.

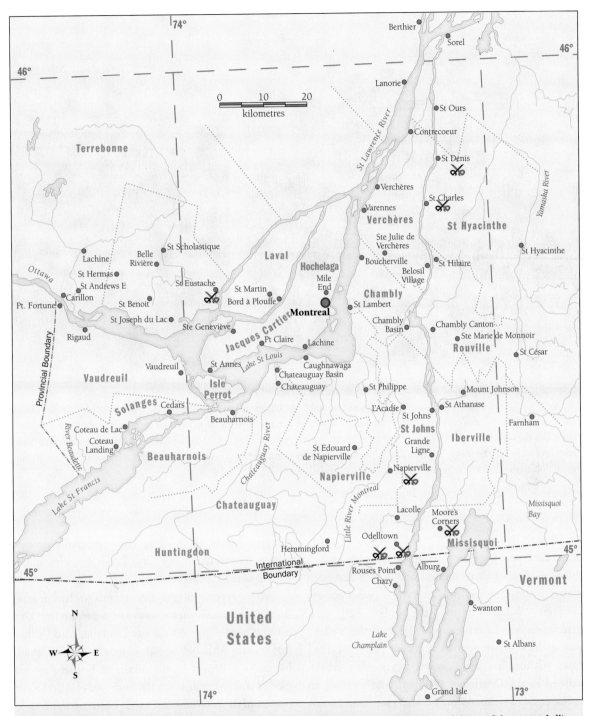

Southwestern Lower Canada in 1837, showing the region of Lower Canada in which the major fighting of the 1837 rebellion occurred. Villages are indicated by dots. The battles, mainly the result of local rural uprisings, are marked with crossed swords. Based on a map from A.D. Decelles's The Patriotes of '37: A Chronicle of the Lower Canadian Rebellion *(1916).*

(above left) *Execution of Lount and Matthews [date and artist unknown]. LAC, C-001242.*
(above right) *"The Insurgents at Beauharnois, Lower Canada," 1838, watercolour by Katherine Jane Ellice (1814–64). The artist was visiting her father-in-law's seigneury at Beauharnois when it was captured by Patriote rebels on the night of 4 November. She made this sketch during the week that she and other members of the household were held hostage before British troops arrived to free them and set fire to the village. The next day, Ellice recorded in her diary that the fire was "still burning; women and children flying in all directions. Such are the melancholy consequences of civil war." LAC, 1990-215-24R.*

In early November 1838, rebellion began again. This second uprising was much more seriously orchestrated in advance than the first one, which had been relatively spontaneous, and involved a secret society (the *Frères Chasseurs*) crossing the border. The government again moved repressively. Most of the leaders, once again, scurried across the border into the United States. Within a few days, however, 753 people had been arrested in the District of Montreal, and starting on 24 November a General Court Martial sat continuously until 8 May 1839, paying only limited attention to the civil liberties of the accused. Murray Greenwood calculates there were at least 25 cases of blatant miscarriage of justice in these treason trials. This tribunal acquitted 72 prisoners, sentenced 99 to death (12 of these were executed, 58 deported to Australia, and 29 conditionally released). Those who paid the supreme penalty were not leaders, but were either guilty of collateral atrocities or died to make a local point.

After reports of the first rebellions had reached Britain, the authorities dispatched a fact-finding commission headed by John George Lambton, Lord Durham (1792–1840). Although he did not remain long in Canada, his famous "Report on the Affairs in British America," filed in January 1839, was a thorough and eloquent examination of the problems in Canada based on information from local reformers. Durham recommended two political solutions: the introduction of responsible government and the unification of the two Canadas. He also wanted changes in land policy, including a general system for the sale of Crown land at sufficient price and the elimination of the proprietorial system in Prince Edward Island.

Historic Sites

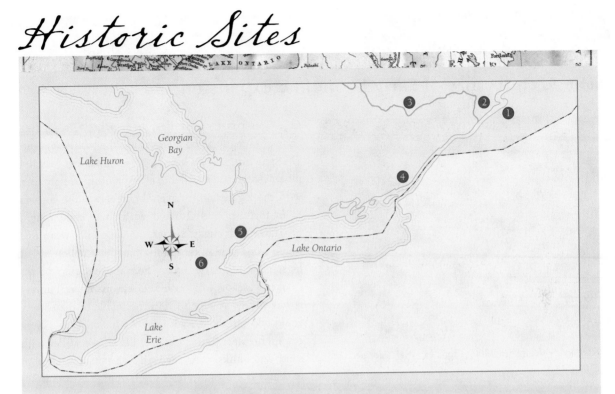

1. **Saint-Denis, Quebec:** A cairn marks the site of Maison Saint Germain, where Patriotes fought the British regulars on 23 November 1837.

2. **Saint-Eustache, Quebec:** Saint-Eustache Church, at 123 St-Louis Street, was the site of a battle on 14 December 1837, where 250 Patriotes attempted unsuccessfully to hold off nearly 2,000 British soldiers. The church was virtually destroyed by cannon and fire in the battle, and has been extensively rebuilt.

3. **Montebello, Quebec:** Here is the Manoir Papineau National Historic Site, encompassing the seigneury on the Ottawa River of Louis-Joseph Papineau, including his stone house and chapel.

4. **Prescott, Ontario:** Fort Wellington National Historic Park contains the 66-foot stone tower built as a windmill and captured by "Patriot Hunters" on 12 November 1838 at the Battle of the Windmill.

5. **Toronto, Ontario:** The Toronto Necropolis, at 200 Winchester Street, is the final resting place of William Lyon Mackenzie and Samuel Lount and contains a 20-foot granite monument to Samuel Lount and Peter Matthews. The monument has a broken peak, symbolizing life cut short.

6. **Scotland, Ontario:** At the corner of Talbot and Simcoe streets is a plaque marking the spot where Charles Duncombe rallied "the Patriots" in 1837.

Conclusion

While the rebellions accomplished little more in the short run than to focus Great Britain's attention on the need for change in her American colonies, Durham's recommendations for the union of the Canadas and for responsible government were adopted over the next few years. Nevertheless, other forces would profoundly help remake British America. Free trade, railroads, economic expansion, and industrialization were, in the end, more powerful engines of change than either political uprisings or constitutional reform.

Historiography

The Architecture of Early Economic Expansion

Interior of shanty, c. 1900. Photo by W.H. Harmer. LAC, C-025718.

As Europeans moved further into the interior and westward from their original colonies on the east coast of North America, they brought with them European ideas of architecture and settlement. When towns and cities took shape, these ideas quickly came to the fore. However, the architecture of the semi-permanent and early settlements was much less confined to "traditional" ideas. Instead, structures were influenced by both sides of the Atlantic, and in adapting these influences the settlers created some very Canadian spaces.

The first indigenously inspired economic expansion occurred in British America between 1815 and 1860. It left a thin but identifiable architectural footprint across the landscape of the several provinces. One distinctively Canadian structure was to be found during the winter months in isolated regions of virgin timber. The "camboose shanty," as it was called, was the bunkhouse, kitchen, and dining room of the timbering crews who pushed ever deeper into the forest in search of the timber that was transported by horse-drawn sleds and then downriver log drives and booms to ports for shipment to Britain. The shanty was an ingenious construction designed to house a logging crew of as many as 60 men during the winter months. The structure was built of large, unhewn logs (usually pine) set atop one another to a height of six to eight feet, with the logs usually dovetail-notched at the corners to fit together and chinked with some combination of straw, mud, sticks, stones, and moss. Flooring was rough wooden planks. The roof, made of hollowed-out logs, included a large square hole above the fire pit for smoke to escape, which worked reasonably well unless it was windy, at which times the inside of the shanty could become choked with smoke. Inside were a large central fireplace (the camboose), i.e., a fire pit filled with sand, and bunks along the walls. The shantymen slept in their clothes and were of a rich fragrance from wood smoke and body odour by the spring of a cold winter. Not until the introduction of the wood stove around 1900 was the shanty replaced.

Another architectural form familiar in western Canada was the fur-trading post, typically located on a grassy knoll overlooking a river. Most posts were called "forts" because they were primitively fortified, usually by the construction of a wooden stockade around the exterior of the building. Encamped outside the walls of the post was a group of Aboriginals, the "Homeguard Indians," mainly women and children since the men were often engaged in trapping and provisioning for the post. Sometimes—on special occasions or for domestic service—the Homeguard Indians were allowed inside the post. These posts were strategically located for commerce and the sites often became centres of population when the fur trade was ended. A less common form of the fur trade era was the post of York Factory, located at the mouth of the Hayes River 200 km south–southeast of present-day Churchill, Manitoba. This wooden structure replaced a stone-and-brick fort, built in the 1790s, which became structurally unsound from the heaving permafrost of the Subarctic region and was razed in the early 1830s. In fact, the fort constructed of wood was actually a series of interconnected buildings, and it served as the headquarters of the Northern Department of the Hudson's Bay Company for most of the nineteenth century. Because of its isolation, York Factory evolved into a self-contained settlement consisting of several hundred males with occasionally the female spouse of a head trader in residence. The post, now a National Historic Site, still survives, but the buildings are both too fragile and too remote to become a tourist attraction.

The lumbermen's shanty, especially, and the early trading posts, because of the methods and materials of construction, were not built to last forever. The shanty, made of round logs, would not last as long as the settler's hewn log cabin because hewing the logs to square them removed the bark and the softer outer wood from the logs. Also, carefully chinked hewn logs, with a sufficiently overhanging roof, did not allow the pooling of water between the logs, as did the hastily built camboose shanty. And, of course, the settler's cabin did not have an open hole in the roof but a stone chimney.

Those in involved in urban commerce, however, wanted their buildings to last and stand as monuments to business (and perhaps to themselves), so stone and brick were the preferred construction materials. The first bank was established in Canada in 1817 by government charter. This Bank of Montreal was initially granted an exclusive right to issue promissory notes as currency. It was soon joined by other similar institutions. Under the terms of their charters they could also issue currency, but the fact that the banking system was essentially in private hands often constrained economic growth. Nevertheless, by 1840 most commercial centres had at least one branch bank, often easily recognizable as a Greek temple, complete with columns. The idea of designing a bank building to resemble a Greek temple had its origins in the United States and quickly spread to Canada, where the classical mode was meant to suggest an institution that was the font of wealth and commercial activity and that had lasted (or would last) for centuries; it still resonates in many cities today.

By the early 1850s Canadian entrepreneurs were beginning to think in terms of larger economic structures. In 1854 John Redpath created a large industrial complex on the Lachine Canal in Montreal that included a seven-storey refinery building, two brick warehouses, and other buildings, thus producing a self-contained industrial complex—one of the first in Canada. It had easy access via the canal to sugar imported from the Caribbean.

Short Bibliography

Brown, Jennifer. *Strangers in Blood: Fur Trade Company Families in Indian Country.* Vancouver, 1980. A fascinating study of family life in the fur trade in the first half of the nineteenth century.

Cadigan, Sean T. *Hope and Deception in Conception Bay: Merchant–Settler Relations in Newfoundland 1785–1855.* Toronto, 1995. A revisionist analysis of socio-economic relations in Newfoundland, based largely on under-utilized court records.

Cameron, Wendy, and Maude McDougall. *Assisting Emigration to Upper Canada: The Petworth Project 1832–7.* Montreal and Kingston, 2000. A recent account of one of the largest assisted emigration schemes of the 1830s.

Creighton, Donald. *The Empire of the St Lawrence.* Toronto, 1958. The classic study of the old mercantile system of Canada.

Errington, Elizabeth Jane. *Emigrant Worlds and Transatlantic Communities: Migration to Upper Canada in the First Half of the Nineteenth Century.* Montreal and Kingston, 2007. A recent synthesis of early migration to one important colony.

Greenwood, F. Murray, and Barry Wright, eds. *Canadian State Trials, vol. 2, Rebellion and Invasion in the Canadas, 1837–1839.* Toronto, 2002. An important collection of essays focusing on the way the law was used in the rebellions.

Greer, Allan. *The Patriots and the People: Rebellion of 1837 in Rural Lower Canada.* Toronto, 1994. An account of the Lower Canadian rebellion of 1837, focusing on the rural community and popular agitation.

Houston, Cecil, and W.J. Smyth. *Irish Emigration and Canadian Settlement: Patterns, Links, and Letters.* Toronto, 1990. A useful study of the emigration of the Irish—from both north and south—to Canada.

Johnston, Hugh. *British Emigration Policy, 1815–1830: "Shovelling Out Paupers."* Oxford, 1972. The standard study of British policy in the era of pauper emigration.

Lower, A.R.M. *Great Britain's Woodyard: British North America and the Timber Trade 1763–1867.* Montreal, 1973. An important analysis of British America's timber trade.

McCalla, Douglas. *Planting the Province: The Economic History of Upper Canada 1784–1870.* Toronto, 1993. An excellent synthesis of the early economic history of a critical province.

McCallum, John. *Unequal Beginnings: Agriculture and Economic Development in Quebec and Ontario until 1870.* Toronto, 1970. A controversial and revisionist study that argues Ontario enjoyed advantages over Quebec because of its agricultural beginnings.

Macdonald, Norman. *Immigration and Settlement: The Administration of the Imperial Land Regulations, 1763–1840.* Toronto, 1939. An old but useful study of land policy and immigration.

Ouellet, Fernand. *Economic and Social History of Quebec, 1760–1850: Structures and Conjunctures.* Toronto, 1985. A provocative survey by the leading scholar of French Canada in the early nineteenth century, based on European historical conceptualizations.

Read, Colin. *The Rising in Western Upper Canada, 1837–8: The Duncombe Revolt and After.* Toronto, 1983. A good corrective to the notion that William Lyon Mackenzie led the only rebellion in Upper Canada in 1837.

Sager, Eric, and L. Fischer. *Shipping and Shipbuilding in Atlantic Canada, 1820–1914.* Ottawa, 1986. An innovative study, based on a massive collaborative project funded by the Social Sciences Research Council of Canada.

Sheppard, George. *Plunder, Profit and Paroles: A Social History of the War of 1812 in Upper Canada.* Montreal and Kingston, 1994. A revisionist analysis of the War of 1812 in the central colony.

Stewart, Gordon. *The Origins of Canadian Politics: A Comparative Approach.* Vancouver, 1986. A provocative survey based on American and British political models.

Taylor, Alan, *The Civil War of 1812: American Citizens, British Subjects, Irish Rebels, and Indian Allies.* New York, 2010. The latest American attempt to subordinate Canadian events to American events during wartime.

Warkentin, Germaine, ed. *Canadian Exploration Literature: An Anthology.* Toronto, 1993. A rich collection of what was probably the most robust writing in British America before 1850.

Wilton, Carol. *Popular Politics and Political Culture in Upper Canada, 1800–1850.* Montreal and Kingston, 2000. A study focusing on popular politics in Upper Canada.

Wynn, Graeme. *Timber Colony: A Historical Geography of Early Nineteenth Century New Brunswick.* Toronto, 1981. A richly rewarding analysis of timbering in early New Brunswick.

Study Questions

1. Why was the relationship between land policy and immigration so critical?

2. How did the British attitude towards emigration change in the first half of the nineteenth century?

3. If you were contemplating immigration to British America in the first half of the nineteenth century, what would be the most important questions you would want answered before you made a decision?

4. Identify the four staple resources in British America at this time.

5. Identify and explain the most important characteristics of the resource economy of British America between 1815 and 1840.

6. How were timbering, shipbuilding, and immigration connected?

7. How did elite society operate in British America in the first half of the nineteenth century?

8. What were the causes of the rebellions of 1837? Were they the same in both Upper and Lower Canada? Would you have supported the rebellions? Why or why not?

9. What were the chief consequences of the rebellions?

Visit the companion website for *A History of the Canadian Peoples*, fifth edition for further resources.

www.oupcanada.com/Bumsted5e

6
Becoming a Nation, 1840–1885

The construction of the Parliament buildings of a united Canada was one of the largest projects of its kind in 1860s Ontario. This photo, from 1862, shows the nearly finished buildings that would become the home of the new Canadian government in 1867. Samuel McLaughlin, LAC, C-018016

Timeline

1841 Union of Upper Canada and Lower Canada proclaimed.

1842 Webster-Ashburton Treaty resolves the New Brunswick border. Great Britain experiments with partially elected, partially appointed legislature for Newfoundland.

1843 Fort Victoria established on Vancouver Island.

1846 Oregon Boundary Treaty settles western boundary. Corn Laws and Timber duties are repealed by British Parliament. St John's, Newfoundland, is destroyed by fire.

1848 Nova Scotia gets responsible government. Lord Elgin concedes responsible government to Canada. Newfoundland reverts to an elected assembly.

1849 Vancouver Island is leased by the British to the Hudson's Bay Company and becomes a Crown colony. Rebellion Losses Bill is enacted, leading to riots in Montreal. Annexation movement flourishes.

1851 James Douglas becomes governor of Vancouver Island. Cable is laid from New Brunswick to Prince Edward Island. Prince Edward Island receives responsible government. Colonial government takes over post offices.

1852 Grand Trunk Railway is incorporated.

1854 Reciprocity Treaty with United States is signed, to last 10 years.

1855 Petroleum is discovered in southwestern Ontario. Newfoundland receives responsible government.

1856 The first legislature meets on Vancouver Island.

1858 British Columbia becomes a colony.

1859 The first steamer is launched on the Red River. First newspaper is established in Red River.

1860 Cariboo Gold Rush begins in British Columbia. Prince Edward Island Land Commission convenes. Royal Tour of Prince Albert suggests that what would become Canada is already, in some senses, a political entity.

1861 American Civil War begins. Montreal and Toronto introduce horse-drawn cars for public transportation.

1862 Cariboo Road is begun in British Columbia.

1863 First non-Native salmon fishery on the Fraser River established.

1864 Reciprocity Treaty is terminated by a vote of the American Senate, to take effect in 1866. Charlottetown and Quebec Conferences are held to discuss union of British North America.

1866 Transatlantic cable laid from Newfoundland to Europe. Union of British Columbia and Vancouver Island implemented, with Victoria as capital.

1867 The British North America Act is passed by British Parliament to take effect 1 July 1867. Emily Howard Stowe obtains a medical degree in the United States, the first woman to do so. British Columbia's legislative council resolves to request that the province be allowed eventual admission into Canada, which officially comes into existence on 1 July under an all-party government headed by Sir John A. Macdonald. Resolutions for territorial expansion are passed by the Canadian Parliament in December. The Americans purchase Alaska from Russia.

Timeline

1857   British Parliament holds inquiry over the future of the Northwest. Palliser and Canadian Exploring Expeditions are sent West to investigate the region. Gold is discovered on the Thompson and Fraser rivers. Ottawa is chosen by Queen Victoria as the site for the capital of the Province of Canada. Canadian legislature passes an Act for the Gradual Civilization of the Indian Tribes in the Canadas.

1868   Canada First is founded in Ottawa. Five hundred and seven Zouaves are recruited in Quebec for the papal army.

1869   Resistance to Canada, led by Louis Riel, begins in Red River. Newfoundland election produces an anti-confederate assembly.

1870   Louis Riel allows execution of Thomas Scott. The Manitoba Act is passed by the Canadian Parliament. The Wolseley Expedition is sent to Red River. Negotiations are begun with British Columbia for admission to Canada. Dominion Notes Act of 1870 is passed.

1871   British Columbia enters Confederation on 20 July 1871. The Washington Treaty is signed with the United States. The Bank Act of 1871 is passed.

1872   In a federal election, Conservatives win 103 seats to 97 for the Liberals. Ontario Society of Artists is formed.

1873   Prince Edward Island enters Confederation. The Macdonald government resigns over the Pacific Scandal. Liberals under Alexander Mackenzie take over federal government.

1874   Liberals win a clear majority in Parliament (133 to 73) over Conservatives. Woman's Christian Temperance Union is founded in December in Picton, Ontario.

1876   Intercolonial Railway is completed, linking Saint John, Halifax, and Montreal. Alexander Graham Bell invents a workable telephone. The first wheat crop is exported from Manitoba.

1877   Saint John fire leaves 13,000 homeless.

1878   Sir John A. Macdonald returns to power as Conservatives elect 137 members to 69 for the Liberals.

1880   Royal Academy of Arts is formed. Canadian government signs contract with the Canadian Pacific Railway.

1881   CPR reaches Winnipeg. The boundaries of Manitoba are expanded. 15,000 Chinese workers are allowed into Canada.

1882   Royal Society of Canada is formed. Conservatives are re-elected, winning 139 seats to 71 for the Liberals, now led by Edward Blake. Macdonald remains Prime Minister.

1883   CPR construction crews discover nickel near Sudbury, Ontario. Canadian Labour Congress is founded.

1884   Louis Riel returns to Canada.

1885   The second resistance led by Louis Riel (the North West Rebellion) is crushed. Riel is executed. The last spike is driven in the CPR.

A seamless web of political and economic expansion, beginning around 1840, brought Canadian Confederation. Between 1840 and 1874, British America became "British North America" and then the "Dominion of Canada," changing from a collection of loosely connected colonies in the northeastern sector of the continent, heavily dependent on the mother country both economically and politically, to a transcontinental nation—at least on paper—with a rapidly diversifying internal economy in the early stages of industrialization. Because the Province of Canada took the lead in national unification, the beginning of the process can be identified as the Act of Union, which joined Upper and Lower Canada in July 1840.

British Americans had witnessed many changes over the centuries since first settlement. But in terms of technology, a settler of 1640 still would have been quite at home in the Canada of 1840. The era of political unification was the first period that experienced substantial technological advances, radically altering perceptions of distance and time in a vast domain separated from Europe by thousands of miles of ocean. With the railroad, travel not only sped up substantially, it acquired a predictable timetable. The invention of telegraphy and the laying of a transatlantic cable from Newfoundland in 1866 affected the perception of time as well as of distance. By 1870 the largest telegraph company in Canada had 20,000 miles (32,000 km) of wire extended across eastern Canada. Communication could take place in seconds instead of months. The ability to operate to a schedule and communicate instantly completely altered the world and the way people operated within it. These changes were not a necessary prerequisite for union, but they were clearly part of the facilitating background. In many respects, modern Canada began not in 1867 with political unification but in the 1840s, the first era of transforming technological change.

The Mobile Society

Throughout the 1840s and 1850s British immigration to North America continued at high levels, although its makeup was now quite different. The proportion of new arrivals from southern Ireland, mainly Roman Catholic, increased and the number of those landing in British America without capital was much higher; the most impoverished were usually forced into the cities since they could not afford to obtain land. Driving immigration were the potato famines in Ireland (and to a lesser extent in Scotland), which peaked in 1846. Between 1840 and 1860 well over 600,000 British immigrants arrived in British North America, many of them seeking land on which to build a new life. They were joined in the 1850s and 1860s by numbers of Germans and Poles deliberately recruited by the Canadian government in the German states.

Combined with the natural population increase within the colonies, the arrival of this horde of new settlers put enormous pressure on available agricultural land, particularly land suitable for staple crop farming for the market. Second-generation farmers accepted less desirable land or moved to the United States, where a more rapid industrialization than in British America had created new employment and where the West was open to settlement. Thus, at the same time as thousands of land-hungry immigrants were moving in, thousands of disillusioned members of the younger generation within the colonies were moving out.

The first sign of serious out-migration came from the seigneurial districts of French Canada, the heartland of French-Canadian culture, language, and religion. Almost any opportunity was superior to a future on a farm of less than 100 acres (40 ha) of worn-out land. Over the course of the 1830s more than 40,000 left Lower Canada for the United States, and that figure jumped to 90,000 in the 1840s and to 190,000 in the 1850s. One clergyman called this population loss "the cemetery of the race." The visitor to New England can still see standing, usually empty and forlorn, the extensive brick buildings that housed the nineteenth-century factories employing these migrants. Thousands of French Canadians also moved into the Eastern Townships of Canada East, originally intended as anglophone enclaves. In the Upper St Francis district of the Eastern Townships, for example, the francophone population grew from 9.7 per cent of the district in 1844 to 64.1 per cent by 1871. Others continued to fill unpopulated regions in the Laurentians and around Lac St-Jean. State and church both promoted colonization of these regions as an alternative to migration to the United States. As well as moving out of the country or into new districts, thousands of French Canadians moved into the cities and expanding towns of the province where they often found employment as manufacturing workers. In Montreal, especially, many of the newcomers were female. Some found employment as domestic servants, but most worked in a few burgeoning industries, particularly clothing manufacture, textile production, and the making of tobacco products.

In Canada West, most of the movement into the United States before 1870 was into the rich agricultural districts of the American Midwest and beyond. A constant stream of Canadians crossed Ohio, Indiana, and Illinois onto the American prairies, contributing to the rapid settlement of Minnesota and the Dakotas. A key factor driving the migrants was the inability of the family farm to accommodate the needs of all family members. Successful farming required several children, but large families also created pressures for the expansion of landholdings and eventually led to the departure of some of the younger generation. In this male-dominated society, only males, as a rule, had expectations of inheritance; hence the tendency in all British North American rural society was to send disproportionate numbers of females (usually between the ages of 15 and 21) into the cities and non-agricultural employ-

ment. Some farms in some districts were more divisible than others, but the pressures were always strong on the younger members of the next generation to seek their fortunes elsewhere. Elder sons (and the women they married) could look forward to becoming pillars of and local leaders in their communities. For most of the children of most farmers, however, coming of age meant moving on. Some new land within Canada West was available to the north. Settlement after mid-century moved rapidly up to Georgian Bay and into the Muskoka country, heedless of the prominent rock outcroppings of the Canadian Shield. For most who chose to remain in Canada West, however, cities and towns were the obvious destinations.

The years before 1860 saw considerable internal expansion in the Atlantic region. Settlers moved on to less desirable and more remote lands, while others

"Roxburgh Place, Residence of A. Marshall, Esq.," 1868. The unnamed artist who painted this farmstead—located in Oxford County, in southwestern Ontario—is thought to have been a local schoolteacher. The painting has probably idealized both the property and the animals in residence on it. On the other hand, the fences are quite accurately portrayed. Courtesy Michael S. Bird.

moved into the major urban centres. Neither expansion nor seasonal migration could, in the end, accommodate the growing population. Many began to migrate, often to the United States. By the 1860s over one-third of the counties in the Maritime provinces were losing people, mostly to the United States, particularly to New England. The correlation between rural counties (with economies largely dependent on fishing and farming) and depopulation was very high. While out-migration was a general phenomenon, Scots and Irish were over-represented in the exodus and Acadians under-represented. Most of those departing were 15–25 years of age.

From Mercantilism to Free Trade

By 1840 the mercantile economy of British North America had reached its apex, and it began to undergo considerable change. That alteration resulted from a number of factors. The most important was clearly the British government's demolition of the imperial trading system, which had prevailed since the seventeenth century. Instead of mercantilism, Britain moved to free trade. In the process, the mother country wiped out protectionist advantages for her colonies. As a result, instead of a transatlantic economy based on the sailing ship, some of British North America began to think in terms of a continental economy. Fortunately, the railway came along at exactly this time, providing possibilities for internal development and internal markets. Equally fortunately, Britain resolved long-standing differences with the Americans, making possible the negotiation of a trade treaty, providing some access for British North America to the lucrative American market. An important factor in the reorganization of the commercial economy was the rise of industrialization. Internal markets within the continent required not raw materials but finished goods. Colonial business sought to oblige.

By the 1840s, the British industrial economy could no longer afford the luxury of protectionism, which limited its access to foreign raw materials and protected markets. The ministry, led by Sir Robert Peel, gritted its teeth and systematically removed protection for corn

and other raw materials, including timber. The British still sought to emphasize importing cheap raw materials and exporting finished goods overseas. Instead of trading with colonies, however, they sought to trade with the entire world. Most colonial merchants appreciated the nature of the revolution that was occurring in Britain. The *Quebec Gazette* summarized several generations of argument in 1842 when it wrote of the timber trade, "Our great ground of complaint is that British Acts of Parliament created the trade, caused capital to be invested in the trade, trusting to these acts, which by the uncertain character they now assume may ruin thousands. We never asked for protection; it was given on grounds of national policy" (quoted in Lower, 1973: 88). British free trade policies would have a tremendous psychological impact on colonial merchants.

In the short run, the British North American rush to export wheat and timber under the old system, before the repeal of the Corn Laws and Timber duties of 1846 took effect, resulted in a collapse of prices in 1847 that would last for the remainder of the decade. Further complicating matters for colonial governments was the arrival of thousands of impoverished Irish immigrants, refugees from the Great Famine of the 1840s. They brought sickness and expense to the colonies along with their anguish. The result of these blows was a conviction that the mother country had subverted the old empire. The crisis seemed much worse in the united Province of Canada because of its reliance on wheat exports. Canadian mercantile policy in the later 1840s was to attempt to come to terms with the Americans. The Canadians continued to improve their canal system. They argued for reciprocal free trade between British North America and the United States in the natural products of each.

Britain's industrial needs also contributed to the need for international peace and bilateral understandings. One of these understandings came with the United States. Since 1815 Britain had sought entente with the Americans, a process that gained momentum during the period of free trade. By 1846 most of the outstanding boundary questions between the two nations had been resolved. In 1842 the Webster-Ashburton Treaty had sorted out the complex eastern boundary issues along the Maine–New Brunswick border. The boundary question was even more complex west of the Rocky Mountains, where the two nations had agreed in 1818 to share occupation until there was a need for a decision. Many Americans had settled in the Oregon Territory south of the Columbia River, and presidential candidate James K. Polk in 1844 had rattled American sabres with his campaign slogan of "54–40 or Fight"; 54' 40" is the latitude of what was the southernmost Russian boundary on the Pacific slope. Under the Oregon Boundary Treaty of 1846, the border across the West from Lake of the Woods continued at the forty-ninth parallel to the Pacific (excluding Vancouver Island). This "compromise" allowed the Americans to possess the state of Washington, in which they had virtually no nationals and which had been occupied chiefly by the Hudson's Bay Company. The forty-ninth parallel artificially bisected the Pacific slope, where mountain ranges and river valleys ran north and south rather than east and west. While the geographical interests of British North America may have been sacrificed by the Oregon settlement, entente was good for business.

Along the way to reciprocity, for a short time some Canadians were seduced by the idea of annexation to the United States. Annexationism gained support after an intense political debate over compensation for Lower Canadians who had not rebelled but had lost property in 1837. It was a far less important movement than that of reciprocity. Both flourished in the economic and political uncertainties of the late 1840s. Many British North Americans saw annexation as the inevitable result of the failure to achieve reciprocity rather than as a desirable end in itself.

Canadians, especially those dependent on the wheat economy, viewed internal markets—which to them meant the United States—as the only alternative to those lost in Britain. The eastern provinces also saw advantages to gaining access to the American market. The Americans displayed no interest until 1852 when the British government decided to toughen its fishery policy. The resultant Reciprocity Treaty of 1854 was hardly a very broad free trade agreement. It removed tariff and other barriers on a variety of enumerated goods, chiefly raw materials common to both countries. It did not remove barriers on finished goods, although the Americans hoped that a more prosperous British North America would buy more American manufactures. The

treaty was potentially much more beneficial to British North America than to the United States. This helps explain why the Americans were so eager to end it at the expiration of its initial 10-year term. It does not appear to have greatly increased trade in either direction while it was in effect. The Reciprocity Treaty of 1854, nevertheless, was of enormous psychological value to British North America.

The Rise of Industrialism

The Reciprocity Treaty encouraged merchants, entrepreneurs, and politicians (mainly in the Province of Canada) to continue reconceptualizing their economic orientation. They moved from an imperial context, in which the British market was critical, to a continental context, in which internal markets were dominant. Supplying the American market in preference to the British one was quite advantageous to the Canadas, especially Upper Canada/Canada West, since these provinces had little open access to the Atlantic Ocean. Once turned from its traditional transatlantic economy to a continental one, Canada began to industrialize. Indeed, one of the principal reasons why American trade in dutiable items did not expand during the 10 years of the reciprocity agreement was that the manufacturing capacity of British North America—again, particularly in the Province of Canada—grew substantially in this period. The internal market permitted agriculture in Canada West to shift partially out of grain cultivation into mixed farming. The concern for modernization led to the elimination of the seigneurial system in the St Lawrence Valley by legislative fiat. A bill replaced traditional seigneurial obligations with a "quit rent," which gave tenants the opportunity to purchase their lands.

The process of economic reorientation was not a uniform one. Canada and the Atlantic region moved in somewhat different directions. While the Canadians became immersed in internal development—even territorial expansion into the prairie West—the Atlantic provinces continued to find the older transatlantic economy quite comfortable. They based their prosperity on a shipping industry committed to the wooden sailing ship, which the region was still successfully producing. The period from 1840 to the early 1870s was the "Golden Age of Sail" in the Atlantic region. With hindsight, it is possible to recognize the long-term technological weaknesses of the wooden sailing ship. So long as vessels that cost less than half as much to produce as iron steamers were more than half as profitable, however, they would flourish. The carrying trade provided employment for thousands. It also produced an outward-looking international orientation rather than one that focused on internal continental development. The Atlantic provinces sought to expand transportation links with Canada (mainly railways) in terms of transatlantic linkages.

The Province of Canada saw railways as a means to continental destinations rather than as transatlantic linkages. Canadian railway expansion would not occur in earnest until after 1850, after the complete demolition of the old imperial trade system. By 1850 only 60 miles (97 km) of track were in use in Canada. The obstacles were not technological; the technology had been available since the 1820s. Finance and psychology were the barriers. Railways were expensive capital investments, few routes in British North America promised to be immediately profitable, and investors shied away until the railway boom of the 1850s. In that decade a mania for internal development totally captured the imaginations of Canadian politicians and investors, encouraged by exaggerated promises of profits resulting from railway expansion. Canadian railway tracks had to be built well on deep beds because of the climate variances that caused heaving. American railroads were less expensive to construct. By 1867 the total cost to Canada of 2,188.25 miles (3,520 km) of track was $145,794,853, or roughly $66,000 per mile. In order to pay for this construction, the railways borrowed on the British exchanges. Governments had to guarantee the loans and make contributions. The Canadian government, by 1867, had incurred a provincial debt on railway construction of over $33 million, and its municipalities added considerably more. The result, however, was the economic linking of cities and towns in a new way.

Vast expenditures brought out the worst in businessmen and politicians, who commonly served together on interlocking directorates and engaged in the various aspects of railway construction. Allan MacNab (1798–1862), who was seven times chairman of the Canadian assembly's railway committee between 1848 and 1857 and served the province as co-premier in 1854–6, was at various times president of three railway companies, chairman of another, and director of two more. Small wonder he once commented, "All my politics are railroads." Bribes to politicians were common. Construction overruns were a way of life. Corruption ran rampant. The most serious problem, however, was that too much construction occurred in advance of a settled population that could sustain a profitable level of traffic. Perhaps the greatest disaster was the Bytown and Prescott Railway, financed by Boston interests in 1852 to carry timber from the Ottawa Valley into the United States but unable to find much other trade. This would always be the Canadian dilemma: trading off development against sustainability.

All railway promoters insisted that their lines would promote manufacturing by reducing transportation costs. Railways not only closed the distance between markets, they also served as a major market for industrial goods, often becoming industrial manufacturers themselves. The Grand Trunk Railway, incorporated in 1852 to build a railway from Toronto to Montreal, began by building its own rolling stock. By 1857 it had decided to produce its own rails as well, constructing an iron foundry and rolling mill in Hamilton. This was the heavy-industry section of the economy. Most railroads relied heavily on carrying Canadian timber, ultimately into the American market. By 1853, no fewer than 51 ports in the Province of Canada were exporting at least a million feet of planks and boards into the United States. As manufacturing grew and required increasing amounts of capital investment, most of the large firms were relatively recent creations. Some of the old entrepreneurs successfully made the shift from the commercial economy. Many others did not. Canadian cities certainly changed in the process.

The growth of industrialization—the introduction of manufacturing and related commerce on a large scale—inevitably made labour relations an increasingly important issue in British North America. The resource economy had employed large numbers of

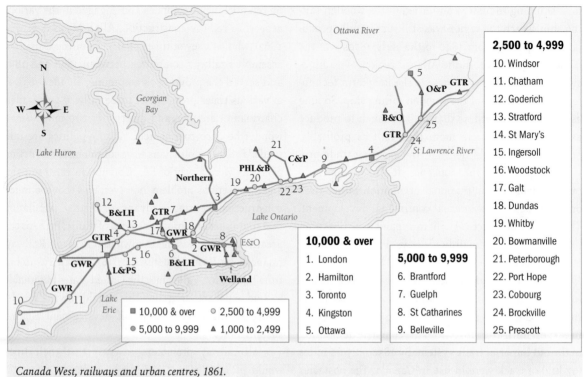

Canada West, railways and urban centres, 1861.
Source: Douglas McCalla, *Planting the Province: The Economic History of Upper Canada 1784–1870* (Toronto: University of Toronto Press, 1993).

men on a seasonal basis, offering little opportunity for organization. Industrialization rationalized and stabilized the labour market. Manufacturing tended to be more continuous, and much of it was conducted indoors. Overhead costs encouraged employers to seek a stable and experienced labour force. The rise of a capitalistic labour market stabilized and settled the workers but did little for their bargaining position. Those with highly developed skills were in the strongest position, and labour organization first developed in industries employing skilled workers, such as printing. Early trade unions emerged in certain skilled industries in various cities. Such unions almost never had any contact with one another. They could achieve only immediate and localized gains.

Like union organization, labour militancy was local and extremely limited. Most industrial action consisted of unsystematic rioting. Employers responded to industrial action of any kind by calling in the police or the military. Before the 1850s there was a tendency for unions to identify with their particular trades rather than with fellow workers in other trades in other places. The development of industry and the rise of factories employing mechanization brought considerable change to the incipient labour movement. A handful of international unions appeared, either British or American in origin. Unions with several local chapters also organized. Although mechanization encouraged unionization, the impersonality of the factory system created problems for labour, particularly when juveniles and women were drawn into the labour market. These workers were hard to organize.

Westward

By mid-century there were signs that the vast territory west of the Lakehead would not forever remain the monopoly of the fur trade. There were also signs of Canadian interest in the West, beginning with editorials in the Toronto *Globe* in 1850. One key development in western settlement was the establishment in 1848 of Vancouver

BACKGROUNDER

Mechanics Institutes

A movement to supply adult educational opportunity for the working classes, who were virtually ignored in the school and university systems, began in Scotland at the end of the eighteenth century and spread to London, where George Birkbeck founded the London Mechanics Institute in 1823. The growth of the movement in Great Britain—over 100 local Institutes by 1826—was facilitated mainly by wealthy businessmen and industrialists, who sought to provide self-improving facilities for working men, thus enabling them to move up the social and economic ladder. The Mechanics Institutes movement was transferred to British America at the end of the 1820s, with the establishment of a Montreal Institute in 1828, one at Toronto in 1830, and one in Halifax in 1831. The movement spread across the colonies in the 1840s, with almost every prominent town and city establishing an Institute and constructing or taking over a building to house the activities of the organization.

Most of the Institutes served three functions: first, they housed libraries and reading rooms publicly accessible to the working classes, who were encouraged to borrow books; many of these facilities eventually provided the basis for public libraries in their respective cities. Second, they provided classroom and lecture space for adult education in the local community; and third, they provided space for local organizations and groups to meet informally. The Institutes offered venues for visiting lecturers and others to speak on important issues and movements of the day, and in the 1840s and 1850s much of public awareness of science in British America was spread by the Mechanics Institutes. Lectures featuring practical exhibitions of scientific principles were common activities at most Mechanics Institutes, and were very well attended. Few Mechanics Institutes remained solvent on the contributions of members of the working classes, relying instead increasingly on government grants and largesse from wealthy benefactors who saw the value of these institutions of adult education.

The Mechanics Institutes seldom served as active sponsors of workingmen's associations or unions, and were more likely to be involved in temperance activity than in labour agitation. Nevertheless, the Mechanics Institutes movement remained a powerful one in Canada throughout the nineteenth century, with more than 300 local Institutes established in Ontario alone before 1900, but the heyday of the Mechanics Institute was between 1840 and Confederation.

Island as a British colony. Until then, Britain had been content to allow the Hudson's Bay Company to act as custodian of all British interests in the West. Earlier, the HBC had sent James Douglas (1803–77) from Fort Vancouver (now in the state of Washington) to establish Fort Victoria on Vancouver Island. This was a fallback position if the Oregon Territory were to be lost, as it was in 1846. In 1849 Vancouver Island was leased to the Company for an annual payment of seven shillings. The HBC would organize the colony there. James Douglas returned to Fort Victoria as chief factor of the Company, subsequently becoming its governor in 1851. Settlement on the west coast was slow. Most newcomers came from the British Isles. They sought to reproduce on the Pacific slope the life of the British gentry. This was not easy. The Colonial Office insisted on encumbering Vancouver Island with unworkable land policies. Land must be high-priced (a pound per acre) and settlement must be led by those who could afford to bring out labourers as settlers to work the lands.

A dour Scot, Kenneth McKenzie (1811–74), was put in charge of farming operations, and he found himself constantly struggling with the social pretensions of the bailiffs. "*Balls & parties* every now & then for farmers in a new country will not do," he admonished one of his underlings, telling another, "It is profits we want at as little outlay as possible" (Ormsby, 1958: 102–3). The HBC was astounded to discover that one of these bailiffs spent eight times his annual salary in 1854 on various expenses and purchases, including 1,606 pounds of sugar and 70 gallons of brandy, rum, whisky, and wine.

In 1838 the British government had extended the Hudson's Bay Company monopoly over the West for 21 years. A major parliamentary inquiry took place in 1857 before the government decided its ongoing policy in regard to the Company. The HBC officials had attempted to argue that the West was inhabitable only in river valleys limited in extent; most of the region was a vast desert too cold and too arid to be settled. The inquiry's report was not very favourable to the HBC. It acknowledged "the desire of our Canadian fellow-subjects that the means of extension and regular settlement should be afforded to them over a portion of this territory" (quoted in Bumsted, 1969: 220). It recommended that the HBC cease to control Vancouver Island. It also encouraged the annexation to Canada of the districts on the Red River and the Saskatchewan River. At the same time, the report maintained that for much of the West the continuation of the trading monopoly of the Company was desirable and appropriate. While the British Parliament was considering the future of the West, two scientific expeditions (one British and one Canadian) set out in 1857 to investigate the region first-hand. The leader of the British expedition was an Irishman, Captain John Palliser (1817–87). The Canadian Exploring Expedition was under the titular command of George Gladman (1800–63), assisted by Simon James Dawson (1820–1902) and Henry Youle Hind (1823–1908). The findings of these expeditions helped to end the public perception of this vast region as utterly unfit for human habitation.

The Great Western Railway station, Hamilton, c. 1850–60. The Great Western Railway initially connected Toronto and Hamilton, but eventually would connect much of the Niagara Peninsula to the rest of Canada. Stations like the one pictured above bound these communities together to help create larger regional and national identities. LAC, C-019415.

Contemporary Views

Letitia MacTavish Hargrave

Born in Edinburgh, Letitia MacTavish Hargrave (1813–54) married fur trader James Hargrave in 1840. The couple spent most of their married life, from 1840 to 1851, living at York Factory, the Hudson's Bay Company trading post on Hudson Bay. Her letters to her family give a vivid account of life at the post.

To Mrs. Dugald MacTavish, York Factory, September 1840

The usual dinner for our mess meaning the 3 ladies & me was—a roast of venison at the top 3 geese at the foot, 4 ducks on one side 6 plovers on the other, a large Red river ham (whole leg) & potatoes & mashed turnips or boiled lettuce. For something green when they have broth they put lettuce [in] & the bitterness is surprizing—They have radish & lettuce after dinner. I am getting a superfine blue cloth gown but I do not see how I am to wear it as I cant bear a cap on my head, the room is so close & the fire quite small. There are 3 windows in it. We have 2 sitting rooms but the kitchen in our house

is not used except in Winter. . . . Our house is a good size, 1 bedroom off each sitting room & men servants rooms off the kitchen a very large closet off the dining. . . . I had nearly forgot my piano. It is a very fine one & the handsomest I ever saw. The wood is beautiful & Mr Finlay[son] is croaking for one the same. Mrs. F does not play except to accompany herself. I was astonished at its appearance as I did not expect the case to be any great thing. The hinge of the lid, & the lock have created a sensation among the geniuses here from the uncommon elegance of their contrivance & mechanism. There was not a scratch upon it nor a note out of tune. The form of the pedal is magnificent & the wood beautifully marked. Mr. Gladman has a barrel organ in wch are a drum & some other instruments. It is never silent, the family imagine themselves so fond of music.

To Mary MacTavish, York Factory, 1st Sep'r 1840

There are 3 windows in each room & 2 in our bedroom so that the sun cant fail to look in when it pleases as they are in all the airts & there is no way of putting on shutters as there is no jut in the windows from the walls being so thin. The stoves are frightful. Mrs Finlayson could not keep the temperature of her rooms lower than 90. . . . I am quite baked with the stove. There are 3 windows open but Gibout [her servant] has made such a fire that the thermometer is 72 & feels like a very warm green house & my eyes are smarting & inflamed. . . . By last years journal the snow began on the 19th of this month but only in showers. There is a small plot of pease in full flourish but they never pod to any size. Indeed the blossoms look more luxuriant than at home but not above half a dozen have formed & they are as flat as a piece of paper. I take them for flowers as there is a great scarcity of such.

Source: Margaret Arnett MacLeod, ed., *The Letters of Letitia Hargrave* (Toronto: The Champlain Society, 1947), 61–3, 72, 74.

The Aurora gold mine, Williams Creek, BC, 15 August 1867, by Frederick Dally. Courtesy of Toronto Public Library, T14321. Note the ramshackle condition of the buildings, typical of the sense of impermanence in mining country.

Both expeditions produced reports acknowledging the great agricultural potential of the West, once opened by a railway.

Meanwhile on the west coast, sheer serendipity brought the region to the attention of the world. In 1857 the discovery of gold on the mainland, along the Thompson and Fraser rivers, attracted fortune hunters from around the world. The amount of gold easily available was quite small by earlier California standards. The ensuing rush was a pale imitation of the American one. Nevertheless, hundreds of miners, mainly from California, made their way to the Fraser River in the interior of British Columbia in the spring of 1858. The quiet village of Victoria was transformed overnight into a major port. South of the forty-ninth parallel, talk of American annexation spread rapidly. The British government rushed through legislation putting New Caledonia under the direct jurisdiction of the Crown. The mainland colony of British Columbia came into formal existence on 2 August 1858, with James Douglas as Governor. The two colonies were at first administratively separate. The miners, however rough in appearance, were not really badly behaved and accepted British authority readily enough.

The extraction of most of the gold required proper machinery and capital expenditure. Many of the gold-seekers found employment in other ways, taking advantage of the developmental spinoff from the rush.

The discovery of gold irreversibly altered life for the Indigenous peoples of the Pacific slope. Even remote regions could contain great mineral wealth. The settlers and the government ignored the land claims of Indigenous peoples in the rush to exploit the land itself.

Few settlers disagreed with the view that the "indolent, contented savage, must give place to the busteling [sic] sons of civilization & Toil" (quoted in Fisher, 1977: 105). For the Aboriginal peoples the result was a very serious

Document

Gold Mining in British Columbia

The following account of the pre-industrial techniques of gold mining is taken from Matthew Macfie's *Vancouver Island and British Columbia*. Macfie had journeyed from Britain to British Columbia in 1859.

The metallic sand in which gold is found is primarily sought, and the peculiar quality of earth that contains the amalgam is technically called the "colour." While engaged in the pursuit of this indication of the presence of gold, the miner is "prospecting." The requisites for this task are a "pan" and some quicksilver. When the miner comes to a spot on the bank of the river which he supposes to be auriferous, he proceeds to test the value of the "dirt" in the following manner. Having filled the pan with earth, he gently dips it in the stream, and by the assistance of a rotatory motion which he gives to the contents, loosened by the introduction of water, the black sand with pebbles is precipitated to the bottom. The lighter earth is allowed to pass over the edge of the pan or basin. After all has been removed except the sand and any specks of gold that may be in combination with it, the pan is placed by a fire or in the sun to dry. The lighter particles of sand are blown away, and if the gold be very fine it is amalgamated with quicksilver. By thus ascertaining the value of the remaining particles of gold dust, skilful "prospectors" conclude whether the ground would pay to work. In this rough method of searching for gold the superior specific gravity of that metal over every other, except platinum, is the basis of operations—auriferous particles, on this principle, settling at the bottom.

The readiest and most primitive contrivance for washing gold is the "rocker", which is still used by Chinamen and a few white men, on the banks of the Fraser. The rocker is constructed like a child's cradle, with rockers underneath. The box is $3\frac{1}{2}$ to 4 feet long, about 2 feet wide and $1\frac{1}{2}$ feet deep. The upper part and one end are open, and the sides gradually slope toward the bottom. At the head is a section closely jointed with a sheet-iron bottom, perforated so as to admit of small stones passing through. Along the bottom of the rocker riffles [these are strips of wood or metal arranged after the manner of a Venetian blind] or cleets are arranged to arrest the gold. This apparatus placed on the margin of the river, the upper iron box is fed by one miner with earth, and by another is rocked and supplied with water. The gold and pebbles passing down to the bottom, the water carries away the latter, and the riffles detain the former. In case the gold is very fine, part of a blanket is often laid along the under box, covered with quicksilver to attract the gold dust. By this simple agency from 1 pound sterling to 10 pounds sterling per day and upwards to the hand has been realised. In an ordinary sluice 40 or 50 lbs. of quicksilver is employed daily, and in a rocker from 8 to 10 lbs. But after the gold has been retorted from it, the same quicksilver may be applied several times over.

The next method to be described, and the one most prevailing on the Pacific, is Sluicing. This is a process of mining that can be conducted on any scale and in connection with the labour of an indefinite number of

Continued...

men. It is almost invariably found in conjunction with a system of "flumes" or wooden aqueducts of various extent, running parallel with the claims on a creek or river. It is necessary, in separating the earth from the gold which is mixed with it, that each sluice should be supplied with a fall of water, and if the stream contiguous to the mine run on too low a level to supply this want, miners . . . are often compelled to go considerable distances in quest of water sufficiently elevated to afford the object desired. Flumes are thus brought into requisition, and by openings made in that side of them opposite the mine, water is admitted to the sluice, which is placed at such an angle that the water may have forced enough to carry off the earth, while leaving the gold behind.

Sluice-boxes are of various sizes, and are fitted closely together so as to form a strongly built and extended trough. The fall of the water in the sluice-box is adjusted to allow sufficient time for the riffles and quicksilver to arrest the gold as it passes, and the supply from the flume is regulated by a slide in the opening on the side of it. The bottom of each sluice is usually intersected with strips of wood, and in the interstices of this grating quicksilver is spread to intercept the fine gold in its descent, nuggets and grains of coarse gold being caught by the grating itself. The sluice is supported on trussels so as to raise or lower it to the level convenient for shoveling in the earth. Several miners introduced "dirt" on either side, and others assist in loosening the heap and removing large stones, so that the gold may be easily precipitated. . . .

Source: Matthew Macfie, *Vancouver Island and British Columbia: Their History, Resources and Prospects* (London: Longman, Green, Longman, Roberts & Green, 1865), 267–70.

cultural disruption, recovery from which would be extraordinarily difficult, if not impossible.

The Fraser River gold rush presaged a new element in the resource economy of British North America: exploitation of the rich mineral wealth of the northern part of the continent. New technologies provided a constantly expanding market for British North America's mineral wealth. They also brought new means of extracting it from the ground. By the 1850s copper ore was being mined along Lake Superior, and petroleum was discovered in southwestern Ontario in 1855. Production of crude oil in Canada by 1863 ran to 100,000 barrels a year. Unlike timbering, mineral production tended to be extremely capital-intensive, requiring specialized scientific knowledge. Until the twentieth century, production involved only a few minerals located conveniently for transportation in bulk. Coal seams on both coasts were obvious targets. The continent's burgeoning industrialization would demand ever-larger quantities of minerals, and the future potential was indisputable.

Responsible Government and the Reorientation of Politics

The British government gradually resolved the constitutional problems of the commercial period in British North America over the decade following the unification of Upper and Lower Canada in July 1840. Legislative union did not by itself satisfy Lord Durham's other major recommendation for Canada, the right of the assembly to decide policy and its implementation through control of "the persons by whom that policy was to be administered" (quoted in Craig, 1963: 141). Part of the problem was that nobody at the time understood the importance of political parties or how they could work in responsible government. Colonial governors served as party brokers rather than conceding responsible government. Finally, in 1848 the governor of Canada, Lord

Elgin (1811–63), called on the leaders of the Reform parties, recently successful at the polls, to form a ministry. Louis LaFontaine (1807–64) and Robert Baldwin (1804–58) had allied their respective parties in 1842 on a Reform platform. In placing himself, as a representative of the Crown, above party politics and leaving government in the hands of leaders selected by their parties, Lord Elgin inaugurated responsible government in the Province of Canada.

The victory of responsible government in Canada did not begin the story or end it, however. Nova Scotia—where Joseph Howe had been agitating for responsible government as a Reformer since 1836—finally achieved it after an election on 5 August 1847, which focused on that single issue. The Reformers were victorious, and when a Reform administration took office in late January 1848, the province became the first colony to achieve responsible government. Prince Edward Island acquired responsible government in 1851 and New Brunswick in 1854. A British attempt at alternative constitutional arrangements complicated the situation in Newfoundland. In 1842 Britain gave the colony a legislature composed partly of elected and partly of appointed members, thus amalgamating the old council and assembly into one body. The experiment was not popular and never had a proper chance to work. The older Constitution returned in 1848. Newfoundlanders immediately began agitating for "a form of Government . . . with a departmental Government and Executive Responsibility similar in character to that form lately yielded to . . . Nova Scotia" (quoted in Gunn, 1966: 315). The British reluctantly gave in to this demand in 1855.

The lower provinces, even including Newfoundland, were sufficiently homogeneous to be able to live with a two-party system. Canada was not so fortunate. It could and did create four parties, two for each section. The Reform alliance of Baldwin and La Fontaine was largely illusory. It quickly transpired that Canada East (the unofficial designation for the former Lower Canada) had slipped back into old voting patterns removed from Reform. The principle of governing by a coalition from each of the two sections of the united province was inherently unstable. By the mid-1840s the French had become enamoured of the principle of the "double majority," in which the province would be governed by

an assembly majority in each of its two main sections. Such an arrangement naturally appealed to French Canada's growing sense of nationality. It also required the parallel growth of political parties in the two sections. Two factors emerged to complicate matters for the Province of Canada.

One was the rise of a new political movement in Canada West at the end of the 1840s. A radical Reform group known as the Clear Grits, with whom the moderate Reformers gradually merged, appeared under the leadership of George Brown (1818–80). Centred in the western districts, the Grits were the heirs of William Lyon Mackenzie rather than of Robert Baldwin. They were democrats, populists, geographical expansionists, and opponents of close connections between church and state in a Protestant rather than a true secularist sense. Furthermore—and ominously—they were hostile to French Canada in traditional anglophone ways. In 1840, when the population of Canada East had been greater than that of Canada West, each section of united Canada got 40 seats in Parliament. When the census of 1851 showed that the population of the anglophone section was growing more rapidly, George Brown adopted "representation by population"—"rep by pop"—as a campaign slogan when he stood as an independent Reformer in the general election of that year. He won easily. "Rep by pop" came to epitomize the brassy reformism of the Clear Grits.

The growing pressures of the Grits contributed to, but did not by themselves produce, the second development of the 1850s. This was the gradual withdrawal of French Canada into its own agenda, centred on the development of nationalist aspirations and the preservation of French-Canadian culture and society. The leaders of the Catholic Church took upon themselves the mantle of nationalism. They used the Grits to separate nationalism from reform. In the context of Canada West, the Grit espousal of "voluntaryism"—the separation of church and state—was directed chiefly against the Anglican Church. Such ultra-Protestantism had even more implications for the Catholic Church. Voluntaryism was not quite the same as secularism. The voluntaryists sought to free the state from "religious privilege," but could contemplate with equanimity the passage of legislation controlling the availability

Sir Samuel Leonard Tilley

Samuel L. Tilley, politician, Montreal, QC, 1864. William Notman photo, I-13477.1. © McCord Museum.

Probably the least well known of the principal "Fathers of Confederation," Samuel L. Tilley (1818–96) was born in Gagetown, New Brunswick, the son of Loyalist parents. He was locally educated at the Church of England's Madras school and then a grammar school before apprenticing as a druggist in Saint John, opening a drug store in the city in 1838. Tilley entered public life as a consequence of his religious beliefs, which demanded that he support various reforms, particularly the elimination of alcohol from society. He became in 1847 a leading figure in the New Brunswick branch of the Sons of Temperance, originally an American organization, which expanded into British America, utilizing

his earlier experience with the Saint John's Mechanics Institute to great effect. For Tilley, prohibition and support for the local business community went hand in hand. He supported protection for infant industries, railway construction, and the New Brunswick Colonial Association (which debated a "Federal Union of the British North American Colonies" and advocated honest government for the province). Tilley entered provincial politics in 1850 as a Reformer, and became provincial secretary when Reform won a majority in 1854. In office, he fought for financial control of the province by the Executive Council and for prohibition, becoming so unpopular that he was defeated in the election of 1856. Unhappy out of politics, however, he ran successfully for the legislature as a Reformer in 1857, returning to the office of provincial secretary in a government headed by Charles Fisher. As secretary, Tilley proved an industrious administrator and demonstrated a real skill at financial management. In 1861 he led a cabinet revolt against Fisher (who had been involved in an unsavoury land scandal), ending up as Premier.

In the early 1860s, Tilley joined Nova Scotia's Joseph Howe as a principal promoter of Maritime railroads, particularly for a rail connection between the region and the province of Canada. His efforts on behalf of an intercolonial rail line led him inexorably to advocacy of the political union of the British American colonies. In August of 1864 he insisted that the colonies should be bound together from Atlantic to Pacific, for "that was the destiny of this country and the race which inhabited it." He attended both the Charlottetown and Quebec Conferences in 1864. Not surprisingly, he opposed Maritime Union and seconded John A. Macdonald's motion at Quebec for a federal union. Although he returned from Quebec aware that there was "a strong current running against Federation," he was surprised at the extent of the government's defeat (and his own) in the election of 1865. Tilley led the pro-Confederation forces in the 1866 "union or disunion" election, backed by the British government and the Roman Catholic Church, and in a negative sense by a Fenian raid at the mouth of the St Croix River in April. One Nova Scotia confederate wrote him, "All the Saints in the Calendar must have been on your side." He took pro-Confederation resolutions passed by the New Brunswick legislature to England in July 1866, and then had to wait impatiently for the Canadians to join him. Tilley's reward for his service was the inferior post of Minister of Customs in the Macdonald government. Nevertheless, Tilley operated efficiently with the customs until 1873, when he briefly became Minister of Finance before the government fell. He then returned to New Brunswick as its lieutenant-governor. In 1877 he re-entered politics, winning a seat in Saint John in 1878 and becoming Minister of Finance in the Macdonald government, a post in which he served until 1885. Tilley's second term as Minister of Finance saw him put in place the tariff structure that implemented the "National Policy," and he was a strong supporter of the CPR. He was appointed again as lieutenant-governor of New Brunswick in 1885, serving until 1893. Tilley was never very well known outside his native province during his lengthy public career, but his persistent advocacy of political union and his financial skills made him essential both to New Brunswick and to Canada.

of alcoholic beverages during the Sabbath (which they held sacrosanct). While God might not be eligible to hold land or be exempt from taxation, he could be used to justify state intrusion in matters of morality. Such ideas were very much at odds with the principles of French-Canadian religious nationalists. The result was an alliance between the latter and the Upper Canadian opponents of the Grits.

The rise of denominational divisions as major factors in politics was not confined to the Canadas, although the sectional situation—Roman Catholicism in Canada East and evangelical Protestantism in Canada West—gave such matters a special edge in that province. To a considerable extent, denominational politics reflected the growing democratization of the political process. As the interest, involvement, and size of the electorate grew, politicians turned to issues that appealed to the voter. Denominations also reflected ethnic background and regional strengths. Infighting among religious denominations constantly tussling for advantage transferred easily into the political arena. In Nova Scotia such struggles had occurred for years over the creation of institutions of higher learning. No denomination could allow another an educational edge, and the result was the creation of a series of colleges and universities, one for each major denomination (and one for each ethnic branch of Catholicism in the province). By the 1850s the venue for denominational disagreements had shifted to public education. In Prince Edward Island the question began over Bible-reading in the schools, a practice pressed by the evangelical Protestants and opposed by the Roman Catholics. The "Bible Question" helped realign Island politics as Catholics and liberal Protestants, backed by the old Tories, joined against evangelical Protestants. By 1858 the principal issue in that year's election was between Protestantism and Romanism, and the result was a Protestant party and a Catholic party. In Newfoundland as well, the contending political parties wore denominational as well as ethnic faces, the Liberals backed by the Irish Roman Catholics and the Tories supported by the English Protestants.

In Canada, John A. Macdonald (1815–91), the Scots-born lawyer from Kingston, came gradually to dominate the anglophone Conservatives. Macdonald was not a man to allow abstract principle, such as the double majority, to stand in the way of power. In 1856 he was able to forge a new coalition among the moderate (some said very pragmatic) Tories he led and the Bleus of French Canada, led after 1859 by George-Étienne Cartier.

This alliance enabled the Tories to remain in power despite Grit victories in Canada West. It also led George Brown's *Globe* to comment in August of 1856 that "If Upper and Lower Canada cannot be made to agree, a federal union of all the provinces will probably be the result." By 1863 most of Canada's leading politicians had come to concur on the need for some other form of union.

George-Étienne Cartier

Sir George-Étienne Cartier. Notman & Son, LAC, C-02162.

Born at Saint-Antoine-sur-Richelieu, Lower Canada, George-Étienne Cartier (1814–73) attended the College of Montreal beginning in 1824 and started legal training in 1831. Becoming a lawyer in 1835, he had already gravitated towards the radicals, and he was clearly a Patriote in 1837, present at the battle of St-Denis. He then fled to the United States until October 1838, when he returned to Montreal and apparently was rehabilitated.

After a number of years of feverish legal activity, he entered the legislature in 1849 and subsequently worked increasingly for the Grand Trunk Railway, with which his name was always associated. He did not enter the debate on the Rebellion Losses Bill. Cartier became associated with the moderate reformers and entered the MacNab-Taché government as provincial secretary for Canada East in 1855. He won an election caused when his acceptance of office required him to seek a fresh mandate from the voters after vociferous opposition from the radical Rouges, and in the Taché-Macdonald cabinet of 1856 he became Attorney General for Canada East. When Taché withdrew from politics in 1857, he joined with John A. Macdonald to form a government. The two remained close political associates until his death. He was part of the "double shuffle" of 1858, in which a defeated government returned to office by briefly accepting different portfolios and then resuming their former ones. In the years before 1862, when he and Macdonald were defeated on a militia bill, he was the guiding force behind a number of legislative measures that reshaped united Canada, including municipal reform, educational reform, and legal reform.

He returned to power in 1864 and became part of the Grand Coalition committed to the unification of British America. He was the chief spokesman for French Canada in the various discussions that produced the Quebec Resolutions, maintaining that only Confederation would do as an alternative to American annexation and insisting on the importance of a separate province for French Canada in which religious and linguistic rights would be preserved. He was also, of course, a strong advocate of a transcontinental railroad. When he entered the first cabinet of the Dominion he refused an honour inferior to Sir John A. Macdonald's knight of the Order of the Bath, and subsequently accepted a baronetcy. He served initially in both the federal and the provincial houses of Parliament, but was clearly Macdonald's chief lieutenant in Quebec and co-leader of the government.

Cartier played a central role in the negotiations that brought the Red River Settlement into Canada, and was unquestionably more sympathetic to Louis Riel and his "rebellion" than were most of the Macdonald cabinet members in 1870. He probably made promises to the delegates from Red River that he could not honour, but he was unable to gain approval for an amnesty for Riel and his government, despite Riel's relinquishment of a nomination to Parliament in 1872 in his favour. Cartier was a genial man who at the same time brooked no opposition to his will, especially in terms of political and religious innovation.

The New Imperial Relationship

The imperial government conceded responsible government in British North America because it had little choice, given its unwillingness in the era of free trade to devote unnecessary amounts of money to colonial administration. There was a feeling in both the Colonial Office and in the Parliament that the separation of colonies, particularly colonies populated with large numbers of British emigrants, was inevitable when those colonies had reached a point of sufficient "maturity." An equally strong feeling was that the costs of imperial administration were an unnecessary drain on the public purse. Britain was responsible for the direction and financing of the land and sea defences of British North America. Under free trade and responsible government, Britain reduced its military establishment in British North America and attempted with mixed success to convince the colonials to take up the burden. When the American Civil War endangered the stability of the continent, the imperial authorities would respond by attempting to strengthen colonial defence through political and constitutional revisions. The "mother country" also had considerable authority in the West, and was in charge of Aboriginal policy everywhere.

John A. Macdonald, c. 1883–4, oil portrait by Thomas Horsburgh, from a photograph by William James. LAC, C-097288.

Victorian Society

The relationship between political unification and social change was a complicated one. There were some obvious connections, however. A number of major themes dominated the society of these years. First, there was an unmistakable sense of geographical movement, as we have already discussed, mainly out of the older and more settled rural districts. Second, the class structure of society began to take shape and to solidify. The chief changes were the appearance of a new business class, the emergence of a working class associated with urbanization and industrialization, and the rapid professionalization of certain educated and skilled segments of the middle class. Along with the development of social classes went a strengthening of certain caste lines associated with class but not identical with it; many of these lines emphasized ethnicity. Finally, an enormous expansion of voluntary organizations of all sorts occurred, at least partly to maintain personal identities and a sense of belonging in a time of great mobility and social change.

Most British North Americans uprooted themselves at least once, and many were constantly on the move. Wilson Benson, an immigrant of the 1830s, tells the story in his autobiography. Beginning in Ireland at age 15, Benson changed his district of residence 11 times (six times in Ireland and Scotland between 1836 and 1838 and five times in Canada West between 1838 and 1851) before finally settling on a farm in Grey County in 1851 at age 30. He bought the farm not with his savings but with an inheritance from Ireland. Benson had changed jobs 29 times in those years and apprenticed to at least six different trades in the 1830s and 1840s before finally settling down to farming. In his later years, he also kept a store in his community. On the whole, transients like Wilson Benson were not economically successful. In both urban Hamilton and rural Peel County, Upper Canada, there was a remarkable correlation between transience and poverty. Whether such people failed because they were continually on the move, or constantly moved in search of a better life they never found, is debatable. So, too, is the question of whether their failure was so deep-rooted as to be transmittable to

BACKGROUNDER

The Orange Order

The Orange Order was founded as the Loyal Orange Association in the 1790s in County Armagh in response to the increasing disorder in Ireland. Protestants in Ulster created local societies devoted to the memory of William of Orange, who had intervened in Ireland militarily in 1688 to replace James II and to guarantee the Protestant succession in England, thus guaranteeing the position of the Protestant minority in Ireland. William's great victory at the Battle of the Boyne in 1690 was celebrated every 12 July with a parade and commemoration, including the festooning of everything imaginable in the colour orange.

In Ulster the Order existed as a hierarchy of local lodges devoted to the maintenance of the Protestant faith and loyalty to the Crown of England, and included a good deal of secrecy and costumed ritual similar to the Masons. In British America the Order downplayed its secrecy and emphasized various fraternal aspects, including life insurance and support for families of members. The first lodge in Canada was founded in Brockville, Upper Canada, in 1830 by Ogle Gowan, and thereafter it spread rapidly. By the later 1830s the Order had over 100 lodges, most of them in Upper Canada. Probably the most important ingredients in its Canadian spread were its transcendence of Irish ethnicity in favour of a non-denominational Protestantism encompassing immigrants from all over the British Isles, its identification with deep-seated fears of Roman Catholicism in many parts of British America, and its various fraternal aspects.

At its height the Orange Order probably had no more than 50,000 actual members, but its degree of popular support in Newfoundland and New Brunswick, as well as in Protestant Upper Canada/Ontario, made it seem much more ubiquitous. The Order had begun by opposing Irish Roman Catholicism through demonstrations and violence. Its leaders insisted that its enthusiasm was mainly a display of support for the Crown, but the Crown during the 1860 visit of the Prince of Wales to British America made clear that waving an orange flag did not find any favour with the monarchy. The Order gradually transferred its hostility from Irish to French-Canadian Catholics and, in Manitoba especially, to the Métis led by Louis Riel. After Confederation the Orange Order became much more constrained in its public demonstrations, but it always maintained a stance of hostility to Roman Catholicism and support for British values (especially the monarchy) in Canada.

their children. In any case, the success stories in terms of the accumulation of wealth usually involved those who remained more or less permanently in one place.

The need for a sense of belonging in an era of change and mobility helps explain the enormous expansion in the number of private associations devoted to non-occupational and non-economic goals. Despite the growth of the state, even in Canada it did not weigh heavily on the lives of British Americans. Political allegiances were not as important to the average person as family, religion, and fraternal commitments. Churches continued to be important. They were increasingly dominated—especially on the Protestant side—by women, who made up the bulk of the attending congregations. Women also supported their own religious organizations with their own money, kept separate from the larger funds of the church, and these organizations offered many women their first glimpse of independent administration. British Americans also found a place in the temperance societies, which had begun in the 1820s but really expanded in the 1840s under the Sons of Temperance, a fraternal organization that served "no liquor stronger than tea." The temperance movement crusaded against drunkenness, but it was also a way of reacting against new immigration—mainly Irish—and asserting a sense of Protestant hegemony.

By 1870 few British Americans—whether urban or rural—could be found who did not belong to a good number of voluntary societies beyond their churches. In earlier eras, private fraternal organizations had supplemented or provided public services such as water, light, fire protection, and library facilities. By 1870, many organizations had virtually relinquished charitable and public goals in favour of entertainment and companionship for their members. Some of the new societies were created to provide a framework for sporting activities such as curling, lacrosse, or baseball.

Rural overpopulation produced some migrants who would settle and tame undeveloped regions and others who would provide a labour force for industrialization. While the farming pioneers remained small-scale commodity producers indeterminately related to the class structure, the urbanized workforce swiftly turned into a landless working class. At the other end of the scale, merchants turned into bankers, financiers,

and industrialists, and became far wealthier. Over the middle decades of the nineteenth century, the older social structure of elites and non-elites disappeared, to be replaced by one far more clearly stratified.

Successful businessmen were highly esteemed in the era of economic transformation, achieving their high status partly by self-ascription and partly by their acknowledged economic and political power. Nowhere was the power more evident than at the municipal level, where businessmen formed a mutually supportive coterie that took the lead in all aspects of life in the city, including its development and land market. Most business leaders in this period were self-made men, not in the sense that they had risen from rags to riches, but in that they had achieved their position in the community by their own efforts. Scots were over-represented in business ranks, where Protestantism predominated. The new wealth was in finance and manufacturing. The wealthier business leaders of Montreal and Toronto began to adopt extravagant lifestyles that were in many respects comparable to those of their American counterparts.

As Canadian cities began the shift from commercial entrepôts to industrial and financial centres, they already contained significant inequalities in terms of wealth and income. In Hamilton, for example, the most affluent 10 per cent of the city held 88 per cent of its propertied wealth, drew nearly half its income, and controlled about 60 per cent of its wealth. On the other hand, the poorest 40 per cent earned only about 1 per cent of the city's total income and controlled about 6 per cent of its total wealth. A close relationship existed between wealth and emerging class status, and between class status and ethnicity. The last was an important determinant of status both because ethnic groups like the Southern Irish carried over their Old World poverty into the New World and because the poorer immigrants tended to arrive later when opportunity was less fluid. The Irish were by far the largest element of the working-class poor in Hamilton and were the most substantial non-Francophone part of the poor in Montreal.

Nevertheless, before 1860 rich and poor in both Hamilton and Montreal lived in close proximity to each other. Only as cities grew larger and developed an expanding middle class that could afford to move out of the urban centre and a working class desperate for housing would the industrial city emerge with its clear divisions between rich and poor and between one economic function and another. In the pre-industrial city the role of women and children in the labour force was fairly limited. Industry could and did employ both women and children for some of the simple repetitive tasks that supplemented the machines, however. Factory owners found that children worked for low wages. Families often insisted that employers take on the entire family, so they would earn enough to live, and the income of all members of the family—including older children—was crucial for survival. In the last analysis, the major characteristic of families on the unskilled side of industrialization was their vulnerability to poverty. Not all the working-class poor worked in factories. Opportunities for women were strong at the lower end of the labour force in domestic service, and increasingly as well as in business and clerical occupations. The mid-Victorian Age saw changes in the retail trade as well as in manufacturing. In 1840 retail establishments were relatively small. By 1870 general merchandising had begun to spawn the department store: the T. Eaton Company was founded in Toronto in 1869.

The relatively small physical size of cities before 1865 made residential segregation relatively difficult, and as various British ethnic communities turned into British North Americans, they came to share loyalty to their new homeland and to a common Empire and monarchy. At the same time, an increase of certain forms of ethnic conflict was imported from the British Isles. Ireland was a major arena for such conflict, as Protestants and Catholics in that land became constantly more aware of their antipathies for one another. The success of the Orange Order was a sign of the problem. As Irish immigration turned into a flood—especially after the potato famine drove thousands of impoverished and embittered Irish Catholics across the Atlantic—the Irish groups were increasingly forced into contact with one another. Irish ethnic differences were not simply confessional or geographical. They also were class-driven. In most places the Catholic Irish were both the latest and the poorest arrivals, forced to take the worst lands (often as tenants) in the countryside or the worst jobs in the cities. The Irish were looked down upon, and often

responded with anger to their treatment. The Irish had a long-standing tradition of parades and public events to celebrate their major ethnic holidays, a tradition they brought to North America. Such occasions, particularly in New Brunswick, the Ottawa Valley, and the city of Toronto, which had especially large Irish Catholic populations, produced continual ethnic tensions.

Between rich and poor, the middle class—although it ranged from small urban merchants to small-town industrialists to well-to-do rural farmers—came increasingly to be anchored by members of the educated professional occupations. Professionals' relative dependability of income tended to set them apart. Guaranteeing that dependability through professionalization was the chief development within the middle classes in this period. The numbers of qualified practitioners were increased through formal education, and at the same time stringent licensing requirements were imposed, often set by the occupation itself. The doctors took the lead. An attempt to legislate the creation of a College of Physicians and Surgeons of Upper Canada failed in 1840, although another similar attempt in Canada East in 1847 was more successful. Perhaps significantly, doctors were one of the first groups to organize nationally: the Canadian Medical Association formed in the very year of Confederation. Lawyers engaged in a similar policy, with most provincial law societies formed between 1846 and 1877.

Outside the class structure entirely were women, Aboriginal peoples, people from Asia, and blacks (or Negroes, as they were then called). In Victorian Canada the woman, as the bearer and nurturer of children, was regarded as belonging in the home as wife, helpmate, and mother. Women had few legal rights. A woman could not expect automatically to inherit a deceased husband's property. In most provinces, a husband could sue a wife for divorce on grounds of adultery, but a wife could sue a husband only if he were adulterous and had committed some other heinous offence. The courts expected women to reform violent husbands rather than to prosecute them. Mothers had a better chance to rights of guardianship over children even if they were unwed. Despite the domestic ideal, many women worked. The most invisible women workers were the domestic servants. The typical domestic servant in the census of 1871 was a single woman in her twenties who lived in the house and could both read and write. The most prestigious occupation to which most women could aspire was that of schoolteacher. Actively recruited into the teaching ranks, they then remained at the lower end of the ranges of both salary and responsibility. There was little opportunity for entry into the professions. Emily Howard Stowe (1831–1903) obtained a medical degree from the New York Medical College for Women in 1867, but she could not achieve proper accreditation until 1880. The first woman lawyer would not appear until the next century.

Blacks and Chinese joined the Aboriginal peoples in suffering from widespread racial prejudice and discrimination in British North America. Chinese migration before 1870 was relatively small, and confined to British Columbia. But thousands of blacks fled the United States for freedom north of border, often encouraged by blacks like Harriet Tubman. After 1840 governments pressured the Indigenous peoples of the settled provinces to become freehold farmers. While governments recognized some Native rights, that alone did not lead to much protection. In 1850 the Canadian Parliament passed legislation

Orange Order parade along King Street, Toronto. Parades were important public occasions in nineteenth-century British America, and were often the occasion for violence. Courtesy of Toronto Public Library, T13222.

that operationally defined who was and who was not an "Indian" within the meaning of the Acts involved. The process of legislating for Aboriginals rapidly escalated after 1850. In 1857 the legislature of Canada passed the Act for the Gradual Civilization of the Indian Tribes in the Canadas. It contained many provisions that ran against the expressed wishes of the Aboriginals. Canadian policy became devoted to removing Natives from the paths of settlement, by coercion and compulsion if necessary. Most of these policies—which defined "Indians," made them citizens when properly educated, and provided for land grants—passed on to the Dominion of Canada from the Province of Canada in 1867.

Few British North Americans believed that the state would come to their assistance in times of trouble. For some, politics and government were a source of employment or patronage, but for the average person the government (whether local, provincial, or federal) existed mainly to act as an impartial and somewhat distant umpire. Government mostly affected events outside the citizen's personal experience. Nevertheless, the exodus from older settled districts with traditional agrarian and resource-oriented economies into towns and cities demonstrated two points. First, it showed the extent to which the older mercantile economy was failing to support the rate of population growth. Second, it showed the extent to which new economic development was essential. By the 1860s politicians were extremely conscious of out-migration, particularly to the United States. Territorial expansion westward was one solution. A more sophisticated economy was another. In the view of many political leaders across British North America both seemed to require new political arrangements.

The Creation of Cultural Infrastructure

The conscious cultivation of mind, creativity, and aesthetic taste—which is what most people have in mind when they think of "culture"—is obviously something that does not come easily to a pioneer society living on the edge of a vast wilderness and spending most of its energy on survival. Such culture requires a complex infrastructure in order to flourish. While small parts of that infrastructure had been in place almost from the beginning of settlement in North America, the elaboration of substantial institutional support for culture was slow to develop. The years between 1840 and 1870 were important in terms of that elaboration, if only because they witnessed such a striking growth in urban populations. Only a few illustrative examples can be discussed here.

Until the 1830s most newspapers had been published weekly, but biweekly editions for papers in the larger cities began in the late 1830s. The Saint John *News* introduced a penny edition in 1839, and dailies started in the 1850s. Most early papers were four page-sheets and had relatively small circulations, printing no more than 1,000 copies, although readership could be far greater. Susanna Moodie described the typical newspaper of her day as "a strange mélange of politics, religion, abuse, and general information," adding that it "contains, in a condensed form, all the news of the Old and New World, and informs its readers of what is passing on the great globe, from the North Pole to the Gold Mines of Australia and California" (quoted in Rutherford, 1982: 38). One modern content analysis of four papers from this era corroborates this description (Rutherford, 1982: 39). George Brown published the first daily in 1853, printing it on a steam-powered cylinder press, and he reached a hitherto unheard of circulation of 28,000 by 1861. In British North America Brown was a pioneer in the regular serialization of popular fiction, including the works of Charles Dickens. He also aggressively covered the arts, especially in the local community. All newspapers, especially the dailies, benefited from the introduction of telegraphy to British America in the late 1840s.

In history everything connects. Critical to the emergence of the daily newspaper and the development of a larger and more sophisticated arts community was the introduction of mass education. This began in the 1840s, especially in anglophone British North America. Mass education was a product of the introduction of publicly supported schooling combined with the principle of universality. The result was that increasing numbers of people learned to read and write, and this increased the

Petition of a Number of Colored Inhabitants of the City of Montreal

One way of showing loyalty to Canada in the nineteenth century was by offering to organize a militia company, as did a number of blacks in Montreal in 1860. We do not know whether the petition was successful.

To His Excellency Sir Edmund Walker Head, Governor General of British North America and Captain General and Governor in Chief of the Provinces of Canada, New Brunswick, Nova Scotia, and the Island of Prince Edward, &c. &c.

The humble Petition of a number of the Colored Inhabitants of the City of Montreal, Canada East,—Montreal, 19th February 1860.

Respectfully Sheweth,

That the undersigned Petitioners, loyal and dutiful subjects of Her Gracious Majesty Queen Victoria, and residing in the City of Montreal, Canada East, are desirous of proving their attachment to the British Crown under which they hold their rights and privileges as Free Citizens, in common with their brethren of European origin, humbly and respectfully solicit the Authority of Your Excellency as the Representative of Her Majesty in this part of Her Dominions, to allow your Petitioners to raise and organize from themselves a Volunteer Militia Company of Foot, in class B, to be dominated, if it should please Your Excellency, the Colored Company of Montreal Volunteer Rifles; to be drilled & exercised in conformity with the regulations of the Service in all respects.

That Your Petitioners pledge themselves should Your Excellency feel disposed to favor their views, to cloth themselves at their own expense, in a neat and appropriate uniform (subject to the approval of Your Excellency), and to conform in every way to the Militia Rules & Regulations,

That Your Petitioners venture most respectfully to bring to Your Excellency's notice, that in the West India Island belonging to Her Majesty, there exist many Companies of Militia composed entirely of the Colored population, who have at all times been found ready to do their duty when called on; and that the Regular Colored Colonial Regiments in the West Indies volunteered their Services to a man on the outbreak of the Indian Mutiny; thus proving that the Colored race, under a free and enlightened Government like that of Great Britain, are second to none in loyalty, fidelity and truthfulness to their Country and their Queen.

Your petitioners, in conclusion, would most respectfully entreat Your Excellency to grant them a favorable reply to this their earnest Petition, to be allowed to participate as Citizens, in the duties of the Militia Force of this valuable Colony; and should your Excellency under all the circumstances of Your Petitioners case, view the same in a favorable light, they, as in duty bound will ever pray—

Proposed Strength of Company

1 Captain	3 N.C. Officers
1 Lieutenant	1 Bugler
1 Ensign	59 Rank & File

[signed with 38 names]

Source: Gary Collison, *Shadrach Minkins: From Fugitive Slave to Citizen* (Cambridge, Mass.: Harvard University Press, 1997), 227–8.

François-Xavier Garneau

François-Xavier Garneau. Bibliothèque et Archives Nationales du Québec.

François-Xavier Garneau (1809–66) was born in Quebec (City) into a quite poor family, his father a man of shifting occupations. He was educated at local schools until age 12, when he entered a Lancastrian school for two years. His family was unable to afford the Séminaire de Québec, and Garneau instead became an assistant to the clerk of the Court of King's Bench before apprenticing as a notary in 1825. Throughout his life he was conscious of his lack of formal education. While an apprentice, he read widely and taught himself Latin, Italian, and English. In 1828 his employer recommended him as a travelling companion for an Englishman who visited the United States. Three years later, on his own initiative, he visited England and France. While in London, he accepted an appointment as Denis-Benjamin Viger's secretary, meeting many of the leading politicians of the time. He returned to Lower Canada in 1833, publishing

poetry and briefly editing a newspaper. Then, in 1834, he returned to the practice of notary and became an ardent nationalist.

By 1837 Garneau had determined to write the history of Canada, but he was apparently not active in the rebellions. In 1842 he was appointed as French translator to the Legislative Assembly, a post that gave him much free time and access to a number of libraries. Locating sources was one of the hardest problems for a historian when Garneau began his work. The first volume of his *Histoire du Canada*, taking events to 1701, appeared in August of 1845. It was heavily criticized for being unsympathetic to religion. At about this time he used his friendship with Edmund O'Callaghan (a Patriote who somehow became state archivist in New York) to consult documentary material copied from French archives. The new documents greatly enhanced the second volume of the *Histoire*, published in April 1846. Continued publication was hampered for some years by ill health, but volume 3 of the *Histoire* appeared in 1849, getting the story to 1792. Garneau disarmed his critics in this volume by declaring the unity of religion and nationality. For several years he worked on revision of the first three volumes (published in 1852, with an account of the period 1792–1840 appended). Here Garneau offered a narrative sympathetic to the Patriotes and highly critical of the Union of the Canadas. In 1855, Francois-Marie-Uncas Maximilien Bibaud, the son of Michel Bibaud, who had written a history hostile to the Patriots, wrote a piece attacking Garneau, referring to his work as "charlatanism in history." This attack could not undermine his growing reputation as French Canada's leading historian. Garneau, with the help of his son, prepared one more edition of the *Histoire*. It appeared in 1859, polishing the style and adding more documentation. A year later Andrew Bell produced an English translation. Garneau complained that the translation was too free and distorted his work, but it remains the version by which Garneau is known to English Canada. Self-taught and extremely conscious of his formal educational deficiencies, Garneau saw the history of French Canada as one of survival against "the Anglo-Saxon race." His work stood at the time as a denial of Lord Durham's sneering remarks about the lack of culture in French Canada. He remains today, for most French-speaking Canadians, the leading French-Canadian author of the nineteenth century and French Canada's greatest historian.

The Victorian era was fond of graphic illustrations of progress. Here four schoolhouses illustrate the improvements made from the early days of settlement to the 1860s. Such images were intended to show not just that education was available in the early settlements, but also to show how quickly it came into line with that of established communities, evolving from one-room structures to more significant structures. Beyond the buildings themselves, what other elements of these illustrations suggest that progression? Top: two "First Settlers' School-houses"; bottom left: "Country District School-house"; bottom right: "Village School-house." From H.Y. Hind, The Dominion of Canada: Containing a Historical Sketch of the Preliminaries and Organization of Confederation *(1869).*

audience and market for the arts and culture. Census data from 1861 suggest that more than 90 per cent of the population of Canada West could read, a tribute to the early introduction of free schooling. The figures were lower in Canada East, where over one-third of the population could not read in 1861, and in the Maritimes, where 22.6 per cent could not read and 32.7 per cent could not write. The 1871 census indicated that only just over 12 per cent of Ontarians could not write; the figure for Quebec was 45.8 per cent and for the Maritimes 23.3 per cent. The data suggest that French Canada remained a much more oral society than English Canada. Naturally, the younger members of society were more literate than their elders, and males in most places were more literate than females. Raw literacy data do not tell us much about how individual people employed their skills, but combined with increases in the number of libraries and the availability of books and newspapers, the figures suggest a marked increase in the audience for cultural productions.

The Road to Confederation

The political problems of the Canadas were the immediate stimulus for Canadian politicians to begin to explore the possibility of a larger union with the eastern provinces, beginning at the famous Charlottetown Conference of September 1864. Such a solution did not come out of thin air, however. Politicians had discussed the political unification of the provinces of British North America on and off since the days of the Loyalists. Few of the early proposals were very elaborate. Most gave no consideration to whether the proposed union would result in an independent national state. Most came from Tories concerned with enhancing the power of the Crown or providing a basis for economic development. By the 1850s, however, particularly in the Canadas, some sense was emerging of "a true Canadian feeling—a feeling of what might be termed Canadian nationality, in contradistinction to a feeling of mere colonial or annexation vassalage," as the Montreal *Pilot* put it on 6 April 1850. Sometimes these sentiments were couched in high-flown rhetoric. Often economic

or cultural protectionism dominated the phraseology, but a new Canadian nationalism was growing in power after mid-century. It flourished partly on changing communications technology that made it possible to transmit fast-breaking news across the provinces in moments. The royal tour of Prince Albert in 1860 suggested that British North America was already in some senses a political entity.

Neither the bind of the double majority nor the beginning of national sentiment was sufficient, however, to propel British North Americans to national unification. As so often had been the case, events in the United States provided the catalyst. The American federal union broke apart with surprising suddenness in 1861. The southern states seceded into their own Confederacy. The American Civil War began. Many Canadians quietly rooted for the Confederacy despite its maintenance of slavery. Britain adopted an official policy of neutrality. The British watched warily while public opinion in the northern states, whipped up by American newspapers, talked openly of finding compensation for the lost Confederacy by annexing British North America.

Britain could hardly leave its North American colonies unprotected. Defending them at great expense was not something the British faced with relish, however. By the 1860s the British ruling classes believed that colonies like British North America would inevitably separate from the mother country. Why not hasten the process and save money? An independent British North America could organize its own defences. In 1864 the military situation in the United States turned more dangerous for British North America, as the Union forces gained clear victories over the Confederacy. In several respects the efforts of the Canadians to create a larger union fitted very well with British desires for reduced colonial responsibility and expense. The full weight of the still considerable influence of the British colonial system came down on the side of unification.

In Canada the difficulty of agreeing to military mobilization was one of the many factors that led George Brown to propose a political coalition with his enemies. The understanding rested on a commitment to a British–American federal union. This Great Coalition—a ministry formed by a union of the Conservatives under

Blackfoot Shirt

This hide shirt, with its quillwork rondell, was part of the formal attire of the Blackfoot. Worn for ceremonial occasions and in warfare, the shirt displays the honours and history of the wearer. Pitt Rivers Museum, University of Oxford, 1893.67.2.

The Blackfoot Confederacy, or the *Siksikaitsitapi*, lived a nomadic lifestyle bounded by the Great Sand Hills of Saskatchewan and the Rocky Mountains. Buffalo hunters, the Blackfoot were one of a number of western First Nations who came into contact with European material culture long before they encountered a person of European origin. As with many Plains tribes, the most important of these was the horse. The horse and other objects of European origin were adapted to fit into their daily lives.

One of the best ways to see that adaptation is in the clothing they wore. The Blackfoot made intricately beaded shirts that were intended to show their accomplishments and prowess. Used to display identity, the shirts, originally made of hide, sinew, and other animal materials, eventually began to incorporate European materials such as beads and

cloth. European tools, like scissors, came to be used in the construction of these objects, and images of guns and other trade goods were incorporated in the quillwork and patterns displayed on the shirts themselves. Quillwork was incredibly difficult to produce, and was considered a sacred, female art among the Blackfoot. The patterns and preparation of quills required exceptional skill. Some shirts were also painted, with details of horses captured and enemies defeated.

The histories of those shirts that survive are complicated. The one pictured above, for example, is today a part of the Pitt Rivers Museum's ethnographic collections. It was given as part of a clothing exchange to Sir George Simpson of the Hudson's Bay Company at Fort Edmonton in 1841. The shirts sometimes were exchanged for "chiefs' coats," often scarlet cloth coats with lace on cuffs and collars. The exchange of garments was part of creating diplomatic trade and political alliances between groups.

While tensions still arise surrounding the ownership and repatriation of material culture of this type, collectors and collections like the one at Pitt Rivers Museum are responsible for the survival of many of these forms of First Nations heritage. Simpson's secretary, Edward Hopkins, ended up in possession of these shirts, and after he took them back to England in 1870 they were purchased in 1893 by the museum. Today, these objects are being given new life, informing groups like the Blackfoot of the skills and traditions of their ancestors. Modern technology has allowed the plant materials used for quill dying to be identified. They have also allowed the Blackfoot to reclaim the history and narratives of some of their ancestors, as the shirts serve as a form of document into the owner's history.

Source: Laura Peers, "Kaahsinnooniksi Ao'toksisawooyawa: Reconnections with the Historic Blackfoot Shirts," Pitt Rivers Museum, http://web.prm.ox.ac.uk/blackfootshirts/index.php/about-the-shirts/index.html.

Macdonald and the Bleus under Cartier, with the Grits led by Brown, announced in the Canadian Parliament on 22 June 1864—broke the political deadlock. The new government moved on a variety of fronts over the summer of 1864. Most important was to prepare the outlines of federal union for a conference of Maritime delegates called at Charlottetown in September to discuss Maritime union. The Maritime region contained a good deal of abstract support for unification with Canada, tempered by two realities: any Maritime participation in a larger union must not work to the disadvantage of the provinces, and many felt strongly that the Maritimes were doing pretty well within the existing imperial structure. Historians sympathetic to central Canada have tended to view the Maritime defence of local interests as parochial. Such an interpretation misses the point. One problem with the Canadian initiative was that Canada was so much bigger and more powerful than the other provinces that almost any union would seem more like annexation than confederation. The Maritimes, moreover, were already part

of a larger political and economic system known as the British Empire. Many Maritimers had travelled on sailing ships to the far corners of the world, and in many ways Maritime voters were far more cosmopolitan than the Canadians. At the time, the case against Confederation was quite reasonable. Unification seemed an impracticable visionary scheme, proposed by politicians in the Province of Canada to meet their needs. It was not necessarily in the best interests of the other colonies.

Considerable ingenuity was required in 1864 to explain to delegates from smaller constituencies how the Canadian proposal really worked to their benefit. The union as finally developed was somewhat different from the one initially proposed. The biggest difference was in the place of the provinces. The Canadians originally intended to create a strong central government by consolidating all the provincial legislatures (and their powers) into one grand Parliament. This procedure of legislative union was how Great Britain had earlier incorporated Scotland and Ireland. The Canadians

The Charlottetown Conference, September 1864. Charles Tupper is standing against the pillar on the left and D'Arcy McGee against the pillar second from the left, with George-Étienne Cartier in front of him; seated next to Cartier is John A. Macdonald. George P. Roberts, LAC, C-000733.

granted the need for local governments to deal with local matters. They did not intend those local governments to be fully articulated provincial governments, certainly not provincial governments capable of forming a counterweight to the central federal one. Neither Scotland nor Ireland (after union) had separate political administrations based upon legislatures, although both still had local governments. The Maritime delegates at Charlottetown responded to visions of greatness, fuelled by food, drink, and much convivial conversation. They agreed to the Canadian scheme. By the time of the Quebec Conference a month later, many had sober second thoughts.

Prince Edward Island took the lead at Quebec against the Canadian steamroller. The smallest province of British North America, the island had fought annexation to Nova Scotia for almost a century. It found it hard to give up its autonomy to proposals that reflected Canadian dominance. When John A. Macdonald moved that the three sections of British North America—Canada West, Canada East, and the four Atlantic provinces—each have 24 members in the Senate, he gave away the game. In the American Senate, each state had two senators regardless of population; in the Canadian Senate, the four smaller provinces would have only one-third of the senators among them. Eventually the Quebec Conference in October 1864 accepted this arrangement, offering Newfoundland an additional four senators. Prince Edward Island also made a big issue—without any success—over getting one more member of the House of Commons than its population allowed (six instead of five). A further and telling debate came over the power of the local governments. The majority case was that Canada's fundamental principle had always been that "all the powers not given to Local should be reserved to the Federal Government" (quoted in Waite, 1962: 95). But a number of Atlantic delegates were not happy. The subsequent debate over the Quebec resolutions was not over the principle of union but over its terms. While it would be convenient to see the matter of terms as a petty haggling over details, some of the details were fairly important.

Another Canadian principle was legislative sovereignty. "We the People" would not create this union, as in the United States. Instead, an Act of the British Parliament would create Canada. Conveniently enough, this denial

of popular sovereignty meant that Confederation did not go before the public in the form of an election, a ratification convention, or a referendum/plebiscite. But at the same time, the union had been worked out totally in a parliamentary context. The public debate on the Quebec resolutions did not always take into account the niceties of political theory. Critics understood the basic thrust of the proposals well enough, however, and the debate did affect their interpretation and ultimate implementation. While the Canadians had initially intended to reduce the provincial governments to municipal proportions, both French Canada and the Maritimes made clear that the provinces would have to survive relatively intact. The proponents of union in Canada East emphasized that Confederation meant giving French Canadians their own province, with—as the *Courrier de St-Hyacinthe* put it in September 1864—the two levels of government both "sovereign, each within its jurisdiction as clearly defined by the constitution." An informal adjustment addressed this matter. On the other hand, the opposition fulminated unsuccessfully to the end over the refusal of the proponents of Confederation to take the scheme to the people.

Newspapers, pamphlets, and debates held in the legislatures of each of the provinces discussed the Quebec resolutions. What these demonstrated most of all was the success of the proponents of union in capturing most of the positive ground. Critics could reduce the proposals to rubble, but had little to put in their place. For Canada, the absence of alternatives was particularly striking. The debates also demonstrated that the Quebec resolutions were, on the whole, far more acceptable to Tories than they were to Reformers. Although the debates in the Canadian Parliament were lengthy and long-winded, the ultimate result was approval. The eastern provinces could stand pat, however, and some did. Newfoundland—convinced it would be little more than "the contemptible fag-end of such a compact" with Canada after an election fought on the question in 1869—remained outside Confederation until 1949. Prince Edward Island felt insufficiently compensated for "the surrender of a separate Government, with the independent powers it now enjoys." It would not join until 1873.

The situation in New Brunswick and Nova Scotia was more complex. In the former province, a coalition of

Contemporary Views

Charles Tupper to Lord Carnarvon, 28 July 1866

Charles Tupper, Premier of Nova Scotia, explains his province's resistance to union with Canada.

In Nova Scotia Mr. Howe has organized an active and formidable opposition to the Union of the Lower Provinces with Canada and although Messrs. Archibald and McCully who have been the leaders of that opposition to the present government have co-operated with us most earnestly and are sustained by the uncommitted group of that party, yet the great body of the opposition will unite with Mr. Howe to defeat confederation and obtain power. On the other hand the Government have rendered themselves and many of their supporters extremely unpopular by carrying a measure providing for the support of education by direct taxation. Many of the Bankers and most wealthy merchants who formerly sustained us[,] under the impression that confederation will injure their position[,] have transferred their support to Mr. Howe. The financial position of Nova Scotia is in the most flourishing condition and the opponents of confederation excite the masses of the people by the assertion that their taxes will be increased to sustain the extravagance of a Canadian Government and to defend the long line of exposed Canadian frontier while the best interests of the Maratime [sic] Provinces will be sacrificed by a Government in whose Legislature their influence will be overborne by numbers. Just at the time when the friends of confederation were endeavouring to meet these arguments Mr. Galt proposed a Bill largely increasing the expenditure and the people of Nova Scotia are deeply annoyed at finding that the fisheries of the Maratime [sic] Provinces have been sacrificed by the adoption of the Canadian policy to issue fishing licenses to foreigners. Able agitators thus effectively armed with the means of inflaming the popular mind against Canada are obtaining numerously signed petitions to the Imperial Parliament against confederation and there can be no doubt that an appeal to the people would result in the reversal of the resolution to the Legislature in favor of the Union and the defeat of the measure for many years. Indeed so strong is the feeling against Canada on the question of the fisheries that I have reason to fear that any delay in consummating the Union may involve the members of the Legislature by whose votes a majority was obtained to sanction the Union memorialising Her Majesty in opposition to any action being taken thereon until it has been submitted to the people.

Source: G.P.L. Browne, ed., *Documents on the Confederation of British North America* (Toronto: McClelland and Stewart, 1969), 192–3.

opponents to union headed by A.J. Smith (1822–83) blew away the pro-Confederation government of Samuel Leonard Tilley (1818–96) in an 1865 election. A year later another election was held against the background of threatened invasion by thousands of Irish nationalists (the Fenians), many of them veterans of the American Union army who had kept their arms when disbanded. The threat was sufficient to return Tilley to office. The new administration moved an address favouring Confederation, not, it must be noted, as embodied in the Quebec resolutions but "upon such terms as will secure the just rights and interests of New Brunswick, accompanied with provision for the immediate construction of the Intercolonial Railway." When this motion carried, opposition disappeared.

In Nova Scotia, which owned one ton of sailing ship for each of its 350,000 inhabitants, there was much concerted opposition to union. Joseph Howe led the opponents of Confederation. He attacked the union's Canadian origins from the vantage point of someone perfectly content with the British Empire. Confederation smacked too much of Canadian self-interest. It gave Upper Canada rep by pop and Lower Canada provincial autonomy, but offered nothing to Nova Scotia. The Nova Scotia legislature never did approve the Quebec resolutions. The government, led by Charles Tupper (1821–1915), introduced a motion calling for a "scheme of union" in which "the rights and interests of Nova Scotia" would be ensured (quoted in Pryke, 1979: 27). It passed by a vote of 31 to 19. Unlike their counterparts in New Brunswick, the opponents of Confederation in Nova Scotia did not melt away. They eventually went on to elect full slates of candidates provincially and federally that promised to take Nova Scotia out of the union in which it had become involved.

Although neither Nova Scotia nor New Brunswick ever actually approved the Quebec resolutions—which all but the most ardent unionists recognized would consign the smaller provinces to national impotence—the fundamentals laid down at Quebec became the basis of the new Constitution. Small wonder that the region later complained about the deal they had made. In November 1866 delegates from Canada, Nova Scotia, and New Brunswick met in London to work out the final details, essentially the Quebec resolutions with more money for the Maritimes and the Intercolonial Railway. All agreed that the name of the new country should be that of its principal progenitor, thus openly declaring the primacy of Canada in the arrangement and causing confusion ever afterwards for students of Canadian history. The resulting legislation, the British North America Act, passed quickly through the British Parliament in 1867. The MPs barely looked up from the order paper as they voted. The Queen signed the bill into law on 29 March 1867, with the date of proclamation 1 July. Governor General Lord Monck (1819–94) called upon John A. Macdonald, the man everyone most closely associated with the union, to be the first Prime Minister.

On the morning of 1 July—a day of celebration and military parades in all four provinces—the new country was proclaimed in the recently completed Parliament buildings in Ottawa. Macdonald received a knighthood. The ceremonial launching of the new nation did not, however, guarantee its success. Much work still would be needed to make Canada an integrated nation.

The road to Confederation was a complex one, with many paths coming together. The British cut British North America free from their mercantile system. The British North Americans naturally were drawn to the continental economy, and began to build railroads and industrialize. The Province of Canada cast covetous glances westward, where the hold of the Hudson's Bay Company was weakened by the beginnings of settlement. A unified Canada was not only more powerful but also a leader in achieving responsible government and in producing a new imperial relationship. Immigration to British North America continued, producing much mobility, which in turn led to a need for roots. Population growth brought a new cultural infrastructure. By the 1860s, the Canadians were ready to take the lead in creating an expanded nation, which they did against the judgement of many in the Atlantic region.

Although 1 July 1867 would be celebrated a century later as the date for Canada's 100th birthday, it was in the larger sense only an interim point. The new union consisted of four provinces—Ontario, Quebec, Nova Scotia, and New Brunswick—carved from the three that had created it. Sir John A. Macdonald's government was conscious that a lot of British territory on the continent had been excluded. The new government was also quite obviously the old Canadian coalition, with a few Maritime faces added. Its organization was the former Canadian departments. It used buildings erected in Ottawa for the old Province of Canada. If the new administration seemed familiar, so did many of its policies.

Adding New Territory

One of the earliest legislative actions of the new Canadian government in December 1867 was the passage of resolutions calling for transcontinental expansion. Most of the legislators regarded such expansion as the nation's inevitable right, a sort of Canadian version of manifest destiny. As a result, in 1868 a ministerial delegation went to London to arrange the Hudson's Bay Company's transfer of the Northwest to Canada. While complex negotiations continued, the Canadian government began building a road from Fort Garry to Lake of the Woods. This was part of a proposed road and water system linking Red River with Canada. The road builders established informal connections with Dr John

Christian Schultz (1840–96), the influential leader of the local faction that had been agitating for Canadian annexation for years. Nobody paid any attention to the Métis who constituted the bulk of the local population of the settlement. The Canadian delegation in London finally worked out a deal for the transfer. The British government received the territory from the Hudson's Bay Company (the Canadians put up £300,000 and agreed to substantial land grants for the Company) and subsequently transferred it intact to Canada.

Since the arrangements for the West were made without bothering to inform the Red River people of their import, it was hardly surprising that the locals were suspicious and easily roused to protest. The Métis were concerned on several counts. The road-building party had been involved in a number of racist incidents. There was transparent haste on the part of the Canadian government to build a road and to send in men to survey land. This rush suggested that Canadian settlement would inundate the existing population without regard for their "rights." Canada made clear that it intended to treat the new territory as a colony. Furthermore, some of the road builders bought land cheaply from the Aboriginal peoples—land that the Métis thought was theirs. The Métis quickly perceived the Canadians as a threat to their way of life, perhaps even to their existence. The Canadian government received a number of warnings in 1869 that trouble was brewing. The warnings came from the Anglican archbishop of Rupert's Land, Robert Machray (1831–1904); from the governor of the Hudson's Bay Company, William Mactavish (1815–70); and from Bishop Alexandre Taché (1823–94), the Catholic bishop of St Boniface. Ottawa received all such reports with little or no interest. Subsequent events were largely a consequence of avoidable Canadian blunders and insensitivities. In colonial thralldom itself until only a few years previously, Canada had little experience in managing imperial expansion. It handled the project very clumsily, and the entire nation would pay dearly for its mistakes.

In October 1869 a leader of the Métis emerged in the person of Louis Riel (1844–85), a member of a leading family in the community. His father, for whom he was named, had successfully led a Métis protest in 1849 against the Hudson's Bay Company,

which had won the right to trade freely in furs. The young Riel spoke out publicly against the surveys. He then led a party that stood on the surveyors' chains and ordered them to stop. In the meantime, William McDougall (1822–1905) was on his way from Canada to assume office as lieutenant-governor of the North-West. A newly formed National Committee of the Métis resolved that McDougall should not be allowed to enter the country. The Métis made it clear that they would oppose him by force if necessary. Canada responded to the unrest by refusing to take over the territory until it was pacified. Riel escalated the conflict. In early November he and a large band of armed Métis took possession of Upper Fort Garry, the Hudson's Bay Company central headquarters. The Métis then invited the anglophone inhabitants of the settlement, most of whom were mixed bloods themselves, to send delegates to meet and co-ordinate policy. Riel managed to get tacit consent for the establishment of a provisional government and approval of a "list of rights." On 7 December he and his men surrounded Dr Schultz's store, taking Schultz and 48 Canadians to Fort Garry as prisoners. The next day Riel issued a "Declaration of the People," announcing a provisional government. He declared that the people of Red River wanted to be allowed to negotiate their own entry into Confederation on the basis of the "rights" already agreed to by the residents. William McDougall made a fool of himself with an illegal proclamation of his government—Canada having refused to take possession of the territory—and then returned home.

Louis Riel marshalled his forces brilliantly. A convention of 40 representatives, equally divided between the two language groups, debated and approved another "list of rights." The convention endorsed Riel's provisional government. It appointed three delegates to go to Ottawa to negotiate with the Macdonald government. So far, so good. But in early March, Thomas Scott, a prisoner who was an Orangeman, got into trouble with Riel and his guards. A Métis court martial condemned Scott to death without offering him a chance to be heard. Riel accepted the sentence, commenting, "We must make Canada respect us." The "murder" of Scott would have enormous repercussions in Orange Ontario, which was looking desperately for an excuse to condemn the Red River

A Red River Letter

Louis Riel, a carte-de-visite portrait taken in Ottawa following his election as member of Parliament for Provencher, Manitoba, in 1873. Notman Studio, LAC, 1957-049, C-002048.

This letter, dated 6 October 1869, represents the earliest written statement of the Métis case for opposition to Canada. The letter was probably drafted by Louis Riel. It claims no authority except "the people themselves," meeting in an assembly composed of two representatives of each parish. The letter claims "indisputable rights" that are unspecified.

St Boniface, 6 Oct., 1869
Dear Mr Editor,

. . . Several newspapers of Upper and Lower Canada have freely published their views on what inconveniences might arise in the organization . . . [of a territorial government by Canada for Red River]. And now that the Canadian people have heard these different discussions, would they not be glad to know what the people of Red River themselves think of all that? Here it is:

They do not appear to be at all ready to receive a Canadian governor. A Council chosen and constituted outside the country cannot hope, we think, to see its decrees highly respected. One perhaps can judge by the demonstrations which the Métis population of Red River has just made. Each parish has elected two representatives in order that they might pronounce in its name on the proceedings of the Canadian government with respect to the people of Red River, and the following are the resolutions that these representatives have passed in their first assembly:

1. These representatives declare in the name of the Métis population of Red River that they are loyal subjects of Her Majesty the Queen of England.

2. These representatives acknowledge themselves, in the name of the Métis population of Red River, beholden to the Honourable Hudson's Bay Company for the protection which they have received under the government of that Company whatever the nature of that government may have been.

3. The people of Red River having till now upheld and supported the government of the Honourable Hudson's Bay Company, which has been established in the country by the Crown of England, the said representatives declare, in the name of the Métis population of Red River, that Snow and Dennis have disregarded the law of nations in coming to carry out public work here in the name of an alien authority without paying any attention to the authority to-day existing in the country.

4. The Honourable Hudson's Bay Company being about to lay down the government of Red River, the said representatives declare, in the name of the Métis population of Red River, that they are ready to submit to that change. But at the same time, being settled, working and living on the lands which they have assisted the Company [to open

Continued...

up, the people] of Red River, having acquired in the above manner [indisputable rights in that country,] the representatives of the Métis population of Red River loudly proclaim those rights.

5. The colony of Red River having always been subject to the Crown of England, and having developed in isolation, through all the hazards of its situation, the said representatives declare in the name of the Métis population of Red River, that they will do everything necessary to have the privileges accorded so liberally by the Crown of England to every English colony respected on their behalf.

There, Mr Editor, is what we would like to communicate to you. And those who take the liberty to send these things to you will not be the last to ensure that the rights of the people of Red River may be respected.

—TWO MÉTIS SETTLERS OF RED RIVER

Source: *Courrier de Saint-Hyacinthe*, 28 Oct. 1869, as translated in W.L. Morton, ed., *Alexander Begg's Red River Journal* (Toronto: The Champlain Society, 1956), 411–13. Reprinted by permission of the publisher.

This photograph shows Louis Riel at the centre of his provisional government sometime in early 1870. In the top row, left to right, are Bonnet Tromage, Pierre de Lorme, Thomas Bunn, Xavier Page, Baptiste Beauchemin, Baptiste Tournond, and Thomas Spence. In the middle row are Pierre Poitras, John Bruce, Louis Riel, John O'Donoghue, and François Dauphenais. In the front row are Robert O'Lone and Paul Proulx. Although Canada had not annexed Red River in December 1869 as planned, it never admitted that the provisional government was legal. LAC, PA-12854.

BACKGROUNDER

Canada First

In April of 1868, a young man named Charles Mair headed to Ottawa to see his first book through the press. He soon fell in with an old friend, Henry J. Morgan, a clerk in the office of the secretary of state and author of the 1862 book *Sketches of Celebrated Canadians*. Morgan introduced Mair to three other visitors to Ottawa: George Taylor Denison III, William Alexander Foster, and Robert Grant Haliburton. All five men were writers, all were bachelors, and only Haliburton was over 30. They quickly discovered their common interests and fell into the habit of spending the early evening listening to the parliamentary debates in the House of Commons before returning to Morgan's rooms at the Revere Hotel to discuss public affairs over smokes and drinks. During the period between 15 April and 20 May 1868, the five young bachelors formed a secret society later called "Canada First." Inspired by the assassination of D'Arcy McGee, they agreed on the evil of provincialism and the need to inculcate a new "national spirit." They also agreed on the necessity of securing for the new Dominion the vast territory west of Ontario. Except for Haliburton, who was from Nova Scotia, the remaining four were Upper Canadians who were sensitive about being colonials and who wanted increased Canadian autonomy under an imperial umbrella.

Like many Canadians of their day, the five young men also believed in the innate superiority of white Anglo-Saxon Protestants. Haliburton was one of the earliest exponents of the notion that Canadians were the heirs of the Aryan northmen of the Old World. He told the Montreal Literary Club in March 1869 that the new Canadian nationality comprised "the Celtic, the Teutonic, and the Scandinavian elements," and embraced "the Celt, the Norman French, the Saxon and the Swede." Canada Firsters looked down their noses at Aboriginal peoples and the Métis. They saw the French as the great "bar to progress, and to the extension of a great Anglo-Saxon Dominion across the Continent," as the Toronto *Globe* put it on 4 March 1870. They were utterly contemptuous of "half-breeds."

Canada First remained only a debating society until the spring of 1870, when it determined to orchestrate public sentiment to the execution of Thomas Scott by the provisional government of Red River headed by Louis Riel. The reaction in Ontario to Riel before Scott's death had been fairly quiet, but by denouncing the execution of Scott, a member of the Orange Lodge, in editorials planted in leading newspapers—it was "like putting a match to tinder," George Denison later wrote—the Canada Firsters managed to inflame Protestant Ontario against Louis Riel and his Métis followers.

In a huge public meeting in Toronto in April, Canada First introduced three resolutions that were passed easily. The first endorsed resistance of the usurpation of power by "the murderer Riel." The second advocated decisive measures to suppress the uprising, and the third declared that it would be gross injustice to negotiate with emissaries of a government who "have robbed, imprisoned and murdered loyal Canadians, whose only fault was zeal for British institutions, whose only crime was devotion to the old flag." As a result of the Canada First intervention, negotiations between Ottawa and Red River had to be conducted unofficially, the military expedition to Red River was allowed to go forward, and the leaders of the Red River resistance received no amnesty for their deeds in 1869–70.

uprising. The three-man delegation from Red River, headed by Abbé Noël Ritchot (1825–1905), gained substantial concessions from the Canadian government. If honoured, they would guarantee some protection for the original inhabitants of Red River against the expected later influx of settlers and land speculators. In what the Canadians always regarded as an act of extortion at the point of a gun, the Métis obtained the Manitoba Act of 1870. This legislation granted provincial status to a Manitoba roughly equivalent to the old Red River settlement, with 1.4 million acres (566,580 ha) set aside for the Métis and bilingual services guaranteed. The remainder of the North-West became a territory of Canada. One of its government's principal tasks was to extinguish Aboriginal title through the negotiation of treaties with the Indigenous peoples. These agreements would open the way for settlement by people of European origin.

In May 1870 the Canadian government sent a so-called peaceful military expedition to Red River. The troops occupied the province for Canada in late August, forcing Riel and his associates to flee for their lives. The Scott execution provided the Canadian government with the excuse to deny Riel and his lieutenants an official amnesty for all acts committed during the "uprising." Those who negotiated with Canada always insisted that such an amnesty had been unofficially promised. The result was that Louis Riel went into long-term exile instead of becoming premier of the province he had created. (An amnesty was granted Riel in 1875, on the condition that he be banished from the country for five years.) Whether the government would keep better faith over its land guarantees to the Métis was another matter.

After the postage-stamp province called Manitoba was taken out, the remainder of the territory transferred to Canada by the Hudson's Bay Company—the North-West Territories—was initially administered under the original legislation passed by the Canadian Parliament in 1869 to deal with the West. It clearly envisioned a region held in colonial tutelage, with both government and natural resources under the strict control of Canada. The lieutenant-governor of Manitoba also served as lieutenant-governor of the Territories. The temporary legislation of 1869 was renewed without change in 1871. Not until 1872 were the Territories actually given even an appointed council. It consisted of 11 members, only two of which resided in the region. The other nine lived in or near Winnipeg, and initial meetings of the council were held there. Only in 1905—long after a second rebellion, in 1885—was provincial status finally granted to the Territories, which became Saskatchewan and Alberta.

While the question of Rupert's Land dragged slowly to its conclusion, the Canadian government was presented with an unexpected (although not totally unsolicited) gift. It consisted of a request from British Columbia—to which Vancouver Island had been joined in 1866—for admission into the new union. The initiative from the Pacific colony had originated with the Nova Scotia-born journalist Amor De Cosmos (William Alexander Smith, 1825–97), a member of the colony's legislative council. As early as March 1867 he had introduced a motion that the British North America Act, then about to be passed by the British Parliament, allow for the eventual admission of British Columbia. Entry into Confederation would introduce responsible government and resolve the colony's serious financial difficulties, which resulted partly from the interest on debts incurred for road building during the gold rushes. Union with Canada received an additional impetus when—coterminous with the passage of the British North America Act but quite independent of it—the American government purchased Alaska from the Russians. The purchase touched off demands in the American press for the annexation of British Columbia as well. Officially the British notified the colony in November 1867 that no action would be taken on its relationship with Canada until Rupert's Land had been duly incorporated into the new nation.

Union with Canada was debated by the British Columbia Legislative Council in March 1870. This debate was different from earlier ones in the eastern legislatures, for the British North America Act was already in place and in operation. British Columbia could not hope to influence the shape of Confederation, only to decide whether it would enter the union and upon what terms. The debate was a bit curious. The opponents of Confederation wanted the issues of popular elections (in an elected assembly) and responsible government cleared up in advance of union, while the pro-confederates—the government party—were quite satisfied with the local status quo.

Negotiations between British Columbia and Canada took place in the late spring of 1870. The Canadians were generous to a fault. Of course, British Columbia could have responsible government. Of course, the debt would be wiped out. Of course, there would be subsidies and grants, as well as federal support for the naval station at Esquimalt. And, of course, British Columbia could have a rail link with Canada, to be begun within

Confederation Complete

To-day, British Columbia passed peacefully and, let us add, gracefully into the confederated empire of British North America. Perhaps it would be more proper to put it thus: To-day the confederated empire of British North America stretches to the shores of the Pacific, "whose limpid waters" to quote the poetic language of Mr. J. Spencer Thompson, "leave in baptismal welcome to brow of the new-born Province which forms the last link in the transcontinental chain—the last star in the constellation which is destined hereafter to shine so brightly in the northern hemisphere." To-day the great scheme of Confederation in British North America may be regarded as practically complete. It is true that two islands of the Atlantic (Prince Edward and Newfoundland) still stand aloof. But Confederation can get on without them much better than they can get on without it. . . . To-day British Columbia and Canada join hands and hearts across the Rocky Mountains, and John Bull the younger stands with one foot on the Atlantic and the other on the Pacific—with his back to the North Pole and his face looking southward—how far we will not now venture to predict. Let the larger political union which we celebrate to-day be symbolic of a union of parties, of purpose and of action. Let the people of this Pacific Province accustom themselves to think of the Dominion as a second edition of Great Britain, and let all learn to regard each other as a band of brothers upon whom has devolved the honor and the responsibility of laying the foundations of empire. There is a feeling in the minds of some that the day which celebrates the nuptials of British Columbia and Canada at the same time celebrates the divorce of the former from the parent empire, and this feeling may tend to damp the enthusiasm of such as are the subjects of it: and we readily confess that, did not ground for the idea exist, we would sympathise with the feeling it is calculated to beget. Not only is there no ground for the idea, but the reverse is actually true. Instead of the union we celebrate weakening those bonds which connect us with the parent empire, it will impart additional strength and vitality to them. It will release us from the red tape and sealing wax of Downing street, it is true—but then, it will draw us nearer to the throne. It will do more. It will draw together all the peoples of British North America into one common brotherhood and beget a national sentiment, a sentiment more truly British than would be compatible with isolation and discontent. Let the union we celebrate be suggestive of a drawing together, a harmonizing and a nationalizing of all those sometime discordant elements which have culminated in local faction; and while joining hands with Canada in the grand and patriotic work of building up a second British Empire on this continent, let us join hands among ourselves in a friendly but firm resolve to begin our new political life a united and harmonious band for the purpose of making British Columbia—what Nature designed her to be—the Queen Province of the Dominion. With one common nationality, one common interest, one object should now actuate every heart and obliterate all those lines created by the factions of the past.

Source: From *The British Colonist* (Victoria), 20 July 1871

under control; they had to get the voters up and were responsible therefore. The cry went round that both sides had a number of voters locked up and were feeding them with whisky, to get them into proper trim; altho this accusation was not strictly true, still voters came to the polling place, where the Courts of Justice now stand, in files. Notwithstanding all this there were no rows outside the polling places, the matter was too serious for this. At length 4 o'clock struck—the polls closed; everyone tired—thirsty, hoarse and expectant. The Anti-confederates had won handsomely. . . .

two years and completed within 15 years. The promise was audacious, although Canada obviously needed a transcontinental railroad to match the lines rapidly being constructed across the United States. The terms were far better than expected, and on 20 July 1871 British Columbia entered Confederation as the sixth province. While in most respects the new province remained isolated until the completion of the rail link in 1885, Confederation encouraged the development of a new land policy for the province. The provincial government opened its Crown lands to massive pre-emption and free land grants; the largesse of British Columbia would far exceed that of the federal government.

Prince Edward Island's acceptance of terms in 1873 was almost anticlimactic. The tiny province had tried to survive without much support from the British, who made clear their lack of enthusiasm for a Crown colony. The imperial refusal to pay the salary of the lieutenant-governor was seen as a "confederate screw unfairly put upon us." Both the Americans and the Canadians actively wooed the island. In the end, it entered Confederation in the wake of a profligate policy of railway construction, which many saw as a scheme to force it into union. As well as offering to take over the debt and the railway, Canada agreed to guarantee continuous communication with the mainland and to help buy out the last of the old landed proprietors. Only one island MLA, the crusty farmer Cornelius Howatt, refused to vote for the Canadian offer.

Unlike Prince Edward Island, Newfoundland was not persuaded to join the union at all. In 1869 Newfoundland held an election fought on the issue of Confederation with Canada. The economy improved in the period before the election, while the opponents of Confederation employed every argument in their rhetorical arsenal. These included rumours that Canada would use Newfoundland children as wadding for their cannons. The 1869 election went decisively against the pro-confederates. The island's Catholics opposed union. In one Catholic area, a pro-confederate candidate was greeted by priest and populace carrying pots of pitch and bags of feathers. The Protestant vote split equally. In the end the election returned nine confederates and 21 antis. The confederates blamed their defeat on the nasty campaign tactics of the opposition, but Newfoundland's union with Canada was not a matter of high priority for anyone. Both the British and Canadian governments acquiesced in Newfoundland's continued autonomy—despite sporadic union discussions as in 1887 and 1895—until 1949.

While adding new territory, the Canadian government also had to pacify Nova Scotia and New Brunswick. This was especially true of Nova Scotia, where pledged anti-confederates took both federal and provincial seats in the election that accompanied union. The British government refused to allow reconsideration of the initial decision to join Canada, chiefly on the grounds that such important political actions should not be taken at the whim of local electorates. The leading anti, Joseph Howe, eventually accepted that there was no alternative to accepting confederation. In February 1869 Howe ran as a pro-confederate in a federal election in Hants County, which was hotly contested. He won with a comfortable majority and headed off to Ottawa, joining the federal cabinet within weeks. In some ways this grudging acquiescence in a situation with which he did not

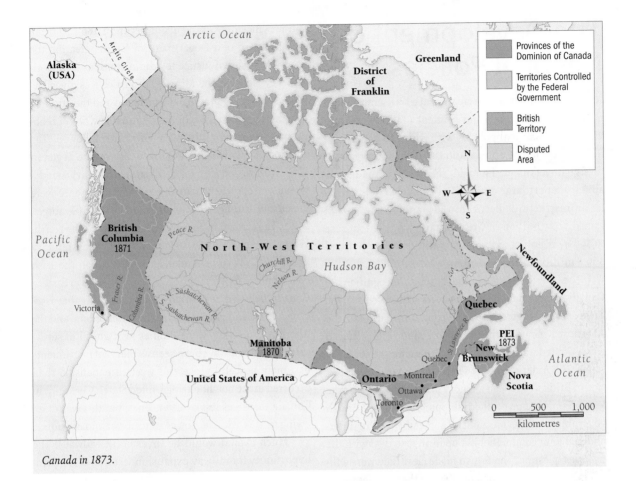

Canada in 1873.

agree may have been the most important political act of his career.

By 1873 Canada as a nation stretched from east coast to west coast, but not from the American border to the Arctic. Early in 1874, however, the British government received inquiries about the ownership of the Arctic Islands in Cumberland Gulf. Uncertain about its claim to sovereignty, the Colonial Office decided to transfer the land of the Arctic Islands to Canada, providing Canada was "prepared to assume the responsibility of exercising surveillance over it as may be necessary to prevent the occurrence of lawless acts or other abuses." The Hudson's Bay Company denied that it had ever claimed the territory, and so had not sold it to Canada in 1870. The government of Alexander Mackenzie told Britain in November of 1874 that it was "desirous" of assuming Arctic responsibility, but wanted more information. The

documents relating to the transfer were finally tabled in the Canadian House of Commons in 1878, and a joint address to the Queen from the Canadian Senate and House of Commons accepted the transfer, but asked for an imperial Act of Parliament with precise details about the boundaries. Still uncertain about title, the British were not anxious for imperial legislation, and Canada ultimately agreed to an Order-in-Council, which stated that as of 1 September 1880 all British territory in the North, except Newfoundland and its dependencies, was "annexed to and form part of the . . . Dominion of Canada." The Canadian government was not told about the British reservations over title, and would not learn of them for another 40 years. On the other hand, during the years after 1880 Canada did not do much to exercise sovereignty over the vast region of the North it had apparently acquired.

The Development of National Policies

As well as completing the creation of a transcontinental nation, the Macdonald government gradually improvised some national policies with which to govern the new Dominion. Confederation was encouraging to foreign investment. From its inception, Canada was able to import large amounts of capital to help create its infrastructure. Between 1865 and 1869 Canada raised $16.5 million in Great Britain, a figure that rose to $96.4 million in 1870–4, $74.7 million in 1875–9, and $69.8 million in 1880–4.

The government obtained some recognition of Canadian diplomatic autonomy by its acquiescence to the Treaty of Washington in 1871. Outstanding issues with the Americans included the *Alabama* claims. The *Alabama* was a Confederate raider built in Britain for the southern states. The Americans, half-seriously, demanded the cession of British-American territory in compensation for the losses it inflicted on northern shipping. In 1871 the British government made Macdonald a member of an international joint commission set up in 1870 to deal with the fisheries question. The British made clear they were willing to surrender Canadian interests in the fisheries to settle outstanding Anglo–American differences. Macdonald signed the resulting treaty. On the domestic front, the banking system of the new nation grew rapidly from 123 chartered bank branches in 1869 to 279 in 1879 and 426 by 1890. Two major pieces of national legislation were the Dominion Notes Act of 1870 and the Bank Act of 1871. The former allowed the government to issue circulating notes of small denominations, only partly backed by specie. The latter exerted control over the banking system. The Bank Act specified capital requirements for banks, prohibited new foreign-owned banks, and supplied general regulation. Canada accepted the international gold standard, but the government would share the issuance of currency (and the control of the creation of money) with the banks until well into the twentieth century.

One of the major new developments of the Macdonald government was a new federal system of justice for the new nation commensurate with Confederation's division of the administration of justice between federal and provincial governments. It began in 1868 with the establishment of a Department of Justice, creating the post of Minister of Justice to administer it as well as an Attorney General; the Minister of Justice was given the task of reviewing provincial legislation and the attorney general the supervision of the criminal law. Other renovations to the administration of justice followed. The creation of a national penitentiary system also began in 1868, with the enactment of a statute that envisioned a prison system where punishment and deterrence were meted out through discipline and rewards (Swainger, 2000). The Canadian government established the North-West Mounted Police in 1873 to act as its quasi-military agent in the West. It modelled the NWMP on the Irish constabulary. Its officers, drawn from the elites of eastern Canada, believed in a notion of public stability that associated crime and violence with the "lower orders" and the Aboriginal peoples. The Mounties kept ahead of settlement and have always been seen as the chief instruments of a more peaceful process of western expansion than occurred in the neighbouring United States. Certainly, in Canada there was less overt violence, but this was often owing to the early exertion of state power and control.

Much capital would be invested in railways. The opportunity for railway expansion was one of the principal arguments for Confederation. Railways were a prime target of foreign investors. The Macdonald government was slow to move on a transcontinental line, chiefly because of the enormous expense involved in building so far ahead of population needs. To some extent, the offer to British Columbia cast the die. There followed an unseemly scuffling over a charter, awarded in 1873 by Parliament to the Canada Pacific Railway Company of Sir Hugh Allan (1810–82). Then the Pacific Scandal broke. Allan had provided the government with money for its 1872 election campaign. Macdonald was unable to steer totally clear of the corrupt dealings. In November 1873 the government resigned. Replacing it was a Liberal government headed by a Scottish-born former stonemason, Alexander Mackenzie (1822–92). He sought to build a transcontinental line more gradually, using public funds. He also encouraged private interests to hook up with American western lines. Trains began running from Minnesota to Winnipeg late in 1878.

(Dominick) Edward Blake

Edward Blake. LAC, D #20738, Ewing, C-30444.

Born in London, Upper Canada, to evangelical Anglican parents from Northern Ireland, Edward Blake (1833–1912) attended Upper Canada College and the University of Toronto (BA, 1854), where he developed a reputation for fierce intellectuality and intensely hard work. These would combine with a moral rigidity to disable him frequently in later life. Becoming a lawyer specializing in equity, he became highly successful and wealthy at an early age; he was lecturing in equity at the University of Toronto before his thirtieth birthday. A conscience-driven Anglican, he was soon sought after as a politician, winning both provincial and federal seats in the first elections after Confederation. In 1869 he introduced into the Ontario legislature motions opposing change to the British North America Act without consultation with the provinces, an early statement of provincial rights.

In 1871 he became Premier of Ontario, but in 1872 was forced to decide between federal and provincial politics when dual representation was abolished. He chose the Dominion, and began a curious federal career of refusing to take on positions of responsibility that he desperately wanted, beginning with the leadership of the Reform Party in March 1873. His problem was continual nervous collapse, brought about by overwork and personal anxiety—contemporaries said he suffered from neurasthenia—exacerbated by aggravation at not being offered positions he thought he deserved because of concerns about his instability. Given his extreme ego, this was a recipe for trouble. During the 1870s he consorted with the Canada First movement and was a firm opponent of Louis Riel, but he would temporize on Riel in 1885–6. In 1874 he made an unsuccessful attempt to replace Alexander Mackenzie as Prime Minister, following up with a notorious speech at Aurora, Ontario, which staked out his political creed, including expanded suffrage, imperial federation, and Senate reform. In 1875 he became Minister of Justice, subsequently declining the appointment as first Chief Justice of the newly created Supreme Court. He resigned his post in 1877 because of ill health, returning to politics in 1880 as leader of the Liberal Party. As leader he dealt unsuccessfully with the discontent of Catholics and French Canadians, continually threatening resignation until finally stepping down in June 1887. Out of office, he became a firm opponent of the unrestricted reciprocity that captured many Liberals at this time. In 1892 he unexpectedly removed himself from Canadian politics by accepting a seat in the British Parliament as an Irish Nationalist, serving until 1907. Blake's weaknesses were many, and could not be overcome by sheer intelligence and hard work.

Mackenzie's government was also largely responsible for the initial funding of western railway construction. It gave the railway companies large land grants along the right of way. Although Canada developed a seemingly generous homestead policy by which pioneers could receive free land grants in return for developing the land, the generosity was deceptive. Almost no homestead land was available within easy access to the rail lines. Most early settlers ended up purchasing their land, either from the railways or from the Hudson's Bay Company.

Mackenzie's government had a number of positive achievements to its credit. It resolved the Louis Riel question in 1875 by granting the Métis leader an amnesty, conditional on his residence in exile for five years. It established the Supreme Court of Canada that same year, and subsequently created the office of the Auditor General. But the real importance of the Mackenzie government was its demonstration that the nation could be governed without serious upheaval by another political party with different policies from the one led by Sir John A. Macdonald. Mackenzie was a man without charisma, however, and many critics thought he spent too much energy micromanaging the budget.

The probity of his government did not save Alexander Mackenzie in 1878. Sir John A. Macdonald returned to power. Recognizing the temper of the times, Macdonald worked hard to restore in the public mind a sense of identification between his party and the process of nation-building. Decisiveness and flamboyance were part of the image. Even before the election was called, Macdonald had his platform. He introduced into the House of Commons a resolution "That this House is of the opinion that the welfare of Canada requires the adoption of a National Policy, which, by a judicious readjustment of the Tariff, will benefit and foster the agricultural, the mining, the manufacturing, and other interests of this Dominion" (quoted in Easterbrook and Watkins, 1962: 238). The Tory leader invented neither the policy nor the term used to describe it. Both went well back into the history of the Province of Canada, which had begun using a tariff as an instrument of both protection and revenue in the late 1840s. Nor did John A. Macdonald ever articulate the version of the National Policy as it was later lovingly described by economic historians and textbook writers. But he certainly rec-

ognized some relationship involving tariffs, manufacturing, employment, and national prosperity. He also wanted a transcontinental railway and the accompanying western settlement necessary to make it a reality. All these features had been and remained a traditional part of Canadian economic expansionism.

What Macdonald achieved was masterful in its own way. He succeeded in persuading a large number of Canadians in all provinces that policies strongly driven by the economic self-interest of some of the people in some of its constituent parts were in the best interest of the nation as a whole. He then persuaded the electorate that his party was the one that had successfully built the nation and would continue to do so. The fact that the opposition party took the lead in developing a different and less overt version of nation-building helped in this identification.

The responsibility for immigration policy had been divided between the Dominion and the provinces by the British North America Act. Both the Macdonald governments and the Mackenzie government sought to develop federal supremacy over immigration policy, in large measure to make possible the rapid settlement of the West. The Dominion also began to set rules indicating which immigrants would be acceptable. The federal Parliament passed its first immigration legislation in 1869 and, in 1872, prohibited the entry of criminals and other "vicious classes." That same year Parliament passed the Dominion Lands Act, which created homesteading privileges on western lands. The Dominion then began extensive advertising in Europe for new settlers. While the Canadian government discouraged the Métis from settling in concentrated blocks of land, in the mid-1870s it negotiated with several European groups, including the Mennonites and the Icelanders, for group settlement in Manitoba.

The first successful arrangements for block settlement were conducted by the Canadian government with Russian Mennonites beginning in 1872 and 1873. These Mennonites were European Quakers committed to pacifism who had originated in Prussia and Poland in the sixteenth century. They were driven out of their homes by threats of military conscription in Frederick the Great's Prussia, finding an asylum in Russia, where Catherine II offered them generous conditions of resettlement, including land, freedom of religion, their own schools, and permanent exemption from military service. By 1870s the Mennonites were again threatened, this time by a rising Russian nationalism that resented a people set apart. The Canadian government offered inducements similar to the earlier Russian ones: exemption from military service, religious liberty, control of education, free homesteads of 160 acres, and the right to purchase additional land at one dollar per acre. Canada set aside two blocks of townships for the Mennonites in southern Manitoba. One block of eight townships was on the east side of the Red River southwest of Winnipeg, and another block of twelve townships ("The West Reserve") was located along the international boundary west of the Red River. The blocks of reserves signalled to the Mennonites that they could live in their own communities (and hold land in common) apart from their neighbours; about 8,000 Mennonites settled in 1874 in southern Manitoba.

In 1879, a federal Order-in-Council prohibited the entrance of paupers and destitute immigrants. Not long afterwards, the government began to admit large numbers of Chinese immigrants (over 15,000), approximately half of them as labourers on the transcontinental railroad. In 1882, a public response to Russian pogroms led to the admission of a contingent of 247 Jews leaving London for Manitoba and the North-West to establish a "New Jerusalem" in what would become Saskatchewan. They did not receive land until 1884, by which time their numbers had been greatly reduced, and the settlement soon failed. By the early 1880s demands for further restrictions on the number of immigrants surfaced in Canada, particularly of those outside previous Canadian experience regarded as "unassimilable." Sir John A. Macdonald told the House of Commons in 1883 that "It will be all very well to exclude Chinese labour, when we can replace it with white labour, but until that is done, it is better to have Chinese labour than no labour at all" (quoted in Magocsi, 1999: 359). As soon as the railroad was completed, Macdonald gave in to pressures from British Columbia and elsewhere to deal with the Chinese, who were blamed for a variety of social and economic evils. A Royal Commission on Chinese immigration in 1885 recommended restrictions on the number of Chinese workers, and Macdonald instituted a head tax of $50 on every Chinese person entering the country. His legislation also restricted the number of Chinese people who could be carried on individual vessels entering Canadian ports. (On 22 June 2006, Prime Minister Stephen Harper formally apologized to the Chinese community for this policy, which continued until 1923.) The federal legislation was added to numerous provincial statutes (especially in British Columbia) to limit the rights of the Chinese in Canada.

The Quest for Regional and National Identity

The British North America Act had no guarantees that political unification would necessarily create a nation. After 1867 Canadians made various attempts to locate themselves in their world. Some of these attempts were political and constitutional. Others were cultural, with intellectuals and artists playing their part by providing rhetorical flourishes as well as creating national institutions in which the arts could operate.

The development of nationhood in the years after 1867 did not mean that all Canadians shared in the same vision (or version) of the meaning of the nation. One of the major questions was whether Canada was an indissoluble new creation or the product of a compact among the provinces that they could modify or even leave. Since the time of the debate over Confederation in the 1860s, people had disagreed over the nature of the union. While most Canadians in 1867 saw the British North America Act as creating a strong central government, provincial legislatures still existed. They would quickly assert more than the merely local power accorded them by the Quebec resolutions. One of the arch-critics of Confederation, Christopher Dunkin (1812–81), had prophesied in 1865 that "In the times to come, when men shall begin to feel strongly on those questions that appeal to national preferences, prejudices and passions, all talk of your new nationality will

BACKGROUNDER

The Republic of New Iceland

People from Iceland had been coming to Canada from the early 1870s, prompted by both volcanic eruptions and grassland shortages in their homeland and a general population excess pressing on available resources. The first arrivals had come to Ontario and Quebec, but were attracted west by promises from the Canadian government of an autonomous settlement in the west. The land they chose was on the west side of Lake Winnipeg, about 15 miles wide and 40 miles long stretching from present-day Selkirk to Hecla Island and including the modern community of Gimli. This territory was beyond the then northern boundary of the province of Manitoba, and the newcomers were allowed autonomous settlement, "the Republic of New Iceland," with its own laws and judicial system. The Canadian government accepted a provisional council ("Thing") set up by the Icelanders, and allowed them to produce a fully articulated system of self-government. This entity became part of Manitoba when the boundaries of the province were expanded in 1881, but self-government remained until 1887. Although the territory the Icelanders chose was good for fishing on Lake Winnipeg, it contained some of the poorest agricultural land in the region. The Icelanders were struck by epidemic disease and spring flooding, and in the later 1870s a religious dispute emerged as well. Many moved to the United States or to Winnipeg. Most who remained made a living by fishing. Icelanders were generally well-educated and committed to preservation of their language. Schools and newspapers were established in New Iceland within months of settlement, and the community over the next half-century would produce a number of poets, journalists, and writers who employed the Icelandic language before the area was absorbed gradually into Manitoba.

Many Icelanders who settled in Manitoba hoped to make a living through agriculture, but due to flooding and disease, as well as settlement on marginal land for farming, most were unsuccessful. Archives of Manitoba, New Iceland 312 (N11314).

sound but strangely. Some older nationality will then be found to hold the first place in most people's hearts" (quoted in Waite, 1963: 511). Even Sir John A. Macdonald had admitted in Parliament in 1868 that "a conflict may, ere long, arise between the Dominion and the States Rights people" (quoted in Cook, 1969a: 10).

Ontario initially spearheaded the provincial-rights interpretation of the new union. The seeds of this interpretation were inherent in the constitutional arrangements, and the movement could have begun anywhere. As early as 1869 Ontario became distressed at "the assumption by the Parliament of Canada of the power to disturb the financial relations established by the British North America Act (1867), as between Canada and the several provinces" (quoted in Cook, 1969a: 11). Not surprisingly, the old Reform Party of Canada West, in the persons of George Brown, Edward Blake (1833–1912), and Oliver Mowat (1820–1903), took the lead. They demanded—in Blake's phrase of 1871—"that each government [Dominion and provincial] shall be absolutely independent of the other in its management of its own affairs" (quoted in Cook, 1969a: 13). The Rouges of Quebec soon joined in the same call, adding the identification of French-Canadian "national" rights to Ontario's "provincial" ones. Before long, Liberals in most provinces—many of whom had either opposed Confederation or been lukewarm about it—had embraced provincial rights.

Provincial rights often seemed interchangeable with Ottawa-bashing for local political advantage, lacking in any other principle than the desire to pressure Ottawa into fiscal concessions. In its early years, Quebec did not dominate the movement. There was little insistence that Confederation was a cultural deal between two distinct societies. In 1884, for example, the Honourable Honoré Mercier (1840–94) tabled resolutions in the Quebec legislature stating merely that "the frequent encroachments of the Federal Parliament upon the prerogatives of the Provinces are a permanent menace to the latter" (quoted in Cook, 1969a: 31). The ensuing debate involved no more cultural nationalism than one backbencher's assertion that "le Québec n'est pas une province comme les autres" (quoted in Cook, 1969a: 33). Although the Riel affair of 1885 (discussed

later in this chapter) pushed Quebec towards the brink of arguments of cultural distinctiveness, when Mercier (by this time Premier of Quebec) invited the provinces to the Interprovincial Conference in 1887 to re-examine the federal compact, broad agreement could be reached on demands for better terms and constitutional change by the five provinces attending without the need for such concepts.

Provincial rights involved on one level a political-constitutional struggle over revenue and power. On another level they were a reflection of the continued identification of the people of Canada with their province of residence as much as, if not more than, with their nation. The educational structure of Canada certainly encouraged this identification. In all provinces education passed from private to public financial support at the same time that schooling became increasingly universal. However, section 92 of the British North America Act left education completely in the hands of the provinces. It is almost impossible to talk about any integrated national movements. Indeed, education would become one of the most divisive issues in the new nation. A major question was whether provinces would have a single public school system for all students or would support separate religious (and linguistic) education as well. Educational diversity was still the norm after Confederation. There were, at best, provincial educational systems and norms, not national ones.

Although a sense of nationalism was beginning to develop, it did not pose a serious challenge to provincial loyalties. The movement calling itself Canada First, for example, did not have a program that was particularly attractive outside Protestant circles in Ontario. Canada First was an exclusive secret society rather than a broad-based organization. It did not help that its vision of Canada was really that of Canada West writ larger. While Canada First's notions were compatible, to some extent, with the westward thrust of Canada West, they were, fortunately, not totally typical of the conscious development of Canadian nationalism. The French-Canadian poet Octave Crémazie (1827–79), for example, lamented ironically that Canada's major literary languages were entirely of European origin. He continued: "if we spoke Huron or Iroquois, the works of our writers would attract the attention of the old world. . . . One would be overwhelmed by a novel or a poem translated from the Iroquois, while one does not take the trouble to read a book written in French by a native of Quebec or Montreal" (quoted in Rasporich, 1969: 225). The search for an essential "Canadian-ness" went on in many corners of the new Dominion. It was nowhere so successful as in the somewhat remote New Brunswick town of Fredericton, home of the University of New Brunswick. There the rectory of St Anne's Parish (Anglican) produced Charles G.D. Roberts (1860–1943), while not far down the road lived his cousin Bliss Carman (1861–1929). Along with Ottawa's Archibald Lampman (1861–99) and Duncan Campbell Scott (1862–1947), these men comprised the first school of Canadian poets, designated "Confederation Poets" by modern literary critics. Roberts, Lampman, Carman, and Scott brought Canadian themes into their writing, notably the local or regional landscape, with some degree of skill and sensitivity. As Crémazie had suggested, however, the European origins of their literary influences limited their efforts.

While many intellectuals and artists sought ways to articulate Canadian-ness in their work, others took a more prosaic route towards the realization of a Canadian national identity. Curiously enough, it was the painters, not normally known for their political acuity, who took the lead in organizing national groups to maintain professional standards and publicize Canadian achievement. The Ontario Society of Artists, formed in 1872 and incorporated in 1877, was at the forefront of this effort. The OSA was instrumental in the formation of the Royal Canadian Academy of Arts in 1880—in collaboration with the Governor General, Lord Lorne (1845–1914)—and in the establishment that same year of the National Gallery of Canada. One of the founders of this organization wrote, "We are bound to try to civilize the Dominion a little" (quoted in Williamson, 1970: 64). The year 1880 was doubly important in art circles, for in that year the Canadian Society of Graphic Art was also founded.

The first president of the Royal Canadian Academy, the painter Lucius O'Brien (1832–99), was art director of an elaborate literary and artistic celebration of the young nation. *Picturesque Canada* (1882) was based on the highly successful books *Picturesque America and Picturesque Europe*. It was the idea of two Americans, the Belden brothers, who had established themselves in Toronto. The editor of the project—George Monro Grant (1835–1902), principal of Queen's University—stated in the preface: "I believed that a work that would represent its characteristic scenery and history and life of its people would not only make us better known to ourselves and to strangers, but would also stimulate national sentiment and contribute to the rightful development of the nation." The two large volumes of *Picturesque Canada*—which can sometimes be found in second-hand bookshops—contain 540 illustrations. They included wood engravings based on paintings and, for the West, photo engravings of photographs that offered serene vistas fulfilling the promise of the title. The descriptive texts by Grant, Charles G.D. Roberts, and others presented an idealized, complacent view of the cities, towns, and regions of Canada, praising the present and pointing to a glorious future.

The Royal Society of Canada was founded in 1882 to promote research and learning in the arts and sciences. Lord Lorne again provided much of the impetus, replicating a British institution to establish the importance of cultural accomplishments in creating a sense of national pride and self-confidence. The first president, J.W. Dawson (1820–99), principal of McGill University (another Nova Scotian transported to central Canada), emphasized in his presidential address a sense of national purpose. Dawson stressed especially "the establishment of a bond of union between the scattered workers now widely separated in different parts of the Dominion" (quoted in Royal Society of Canada, 1932: 91–2). Thomas Sterry Hunt (1826–92), a charter member and later president, observed that "The occasion which brings us together is one which should mark a new departure in the intellectual history of Canada" (Royal Society of Canada, 1932: 91–2). He added that "the brightest glories and the most enduring honours of a country are those which come from its thinkers and its scholars" (Royal Society of Canada, 1932: 91–2). However romantic that praise might sound, what mattered was Hunt's emphasis on the country as a whole. Like the Royal Canadian Academy, the Royal Society had its headquarters in Ottawa.

Religion and the Churches

The mid-Victorian period was a crucial era for Roman Catholicism in Canada. Within French Canada the period witnessed the emergence of the Church as the leading voice of French Canada's national aspirations and the assumption of local leadership by the *curé*. It also saw the Church take on the ultramontane character that would remain with it for many years. In Quebec, the man who symbolized the ultramontane Church in the mid-Victorian period was Bishop Ignace Bourget (1799–1885). Bourget was consecrated coadjutor to the Bishop of Montreal in early 1837, on the very eve of rebellion, and succeeded to the see in 1840. He died in June 1885, on the eve of the second Riel uprising, although he had retired a few years earlier. Bourget was always an active defender of both the papacy and the position of the Church in Canada. He introduced the Roman liturgy and fervently opposed the principles of the European revolutions of 1848. Gradually, he became the leading opponent of liberal thinking in the province, particularly as it was represented by the Institut Canadien in Montreal. Bourget carried on a lengthy battle against the Institut and especially its library, which contained many prohibited books. Equally important was his expansion of the ecclesiastical administrations of his diocese, so that nearly every parish had a priest and nearly half the priests had an assistant. The clergy were now able to mobilize public opinion, and they did in 1868 when they helped raise 507 Zouaves in Quebec (and over $100,000 to support them) to serve in the papal army. Quebec bishops strongly supported the doctrine of papal infallibility at the First Vatican Council in 1870.

English-speaking Catholicism had succeeded by 1840 in separating itself from francophone control. At about the same time, the hierarchy had also re-established its control over the laity, which had previously assumed considerable autonomy in the absence of local bishops and clergy. Anglophone bishops from the Maritime region were among those who attempted unsuccessfully to prevent the issue of papal infallibility from being decided at the Vatican Council. Contemporaries often overlooked the importance of Anglophone Catholicism in the nineteenth century.

Only in Canada West/Ontario were Protestants in such a clear numerical ascendency and position of power that the regional culture assumed obvious Protestant dimensions. This Ontario culture, especially as it expanded westward onto the prairies, began to be confused with Canadian culture in some circles.

By 1840 Protestantism everywhere in British North America had largely cut itself free from its foreign origins in either Great Britain or the United States. The major development of the mid-Victorian period, notably in an Ontario where Protestantism emerged as a distinct and all-embracing culture, was the construction of a broad alliance among the major denominations: Anglican, Presbyterian, and Methodist. The gradual elimination of the major points of public friction between the established churches and the dissenters made this possible. The result was a Victorian Protestant culture in Ontario that emphasized the relationship between social stability and Protestant morality. A firm belief in God and his millennium formed the basis for the latter. Gradual social change was progressive, offering a way of understanding the events and changes that swirled around the individual in the Victorian era. The moral code was strict, but chiefly voluntary and individualistic.

The churches, especially the Protestant ones, were also a key to the growth of a vast network of clubs, societies, and charities. By the mid-nineteenth century women members were implicitly challenging the male governance of the churches. Evangelically oriented churches frequently employed their ladies auxiliary groups to sponsor missionary activity. By 1885 there were 120 Baptist Women's Missionary Aid Societies scattered across the Maritimes. Women generally used their own money to support their religious organizations, which kept separate accounts and offered many women their first opportunity at independent administration.

Cultural Life

The creation of the nation did not directly affect all aspects of cultural life. Indeed, most culture in Canada existed quite apart from political considerations. Despite their new self-consciousness about the need for cultural achievements to match their political accomplishments, most Canadians probably did not appreciate how much progress was being made in many cultural spheres. Only a brief sampling of cultural activity in Victorian Canada—focusing on painting, theatre, music, organized sports, and literature—can be included here.

Painting was the most vibrant and productive of the arts in the era immediately after Confederation, with many artists producing large numbers of canvases, some of them key works in the history of Canadian painting. The beginning of the period coincided roughly with the end of a tradition of landscape painting that had become dominant partly in response to the developing quest for national identity and the topographical beauties of the new country that were still being discovered. Lucius O'Brien (1832–99) and John A. Fraser (1838–98) were two of numerous painters who travelled west in 1880 at the invitation of the Canadian Pacific Railway to paint the Rockies. O'Brien's most famous painting, however, is *Sunrise on the Saguenay* (1880). It is a remarkable depiction of the sublime in nature, while in its poetic, moody treatment of the romantic scene it is also an outstanding Canadian example of a style, popular in the United States, that came to be called "luminism." This painting was hung in the inaugural exhibition of the Royal Academy, of which O'Brien was the first president, and deposited in the new National Gallery of Canada.

Homer Watson (1855–1936) and his friend Horatio Walker (1858–1936) both came to concentrate on Canadian landscapes that romanticized rural scenes. Oscar Wilde, after seeing Watson's work in Toronto, called him "the Canadian Constable." In fairness to Watson, he was no imitator, since at the time he had never heard of Constable. Walker, who was born in Listowel, Canada West, wintered in New York and summered on the Île d'Orléans just north of Quebec in the St Lawrence. He specialized, with great commercial success, in striking, sentimentalized interpretations of Quebec farm life in the style of the French painter Jean-François Millet. Walker himself described his preoccupations:

The pastoral life of the people of our country-side, the noble work of the Habitant, the magnificent panoramas which surround him, the different aspects of our seasons, the calm of our mornings and the serenity of our even-

ings, the movement of ebb and flow of our tides which I have observed on the shores of my island which is truly the sacred temple of the muses and a gift of the gods to men: such are the preferred subjects of my paintings. I have passed the greatest part of my life in trying to paint the poetry, the easy joys, the hard daily work of rural life, the sylvan beauty in which is spent the peaceable life of the habitant, the gesture of the wood cutter and the ploughman, the bright colours of sunrise and sunset, the song of the cock, the daily tasks of the farmyard, all the activity which goes on from morning to evening, in the neighbourhood of the barn. (Quoted in Harper, 1966: 204)

By 1880 young Canadian painters sought to study in the academies of Paris, the centre of the art world of the time. There they learned to paint large, richly detailed, subtly coloured, naturalistic canvases featuring the human figure and sentimental subtexts. Robert Harris's studies of everyday life were exemplars of this approach. They included: The *Chorister* (1880), showing a young man singing in a church choir; *Harmony* (1886), a portrait of a young woman (his wife) playing the harmonium, a popular musical instrument in rural Canada; and *A Meeting of the School Trustees* (1885), in which a young Prince Edward Island teacher, identified as Kate Henderson, doubtless with "new-fangled ideas," faces the suspicious gazes of four male trustees.

Perhaps the most important development in Canadian theatre in this period was the extension of railroad construction, which would make possible extensive touring across the nation by theatrical and vaudeville companies. By the 1880s, most Canadian cities could look forward to visits by professional performers, which undoubtedly raised the standard of presentation and provided models worthy of emulation. At the same time, the arrival of professionals and the raising of standards could be damaging to local amateurs, who had previously dominated the theatrical scene and occasionally even produced home-grown plays and musicals.

Although only a few trained musicians existed in British North America, the mid-Victorian era saw the

Luminism was a North American style that focused on detail and emphasized the striking vistas of the continent. The vastness of the natural landscape compared to the human element of the boats, especially when compared to the growing industrial cities of Europe, made Canada seem wild and vast. "Sunrise on the Saguenay," oil on canvas, 1880, by Lucius O'Brien. National Gallery of Canada, Ottawa. Photo © National Gallery of Canada, 113.

development of a widespread musical life. Garrison bands and choral groups were the chief components. In British Columbia the band of the Royal Engineers brought new standards of musical performance when it arrived in the colony in 1859. From that year until 1863 (when it was reposted to Britain) it entertained as militia band, fire-brigade band, brass band, and even a dance band. In British Columbia, as elsewhere, brass bands were the most common and popular instrumental ensembles throughout the nineteenth century. Few band musicians were professional or professionally trained. A number of brass bands were organized in the province in Aboriginal communities and residential schools. At least 33 sprang to life between 1864 (when the Oblates

founded the St Mary's Mission Band near Mission City) and the end of the century. In Red River, a brass band from St Boniface played as the Métis provisional government raised its new flag in December 1869.

By the time of Confederation, larger cities were producing substantial numbers of musical societies, chiefly choral in their orientation. In 1864, for example, the Mendelssohn Choir and the Société Musicale des Montagnards Canadiens, as well as Les Orphéonistes de Montréal, joined the Montreal Oratorio Society. Montreal also helped produce the first well-known Canadian composer, Calixa Lavallée (1842–91), best known today for the music to "O Canada." He made his debut at the piano in Montreal at age 13, spending much time in the United States until he went to Paris in 1873. Returning to settle in Quebec, Lavallée wrote a grand cantata for the reception of Governor General Lord Lorne and his wife. It concluded with a stirring contrapuntal arrangement of "God Save the Queen" and "Comin' thro' the Rye." Unable to make a living in Canada, the composer spent the last years of his life in exile in the United States. Although Canada was not often generous to its professional musicians, it embraced amateur musical performance with gusto. Most music-making occurred in the home, with people gathering around the piano to sing hymns and popular songs of the day.

The mid-Victorian period in Canada saw a continued development of organized sports and games. Most were imported, although some (like lacrosse) had local origins. Lacrosse had begun as an Aboriginal game called *baggataway* or *tewaarathon*, and was played by many tribes under various rules. In 1833 the First Nations near Montreal played lacrosse, and in 1856 the Montreal Lacrosse Club was organized, to be joined by two others before 1860. A Montreal dentist, William George Beers (1843–1900), codified the game in Montreal and promoted it across the country. Lacrosse flourished between 1868 and 1885, achieving great success as a spectator

"A Meeting of the School Trustees," oil on canvas, 1885, by Robert Harris. National Gallery of Canada, Ottawa. Here the artist captures the dynamic of many a school district in Canada in this period. Purchased 1886, #6. Photo © National Gallery of Canada, 6 R.

sport until it was overtaken by baseball and hockey. Snowshoeing, which became very popular as an organized winter activity in the 1860s (often among the summer lacrosse crowd), was another obviously Aboriginal development. The Montreal Snow Shoe Club was organized in 1843, and in Winnipeg a snowshoe club, begun in 1878, was the major winter diversion for members of the city's elite by the early 1880s.

The formulation of rules for these and other sports occurred in most cases between 1840 and 1880, which was the great era of codification of sports. Precise dates are very contentious, with many communities advancing their own claims for "firsts." Certainly by 1880 most sports and games familiar to us today had reached a stage of rule development that would have made them comprehensible to a modern Canadian. What is important about the development of sports is not simply the introduction of standardized rules, techniques, and equipment, but the sheer scope and ubiquity of sporting activity on the part of both participants and spectators. While many Canadians participated, many more gathered to watch sporting activity. The development of any of the major games followed roughly the same path of regularization, which made it possible for teams from one place to play teams from another.

By 1885 two aspects of sports in Canada had evolved: participation and spectacle. Sports still had not achieved an overt political meaning. There was not yet the creation of either national leagues or national teams to play in international competitions. Expansion, sophistication, and growing organization matched the development of the nation. The mobility of the population moved various sports and games around the country and made the standardization of rules both possible and necessary. The development of official rules and growing hierarchies of teams and players pointed to the future.

The Struggle for the West

Sincere efforts were made in the new Dominion to encourage a sense of nationhood transcending the linguistic barriers between French and English and the geographical barriers of the provinces and the regions. Nevertheless, the new Canadian nationality remained fragile, more than a bit artificial, and very racist. In addition, at least outside French Canada, it tended to express the prejudices and values of British Ontario. The crucible for the new Canada, many believed, was in the vast expanse of territory west of the Great Lakes. Here its limitations were most clearly evident.

The interests of the Canadian government in the North-West Territories, especially under Sir John A. Macdonald, were focused on agricultural settlement. This would provide both an outlet for excess eastern population and the means of encouraging the development of a truly transcontinental nation. The process of settlement and government policy pushed the Aboriginal inhabitants of the region out of the way as quickly as possible. The federal government continued the pre-Confederation policy of the Canadas by establishing an Indian Department and insisting on the rule of law in its westward expansion and in its dealings with the Native peoples. Foremost in the rule-of-law approach were the creation of the North-West Mounted Police and the working out of treaties with the First Nations that extinguished Aboriginal claims to the land as first inhabitants in exchange for reserves on the most marginal and least attractive land. Eleven "numbered" treaties were negotiated between 1871 and 1930, the first five of which were land cession agreements covering most of the Canadian West, except for British Columbia. As well as reserves, the Aboriginals received cash money, allowances for blankets and tools, seed and livestock, and the right to hunt on land not otherwise used by Canadians. The government's hope was to convert the First Peoples into settled farmers, and its rhetoric featured an insistence on its humanitarianism and paternalism, under which a good deal of racism and prejudice flourished. As one Indian Commissioner wrote in 1887, the government was engaged in "the slow and tedious work of uplifting a savage race and eradicating the nomadic and other inherent tendencies which centuries of a wild and barbarous life have firmly planted" (quoted in Titley, 2009: 207). While the Aboriginal people might eventually aspire (with Canadian government assistance) to full citizenship by assuming all the characteristics of

Caughnawaga (Kahnawake) Mohawks, lacrosse champions of Canada, 1869; photo by James Inglis. This photograph makes clear that Aboriginals were skilled and successful lacrosse players. James Inglis, LAC, C-001959.

the European colonizers, in the meantime they would be denied full citizenship and given a special inferior status experienced by no other Canadians.

Administration of the treaties and of Dominion "Indian policy" in the West left a good deal to be desired. The Aboriginal peoples were obviously caught in an inexorable process that was going to change forever their traditional way of life. The buffalo were rapidly disappearing, the victims of overhunting and of the arrival of settlement and new technology. Most Aboriginal leaders saw the handwriting on the wall clearly enough. They did not get anywhere near enough help from the Department of Indian Affairs, however. The government expected the Aboriginals to be able to become self-sufficient virtually overnight. It did not supply the reserves with enough food to prevent starvation and disease, and it complained when the Natives slaughtered their livestock for something to eat. The reserve land tended to be marginal, the assistance supplied was inadequate—

often for financial reasons—and the attitude of many of the government's Indian agents was unsympathetic. By the early 1880s, the North-West was a virtual powder keg of Aboriginal discontent. Cree leaders in what is now Alberta sent a letter to John A. Macdonald (who was Minister of the Interior and head of Indian Affairs as well as Prime Minister) complaining of destitution and noting that the motto of their people was: "If we must die by violence let us do it quickly." The winter of 1883–4 was particularly harsh and severe, and many were starving. Some Indian agents wrote to Ottawa, but nothing was done. In June 1884, Big Bear and his followers, with many others, travelled to Poundmaker's reserve to hold a big meeting. They discussed the serious state of affairs, after which some 2,000 Aboriginals held a Thirst Dance, a religious ritual.

Like the First Nations, settlement drove the Métis to the margins. By 1885 Ontario-born settlers outnumbered the Métis five to one in Manitoba, and only 7 per cent of

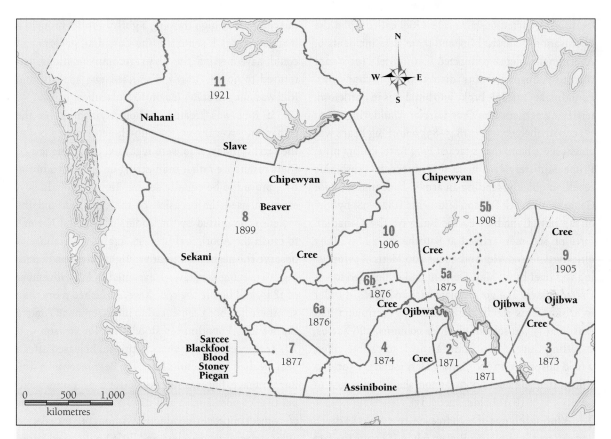

The numbered treaties, 1871–1921. Adapted from J.R. Miller, Skyscrapers Hide the Heavens: A History of Indian–White Relations in Canada, *rev. edn (Toronto: University of Toronto Press, 1991), 166.*

the population of the province was of mixed-blood origin. Many Métis drifted farther west, to the Saskatchewan Valley, where they formed small mission settlements including Qu'Appelle, Batoche, and Duck Lake. The buffalo were becoming scarce everywhere. Government surveyors caused uncertainty and fear, as they had in Red River a decade earlier. Over the harsh winter of 1883–4, many Métis and Aboriginals starved. The Métis turned in despair to Louis Riel. He had apparently put his life back together after years of exile in the United States and hospitalization for mental disturbance in 1876–8 at Longue Pointe, Quebec. He became an American citizen and was teaching in St Peter's, Montana (where he had married), when a delegation from the Saskatchewan country visited him on 4 June 1884. They told him of the grievances that were burdening the peoples of the region, explained that agitation was developing against the Canadian gov-

ernment, and pleaded with him to return to Canada to lead them. Why Riel agreed to do so is one of the many mysteries surrounding his life. However, within a month he and his family were in Batoche. By December 1884, Riel and W.H. Jackson (secretary of the Settlers' Union) had finished drafting a long petition (with 25 sections), which they sent to Ottawa. It concluded by requesting that the petitioners "be allowed as in [1870] to send Delegates to Ottawa with their Bill of rights; whereby an understanding may be arrived at as to their entry into confederation, with the constitution of a free province." Ottawa acknowledged the petition, but gave no other response.

In March 1885 events took a menacing turn. Riel's military leader, Gabriel Dumont (1836–1906), intercepted a small NWMP detachment near Duck Lake. The engagement turned into a full-fledged battle in which fatalities occurred on both sides. Riel called upon the First Nations to assist him, and there were incidents of Aboriginal violence connected less to Riel's resistance than to younger warriors' discontent with conditions. Poundmaker's people broke into buildings in Battleford, terrifying settlers. The Cree warrior, Wandering Spirit (Kapapamahchakwew, *c.* 1845–85), one of Big Bear's war chiefs, led a band that attacked Frog Lake, killing nine. Prime Minister Macdonald determined to crush this rebellion quickly, sending an armed force under Major General Frederick Dobson Middleton (1825–98) by way of the new Canadian Pacific Railway. The Canadian force of 800 men arrived at Batoche on 9 May. They quickly defeated Riel and about 200 Métis. The uprising was over by 12 May. Dumont and others fled to the United States. The government arrested Riel. In order to achieve this result, the Canadian government had mustered "5,546 soldiers in three columns, 586 horses, 2 Gatling Guns, 6,000 Snider Enfield, 50 calibre rifles, 2 field hospitals, 70,000 Gatling Gun rounds, 1,500,000 rifle cartridges and 2,000 cannon shells," at a cost of $4,451,584.38 (Barnholden, 2009: 13).

A formal charge of high treason, carrying the death penalty, was laid against Riel on 6 July. (Despite the fact that Riel was an American citizen, the Canadian government held with the British government that he was also a British subject, since British citizenship acquired through birth could never be renounced.) Even if Riel was a foreign national, however, he could still be tried for treason. The government chose to focus responsibility for the rebellion on Riel, which would allow leniency towards most of his followers. The trial began on 28 July in Regina, where feelings ran high. It was a political trial, infamously coloured in many ways by Macdonald's determination to have Riel found guilty and executed.

Riel passionately denied a plea of insanity introduced by his lawyers, realizing that to be declared insane (i.e., not responsible for his actions) would devastate his reputation and impugn his honour. The six-man jury (operating under the law of the North-West Territories) found him guilty but recommended mercy. It is not clear whether the jury brought in the mercy recommendation because it felt Riel's resistance was partially justified or because it did not really believe that he was responsible for his behaviour. In any case, because the charge was high treason, a guilty verdict brought a mandatory death sentence. The Canadian government could have heeded the jury's recommendations, but refused to do so. Ottawa dismissed two appeals, and Riel was hanged at Regina on 16 November.

If Riel was treated without sympathy by the Canadian government, the punishments meted out to the First Nations, who were regarded as having joined Riel's resistance rather than acting on their own initiative, proved to be equally severe. The Macdonald government used the occasion of the rebellion and the violence committed by the leaders of the First Nations to crush the Aboriginal protests against the failure to observe the negotiated treaties. Eight warriors, including Wandering Spirit, were executed in late November of 1885, and before the courts were finished more than 50 others had been sentenced to imprisonment. Among the leaders, Poundmaker stood trial for treason and was sentenced to three years in prison. Released after a year, he died four months later. Big Bear received a similar sentence, but was released after a year and a half because of poor health and died soon after. The trials were most improper, conducted without full translation against people who understood little English and less of the law being employed. Few were properly represented in court. Most First Nations leaders and people tried to remain clear of the Métis uprising, but this did not save them from a subsequent campaign of repression by Assistant Indian Commissioner Hayter Reed, who argued that the rebellion had abrogated the treaties and who introduced a series of policies that made the First Nations totally dependent on the largesse of Canada.

The execution of Louis Riel had a lasting impact on Canada. In Quebec it strengthened French-Canadian nationalism and helped turn voters away from the Conservative Party, which they had supported since Confederation. On 22 November 1885, at a huge gathering in the public square in Montreal called the Champ de Mars, Honoré Mercier, the Liberal leader in Quebec, joined Wilfrid Laurier in denouncing the government action. Mercier insisted: "In killing Riel, Sir John has not only struck at the heart of our race but especially at the cause of justice and humanity which…demanded mercy for the prisoner of Regina, our poor friend of the North-West." Laurier added: "Had I been born on the banks of

Biography

Big Bear (Mistahimaskwa)

The fact that little is known of Big Bear's lineage—his parents were probably Salteaux but he became a leader among the Cree—tells us much about the fluidity among First Peoples on the Canadian Plains in the nineteenth century. Big Bear (*c.* 1825–88) was apparently brought up in a "homeguard" family near Fort Carlton in present-day central Saskatchewan, later moving as a chief to reside near Fort Pitt. Around 1870 he moved south to the Plains, and reportedly participated in the last major Aboriginal battle in the region at Belly River (near present-day Lethbridge, Alberta) in October of that year. He was one of the few chiefs who rejected friendly overtures from the Canadian government in the 1870s, suspecting that the next step would be peace treaties in which the First Nations would surrender land and end up on reserves. Regarded as a troublemaker, he did not attend the negotiations for Treaty Six in August 1876, and was the first important chief to refuse to sign a treaty. Increasing numbers of dissident warriors joined him over the next few years as the number of buffalo coming north decreased, and then, after 1879, disappeared from the region. Still resistant, Big Bear and his people moved to Montana and hunted the remaining buffalo until late in 1882, when Big Bear capitulated and signed Treaty Six in return for food. For the next several years, he argued with Indian Department officials before hosting a Thirst Dance, a ritual explicitly forbidden by the Canadian government, at Poundmaker's reserve in April 1884. Several thousand First Nations warriors gathered, many later confronting the RCMP and nearly provoking an open battle. Big Bear made clear in August of 1884 that he wanted the signed treaties revised and renegotiated by one chief speaking for all the tribes. That same month he met with Louis Riel. But the government paid little attention.

When news of a Métis victory at Duck Lake reached the First Nations camped at Frog Lake, Big Bear's son, Ayimasis (Little Bad Man), and the war leader Wandering Spirit emptied the Catholic church and despite Big Bear's shouts of "Stop! Stop!" killed most of the worshippers and priests present. The subsequent trial (for treason-felony) was told that Big Bear had said afterwards, "it is not my doings and the young men won't listen, and I am very sorry for what has been done." Others testified that the warriors paid no attention to Big Bear. The judge instructed the jury of six that the old chief could be called innocent only if he had removed himself from the band when it rose up in violence. The jury took 15 minutes to bring in a sentence of guilty, with a recommendation for mercy. Big Bear was sentenced to three years in the Stony Mountain prison near Winnipeg, dying shortly after his release in 1887, probably of tuberculosis. He was one of the last of the traditional chiefs to oppose European civilization, but despite his conviction and jail sentence, he had not done so with guns.

the Saskatchewan . . . I would myself have shouldered a musket to fight against the neglect of governments and the shameless greed of speculators." The two leaders disagreed over Mercier's proposal that French Canadians leave the two major parties and form one of their own. Laurier insisted that Mercier's proposal would destroy Confederation. Symbolically, French Canada took the execution of Riel to represent the final exclusion of the francophone from the West. Few spoke of the symbolic meaning for the Aboriginal peoples of the shearing of Big Bear's long hair when he was in captivity, or of the execution of Wandering Spirit.

The military defeat of the Métis, the humiliation of the First Nations, and the public execution of Louis Riel in November 1885 were only part of the reason why that year and that month were so significant, not only

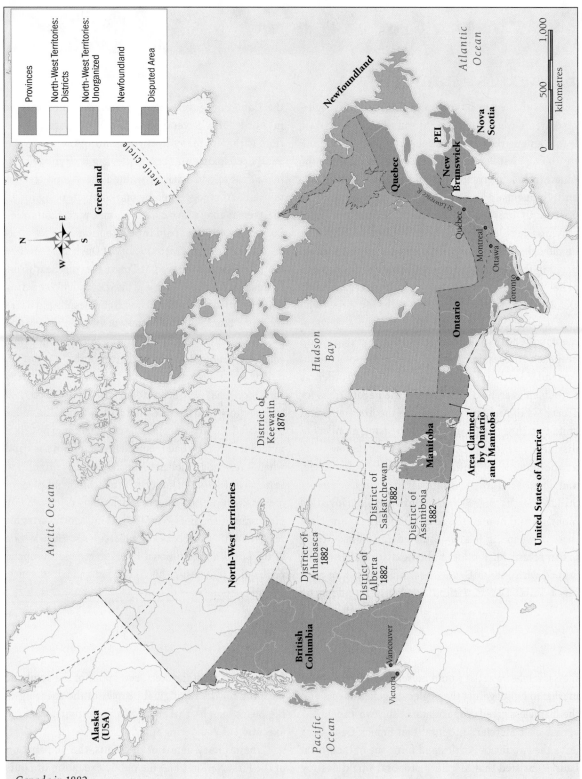

Canada in 1882.

"All That I Used to Live on Has Gone"

At a meeting with the visiting Governor General of Canada, the Marquess of Lorne, at Fort Carlton in 1881, Chief Ahtahkakoop of the Plains Cree addressed Lord Lorne.

I have reason to be thankful to see His Excellency and since this [treaty] medal was put on my neck from the Great Mother I am thankful—& all my tribe—to see the Great Mother's representative here that I will speak for her as I speak for my children. I am a poor man and now will express my views on this subject, but as I look round I do not see anything I could live by. I see nothing, all that I used to live on has gone. Where I used to get my [living] was the animal the buffalo, and also I had horses, now the buffalo and the horses have left me. I say with that I am a poor man.

You may have seen the poverty of the land as regards the animal—that was my hunting ground. I used to find them all I wanted. Now it is a solitary wilderness. I find nothing there, when I look at all this I see but one thing left, that is to work the ground. I am too old to work but I think of my children & grandchildren they may learn.

The first thing [we want] is some strength, i.e., farm implements & cattle—these are necessary. If we don't progress faster than in the past years, we shall move very shortly and my Grandchildren will not see it for we walk very slowly now. Why I say this is that the crops we have raised the half was spoilt as sickness came on us and my people could not work. I remember right on the treaty it was said that if any famine or trouble came the Government would see to us and help. My trouble arose from partly starvation and sickness. The remedy I ask for now. We want nets, we want guns. I ask for these only for living. There is another thing we lack. When I take a flail to thrash I lose part of my wheat. I want a thrashing machine. A thrasher and a reaper and the power to work them. There is no end to my losses. I loose [lose] in the thrashing. I have miles sometimes to go through the snow to have my grain ground, and I am only about to bring back a handful. I make no doubt that his Excellency will sympathize with us, that he will open his heart towards the trouble of his Indian Children. What we want is speedy help on my farms. I have no more to say. I wish to be remembered to the Great Mother & to the Princess and please remember me in the cold winter days & give me covering for my women and children.

Source: "Report of the Marquis of Lorne's Trip," quoted in Deanna Christensen, *Ahtahkakoop: The Epic Account of a Plains Cree Head Chief, His People, and Their Struggle for Survival 1816–1896* (Shell Lake, Sask.: Ahtahkakoop Publishing, 2000), 422–3.

in the history of the West but in the history of Canada. In November 1885 workers drove the last spike at Craigellachie in eastern British Columbia, marking the completion of the Canadian Pacific Railway. The CPR had been resurrected in 1881 as a hybrid corporation controlled by private capitalists and financed largely by the state, which, along with public subsidies, gave it about 25 million acres (10,117,500 ha) of land along its right of way. Contemporaries actively debated the question of building in advance of settlement, particularly given the inducements needed to persuade hard-headed businessmen to proceed with construction. The Macdonald government defended the railway on the grounds of national interest. Since this concept is not measurable in dollar amounts, it is impossible to know whether the price was too high. Even before the line was completed, Macdonald used it to send troops west to help suppress the Métis uprising of 1885.

BACKGROUNDER

The Battle of Batoche

With rumours of armed trouble rife across western Canada, a contingent of militia from Winnipeg was mustered and ordered west before the encounter at Duck Lake near Prince Albert, where a column of Mounties and special constables were badly beaten by a force of Métis commanded by Gabriel Dumont. After Duck Lake, Major General Frederick Middleton, arriving in Winnipeg via American rail lines, left the city with the 90th Rifles, 260 strong and badly equipped. The railroad got the troops only as far as Qu'Appelle, whence they marched north to Fort Qu'Appelle to practise firing rifles before heading further north to Batoche, a village on the east bank of the South Saskatchewan River, where Middleton had decided to confront the Métis.

The troops made about 25 miles a day under adverse conditions. It was over 200 miles from the end of the railway line to the Métis strongholds, and so the CPR played very little active role in the campaign. By 24 April they had made Fish Creek and found signs of smouldering Métis campfires in a ravine between bluffs. The troops suffered heavy casualties from a crossfire from Métis sharpshooters, who disappeared into the bush of a ravine and withdrew as their ammunition ran out. Middleton camped on the site of this first battle for 12 days, waiting for reinforcements from eastern Canada and a detachment manning a Gatling gun.

The village of Batoche was a scattered settlement of houses and outbuildings on both sides of the river, connected by a ferry operated on a cable. On 5 May the paddlewheel steamer the *Northcote* arrived on the river and was ambushed by the sharpshooters, then damaged severely when its smokestacks hit the ferry cable. Middleton had 800 men, most of them infantry but including about 100 horsemen. He also had four field guns and the Gatling gun. Gabriel Dumont later estimated he had 200 effectives (Métis), and perhaps 200 Aboriginal warriors to fight with him. Louis Riel and Dumont disagreed over tactics. Riel prayed for divine assistance, while Dumont dug into rifle pits across a two-mile front.

The initial encounters impressed General Middleton, but he was afraid to fall back because he doubted his inexperienced troops could sustain their discipline in retreat. The Canadians held their ground, constructing a little fort of wagons in the midst of the prairie. Middleton wanted a decisive victory and was prepared, if necessary, to starve out Batoche. He ordered his troops to fire away, but did not yet order an assault. Finally Middleton ordered a battle plan for 12 May. He would attack the village from two sides, using mounted troops from the north and the infantry from the south. The men on horseback were to be the feint, the infantry assault the major attack. The feint went well, but the infantry attack did not occur, apparently because the order to advance had not reached Colonel van Straubenzie, the officer in charge.

In the meantime Middleton had met emissaries from Riel, asking him to stop shelling the

The construction of the CPR was a spectacular feat of engineering, partly thanks to the managerial skills of William Van Horne (1843–1915). The CPR was built chiefly on the backs of 6,500 Chinese coolie labourers especially imported for the job. Many died, and those who survived were summarily discharged when the work was completed. With the CPR finished, the Canadian government moved swiftly to limit Chinese immigration. With the Plains peoples and their Métis allies totally subjugated, Canada was open for settlement from coast to coast.

houses harbouring women and children. Middleton responded by telling them to gather the women and children in a house marked with a white flag, which would not be shelled. But he would not negotiate and would only accept unconditional surrender. It was never clear who gave the infantry the order to advance, but once the order was given the troops quickly overran the rifle pits and headed for the village. The battle was over within half an hour. Batoche was taken and the resistance melted away.

On this last day the army lost five dead and 25 wounded, while the Métis casualties were never counted. Mounted riders quickly brought the news of the victory back to the telegraph lines and then east to a victory-starved Canada. The army soon rounded up the Aboriginals who were independently fighting the settlers, the NWMP, and the Canadian military. The Last Stand of the Aboriginal West had ended.

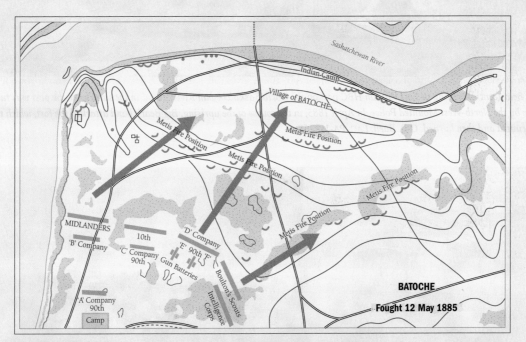

Battle of Batoche. The battle took place over several days, and included several different stages. What does this map/diagram tell us about the battle?

Source: Bruce Tascona and Eric Wells, *Little Black Devils: A History of the Royal Winnipeg Rifles* (Winnipeg: n.p., 1983), 50). Courtesy of The Royal Winnipeg Rifles.

Conclusion

By the 1860s the united province of Canada was ready to take the lead in creating an expanded nation. The two Maritime provinces of New Brunswick and Nova Scotia were reluctantly joined to the new union (with Prince Edward Island soon following suit), and United Canada itself became the two provinces of Ontario and Quebec. Now Canada began casting covetous glances westward, and over the next few years produced a transcontinental nation. The West was to be

Historiography

Confederation and the Canadian Senate

One of the curious features about Canadian Confederation is that it has generated virtually no historiography. A handful of books and articles appeared during the Centennial years of the 1960s, but those were mainly interested in explaining how a bunch of disparate colonies had managed to achieve unification rather than exploring historical questions in any depth. There was much learned discussion of the federal principle. After this spate of material there was virtual silence until Christopher Moore's 1997 study, *1867: How the Fathers Made a Deal*. This strange history helps to explain, as Moore observed, why the existing studies failed to address usefully issues of current interest. One of those questions is: why is the Canadian Senate so useless? The simple answer is: because the Fathers designed it that way. Why they did so is a rather more complicated and interesting business.

The delegates to the Quebec Conference met on Monday, 10 October 1864, in the second-floor library of the Legislative Council. The conference continued a dialogue begun at Charlottetown a month earlier between representatives of Canada and those of the Maritime provinces of British America, with a view to unification. The dialogue was in some ways unequal. The Canadians met regularly in caucus and planned their moves in concert. The average Maritime delegates had no such organizational support. As a result, the Maritimers were often simply overwhelmed—or bullied—into agreement by the force of Canadian prior agreement, perhaps chivvied along a bit by champagne and rich dinners. According to PEI's Edward Palmer, "for the first few days, the leading delegates of the lower provinces exhibited caution and vigilance upon every question affecting the interests of these provinces." But after the Senate debate, compromise in favour of Confederation was much more common. Many thought Charlottetown had resolved the broad outlines of a scheme to establish a new nation; all that remained were the details. But these details were not easily agreed upon. The biggest problem faced by the delegates was the disparity in size between Canada and the lower provinces, even when the latter were combined. Maritimers understandably feared being swallowed up by the behemoth. To assuage Maritime concerns, Canada had conceded at the outset that it would forgo its preference for a single elected legislature to form a two-tiered (or bicameral) structure, with an upper house formed on principles more favourable to the Maritimes.

On 16 October John A. Macdonald introduced the Canadian proposal for the Senate, offering sectional equality among Ontario, Quebec, and the Maritimes combined into one unit. The Maritimers seemed to accept unification, but argued for more senators. As Andrew Macdonald of PEI insisted, if there was to be representation by population in the elected chamber, "the upper house should be more responsible of the smaller provinces, as it was to be the guardian of their rights and privileges." He proposed that each province should have an equal number of representatives, as was the case in the American Senate. Why Macdonald's proposal did not win more favour from the Maritimes contingent is not clear, Instead, Canada proposed additional seats if Newfoundland joined the union. After several more days of debate, the delegates unanimously agreed that senators would be appointed for life by the federal government. As Christopher Moore observes, such a method of appointment would assure that the Senate would not be a powerful independent body. And such, it turned out, was exactly the point. In the 1850s most provinces had toyed with the idea of an elective upper house—Canada had even accepted one in 1856. But most British Americans were still fascinated by the concept of responsible government, and responsible government could not work properly if both houses of a bicameral legislature were equally powerful. Money bills had to originate in the House of Commons. The delegates could accept an upper house of "sober second thoughts," but not a strong Senate.

As George Brown argued in Toronto shortly after Quebec, he doubted whether "two elective chambers, both representing the people and both claiming control over the public finances," could possibly work in continual harmony. There was considerable agreement—indeed virtual unanimity—at Quebec that the demands of responsible government could only be met by constructing a weak Senate, and such was what the Fathers of Confederation put together, however strange a legislative body resulted from their efforts.

an anglophone colony of Canada. Not only were First Nations, Métis, and Chinese cast aside as quickly as possible, but French Canadians were not expected to settle there in any substantial numbers. National consolidation was arguably complete in 1885, but much Canadian "nationalism" still bore the distinctive mark of the Ontario WASP. Two cultures, French and English, were in firm opposition to each other, and other cultures were thoroughly marginalized. Trying to satisfy the nation's two main components would continue to be the most challenging task facing the Canadian government for many years.

Short Bibliography

Bolger, Francis. *Prince Edward Island and Confederation, 1863–1873*. Charlottetown, 1964. The standard study.

Bradbury, Bettina. *Working Families: Age, Gender, and Daily Survival in Industrializing Montreal*. Toronto, 1993. An exciting work on early industrialization in Montreal from the twin perspectives of women and the working classes.

Buckner, P.A. *The Transition to Responsible Government: British Policy in British North America 1815–59*. Westport, Conn., 1985. Now the standard study, based on detailed research and elegantly argued.

Bumsted, J.M. *The Red River Rebellion*. Winnipeg, 1996. A revisionist account.

Courville, Serge, and Normand Séguin. *Rural Life in Nineteenth-Century Quebec*. Ottawa, 1989. A middle-level synthesis of an important topic.

Curtis, Bruce. *Building the Educational State: Canada West, 1836–1871*. Sussex and London, 1988. A revisionist work that argues the importance of educational policy for state formation in this period.

Daschuk, James. *Clearing the Plains: Disease, Politics of Starvation, and the Loss of Aboriginal Life*. Regina, 2014. A controversial study arguing that the First Nations were deliberately starved in the West in the 1870s and 1880s.

Gagan, David. *Hopeful Travellers: Families, Land, and Social Change in Mid-Victorian Peel County, Canada West*. Toronto, 1981. The product of a huge quantification project, this book attempts to explain the relationship between land and mobility in rural English Canada.

Galbraith, John S. *The Hudson's Bay Company as an Imperial Factor*. Toronto, 1957. The classic statement of the imperial role of the Hudson's Bay Company in the nineteenth century.

Grant, Shelagh D. *Polar Imperative: A History of Arctic Sovereignty in North America*. Vancouver, 2010.

Greer, Allan, and Ian Radforth, eds. *Colonial Leviathan: State Formation in Mid-Nineteenth Century Canada*. Toronto, 1992. A collection of essays informed by international thinking about the nineteenth-century state.

Hodgetts, J.E. *Pioneer Public Service: An Administrative History of the United Canadas, 1841–1867*. Toronto, 1955. A pioneer work decades ahead of its time.

Katz, Michael. *The People of Hamilton, Canada West: Family and Class in a Mid-Nineteenth-Century City*.

Cambridge, Mass., 1975. The first attempt to apply American quantitative methodology on a large scale to a Canadian subject.

Lewis, Robert. *Manufacturing Montreal: The Making of an Industrial Landscape, 1850 to 1930.* Baltimore, 2000. A study from a geographer's perspective of the growth of industrial Montreal.

Lucas, Sir Charles, ed. *Lord Durham's Report on the Affairs of British North America*, 3 vols. Oxford, 1912; reprinted New York, 1970. The scholarly edition of the complete Durham Report.

Masters, D.C. *The Reciprocity Treaty of 1854.* Ottawa, 1963. Still the standard account of this important treaty.

Metcalfe, Alan. *Canada Learns to Play: The Emergence of Organized Sport 1807–1911.* Toronto, 1987. An important work that documents the development in Canada of organized sport in the nineteenth century.

Monet, Jacques. *The Last Cannon Shot: A Study of French-Canadian Nationalism.* Toronto, 1969. The classic study of the emergence of nationalism, under the watchful eye of the Church, in Lower Canada/Canada East.

Pryke, Kenneth. *Nova Scotia and Confederation 1864–1873.* Toronto, 1979. The standard account.

Saddlemyer, Ann, ed. *Early Stages: Theatre in Ontario 1800–1914.* Toronto, 1990. A collection of pioneering essays that demonstrate how much is to be learned about Canadian culture in the nineteenth century if one chooses to look.

Shelton, W. George, ed. *British Columbia and Confederation.* Victoria, 1967. A useful collection of essays.

Shippee, L.B. *Canadian–American Relations 1849–1874.* New Haven, 1939. Still the best overall study of the topic.

Tucker, Gilbert. *The Canadian Commercial Revolution 1845–1851.* Ottawa, 1970. The most useful survey of this question.

Waite, Peter B. *The Life and Times of Confederation, 1864–1867: Politics, Newspapers, and the Union of British North America.* Toronto, 1962. Still the best account of the central period of unification.

Winks, Robin. *Canada and the United States: The Civil War Years.* Montreal, 1971. Old, but still the standard work; a thorough account of Canadian–American relations during the war years.

Zeller, Suzanne. *Inventing Canada: Early Victorian Science and the Idea of a Transcontinental Nation.* Toronto, 1987. A work with a controversial argument—that science helped unite British North America—and a good deal of material on colonial science.

Study Questions

1. Explain how Britain's espousal of the free trade doctrine affected markets for Canadian wheat in the late 1840s.

2. Explain why the free trade doctrine led to the Reciprocity Treaty between British North America and the United States. How did this lead to more railway-building and the rise of industrialism in British North America?

3. Identify three reasons why people in Canada West were so anxious to move into the Canadian West.

4. Outline the political consequences of the move to responsible government in Canada East.

5. Why did volunteer and fraternal organizations become so popular in British North America?

6. Explain how the infrastructure of an educational system and a publishing industry contributed to Canadian cultural production during this period.

7. What is important about George Brown's observation that the Maritime delegates agreed that union was desirable "if the terms of union could be made satisfactory"?

8. Give two reasons to explain why people in the Maritimes might think of Confederation as a "Canadian plot."

9. How would you have felt about Canadian policy towards the West if you were a settler living in Saskatchewan in 1885? If you were an Aboriginal person?

Visit the companion website for *A History of the Canadian Peoples*, fifth edition for further resources.

www.oupcanada.com/Bumsted5e

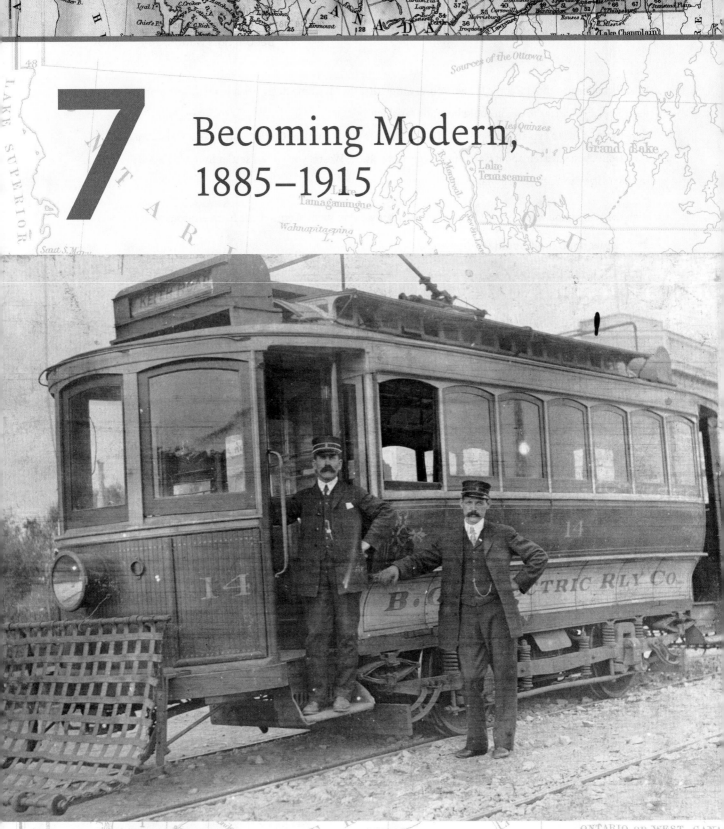

7 Becoming Modern, 1885–1915

Trolley cars became a principal mode of urban transport in the 1890s. The single-truck car shown here is from the Lower Mainland of British Columbia. Trolleys varied from city to city and were adapted to their specific urban environments. Note that this car has a mesh guard attached to its front and to its back, suggesting that there was a reasonable chance that it would encounter humans or animals on its tracks. City of Vancouver Archives, H-303

Timeline

1886 W.S. Fielding introduces legislation in Nova Scotia calling for secession from the union. The first CPR transcontinental arrives in Manitoba.

1887 Honoré Mercier leads *nationaliste* Liberals to victory in Quebec. St Catharines opens first electric streetcar system in Canada.

1890 Manitoba government abolishes public funding for Catholic schools. CPR builds rail line through Maine to connect Moncton with Montreal.

1891 Sir John A. Macdonald dies.

1892 A great fire destroys St John's, Newfoundland.

1896 Wilfrid Laurier leads the Liberal Party to a national electoral victory. Gold is discovered in the Klondike. The Manitoba Schools Question becomes a national issue.

1898 A national referendum is held on prohibition of alcoholic beverages. Newfoundland completes a railway across the island.

1899 Canadian Northern Railway is incorporated. Alaska Boundary Dispute is referred to an international tribunal. Canada agrees to send volunteer troops to South Africa.

1900 Art Museum of Toronto is founded. Prohibition legislation is passed on Prince Edward Island.

1901 The first wireless message transmitted across the Atlantic is received on Signal Hill near St John's, Newfoundland.

1902 Ernest Thompson Seton founds Woodcraft Indians.

1903 Alaska Boundary Dispute between Canada and the United States is handed over to a joint commission of six "impartial jurists of repute."

1905 Saskatchewan and Alberta are created as provinces out of the North-West Territories. Ontario Conservatives finally win political control of the province.

1906 Ontario Hydro-Electric Commission is created.

1907 Development of Marquis wheat. Canadian Department of Interior begins paying bonuses to European immigrant agents for labourers. Canadian Art Club is founded in Toronto.

1908 Border crossings established at 38 points across the US–Canada border.

1909 Department of External Affairs is created.

1910 Steel Company of Canada is created by an amalgamation of smaller firms.

1911 Robert Borden's Conservatives take over federal government in the Reciprocity Election. Marius Barbeau is appointed as anthropologist in the Museum Branch of the Geological Survey of Canada. Noranda gold/copper mine opens in Quebec.

1912 Social Services Council of Canada is organized. Quebec's boundaries are extended to Hudson Bay.

In the years after Confederation, Canada became one of the richest nations in the world in terms of gross national product and per capita income. Given the advantage of hindsight, historians from comparably sized countries—such as Mexico, Brazil, or Argentina—can only envy Canada's privileged position of wealth, if not power, in this critical period. From the late 1870s to the end of World War I, Canada was among the top 10 of the world in industrial development. Though the country possessed rich agricultural and natural resources, much of the key to its success lay in the exploitation of these advantages by a burgeoning industrial sector. Canadians often saw only the weaknesses of the Canadian economy. From the vantage point of most of the world, however, Canada was rich, powerful, highly industrialized, and "progressive," even if still a part of the British Empire. It possessed a vibrant labour movement. Before the Great War, Canada had created a self-sustaining internal economy and a dynamic foreign trade. While the nation was transforming its economy, it was also altering its society and culture. There was another round of immigration, and Canada became an increasingly urbanized country. This was also the great era of reform, both political and social. As well, there was a great national debate over Canada's place within the British Empire. The political system that made all these developments possible operated through the mediating influence of political parties.

As a result of both its geographical position and its colonial situation, Canada before 1914 was able to enjoy relative isolation from the turmoil of international politics, concentrating on its own domestic development. Like Americans, most Canadians were relatively inward-looking, even isolationist, in their attitudes towards the wider world. Most French Canadians saw themselves as an autonomous people without close European or international connections, while Canadians of British origin felt varying degrees of loyalty to Great Britain, which looked after most international affairs in the name of the Empire. Canada's corps of diplomats was tiny, confined to Washington, London, and Paris. After 1909 a small Department of External Affairs supervised and co-ordinated the nation's sporadic formal relations with the world. While most Canadians felt no need to be citizens of the world before 1914, they were not necessarily ignorant of it. The larger daily newspapers covered foreign affairs far more assiduously than their modern equivalents, for example.

The Developing Political and Constitutional System

The Fathers of Confederation had not written political parties into the Canadian Constitution. Nevertheless, by the mid-1880s a two-party system had evolved at both the federal and provincial levels that would remain unchanged until World War I. Indeed, this period was in many respects the golden age of Canadian party politics. Party affiliation was a serious matter. Being a Liberal or a Conservative was a commitment passed on from father to son; small towns had parallel Liberal and Conservative business establishments, including funeral parlours. The seeming vitality of the two-party system disguised, to some degree, the underlying tensions of Canadian federalism. Before 1914, however, the parties appeared flexible enough to contain various currents of conflict and disagreement. Both national parties developed consensual systems capable of holding together differing ideologies, sections of the country, and interest groups.

The key to the successful functioning of the national parties—and the allegiances of their adherents—was in large part the power of patronage. Both parties, in office, distributed honours and jobs to their leading supporters, carefully apportioning rewards to those whose qualifications were judged solely in terms of political service and loyalty. The patronage system rewarded chiefly those members of the Canadian professional and business elites (mainly from the so-called middle class) who ran the two parties. The system diminished ideological and regional differences, offering French Canadians their own opportunities for advancement. Patronage thus encouraged a stable party system in which matters of principle were less important than the division of the spoils of victory.

Despite their consensual utility, Canadian political parties had considerable difficulty in mediating the relationships between the federal and provincial levels of government. The rise of a strong movement for provincial rights, initiated by Ontario, joined by Quebec, and supported on occasion by all provinces, was almost inevitable. The chief, although not sole, bone of contention would be economic development. Provinces insisted that they, not the federal government, should control development within their boundaries. What was unexpected was the support for provincial rights provided by the Judicial Committee of the British Privy Council, the court of last resort for federal–provincial disagreements. In a series of landmark decisions stretching from the 1880s to the Great War, the Judicial Committee consistently reduced the power of the federal government and enhanced that of the provinces. Both anglophone and francophone voters tended to support this readjustment of Confederation. They saw the provinces as a check on the federal government's power, and they consistently supported provincial parties that wanted to confront Ottawa. Thus there was nothing unique about the 1887 victory in Quebec of the *nationaliste* Liberal government of Honoré Mercier (1840–94). W.S. Fielding (1848–1929) had won for the Liberals in Nova Scotia in 1884 on a platform of provincial rights. In 1886 Fielding introduced legislation calling for the secession of Nova Scotia from the union. Obviously, provincial parties could not afford too close an identification with their federal counterparts, particularly while the latter were in power. Only with the success of Laurier's Liberals in 1896 did the Ontario Tories escape the albatross of a federal Conservative Party, for example. By 1905 they won control of the province, which they would seldom relinquish over the remainder of the century.

A great irony of Confederation was that French Canada continued as the region upon which national political success had to be built. Until the death of Sir John A. Macdonald in 1891, the Conservatives had successfully appealed to Quebec with a judicious combination of local political patronage and national political policies. The execution of Louis Riel late in 1885 threatened that appeal, but the government's Quebec ministers held firm. The Grand Old Man's successors, including

J.J. Abbott (1821–93), John S. Thompson (1844–94), and Charles Tupper (1821–1915), simply did not have the magic. In 1896 Wilfrid Laurier (1841–1919) became the national *chef*. He had put together a coalition of provincial Liberal parties by softening the potential issues of division. Laurier's agonizing over the Manitoba Schools Question of the early 1890s, when his distaste for a unilingual policy for Manitoba schools was matched only by his refusal to prevent provinces from running affairs within their own general mandate, was a pure reflection of his approach. Laurier saw national unity and national harmony as identical and, not surprisingly, viewed a bicultural state as essential.

The Conservatives of Robert Borden (1854–1937) replaced Laurier's Liberals in 1911. The Tories split the Quebec vote while sweeping Ontario, thanks in large measure to the support of the Ontario provincial party. Key issues in the 1911 election were American reciprocity and imperial naval defence. Borden's victory was a triumph for Canadian imperial sentiment, anti-continentalism, and middle-class reform. Borden had set out his Halifax Platform in 1907, calling for civil service reform, public ownership of telephones and telegraphs, a reformed Senate, and free mail delivery in rural areas. Borden spoke for the "progressive" forces of Anglo-Canadian society and reform, which had been marshalling strength since the mid-1880s. Laurier had enacted some of Borden's planks, including civil service reform in 1908, but the Conservatives still claimed the close imperial connection and had added the progressive mantle. Borden achieved some of his imperial vision only with the beginning of the Great War. The Conscription Crisis of 1917 completed the process, which began in 1911 with the defeat of Laurier, of the political isolation of French Canada. At the same time, neither the West nor the Maritimes were content, as events after the war's end soon demonstrated.

The Economic Infrastructure

Control of capital through chartered banks headquartered chiefly in central Canada was one of that region's great advantages. Unlike the United States, Canadian banking was always highly centralized. In 1914 in Canada there were only 26 banks operating 2,888 branches. Some of the larger banks (the Royal Bank, the Bank of Commerce) had more than 300 branches each. From the beginning, Canadian chartered banks focused less on serving local customers than on facilitating the transfer of commodities and funds. Their credit facilities, especially for outlying districts of the nation, were quite limited. The banking industry itself wrote Canadian banking legislation. The Canadian Bankers' Association was an organization of a few powerful men.

Although in 1913 Montreal-headquartered banks held half of the assets of all Canadian banks ($788 million of $1.55 billion), Quebec contained considerably fewer branch banks per capita than the remainder of the nation. The result was the founding by Alphonse Desjardins (1854–1920) of the caisses populaires, often run by *curés* in association with Catholic parishes. Financial institutions to compete locally with the chartered banks did develop, not only in the form of caisses populaires but as government savings banks, local savings banks, and credit unions. Their economic power was limited, however, and the chartered banks continued to grow. Banks with head offices in central Canada refused to make local loans and

Biography

Sir Wilfrid Laurier

Wilfrid Laurier, c. 1882. Topley Studio Fonds, LAC, PA-013133.

The family heritage of Wilfrid Laurier (1841–1919), born in a small Quebec village outside Montreal, dated back to seventeenth-century Quebec. As part of his education,

Laurier lived for two years with an English-speaking family and attended an English-speaking school. His facility in both languages was subsequently one of his great political strengths. After education at l'Assomption College and McGill University, he was called to the Quebec bar.

From his earliest days Laurier was a Liberal, and after election to Parliament in 1874 he soon joined the Mackenzie cabinet. Laurier was an outspoken critic of the ultramontane wing of the Catholic Church in Quebec and defender of both the Liberals as a party of moderation and of the laity as entitled to make their own choices free of clerical pressure. Like many French-Canadian Liberals of his generation, he not only wanted a non-denominational party but was also attracted to British history and to the British Constitution.

Somewhat chastened by political failure in the early 1880s, his career was rejuvenated by the execution of Louis Riel, whose constitutional grievances he championed. But Laurier resolutely refused to become a racial and religious nationalist, and he advocated conciliation between French and English. He exploited the clumsiness of both the Conservatives and French-Canadian set local interest rates at high levels. Sir Edmund Walker (1848–1924), president of the Bank of Commerce, labelled regional complaints "local grievances against what we regard as the interests of the country as a whole" (quoted in Naylor, 1975, I: 103).

Transportation continued to be an essential ingredient of development. As in the age of the first railway boom of the 1850s, railways were both a means of development and a field of investment. Substantial railway construction involved significant public subsidies, often in the form of land grants along the right of way, as well as other boons. The Canadian Pacific Railway (CPR) received from the government the completed line from Fort William, Ontario, to Selkirk, Manitoba, as well as the line from Kamloops to Port Moody in BC. Moreover, it received a cash payment of $25 million, plus 25 million acres (10,117,500 ha) "fairly fit for settlement," and various tax exemptions on its land. In addition, it had a monopoly position. Nor was the Canadian Pacific the only railway so favoured. Dozens of railways incorporated in Canada during these years. Local communities fought desperately for railways, seeing them as links to a prosperous future. Sir William Mackenzie (1849–1923) and Sir Donald Mann (1853–1934) constructed a second transcontinental line, the Canadian Northern Railway, which passed considerably to the

clerics over the Manitoba Schools Question, insisting that he could effect a satisfactory compromise, which he did.

Once elected to office as Prime Minister in 1896, with the strong backing of Quebec voters, he appointed a strong cabinet composed mainly of provincial leaders with progressive ideas. Fortunately for the Liberal government, Canada was entering a period of great growth and economic boom, especially in the West, providing a tide upon which almost any government could have ridden successfully. The Liberals became involved with Canadian big business interests over the construction of two new transcontinental railroads, but eventually came to grief over military and imperial policy, issues that still divided English and French Canada. Laurier survived the Boer War by allowing English Canadians to participate as volunteers and by stifling all initiatives for closer imperial co-operation. He even managed to deal with the problem of increased German naval construction by introducing a Canadian navy instead of Canadian contributions to the British one.

One issue that helped defeat his government in 1911 came unexpectedly, when the United States offered Canada a reciprocal economic arrangement and Laurier accepted it enthusiastically. To its surprise, the Liberal government discovered that Canadians were not willing in boom times to pay the price of a potential loss of national sovereignty in return for American advantages, although the loss of Quebec support on imperial issues was probably more important, as was a perception that the Liberals had lost their reformist edge and were less progressive on social issues than were the Conservatives. Laurier supported Canadian entrance into World War I wholeheartedly, but refused to co-operate in 1917 with the government over conscription or to join a coalition government committed to the question. He was deserted by many English-speaking Liberals, and in the election of November 1917 his support was reduced almost solely to Quebec seats.

Laurier was well known as a conciliator who sought compromise and opposed political extremism and sectional division in word and deed. In retrospect, one of his most important achievements may have been his refusal to allow his nation to become more closely integrated into the British Empire.

north of the CPR. Everyone outside central Canada complained about the high costs of freight, but all Canadians relied on the railway. Passenger travel was swift and relatively inexpensive.

Energy was another essential. Canada always possessed rich potential energy resources. Coal never provided much advantage, but abundant water power did. Changing technology at the close of the nineteenth century enabled major natural waterfalls to be harnessed and others to be created through dams. Development for hydroelectric power was substantial in the early years of the twentieth century. No province had greater potential for hydroelectricity generation than Quebec. Unlike Ontario, which established the Ontario Hydro-Electric Commission in 1906 under the chairmanship of Sir Adam Beck (1857–1925), Quebec permitted its hydroelectric development to be carried out by private enterprise. The process of exploiting electricity, both for light and for power, was one of the great unsung technological developments of the age. Industry could use water power as an alternative to fossil fuel. Cheap hydroelectric power became an advantage for Canadian industry. The manufacturing community saw cheap power as essential to its growth and development. Hydroelectricity lit Canadian homes at relatively low cost. It fostered the growth of electric-powered public transportation, such as the tram and the trolley.

The period between 1880 and 1919 was a great age of science and technology throughout the Western world. Most fields of scientific endeavour transformed out of all recognition the basic theoretical assumptions that had dominated humankind for generations. The number of inventions that altered in practical ways how people lived and worked was astounding. Canada played little role at the frontiers of pure science. Its record in the technical application of science was somewhat better, as the activities of the Dominion Experimental Farms system (created by Ottawa in 1886) demonstrated. The great achievement of Canadian agricultural research in this period was the development of Marquis wheat in 1907 by Charles Edward Saunders (1867–1937). In both science and technology, however, Canada was fortunate to be able to borrow heavily from Great Britain and the United States. Most Canadian technical accomplishment came through adapting imported technology to Canadian conditions, although a number of useful Canadian inventions were introduced in this period.

Population growth was also necessary for economic development. Immigration provided much of that growth for Canada in this period, as in others. Between 1880 and 1920 nearly 4.5 million immigrants arrived in Canada, mainly although not exclusively from Europe and the United States. Beginning in the mid-1890s, the origins of the newcomers shifted perceptibly. Most of the earlier immigrants came from the British Isles, while after 1896 large numbers came from Eastern and Southern Europe. In addition, Americans again began arriving in Canada in large numbers, their destinations the "Last Best West" in Alberta and Saskatchewan. By 1901, 34 per cent of the newcomers to the prairie West came from other countries than Canada, with 33 per cent from the United States and 22 per cent from Britain. During the peak decade of immigration (1905–14), nearly 2.8 million people immigrated to Canada, with the numbers about equally divided among Central and Eastern Europe, the United States, and the British Isles. (A small number of Asians and people from the Near East were included in the total. Most of the Near East immigrants came from Lebanon and were listed as "Syrians" in the official records. (Many of the victims in April 1912 on board the ill-fated passenger liner *Titanic* were "Syrians" travelling in steerage on their way to Canada.) Between 1901 and 1911 alone, the Canadian population grew by 43 per cent. In the 1911 census, over 20 per cent of all Canadians enumerated had been born abroad. While many of the newcomers settled on farms, fully 70 per cent joined the labour force in industry and transportation. Canadian business and government specifically recruited many of the newcomers, often on a contract basis, to provide an industrial workforce. In 1907 the Canadian Department of the Interior began paying bonuses to European immigration agents for people who had labour experience, such as farmers, navvies, or miners. Much of this industrial workforce ended up in Canada's cities.

While the typical newcomer to Canada in these years continued to be the unassisted immigrant, arriving under his or her own power, either alone or as part of a family group, several other categories need to be singled out for special attention, particularly British "orphans" and European contract labourers.

The Canadian Bank of Commerce building at 25 King Street West, designed by R.A. Waite and erected in 1889–90, was one of several new office buildings in Toronto that had some claim to architectural distinction and even grandeur. At seven-and-a-half storeys, it soared over neighbouring three- and four-storey buildings, and reflected the influence of the first skyscrapers in New York and Chicago. City of Toronto Archives, Fonds 1497, Item 21.

Canadians were generally more willing to accept immigrants from the British Isles than from any other place, although resentment was common against those Britons who looked down their noses at their "colonial cousins." On the other hand, many Canadians objected to the activities of British philanthropists and philanthropic institutions in employing Canada as a dumping ground for unwanted children of the urban poor. These children were recruited as cheap labour, mainly for Canadian farms and as domestic servants. The majority were young boys, but a substantial number were young girls. Nearly 100,000 of these "home children" were sent to Canada before the Great War, most of them recruited in British slums. Many were encouraged to go by their parents; others were literally seized from parents and sent overseas "for their own good." The results were

mixed, with the worst experiences probably suffered by children of both genders who were sent into rural homes, where many were badly exploited by their supposed benefactors. This immigration was constantly accompanied by opposition to its continuance. Much of the opposition to child immigration came from the Canadian labour movement, especially between 1888 and 1895. It was concerned less with the treatment of the victims than with their presence as an unregulated low-wage component of the workforce.

Perhaps the most colourful of the philanthropists involved in child "rescue" was the Dublin-born Thomas John Barnardo (1845–1900), who was personally responsible for sending more than 30,000 youngsters to Canada. Barnardo, always known as "Doctor" Barnardo, actually scoured the streets of London for waifs, collecting thousands of pounds from the British public for his charity work. He used the money less to improve existing conditions than to expand the scope of his activities. Barnardo was a lightning rod for complaints of abuse and victimization. His activities were criticized on a number of occasions, and he came to take care that records were kept, using photographs and letters from children to demonstrate how well they were getting on. As for the children, one modern study of Barnardo children has concluded that some evidence exists that 9 per cent of the boys and 15 per cent of the girls were actually abused (Parker, 2009: 221). (In February 2010, British Prime Minister Gordon Brown met with a group of former immigrants and others to apologize for their treatment [Boycott, 2010].)

Despite the emphasis on agricultural settlement and the concerns about the assimilability of non-British immigrants, a number of Canadian corporations insisted on their need for willing workers. For these companies, headed by the railroads, British immigrants were not desirable because they complained about wages and working conditions; farmers were unsuitable because they left their jobs at harvest time. The CPR turned increasingly after 1901 to contract workers, often from southern Italy. According to Donald Avery (1995: 30), these workers—supplied by labour agents working in Europe—could "live for a year on the wages they earn in six months." The railroads liked Bulgarians, Poles, and Italians because by working hard and living simply, they were "peculiarly suited for

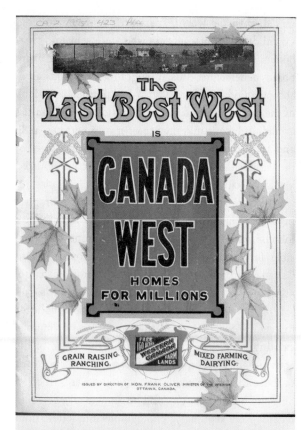

A 1907 poster exhorting immigrants to settle in western Canada. This poster well illustrates the mentality of western development in the first years of the new century. How would you describe this mentality? LAC, C-30621.

the work." A massive national railway construction program between 1900 and 1914 was sustained by 50,000 to 70,000 immigrant navvies (unskilled construction workers) per year. Mining corporations were equally attracted to Slavic and Italian workers, and by 1913 more than 300 labour agencies were recruiting more than 200,000 workers per year from abroad for labour in Canada. Several foreign governments protested the treatment of their nationals by labour agencies and Canadian employers, and both organized labour and nativist groups opposed the contract workers as being scabs. More than half of these workers were sojourners, who intended to use the savings from their earnings to return to their homelands, but a substantial minority would remain in Canada permanently. The Italians brought several new elements in their cultural baggage. Several secret societies mod-

elled on the Sicilian Mafia and the Calabrian 'Ndrangheta provided a range of services to immigrants, sometimes also engaging in extortion activities that were attributed by the Canadian media to the "Black Hand." A few Italians were also anarchists; one of their leaders, Luigi Galleani, was deported from Canada in 1903.

Another Round of Industrialization

Financial centralization and growing industrial capacity, particularly the shift from the processing of primary goods into the secondary manufacturing of finished goods, were major economic developments in Canada in the years 1880–1919. Continued industrialization always involved more than the construction of new and larger factories. Canadians needed to extend and rationalize transportation facilities. They had to mobilize investment, exploit resources, and recruit a labour force. Despite the National Policy, Ottawa did not maintain control over, or ownership in, the Canadian economy. The country's emergence on the international scene increased its vulnerability to world economic conditions and economic cycles. Moreover, its industrial development was distinctly uneven, with industrial growth well above the national average in Ontario, at the national average in Quebec, and well below the national average in the Maritime and western provinces. Larger urban centres, such as Montreal and Toronto, expanded constantly, while smaller communities fell steadily behind.

One of the keys to Canadian economic growth between 1885 and the Great War was an influx of foreign investment. Few nations depended so heavily on foreign capital to fuel economic growth as has Canada throughout its history. Investment in this era—particularly in the boom years 1900–13—was significant. Like other countries, Canada used most of its imported capital to finance large development projects, such as railways and hydroelectric generation. Canada's imports of capital came in the two forms of indirect (portfolio) investment and direct investment. These two types of investment reflected the respective activity of Canada's two largest financial partners. Much of the portfolio investment came from Great Britain. Much of the direct investment came from the United States. In terms of the foreign domination of the economy that resulted, the two types of investment were quite different. Direct investment resulted in far greater control. At the time few Canadians agonized overly much about the extent or the origin of foreign ownership. Foreign control did not become a serious issue in Canadian economic theory or public life before the late 1950s. Until then, almost all Canadians might have agreed with the American entrepreneur Frank Clergue, who declared in 1901 that "foreign money injected into the circulating medium of Canada" would "remain forever to the everlasting blessing of thousands of its inhabitants" (quoted in Bliss, 1972: 38).

As students now learn routinely in introductory economics courses, portfolio investment represents money borrowed against securities, in this period mainly bonds. Bonds are a relatively safe investment. They do not carry management implications. The British preferred portfolio investment in Canada because their prosperous citizens wanted to clip coupons in their old age. Government (federal, provincial, municipal) and the railways did most of Canada's borrowing in Britain. The money went to finance transportation networks and public works. Little was available for private enterprise, almost none for venture capital. In the first years of the twentieth century, Canadian entrepreneurs exploited the British investment market in new ways. The chief innovation was the promotion of bond issues for giant industrial operations created from the merger of smaller companies. Nobody was more successful at merging than William Maxwell Aitken (1879–1964, later Lord Beaverbrook), son of a New Brunswick Presbyterian minister. His great triumph came in 1910 with the creation of the Steel Company of Canada (Stelco), the bonds for which his Royal Securities firm sold in London. "I believe in consolidations," Aitken told *Maclean's* magazine in 1911. "They are more efficient. They give better service to the consumer. In a large country such as Canada, they reduce the distribution costs. They are good for the consumer" (quoted in Marchilson, 1996: 181). He was the most visible and sharpest oper-

ator in a movement that saw 58 giant corporations created in Canada between 1909 and 1912.

The United States was an importer of British capital before World War I and had little available for overseas portfolio investment. The Americans invested directly in Canada to gain access to Canadian raw materials and the Canadian market. They went heavily into the resource sector. They also invested in Canadian manufacturing to gain maximum access to the Canadian market. Less than half of American direct investment was in manufacturing, but the total amount involved was over $100 million by 1910. The protective tariff played an important role in encouraging American branch-plant investment. Early Canadian protectionism sought to foster employment. Canadians did not worry much about the outflow of profits or the influx of foreign managers. Canadians generally accepted that Canadian businessmen and investors were not very adventurous, preferring familiar fields and allowing the Yankees to take the chances. Far from endangering the Canadian identity, American investment fostered it. The alternative was immigration to the United States.

The Americans preferred to locate their branch plants in southern Ontario. This choice came for a variety of reasons. Americans were active in the heavy industries of Ontario, partly because Ontario was so close to the industrial heartland of the United States south of the Great Lakes. Moreover, Ontario deliberately encouraged Americans to invest in the processing of raw materials by allowing them virtually free access to the province's natural resources. Ontarians believed that they had all the requirements for self-sufficiency within their own borders. The province required that resources taken on Crown land be processed in Canada. "Debarred from the opportunity of cutting logs for export, it is an absolute certainty that the American lumberman, in default of other sources of supply, will transfer his sawmill enterprises to Canadian soil" (quoted in Nelles, 1974: 217). American preference both contributed to and reflected the industrial development of Ontario.

After 1885 manufacturing replaced commerce as the chief propellant of urban growth in Ontario. Much of the new industrial plant involved sophisticated technological applications, often imported from the United States. Ontario became the centre of the Canadian iron

Workers at looms, c. 1908. As this photograph indicates, most workers in the textile industry were women, working in crowded conditions on the shop floor. City of Toronto Archives, James Collection, Fonds 1244, 137.

and steel industry. The transformation of the older iron industry into the steel industry was symptomatic of the process that was occurring. Coal replaced charcoal as the source of heat. The refining process turned into two steps, first involving open-hearth furnaces and then a steam-driven rolling mill. The result was a product with a slightly higher carbon content. Its name was steel. Mechanization occurred at every step in the manufacturing process. "Gigantic automation" was the watchword at huge installations like Stelco's Hamilton plant and Algoma's Sault Ste Marie operation. Steel rails were the most common standard product. Ontario's manufacturing grew in a number of smaller urban centres.

Quebec manufacturing relied far less on heavy industry (and vast capitalization) than did manufacturing in Ontario. It depended far more on an industry based on labour and fussy mechanization, such as clothing, wood products, textiles, and food processing. Part of the explanation for the difference may reside in labour availability. Part may have been the availability of cheap hydroelectric power in Quebec after 1900. Quebec had eliminated Ontario's early advantage in secondary over primary manufacturing by 1915. Montreal provided the greatest concentration of Quebec's manufacturing sector. By 1900 workers in that city represented about half the manufacturing labour in the province. It is easy to overemphasize the notorious lag between the two central Canadian provinces. They were more like one another than they were like the remainder of the nation. The industrial disparity between the

Manufacturing Output, 1870–1890

One of the developments of the post-Confederation period was the tendency for the industrial output of the Maritime region to lose ground to Ontario and Quebec. The following table documents the change in output by province in various industrial sectors between 1870 and 1890.

Percentage Change in Manufacturing Output, 1870–1890

Industry	Nova Scotia	New Brunswick	Quebec	Ontario
All factories	128	42	104	116
Farm production (butter, cheese, and cloth)	60	67	50	34
All manufacturing	120	44	101	113
Consumer goods	160	95	100	119
Durable goods	30	−10	83	61
Intermediate goods	214	50	120	162
Chemical products	210	3	149	410
Clothing	224	49	125	277
Coal & petroleum products	164	321	365	−5
Food & beverages	361	292	122	82
Iron & steel products	142	21	92	90
Leather & fur products	−1	−12	50	41
Nonferric metal products	348	204	191	854
Nonmetallic mineral products	114	121	186	215
Printing	54	111	86	177
Paper products	48	−52	313	254
Rubber goods	n.a.	n.a.	202	4,311
Transport equipment	3	−38	154	26
Tobacco products	−78	64	162	263
Textiles	505	443	406	150
Wood products	213	2	64	153

Source: Kris Inwood, "Maritime Industrialization from 1870 to 1910," Acadiensis 21, 1 (Autumn 1991): 147. Reprinted by permission.

central provinces and the others grew continually in the years before 1914.

While the absence of industrialization in the Canadian West was a consequence of the recentness of its settlement, this did not apply to the Maritime region. Here rural stagnation joined a crisis in the shipbuilding industry. The growth of new technologies was partly to blame, but the problem was mainly a failure of the Maritime shippers' nerve. The shippers always viewed their ships as instruments of trade. Instead of reinvesting their capital in a modern shipbuilding industry, they and the business community of the region made a desperate effort to exploit the internal market. They accepted the National Policy and tried to work within it. The attempts at continentalism seemed initially successful in the 1880s, but rapidly turned to failure.

The reasons for the ultimate Maritime failure remain uncertain. Most Maritime entrepreneurs seemed to lack the financial resources to withstand the ups and downs of the economic cycles. They tended to blame many of their problems on high railway freight rates. At about the same time that the region's business community was moaning about railway rates, outside capital moved in and began buying up locally based companies. Montreal capitalists did most of the damage. They bought up and dismantled many burgeoning industries still servicing the local market.

Maritime entrepreneurs, convinced that they were at a substantial geographical disadvantage in competing with central Canada, ceased trying in most sectors after 1895. Instead, the region turned to the panacea of iron and steel. Surely the presence of local raw materials would make this industry a competitive one. Unfortunately, central Canadian interests soon took over the Maritime steel industry. By 1911 Montreal controlled much of the region's industrial enterprise. Toronto, on the other hand, moved into the region's wholesale and retail marketing sector. Between 1901 and 1921 the number of regional businesses that were branches of central Canadian firms more than doubled, from 416 to 950. The net result of both sorts of takeovers was a regional loss of economic autonomy. Outsiders siphoned capital away from the Maritimes, and when times got tough they closed stores and factories. The region was systematically deindustrialized and decommercialized. It would never recover its economic vitality.

Most of the businessmen who operated the industrializing economy were immigrants or sons of immigrants, with Scots farmers over-represented in both categories. Few had begun at the bottom of the social scale. French Canadians were seriously under-represented among large-scale entrepreneurs and industrialists, even within their own province. Most French-Canadian busi-nesses remained small in scale, family-controlled, and confined chiefly to the province of Quebec. These businessmen did share an overall philosophy. They insisted on government involvement in large schemes of public development, such as railways. They accepted government power to grant monopolies of public service through charters or access to Crown lands through advantageous leases. They sought to minimize competition wherever possible, even if public regulation was the price paid for the reduction. Small businessmen who could not combine institutionally to control trade, such as the small retailers, fought hard for early closings and price-fixing. Business rhetoric about competition had less to do with extolling the virtues of free enterprise than with complaining about unfair competition. The business community insisted that what it wanted was a "living profit," a reasonable return on investment of time and capital.

While few business leaders believed in policies of laissez-faire in the relationship between the state and business, the situation was quite different when it came to labour organizations. From the view of business, organized labour was an illegitimate combination designed to erode the right of the individual to run his business as he saw fit. Nevertheless, the growth of industrialization was conducive to expanding worker militancy. The Canadian state proved relatively receptive to the rights of labour to organize. Whereas in the United States public policy was almost universally hostile to labour organization, in Canada laws that legalized union activity were put on the books beginning in the 1880s. Many of the late nineteenth-century labour organizations in Canada were foreign imports, chiefly from the United States. If Canadian labour got much of its structure from the Americans, it drew much of its practical experience from Great Britain. The Noble and Holy Knights of Labor spread from the United States across Canada in the 1870s.The Knights were all-inclusive reformers, as their agenda suggested. For Canada as a whole, the Canadian Labour Congress formed in 1883 as an umbrella organization for local trade councils, and in 1892 it became the Trades and Labor Congress of Canada.

In this period most labour conflict revolved around the right to organize and the recognition of unions. Government acceptance of union activity in some ways

Declaration of Principles of the Knights of Labor (1883)

1. To bring within the fold of organization every department of productive industry, making knowledge a standpoint for action, and industrial moral worth, not wealth, the true standard of individual and national greatness.

2. To secure to the toilers a proper share of the wealth that they created; more of the leisure that rightfully belongs to them; more society advantages; all of the benefits, privileges and emoluments of the world; in a word all those rights and privileges necessary to make them capable of enjoying, appreciating, defending and perpetuating the blessings of good government.

3. To arrive at the true condition of the producing masses in their educational, moral and financial condition, by demanding from the various governments the establishment of bureaus of labor statistics.

4. The establishment of co-operative institutions, productive and initiative.

5. The reserving—of public lands—the heritage of the people—for the actual settler. Not another acre for railroads or corporations.

6. The abrogation of laws that do not bear equally upon capital and labor; the removal of unjust technicalities, delays and discriminations in the administration of justice; and the adopting of measures providing for the health and safety of those engaged in mining, manufacturing and building pursuits.

7. The enactment of laws to compel chartered corporations to pay their employees weekly, in full, for labor performed the preceding week, in the lawful money of the country.

    The enactment of laws giving mechanics and laborers the first lien on their work for their full wages.

8. The abolishment of the contract system on national, state and municipal roads or corporations.

9. The substitution of arbitration for strikes, whenever and wherever employers and employees are willing to meet on equitable grounds.

10. The prohibition of the employment of children in workshops mines and factories, before attaining their fourteenth year.

11. To abolish the system of letting out by contract the labor of convicts in our prisons and reformatory institutions.

12. To secure for both sexes equal pay for equal work.

13. The reduction of the hours of labor to eight per day, so that the laborers may have more time for social enjoyment and intellectual improvement, and be able to reap the advantages conferred by the labor-saving machinery which their brains have created.

Source: *Labor Union* (Hamilton), 1883, as quoted in Gregory S. Kealey and Bryan D. Palmer, *Dreaming of What Might Be: The Knights of Labor in Ontario, 1880–1900* (Cambridge: Cambridge University Press, 2004), 399–400.

increased the frequency of conflict. Moreover, the civil authorities frequently intervened in labour conflicts, usually in the name of public order and often on the side of management. Such intervention often produced violence. Strikes were certainly common everywhere in Canada, especially after 1900. In Ontario's 10 largest cities, between 1901 and 1914, there were 421 strikes and lockouts involving 60,000 workers. In the Maritimes, 324 strikes occurred between 1901 and 1914. Except in the Far West, the majority of the workers involved in these confrontations were skilled rather than unskilled. By 1914 approximately 155,000 Canadians belonged to

"Steel mills at Sydney, Cape Breton," oil on canvas, 1907, by the railway magnate Sir William Cornelius Van Horne. Built between 1900 and 1905, these two plants attracted hundreds of workers, creating an instant city. The Montreal Museum of Fine Arts, gift of the artist's grandson, William C. Van Horne. Photo: The Montreal Museum of Fine Arts, Brian Merrett.

organized labour unions, many of them affiliated with American internationals.

Natural Resources

If Canada was to avoid eternal international balance-of-payment deficits (the plague of Third World countries in our own era) it obviously needed commodities to export. It found many of these in the natural resources sector. To a considerable extent Canada's resources were the old mainstays of the colonial staple economy, now produced under different guises. Resources not

only earned money abroad, they encouraged manufacturing at home.

Agriculture

As if on some master schedule, the Canadian wheat economy continued to expand without pause. Fields of operation moved from central Canada to Manitoba and slightly later to the North-West Territories (which became the provinces of Saskatchewan and Alberta in 1905). Between 1870 and 1890 thousands of farmers, chiefly from Ontario, poured into the West. The number of acres of occupied land went from 2.5 million to over 6 million (1,011,750 to 2,428,200 ha) in the years 1881–91, while the acres of land under cultivation exploded from 279,000 to 1,429,000 (112,911 to 578,316 ha) in the same 10-year period. The opening of the CPR was critical for the production of western wheat. So, too, was the appearance of new wheat strains capable of maturation in the short prairie growing season.

Before the mid-1890s the typical prairie settler was an Ontario-born farmer who came west to make a new start. Despite the passage of the Dominion Lands Act of 1872, which made a fair amount of homestead land available, most farmers preferred to purchase land from companies set up by the great corporate benefactors of government land grants, especially the railways. Farmers believed (with some legitimacy) that homestead land was less likely to acquire rail transportation than was land owned by the railway itself. Although homestead land was free to the male settler (women could not apply for homesteads), successful farming still required substantial capital investment. Conservative estimates of the costs of "farm-making" ranged from a minimum of $300 (the annual wage for an unskilled labourer) to $1,000. Most farmers brought money with them from the sale of land back east. The western farmer was a market farmer. Although the family grew as much food as possible for personal consumption, the farmer's instinct was to increase constantly his acreage under production. Before World War I, mechanization was limited mainly to harvesting. Animals (horses and oxen) did most of the ploughing and cultivation. Nevertheless, the individual farmer managed to cultivate considerable quantities of land, limited mainly by the size of his labour force. In 1898 Ontario-born A.J. Cotton (1857–1942) harvested a crop of over 17,000 bushels of top-grade wheat in Treherne, Manitoba.

Before the 1890s, western settlement was hampered by several factors. In the first place, the American West seemed a more attractive option to most potential new arrivals, with a longer growing season and better transportation networks. Between 1871 and 1891, more people from Canada had departed to the United States than had come to Canada from abroad. In the second place, Canadian immigration authorities had concentrated on recruiting British farmers, with only limited success. People with agricultural backgrounds in Britain were, on the whole, doing well and not anxious to move. Finally, the large private land companies that had received large land grants were not anxious to select their lands and release them onto the market, speculating that land would increase in value after the country was better settled. Beginning in the 1890s an open and aggressive Canadian immigration policy, conducted by both the federal and provincial governments, brought new settlers to the prairies. In 1896 a new Minister of the Interior (with responsibility for immigration) took office. Clifford Sifton (1861–1929) was an Ontario-born Manitoban who believed in massive agricultural immigration as the key to Canadian prosperity. The trick, he held, was to find suitable immigrants and to get them onto the land. Sifton decided to take his immigrant farmers from wherever in the world he could find them, rather than concentrating on people from the United Kingdom. He was prepared to recruit in Eastern Europe, especially on the steppes of Russia where grain cultivation was well established. Sifton saw a quality immigrant as a "stalwart peasant in a sheep-skin coat born on the soil, whose fore-fathers have been farmers for ten generations, with a stout wife and a half-dozen children" (quoted in Petryshyn, 1985: 21). He was also prepared to recruit in the United States, which no longer had an unsettled frontier of its own, despite a previous Canadian reluctance to encourage American settlement. Changing conditions in both Eastern Europe and the United States worked to Canada's advantage.

The Ukrainians and Doukhobors

Ukraine is a vast territory on the central and southern plains of Eastern Europe, and during the later nineteenth century 85 per cent of this territory was part of the Russian Empire, while 15 per cent belonged to the Austrian Empire. The first settlers from Ukraine to Canada had come in the early 1890s, joining Mennonites and Hungarians as early arrivals from these European empires. In 1895, Dr Joseph Oleskiw, a Ukrainian academic who taught agriculture, visited Canada and proposed an extensive Ukrainian immigration to the Canadian West, which Clifford Sifton did his best to implement. Between 1896 and 1914, about 170,000 Ukrainians—chiefly from the overpopulated Austrian

In western Canada, farmers' instincts were to increase acreage as much as possible, creating large, profitable farms. Here, farmers are seen breaking land in Pincher Creek, Alberta. Despite the width and size of the plows illustrated here, they are still being drawn by horses. Note the size of the crew apparently required for this operation. Glenbow Archives, NA-2382-9.

provinces of Galicia and Bukovyna—entered Canada, mainly settling on the prairies. In their homeland, these people had been experiencing increasing subdivision of their land and declining productivity because of lack of capital resulting from heavy taxation. By 1900, half of the landholdings in the provinces of Galicia and Bukovyna were less than two hectares in extent, and many small landholders were heavily in debt. The Ukrainians would probably have preferred to go to the United States, but they faced increasing immigration restrictions and an often hostile reception from the Americans, who no longer had any unsettled agricultural land to distribute to newcomers. Many of the immigrants came to Canada because of a secret agreement between the Canadian

government and the North Atlantic Trading Company, which directed immigrants to Canada in return for under-the-table payments on a per capita basis. Indeed, steamship and railway companies were probably more successful recruiters of immigration outside the British Isles than was the Canadian government.

Canada may have been a second choice, but at least it encouraged Ukrainians to settle and it could make land available to them. Most Ukrainian immigrants were poor but not destitute. Like generations of immigrants before them, they had sold their land and possessions to purchase their passage. Like all immigrants of the time, they found the transatlantic passage in steerage to be a difficult experience. As their own historians have emphasized, the situation the Ukrainians entered in Canada was little different from that at home: bare survival on the land and an early death for those who failed. But they were stubborn—and hopeful. Many new arrivals found the quarter-section homestead concept—160 acres or one-fourth of a square mile township, the standard survey unit in the West—to be beyond their comprehension, partly because of its size and partly because of the difficulty of reproducing compact village communities like the ones they had left.

The first Ukrainians typically emigrated without many of their natural leaders, especially parish clergymen. They were particularly assisted by three members of the Ukrainian intelligentsia—Joseph Oleskiw, Kyrole Genik, and the Reverend Nestor Dmytriw—employed by the Canadian government as "overseers" and advisers. These three men produced a substantial body of writing to assist the new arrivals. They emphasized the need for capital to establish a farm, the adoption of Canadian styles of dress, and the acquisition of free land. Canadian society received the Ukrainians with considerable suspicion, chiefly because they were obviously non-British "foreigners" who spoke an alien language and practised different customs. Those who settled in the cities (especially Winnipeg's North End) in ethnic slum communities were almost visible. But the willingness of the new arrivals to work hard was in their favour, at least before the onset of the Great War. After 1914, Austria-Hungary joined Germany as the enemy, and many Ukrainians in Canada became "enemy aliens."

Usually considered separately from the Ukrainians, although originating from the same region, the Doukhobors were a sectarian movement that broke away from the Russian Orthodox Church in the eighteenth century. The Doukhobors (the term literally means "spirit wrestlers") became a Quaker-like pacifistic group that emphasized the brotherhood and sisterhood of all men and women and the validation of their beliefs not in books but in the "book of life." With the aid of Russian novelist Leo Tolstoy, the Doukhobors came to western Canada in search of refuge from Russian persecution. The first contingent was granted recognition as conscientious objectors by the Canadian government on 6 December 1898. Over the next few years, more than 7,500 Doukhobors arrived in Canada to settle on tracts reserved for them in

what would become Saskatchewan and Alberta. They were joined by their leader, Peter Verigin (1859–1924), in 1903. In 1907 the Canadian government backed away from an earlier commitment to allow the Doukhobors to live and work communally, insisting instead on individual homesteading and an oath of allegiance. As a result, under the leadership of Verigin, communal-living Doukhobors bought land in the Interior of British Columbia and moved into the Kootenay region, where they would subsequently struggle with the authorities over their beliefs.

The Americans

Although the Canadian press would occasionally complain about the "Americanization" of the West and other places, most Americans had always been regarded as desirable settlers who "understood the ways of the continent and its institutions" (Troper, 1972: 12). Many Americans, of course, had started their lives in British America before moving to the United States earlier in the century. Some exceptions to the favourable attitude towards Americans prevailed, however. Many Canadians objected to the polygynous marriage practices of the Mormons, who were one of the earliest groups of immigrants into Alberta in the 1880s, and few Canadians showed any enthusiasm for the admission into their country of American blacks from Oklahoma and elsewhere. In addition to the Mormons, American cattle and sheep ranchers arrived before the 1890s, but following the well-publicized "closing of the frontier" in the United States during that decade the Canadian government made a real effort after 1896 to recruit American farmers of European origins for what would become known as "The Last Best West."

Canadian agents openly sought wealthy immigrants. One common form of recruitment was through personal correspondence from successful settlers to prospective ones, organized by the Department of Immigration. Much of the settlement in Saskatchewan and Alberta occurred in the so-called Palliser's Triangle, a dry-belt region with marginal rainfall. American farmers were alleged to be the best settlers of such land, as they were familiar with the techniques of dry-land farming. In a series of land rushes, thousands of American farmers settled the dry belt in the years between 1906 and 1914. They prospered because there was adequate rainfall during this period, but later they abandoned the region when drought conditions returned.

By 1921 over 44 million acres (17,806,800 ha) of the prairies were under cultivation. According to one set of calculations, the wheat economy in 1901–11 contributed over 20 per cent of the growth in per capita income in Canada. While wheat was the big prairie crop, other crops were possible. Before the arrival of farmers, much of southern Alberta and southwestern Saskatchewan was the domain of ranchers, who grazed their cattle on open range leased from the federal government. At the height of the cattle boom in 1898, Canadian ranchers exported 213,000 live head. Most cattlemen were American, but a

substantial minority were British, and polo-playing was common in early Alberta. Although ranchers insisted that much of the range land was unsuitable for farming because of water shortages, their obvious self-interest in an open range negated the force of much of their argument. Nevertheless, water remained a major potential problem in much of the West.

Mines and Timber

In 1890 Nova Scotia was the leading mining province in Canada, chiefly because of its rich coal resources. After that year, three factors hastened a great shift in Canadian mineral extraction. One was the development of new

Ukrainian (Galician) immigrant family in Quebec, 1911. While immigrants came from many parts of the world to Canada, a number of programs were directed at Eastern Europeans. Minister of the Interior Clifford Sifton desired these "stalwart peasants in sheep-skin coats," such as those pictured here, to farm the West. Photo by W.J. Topley, LAC, PA-10401.

technologies to extract ore. Another was the increasing availability of railway transportation to remote areas. Most important of all, the international market created a new demand for metals that Canada had in abundance: copper, nickel, and silver. Almost overnight, Ontario and British Columbia became the leading mineral producers.

Although the most famous mining rush of the period was to the Yukon's Klondike district for gold, the Klondike was hardly typical of the mining industry. More representative were the mining towns that suddenly sprang up and equally rapidly closed down in the mountains of British Columbia and Alberta. Like most Canadian mines, these required considerable machinery and expertise to exploit, well beyond the resources of the individual miner. Well-capitalized corporations opened such mines, employing money and technology often imported from the United States. In Quebec, the most buoyant segment of the mineral industry between 1900 and 1920 was asbestos fibre, used chiefly in construction material consumed in the United States. The Canadian mining industry greatly benefited from the military requirements of the Great War.

In the forest industry, the decline through permanent depletion of the white pine forests of eastern Canada pushed the centre of activity to the West. British Columbia had millions of acres of Douglas fir and cedar. The province started harvesting in the coastal regions close to water, but soon pushed inland. Most of its production went to American markets. The remaining forests of eastern Canada proved valuable for their softwood. The pulp and paper industry expanded rapidly, driven by an insatiable American demand for inexpensive newsprint. By 1915 wood pulp and paper represented one-third of the value of Canadian exports, virtually equal to wheat and grain in the overseas market. Quebec produced nearly one-half of Canada's wood pulp and paper.

The resource sector produced its own version of labour militancy. The sector was difficult to organize by traditional means. In mines and lumber camps, the distinction between skilled and unskilled labour had little meaning. Nevertheless, worker alienation was often extreme. In British Columbia, unrest was particularly strong among miners, who worked for large absentee corporations under difficult conditions. In this kind of environment, syndicalists and radicals (such as the Wobblies or the Impossibilists) did very well. They preached the need for the organization of all workers into general unions and the destruction of capitalism by revolution.

Urban and Rural Canada

In 1881 Canada had a population of 4,325,000, of whom 3,349,000 lived outside urban centres. Forty years later, of the nation's 8,788,000 inhabitants, only 4,811,000 resided in non-urban areas, and 1,659,000 lived in cities with populations over 100,000. While the non-urban population had grown over these years from 3,349,000 to 4,811,000, the number of city dwellers had burgeoned from 974,000 to 3,977,000. Urban growth was obviously a major trend of the period 1880–1918. Canada developed some very large metropolitan centres, but their residents did not constitute the entire urban population. If 1,659,000 Canadians lived in cities of over 100,000 in 1921, another 2.2 million lived in smaller centres, with 1,058,000 in towns of 5,000 to 29,999 people and 765,000 in towns of 1,000 to 4,999. Canadian urban growth in this era produced all sorts of new problems for the nation. At the same time, urban development was not the entire story for these years. As the statistics well demonstrate, before 1921 more Canadians continued to reside in rural than in urban areas. Rural Canada, although its earlier dominance was gradually eroding away, was still very important to the national ethos. Moreover, the very sense of the gradual loss of traditional rural values was critical for the Canadian psyche.

The City

As with most other aspects of Canadian development in this period, urban growth was uneven across the regions. Maritime cities grew fairly sluggishly. None could establish regional dominance. Indeed, Halifax lost ground as central Canada siphoned off its financial

BACKGROUNDER

Child Labour in Victorian Canada

The 1889 Royal Commission on the Relations of Labor and Capital documented through first-person testimony that a substantial number of children of both sexes between the ages of 10 and 14 were employed full-time (10 hours a day, six days a week) in the factories of Ontario and Quebec. They were paid between $1.00 and $2.00 per week, depending on their age and production during a time when the typical working-man earned $7.00 per week and females somewhat less. These children were subjected to heavy discipline, including corporal punishment. They were frequently fined when they fell behind quotas, and one factory even had a "black hole" in which a child could be confined for hours or even days. Laws against the use of child labour, especially children under the age of 14, existed but were not enforced any more than were the laws calling for compulsory school attendance. Parents supported the employment of their children, even insisted upon it, as part of a "family economy" that helped sustain many in the working classes of the nation. The absence of any clear concept of childhood beyond the early years helped contribute to the presence of children in factories and elsewhere in the Canadian industrial workforce, but such a pattern was only the tip of the iceberg when it came to the employment of children in Victorian Canada. Most of Canada remained agricultural, and in this sector of the economy the dominant economic institution was the family farm, which operated on the assumption that every family member beyond the earliest years worked to contribute to its survival and prosperity.

Unlike the child factory workers, many of whom probably turned their earnings over to their families, the children working on the farm received no wages. Also unlike those employed in factories, of course, some of those children who worked on the family farm had a prospect of an inheritance at the end of the day, although usually only the older males and almost never the females benefited in this way. According to one recent study of prairie child labour in the Victorian period, the Canadian West could not have been successfully settled without the heavy use of child labour. "Children contributed to production, took part in paid employment or other money-raising activities, worked at domestic and subsistence tasks, and thereby increased the supply of cash, food, and other necessary commodities to the family" (Rollings-Magnusson, 2009: 133–4). Indeed, settlement in Canada in any period was based on the exploitation of the unpaid labour of the family, including both women and children.

Although there were laws in place to protect child labourers, such as the children seen here separating the ore from the rock in a Quebec copper mine, these laws were not enforced. © McCord Museum.

institutions. In Quebec, Montreal continued its path to the status of the Dominion's premier city, with Quebec City and other towns lagging far behind. In Ontario, Toronto was clearly the "Queen City," although a number of smaller cities (Hamilton, London, and Kingston) were vibrant. Ottawa inhabited a world of its own as the nation's capital, as it always would. The most spectacular urban growth rates were in the West, which in this era spawned two major cities, Winnipeg and Vancouver, and two contenders for such a rank, Edmonton and Calgary. While western settlement usually suggests farms and agriculture, urban development in the West was strong from the outset. Land speculation drove local pretensions, and many communities aspired to be regional entrepôts. In the Prairie provinces the urban population grew from 103,000 to 606,000 between 1900 and 1916. City dwellers, who represented 25 per cent of the region's population in 1901, had increased to 35 per cent only 10 years later. By 1921 in British Columbia, Vancouver (117,217) and Victoria (38,727) contained 25 per cent of the population of that Pacific province.

The larger cities of Canada most clearly exposed the social problems of the later Victorian and subsequent Edwardian eras. The greatest problem was poverty. Existing evidence suggests that up to half of the Canadian urban working class lived below, or at best around, the poverty line. Most working-class families were glad to supplement the father's income with the earnings of wife and children in menial occupations. Given the grinding conditions of their lives, it is not surprising that many sought refuge in alcohol. Unbalanced diets and malnutrition were only the start of the problems of the poor. Their housing was typically overcrowded, with poor sanitation and a lack of open yards and spaces.

Home ownership was difficult, even for the middle classes, because mortgages were hard to obtain and were only of short duration, often no more than three or four years. Malnutrition and deplorable housing conditions combined to produce high overall death rates and high infant mortality rates in Canada's largest cities. The mortality differentials between the poor and the prosperous were substantial, ranging from 35.51 deaths per 1,000 in 1895 in one working-class ward in Montreal to less than 13 per 1,000 "above the hill." Infant mortality rates in Canadian cities were little different from those in places like Calcutta and Bombay. The children of the urban poor often got little schooling. Moreover, the poor resisted pressures for compulsory education.

If the city had social problems, it also made possible a rich and varied cultural life. Before 1918 cultural life maintained an amateur tradition of considerable vitality. The major development in Canadian urban culture in this era was not so much the appearance of first-rate artists as the creation of an institutional infrastructure that might eventually enable them to emerge. The city made possible the development of cultural institutions in the form of both organizations and buildings to house them. The construction of museums, for example, was characteristic of the age. The Art Museum of Toronto appeared in 1900, the Royal Ontario Museum in 1912 (it opened in 1914). Equally characteristic of the era was the formation of artistic organizations. The Canadian Art Club (1907) was organized in Toronto, although its founders had no idea how to achieve their goal of introducing new Canadian painting to the entire nation. Formal art and music schools were organized in most of the larger urban centres, offering regularized instruction to neophyte painters and musicians. Theatrical buildings became a measure of a city's status. As early as 1891 Vancouver had a 1,200-seat opera house. Toronto's Royal Alexandra Theatre (1906–7) seated 1,525, and Winnipeg's Walker Theatre (1907, recently renovated as a theatrical venue) seated 2,000 in splendid comfort. These buildings operated continuously, housing mainly professional touring companies and local amateurs. Homegrown professional theatre emerged first in Montreal. There were 10 different professional companies at work in Montreal in the 1890s. In 1899 alone these companies gave 618 performances of 109 plays.

The extent of the growth of urban Canada between 1880 and 1919 was largely unanticipated. The large city cut against most of the dominant ideologies of the time, which were traditional and rural. The institutions of urban government were not well integrated into the overall Canadian political system. The British North America Act did not leave much room for the governance of cities that would have budgets and revenues as large as those of the provinces in which they

The "foreign" quarter of Winnipeg, c. 1909. Archives of Manitoba, Immigration 17, N7936.

were located. Urban government and urban politics operated outside the structures of Confederation, with their own agendas and distinct party labels. Most cities were slow to abandon property qualifications for voting. Local merchants and real estate promoters tended to dominate city councils, even in cities with a relatively democratic franchise. The ward system produced municipal politicians who curried favour with the electorate through corrupt practices ranging from the purchasing of votes to offers of "jobs for the boys."

No urban centre could expect to prosper in this era if it was not on a main-line railway. Contemporaries clearly recognized this reality. During the several outbursts of railway expansion—particularly between 1906 and 1915, when more than 14,000 new miles (22,530 km) of railway track were laid in Canada—efforts by aspiring communities to become depots and junction points were prodigious. Conversely, rumours of new railway construction were sufficient to create a village where none had existed previously. The extremes to which communities would go to publicize themselves in order to attract railways were occasionally ludicrous and often

expensive. Agricultural fairs, as well as the presence of town bands and sports teams, publicized communities. A marching brass band and a baseball team were two of the best advertisements an "up-and-at-'em" town could enjoy. "Bonusing"—financial inducements for railways and business entrepreneurs alike—was a way of life in this period.

If urban growth relied on railway networks, it operated in a context of fairly blatant and open land speculation. The attempted creation of every new city in western Canada began with a land boom. This stage of development usually ended with a collapse in land prices that required years of recovery. Many small businessmen in the West made a decent living selling out in one community just ahead of the bust and moving to a new townsite further down the rail line. The false fronts on western small-town stores were symbolic of the transitory nature of commitment. Speculation in land involved not merely businessmen—or the West. Almost all segments of local communities across Canada joined in real estate speculation whenever they could. Indeed, the attempt to turn a profit by investing in undeveloped

Interior of slum home, Winnipeg, c. 1915.What assumptions can we make about the subjects and surroundings in this photograph?
Archives of Manitoba, Foote 1491, N2438.

land must surely be one of the most enduring features of Canadian life. Speculation was different from development. The former involved the holding of land for future profit, the latter the translation of land—often acquired at bargain prices—into immediate profit as sites for houses or factories.

Town and Suburb

In the larger urban centres land speculation and development were inseparable from the process of suburbanization. This trend combined with urban expansion away from the commercial core of most cities. There were three distinct motives for suburban expansion. Different types of suburbs were the result. The first motive dominated among the prospering business and professional classes, who moved to new residential suburbs to escape the noise, odours, and bustle of the central city. Horse droppings on busy city streets, for example, were a major problem before the Great War. Some of these suburbanites were attempting to separate themselves from the growing slums of the industrializing city. The architectural style most closely associated with the new suburban elites grew out of the English Arts and Crafts movement and became known as the English Domestic Revival. A second motive for suburban growth was the quest for lower land costs and lower taxes outside the central city. The result was the development of a number of industrial suburbs, such as Maisonneuve in Montreal, which flourished outside the city but were still within its orbit. The third motive was proximity to work. As industrial development moved into the cheaper outskirts, workers were forced to follow their jobs into often inadequate new housing. During this period, most large cities in Canada grew by a continuous process of absorbing outlying communities.

The genuine Canadian small town tended to fit one of two models. It was either a community serving a surrounding rural area, sometimes with a manufacturing plant or two, or a single-resource community, often remotely located, that had formed around a mine or

mining/smelter operation. The resource town consisted almost exclusively of single males, with only a handful of women. There were precious few sources of entertainment other than booze and gambling. Many resource towns, though not all, were company towns. Such communities were both violent and restive, often centres of labour unrest.

The service community, on the other hand, was the centre of economic, social, and recreational life for its district. Before the advent of radio and television, the social life of small-town Canada bustled impressively. Organizations of all kinds proliferated and flourished. Most towns had a variety of lodges and an endless round of meetings, dances, and "occasions." These occasions included concerts, plays, sermons by visiting evangelical

Contemporary Views

Herbert Brown Ames on Poverty in Montreal

In 1897 the Montreal businessman Herbert Brown Ames published a series of articles in the *Montreal Star* that subsequently appeared as a book. The articles were based on his careful survey of social conditions in part of the west side of Montreal. The district he had selected probably offered a fair sample of working-class residences in Montreal at the end of the nineteenth century.

It will be remembered that, according to our industrious census, the total number of poor families was reckoned at 888 in "the city below the hill." Half of this number were by the writer selected as material for a second and more searching investigation, with a view of more fully examining the characteristics, conditions and causes of our west-end poverty. Four hundred and thirty-six families were sought for, and the first fact that was brought to the notice of the investigator was that 46 families, or 10 1/2 per cent of the above number, had left their former abodes, within the two months between the first and second canvass, drawing attention to one of the sad features of poverty's lot, viz., the constant necessity to move on because of inability to satisfy the claims of

the landlord. If this ratio were maintained, and each month saw 5 per cent of the poor evicted, in a year not half these families could be found at the former addresses.

A second fact, made apparent by the special investigation, was that our west-end poverty was not the result of recent immigration. Quite the reverse from what would have been the case in New York or Chicago, hardly a dozen families were discovered that had not been residents of the city for at least three years. The vast majority were old residents who had lived in Montreal for the greater part of their lives. The presence of poverty, then, in the nether city is not chargeable to any considerable influx of foreign elements.

preachers, and lectures on temperance or exotic places. By the end of the Great War, most towns had a "movie house" or a hall that exhibited motion pictures on a regular basis. Many small towns had exercised the local option permitted by liquor legislation and "gone dry." Small-town social relations were often strained, particularly between the middle classes and those who worked in the factories that many eastern small towns possessed. In the West, class conflict often pitted farmers against hired hands or the crews of threshing contractors. The possibility of outbreaks of violence was never far away.

Even more serious were the gender constraints inherent in the structure of small towns. Masculinity dominated the life of the town, in terms both of family relationships and especially of extracurricular activity. Local sports were controlled by notions of manliness, and most athletic organizations catered only to men. Local fraternal organizations were equally masculine and exclusionist, although occasionally they had women's auxiliaries. One of the most important underlying tensions in many (although not all) small towns was between church-related and other voluntary organizations. The church organizations were dominated by women and often sought reform, including prohibition of alcohol and elimination of gambling. The masculine-dominated voluntary structure was often, by implication, the chief target of these reformers. The attentive and careful reader can find all these tensions exhibited in the novels of small-town life that dominated Canadian literature in these years.

In the case of 323 families inquiries were made as to the causes, assigned by the people themselves, for their indigent condition. With 109 families, or 34 per cent the reply was "irregularity of work." The wage-earners were not without vocations but their employment was intermittent and often work ceased altogether for considerable periods. With 87 families or 28 per cent the answer was that the wage-earners had no work whatever, nor did there seem to be any immediate prospect of getting any. With 27 families, or 9 per cent, old age had unfitted and with a like number sickness had prevented the worker from earning the requisite support. Out of these 323 families, among the poorest of the poor, 62 per cent claimed to be able to better their condition were employment regular and abundant. That a certain percentage of the answers given did not state the real facts of the case is quite probable. Few are the families that will admit to a stranger that drink, crime or voluntary idleness is the cause of their misery, though in 7 per cent of the cases visited drunkenness was clearly at the bottom of the trouble. Still it is the belief of the investigator that the undeserving among the poor form a far smaller proportion than is generally imagined.

As to the composition of the family, out of 390 families, 86 were found wherein the head of the household was a widow, and 54 cases where the husband was too old or too ill to work, making in all 140 families, or 36 per cent of the whole, that might be called "decapitated" family groups. In about two-thirds of the families, or in 64 per cent of the cases examined, there was an able-bodied man in the house, oftimes more than one, a man able to work and professing to be willing to do so. If these proportions may be taken as fairly indicating the average among the families of the poor, it is evident that at least one-third of them are in indigent circumstances through no fault of their own. . . .

Source: H. Ames, *The City Below the Hill*, pp. 74–6. © University of Toronto Press, 1972.

Rural Canada

A number of major changes occurred in Canadian agriculture during the period from 1880 to 1914. The most obvious was the enormous expansion of farming in the prairie West, concentrating single-mindedly on grain cultivation. Elsewhere, the era saw a major shift in eastern Canada towards specialized farming. In central Canada, farmers moved into specialized high-quality consumer production, becoming increasingly dependent on off-farm processing, particularly of cheese, butter, and meat. By 1900 Ontario had over 1,200 cheese factories, which captured over half of the British market. Ontario cheese makers were renowned around the world. Quebec farmers had greater difficulty in making the change because of the marginality of much of their land. Specialty farming was very remunerative for those able to engage in it. The aristocrats of farming were the dairy farmers and the fruit farmers. Along with specialized farming came new technology, although the ubiquitous tractor did not replace the horse until after the Great War. More important were mechanical harvesters, centrifugal cream separators, and the introduction of refrigeration. Technology was essential to specializa-

tion. It was also capital-intensive. Not all farmers could make the shift. Those who could not often stagnated or failed absolutely. Between 1891 and 1921 the Maritime region lost 22,000 farms and 1,556,709 acres (630,000 ha) of farmland under cultivation. Unmodernized farms could not continue to support the entire family. By 1911 the *Farmer's Advocate* could refer to the "perennial debates as to 'Why the Boys Leave the Farm'." While urban migration was one response, another was that farmers—and farm women—moved into the traditional resource industries of the nation. Males went to sea to fish or into the woods to cut timber. Females worked seasonally in factories, processing farm products or fish.

Contemporaries often blamed the growing rural exodus on the social and cultural attractions of the city. While it might thus be tempting to visualize rural Canada as a vast wasteland of isolated and unlettered country bumpkins, such a view would be most inaccurate. Isolation did exist, as did educational limitations. On the other hand, a relatively efficient and inexpensive postal service provided contact with the wider world. People read books and discussed them at clubs that met in local churches. Clergymen often talked about controversial books and topics from their pulpits. Many farm families received at least one daily newspaper through the mail— seldom on the day of publication, but usually only a day or two later. Canadian dailies in this era provided more substantial fare than today. International coverage was much fuller, and many papers saw themselves as "papers of record," often reproducing verbatim accounts of court trials and important meetings. In the spring of 1919, for example, the *Winnipeg Tribune* carried a full stenographer's report of the debates at the labour convention in Calgary, which agreed to "an Industrial Organization of all workers." Most rural folk also relied heavily for their edification on farm journals such as the *Grain Growers' Guide* (1908–28) and more general magazines like the *Christian Guardian*, the voice of the Methodist Church; it was begun in 1829 by Egerton Ryerson and continued under that name until 1925. The wide range of letters to the editor included in most of these periodicals suggests both their circulation and their vitality.

If rural Canadians had access to considerable information, they were also surprisingly able to get together socially with each other. The school and the church

Although most athletic organizations catered only to men, by the turn of the twentieth century, hockey was being regularly played by women as well as men. Here is the Rossland, British Columbia, Ladies' Hockey Team, c. 1900. Rossland Museum Archives, RHMA02-18-997.

The Town Directory of Treherne, Manitoba, 1895

In 1907 Alan Ross, a local poet in Treherne, Manitoba, published a small volume of his verse. It included the following poem, the subject of which is self-explanatory.

Town Directory 1895

E. Hamilton's our high school master;
D. Hamilton puts on the plaster;
Revds. McClung, Fraser and George Fill
On Sundays do our pulpits fill;
T.J. Lamont's our town M.D.;
One blacksmith's name is Thos. Lee;
Rogers sells dry goods and coffees;
Alexander keeps post office;
D. Williams and J.K. McLennan
Sell dry goods, cod, haddock finnan,
Ben Englewain repairs the clocks;
Our miller's name is Jas A. Cox;
James Telford Reid's our legal light
One retired farmer's called John White;
'Tis G.A. Anderson that carried
The business on for Massey-Harris;
And S.L. Taylor sells the pills,
That sometimes cure and sometimes kill;
C.W. Barkwell is town baker;
Ed Roberts is the undertaker;
Tom Roberts helps his brother Ed

Sell furniture and house the dead;
Joe Straube is town hardware man;
In athletics Paulin leads the van;
One livery's kept by the Parker Brothers;
And John Perrie keeps the other;
Jas. Stevenson keeps the "Manitoba,"
With parlor, dining-room, and lobby;
Fred Rocket keeps the "Rocket House";
Our tailor's name is Harry House;
D. Harvie harness makes and collars
Watt Smith irons wagons, sleighs and rollers
And general blacksmith shop controls;
His carriage maker's William Bowles;
Andrew Ross supplies the butcher meat;
Malcolm McClarty shoes the feet;
H. Watson, Senior health inspector;
James McAdam's tax collector;
Claude Somerville's mill engineer;
John Coulter is mill charioteer;
James Emmond sues for delinquent debts,
And William Frame does serve the writs;
Robson deals in lumber, lime, and bricks . . . .

Source: Alan Ross, *Poems* (Treherne, Man.: The Treherne Times, 1907), 18.

were two local institutions that served other functions besides providing formal education and worship services. School districts were usually the only sign of public organization in vast regions of rural Canada that were otherwise politically unorganized. The community jealously guarded its schoolhouse, which, from coast to coast, was typically of one room. The most common Quebec school in the 1913 census had one room, built at a cost of $1,200. Whether Protestant or Catholic, francophone or anglophone, rural Canadians took their religion seriously. Sermons provided topics for daily conversation. The activities of various auxiliary groups connected with any church, particularly the picnics and socials, were very popular. Winter did not shut down social life in rural areas, but permitted it to flower. The demands of the farm were much lighter in winter, while snow and ice provided a decent surface for horse-drawn sleighs and carrioles to travel about the countryside. "A working day . . . was from about 4:30 a.m. to 11 o'clock at night," reported one western farmer, "but this was only in seeding and harvesting time. In the winter we used to really have fun" (quoted in Voisey, 1988: 158).

A number of diaries and journals kept by rural Canadians in this period have recently appeared in print. They provide two revelations for the modern reader. The first is the sheer volume of social interchange, especially among the young, that actually occurred. The second is the extent to which Canadians of this era actively participated in their own entertainment rather than being amused as passive spectators by the activities of others. Canadians of both sexes and all ages routinely spent social evenings singing hymns and other songs. They created and performed their own skits and joined together in active games such as charades.

Rural life was not all bucolic pleasure, of course. The real reason for the rural exodus was not isolation but exploitation and lack of economic opportunity. The underside of life on the family farm was the exploitation and abuse of those who would not in the end inherit a substantial share in the property. The system was particularly hard on women, who usually did not share in the ownership of the farm and who seldom received remuneration for their labour. Western farmers especially were hostile to "anachronistic" legal concepts such as dower rights. The homesteading system was generally unsympathetic to the rights of women to set up as independent farmers. For many women everywhere in Canada, the daily routine was even more continually demanding than it was for men. Women's responsibilities included not only the kitchen garden and the smaller livestock, such as chickens and pigs, but care of the family itself. One consequence of the shift into specialized farming was that parts of the farm operation previously consigned to women that provided them with a small income ("egg money") were taken over by the males. Canadian rural society continued to be inherently patriarchal in its organization. Men owned the land and usually made the decisions, including when to uproot and resettle, often against the wishes of their wives. The figure of the rural patriarch as an intensely self-righteous, land-hungry, materialistic tyrant became a common motif in Canadian fiction of this and a slightly later period.

Despite the darker side, a vast majority of Canadians continued to hold rural values and to think of the nation largely in pastoral terms. Those who read Canadian poetry or looked at Canadian art found little but Canadian nature. Foreigners inevitably saw Canada as a completely undeveloped country and Canadians as an agricultural people. In the hands of the poets, Canadian nature was chiefly benign. Writers of prose sometimes depicted nature differently, often in terms of the victory of hardy settlers over the harsh landscape and climate. Many Canadian writers and painters of this period romanticized the farm and farming, none more so than Lucy Maud Montgomery. *Anne of Green Gables* summed up a major conflict of the era: the problem of reconciling the bucolic beauty and tranquility of the rural landscape with the need to leave it in order to fulfill one's ambitions. For large numbers of Canadians of this era, growing up meant leaving the farm.

Another form of romanticization of rural life was the collection of its folklore and folksongs. Marius Barbeau (1883–1969) was the first great Canadian collector of folk traditions, beginning in 1911 when he was appointed an anthropologist at the Museum Branch of the Geological Survey of Canada (now the National Museum of Canada). Barbeau recorded and preserved in archives thousands of songs and narratives that document not only the folk traditions of rural Quebec but also those of the Aboriginal peoples in British Columbia. The folkways and songs that Barbeau and others collected were part of the traditional rural experience of Canada. They preserved almost nothing of urban origin. The collectors desperately gathered up dialects, riddles, tall tales, and children's rhymes, all of which told more of the daily life of the people than most other historical evidence. Underlying the desperation was the fear that these traditions would disappear in the rapidly changing society of the period.

The dominance in Canada of the myth of agriculture carried over into the various efforts of the period to turn Aboriginal peoples into "peaceable agricultural labourers." Agrarian ideology had the advantage of both justifying the dispossession of the Native peoples of their hunting grounds and providing them with an alternate way of life. Before the Great War most Canadians regarded agriculture as "the mainspring of national

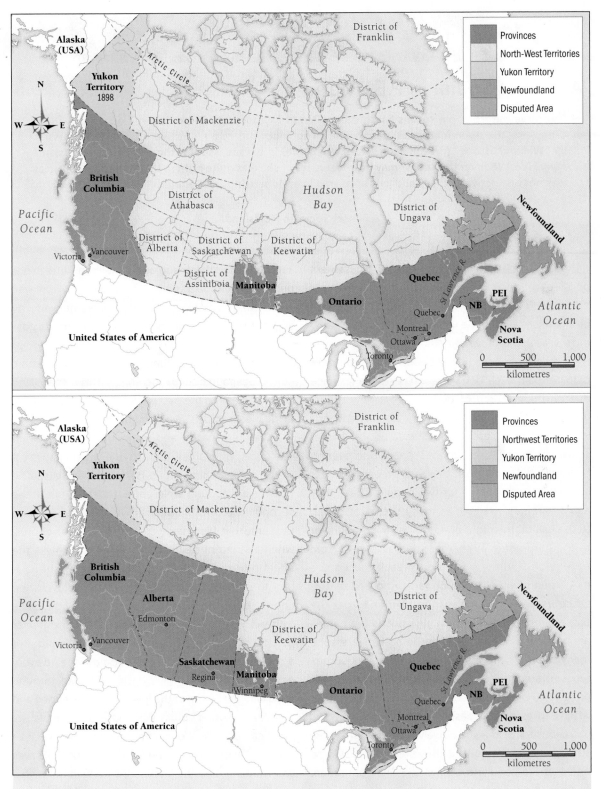

Canada in 1898 and 1905.

"A Basket Social in P.E. Island"

"Preserve me from 'pie socials'," wrote Lucy Maud Montgomery in her journal on 4 April 1899. "They are the abomination of desolation." The following more positive view was expressed by "Welland Strong" (presumably a *nom de plume*) in a 1901 issue of the *Prince Edward Island Magazine*. Whoever the author may have been, he or she was quite right in thinking that the social was not distinctive to the Island, but appeared everywhere in rural Canada.

A Basket Social in P.E. Island
by Welland Strong

Basket socials may not be a form of amusement peculiar to Prince Edward Island, but in all events, I have never seen a place where they attained to such prominence, among the various schemes for getting money, as in this province. . . .

Often it happens that in country villages a debt is to be paid by a congregation, either a balance due on their church or perhaps for a new organ. Instead of raising the necessary amount by private subscription, the people decide upon a basket social, and word is sent to everyone. Upon hearing this the young ladies all begin to prepare baskets containing ample lunch for two people. These they carry, carefully wrapped in many sheets of paper, to the hall on the night of the social, and hand over to the committee in charge. The baskets are sold by auction, and the purchaser of each must share its contents with the young lady who brought it. Of course every young man is anxious to get the basket prepared by his "best girl": but as the names are not announced until after the baskets are sold, many mistakes are made, and the remarks sometimes uttered, by fond lovers who have paid a high price for the wrong one, look much better in print when expressed by a dash.

Let us try to imagine ourselves in a hall in almost any country settlement on the evening devoted to one of these popular meetings. . . . The committee, composed of elders of the church, were kept busy finding seats for the ladies; taking care of the bas-

kets handed to them, and doing the many little things necessary at all such entertainments. Now, however, we see them placing a row of chairs on the platform, and pushing the organ into a more convenient position. Hardly had this been done when there enter from a side door a number of ladies and gentlemen, who proceed to occupy the chairs. This is the village choir, and during the past week they have been practicing pieces to be sung to-night. . . .

Cheers, whistles and stamping of feet greeted the choir, who arose and, to the accompaniment of a hard-breathing organ, sang "Jingle Bells." The first verse was sung amid perfect silence, but in the second the crowd caught the rhythm of the piece and kept time to it with their feet, especially in the chorus, when a string of sleigh bells was used to make the effect more realistic. A recitation, "Curfew shall not ring to-night," given by a young lady, followed the chorus, but as most of the audience knew the piece by heart, very little attention was paid, and the greater portion of the piece remained almost unheard. But amid the din the speaker's voice could be heard every now and then, and bravely she struggled through until, with the saving of the lover, the piece ended and the "Amen corner" burst into thunderous applause. Then came a fine-looking soloist—tenor in the choir and local auctioneer. He began "Ten thousand leaves are falling," but having pitched the song in too high a key, his voice broke and he stopped, his failure being greeted by frantic howls and advice from one of the small boys to "start her at five thousand." The programme went on; chorus following reading, and solo, chorus, the last few numbers being rendered 'midst an almost deafening noise and shouts of "Bring on the baskets."

When it ended the choir moved to one side of the platform, the schoolmaster who was to act as secretary and treasurer took his place at the table, and the auctioneer stepped forward holding in his hand the first basket, now unwrapped and decorated in a most fantastic manner with flags, flowers and coloured tissue paper. . . . After all the baskets have been sold, the names of the purchasers and ladies are read off by the secretary, and the baskets opened by them. Usually besides various kinds of cake and pie, the basket contains glasses and a bottle of home-made wine; but in case this has been left out, and also for the benefit of the older people, the committee furnish plenty of tea. When the lunch has been disposed of, the men go to the nearest stables for their horses, which have been left there, while the young ladies gather their belongings, get muffled up ready for the drive home and, while waiting for their friends, sing a verse of "God save the King."

Sleigh after sleigh drives up to the door, the women and girls depart, and in a very few minutes no one remains in the hall save the members of the committee—counting over the money they have made and writing a report of the social to be published in the papers next day.

Source: *The Island Magazine* 46 (Fall/Winter 1999): 7–12. Reprinted with permission.

greatness" and farming as a way of life that uplifted one "morally and emotionally" (Carter, 1990: 20). Scientists saw agriculture as a crucial step in the ladder of progress. They perceived other ways of using the land, such as mining or lumbering, as tainted and inferior. The government displaced Aboriginals by treaties, then removed them to reserves and encouraged them to farm. Exhortation was not the same as useful practical assistance. Native Canadians on the prairies needed a good deal of help to shift from a semi-nomadic hunting/gathering existence to a settled agricultural one, and they did not consistently receive assistance. Government aid was sporadic, cheese-paring, and patronizing. After 1885 coercion replaced subsidization as the federal government's major weapon to impose agriculturalism on the reserves. Not surprisingly, the policy failed.

A final illustration of nature's appeal for Canadians came in the various back-to-nature movements. One form involved mounting crusades to preserve Canada's natural environment in the face of encroaching civilization. The fight for the conservation of Canadian wildlife involved the establishment of game reserves and legislation to curb indiscriminate hunting. The crusade's major victories came with the establishment of large numbers of national and provincial parks across Canada in the years before the Great War. Another expression of the back-to-nature movement was the summer cottage, which flourished among urbanites who could afford one by the early years of the twentieth century. Many refugees from the farm resolved their ambivalences through the summer cottage or summer travel, often into the wilderness. Thus, alongside the burgeoning Canadian cities came the growth of summer cottages and resort hotels, located at lakeside or seaside, and frequently directly served by rail. Weekend train services poured middle-class Canadians by the thousands into the Laurentians of Quebec, the Muskoka, Algonquin Park, and Haliburton districts of Ontario, and from Winnipeg into the Lake of the Woods district. The Canadian fascination with the summer cottage had taken firm hold before the Great War. During this same period, the establishment of a national park system had begun with the creation of Rocky Mountain Park (later Banff National Park) in 1885, and this and other parks in the Rocky Mountains (Yoho, Glacier, Jasper, Waterton Lakes) of British Columbia and Alberta were conveniently reached by rail and, in some cases, the railways built expensive, sumptuous hotels to accommodate sojourners from the city.

While some Canadians settled temporarily into cottage or tourist hotel, others became fascinated with the recreational possibilities of wilderness travel. The waterways of Ontario and Quebec grew crowded

Sadie Allen's Diary, Summer 1892

Wed. June 29 [1892]. Well here it is just a beautiful day, fine and just warm enough to be pleasant. This is the third day of our holidays and I can't say I have enjoyed them very much so far. Yesterday it poured rain from dinner time until tea time, but still I was not very lonely because there is such a houseful of us. Besides, Aunt Rose (who came over a week ago tomorrow) came up and stayed all day, and she is just splendid company. In the morning I did my housework up and then trimmed May's sailor hat, and after dinner I got Winnie's ready for trimming and then made lemon filling for my Washington pie which I made yesterday and made frosting for it also. And I practised some and read some of a book called *Little Journey in the World* by the same author of *Baddeck and That Sort of Thing*. Mr. Bailey and Eddie White, Fred Henderson and Leonard Webster came up and spent the evening. We had lots of fun as usual over those Tiddlywinks. We had two tables, and when one side missed they had to go to the other table, and the best players kept their same places. There were Mr. B. and Nell, Win and Fred, Leonard and Bois, and Eddie and I. After playing we had a lot of music. Leonard sang "They are After Me" and some other songs, and Mr. Bailey gave us a solo, then we had some Charades. We also made up an orchestra just for fun. Mr. B. played on the mouth organ (he plays just beautifully on it), and Leonard had the tambourine, Bois a tin whistle, Eddie another, and May the table bell, and Winnie played one piano and Nell accompanied her on the other, while I had the zither. Oh but we had fun over that.

Monday morning (day before yesterday) was fine but the afternoon was wet. I wrote a long letter to Ted before dinner. She wrote Nell and I while she was on her journey that they had stopped for a while at a little place a hundred miles from Port Arthur. Her mother told me yesterday that they both liked it in Winnipeg very much and Lottie was feeling very well only tired and sleepy. It is just three weeks I think from Monday since they left. For the past month back, part of the Lodge members were getting up a drama for the Lodge called *The Social Glass*. Nettie Evans, Mrs. Lodge, and Floss White and Eddie McDonald, Mr. Russell, Mr. Butler, Mr. Colwell, and Mr. Belyear and Es Hamilton are the ones that took part in it. So they gave it to the public last Monday evening. It was just fine. They had a full house and the band played between every act, some very pretty selections. They all took their parts splendidly. Hardly anybody knew Flo, when the curtain rose, and she was dressed as a bride in a light blue dress and her hair done up and flowers in it and she looked just sweet but so womanly. Es Hamilton was too comical for anything as Bob Brittle. Oh he was grand. Nettie Evans as Nettie Nettlebee could not have been better. It just suited her to a tee. "She did love to make folks happy." Will Butler was splendid as Fairly. He acted the delirium tremens fine and all the rest were good too. Though it was ridiculous and comical in lots of places, yet it was sad when you thought it was just real life. This social glass at first and then it gets to more and more until your own life is ruined by it and many many others.

Source: Mary Biggar Peck, ed., *A Full House and Fine Singing: Diaries and Letters of Sadie Harper Allen* (Fredericton: Goose Lane Press, 1992), 66–7.

with weekend canoeists enjoying a brief respite from the pressures of the city. Ernest Thompson Seton (1860–1946), who founded an organization called Woodcraft Indians in 1902, promoted a junior version of this outdoor activity from his apartment in New York City. Some of the best publicists for the canoe and the wilderness were painters, especially those who eventually formed the Group of Seven in 1920. Its members,

"Odabin Cottage," the summer house of Charles Howard Millar, the local postmaster, Drummondville, Quebec, c. 1903. Canadians' fascination with the summer cottage had already taken hold before 1914. Except for some ostentatious present-day "cottages" on some lakes, this cottage of more than a century ago is little different from those that Canadians rush to in the summer months today. Such cottages are perhaps most notable for how they blend into—as opposed to stand out from—the surrounding natural environment, in this case even with the decking built around small trees. © McCord Museum.

mainly English-born Torontonians making a living as commercial artists, had begun travelling north into the Georgian Bay and Algonquin wildernesses as early as 1911. This group captured the iconographic essence of wilderness Canada: a bleak and sombre but none-theless curiously beautiful landscape of Jack pines, rock outcroppings, and storm-driven lakes, totally uninhabited by people.

Other Identities

We can easily make too much of the political and religious arena. The elaboration of competing and occasionally incompatible identities by and for its cit-

izens characterized the Victorian Age. As well as their national and provincial loyalties, most Canadians had firm allegiances to their ethnic origins, whether these were French Canadian, Acadian, or British. French Canada further elaborated its cultural identity in this period, and the Acadians began self-consciously to develop one. As for those people whose origins were in the British Isles, they simultaneously thought of themselves as British as well as Welsh, Scottish, Irish, or English. Indeed, British Canadians may well have thought of themselves as more British (as opposed to Welsh or Scottish) than did their compatriots at home.

The state did not weigh heavily on the daily lives of most Canadians in this era, although the administrative state had begun its development before Confederation.

Taxation had not yet become ubiquitous and occurred mainly as tariffs and duties. Moreover, the state—as represented by province, nation, or city—did not normally provide social benefits or solace when people got sick, lost jobs, retired, or died. For some, politics and government were a source of employment or patronage. For most Canadians, however, government had very little to do with their lives. For many people, political allegiance to the state was therefore not as important as loyalty to the caring institutions: family, ethnic group, religion, and fraternal organization. Churches and religion were most important. Canada was a Christian country and few of its citizens openly defied Christian norms and values. By the 1880s the mobility of many Canadians contributed to the tendency to belong to a good many other voluntary organizations beyond the church. In an earlier period, voluntary organizations supplemented or provided municipal services such as water, light, fire, and libraries as well as charity. By the 1880s some organizations had begun providing entertainment and companionship for their members.

Technically independent of the churches, but closely connected in overlapping membership and social goals, were reform organizations like the Woman's Christian Temperance Union. Letitia Youmans (1827–96), a public school teacher and Sunday school teacher in the Methodist Church, founded the first Canadian local of the WCTU in December 1874 in Picton, Ontario. The WCTU spread rapidly across Canada in the 1880s, preaching that alcohol abuse was responsible for many of the social problems of contemporary Canada and campaigning for public prohibition of the sale of alcoholic beverages. Most of its membership came from the middle class, and much of its literature was directed at demonstrating that poverty and family problems among the lower orders could be reduced, if not eliminated, by cutting off the availability of alcohol to the male breadwinner.

Canadians of the time tended to associate Orangeism with political matters—organizing parades on 12 July, opposing Roman Catholics, objecting to the 1870 execution of Thomas Scott—and with the Irish. Nevertheless, the Orange Order's real importance and influence continued to rest on the twin facts that its membership united British Protestants of all origins and that it served as a focal point on the local level for social intercourse and conviviality. As a "secret" society, it had elaborate initiation rites and a ritual that appealed to men who spent most of their lives in drudgery or dull routine. Lodges provided a variety of services for members, including an elaborate funeral. But if local fraternity was the key to Orangeism's success, its public influence was enormous. In 1885 John A. Macdonald's government would prefer to risk alienating Quebec by executing Louis Riel than alienating Orange Ontario by sparing him.

The Orange Order was not the only fraternal organization that grew and flourished in Canada. Because most of these societies were semi-secret, with rites based on Freemasonry, they appealed mainly to Protestants. The Masons themselves expanded enormously during the mid-nineteenth century. They were joined by a number of other orders, such as the Independent Order of Oddfellows (founded in England in 1813 and brought to Canada by 1845), the Independent Order of Foresters (founded in the United States in 1874 and brought to Canada in 1881), and the order of the Knights of Pythias (founded in Washington, DC, in the early 1860s and brought to Canada in 1870). The Knights of Labor was an all-embracing labour organization that owed much to the lodges. Fellowship and mutual support were the keys to the success of all of these societies. Their success led to the formation in 1882 of the Knights of Columbus as a similar fraternal benefit society for Roman Catholic men, although the first chapters in Canada were probably not founded until the early 1890s. While few of these societies admitted women directly, most had adjunct or parallel organizations for women. By the 1880s many Canadians belonged to one or more of these societies. Membership offered a means of social introduction into a new community, provided status and entertainment to members, and increasingly supplied assurance of assistance in times of economic or emotional crisis.

Culture

In the Victorian and Edwardian eras, most Canadians continued to amuse themselves at home by making music and playing numerous parlour games. Outside the home, the amateur tradition remained strong. In most fields of artistic endeavour, Britain and the United States remained the dominant influences. Perhaps the outstanding original achievements in Canadian cultural production in this period occurred in fiction. Three developments stand out. One was the creation of the Canadian social novel. A second was the rise of a major figure in Canadian humour to carry on the earlier tradition of Haliburton and McCulloch. The third development, related to the previous two, was the emergence of several Canadian authors as international bestsellers. Some of these authors were women. All the successful authors were at their best in writing about the values of rural and small-town Canada at the end of the nineteenth century.

The best example of the social novel—also a novel of ideas—was *The Imperialist* by Sara Jeannette Duncan (1862–1912). Duncan had been born in Brantford and educated at the Toronto Normal School. She then became a pioneering female journalist, working for a long list of newspapers in the United States and Canada. In 1888 she and a female friend began a trip around the world, which she subsequently fictionalized. In 1904 she produced *The Imperialist*, a novel intended to describe the Imperial Question from the vantage point of the "average Canadian of the average small town . . . whose views in the end [counted] for more than the opinions of the political leaders" (quoted in Klinck, 1965: 316). Duncan drew on her childhood experiences in Brantford to describe conditions in Elgin, a "thriving manufacturing town, with a collegiate institute, eleven churches, two newspapers, and an asylum for the deaf and dumb, to say nothing of a fire department unsurpassed for organization and achievement in the Province of Ontario" (Duncan, 1971 [1904]: 25). The opening chapter began with an account of the celebrations in Elgin on 24 May, the Queen's Birthday. Duncan interwove the issue of imperialism with the social values of late Victorian Canada. For her protagonist, young politician Lorne Murchison, Canada's continuation as a British nation was of moral rather than strategic importance.

Duncan was perhaps the first Canadian writer to recognize the literary potential of small-town Canada, especially for satirical purposes, but she was not the greatest.

Lucy Maud Montgomery (1874–1942) sold the rights to her highly successful novel Anne of Green Gables to an American publisher for $500. Anne has gone on to become a mythic Canadian heroine, equally popular in Japan as in Canada itself. Public Archives and Records Office of Prince Edward Island. Lucy Maud Montgomery 3110-1.

Stephen Leacock (1869–1944) had been born in England, but grew up on a farm near Lake Simcoe. Educated at Upper Canada College, the University of Toronto, and the University of Chicago, Leacock published a successful college textbook, *Elements of Political Science*, in 1906. He produced his first volume of humorous sketches, *Literary Lapses*, in 1910, and two years later published *Sunshine Sketches of a Little Town*. This was an affectionate satirical look at life in Mariposa, a fictionalized version of Orillia, the nearest town to his boyhood home. Leacock perfectly captured the hypocrisy, materialism, and inflated notions of importance possessed by Mariposa's residents. He followed this triumph with a much more savage satire of a North American city, obviously the Montreal in which he lived and taught (at McGill University). The work was entitled *Arcadian Adventures with the Idle Rich* (1914). In this book, which he pretended to set somewhere in the United States, Leacock began the transference of his satire from Canada to North America. He moved on from these early works to produce a volume of humorous sketches virtually every year, increasingly set in an international milieu. His books were very popular in Britain and the United States. Many critics feel that Leacock's best work was his early Canadian satire, in which he scourged Canadian pretensions.

Duncan and Leacock both achieved international reputations as writers of fiction, and they were joined by several other Canadians in the years between 1900 and 1914. One was the Presbyterian clergyman Charles W. Gordon (1860–1937), who under the pseudonym "Ralph Connor" was probably the best-selling writer in English between 1899 and the Great War. Born in Glengarry

Document

The Spell of the Yukon

British-born Robert W. Service (1874–1958) was the most popular poet in Canada at the end of the nineteenth century, best known as the "poet of the Yukon." His poem, "The Spell of the Yukon," reprinted below, suggests his attraction.

The Chilkoot Pass. This iconic photograph suggests some of the difficulties gold seekers endured to reach the Yukon. © World History Archive/Alamy.

I wanted the gold, and I sought it,
I scrabbled and mucked like a slave.
Was it famine or scurvy—I fought it;
I hurled my youth into a grave.

I wanted the gold, and I got it—
Came out with a fortune last fall,—
Yet somehow life's not what I thought it,
And somehow the gold isn't all.

No! There's the land. (Have you seen it?)
It's the cussedest land that I know,
From the big, dizzy mountains that screen it
To the deep, deathlike valleys below.
Some say God was tired when He made it;
Some say it's a fine land to shun;
Maybe; but there's some as would trade it
For no land on earth—and I'm one.

You come to get rich (damned good reason);
You feel like an exile at first;
You hate it like hell for a season,
And then you are worse than the worst.
It grips you like some kinds of sinning;
It twists you from foe to a friend;
It seems it's been since the beginning;
It seems it will be to the end.

County, Canada West, and educated at the University of Toronto and Edinburgh University, Gordon became minister of a Presbyterian church in Winnipeg, where he lived for the remainder of his life. Ralph Connor's first three books, published between 1899 and 1902, sold over five million copies. One of these, *Glengarry School Days: A Story of Early Days in Glengarry* (1902), was probably the best book he ever wrote. Like Duncan and Leacock, Connor excelled at the evocation of small-town life and mores, drawing from his personal experiences as a boy. He was not a great writer but knew how to sustain a narrative and to frame a moral crisis. Some of his work—including novels in which clerical examples of muscular Christianity faced a variety of frontier challenges—obviously struck a responsive chord in an international audience. Connor's heroes triumphed over sin, anarchy, and unregenerate people by sheer force of character, Christian conviction, goodness, and even physical strength; they represented

I've stood in some mighty-mouthed hollow
That's plumb-full of hush to the brim;
I've watched the big, husky sun wallow
In crimson and gold, and grow dim,
Till the moon set the pearly peaks gleaming,
And the stars tumbled out, neck and crop;
And I've thought that I surely was dreaming,
With the peace o' the world piled on top.

The summer—no sweeter was ever;
The sunshiny woods all athrill;
The grayling aleap in the river,
The bighorn asleep on the hill.
The strong life that never knows harness;
The wilds where the caribou call;
The freshness, the freedom, the farness—
O God! how I'm stuck on it all.

The winter! the brightness that blinds you,
The white land locked tight as a drum,
The cold fear that follows and finds you,
The silence that bludgeons you dumb.
The snows that are older than history,
The woods where the weird shadows slant;
The stillness, the moonlight, the mystery,
I've bade 'em good-by—but I can't.

There's a land where the mountains are nameless,
And the rivers all run God knows where;
There are lives that are erring and aimless,
And deaths that just hang by a hair;
There are hardships that nobody reckons;
There are valleys unpeopled and still;
There's a land—oh, it beckons and beckons,
And I want to go back—and I will.

They're making my money diminish;
I'm sick of the taste of champagne.
Thank God! when I'm skinned to a finish
I'll pike to the Yukon again.
I'll fight—and you bet it's no sham-fight;
It's hell!—but I've been there before;
And it's better than this by a damsite—
So me for the Yukon once more.

There's gold, and it's haunting and haunting;
It's luring me on as of old;
Yet it isn't the gold that I'm wanting
So much as just finding the gold.
It's the great, big, broad land 'way up yonder,
It's the forests where silence has lease;
It's the beauty that thrills me with wonder,
It's the stillness that fills me with peace.

CANADA   Material Culture

St Mary's Church, Indian River, Prince Edward Island

St Mary's Church. © Bill Gozansky/Alamy.

A wooden church in the French Gothic style located on Prince Edward Island, St Mary's Church in Indian River was designed by William Critchlow Harris (1854–1913), perhaps the leading architect in the Maritime provinces in the late nineteenth and early twentieth centuries. Harris was born near Liverpool, England, and immigrated with his family to the Island in 1856. One of seven children, he attended Prince of Wales College and spent his life in the Maritimes, a residential choice that may have cost him the opportunity to achieve a national or even international reputation as did his elder brother Robert Harris, the painter. Harris began designing churches in 1880, most of them located on PEI or in Nova Scotia. Although he frequently built with stone, his most characteristic and iconic churches are, like St Mary's, renderings in wood of buildings in the Gothic style. Indeed, his adaptation of wood to a Victorian vocabulary was his most original contribution to the architectural landscape of the region. The buildings stand out today partly because they are painted in bright colours. Harris began working in High Victorian Gothic, but gradually shifted to French Gothic, as exemplified in St Mary's. A keen amateur musician, Harris's churches were invariably acoustical triumphs, in effect musical instruments rendered as buildings. This church was decommissioned by 2009 and is presently used as a concert hall. Harris's designs were distinguished by multi-paned pointed-arch Gothic windows and often by circular side-towers, as well as clipped gable roofs and bargeboards with drilled holes as decoration. The tower at Indian River also contains representations of the 12 apostles, perhaps a tribute to the Cathedral at Chartres. Harris's willingness to adapt wood to the Gothic style is an obvious repurposing of a specific material culture tradition to Canada. The use of classic architectural forms to produce distinctively regional churches is a repeated theme of colonial encounters, but in St Mary's we see that trend continuing even after Canada has become an established nation. That the building now hosts concerts and other musical events is a holdover from the interests of its architect, but also an adaptation of the space to present needs.

what his generation saw as the forces of civilization and progress. Fellow Presbyterian Nellie McClung (1873–1951) also had great success with similar material, even less artfully rendered, in books such as *Sowing Seeds in Danny* (1908); her fame was more in the political arena.

A much superior artist was Lucy Maud Montgomery (1874–1942), whose *Anne of Green Gables* also first appeared in 1908. Montgomery's books lovingly described rural life and presented some of the standard dilemmas faced by her readers, ranging from growing up to having to leave the farm.

Imperialism, Reform, and Racism

Contemporaries often characterized Canadian political life in this era in terms of its lack of ideology and its predilection for what the French observer André Siegfried called the "question of collective or individual interests for the candidates to exploit to their own advantage" (Siegfried, 1907: 142). Lurking only just beneath the surface, however, were some serious and profound issues. First was the so-called Canadian question, which bore in various ways upon the very future of the new nation. It often appeared to be a debate between those who sought to keep Canada within the British Empire and those who wanted it to assume full sovereignty. Into this discussion other matters merged subtly, including the "race" question and the reform question. The former involved the future of French Canada within an evolving Anglo-American nation. The latter concerned the institution of political and social change through public policy. Debate and disagreement over the three loosely linked issues—imperialism, Anglo–French antagonisms, and reform—kept political Canada bubbling with scarcely suppressed excitement from the 1880s to the beginning of the Great War. Canada's involvement in the military conflict of Europe would bring those issues together, although it would not resolve them.

Imperialism

The period from 1880 to 1914 saw a resurgence of imperial development around the world. The French, the

Germans, even the Americans, took up what Rudyard Kipling called the "White man's burden" in underdeveloped regions of the world. About the same time, Great Britain began to shed its "Little England" free trade sentiments. The world's shopkeeper discovered that substantial windfall profits came from exploiting the economies of Asia, Latin America, and Africa, especially the last. Canada first faced the implications of the resurgence of Britain's imperial pretensions in 1884 when the mother country asked it to contribute to an expedition to relieve General Charles Gordon, besieged by thousands of Muslim fundamentalists at Khartoum in the Egyptian Sudan. Sir John A. Macdonald's immediate response was negative, but he ultimately found it politic to allow Canadian civilian volunteers to assist the British army. By the end of the century Joseph Chamberlain at the Colonial Office in London was advocating that Britain's old settlement colonies be joined together in some political and economic union, the so-called Imperial Federation.

Encouraged by a new infusion of immigrants from Britain—nearly half a million between 1870 and 1896 and a million between 1896 and 1914—many anglophone Canadians began openly advocating Canada's active participation in the new British Empire. Their sense of imperial destiny was not necessarily anti-nationalistic. They saw no inconsistency between the promotion of a sense of Canadian unity and a larger British Empire. "I am an Imperialist," argued Stephen Leacock in 1907, "because I will not be a Colonial." Leacock sought "something other than mere colonial stagnation, something sounder than independence, nobler than annexation, greater in purpose than a Little Canada" (quoted in Bumsted, 1969, II: 78). Such pan-Britannic nationalism came to express itself concretely in demands for Imperial Federation. It was most prevalent in the province of Ontario.

Unfortunately for the imperialists, not all Canadians agreed with their arguments. Several strands of anti-imperial sentiment had emerged by the turn of the century. One strand, most closely identified with the political journalist Goldwin Smith (1823–1910), insisted that the geography of North America worked against Canadian nationalism. Smith advocated Canadian absorption into the United States. Fear of this development led many Canadians to oppose a new reciprocity agreement with

Biography

Nellie Letitia McClung

Nellie McClung. CP PHOTO.

Born in Chatsworth, Ontario, Nellie McClung (née Mooney) (1873–1951) moved with her family to Manitoba in 1880. After attending normal school in Winnipeg, she taught in rural Manitoba for many years. She was active in temperance work and in suffrage agitation. In 1896 she married Robert Wesley McClung, a druggist, who promised, Nellie later reported, that "I would not have to lay aside my ambitions if I married him." Her emergence to prominence began when she entered an American short story competition in 1902 and was encouraged by an American publisher to expand the story into the novel that became *Sowing Seeds in Danny*, a lighthearted look at village life on the prairies published in 1908. The book sold over 100,000 copies, was in its seventeenth edition at the time her death, and brought her both fame and fortune.

She and her husband moved to Winnipeg with their four children in 1911, where she helped organize the Political Equality League in 1912. Frustrated with the difficulty of arousing male politicians to suffrage reform, after some humiliating experiences she turned herself into a first-rate platform speaker. In 1914 she organized the Mock Parliament of Women, in which women played all the political roles. McClung herself was Manitoba Premier Rodmond Roblin, one of the major opponents of women's right to vote. McClung and her associates, supporting the Liberal Party, were unable to defeat Roblin's government in the 1914 election, but it soon fell under the weight of a construction scandal. The Liberal government of Tobias Crawford soon made Manitoba the first province in Canada to grant women the right to vote.

Meanwhile, the McClungs had moved to Edmonton, where Nellie again led the fight for female suffrage. She was also a strong supporter of the war effort and the Red Cross. In 1921 she was elected to the Alberta legislature, where she championed a host of radical measures of the time, ranging from mothers' allowances and dower rights for women to sterilization of the mentally unfit. She was defeated in 1926 when her temperance stance became unpopular. Nellie subsequently helped in the successful fight for Canadian woman senators. The McClungs moved to Victoria in 1933. In her west coast years, she became a CBC governor (1936–42), a delegate to the League of Nations (1938), and an advocate of divorce reform.

Throughout her life she was an active Methodist and subsequently a member of the United Church, and was prominent at the national and international levels in her church work. Apart from her first novel, none of her subsequent fiction has withstood the test of time very well. McClung did better with her autobiographical memoirs, all of which were highly regarded and reprinted. Like many early feminists, she was clearly a figure of her own time. She supported the Great War with almost bloodthirsty enthusiasm and was an active advocate of eugenics.

the United States in 1911. Another strand, led by John S. Ewart (1849–1933), insisted on Canada's assumption of full sovereignty. Ewart argued that "Colony implies inferiority—inferiority in culture, inferiority in wealth, inferiority in government, inferiority in foreign relations, inferiority and subordination" (Ewart, 1908: 6). Yet another perspective was enunciated by Henri Bourassa (1868–1912), who advocated a fully articulated bicultural Canadian nationalism. He wrote, "My native land is all of Canada, a federation of separate races and autonomous provinces. The nation I wish to see grow up is the Canadian nation, made up of French Canadians and English Canadians" (quoted in Monière, 1981: 190). The Bourassa version of nationalism was considerably larger than the still prevalent traditional nationalism of French Canada. As the newspaper *La Vérité* put it in 1904, "what we want to see flourish is French-Canadian patriotism; our people are the French-Canadian people; we will not say that our homeland is limited to the Province of Quebec, but it is French Canada."

The most common confrontations over the role of Canada within the Empire occurred in the context of imperial defence. At Queen Victoria's Jubilee celebration in June 1897, Laurier had fended off a regularization of colonial contributions to the British military. The question arose again in July 1899 when the mother country requested Canadian troops for the forthcom-

Professor Stephen B. Leacock, Montreal, 1914. Leacock was both a successful Canadian writer of humorous fiction and a skilled polemicist on the subject of Imperialism for Canada. © McCord Museum.

ing war in South Africa against the Boers. When the shooting began on 11 October 1899, the popular press of English Canada responded with enthusiasm to the idea of an official Canadian contingent. But newspapers in French Canada opposed involvement. As *La Presse* editorialized, "We French Canadians belong to one country, Canada: Canada is for us the whole world, but the English Canadians have two countries,

Contemporary Views

On Imperialism and Nationalism

One of the opponents of Canadian imperialism was Henri Bourassa (1868–1952). In 1912 he explained his position in an address to the Canadian Club.

We speak of "our Empire." Have you ever considered how little we Canadians count in that Empire, the most wonderful fabric of human organization that has ever existed. Of course, as far as land is concerned, and water, and rocks, and mines, and forests, we occupy a large portion of the Empire. As to population we are only seven millions out of over four hundred millions. As to imperial powers, we have none. The people of

the British Kingdom, forty millions in number, possess as their sole property the rest of that Empire. Suppose you except Canada with her seven millions, Australia with her four millions and a half, New Zealand with one million, and South Africa, with a little over one million of white people: apart from those semi-free states, the whole empire of India, the hundreds of Crown colonies, and those immense protectorates in Africa or Asia, no

Continued...

more belong to us than they belong to the Emperor of Germany, or to the President of the French Republic. We have no more to say as regards the government, the legislation, the administration, the revenue and the expenditure, and the defence of that territory, comprising four-fifths of the total population of the Empire, than have the coolies of India or the Zulus of Matabeleland! I am not saying this in disparagement of the system; I am simply putting our position as it is. At the present time, the seven millions of people in Canada have less voice, in law and in fact, in the ruling of that Empire, than one single sweeper in the streets of Liverpool, or one cabdriver on Fleet Street in London; he at least has one vote to give for or against the administration of that Empire, but we, the seven million Canadians, have no vote and no say whatever.

When I hear splendid phrases, magnificent orations, sounding sentences, about that "Empire of ours," I am forcibly reminded of the pretension of a good fellow whom I had hired to look after the furnace of a building of which I had the management in Montreal. Every year, when the time came to purchase the coal for the winter, he used to exclaim, with a deep sense of his responsibilities: "How dear it costs us to keep up our building!" Our right of ownership, of tutelage, of legislation, in the British Empire is exactly what the right of partnership of that stoker was in that building.

. . . [A]t the sixth Imperial Conference, the delegates from Australia, representing a courageous, intelligent, progressive British community, with a high sea trade amounting in imports and exports to $650,000,000 a year, asked the representatives of the British Government why the British authorities, without even thinking of asking the opinion of Canada, of Australia, of South Africa, and of New Zealand, had concluded with the great maritime powers the international treaty known as the Declaration of London, which may affect beneficially or otherwise the trade of the world in future naval wars. They enquired also if it would be possible to have at least one representative from the self-governing British colonies on the Board of Arbitration, eventually to be constituted, under the terms of that treaty, to adjudicate upon the seizures of trade and ships in times of war. Sir Edward Grey, undoubtedly one of the ablest men in British public life to-day, showed there, I think, his great tact and his extraordinary command of words and of diplomatic means. But, when all the courteous terms and all the frills were taken off, his answer amounted to this: On that board the negro President of Hayti could sit, the negro President of Liberia could sit, but the Prime Minister of Canada or of Australia could not sit, simply because Hayti and Liberia are nations, whilst Canada or Australia are not nations. He explained that the colonies were not consulted because they exist only through Great Britain, and that the moment Great Britain accepted that treaty it applied to us as to her. Undoubtedly true and another evidence, I think, to show that in the "imperial partnership," in the enjoyment of that imperial citizenship of which we hear so much, there still remains a slight difference between the British citizen in England, Scotland and Ireland, and the British citizen of Canada: one is a member of a sovereign community, the other is the inhabitant of a subjected colony.

Source: H. Bourassa, *Canadian Club Addresses 1912* (Toronto: Warwick Bros & Rutter, 1912), 78–80.

one here and one across the sea." The government compromised by sending volunteers, nearly 5,000 before the conflict was over. The defence issue emerged again in 1909, this time over naval policy. Under imperial pressure, Canada finally agreed to produce a naval unit of five cruisers and six destroyers. Both sides attacked Laurier's compromise Naval Service Bill of January 1910. The anglophone Tories insisted it did not provide enough assistance for the British, while in Quebec nationalists and Conservatives joined forces to fight for its repeal.

Reform

The reform movement of this period was rich and varied in its interests. It ranged from the women's suffrage movement to various efforts at social and humanitarian change. Mainstream Canadian reform movements had some features in common, however. Their leaders were members of the middle and professional classes who shared assumptions of the age about regeneration and social purity. Those of Protestant backgrounds tended to predominate, particularly in temperance/prohibition, public health, education, and women's suffrage. Women, because of their general nurturing role in society, played a major role in most reform movements. These women were often less concerned with restructuring gender roles in society than with the need for inculcating middle-class virtues or with helping the poor. French-Canadian women were significantly under-represented in most national reform movements, partly because of the political isolation of Quebec and partly because the

Contemporary Views

A Few General Rules Regarding Diet for School Children

Adelaide Hoodless (1858–1910) was the leading advocate of domestic science in Canada before the Great War. She was also the inspiration for the organization of Women's Institutes, and with her friend Lady Aberdeen (the wife of the Governor General) she was the co-founder of the National Council of Women of Canada, the national YWCA, and the Victorian Order of Nurses. In 1898 she published a textbook entitled *Public School Domestic Science*, from which the following is an excerpt.

The average age of school children is from six to sixteen years. During this time both mind and body are undergoing development. Throughout school period the growth of the body is continued until almost completed. There are unusual demands, therefore, upon the functions of absorption and assimilation. The food must be abundant, and of the character to furnish new tissue, and to yield energy in the form of heat and muscular activity. The food should also contain salts of lime to meet the requirements of formation of the bones and teeth. Many children acquire habits of dislike for certain articles of food, which become so fixed in later life that they find it very inconvenient, especially when placed in circumstances, as in travelling, where one cannot always obtain the accustomed diet; it therefore is unwise to cultivate such habits, which are often a serious obstacles to normal development. . . . An important consideration in school diet is to avoid monotony, which becomes so common from economic reasons, or more often from carelessness. It is much easier to yield to routine and force of habit than to study the question. The hours for study and for meals should be regulated that sufficient time will be allowed before each meal for children to wash and prepare themselves comfortably without going to the table excited by hurry, and they should be required to remain at the table for a fixed time, and not allowed to hastily swallow their food in order to complete an unfinished task or game. An interval of at least half an hour should intervene after meals before any mental exertion is required. Constant nibbling at food between meals should be forbidden; it destroys the appetite, increases the saliva, and interferes with gastric digestion. . . . [C]hildren should have their meals made tempting by good cooking and pleasant variety, as well as an agreeable appearance of the food. Meat which is carved in unsightly masses and vegetables which are sodden and tasteless will be refused, and an ill attempt is made to supply the deficiency in proper food by eating indigestible candy, nuts, etc. Children often have no natural liking for meat, and prefer puddings, pastry or sweets when they can obtain them; it is therefore more important that meat and other wholesome foods should be made attractive to them at the age when they need it.

ideology of the traditional society greatly limited the place of women in that province.

The suffrage movement did emphasize the gender question. It addressed women's political powerlessness by attempting to win for them the right to vote. The movement was chiefly an urban one, dominated by well-educated women who saw political power as necessary to bring about other legislative change. The suffragist leaders were almost exclusively Canadian or British-born and belonged to the mainline Protestant churches. Well over half of these women were gainfully employed, mostly in journalism and writing. The suffragists gradually lost contact with working-class women, who were suspicious of the class biases in both the suffrage and reform movements. They also failed to gain the support of farm women because they did not understand rural issues, especially the concern over rural depopulation. Many rural women became involved in their own organizations designed to deal with their own problems, such as the Women's Institutes. Adelaide Hoodless (1858–1910) founded the first Institute at Stoney Creek, Ontario, in 1897. (In Henry James Morgan's biographical compilation *The Canadian Men and Women of the Time*, 2nd edn, 1912, Hoodless is listed under the entry for her husband John, who was an obscure furniture manufacturer in Hamilton.) Women's Institutes promoted appreciation of rural living, as well as encouraging better education for all women for motherhood and homemaking. In 1919 the Federated Women's Institutes of Canada organized with its motto "For Home and Country."

One female reform organization, the Woman's Christian Temperance Union, had both rural and urban memberships. Founded in 1874 in Picton, Ontario, the WCTU claimed 10,000 members by 1900 and had an influence far beyond that number. Despite its name, the WCTU wanted prohibition, soon seeing the elimination of alcoholic beverages as a panacea for many of the ills currently besetting Canadian society, such as crime, the abuse of women and children, political corruption, and general immorality. The WCTU was only one of several members of the Dominion Alliance for the Total Suppression of the Liquor Traffic. Like most Canadian reform movements, prohibition required state intervention to be effective, and this eventually led some of its supporters to women's suffrage. Laurier held a national referendum on prohibition in 1898. Although its supporters won a narrow victory, the Prime Minister refused to implement national legislation because only 20 per cent of the total electorate had supported the principle. The prohibitionists turned to the provinces, succeeding in getting legislation passed in Prince Edward Island in 1900 and in Nova Scotia in 1910. The local option was even more effective, since it involved local communities where prohibitionist sentiment could be strong. Prohibitionism exemplified both the best and the worst features of reform. It had little Catholic or urban working-class support. Moreover, it tended to clothe its single-minded arguments with intense moral fervour, often of the social purity variety.

Humanitarian reform, usually of urban abuses, often focused on the human victims of disastrous industrial social conditions. One of the main spearheads of such reform was the social gospel. Beginning in the Methodist Church and expanding to all Protestant denominations in Canada, the social gospel saw Christ as a social reformer and the institution of the Kingdom of God on earth as its (and his) mission. The growth of city missions and church settlement houses led to the establishment of the Social Services Council of Canada in 1912. The most prominent social gospeller was J.S. Woodsworth (1874–1942). Another branch of humanitarian reform involved various professionals who became concerned with social problems through their professional practices. Thus doctors, for example, were active in promoting a public health system and in recommending ways of improving public health care. Among the medical profession's public health recommendations was compulsory medical inspection of schoolchildren.

Schools and members of the teaching profession were also in the front lines of humanitarian reform. In this period educators pushed not only for improved schooling but for the schools to assume much of the burden of social services for the young by acting *in loco parentis* for the children of slum and ghetto dwellers. The pressure for compulsory school attendance legislation, extended on a province-by-province basis across the nation by 1914, was partly reformist in nature. Regular school attendance would provide a more suitable environment for children than roaming the streets or working in factories. The children might learn skills that would lift them out of their poverty and (in

The Americanization of Canada

In 1907 the American journalist Samuel E. Moffatt published a book entitled *The Americanization of Canada*, which extended Goldwin Smith's earlier arguments about the extent of Canadian integration into the United States.

In 1850, 147,711 persons of Canadian birth were living south of the border—about one-sixteenth of the number of people living in the British possessions at the same time. In 1860 the Canadian-born population of the United States had increased to 249,970, a gain of 76 per cent, while the general population of the Union was increasing at the rate of 35.6 per cent, and that of the British provinces at about 33.6. In 1870 there were 493,464 Canadians in the United States, an increase of 97.4 per cent for the decade against 22.6 per cent for that of the population of the Republic as a whole, and 16.2 per cent for that of the British colonies, now united in the Dominion of Canada.... While the population of the Republic was a little more than tripling in fifty years, and that of Canada was being multiplied by less than two and a half, the little Canada south of the boundary line saw the number of its inhabitants multiplied by eight. Of all the living persons of Canadian birth in 1900, more than one-fifth were settled in the United States. But if the statement stopped there it would be incomplete. In addition to the native Canadians in the United States in 1900, there were 527,301 persons of American birth but with both parents Canadian. There were also 425,617 with Canadian fathers and American mothers, and 344,470 with Canadian mothers and American fathers. Thus there were in all 2,480,613 persons in the United States of at least half Canadian blood, which is more than half the number of similar stock in Canada....

In density of Canadian population, ignoring all other elements, Massachusetts stands first, exceeding any province of Canada, and Rhode Island second. The relative rank of the various Provinces and States previously named on this basis is:

Canadian population per square mile

1	Massachusetts	64.2
2	Rhode Island	64.0
3	Prince Edward Island	45.36
4	Nova Scotia	20.6
5	New Brunswick	11.2
6	Connecticut	10.9
7	New Hampshire	10.8
8	Ontario	8.4
9	Michigan	7.1
10	Vermont	6.8 ...

Classified in the same way, the principal Canadian cities in 1900–1 were:

1	Montreal	267,730
2	Toronto	208,040
3	Boston	84,336
4	Quebec	66,231
5	Chicago	64,615
6	Ottawa	49,718
7	Detroit	44,592
8	New York	40,400 ...

Source: Samuel Erasmus Moffatt, *The Americanization of Canada* (1907).

the case of immigrants) they would become assimilated to the values of Canadian society.

Educators clearly believed that using schools for reform purposes was in the best interests of Canadian society. It was also in their best interest. Compulsory education opened more employment and introduced the educator as social expert, a professional who knew more about what was important for children than

Sample Questions for Junior Grade Examinations, May 1911

1. If there are before you two tumblers of colorless liquid and you are told one contains water and the other alcohol, by what four tests can you determine which contains alcohol?

2. Explain how the juices of raspberries, cherries and currants are turned into wine. Why is the use of such home-made wines objectionable?

3. Explain the real cause of the so-called "stimulating" effect of alcohol on the heart.

4. Explain why employers do not wish to employ persons who use alcoholic liquors, tobacco or narcotics.

5. Why is alcohol which quickens action, hurtful, while exercise, which does the same thing, useful?

6. What is sleep? Show the necessity for it, and the evil effects of narcotics upon it.

Source: *Canadian White Ribbon Tidings*, May 1911, as quoted in Sharon Anne Cook, *"Through Sunshine and Shadow": The Woman's Christian Temperance Union, Evangelicalism, and Reform in Ontario, 1874–1930* (Montreal and Kingston: McGill-Queen's University Press, 1995), 121.

parents, particularly the parents of the disadvantaged. Compulsory education, medical examinations, school nurses, and lunch programs all were part of a new form of social engineering that would only increase in emphasis over the century.

In the course of time, many of the private agencies of reform became conscripted as quasi-public ones under provincial legislation. They served as arms of the state in the intermediate period before the establishment of permanent government bureaucracies. Thus private child welfare programs became officially responsible for abandoned, abused, and delinquent children. Despite this trend towards a public approach, the framework remained that of individual morality. The humanitarian reformers commonly linked vice, crime, and poverty. Even those who focused on poverty tended to attribute it to almost every other cause than the failure of the economic system to distribute wealth equitably. The concept of a basic minimum standard of living as the right of all members of society was slow to develop in Canada. Attacks on poverty in this period retained a certain class overtone, with a "superior" class helping an "inferior" one.

Another whole category of reformers sought structural alteration within the Canadian system. Their model was often sound business practice, for the leaders of this movement were usually successful businessmen. They sought the elimination of wasteful graft and corruption through political reform, the creation of publicly operated (and profitable) utilities to reduce unnecessary taxation, and the introduction of public planning. They tended to focus on the big city, although they spilled over in various directions. These reforms, which in the United States were associated with the Progressive movement, all found allies within associated middle-class and professional groups. The City Beautiful Movement, for example, received much of its support from an expanding community of professional architects, who combined an urge to plan the city as a whole with aesthetic considerations of coherence, visual variety, and civic grandeur. Like Americans, many Canadians saw cities as the culmination of civilization, and many grand plans made their appearance on paper. Cities settled for a few monumental new buildings, such as the imposing legislative structures completed in many provinces before the war. Political reform of municipal government concentrated on "throwing the rascals out," combined with structural changes to reduce the damage they could do when they were in. The changes often included the replacement of

Clara Brett Martin

Clara Brett Martin, first female lawyer in the British Empire. Law Society of Upper Canada Archives, Archives Department collection, "Photograph of Clara Brett Martin," P291.

The pioneering woman in the Canadian legal profession was Clara Brett Martin (1874–1923), who graduated with high honours in mathematics from Trinity College, Toronto, in 1890. In 1891 she petitioned the Law Society of Upper Canada to be registered as a student. The petition was denied, and she was advised to "remove to the United States," where more than 20 states admitted women to the bar. Instead of leaving the country, Martin found an Ontario legislator willing to introduce a bill into the provincial legislature that would explicitly define the word "person" in the Law Society's statutes as including females. This initiative was supported by Dr Emily Stowe, leader of the Dominion Woman's Enfranchisement Association, who gained the approval of Premier Oliver Mowat for the new legislation. By the time it was passed in 1892, the legislation was emasculated so that women could only become solicitors (not barristers), and then only at the discretion of the Law Society.

The Law Society subsequently again refused admission to Martin, and Oliver Mowat himself attended the next Law Society Convocation to move her admission. The Law Society agreed by the narrowest of margins, and Clara Martin became a student-at-law, accepted as an articling student by one of the most prestigious law firms in Toronto. Martin met much disapproval from within her law firm and was forced to change firms in 1893. She was also harassed in the lecture halls of Osgoode Hall and missed as many lectures as she possibly could. She eventually completed her degree and easily passed the bar examinations. Martin also pressed for revision of the legislation that allowed women to act only as solicitors, not barristers. She won this battle, too, and then had to face the Law Society again. A final controversy came over the dress code for female barristers, when women were required to wear their gowns over a black dress. Martin was finally admitted as a barrister and solicitor on 2 February 1897, the first woman in the British Empire entered into the legal profession. She practised for most of her legal career in her own firm in Toronto.

elective councils with more professional government by commission. Businessmen reformers also fought fierce battles over the question of the ownership of utilities. While the utilities barons complained of the attack on private enterprise, the corporate reformers countered by arguing that utilities were intrinsic monopolies that should be operated in the public interest. Much of the impulse behind reform of all sorts came from fear of class warfare and moral degeneration. The reformers did *for* the poor rather than *with* the poor. The results were a vast increase in the public concerns of the state and the beginning of the growth of a public bureaucracy to deal with social matters.

Racism: The Darker Side of Canada's Growth

Racialist thinking was at its height during this period. Part of the "race question" in Canada was not about "race" at all, of course, but about the conflict between French and English Canada. While there was no racial barrier between French and English, contemporaries accepted race-based arguments and analyses as "scientific." Many imperialists regarded the historical progress of the United States, Great Britain, and Canada as evidence of the special genius of the "Anglo-Saxon race." The French were acceptable partners because they, too, were a northern people. Out of the scientific theories of Charles Darwin came the conviction that inheritance was the key to evolution. Races were formed by natural selection, exhibiting quite unequal characteristics. In almost everyone's hierarchy, the dominant Canadian population was at the progressive top of the racial scale. Newcomers who could not or would not assimilate would inevitably lower the Canadian "standard of civilization." Sexual morality was an important component of the racism of the time.

Canadians saw the new immigration after 1896 as particularly troubling. Even that secular saint J.S. Woodsworth, the Methodist minister and social worker in Winnipeg who would become a leftist federal parliamentarian and the first leader of the Co-operative Commonwealth Federation (CCF), associated criminality with the newcomers. Many feared the potential degeneracy of the "great northern race" through commingling with lesser stocks. Others concentrated on the campaigns for social purity, mixing restrictions on the consumption of alcoholic beverages with hostility to prostitution, venereal disease, and sexual exploitation. The first serious efforts at large-scale immigration restriction, designed mainly to keep out the "degenerates," began in the early years of the century. Campaigns for social purity, immigration restriction, and exclusion

of Asians all came out of the same stock of assumptions about heredity and environment that informed many other reform movements of the period. The reformers often emphasized social and moral aspects, directing their efforts chiefly against newcomers.

Immigration restrictions came in three senses. One was an insistence on the good health, good character, and resources of the individual immigrant. A second was an equally strong insistence on preventing group immigration by certain peoples deemed unassimilable, headed by Asians but also including American-born blacks. Efforts at a broader exclusionary practice involved bilateral negotiations with foreign nations to restrict the departure of their nationals, such as an exclusionary agreement with Japan in 1907 that followed anti-Asian riots in Vancouver. The third involved provincial legislation, mainly in British Columbia, to limit the rights of the unwanted. By 1907, the British Columbia legislature had disenfranchised nationals of China, Japan, and imperial India. Federal immigration policy was expressed mostly in informal ways before 1906, but thereafter, immigration authorities became much more concerned with formal regulation of the flow of newcomers, emulating the Americans in this regard.

In 1906 a new Immigration Act consolidated many earlier laws, barring large categories of people, including prostitutes and pimps, the insane, the mentally retarded, epileptics, and the "deaf and dumb." An expanded immigration service in 1908 for the first time began to monitor the border with the United States at 38 border crossings across the continent—before this time the border had been wide open with little checking of those crossing it in either direction—and was allowed to deport individuals who belonged to prohibited categories or become public charges. In 1908, another amendment to the Immigration Act provided that all immigration to Canada had to come via a continuous journey on a through ticket from the country of origin. This "continuous journey" proviso was intended to make it more difficult for immigrants to Canada to evade immigration restrictions placed by the governments of their homelands, often established at Canadian insistence, and it effectively cut off immigration from India. Another restrictive Immigration Act in 1910 gave the cabinet the power to regulate immigration according to race and to keep out "prohibited and undesirable classes." Any group deemed unsuited to the climate or requirements of Canada could be deported on grounds of political or moral undesirability. Political grounds for rejection included the advocacy by a person not a Canadian citizen of the overthrow by force or violence of the government of Great Britain or Canada. The Act also introduced a head tax on all immigrants except the Japanese, who had been paying $500 since 1903 (9–10 Edward VII Chap 27, An Act respecting Immigration).

Perhaps the most extreme example of Canadian exclusionism occurred in May of 1914, when the Japanese vessel *Komagata Maru* arrived in Vancouver harbour with 376 passengers aboard. Of these, 165 had boarded at Hong Kong, 111 at Shanghai, 86 at Maji, and 14 at Yokohama. Of the passengers, 340 were Sikhs, a people who had been arriving in British Columbia for more than a decade. Most had been males from the Jat Sikh community in rural Punjab who came to Canada as sojourners, intending to return to their homes; according to official Canadian statistics, the number of East Indian adult females who entered Canada over the years 1904–7 was 14, and the number of children was 22. The East Indian community soon began to become organized and articulate. The Khalsa Diwan Society, a fraternal organization with nationalist overtones, was organized in Vancouver in 1907. East Indian revolutionary agitators began their work in North America, including Canada. Separating the activities of Indian nationalists into those directed at abuses at home and in host countries is not easy. Much of our knowledge about the nationalists comes from information collected by police undercover agents, and must be understood in this context. The agents were convinced that the leading nationalists were advocates of violence and terrorism.

The *Komagata Maru*'s organizer expected that the Canadians would overlook the continuous voyage requirement when the ship docked in Vancouver and that the local community would raise the money for the head tax. He was right on the second count but wrong on the first. The Canadian government—backed by Vancouver municipal authorities and the British Columbia government, both of which became quite hysterical—refused to allow the passengers to land. Conditions on board ship deteriorated rapidly, and the incident quickly became an international one. Canadian immigration authorities attempted to storm the vessel by force but were driven off. Eventually the ship sailed out of Vancouver harbour under naval escort and headed back to India, a powerful symbol of Canada's exclusionism.

Canada's Entrance into the Great War

The sudden arrival of the Great War in September of 1914 would subsume events such as those in British Columbia, as it would virtually everything in Canadian life. Canada officially went to war at 20:45 hours (Ottawa time) on 4 August 1914, as an automatic consequence of the British declaration of war on Germany. If Canada had no voice in the decision to go to war, it did have some control over the extent of its involvement, and it chose to plunge into the maelstrom quickly and completely. The Canadian Minister of Militia was Colonel Sam Hughes, who had long expected that Canadians would eventually meet Germans on the battlefield. On 10 August, an Order-in-Council permitted him to call 25,000 men to the colours. By this time, some militia units had already begun appealing for recruits. In Winnipeg, for example, Lieutenant-Colonel J.W. de C. O'Grady had mustered his unit, the 90th Winnipeg Rifles, in their drill hall and announced that he had promised that the regiment would turn out "not only [in] full strength but one thousand strong. Who goes?" (Tascona and Wells, 1983: 63). The response was overwhelming, and on 9 August— the day before the Order-in-Council—the Rifles held a recruiting parade on the streets of Winnipeg. When formal sign-ups began after 10 August, one of the rules was that married men had to have the permission of their wives, many of whom dragged their spouses out of the ranks while brandishing their marriage certificates. These early volunteers had virtually no uniforms or equipment, and were sent for first training aboard trams.

By the time the Canadian Parliament met on 18 August the die was cast. Canadian volunteers would participate in the war on a massive scale. On 22 August Parliament passed "An Act to confer certain powers upon the Governor in Council in the event of War, Invasion, or Insurrection"—the famous War Measures Act—enabling the government to act in the defence of the realm without consulting Parliament. Before August was over,

Sam Hughes had created a vast training camp northwest of Quebec City at Valcartier—a tent city capable of housing 32,000 men. Before the end of September the first contingents of soldiers from Valcartier were boarding the passenger liners that would take them to Britain. The fleet sailed on 3 October and arrived at Plymouth 11 days later. "Canada's Answer," as the British called the new arrivals, numbered 31,200. Sent to bivouac on Salisbury Plain, they were finally reviewed by King George V on 4 February 1915, and before the end of the month they were suffering their first casualties on the front lines in France. One of the advantages of the breathtaking speed with which Hughes had moved to create Canadian regiments was that Canadian troops were kept together as units rather than being broken up and integrated into the British forces.

World War I brought to fruition several major trends of the period between 1885 and 1914. It marked a triumph of sorts for Canadian imperialism, for example, as Canada subordinated its substantial military effort to the needs and direction of Great Britain. It also rejuvenated Canadian reform. The patriotic fervour of the war and the eventual political isolation of French Canada made possible a sweeping program of reform, much of which French Canada had opposed. Reform has always required an active state, and wartime conditions encouraged the Canadian government to intervene in almost all areas of life and work.

Historiography

How History Has Changed: Aboriginal Peoples and Christian Missions

Susan Neylan, Wilfrid Laurier University

For a long time, histories of Christian missions to Aboriginal peoples in Canada privileged the churches' perspectives and valorized heroic missionaries. They highlighted conversion experiences and, for the nineteenth and early twentieth centuries, emphasized what was termed the "civilizing" project. Historians told the story of how Aboriginal people encountered Christianity through the teachings of Euro-Canadian missionaries and cast aside former belief systems for the new religion and, often, its Western associations. Aboriginal spiritualities and Christianity were cast in opposition to one another.

Parallel to the rise of Native history as a distinct field of Canadian historical scholarship in the 1970s and 1980s, a new generation of mission historians arose who gave far more attention to the role of Aboriginal peoples. Scholars stressed either their agency or victimization by casting a critical eye on the churches and missionaries. John Webster Grant's *Moon of Wintertime* (1984) argues that Aboriginal peoples accepted Christianity at a moment of severe cultural disruption; as missionaries arrived on the scene bent on transforming Aboriginal cultures, Native spiritual systems were thrown into crisis. First Nations were not helpless in this encounter, yet they had little input beyond the local context.

However, this generation of scholars also highlighted the importance of First Nations, Inuit, and Métis in the narrative. Many actively resisted the encroachment of missions through rejection and opposition; others embraced elements of Christianity and assumed roles of leadership within the missions and churches. Such latter individuals were cast as cross-cultural mediators who enabled the transmission and the translation of religious ideas. Accordingly, biographies of Aboriginal men and women abound in the literature, ranging from those who enthusiastically spread the gospel as mission employees to others who walked in two worlds. Winona

Wheeler's study (2003) of Askeenootow (Charles Pratt) demonstrates how adopting Christianity was never a clear-cut replacement of his Cree-Assiniboine identity with the Christian one.

The third scholarly generation was influenced by the so-called "cultural turn" of the 1990s that drew on theories from anthropology, cultural studies, linguistics, and literary studies, notably post-colonial literature. It encouraged historians to look at the big picture, particularly when it came to culture, and the socially constructed nature of all human reality. Historians recognized the place of missions within older frameworks of Indigenous histories of change and continuity and broader patterns of systemic colonialism. Accordingly, the encounter between Aboriginal peoples and Christians came to be represented in far more nuanced terms than the mission hagiographies of the first generation or the agency/victimization or Aboriginal spirituality/Christianity models of the second.

Scholars proceeded from the idea that Christianity can be translated and incorporated as an integral part of an authentic Indigenous identity without having to wholly replace what came before. Adopting a post-colonial interpretation, Aboriginal spiritual practices were seen to have altered Christianity itself. Hence the Aboriginal–Christian encounter could be studied from points on meeting and similarities, instead of only underscoring distance and differences. Susan Neylan (2003) studies the role in mission work of the first generation of Aboriginal Christian converts, highlighting their contributions to mission forms in ways that did not forsake older spiritual traditions, despite the negative effects of missions. Many turned to Christianity for more than its spiritual appeal and resonance. They were seeking citizenship in a wider Western framework that would allow them to survive as Indigenous people regardless of the political, economic, and cultural changes instituted under colonialism.

Third-generation scholars demonstrate Aboriginal creativity and initiative alongside missionary coercion and dogma, and analyze the impact of the Indigenization (whereby Christianity is made culturally relevant and naturalized as their own), syncretism (the creation of new beliefs and practices through the compatibility of religious forms and traditions), and genuine conversion. However, there is no denying the part Christian churches played in the colonial process itself, which included the attempted destruction of Aboriginal cultures, identities, lands, and resources. Aboriginal residential schools are probably the best-known tool of Christian colonialism. J.R. Miller's *Shingwauk's Vision* (1996), John Milloy's *A National Crime* (1999), and studies authored by residential school survivors expose this dark, shameful aspect of Aboriginal–Christian relations.

Whether talking about first-generation scholars or those of the twenty-first century, the trajectory of this historical scholarship has also been heavily influenced by changes in methodologies. Initially, church records and missionary accounts comprised the bulk of the primary sources used as evidence. There were Aboriginal voices within this colonial archive, but usually very few, or the materials had to be read closely "against the grain" to find Aboriginal perspectives. This changed with the application of ethnohistorical methodologies. Ethnohistory is an approach to the study of the Aboriginal–non-Aboriginal encounter that considers textual, oral, and material sources in its analysis. Scholars sought to evaluate Native responses to Christian missions in as much detail as they had invested in the examination of missionary goals and criteria.

More recently, ethnohistorians have turned from colonialism as the only way to assess the encounter between the colonizers and the colonized. Change, even when it first appears to be evidence of colonialist successes at work, can simultaneously exemplify cultural continuities. Canadian history can also be situated within Aboriginal history and chronologies. Research *with* rather than *about* Aboriginal peoples, employing Indigenous research methodologies, has served to accentuate Aboriginal voices, world views, and conceptualizations of the past. *Standing Up with Ga'axsta'las* (2012) reconsiders one Christian Aboriginal woman's life in the context of both Kwakwaka'wakw systems of prestige, knowledge, and status and colonial political histories. By prioritizing Indigenous insights and written as a collaboration, the study shifts from merely an analysis of Aboriginal–Settler interactions to one that

Continued...

shows internal community dynamics and tension. After all, history is also negotiated in the present.

Bibliography

Agnes, Jack, ed. *Behind Closed Doors: Stories from the Kamloops Indian Residential School*, rev. edn. Penticton, BC, 2006.

Axtell, James. "Some Thoughts on the Ethnohistory of Missions." *Ethnohistory* 29, 1 (1982): 35–41.

Bradford, Tolly. *Prophetic Identities: Indigenous Missionaries and British Colonial Frontiers, 1850–75*. Vancouver, 2012.

Carlson, Keith Thor. *The Problem of Place, the Problem of Time: Aboriginal Identity and Historical Consciousness in the Cauldron of Colonialism*. Toronto, 2010.

Furniss, Elizabeth. *Victims of Benevolence: The Dark Legacy of William Lake Residential School*, 2nd edn. Vancouver, 1995.

Grant, John Webster. *The Moon of Wintertime: Missionaries and the Indians of Canada in Encounter since 1534*. Toronto, 1984.

Gray, Susan Elaine. *"I Will Fear No Evil": Ojibwa–Missionary Encounters along the Berens River, 1875–1940*. Calgary, 2006.

Haig-Brown, Celia. *Resistance and Renewal: Surviving the Indian Residential School*. Vancouver, 1988.

Johnston, Basil H. *Indian School Days*. Toronto, 1988.

Lutz, John Sutton. *Makúk: A New History of Aboriginal–White Relations*. Vancouver, 2009.

Miller, J.R. *Shingwauk's Vision: A History of Native Residential Schools*. Toronto, 1996.

Milloy, John. *A National Crime: The Canadian Government and the Residential School System, 1879–1986*. Winnipeg, 1999.

Neylan, Susan. *The Heavens Are Changing: Nineteenth-Century Protestant Missions and Tsimshian Christianity*. Montreal and Kingston, 2003.

Regan, Paulette. *Unsettling the Settler Within: Indian Residential Schools, Truth Telling, and Reconciliation in Canada*. Vancouver, 2010.

Robertson, Leslie A., with the Kwagu'ł Gixsam Clan. *Standing Up with Ga'axsta'las: Jane Constance Cook and the Politics of Memory, Church, and Custom*. Vancouver, 2012.

Rutherdale, Myra. *Women and the White Man's God: Gender and Race in the Canadian Mission Field*. Vancouver, 2002.

Sellars, Bev. *They Called Me Number One: Secrets and Survival at an Indian Residential School*. Vancouver, 2012.

Smith, Donald. *Sacred Feathers: The Reverend Peter Jones (Kahkewaquonaby) and the Mississauga Indians*, 2nd edn. Toronto, 2013 [1987].

——. *Mississauga Portraits: Ojibwe Voices from Nineteenth-Century Canada*. Toronto, 2013.

Wheeler, Winona. "The Journals and Voices of a Church of England Native Catechist: Askenootow (Charles Pratt), 1851–1884." In Jennifer S.H. Brown and Elizabeth Vibert, eds, *Reading Beyond the Words: Contexts for Native History*, 2nd edn, 237–61. Peterborough, Ont.: Broadview Press, 2003 [1996].

Short Bibliography

Avery, Donald. *Reluctant Host: Canada's Response to Immigrant Workers, 1896–1994*. Toronto, 1995. The best synthesis of the topic.

Bacchi, Carole. *Liberation Deferred? The Ideas of the English-Canadian Suffragists, 1877–1918*. Toronto, 1983. An analysis of English-Canadian suffragism, emphasizing the distinction between maternal and radical feminism.

Berger, Carl. *The Sense of Power: Studies in the Ideas of Canadian Imperialism, 1867–1914*. Toronto, 1970. The pioneer study of these ideas in Canada, and still easily the best.

Bliss, J.M. *A Living Profit: Studies in the Social History of Canadian Business, 1883–1911*. Toronto, 1974. A collection of stimulating essays on Canadian business in a critical period.

Bradbury, Bettina. *Working Families: Age, Gender, and Daily Survival in Industrializing Montreal*. Toronto, 1993. A valuable study on the effect of industrialization on the family and its strategies.

Carbert, Louise. *Agrarian Feminism: The Politics of Ontario Farm Women*. Toronto, 1995. The first full-length analysis of what farm women were up to before 1914.

Christie, Nancy. *Engendering the State: Family, Work, and Welfare in Canada*. Toronto, 2000. A controversial work that locates the origins of the Canadian welfare state in the quest for stability for the family.

Copp, Terry. *The Anatomy of Poverty: The Condition of the Working Class in Montreal 1897–1929*. Toronto, 1974. An early study of the urban working class in Montreal, probably still the best analysis available.

Courville, Serge, and Normand Séguin. *Rural Life in Nineteenth-century Quebec*. Ottawa, 1989. A synthesis of a good deal of secondary literature, which emphasizes how similar rural French Canada was to English Canada.

English, John. *The Decline of Politics: The Conservatives and the Party System, 1901–20*. Toronto, 1977. The best study of politics before the Great War.

Heron, Craig. *Working in Steel: The Early Years in Canada, 1883–1935*. Toronto, 1988. A brilliant account of the origins of steelmaking in Canada, especially strong on labour issues.

Johnston, Hugh. *The Voyage of the Komagata Maru: The Sikh Challenge to Canada's Colour Bar*. Delhi, 1979. A dispassionate recounting of the story.

Linteau, Paul-André. *The Promoters' City: Building the Industrial Town of Maisonneuve, 1883–1918*. Toronto, 1985. A wonderful study of the creation of an industrial suburb in French Canada.

McCormack, A.R. *Reformers, Rebels, and Revolutionaries: The Western Canadian Radical Movement, 1899–1919*. Toronto, 1977. A work that resurrects and brings to life a collection of radicals previously neglected in the traditional literature.

McDonald, R.J. *Making Vancouver: Class, Status, and Social Boundaries, 1863–1913*. Vancouver, 1996. Urban social history that takes advantage of all the latest conceptualizations.

Magocsi, Paul Robert. *Encyclopedia of Canada's Peoples*. Toronto, 1999. A co-operative project by dozens of scholars providing a vast compendium of material on Canadian ethnicity.

Miller, Carman. *Painting the Map Red: Canada and the South African War, 1899–1902*. Montreal, 1993. The best study of Canada and the Boer War.

Parker, Roy. *Uprooted: The Shipment of Poor Children to Canada, 1867–1917*. Vancouver, 2008. A thorough scholarly synthesis of an emotive subject.

Petryshyn, Jaroslav. *Peasants in the Promised Land: Canada and the Ukrainians, 1891–1914*. Toronto, 1985. A careful study of the early Ukrainian migration.

Rollings-Magnusson, Sandra. *Heavy Burdens on Small Shoulders: The Labour of Pioneer Children on the Canadian Prairies*. Edmonton, 2009. A recent study that suggests how much the settlement of the West depended on the work of children.

Sager, Eric, with Gerald Panting. *Maritime Capital: The Shipping Industry in Atlantic Canada, 1820–1914*. Montreal, 1990. A study, based on quantitative data, of an important industry.

Troper, Harold Martin. *Only Farmers Need Apply: Official Canadian Government Encouragement of Immigration from the United States, 1896–1911*. Toronto, 1972. The standard work on the topic.

Valverde, Mariana. *The Age of Light, Soap, and Water: Moral Reform in English Canada, 1885–1925*. Toronto, 1991. One of the few overall syntheses of the reform movement, focusing particularly on its moral dimensions.

Voisey, Paul. *Vulcan: The Making of a Prairie Community.* Toronto, 1988. Probably the best historical community study ever executed in Canada.

Walden, Keith. *Becoming Modern in Toronto: The Industrial Exhibition and the Shaping of a Late Victorian Culture.* Toronto, 1997. A work in cultural studies that deconstructs the Toronto Industrial Exhibition.

Study Questions

1. What role did the patronage system play in Canadian political parties in the years before the Great War?

2. How did the industrialization of the period 1885–1914 differ from that of the 1850s and 1860s?

3. Compare the major problems of urban and rural life in Canada in the early years of the twentieth century.

4. Are the differences between child labour in factories and on farms significant?

5. What does the poem "Town Directory" tell us about Treherne, Manitoba, in 1895?

6. How was Canada selling the western region to newcomers in 1907?

7. Discuss the relationship between the small town and the development of Canadian fiction, 1890–1914.

8. What were the linkages among imperialism, reform, and racism before the Great War?

9. Was Canada a country truly open to immigrants in this period? What were the limitations?

Visit the companion website for *A History of the Canadian Peoples*, fifth edition for further resources.

www.oupcanada.com/Bumsted5e

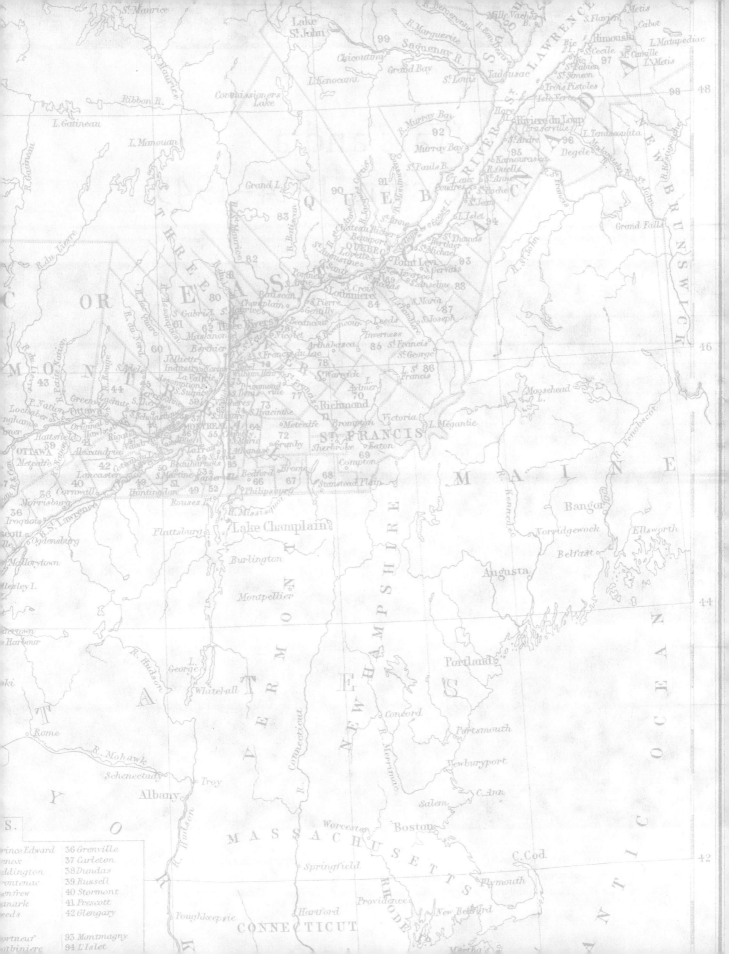

8 Two Wars and a Depression, 1914–1945

During World War II, thousands of women worked in Canadian industrial plants manufacturing war materials. Taken in December of 1943, this picture shows Cecilia Butler working in a munitions plant in Toronto, Ontario. Obviously staged, the photograph presents war-time Canada as a racially tolerant, multi-ethnic society. National Film Board of Canada. Photothèque, LAC, e000761869.

Timeline

1914 Canada and Newfoundland enter the Great War.

1925 United Church of Canada is formed. Pacific Coast Hockey League folds.

1915 Canadian Expeditionary Force fights in the first Battle of Ypres. Ontario introduces Regulation 17.

1926 Governor General Byng refuses Prime Minister King a dissolution for a new election; a constitutional crisis ensues.

1916 Canada introduces a business profits tax. The Newfoundland Regiment is decimated at Beaumont Hamel.

1929 Stock market collapses. Aird Commission report on public broadcasting favours nationalization of radio.

1917 Canadian Expeditionary Force suffers heavy losses at Vimy in April. Canada introduces an income tax. Conscription crisis emerges over introduction of Military Service Act. Much of Halifax is destroyed in an explosion.

1930 Great Depression begins. R.B. Bennett's Conservatives are elected to power in Ottawa.

1918 The Great War ends. Spanish influenza epidemic begins.

1931 Canadian government arrests and imprisons eight leaders of the Communist Party.

1919 "Red Scare" begins. Government suppresses Winnipeg General Strike. First Congress of the League of Indians meets in Sault Ste Marie. *Canadian Bookman* is founded.

1932 Co-operative Commonwealth Federation is founded in Calgary. Bennett government forms the Canadian Radio Broadcasting Commission.

1933 Depression sees huge unemployment rolls. Regina Manifesto is adopted by the CCF. Maurice Duplessis becomes leader of the Conservative Party of Quebec. T. Dufferin Pattullo wins election in British Columbia.

1920 Progressive Party is formed. First issues of *Canadian Forum, Canadian Historical Review,* and *The Dalhousie Review* appear. The Group of Seven holds its first exhibition of paintings.

1921 In a federal election, the Progressive Party wins 64 seats. William Lyon Mackenzie King's Liberals form the government. The Maritime Rights Movement is organized.

1935 R.B. Bennett announces a "New Deal" for Canada, but is defeated by W.L.M. King in the election. Social Credit under William Aberhart sweeps to power in Alberta. Duplessis forms the Union Nationale. The On-to-Ottawa Trek is suppressed at Regina.

1923 Famous Players' Canadian Corporation takes over Allen Theatres.

1936 Canadian Broadcasting Corporation is formed.

1924 William Aberhart begins the Prophetic Bible Institute broadcasts over Calgary's CFCN.

1937 General Motors strike in Oshawa. Royal Commission on Dominion–Provincial Relations is appointed. Lord Tweedsmuir creates the Governor General's awards.

1939 Canada declares war on Germany. British Commonwealth Air Training Plan is founded.

1942 Dieppe raid sees 2,700 Canadians killed or captured. National plebiscite held to release government from non-conscription pledge.

1940 Royal Commission on Dominion–Provincial Relations recommends restructuring of public finances.

1943 Marsh report on social security is tabled in the House of Commons.

1941 Emily Carr wins Governor General's award for *Klee Wyck.* Hong Kong surrenders to Japan. Pearl Harbor attacked.

1944 Family Allowances Act and National Housing Act are passed.

The entrance of Canada into World War I marked a triumph of sorts for Canadian imperialism, as one journal emphasized in 1915:

Your Birthright

There is one race that is fast dominating the world—the Anglo-Saxon race, represented by Great Britain and the USA, born rulers, exceeding all others in the capacity for governing. The only Empire of the present day which answers to this is the British Empire, a Christian Empire, which includes strong young nations that are federating into a company—which carries the gospel to all lands, in all languages—and which is growing and growing—and bids to fill the earth. Do you belong to the British Empire? Then you belong to the blessed race, the blessed Empire—God's chosen rulers of the world. (*Canada's White Ribbon Bulletin*, August 1915, in Cook, 1995: 107)

Canada did not make its own declaration of war, but simply joined the British war effort. Before it ended, the war would inflict extremely heavy Canadian casualties: 60,661 killed in action and 172,000 wounded out of some 620,000 Canadians in uniform drawn from a population of only 8 million. The war gradually isolated French Canada and made possible sweeping national reforms on several fronts. Reform had always implied an interventionist state, and wartime conditions encouraged the Canadian government's intrusion into many new areas of life and work. The government's expenditures were enormous, but it managed to find the money to keep going, mainly through extensive borrowing. One of the new developments was a business profits tax, retroactive to the beginning of the war, introduced in 1916. Another was an income tax, first levied in 1917. Yet another was the nationalization of the railways. The war also accelerated and distorted virtually every economic development that Canada had experienced during the previous 40 years.

Canadians entered the war with no idea of its ultimate length, intensity, or futile savagery. The initial enthusiasm of English-speaking Canadians assumed a swift defeat of Germany and its allies. By 1917 support for the war effort emphasized the extent of the sacrifices already made. Families of the dead soldiers could emotionally rationalize their losses only by calling for more effort towards a final victory. Canada's military contribution was substantial. Nevertheless, Canadians who fought in Europe were almost exclusively volunteers. Serving as the shock troops of the British Empire, Canadians achieved an enviable reputation for bravery and fierceness. Their commanders continually placed them in the most difficult situations, and they performed well. The list of battles at which they fought heroically (and at heavy cost) was a long one, beginning at Ypres in 1915 and continuing through to the Belgian town of Mons, where fighting ended for the Canadians at 11 a.m. on 11 November 1918.

Life in the trenches—which was the main battle experience of most Canadian soldiers in World War I—was a nightmare, so hard to describe that most returning veterans did not really try. Loved ones at home seldom heard accounts of the trench experience, either in letters from the front or after the war. The social world of the trenches was a bizarre, surrealistic experience like no other to be found anywhere in the world. It is true that troops were rotated in and out of the front lines, but almost all experienced the danger and discomfort of life in the trenches at some point. Artillery shelling was constant, and reserves in the secondary and tertiary lines of fortifications were if anything shelled more heavily by large guns than those in the front lines; artillery crews always fired at longer-range targets for fear of hitting their own men. Periods of rotation were not standardized, and during times of crisis the stay in the front line could seem a lifetime. Actual attacks and offensives were relatively rare, but life in the trenches was extremely wearing; men faced not only the shelling and continual risk of sniper fire but difficulties in sleeping, bad food, and the ubiquitous mud, in which many men drowned. The worst thing about the mud was having to move through it. Most Canadian soldiers carried more than 60 pounds (27 kg) of equipment, and a mud-soaked greatcoat could weigh another 50 pounds (23 kg).

While in the front trenches, soldiers had to be constantly on the alert. They were regularly employed on "fatigues," moving rations, stores, and wounded men, and repairing the trenches. Sleep deprivation was common.

Soldiers suffered from the heat in summer and the cold in winter, and from rain virtually year-round. Corpses lay everywhere in the trenches and outside them, attracting rats and lice in great numbers. One Canadian remembered, "Huge rats. So big they would eat a wounded man if he couldn't defend himself" (quoted in Ellis, 1975: 54). The trenches also stank of chloride of lime (a disinfectant), creosol (for the flies), human excrement and human sweat, and the putrefaction of decomposing bodies. Most soldiers were conscious not only of the stench but of the noise, especially the sounds of various sorts of artillery fire that were part of the continual bombardment in the trenches, particularly during offensives. Some could distinguish the various weapons by the noises they made. Dr Andrew Macphail, who served at the front with the 7th Canadian Field Ambulance, commented in his diary:

> I amuse myself finding words to describe the sounds made by the various classes of guns. The 18 pounders thud, thud. The 4.7s bark like an infinite dachshund. The howitzers smash. The machine-guns rat-tat like the wood-pecker or the knocker of a door. A single rifle snaps like a dry twig when it is broken. Rapid rifle fire has a desolating sound; it is as if a load of small stones was being dumped from a Scotch cart. A large shell sounds exactly like a railway train; and shrapnel bursts as if boiler-plate were being torn into fragments, or as if the sky were made of sheet-iron, and had been riven by a thunderbolt. The whistle of the passing rifle bullet is unmistakable. (Macphail, 1915)

Many thought the worst things about the guns were the vibrations and the "solid ceiling of sound." By 1918 soldiers were also exposed to aerial attacks and bombardments. The Great War produced a new form of nervous illness, which came to be called "shell shock," but which was really a combination of various assaults on the human nervous system.

Given the conditions under which the men operated, it becomes easier to understand how they could, from time to time, be led "over the top" in open mass assaults or in raids in small parties—either way to risk

death. Sleep-deprived and in a constant state of shock, most troops who actually engaged in battle were numb to virtually everything going on around them. They fought in a zombie-like state, and those who managed to return were totally exhausted. High command never really understood what the war was like in the trenches. The generals never appreciated that defensive firepower from a dug-in enemy meant that most attacks were nothing but human carnage. Field officers believed in the mystical value of intestinal fortitude. In April 1915, a Canadian regiment at Ypres withstood one of the first poison gas attacks, using for protection nothing but handkerchiefs soaked in urine. After beating back the enemy at great human cost and with other units retreating all around them, the regiment's colonel, supported by those remaining of his junior officers, volunteered to hold the line. He telephoned divisional headquarters and reported modestly, "The 90th Rifles can hold their bit." And they did. The casualties in this one unit in this one battle ran at 20 officers and 550 men killed, wounded, missing, or gassed—out of a total complement of 900.

While dispatches spoke reassuringly of the value of the assaults and the heroism, the soldiers knew perfectly well that their sacrifices were achieving very little. Canadian casualties, like those of other settlement colonies, tended to run considerably higher than those of the armies of the European allies. Whether the colonials had less experience as soldiers, or were placed in the most dangerous places, or simply fought more savagely, is not entirely clear. On one horrible day in 1916 at Beaumont-Hamel, 780 Newfoundlanders were trapped by barbed wire and mowed down by German machine guns; 310 died. While it was possible to be invalided back to Britain ("Blight") or even Canada with a serious enough wound (often called "a blighty"), most of the Canadian soldiers sent to Europe either died on the battlefield or remained on the lines until the Armistice.

Despite these sacrifices, the Canadian government had to fight hard for a voice in imperial war policy. It also worked hard to maintain separate Canadian unit and command structures. The arguments for autonomy—and the manpower necessary to sustain them—dragged the government ever deeper into the quagmire. By the time of Vimy in April 1917, Canada could no longer recruit new volunteers to replace the mounting casualties.

Lucy Maud Montgomery and the War

The following are excerpts from Lucy Maud Montgomery's journal for late 1914.

Monday, Dec. 7, 1914
  Leaskdale, Ont.

A *Globe* headline today was "The Germans Capture Lodz."

This war is at least extending my knowledge of geography. Six months ago I did not know there was such a place in the world as Lodz. Had I heard it mentioned I would have known nothing about it and cared as little. To-day, the news that the Germans have captured it in their second drive for Warsaw made my heart sink into my boots. I know all about it now—its size, its standing, its military significance. And so of scores of other places whose names have been lettered on my memory in blood since that fateful 4th of August—Mlawa, Bzura, Jarolwav, Tomaskoff, Yser, Lys, Aisne, Marne, Prysmysl. At the last mentioned the newspaper wits have been poking fun since the siege of it began. Nobody seems to know how it is pronounced. I daresay the Austrians would think that Saskatchewan and Musquodoboit were about as bad.

  The Manse, Leaskdale, Ont.
  Thursday, Dec. 10, 1914

To-day at noon Ewan [her husband] came in jubilantly. "Good news!" he said. I snatched the paper and read that a German squadron had been totally destroyed by a British one off the Falkland Isles. Coming after the long strain of the recent series of Russian reverses I rather went off my head. I waved the paper wildly in air as I danced around the dining room table and hurrahed. Yet hundreds of men were killed in the fight and hundreds of women's hearts will break because of it. Is that a cause for dancing and hurrahing? Oh, war makes us all very crude and selfish and primitive!

  Saturday, Dec. 12, 1914

To-day's war news was better than it has been for some time—the second German invasion of Poland seems to have been definitely checked. Ever since it began—a fortnight or so ago—I have been wracked with dread. If Germany should smash Russia and then her victorious army back against the French and British lines! That thought was the Dweller on my Threshold. All through the forenoons I could manage to work and hold my dread at bay. But when at twelve I saw Ewan going out for the mail my nerve invariably collapsed. I could not do anything—it was of no use to try. I could not even read. I could only pace the floor like a caged tiger, nerving myself to meet the worst. Then when he came back I would snatch the *Globe* and desperately tear over the headlines. It has been agonizing.

Source: Mary Rubio and Elizabeth Waterston, eds, *The Selected Journals of L.M. Montgomery, vol. 2, 1910–1921* (Toronto: Oxford University Press, 1987), 157–8. Reprinted by permission of the publisher.

The government saw conscription as the only solution. Conscription was a policy intensely opposed by many French Canadians. From the standpoint of Anglo-Canadians, French Canada had not borne its fair share of the burden of war. English Canada argued that less than 5 per cent of the Canadian volunteers had come from French Canada. On the other hand, French Canadians came to feel increasingly under attack by English Canada. As a symbol of their position they focused on the plight of francophones in Ontario, where in 1915 Regulation 17 had seemingly imposed unilingualism on the elementary school system. Virtually all

In the Trenches

Charles Yale Harrison (1898–1954) was a Canadian writer who served with the Royal Montreal Regiment and was wounded at the Battle of Amiens in 1918. He wrote a powerful novel about his experiences in the war.

The sergeant comes into the bay again and whispers to me: "Keep your eyes open now—they might come over on a raid now that it's dark. The wire's cut over there—" He points a little to my right.

I stand staring into the darkness. Everything moves rapidly again as I stare. I look away for a moment and the illusion ceases.

Something leaps towards my face.

I jerk back, afraid.

Instinctively I feel for my rifle in the corner of the bay.

It is a rat.

It is as large as a tom-cat. It is three feet away from my face and it looks steadily at me with its two staring, beady eyes. It is fat. Its long tapering tail curves away from its padded hindquarters. There is still a little light from the stars and this light shines faintly on its sleek skin. With a darting movement it disappears. I remember with a cold feeling that it was fat, and why . . .

The sergeant rushes into the bay of the trench, breathless. "Minnies," he shouts, and dashes on.

In that instant there is a terrible roar directly behind us.

The night whistles and flashes red.

The trench rocks and sways.

Mud and earth leap into the air, come down upon us in heaps.

We throw ourselves upon our faces, clawing our nails into the soft earth on the bottom of the trench.

Another! . . . Still they come.

I am terrified. I hug the earth, digging my fingers into every crevice, every hole.

A blinding flash and an exploding howl a few feet in front of the trench.

My bowels liquefy.

Source: Charles Yale Harrison, *Generals Die in Bed* (Waterdown, Ont.: Potlatch Publications, 1995), 22–4.

French-Canadian members of Parliament opposed the Military Service Act, which became law in August 1917. In its wake, and with a federal election coming, a Union government was formed out of the Conservatives and those English-speaking members of the Liberal Party who had broken with Laurier over his opposition to conscription.

French Canada was not alone in becoming isolated by the war. Members of Canada's other ethnic minorities, many of them originating in parts of Germany and the Austro-Hungarian Empire, found themselves under attack. The government became increasingly repressive as the war continued. It interned "aliens" by Order-in-Council and suppressed much of the foreign-language press. The Wartime Elections Act of September 1917 ruthlessly disenfranchised Canadians of enemy origin. Organized labour found itself shackled. The government introduced compulsory arbitration into all war industries in 1916. In the crisis year of 1917, the government announced its intention to outlaw all strikes and lockouts. The Union government was simultaneously bipartisan and sectional. It was able to implement several national reforms favoured by its Anglo-Canadian supporters. Many provinces had allowed women the vote earlier in the war. The Wartime Elections Act in 1917 granted the federal electoral franchise to women with close relatives in the war. In 1918 all women got the vote federally. Prohibition also triumphed nationally in 1918, not only to keep the soldiers pure and to ensure that the country to which they returned would

Material Culture

The Sopwith Camel

Sopwith Camel. © Chronicle/Alamy.

The Sopwith Camel was a single-seat biplane airplane in service between June 1917 and 1920. Although tricky to fly, it was extremely manoeuvrable in the hands of a skilled pilot, and was responsible for nearly 1,300 "kills" (enemy planes destroyed), more than any other Allied aircraft. The Camel weighed 420 kilograms empty and was powered by a nine-cylinder rotary engine rated at 130 horsepower (by comparison, the World War II Spitfire weighed almost 2,300 kilograms empty and had a 1470 horsepower engine). The light weight was achieved by a flimsy construction, with plywood panels around the cockpit, and with fuselage, wings, and tail covered with fabric. Obviously there was no protection for the pilot, and the contemporary joke was that it offered "a wooden cross, a Red Cross, or a Victoria Cross." The plane had two .303 Vickers machine guns mounted for synchronized fire in front of the cockpit. Nearly 5,500 Camels were built. Many were diverted to home defence against German bombers, and the Camel proved capable of flying at night when the enemy shifted to night bombing. Towards the end of the war the Camel was limited by slow speed and poor performance at high altitudes, but was used as a ground attack weapon, destroying many enemy aircraft by strafing runs at low altitude. It was the favourite aircraft of Major William Barker, one of the most decorated Canadian pilots during the war.

The Great War was not a very romantic one, with most destruction involving large numbers of casualties inflicted by anonymous weapons. The war in the air was one of the few places featuring one-on-one combat opportunities and duels between skilled flyers, and a number of fighter pilots, such as Barker and Billy Bishop, developed substantial popular reputations. Canadian pilots flew for the Royal Air Force for most of the war, since a separate Canadian unit (the Royal Canadian Air Force) was not created until September 1918. Nevertheless, Canadians were highly successful in the air, with over 80 "aces" credited with 10 "kills" or more. The Sopwith Camel, itself an adaptation of previous technology to a more war-like purpose, was in fact a conglomerate of early twentieth-century material culture. The biplane, the internal combustion engine, and the machine guns were all recent innovations. War obviously leads to many of these advances, and the material culture of conflict is one that continues to garner interest.

A number of Camels were given to Canada as part of an imperial gift following the war. Primarily used for training and maintaining the skills of new and veteran pilots, all of the Camels were decommissioned by the mid-1920s. While they rather quickly became obsolete for their original purpose, the romanticism of early aerial combat led to these weapons having a more lasting impact on society, and their legacy, both for the skill of Canadian pilots and the nature of this new form of warfare, remained.

be a better place to live but also to prevent waste and inefficiency. Daylight savings added an hour of light to the workday. Previous arguments about infringing personal liberty lost their cogency during wartime.

Canadian industry—at least in central Canada and industrial Nova Scotia—benefited directly from the war. By March 1915 over 200 firms had converted to munitions manufacture. Later in 1915 the government set up the Imperial Munitions Board, chaired by businessman Joseph Flavelle (1858–1939). Canadian munitions production increased dramatically, raising the export of iron and steel products from $68.5 million in 1915 to $441.1 million only two years later. The Canadian munitions industry employed 200,000 workers in 673 factories. By 1917 the Imperial Munitions Board alone had an annual budget three times that of the federal government in 1914. In the latter years of the war nearly 40 per cent of Canadian manufacturing products found export markets. The high point came in 1918 when Canadian manufacturing exports reached $636 million and total exports peaked at $1.54 billion.

As for Canadian agriculture, it could not produce enough in the short run. From 1914 to 1919 in Canada as a whole, agricultural acreage under cultivation doubled. Wheat prices trebled, and western farmers expanded the size and number of their farms. The federal government created a national Wheat Board in 1917 to facilitate marketing. The number of prairie farms actually increased by 28 per cent between 1911 and 1921. Although the sons of Canadian farmers could gain exemption from conscription, by the time the draft was introduced in 1917 there were few young men left on the farms. Rural Canada, especially in the West, had outdone the remainder of the country in volunteer enlistment. The result was an increase in labour costs, which forced farmers to buy more agricultural equipment. Increased production also pushed up the price of land. Farmers therefore increased production by borrowing money at high rates of interest. Farm debt increased substantially. High prices also encouraged farmers to move cultivation onto marginal land while abandoning most of the tested techniques of soil and moisture conservation hitherto practised. The result of all this expansion would be an inevitable disaster when the price of grain and other crops ultimately fell on the international market.

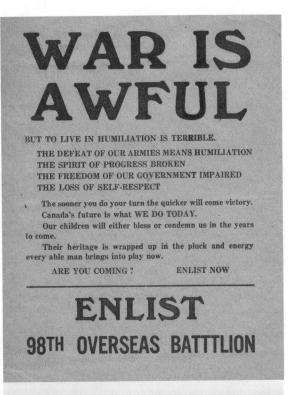

A recruitment poster. Archives of Ontario, MU 2052, #40, F 895 (1915). Recruiting Circulars. What does this poster tell us about public attitudes in Canada towards the war in 1915?

One of many casualties of the war was civil liberty in Canada. The War Measures Act, passed at war's beginning, was a blank cheque allowing the government to censor writing and speech, as well as to arrest, detain, and even deport those regarded as obstructing the war effort. As a nation of immigrants, Canada inevitably contained citizens and residents whose homelands were part of the enemy, the so-called "enemy aliens." Although the bulk of such people were German, most of those persecuted and interned were citizens of the Austro-Hungarian Empire, chiefly people of Ukrainian origin. After 1917 and the Bolshevik Revolution, the activities of radical ethnic organizations came under heavy scrutiny, and the Dominion government was easily persuaded that the Ukrainian community was the centre of Bolshevism in Canada. Thus, on the eve of the Armistice, two Orders-in-Council suppressed the foreign-language press and most socialist/anarchist organizations.

The Great War had a profound impact on Canada in almost all aspects of life. Its rhetorical side was one of

The Newfoundland Regiment, D Company, near St John's, 1915. On 1 July 1916 the Newfoundlanders would see their first action in France. Of the 780 men of the Newfoundland Regiment who entered the fray that day at Beaumont-Hamel, in the first engagement of the Battle of the Somme, more than 700 were killed, wounded, or reported missing. Since 1917, the first of July is observed in Newfoundland as Memorial Day, in remembrance generally of Newfoundland's war dead and specifically of those who were slaughtered at Beaumont-Hamel. The Rooms, Provincial Archives of Newfoundland and Labrador, E 22-45.

present sacrifice for future benefits. This "war to end all wars" would make the world safe for democracy. An era of full social justice would follow the great victory. That the Canadian government had ignored democratic civil liberties in fighting the war was an irony escaping most contemporaries.

The war's conclusion amounted to a triumph for Protestant Anglo-Canada, with little thought given to the tomorrows that would follow the coming of peace. A nation that had drawn heavily on its resources was really not ready to deal with the negative legacies of its efforts.

Only days after the Armistice was declared in November 1918, Prime Minister Sir Robert Borden went to Europe to head the Canadian delegation at the Peace Conference. Canada's participation at Paris beginning in January 1919 was less concerned with the disposition of European and international problems than it was with its own status in dealing with that disposition. This was a policy agreed upon in advance by the Union cabinet in Ottawa, although many Canadians would have preferred that their government stay away from Versailles entirely. Canada and the other dominions banded together to insist on being treated as independent

A Canadian battalion going "over the top," October 1916. W.I. Castle, Canada. Dept. of National Defence, LAC, PA-000648

nations at the Peace Conference rather than as part of the British imperial delegation. The principal opponent to this change of policy was not the British government, but the United States, backed by other participants, who insisted that autonomous dominions would enhance the British voice in the deliberations, which did not answer the dominions' claim that their commitment of manpower (and casualties) during the war entitled them to a separate say in the outcome.

Sir Robert Borden proved to have an influence on the conference greater than Canada's actual power in world affairs. The first breakthrough came in early January 1919, when President Woodrow Wilson conceded a representative from each dominion at the peace table. Sir Robert Borden responded by calling a meeting of the dominions, refusing to accept one representative, and demanding two. Wilson agreed to two representatives from Canada, Australia, South Africa, and India, and one for New Zealand. Newfoundland would have to sit as part of the British delegation. The dominions subsequently got the right to separate membership on new international organizations coming out of the treaty, including the League of Nations, and a separate signature on the treaty and conventions. Membership in the League, of course, implied liability for any commitments undertaken by that organization. Canada had achieved a new status in world affairs. Whether that status justified the numbers of dead and wounded was another matter.

Once the Great War had ended, most Canadians did their best to put the conflict behind them. Many

During World War I, Ukrainians were one of several nationalities dubbed "enemy aliens." Many of these people were imprisoned in Canadian internment camps, such as the camp and internees shown here, at Castle Mountain, Alberta. Glenbow Archives, NA-1870-6.

hoped for the emergence of a more just society. Stephen Leacock well expressed the ambivalence of the post-war period in *The Unsolved Riddle of Social Justice* (1919). Recognizing that industrial society did not normally employ its full potential, Leacock could only hope that the destructive energy of war could be harnessed for peacetime reform. The unsolved riddle was simply stated: "With all our wealth, we are still poor." Every child, Leacock insisted, should have "adequate food, clothing, education and an opportunity in life." Unemployment should become a "social crime" (Bowker, 1973: 74–80). Leacock did not offer specific solutions. Such a collective transformation would not be easy to accomplish. There were too many unresolved economic, constitutional, and social problems. The development of Canada over the next quarter-century demonstrated

that at least in peacetime, Canadians still had great trouble coming to terms with the paradox Leacock had identified in 1919. During the Great Depression especially, the state seemed impotent to improve conditions. The politicians blamed the Constitution. Beginning in 1939, however, Canada would again demonstrate its capacity for waging total war within the constraints of the British North America Act.

Returning to "Normalcy"

During demobilization Canada experienced one of the most devastating epidemics of modern times, the

Document

Sir Robert Borden on Canadian Representation at Versailles

In his *Memoirs*, originally published in 1938 and based on his diaries kept at the time, Sir Robert Borden wrote the following.

The subject [of representation] was first debated informally at conferences between the British and Dominion Ministers, and afterwards in the formal meetings of the Imperial War Cabinet. It was assumed that only five places could be secured for the British Empire at the Peace Conference. The panel system, under which the representation of the British Empire at the sessions of the Peace Conference would be selected from day to day, as the nature of the subject demanded, was not regarded as satisfactory in itself.

Finally, I proposed that in the general representation of the British Dominions, the panel system might be utilized when necessary or appropriate but that there should be distinctive representation for each Dominion on the same basis as was to be accorded to the smaller nations of the Allied Powers. This proposal was eventually accepted at the preliminary conference in London between representatives of the British Empire, France, and Italy.

But all the difficulties had by no means been overcome. When the question of procedure, including that of representation, came before the Peace Conference on January 12, 1919, the proposal for distinctive representation for the British Dominions aroused strong opposition. The subject was further discussed in the British Empire Delegation, which was really the Imperial War Cabinet under another name; and the Dominions, standing firmly upon the principle recognized in London, declined to accept an inferior status. In the result, there insistence prevailed; and through a combination of the panel system together with their own distinctive representation, the Dominions secured a peculiarly effective position.

Elsewhere I have said, and here I emphatically repeat, that Canada and the other Dominions would have regarded the situation as intolerable if they, who numbered their dead by the hundred thousands in the fiercest struggle the world had ever known, should stand outside the council chamber of the Conference, while nations that had taken no direct or active part in the struggle stood within and determined the conditions of Peace. . . .

We were lodged at the Hotel Majestic where I had a very commodious bedroom and sitting-room. The British had brought over an entire staff for the hotel as they were afraid to utilize a French staff, lest important information leak out. As a result, we had typical English meals, altogether too heavy for persons habitually deprived of normal opportunities for exercise. I used to escape the dinners two or three times a week and content myself with an apple, a glass of water, and a long walk. This regimen enabled me to survive. On one occasion I avoided dinner for ten consecutive evenings.

[Feb. 4 1919] That evening, Foster [Sir George Foster] and I went with the Dowager Duchess of Sutherland to dine with Lord Brooke at the Café Escargot, where we had an excellent meal to which we did ample justice except the snails included in the menu. After dinner we attended the Theatre St. Martin to see *Cyrano de Bergerac*, beautifully acted but sad in its ending. We were invited to supper by the leading lady of the piece, "Roxanne," and at her apartment we met Percival Langdon of the *Morning Post*. We had an excellent supper and a most enjoyable time. This was one of the friskiest evenings of Foster's life, as we kept him up until 1:15. I told him I never would have embarked on such an adventure without his presence as chaperon.

Source: *Robert Laird Borden: His Memoirs, vol. 2, 1916–1920* (Toronto: Macmillan, 1938), 908.

Spanish flu outbreak of 1918–19. The situation was so desperate in November 1918 that the government actually attempted, without success, to postpone public celebration of the Armistice for fear of spreading infection. Canadian deaths from the flu ultimately ran to 50,000—only some 10,000 thousand fewer than the number of Canadians who had died in battle. Fatalities had shifted from the trenches to the home front.

Yet another form of infectious epidemic made its appearance in 1919 with the great "Red Scare." The Bolshevik Revolution of 1917–18 in Russia provided the Canadian government and businessmen with an example of what might happen if popular unrest got out of hand. Political paranoia was as catching as the flu. Both the government and the business community became almost hysterical over the possibility that the revolution was nigh. The immediate focus of their concern was the Winnipeg General Strike of June 1919, but it had been preceded by the organization of the One Big Union, formed in Calgary in February amid considerable anti-capitalistic rhetoric. As usual, the Canadian government responded to anything smacking of popular uprising with repression.

Most of the conditions and issues that initially produced labour unrest in Winnipeg in the spring of 1919 were traditional ones exacerbated by the war: workers sought recognition of union rights to organize, higher wages, and better working conditions. A walkout by workers in the city's metal trades and building industries was quickly joined by others (as many as 50,000) in a general sympathy strike. On 15 May the strikers voted to close down the city's services. Much of the rhetoric of the strike sounded extremely radical. Some labour leaders hoped to use the general strike as a weapon to bring capitalism to its knees. Many, but not all, demobilized servicemen supported the strikers. Worried businessmen saw the general strike as a breakdown of public authority. Workers in other cities, such as Toronto and Vancouver, responded with declarations of support and threats of their own strikes. The Canadian government, represented locally by acting Minister of Justice Arthur Meighen (1874–1960), responded decisively. He supplemented the army with local militia, the Royal North West Mounted Police, and 1,800 special constables.

The Canadian Naturalization Act was hastily amended in early June 1919 to allow for the instant deportation of any foreign-born radicals who advocated revolution or who belonged to "any organization entertaining or teaching disbelief in or opposition to organized government" (quoted in Avery, 1986: 222). Most strikers were British or Canadian-born, but the general public was easily persuaded that what was needed was to "clean the aliens out of this community and ship them back to their happy homes in Europe which vomited them forth a decade ago" (quoted in Bumsted, 1994: 66).

Arthur Meighen effectively broke the strike on 17 June when he authorized the arrest of 10 strike leaders on charges of sedition. On the 21st—"Bloody Saturday"—a public demonstration of strikers and returned soldiers, marching towards the Winnipeg city hall, was met by a charge of Mounties on horseback. The result was a violent melee that injured many, killed two strikers, and led to the arrest of a number of "foreign rioters." This degree of violence, precipitated by the authorities, was unusual during the strike, perhaps because provincial prohibition in 1916 had closed bars and beverage rooms, making it difficult to get drunk and disorderly in public. Bloody Saturday happened despite the best efforts of the strike leaders to prevent the demonstration from going forward. The Strike Committee subsequently agreed to call off the strike if a Royal Commission investigated it and its underlying causes. The Royal Commission, called by the province of Manitoba, found that much of the labour unrest in Winnipeg was justified and that the strike's principal goal was to effect the introduction of collective bargaining.

On the other hand, the Manitoba Court of Queen's Bench convicted most of the arrested leaders (who were either British- or Canadian-born) on charges of sedition. The Department of Immigration held deportation hearings for the "foreigners" in camera. The use of the civil arm to suppress radicalism, long a part of the Canadian tradition, was given a new meaning in post-war Winnipeg. Perhaps most significantly, the strike and its handling by the government demonstrated the fragility of the post-war readjustment. The next decade would further emphasize the problems.

Regional Protest in the 1920s

The decade of the 1920s is usually associated with prosperity, but in truth the period faced great economic difficulties. The boom did not begin until 1924 and it was quite limited in its influence. The depression of 1920–3 had seen world prices for resource products fall abruptly, while costs fell much more gradually. Prosperity finally came from substantial growth in new housing construction and a great wave of consumer spending, both understandable after the war and subsequent depression. There was a major expansion of consumer credit facilities to finance the new spending. An advertising industry quickly developed to promote consumerism. Speculative activities—in real estate, in the stock market, and in commodity futures—all flourished. So did gambling, both in the stock market and in games of chance; Canadians bet on almost anything. However, much of the boom was at best internal, at worst artificial. International markets, except in the United States, were very soft. The traditional resource sectors of the economy had suffered most from the worldwide fall in prices, although they recovered somewhat in the latter years of the decade. Only Ontario's economy really prospered, chiefly on the strength of the manufacture of the motor car both for domestic consumption and for export into a British Empire protecting itself against the Americans. The economy of the Maritime provinces

Despite efforts to protect themselves from the Spanish flu outbreak of 1918–19, approximately 50,000 people died in Canada from the disease. CP PHOTO/*National Archives of Canada.*

James Shaver Woodsworth

James Shaver Woodsworth. National Archives of Canada, C-057365.

James Shaver Woodsworth (1874–1942) was born in Etobicoke near Toronto. His father, a Methodist minister, moved the family to Brandon, Manitoba, in 1882, and James became a Methodist minister himself in 1896, subsequently studying at Victoria College and then at Oxford University. In 1902 he moved to Winnipeg and began questioning Methodist teachings. In 1907 he resigned from the ministry, but was instead given the superintendency of All People's Mission in Winnipeg's North End, spending six years working with immigrants and the poor. Two books—*Strangers within Our Gates* (1909) and *My Neighbour* (1911)—resulted from his work at All People's Mission and established his reputation as a social reformer. Beginning in 1913 he spent some years travelling in western Canada, becoming a socialist in 1914 and espousing pacifism during World War I. In 1919 he returned to Winnipeg to become editor of the *Western Labour News* when its editor was arrested for seditious libel. He, too, was briefly arrested but was never charged. The publicity made his reputation as a labour radical and in 1921 he was elected as an Independent Labour Party MP for Winnipeg North. In 1925 Woodsworth used his vote in a deadlocked House of Commons to force the Liberals to promise to create a plan for old-age pensions, later introduced in 1927. In 1932 he helped found a new political party, the Co-operative Commonwealth Federation, based largely on British Fabian socialist principles, although he insisted the party's socialism would be distinctly Canadian. He was easily chosen as first leader of the CCF, and spent the remainder of the Depression attempting unsuccessfully to challenge the two established parties and supplant the Liberals as the major party of the left. When World War II broke out, Woodsworth refused to support it and was repudiated by the majority of his party as a result. He was re-elected to Parliament in 1940, but was old and sick, dying in early 1942. Although Woodsworth advocated many of the major social policies of the modern welfare state, he was largely unsuccessful in implementing any of them, and both his socialism and his pacifism were abandoned by his party and its successors. Nevertheless he is generally venerated as one of the early leaders of the Canadian left.

continued to decline precipitously, since both the power revolution and the new industrialization bypassed them while foreign markets (especially for fish) continued to decline.

Despite the government's brutal suppression of the Winnipeg General Strike, industrial unrest remained high through 1925. The One Big Union, a radical and militant industrial union, flourished briefly in western Canada. In 1921 labour representatives sat in seven of nine provincial legislatures. In the federal election of that year, more than 30 labour candidates ran for office, although only four were actually elected. Labour unrest after Winnipeg was most prevalent in the geographical extremes of the country. There were a number of notable

BACKGROUNDER

The Spanish Flu Pandemic

I had a little bird
And its name was Enza.
I opened the window
And in-flew-Enza.
(children's skipping song of 1918)

The wild card in Canada's post-war experience in late 1918 and early 1919 was the pandemic always known as the Spanish flu. There are no real questions about the incidence, the extent of sickness, or even the number of deaths caused by the disease, which ran rampant across Canada between September 1918 and March 1919. The problem is that it is impossible to document any real correlation between the flu and anything else going on in Canada at the time. Disease has always seemed to exist separately and independently from other historical factors. Contemporaries talked openly about the connection between the high cost of living and popular discontent, for example, but advanced few arguments about any relationship between fatal illness and the socio-political dissatisfaction of 1919.

Few historians dealing with the unsettled conditions in North America in 1919 mention the flu and popular attitudes in the same breath. The flu's almost unthinkable extent and impact across Canada at the end of the war seems to have eluded historical attention, perhaps partly because it was obviously not of human agency and was seldom seen by those who lived through it as anything other than a disease that struck at individuals and families. It was seen by its victims as a danger to their bodies but not as a social problem menacing the body politic. Even the rediscovery of the virulence of the pandemic by historians beginning in the 1980s—resulting in a major increase in information about it—has not produced many attempts to connect influenza in a careful way

to other events occurring at the same time or only a few months later.

The likelihood is that more than one virus was responsible for the epidemic's course worldwide. The likelihood also is that the several viruses either mutated, or became much more virulent, during their travels around the world, or that other strains succeeded in jumping from animals to humans by either adaptation or hybridization. Early evidence of the beginnings of the flu in its milder forms can be seen in various parts of the world. One outbreak occurred in San Sebastién on the northern coast of Spain in February of 1918. The Spanish experience gave the disease its name, unfairly since there was no real evidence that its actual origins were Spanish. In its early incarnations, this "three-day fever"—as the American Expeditionary Force called it—was not terribly menacing. The symptoms were typically flu-like in a way familiar to all of us. The victim suddenly became ill, running a high fever. The face became red, every bone in the body ached, the body perspired considerably, and there was usually an accompanying headache. The period of feeling really sick usually lasted only 72 to 96 hours, during which time the victim was practically comatose, although after rising from his or her bed the victim remained weak for a further seven to 10 days. The disease was highly contagious.

At some point over the summer of 1918, this relatively mild influenza (with low mortality rates), which had affected Europe and the United States up to this point, mutated or morphed into a more virulent disease. The new variety (or varieties) was far more deadly. Some victims became extremely ill almost instantly with symptoms of extreme pneumonia, exhibiting high fevers and lungs full of fluid. Others gradually developed pneumonia after a few days of what appeared to be the ordinary flu. Associated with

Continued…

the new influenza was a cyanosis that discoloured the face and the feet with a dark bluish, almost black, cast and a cough bringing up blood-stained sputum and mucus. Unlike the earlier outbreaks, these new ones were highly fatal. There were reports at hospitals of corpses stacked up like cordwood.

Canadian troops returning home in the late spring and early summer brought the flu back to Canada from Europe. How many of the troops were carrying the earlier strains of the virus and how many the newly mutated ones will never be known, although clearly the virulent form was being introduced into the nation from somewhere. Troop ships, military camps, and soldier movement via the railroads were probably the major means of spreading the flu across Canada. The flu apparently did not usually hit on the whole very hard at the very old and the very young, who were the typical victims of most epidemic diseases. It hit hardest at young adults, who were in most epidemics the most immune.

The flu devastated most large cities in Canada. In the rural districts, where houses were often far apart and isolated but relatively safe from infection unless it was introduced from outside, farm people often did exactly the wrong thing, fleeing to towns and villages to find companionship and medical assistance and thus increasing the likelihood of the spread of infection. Certainly the pandemic hit with especial fury against the First Nations. The death rate from influenza among Canadian Native peoples in these years overall was 37.7 per thousand, while the flu death rate per thousand was 14.3 in Toronto, 16.7 in Winnipeg, and 23.3 in Vancouver. Before it was over in the spring of 1919, approximately 50,000 Canadians had died.

strikes in Cape Breton, Alberta, and British Columbia. In the coalfields, 22,000 miners were on strike in August 1922. Several unions were broken in some of the bitterest labour violence that Canada had ever seen. Tactics in the mining communities made Winnipeg seem like a Sunday school picnic. A number of movements, mainly regionally based, sprang up to protest inequalities in the national system. Their collective inability to effect much change—though they tried a variety of approaches—was, and is, instructive. One of the principal problems was the very difficulty of working together despite common complaints.

Certainly nobody felt harder done by after the Great War than the farmer. The movement of farm protest reached its height in the 1921 election, before the final wheat market collapse and the spread of drought conditions. Farmers in Anglo-Canada disliked inflation and had two specific economic grievances beyond the wheat price collapse of 1920. First, the wartime wheat marketing system had been abandoned by the government in 1919. Second, the government had failed to introduce serious tariff reform to lower the costs of farming. Behind these complaints was a long-standing farmer conviction that the political system operated to the advantage of profiteering central Canadian capitalists. Farmer discontent was national in scope, although western farmers were the most alienated. The new Progressive Party, formed in 1920, won 64 seats in the 1921 federal election in six provinces: 37 on the prairies, 24 in Ontario, one in New Brunswick, and two in British Columbia. Joining 50 Conservatives and 117 Liberals, the Progressives broke the established two-party tradition. But despite occasional farmer–labour alliances, the two major groups of malcontents were unable to unite politically for change

Though they were entitled to become the official opposition, the Progressives were badly divided. Former Liberals wanted free trade, while the farm protestors sought more radical reform. The farm wing, led by Alberta's Henry Wise Wood (1860–1941), wanted to scrap the existing party system. It sought instead to focus on farmer grievances. The only actions the two wings could agree upon were negative. The Progressives would not become the official opposition, and they would not join in coalition with the Liberals, now led by William Lyon Mackenzie King (1874–1950). As a result, the inexperienced farmer MPs were unable to accomplish anything substantial in Ottawa when economic conditions in

The Winnipeg General Strike, 21 June 1919. This photograph shows the crowd gathered in downtown Winnipeg on Bloody Saturday, before the Mounties charged the crowd to break it up. Does this well-dressed crowd appear to be looking for trouble? Provincial Archives of Manitoba, N2771, Foote Collection 1705.

western Canada worsened. The King government provided token programs to gain the support of moderate Progressives. Meanwhile, drought and the worldwide collapse of wheat prices beginning in 1921 produced a widespread inability to meet mortgage payments. Much of the land in the dry-belt region reverted to the state for unpaid taxes. Its inhabitants went either to the cities or, in many cases, back to the United States. Surviving farmers became too disheartened to support a party that had accomplished little in Ottawa, and the Progressives quickly disappeared.

A similar fate befell the major eastern expression of protest, the Maritime Rights Movement. Maritimers had difficulty joining western farmers in a common cause. The easterners sought not free trade but increased protectionism, as well as lower railway freight rates. The region was acutely conscious of its increasing impotency in Confederation, as its population base continued to decline proportionally to central Canada and the West. By the end of 1921, regional discontent found expression in the Maritime Rights Movement, which combined an insistence on from 1931 to 1941 and 50,000 from 1942 to 1945—but the most important feature of the period was the mounting negative attitude on the part of the Canadian authorities and citizens alike towards extensive immigration, with racism expressed against many ethnic groups. Exclusionary policies seemed increasingly in vogue. The main task of the Immigration Department, especially after 1930, seemed to be to figure out ways to keep immigrants out of the country, rather than of developing ways of allowing them to enter.

The Anglo-Canadian tradition had always been to reward soldiers with free land, and the Great War provided no exception. Providing returned veterans with land would support an agricultural community experiencing difficulties after the war, and soldier settlement began even before the war was over. In May 1919 soldier settlement was revamped to expand the amount of land available and to provide for a more generous supply of credit. Land in the West was taken from Indian reserves, and much of this land proved to be only marginally viable. By 1923 the failure rate among soldier-settlers ran at 21.5 per cent. An even larger problem was that soldier settlement absorbed a disproportionate amount of the money spent on veterans'

Strikers from the BC relief camps heading east as part of the On-to-Ottawa Trek; Kamloops, June 1935. LAC, C-029399.

benefits by the federal government. About 4 per cent of the total number of able-bodied Canadian veterans got about 14 per cent of the money allocated for ex-soldiers. In a related vein was Empire Settlement, by which large numbers of Britons were recruited to come to Canada. The Canadian government was never very keen about Empire Settlement (which was an imperial scheme), persuaded as it was that most of those recruited were "defectives" being dumped by the United Kingdom. Despite the arrival of more than 100,000 British immigrants to Canada between 1922 and 1935—especially female domestics (20,000), intending farmers (10,000), and British farm families (3,500 families)—Empire Settlement did not work well, chiefly because the host country did not fully support it. British immigration became somewhat more popular after 1924, when the American government instituted a permanent quota system and exempted Canada from its provisions: between 1925 and 1932 nearly half a million Canadians would move to the United States.

The exodus of Canadians to the United States and boom conditions in Canada led in 1925 to the Canadian government signing an agreement with Canada's two major railroads. The Dominion now agreed that the railroads could recruit genuine European agriculturalists until 1928 from previously "non-preferred" parts of Europe. Over the next half-decade, nearly 200,000 immigrants from Central and Eastern Europe were admitted to Canada, normally by co-operative arrangements among the railroads, their colonization companies, and various ethnic and religious organizations in Canada.

But exclusionary policies and practices were more common between the wars. One example of Canadian laggardness towards new immigrants can be found in the Canadian response to the persecution of the Armenian people by the Turkish government near the end of the Great War. Canadians responded to this genocide by raising hundreds of thousands of dollars to assist the refugee survivors. But the Canadian immigration authorities managed to combine two different standards for exclusion—refugee status and racial classification—to keep the number of Armenians allowed into Canada to a mere 1,200, during a period when 23,000 were admitted to the United States and 80,000 allowed into France. Most Armenians lacked proper passports, and Canada

resolutely refused to recognize special identity certificates in lieu of passports. The Canadian Immigration Service also insisted on treating the Armenians as Asians, bringing into play all of the regulations designed to exclude people from Asia. They were required to have $250 in cash, to come to Canada via a continuous journey, and to meet Canada's occupational requirements as farmers experienced with North American conditions. The 1920s saw a further tightening of Dominion immigration policy directed at Asians, including a new agreement with the Japanese government to restrict the number of their nationals going to Canada to 150 per year and to put a stop to the so-called "picture brides" (Japanese women coming to Canada to marry Canadian Japanese men whom they had never met).

Demographic Trends

Like all industrial countries, Canada experienced profound demographic changes. Some of these had been somewhat disguised by the federal government's failure, until 1921, to keep accurate national statistics beyond the census. Enormous infusions of new immigrants before 1914 also helped prevent the new demographic trends from becoming easily apparent, but they existed. By the 1941 census more Canadians lived in urban rather than rural places, a result of a substantial increase in urban residents, especially during the 1920s. Moreover, the 1941 census would be the last in which rural numbers and farm dwellers grew absolutely in number. Even before 1941, the impact of urbanization and industrialization was apparent.

First, mortality rates declined. In the critical area of infant mortality, the death rate had been steadily declining since the nineteenth century. Infant mortality took another major drop in the 1930s, while the overall death rate drifted perceptibly downward. By 1946 the median age at death was 63.1 for males and 65.3 for females. For the first time, Canadian society had begun to produce substantial numbers of people who would live beyond the age of productive labour; a rise in agitation for old-age pensions in this period was hardly accidental. The main exception to the national trend was in the Aboriginal population. Their death rates ran to four times the national average; infant mortality was at least twice that of Canadian society as a whole. Large numbers of Native mothers died in childbirth. Moreover, Aboriginal people suffered up to three times more accidental deaths than Canada's population overall. They had a high suicide rate. Before 1940 most Aboriginal people died of communicable rather than chronic disease, with tuberculosis as the big killer. The decreasing death rate for Canadians in general resulted from an improved standard of living, including especially improvements in nutrition and hygiene as well as better medical treatment. In the years 1921–6, 270 out of every 1,000 Canadian deaths came from pulmonary and communicable disease. By 1946 such fatalities dropped to just over 60 out of every 1,000 Canadian deaths. Cardiovascular problems, renal disease, and cancer—all afflictions of an aging population—became more important killers.

Then fertility rates declined. The extent to which the fall in the birth rate resulted from conscious decisions on the part of women is not entirely clear, but the two were plainly related. Increased urbanization made large families less desirable. As industrialization took more women out of the home and into the workforce, child care became a serious problem. More women, especially those over 30 years old, began to limit the number of children they bore, practising some form of contraception. Birth rates had begun to fall in Canada before 1919 and continued to fall in the 1920s and 1930s. They recovered from an extremely low point in the middle of the Depression after 1941, increasing sharply after 1945. There were some significant internal differentials. One was between Quebec and the remainder of Canada. The birth rate in French Canada remained substantially higher than in the rest of the country, although it shared in the general decline. There was also a difference between urban and rural areas, with substantially higher birth rates in the latter. A third differential occurred between Catholics and Protestants, although certain Protestant subgroups, such as Mennonites and Mormons, had higher rates than the overall Catholic one. Finally, Aboriginal birth rates were at least twice the national average.

Another important new factor was divorce. The year 1918 saw 114 divorces in all of Canada, a rate of 1.4 per 100,000 people. By 1929 the divorce rate had reached 8.2 per 100,000, rising to 18.4 per 100,000 in 1939 and to 65.3 per 100,000 by 1947. Higher rates occurred partly because more Canadians gained access to divorce courts; Ontario courts obtained divorce jurisdiction in 1930. The increase also reflected changing attitudes, particularly among women, who instituted most divorce actions. Divorce statistics did not begin to measure the extent of marital dissolutions, however. Most dissolutions never reached a court. Especially during the Depression, husbands simply deserted their wives. Many contemporaries saw the increase in divorce as evidence of the disintegration of the Canadian family.

Technological Change

Despite the nation's uneven economic record between 1919 and 1945, Canadians in these years experienced an increase in the rate and nature of technological change. The new technologies had enormous impact on all aspects of Canadian life. On one level they forced governments to adopt a myriad of new policies. On another level they had tremendous psychological impact, particularly by militating against communalism in favour of the individual, family, or household.

One evident area of change was in the mass acceptance of the internal combustion engine in the form of the automobile and the tractor. Before 1920 automobile ownership had been almost entirely an urban phenomenon, but by 1920 it had become more general. In 1904 there were fewer than 5,000 motor vehicles in Canada. By 1920 there were 251,000, most of them built during the war. From 1918 to 1923 Canadian manufacturers, allied to US companies, were the second-largest car producers in the world. Canada was a major exporter, especially to the British Empire. By 1930 only the United States had more automobiles per capita than did Canada. In that year Canada had 1,061,000 automobiles registered. Also significant was the increase in the number of tractors employed on the nation's farms after 1918.

The automobile was individually owned and operated as an extension of a household. It represented private rather than public transportation. No other single product operated so insidiously against communalism as the automobile. It also had tremendous spinoff consequences. Automobiles required roads, which were a provincial and municipal responsibility. More than

BACKGROUNDER

Canada and the Refugees from Nazi Germany, 1933–1939

From Adolf Hitler's assumption of office as German chancellor, it was clear that the Jews would be a target for persecution. Those Jews who could escape Germany did so, although they were unable to flee swiftly enough to escape the German annexations of the Rhineland, Austria, and Czechoslovakia. Most countries sheltering refugees made clear that they were providing only temporary shelter, and Canada felt it could not open its doors to a flood of people from Europe. Canadian policy was put in the hands of Frederick Charles Blair, a lifetime bureaucrat and well-known anti-Semite, who saw Jewish people as unassimilable. Blair kept the Jews out with the full approval of the Canadian cabinet. In 1938 he decided that the few Jews admitted to Canada as farmers were not really agriculturalists. That same year Canada reluctantly attended a conference at Evian, France, sponsored partly by the United States, to discuss the refugee problems of Europe. Canada was a nation with large amounts of vacant land, and many of its politicians and population feared—quite accurately—that the world community would be quite satisfied to resolve its problems with displaced persons by sending them to Canada. From Canada's perspective, there was no reason to become involved in a European mess not of its own making. Unfortunately, isolationism did not suit the times.

A handful of Jewish members of Parliament (there were only three after 1935), with the support of J.S. Woodsworth of the Co-operative Commonwealth Federation, proposed to the Canadian cabinet that Canada offer at this conference to admit 5,000 Jewish refugees over four years, with all costs to be assumed by the Jewish community in Canada, including guarantees that the newcomers would not become charity cases. The cabinet rejected this offer, chiefly on the grounds that such action could serve as the thin edge of the wedge. By 1938, of course, there were at least a million refugees to be dealt with. Canadian Undersecretary of State for External Affairs O.D. Skelton told the Americans that "governments with unwanted minorities must . . . not be encouraged to think that harsh treatment at home is the key that will open the doors to immigration abroad" (quoted in Abella and Troper, 1991: 27). The Evian conference accomplished nothing except to demonstrate to the Nazis the lack of international support available to the Jews, thereby probably spurring further persecution, including the "Kristallnacht" pogrom of late November 1938. On 23 November 1938 a delegation of Jews met with Prime Minister William Lyon Mackenzie King and T.A. Crerar, the Minister of Immigration, to plead for the admission of 10,000 refugees totally financed by the Jewish community. They were rebuffed, and the cabinet on 13 December 1938 agreed to maintain existing immigration regulations, which admitted only farmers with capital. Highly skilled professionals and intellectuals (including doctors, scientists, and musicians) were thus rejected as "inadmissible."

In May of 1939, nearly 1,000 German Jews left Hamburg on a luxury liner, the *St Louis*, some with entrance visas for Cuba. The Cubans rejected most of the passengers, and while Canada sat on the sidelines, the ship was forced to return to Europe. The most that could be said for the Canadian exclusion of Jews was that it was consistent with past national policy, which had never been strongly influenced by humanitarian considerations. But for a nation as limited in world-renowned scientific, intellectual, and cultural talent as Canada, the result was a cruel—if totally deserved—shortfall. Even in the crassest of practical terms, Canadian policy was a disaster. But it was also inexcusable, in a moral sense, on the part of a nation that constantly lectured the rest of the world about its shortcomings.

After being denied entry into Cuba, the SS St Louis was then sent away from the United States and Canada before returning to Europe, where many of its Jewish passengers were killed in the concentration camps. AP Photo, CP Images.

one-quarter of the $650 million increase in provincial and municipal debt between 1913 and 1921 resulted from capital expenditures on highways, streets, and bridges. Road mileage in Canada expanded from 385,000 miles (619,580 km) in 1922 to 565,000 miles (909,254 km) in 1942. Motorists wanted not only roads but properly paved ones. Although in 1945 nearly two-thirds of Canadian roads were still of earth construction, the other third had been paved or gravelled at considerable expense. Automobiles ran on petroleum products. Not only did they encourage petroleum production, chiefly in Alberta, but they also created the gasoline station, the repair garage, the roadside restau-

rant, and the motel—new service industries to provide for a newly mobile population. Door-to-door rather than station-to-station mobility was one of the principal effects of the automobile revolution. Both the automobile and the truck competed with the railways, which began their decline in the 1920s. Although the automobile provided an important source of tax revenue for both federal and provincial governments, neither Ottawa nor the provinces made any serious effort to control the use or construction of motor vehicles, aside from some fairly minimal rules of the road and the issuance of drivers' licences to almost all comers. Despite its importance, the automobile and its 20,000 parts were produced entirely according to manufacturers' standards and consumers' desires, without government regulation. The car quickly became the symbol of North American independence and individuality. It also served as a combined status and sex symbol, and according to some critics, as a "portable den of iniquity."

Unlike the automobile, radio was treated by the federal government as a public matter deserving of regulation. The programs broadcast, rather than the radio receiver itself, became the target of government control. The transmission and reception of sound via radio waves had initially been developed before the Great War as an aid to ships at sea. The 1920s saw the mass marketing of the radio receiver in North America. In order to sell radios, it was necessary to provide something to listen to. By 1929, 85 broadcasting stations were operating in Canada under various ownerships. Private radio broadcasting in Canada was not all bad, but it was uneven. A Royal Commission

on Broadcasting—the Aird Commission, appointed in 1928 and reporting in 1929—recommended the nationalization of radio. Its advice was not immediately taken. The Bennett government eventually introduced the Broadcasting Act of 1932, however, which led to the formation of the Canadian Radio Broadcasting Commission to establish a national network and to supervise private stations. In 1936 this Commission became the Canadian Broadcasting Corporation, with extensive English and French networks, and operated with federal financial support as an independent agency. No other Canadian cultural institution of its day was so closely associated with Canadian nationalism and Canadian culture than was the CBC. The CBC was not only pre-eminent but frequently unique in fostering Canadian culture. Often the battle seemed to be uphill, since Canadians usually preferred listening to the slick entertainment programming produced in the United States.

A Toronto traffic jam, 1924: motorists out for a Sunday drive on the newly built Lakeshore Boulevard. City of Toronto Archives, James Collection, Fonds 1244, 2530.

Prohibition and Church Union

The impetus for social reform died after 1918. To some extent, the movement was a victim of its own successes. For many Canadians, the achievement of prohibition and women's suffrage—the two principal reform goals of the pre-war period—meant that the struggle had been won. To some extent, reform was a victim of the Great War. Reformers had exhausted themselves in a war effort that had produced devastation but no final victory. The war had been a disillusioning experience for many.

The failure of the prohibition experiment symbolized the decline of reform. Despite considerable evidence that the elimination of alcoholic beverages had made a social difference—the jails were emptied in most places, since they were usually filled with prisoners who had committed alcohol-related offences—the supporters of prohibition were unable to stem the tide. The Ontario Alliance for the Total Suppression of the Liquor Trade claimed in 1922 that the number of convictions for offences associated with drink had declined from 17,143 in 1914 to 5,413 in 1921, and drunkenness cases decreased in the province's major cities from 16,590 in 1915 to 6,766 in 1921.

Nevertheless, various provinces went "wet" between 1920 and 1924, and the Liquor Control Act replaced the Ontario Temperance Act in 1927. Opposition to prohibition after the war found a new argument to add to the old one that private conduct was being publicly regulated: attempts to enforce prohibition encouraged people to flout the law and even created organized crime and vice. Too many people were prepared to ignore the law, said prohibition's opponents, who found more acceptable slogans of their own in "Moderation" and "Government Regulation." In many provinces, the possibility of obtaining provincial revenue for tax-starved coffers led to the introduction of government control over the sale of alcohol. Taxing bad habits rather than forbidding them became part of the Canadian tradition.

While prohibition was dying, in 1925 the Methodist, Presbyterian, and Congregational churches (the first two were among Canada's largest denominations) merged as the United Church of Canada. As three of the most "liberal" denominations in Canada, home of much of the social gospel commitment to Christian reform of secular society, they hoped to rejuvenate reform fervour through unification. Not all members of the three denominations were equally enthusiastic. Opposition to union was particularly strong among the

Household Equipment Ownership in Montreal, 1941

Heating		Icebox	65.0
By stove	51.5%	None	5.1
Wood and coal	92.3	Radio	85.5
Cooking Fuel		Bathtub	83.9
Wood and coal	17.7	Telephone	44.9
Gas & electric	80.6	Vacuum cleaner	28.2
Refrigeration		Automobile	15.7
Mechanical	25.1		

Source: Denyse Baillargeon, *Making Do: Women, Family, and Home in Montreal during the Great Depression* (Waterloo, Ont.: Wilfrid Laurier University Press, 2000), 187. Reprinted with permission.

Presbyterians. In the end, congregations could vote to stay out of the union. Thus 784 Presbyterian and eight Congregational congregations so declared, while 4,797 Methodist, 3,728 Presbyterian, and 166 Congregational congregations joined in the United Church of Canada. The new denomination became the most substantial Protestant communion of Canada, generally committed to liberal thinking and reform.

Racism

Canadian society between the wars continued to be profoundly racist. That point was demonstrable in a variety of ways, although it must be emphasized that very few Canadians saw their exclusionary attitudes as either socially undesirable or dysfunctional.

Imported from the United States, the Ku Klux Klan flourished in Canada during the 1920s. In the United States the revived Klan spread anti-black and anti-Catholic hate propaganda under the guise of a fraternal organization. In its secret rituals, fundamentalist Protestantism, and social operations, the Klan appeared to some Canadians to be little different from a host of other secret societies. The Klan assumed a Canadian face, posing as the defender of Britishness against the alien hordes and calling itself the "Ku Klux Klan of the British Empire." Although the Klan had some success everywhere in Canada, it made particular headway in the late 1920s in Saskatchewan, where by 1929 there were over 125 chapters. In that province it found support from a number of Protestant ministers, who objected to the increasingly liberal leanings of the mainline Protestant churches. It also gained acceptance as a way of opposing the patronage-style politics of the provincial Liberal government. Few of its members associated it with American-style cross burning or midnight lynch mobs.

Canada's treatment of its Aboriginal population continued to reflect both belief in the superiority of non-Native culture and antagonism towards the Native peoples. The Department of Indian Affairs assumed that assimilation was the only possible policy. Deputy Minister Duncan Campbell Scott stated in 1920 that "Our object is to continue until there is not a single Indian in Canada that has not been absorbed into the body politic, and there is no Indian question, and no Indian Department." Indian Affairs employed a variety of policies. It forced Aboriginal children into schools, usually residential ones far removed from their families. It forbade and actively suppressed the practice of traditional Native rituals like the potlatch. It carried out the Canadian government's legislative provisions to enfranchise the Aboriginal people, thus in theory making them full citizens and no longer wards of the state. Most of the resistance to these measures was passive, although there was the beginning of organization. The first congress of the League of Indians convened at Sault Ste Marie, Ontario, in September 1919. The League's objectives were "to claim and protect the rights of all Indians in Canada by legitimate and just means" and to assert "absolute control in retaining possession or disposition of our lands" (quoted in Cuthand, 1978: 31–2). The League and its successors met regularly thereafter.

In British Columbia, an anti-Oriental movement flourished during the interwar years. Much of the criticism of the "menace" from Asia came from economic fears, although there was also a general concern for the racial integrity of the province as a white society. The general argument was that the newcomers would not assimilate, although there was considerable evidence that the Japanese, at least, were acculturating rapidly. Moving onto small holdings in the Fraser Valley and into salmon fishing along the coasts, the Japanese appeared to pose a potential military threat should their homeland—which was militarily aggressive in the Pacific from the beginning of the century—attempt to expand into Canada. If people from Asia were highly visible in some areas and in some industries, that fact was partly explained by their exclusion—in law and in practice—from so much of the life of the province.

Women

Canadian women emerged from the Great War with the vote in hand. A few feminist critics had argued that the vote was no panacea for women's second-class position in Canadian society. It did not even assure a high level of political involvement. Between the wars women did not very often run for public office or constitute a recognizable voting bloc. The flapper, with her bobbed hair, short

Charlotte Whitton, the mayor of Ottawa (second from left), at the unveiling of a commemorative bust of Agnes Macphail, the first woman elected to the House of Commons, outside the House, Ottawa, 1955. Also pictured (from left) are MP Margaret Aitken, Senator Cairine Wilson, and MP Ellen Fairclough. Duncan Cameron, LAC, PA-121765.

exercise. As a people Canadians were willing—indeed, active—collaborators in cultural production, both at home and in the United States itself. A closer examination of motion pictures and hockey in this period is instructive.

In the world of film, Hollywood's success was also Canada's, since there was no shortage of Canadian talent involved in the formative years of Tinseltown. Mack Sennett, Sidney Olcott, Louis B. Mayer, Jack Warner, Walter Huston, Mary Pickford, Norma Shearer, and Marie Dressler—some of Hollywood's biggest and most influential names at the time—were Canadian-born. Pickford, Warner, and Mayer founded three of the major Hollywood studios between 1919 and 1924. Canada itself had only the beginnings of a film industry, consisting mainly of the seven films produced by Ernest Shipman, of which *Back to God's Country* (1919) is a Canadian silent film classic. Otherwise filmmaking in Canada was confined chiefly to newsreels and documentaries, which were often appended to American features. By 1922 American studios were including Canadian receipts as part of domestic revenue, and in 1923 Famous Players' Canadian Corporation, a subsidiary of Pickford's studio, took over the leading Canadian cinema chain, Allen Theatres. At the height

of the silent film era, Hollywood succeeded in monopolizing the distribution of film in Canada; Canadian exhibitors and cinema owners were not much concerned about where the product had originated so long as it was profitable.

Other nations around the world took some sort of defensive action against the Hollywood juggernaut, either placing quotas on imported films or providing tax incentives for local productions. Canada did neither, partly because a few of its citizens were so closely connected with the American film industry, partly because Canadians so clearly preferred Hollywood films to the alternatives. During the Great Depression, when the Dream Factory provided blessed release from the cares and woes of everyday life for millions of Canadians, that dream was plainly American. Canadians continued to love American movies despite the inaccuracy with which Hollywood persistently treated Canadian geography, society, and history. Symbolically, the successive and successful film portrayals of that quintessential American, Abraham Lincoln, by two Canadian actors, Walter Huston (1884–1950) and Raymond Massey (1896–1983), only solidified the close identification of Canadians and Americans in the popular mind on both sides of the border.

The situation with professional hockey was equally interesting. The National Hockey Association (NHA) was organized in 1909 in eastern Canada. On the west coast, Frank and Lester Patrick, in 1911–12, formed the Pacific Coast Hockey Association (PCHA), whose Vancouver Millionaires defeated the Ottawa Senators of the NHA for the Stanley Cup in 1915. The next year, the Montreal Canadiens of the NHA outlasted the PCHA's Portland Rosebuds—the first US-based team in the Stanley Cup final. Then, in 1917, the National Hockey League (NHL) formed out of the NHA. The PCHA folded in 1924. That same year, the NHL granted a franchise lease to the Boston Bruins and became the top professional hockey league in North America. The New York Rangers and the Pittsburgh Pirates soon followed, and Chicago and Detroit received NHL franchises in 1927. Most of the American clubs were owned or managed by Canadians, and the players were almost entirely Canadian. Indeed, the Patrick brothers had brought players from their PCHA teams to the American-based NHL teams they acquired in the 1920s. The Toronto Maple Leafs acquired a physical

As for Me and My House

In 1941 (James) Sinclair Ross (1908–96) published a novel in New York entitled *As for Me and My House*. Set in Horizon, Saskatchewan, in the 1930s, the story is told from the vantage point of Mrs Bentley, the wife of a local clergyman.

Sunday Evening, April 30.

The wind keeps on. It's less than a week since the snowstorm, and the land is already dry again. The dust goes reeling up the street in stinging little scuds. Over the fields this morning on our way to Partridge Hill there were dark, foreboding clouds of it.

Service was difficult this morning. They were listening to the wind, not Philip, the whimpering and strumming through the eaves, and the dry hard crackle of sand against the windows. From the organ I could see their faces pinched and stiffened with anxiety. They sat in tense, bolt upright rows, most of the time their eyes on the ceiling, as if it were the sky and they were trying to read the weather. . . .

Philip and Paul and I stood on the school steps till the congregation were all gone. The horses pawed and stamped as if they, too, felt something ominous in the day. One after another the democrats and buggies rolled away with a whir of wheels like pebbly thunder. From the top of Partridge Hill where the schoolhouse stands we could see the prairie smoking with dust as if it had just been swept by fire. A frightening, wavering hum fled blind within the telephone wires. The wind struck in hard, clenched little blows; and even as we watched each other the dust formed in veins and wrinkles round our eyes. According to the signs, says Paul, it's going to be a dry and windy year all through. With the countryman's instincts for such things he was strangely depressed this morning. . . .

I found it hard myself to believe in the town outside, houses, streets, and solid earth. Mile after mile the wind poured by, and we were immersed and lost in it. I sat breathing from my throat, my muscles tense. To relax, I felt, would be to let the walls round me crumple in. . . .

It's the most nerve-wracking wind I've ever listened to. Sometimes it sinks a little, as if spent and out of breath, then comes high, shrill and importunate again. Sometimes it's blustering and rough, sometimes silent and sustained. Sometimes it's wind, sometimes frightened hands that shake the doors and windows. Sometimes it makes the little room and its smug, familiar furniture a dramatic inconsistency, sometimes a relief. I sit thinking about the dust, the farmers and the crops, wondering what another dried-out year will mean for us.

We're pinched already. They gave us fifteen dollars this week, but ten had to go for a payment on the car. I'm running bills already at the butcher shop and Dawson's store. Philip needs shoes and a hat. His Sunday suit is going at the cuffs again, and it's shiny at the seat and knees. I sent for a new spring hat for myself the other day, but it was just a dollar forty-five, and won't be much.

Source: Sinclair Ross, *As for Me and My House* (Toronto: McClelland & Stewart, 1970 [1941]), 37–9.

presence when Maple Leaf Gardens was built as their home. At the opening on 12 November 1931, Foster Hewitt (1902–85) broadcast his first *Hockey Night in Canada*, describing the game from a gondola overlooking the rink. For three decades thereafter, his high-pitched voice—and his excited refrain, "He shoots! He scores!"—*was* hockey for most Canadians. *Hockey Night in Canada* was the one and only Canadian-produced radio program

Emily Carr in the Cariboo region of British Columbia, 1904.

ies and towns, hundreds of high school drama groups, dozens of university drama groups, and innumerable other drama and musical drama organizations sponsored by fraternal organizations, church groups, and labour unions. In most Canadian cities and towns, one group or another was rehearsing a play or a musical at any given time during the winter months. During the darkest days of the Depression, Canadian theatre blossomed, providing relief for many from the grim conditions of their lives. Protracted hard times, while discouraging some artists, also energized others, particularly those who sought cultural directions that would encourage a new spirit of social involvement and commitment.

During the Depression, a theatre of the left emerged in the major cities of Canada, particularly Vancouver, Toronto, Winnipeg, and Montreal, which spread to other places (like Timmins, Ontario) where "progressive" people were to be found. In all of these places, there was a twin emphasis: first, on supplying theatre that spoke directly to its audiences about what was going on in Canada and the world; and second, on exemplifying the ideals of collective experience in theatrical production. The theatre of the left tended to exalt amateur values and participation. It also had far more Canadian content in its plays. The first tour of the Workers' Theatre, for example, included seven short plays, including *Eviction* (written by members of the Montreal Progressive Arts Club), *Farmers' Fight* (also written by the Montreal PAC), *Joe Derry* (written by Dorothy Livesay), and *War in the East* (written by Stanley Ryerson). Interestingly, progressive theatre groups did not shun the establishment-oriented Dominion Drama Festival (DDF) but instead competed frequently, seeking thereby to test their theatrical quality, apart from the political value of their work. The DDF adjudicators, in their turn, were sympathetic to the productions but often unenthusiastic about the doom and gloom of their themes, preferring lighter fare. In 1937, a four-person play entitled *Relief*, written by Minnie Evans Bicknell of Marshall, Saskatchewan, and performed by the Marshall Dramatic Club, was one of the finalists at the DDF. The play was a domestic tragedy performed in a naturalistic style in which the performers dealt with matters that were all too familiar in their daily lives, as

on CBC that consistently outdrew American offerings with the Canadian listeners. Although the Depression benefited professional sports by creating a desperate need for escape, not all Canadians could afford to pay for admission. In Toronto, for example, ticket prices of 50¢ and $1.25 resulted in many empty seats. By 1939 the NHL had suffered the loss of all but two of its Canadian teams, the Maple Leafs and the Montreal Canadiens. The centre of professional hockey power shifted to the United States, although Canadians knew that virtually all the players still came from Canada, where hockey was a way of life on the frozen rivers and lakes of the nation in the winter months.

While Canada's film and hockey successes were mainly in Hollywood and in American arenas, a vital grassroots theatrical movement existed at home between the wars, almost entirely on the amateur level. It consisted of Little Theatre groups in most major cit-

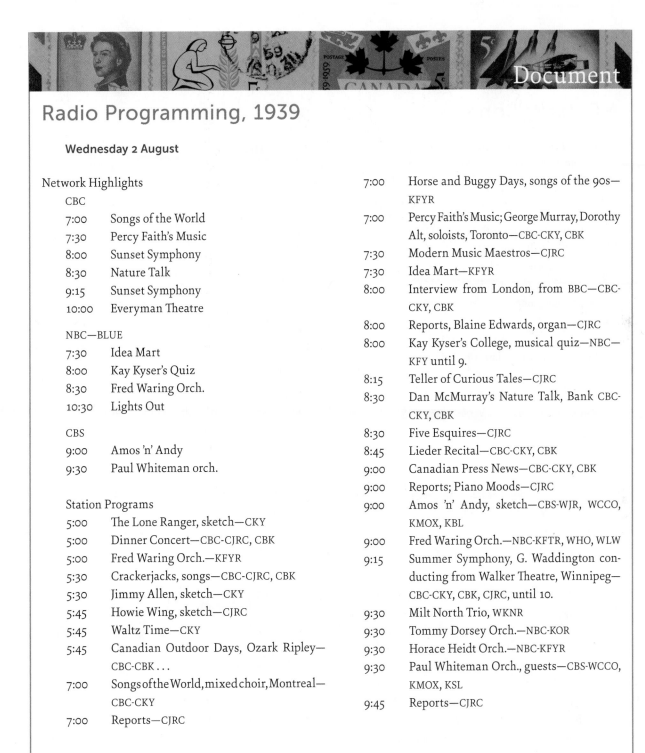

Radio Programming, 1939

Wednesday 2 August

Network Highlights

CBC
7:00	Songs of the World
7:30	Percy Faith's Music
8:00	Sunset Symphony
8:30	Nature Talk
9:15	Sunset Symphony
10:00	Everyman Theatre

NBC—BLUE
7:30	Idea Mart
8:00	Kay Kyser's Quiz
8:30	Fred Waring Orch.
10:30	Lights Out

CBS
9:00	Amos 'n' Andy
9:30	Paul Whiteman orch.

Station Programs
5:00	The Lone Ranger, sketch—CKY
5:00	Dinner Concert—CBC-CJRC, CBK
5:00	Fred Waring Orch.—KFYR
5:30	Crackerjacks, songs—CBC-CJRC, CBK
5:30	Jimmy Allen, sketch—CKY
5:45	Howie Wing, sketch—CJRC
5:45	Waltz Time—CKY
5:45	Canadian Outdoor Days, Ozark Ripley—CBC-CBK . . .
7:00	Songs of the World, mixed choir, Montreal—CBC-CKY
7:00	Reports—CJRC

7:00	Horse and Buggy Days, songs of the 90s—KFYR
7:00	Percy Faith's Music; George Murray, Dorothy Alt, soloists, Toronto—CBC-CKY, CBK
7:30	Modern Music Maestros—CJRC
7:30	Idea Mart—KFYR
8:00	Interview from London, from BBC—CBC-CKY, CBK
8:00	Reports, Blaine Edwards, organ—CJRC
8:00	Kay Kyser's College, musical quiz—NBC—KFY until 9.
8:15	Teller of Curious Tales—CJRC
8:30	Dan McMurray's Nature Talk, Bank CBC-CKY, CBK
8:30	Five Esquires—CJRC
8:45	Lieder Recital—CBC-CKY, CBK
9:00	Canadian Press News—CBC-CKY, CBK
9:00	Reports; Piano Moods—CJRC
9:00	Amos 'n' Andy, sketch—CBS-WJR, WCCO, KMOX, KBL
9:00	Fred Waring Orch.—NBC-KFTR, WHO, WLW
9:15	Summer Symphony, G. Waddington conducting from Walker Theatre, Winnipeg—CBC-CKY, CBK, CJRC, until 10.
9:30	Milt North Trio, WKNR
9:30	Tommy Dorsey Orch.—NBC-KOR
9:30	Horace Heidt Orch.—NBC-KFYR
9:30	Paul Whiteman Orch., guests—CBS-WCCO, KMOX, KSL
9:45	Reports—CJRC

Source: *Winnipeg Tribune*, 2 August 1939, 2.

A Cabaret Song

One of the major songwriters for the cabarets of the left-wing Theatre of Action was Frank Gregory. These cabarets began in 1939 and continued through the early 1940s. The songs were heavily influenced by Tin Pan Alley and Broadway.

We Get Along

We never travel in Café society,
And Winchell never gives us notoriety—
    I guess we must be
    Socially insignificant
But we get along.

You'll never find us at the El Morocco,
We can't afford the latest Broadway socko—
    It seems we are just
    Socially insignificant.
But we get along.

Don't think we're satisfied
To sit and bide
Our time as we are:
    We're not the patient kind.
For in addition
We've got ambition,
But that can't get us far,
    With money and security so hard to find.

So that is why you'll never see our faces
In photographs of all the swellest places:
    You'd think we were born
    Socially insignificant,
But we get along.

Source: Quoted in Toby Gordon Ryan, *Stage Left Canadian Theatre in the Thirties: A Memoir* (Toronto: CTR Publications, 1981), 189. Courtesy CTR Publications.

the critics noted in their reviews. Toronto's Theatre of Action was particularly active in seeking out Canadian themes and Canadian playwrights. The thematic content of the drama preferred by the theatre of the left was undoubtedly one of the factors that limited its popular acceptance. Towards the end of the 1930s, however, influenced by the cabaret theatre of Kurt Weill and Bertolt Brecht as developed by left-wing American theatre groups, progressive theatre in Canada became more interested in musical theatre. Some of the cabaret productions actually featured songs that commented satirically on Canadian politics. This topical humour offered a lighter alternative to the fare presented by the more earnest theatre companies.

World War II

Canada went back to war on 10 September 1939. This time the government waited a week after the British declaration of war against Germany to join the conflict, thus emphasizing Canada's "independent" status. The nation's entry into the war helped complete the process of economic recovery. Unprepared militarily, as in the Great War, Canada proved capable of mobilizing resources remarkably swiftly when required. Canada quickly accepted the British Commonwealth Air Training Plan as its major war commitment. The details of the scheme were agreed upon by Britain and Canada on 17 December 1939. Within months the program's first graduates emerged from Camp Borden, Ontario. It eventually graduated 131,552 Commonwealth airmen from Canada, Great Britain, Australia, and New Zealand (Table 8.1), over half of whom were Canadian, at a cost of $1.6 billion. A nation of less than 12 million people would eventually put over 1 million of them into uniform. Using the War Measures Act, Canada succeeded in mobilizing economic resources in a way that had seemed impossible during the Depression. Tax arrangements between the Dominion and the provinces were restructured during the emergency, with the federal government collecting most of the revenue and making grants to the provinces to recover their operating expenses.

The economy was totally managed and regulated, a process associated with Ottawa's wartime economic czar, Clarence Decatur Howe (1886–1960). By 1943 unemployment was well under 2 per cent, a figure regarded in most quarters as full employment. Federal spending rose from 3.4 per cent of the gross national product (GNP) in 1939 to 37.6 per cent of GNP by 1944, totalling a full $4.4 billion in the latter year. Industrial growth was better distributed across the regions than in 1914–18, inflation was controlled, and consumption was regulated by shortages and rationing. Canada's total GNP rose from $5.6 billion in 1939 to $11.9 billion in 1945. The nation became one of the world's industrial giants, producing 850,000 motorized vehicles and over 16,000 military aircraft during the war. The government borrowed heavily from its own citizens, partly in the form of war bonds. While the achievement was impressive, it suggested that Leacock's "riddle of social justice" remained unsolved. Canada appeared far more capable of efficient use of its productive capacity to fight destructive wars abroad than to battle domestically with poverty and unemployment.

As in the Great War, Canadians fought well whenever called upon. As in the previous conflict, they were often employed as shock troops. In the disastrous landing of the 2nd Canadian Division at Dieppe in August 1942, nearly 2,700 of the 5,000 Canadians who embarked were either killed or captured. Canadians landed on Juno Beach on D-Day, 6 June 1944, and took heavy casualties. The First Canadian Army, formed in 1942 under the command of General A.G.L. McNaughton (1887–1966), was composed of five divisions that were eventually split between Italy and Northwest Europe.

This army was independently commanded, although the Royal Canadian Air Force and the Royal Canadian Navy were mainly integrated with their British counterparts. Canadian flyers became noted for their work in bombers rather than in fighters, as in World War I. Many thousands of Canadians spent most or all of the war years in Britain, and a number brought their British wives back to Canada after the war.

The RCN grew to 365 ships, spending the war mainly protecting convoys on the North Atlantic route and achieving such expertise in this duty that in May 1943 a Canadian, Admiral L.W. Murray (1896–1971), was given command of the Canadian Northwest Atlantic theatre. Many other Canadians and Newfoundlanders served in the Canadian merchant marine, a thankless task that kept them out of the loop for veterans' benefits for many years. Canada ultimately had the third largest navy among the Allied powers, the fourth largest air force, and the fourth largest army. Such a contribution ought to have made it something of a power in the world, although the major powers—Britain, the United States, and the USSR—routinely treated Canada as little different from Allied nations such as Chile and Brazil, which had only token forces in the war. The superpowers admitted France to their council tables almost as soon as the nation was liberated, while ignoring Canada completely.

Canada fought chiefly in the European and North Atlantic theatres. Canadian assistance to American and British efforts in the Pacific and Southeast Asia was fairly minimal. In December 1941, however, two Canadian battalions were involved in the surrender of Hong Kong. The 1,421 men who returned home after years in Japanese prison camps had to fight for 23 years to win proper veterans' benefits from the Canadian government. As in the Great War, casualties in this conflict were heavy, with 42,642 Canadians giving up their lives. On the other hand, this was not a war of stalemate in the trenches. Instead, the establishment of beachheads was followed by a constant advance that involved liberating places held by the enemy. One innovation in this war was the active military service of women. As in 1914–18 large numbers of women were employed in the war industry, but by 1945 over 43,000 women were actually in uniform. A Gallup poll taken in 1944

TABLE 8.1 Final Output of the British Commonwealth Air Training Plan

Trade	RCAF	RAF	RAAF	RNZAF	Total
Pilot	25,646	17,796	4,045	2,220	49,707
Navigator	7,280	6,922	944	724	15,870
Navigator (B2)	5,154	3,113	699	829	9,795
Navigator (W)	421	3,847	30		4,298
Air Bomber	6,659	7,581	799	634	15,673
Wireless Operator/Air Gunner	12,744	755	2,975	2,122	18,596
Air Gunner	12,917	2,096	244	443	15,700
Flight Engineers	1,913				1,913
Total	72,734	42,110	9,706	7,002	131,552

Source: http://www.canadianwings.com/BCATP.

Canadian soldiers, known for their bravery, were instrumental in liberating northwestern Europe from the Germans. Canadian Major David Currie (left, holding pistol) won the Victoria Cross for his role in helping to close the Falaise Gap in August 1944. CWM 20020045-2276, George Metcalf Archival Collection, Canadian War Museum.

indicated, however, that most Canadians, including 68 per cent of the women polled, believed that men should be given preference for employment in the post-war reconstruction. As a result, the machinery for women's participation in the workforce, including daycare centres, was dismantled with unseemly haste at the war's end.

Dissent was met with persecution, as had been the case during the Great War. The Canadian government proved almost totally insensitive to pacifists' beliefs. It interned thousands of Canadians without trial, often for mere criticism of government policy. The most publicized abuse of the state's power was the treatment of the Japanese Canadians. Although the King government did not for a minute believe that Japanese Canadians represented any real military danger, it yielded to pressure from British Columbia and forcibly evacuated most Japanese Canadians from the west coast. Many were sent to internment camps in the

BC Interior, and others were scattered across the country, their land seized and their property sold at auction. "National emergency" was also used to justify the dissemination of propaganda, now called "management of information." Citizens needed to be educated in order to maintain faith and hope and to eliminate "potential elements of disunity," a euphemism for criticism of the government. One major institution of information management was the National Film Board of Canada, under Scottish-born John Grierson (1898–1972), who believed in the integration of "the loyalties and forces of the community in the name of positive and highly constructive ideas." Grierson saw "information services— propaganda if you like" as an inevitable consequence of the government's involvement in the crisis (quoted in Young, 1978: 217–40).

Internally, wartime policies revolved around two major questions: conscription and post-war reconstruction. In a national plebiscite held on the question

Contemporary Views

Owning a Piece of Juno

Many gave their lives on D-Day. Sixty-three in The Queen's Own paid the price. In our section of ten men, seven fell: David Boynton, Fred Eaman, Edward Westerby, Albert Kennedy, John Kirkland, Douglas Reed—all Riflemen—and Corporal John Gibson.
Three of our ten survived: Rifleman Robert Nicol, Corporal Rolph Jackson, and myself.

Although I spent more than twelve hundred days in active service only three were spent on the beachhead. Less than three hours were spent on my feet. The rest was on a stretcher. That first night was in a small building on what is now called rue de la Queen's Own Rifles of Canada. The second night was in the now very well-known orchard where we were taken care of by those wonderful nuns. Then it was a rocky and dangerous ride getting out to an American

LST [landing ship, tank] and back to England.

It was August 1944 before my wound healed and I could get back to the invasion beach and take a look at Bernières-sur-Mer. I found the temporary graves of some of our fallen by the railroad tracks. One of the cleanup pioneers told me bodies were still washing ashore from time to time. I stood facing the beach, heart heavy and mind racing.

A British sergeant began to explain things to me describing what took place on D-Day. It was clearly beyond his imagination. It hurt to listen.

"Were you there?" I asked him. "No." "Well, if you had been there you wouldn't need to say a word. If you weren't, then it's impossible for you to understand.

"You see that beach? My friends and I own a piece of it. And I don't want to hear another word."

Source: Doug Hester (Toronto, Ontario, Queen's Own Rifles, Canadian Third Division), "A War Memoir," http://www. warchronicle.com/canadian_third_div/soldierstories_wwii/hester.htm.

of conscription in the spring of 1942, the nation voted 2,945,514 to 1,643,006 to release the government from an earlier pledge not to conscript for overseas service. Quebec voted strongly in the negative. The conscription issue emerged again in 1944, when the military insisted (as in 1917) that it was necessary to ship conscripts overseas, although they had been drafted with the promise that they would not be required to serve abroad. In the end, while conscripts were sent to Europe, few served as combatants before the war ended in May 1945. For the King government, the increasing threat from the CCF became a problem as nagging as that of Quebec. As early as 1941 many Canadians had apparently come to realize that the failure to make a concerted assault on social injustice had been a result mainly of governments' refusal to act. Canada was now, in wartime, demonstrating how thoroughly the country could be mobilized if the will to do so was present. Public opinion in Anglo-Canada began turning to the social promises of the CCF. Indeed, in the September 1943 federal election, the CCF received the support of 29 per cent of the electorate at the polls, and in 1944 the Saskatchewan CCF wiped out a long-standing Liberal government in an election fought over social services.

Contemporary Views   LE CANADIEN.

The Story of War Bride Ruby McCreight

This narrative of a Canadian war bride begins in the third person but concludes in the first person.

Ruby was a lonely English girl from London, England. She was a widow with a three-year-old daughter. Ruby didn't make friends easily because she was hard of hearing and tended to keep to herself. At the time, she worked in a Legion waiting on tables and helping with the cleaning for the more than 400 soldiers of every nationality who called the Legion home. They could not go to their real homes on leave, so most of them stayed at the Legion.

Every New Year's Eve, the soldiers donned kitchen aprons and waited on the help. Everyone made jokes and enjoyed the antics and the soldier who waited on them.

The Canadian soldier who waited on Ruby spoke to her several times and even put a present on her plate, but she didn't answer him, she just tried to smile. Not many people knew she was hard of hearing.

After all the tables were cleared, the band began to play and couples started dancing. Ruby stood alone, just watching.

Suddenly Ruby's soldier approached her and gave her a note to read: "I know you have trouble hearing. Are you as lonely as you look: I feel the same way; I miss my folks home in Canada. Would you keep me company and dance with me?" She surprised herself and danced with him several times. He saw her home, and after this he continued to see her at work and on the occasional date.

After seeing him for a little over six months, she took him home to meet her parents and her little girl. When the little girl saw him she ran to him and said: "Daddy, you came home!"

She had seen her dad in uniform in a photo on her shelf, and seeing the soldier in uniform, she naturally assumed it was her father.

After the young girl was put to bed and Ruby and the soldier was [sic] alone, he asked, "Well, how about it?"

"How about what?" Ruby asked.

"Being her daddy," he replied.

This was in 1944. We were married in 1945 and came to Canada the next year. We have now been married for 46 years and we have five children—and are still as happy as the day we first met.

Source: David Helwig, ed., *Back Then: Voices of Memory 1915–1945* (n.p: Oberon Press, 1993), 102–3.

King's Liberals had long dragged their heels over serious social welfare reform. Federal unemployment insurance had been introduced in 1940, but other progressive legislation remained on hold. Now, in 1944, King declared in the House of Commons "a wholly new conception of industry as being in the nature of social service for the benefit of all, not as something existing only for the benefit of a favoured few." The introduction of social reform was necessary not only to deal with the threat from the CCF but also to prevent possible public disorder at the conclusion of the war and to assert the authority of the federal government over the provinces. Once the political decision was made to implement social reform, there were plenty of schemes available, including a package in the *Report on Social Security for Canada* tabled in the House of Commons Special

Committee on Social Security by economist Leonard Marsh (1906–82) in 1943. In the end, a full program of progressive legislation was never actually enacted before the end of the war. The Liberal government did introduce the Family Allowances Act of 1944, Canada's first social insurance program with universal coverage. It provided benefits to mothers of children under age 16. In 1944 the Liberals also passed the National Housing Act, described as "An Act to Promote the Construction of New Houses, the Repair and Modernization of Existing Houses, the Improvement of Housing and Living Conditions and the Expansion of Employment in the Postwar Period." The King government turned to the post-war period, however, with intentions of attacking the problem of social justice and the constitutional limitations of the British North America Act simultaneously.

Japanese Canadians being relocated to camps in the Interior of British Columbia, 1942. LAC, C-046355.

Document

Evacuation from Woodfibre, British Columbia, 1942

Takao Ujo Nakano published this account of his wartime experience in 1980.

Pearl Harbor, the opening strike of the Japan–U.S. conflict, shocked Woodfibre's inhabitants. The quiet town was completely transformed as rumours propagated rumours, fed by often conflicting reports. The Japanese community especially was in an uproar.

We Japanese, largely working-class immigrants, were, generally speaking, not given to sophisticated political thinking. Rather we had in common a blind faith in Japan's eventual victory. The extent of our reasoning, decidedly specious in retrospect, went something like this: The burst of energy at Pearl Harbor was exemplary. If the war were short, say of less than two years' duration, Japan stood to win. If it were prolonged, Japan, weakened by over a decade of aggression in Manchuria and China, admittedly might lose. Meanwhile, we kept receiving reports of Japanese victories in the Far East. We therefore resolved to bear the present uneasiness patiently.

In the weeks that followed, life in Woodfibre was indeed changed. I remember especially the compulsory nightly blackout, meant to thwart the activity of Japanese bombers that might fly over British Columbia.

With Canadians thus anxious, some drastic move was inevitable. By mid-January of 1942, some of us faced the prospect of evacuation. At that time it was said that if the Issei [Japanese-born] men aged eighteen to forty-five went to the road camps, then the Issei men over forty-five, the Issei women and children, and all Nisei [Canadian-born of Japanese descent] would be allowed to remain where they were. We Issei men accordingly received an order to depart on March 16.

As the day of departure drew nearer, tension mounted in the Japanese community. The lot of us Issei men was held to be a sorry one indeed. The Rockies were terribly cold in March; some of us would likely freeze to death in the twenty-below temperature. Again, the steep mountains were subject to avalanches; road work in them would be very dangerous. And again, deep in the mountains, men could easily become isolated by the snow and starve when provisions failed to get through to them. With such conjectures, the families of Issei men spent anxious days and sleepless nights. But the order to depart was a government order. To accept it as fate was our sorry resolve. . . .

Source: T.U. Nakano, "Evacuation from Woodfibre, British Columbia, 1942," from T.U. Nakano, *Within the Barbed Wire Fence: A Japanese Man's Account of His Internment in Canada* (Toronto: University of Toronto Press, 1980), 8–10. © University of Toronto Press, 1980.

Conclusion

Despite war fatalities, injustices, and some deprivation, World War II was, on balance, a more unifying and positive experience for most Canadians than the Great War had been. Full employment helped a good deal. Rationing provided a better-balanced diet. Limited leisure time and the absence of big-ticket consumer items, such as automobiles and household appliances, forced many Canadians to save, often by purchasing war bonds and savings stamps. By war's end, a 15-year deferral of expectations had built up a powerful urge among Canadians to enjoy material comforts, free from concern over life's vagaries and hazards. This population was fully conscious of the dangers of assuming that social protection could be left to the private individual. It was equally aware that the state could intervene in the process, if it so desired.

Historiography

Studying Canada's Military Effort in World War I

Roger Sarty, Wilfrid Laurier University

Personal favourites, among many short, introductory accounts, are D.J. Goodspeed, *The Road Past Vimy: The Canadian Corps 1914–1918* (Toronto, 1969) and Terry Copp, Matt Symes, and Nick Lachance, *Canadian Battlefields 1915–1918* (Waterloo, Ont., 2011).

Books about Canada's role began to appear during the conflict[1] and continued to pour forth in the following decades. These included memoirs, popular works, and regimental histories. Many are still very useful. The regimental histories, for example, present detailed accounts of operations and sketches of personalities available nowhere else.[2] Among the most distinguished memoirs are those of the wartime leader, Prime Minister Robert Borden, assembled by his nephew, who drew heavily on Borden's papers.[3]

The project initiated by the Department of National Defence for an eight-volume official history, however, produced only the first volume and a supporting volume of documents. These appeared in 1938 and cover the initial year of the war. Immensely detailed, they are still an essential resource.[4] A full official account of Canadian participation in land warfare—nearly 500,000 Canadian troops served overseas—appeared in a single volume in 1962.[5] Colonel G.W.L. Nicholson, a senior member of the professional Army Historical Section, and the noted academic C.P. Stacey led the team that was organized during and after World War II to work on this history. They drew on the vast archives organized by the original historical section and the book is still the best starting place.

Nicholson produced two other thoroughly referenced, foundational volumes. *The Fighting Newfoundlander: A History of The Royal Newfoundland Regiment* (St John's: Government of Newfoundland, 1964) is the first comprehensive account of the extraordinary sacrifice by this British Dominion, separate from Canada, that did not join Confederation until 1949. Nicholson's

The Gunners of Canada: The History of the Royal Regiment of Canadian Artillery, vol.1, 1534–1919 (Toronto and Montreal, 1967) details the organization and operations of the immensely powerful artillery arm of the Canadian Corps, which was a key element in its formidable striking power.

Canada's large contribution to the air war—the provision of some 20,000 personnel to the British flying services—was the least well recorded part of the military effort. This was belatedly corrected when the Army Historical Section became the tri-service Directorate of History in 1965 and focused on aviation history. S.F. Wise, *Canadian Airmen in the First World War*, The Official History of the Royal Canadian Air Force, vol. 1 ([Toronto], 1980)is still a foremost authority on not just the Canadian role, but on aviation more generally during World War I.

At the leading edge of scholarly work that started in the 1960s with the opening of government archives was Robert Craig Brown's biography, *Robert Laird Borden: A Biography*, 2 vols (Toronto, 1975–80). Another benchmark in superbly researched biography is Michael Bliss's volume on Sir Joseph Flavelle,[6] who headed munitions production in Canada from 1916 to 1918. This is the fullest published account of Canada's industrial effort. Strong in its research on both the home front and the overseas effort is Ronald G. Haycock's life of Sir Sam Hughes, Minister of Militia and Defence from 1911 until 1916, when Prime Minister Borden finally lost patience with Hughes's erratic, scandal-prone administration.[7] General Sir Arthur Currie, the militia officer who succeeded brilliantly on the battlefield and commanded the Canadian Corps in 1917–18, has had three major biographies written about him, all well worth consulting.[8]

Robert Craig Brown joined Ramsay Cook to produce a survey of signal importance, *Canada 1896–1921:*

A Nation Transformed (Toronto and Montreal, 1974). Its chapters on the war draw on the large number of graduate theses recently completed or in progress prior to the book's publication; the book really marks the beginning of sustained scholarship, particularly on the homefront. For further work in the following three decades, see the outstanding collection of papers in David Mackenzie, ed., *Canada and the First World War: Essays in Honour of Robert Craig Brown* (Toronto, 2005), which captures subsequent work on combat and the home front by many of the now senior scholars whose early research informed the 1974 volume by Brown and Cook.

Publication of new scholarly work in the 1970s and 1980s included little on the navy. It raised a total of 9,600 personnel during the war, about 1,700 for service with the British fleet overseas and the rest for the protection of shipping in Canadian waters. Gilbert N. Tucker's detailed *The Naval Service of Canada: Its Official History*, vol. 1, *Origins and Early Years* (Ottawa, 1952) is still a valuable source on many subjects. The volume, however, is circumspect about personalities and silent on important aspects of operations. Michael L. Hadley and Roger Sarty sought to fill these gaps in *Tin-Pots and Pirate Ships: Canadian Naval Forces and German Sea Raiders 1880–1918* (Montreal and Kingston, 1991). The navy had long carried much blame for the Halifax Explosion, the devastation of the city by the explosion of a munitions ship in the Halifax harbour on 6 December 1917. John Armstrong's *The Halifax Explosion and the Royal Canadian Navy: Inquiry and Intrigue* (Vancouver, 2002) explores the navy's role, and challenges its responsibility for the critical lapses with newly discovered archival sources. Mark Hunter's *To Employ and Uplift Them: The Newfoundland Naval Reserve, 1899-1926* (St John's, 2009) covers the service Newfoundland's experienced seamen gave to both the British and Canadian fleets during the war. These works helped lay the foundation for William Johnston, William G.P. Rawling, Richard H. Gimblett, and John MacFarlane, *The Seabound Coast: The Official History of the Royal Canadian Navy, 1867–1939*, vol. 1 (Toronto, 2010), which the Directorate of History (now the Directorate of History and Heritage) undertook because of renewed interest in World War I.

The enormous achievements of the Canadian Corps that fought in France and Belgium, and the heavy losses it bore, have been the subject of the bulk of scholarly research that started in the 1960s and 1970s, gained momentum in the 1980s and 1990s, and continues with the interest aroused by the centenary of the war. Still important are the well-researched books produced by Daniel G. Dancocks in the 1980s, including *Spearhead to Victory: Canada and the Great War* (Edmonton, 1987). One of the first and still leading academic authors is Desmond Morton. Among his numerous, wide-ranging studies, *When Your Number's Up: The Canadian Soldier in the First World War* (Toronto, 1993) perhaps best encapsulates his research on combat. It can profitably be read in conjunction with Bill Rawling's *Surviving Trench Warfare: Technology and the Canadian Corps, 1914–1918* (Toronto, 1992). A comprehensive and insightful treatment of French Canada's part in combat is Jean-Pierre Gagnon, *Le 22e bataillon (canadien–français) 1914-1919: Étude socio-militaire* ([Quebec City], 1986), which was produced by the Directorate of History. The fullest treatment of the divisive conscription issue is still J.L. Granatstein and J.M. Hitsman, *Broken Promises: A History of Conscription in Canada* (Toronto, 1977). The journal *Canadian Military History*, published since 1992 by the Laurier Centre for Military, Strategic, and Disarmament Studies at Wilfrid Laurier University has featured a great deal of the new work on World War I combat. Geoffrey Hayes, Andrew Iarocci, and Mike Bechthold's *Vimy Ridge: A Canadian Reassessment* (Waterloo, Ont., 2007) comprises wide-ranging essays by many of the leading younger scholars on the Canadian Corps' iconic battle. J.L. Granatstein drew on much of the more recent scholarship in *The Greatest Victory: Canada's One Hundred Days, 1918* (Toronto, 2014). One of the foremost younger authors is Tim Cook, who in two substantial volumes presents the whole combat history of the Canadian Corps with the rich personal accounts that have become available since the 1960s.[9]

Notes

1. Max Aitken, *Canada in Flanders. The Official Story of the Canadian Expeditionary Force*, vol. 1 (London, 1916), for example, was a best-seller.

2. For a full listing, see O.A. Cooke, *The Canadian Military Experience 1867–1995: A Bibliography*, 3rd edn (Ottawa, 1997). See also Brian Douglas Tennyson, *The Canadian Experience of the Great War: A Guide to Memoirs* (Plymouth, UK, 2013).

3. Henry Borden, ed., *Robert Laird Borden: His Memoirs*, 2 vols (Toronto, 1938).

4. Archer Fortescue Duguid, *Official History of the Canadian Forces in the Great War, 1914–1919*, vol. 1 (Ottawa, 1938).

5. G.W.L. Nicholson, *Canadian Expeditionary Force, 1914–1919* (Official History of the Canadian Army in the First World War) (Ottawa, 1962).

6. Michael Bliss, *A Canadian Millionaire: The Life and Business Times of Sir Joseph Flavelle, Bart., 1858–1939* (Toronto, 1978).

7. Ronald G. Haycock, *Sam Hughes: The Public Career of a Controversial Canadian, 1885–1916* (Waterloo, Ont., 1986).

8. H.M. Urquhart, *Arthur Currie: The Biography of a Great Canadian* (Toronto, 1950); A.M.J. Hyatt, *General Sir Arthur Currie: A Military Biography* (Toronto, 1982); D.G. Dancocks, *Sir Arthur Currie: A Biography* (Toronto, 1985).

9. Tim Cook, *At the Sharp End: Canadians Fighting the Great War 1914–16*, vol. 1 (Toronto, 2007) and *Shock Troops: Canadians Fighting the Great War, 1917–1918*, vol. 2 (Toronto, 2008).

Short Bibliography

Abella, Irving, and Harold Troper. *None Is Too Many: Canada and the Jews of Europe, 1933–1948*. Toronto, 1982. The standard work on the subject, judicious, fair, and scathing in its critique of Canadian policy.

Baillargeon, Denyse. *Making Do: Women, Family, and Home in Montreal during the Great Depression*. Waterloo, Ont., 2000. An exploration of women's role during the Depression.

Baum, Gregory. *Catholics and Canadian Socialism: Political Thought in the Thirties and Forties*. Toronto, 1980. A stimulating book emphasizing that not all Catholics were unsympathetic to social reform and socialism.

Berton, Pierre. *Hollywood's Canada: The Americanization of Our National Image*. Toronto, 1975. Perhaps Berton's best work, this explores the ways in which Hollywood has dealt with Canada and Canadian subjects.

Bumsted, J.M. *The Winnipeg General Strike of 1919: An Illustrated History*. Winnipeg, 1994. Makes the history of the strike accessible to the general audience.

Fedorowich, Kent. *Unfit for Heroes: Reconstitution and Soldier Settlement in the Empire between the Wars*. Manchester, 1995. Examination of the failed attempts to relocate British ex-soldiers as immigrants to rural areas in Canada and other Anglo countries.

Finkel, Alvin. *Business and Social Reform in the Thirties*. Toronto, 1979. A useful analysis of the relationship between business and social reform in the Depression, emphasizing that many businessmen saw reform as the only alternative to the destruction of capitalism.

Forbes, Ernest R. *The Maritime Rights Movement 1919–1927: A Study in Canadian Regionalism*. Montreal, 1979. A fascinating study of one movement of regional protest that failed.

Kaprelian-Churchill, Isabel. "Armenian Refugees and Their Entry into Canada, 1919–1930." *Canadian Historical Review* 71, 1 (1990): 80–108.

Lévesque, Andrée. *Making and Breaking the Rules: Women in Quebec, 1919–1939*. Toronto, 1994. An important study of women in Quebec between the wars.

MacMillan, Margaret. *Paris 1919: Six Months That Changed the World*. New York, 2002. A Canadian-based historian's massive narrative of the Paris Peace Conference, including Canada's role put in context.

Morton, W.L. *The Progressive Party of Canada*. Toronto, 1950. The classic account, still generally valid.

Owram, Doug. *The Government Generation: Canadian Intellectuals and the State 1900–1945*. Toronto, 1986. A synthesis of secondary literature on the subject to the mid-1980s.

Peers, Frank. *The Politics of Canadian Broadcasting 1920–1951*. Toronto, 1969. A first-hand history of the development of Canadian broadcasting before television.

Safarian, A.E. *The Canadian Economy in the Great Depression*. Toronto, 1959. The standard account of the performance of the Canadian economy in the 1930s.

Stacey, C.P. *Arms, Men and Governments: The War Policies of Canada 1939–1945*. Ottawa, 1970. A useful survey of Canada's military policy during World War II.

Strong-Boag, Veronica. *The New Day Recalled: Lives of Girls and Women in English Canada 1919–1939*. Toronto, 1988. A survey of the changing (or unchanging) role of women in English Canada between the wars.

Sunahara, Ann. *The Politics of Racism: The Uprooting of Japanese Canadians during the Second World War*. Toronto, 1981. A sober and unsentimental account that does not hesitate to call this part of Canadian war policy racist.

Thompson, John Herd, and Allan Seager. *Canada 1922–1939: Decades of Discord*. Toronto, 1985. The best synthesis of the interwar years, rich in detail.

Tippett, Maria. *Making Culture: English-Canadian Institutions and the Arts before the Massey Commission*. Toronto, 1990. Perhaps the only overview of the cultural infrastructure of any part of Canada before 1951.

Trofimenkoff, Susan Mann. *Action Française: French-Canadian Nationalism in the Twenties*. Toronto, 1975. An analysis of nationalism, mainly in Quebec, in the 1920s, focusing on Abbé Groulx and his circle.

Study Questions

1. What was Stephen Leacock's "unsolved riddle of social justice"? How did Canadians address this riddle in the interwar period?

2. Identify three causes of labour unrest in Canada after the Great War.

3. Explain why the Depression was a devastating experience for many Canadians.

4. What social and economic impacts did the automobile have on the Canadian public during this period?

5. Did gaining the vote substantially increase the political power of Canadian women? Explain.

6. In what ways could Canada's exclusionist immigration policy be defended?

7. What does the document "Radio Programming, 1939" tell us about what Canadians listened to in 1939?

8. Why was the theatre of the left more active than the mainstream theatre in presenting Canadian themes during the 1930s?

9. For Canadians, in what ways was World War II a replay of World War I? In what ways was it different? Are the similarities more important than the differences?

10. Are there incidents in this period about which the Canadian government needs to be ashamed? What are they?

Visit the companion website for *A History of the Canadian Peoples*, fifth edition for further resources.

 www.oupcanada.com/Bumsted5e

9 Prospering Together, 1945–1960

Pipers march during the opening ceremonies of the Canso Causeway, 13 August 1955. The causeway, one of the major engineering achievements of the period, linked Cape Breton to the Canadian mainland. There were supposed to be 100 pipers, but some accounts claim that one man refused to play. While not clear from this photo, it does appear that there is a man missing from the second row of the third column (behind the Union Jack). Canada. Dept. of Manpower and Immigration, LAC.

Timeline

1945 Liberal government is re-elected. Dominion–Provincial Conference on Reconstruction is convened. United Nations is founded in San Francisco. Gouzenko Affair. Cold War begins.

1947 Imperial Oil brings in Leduc, Alberta, oil field. Prime Minister King acknowledges Canada's "moral obligation" to refugees and displaced persons in Europe.

1948 Mackenzie King resigns and is replaced by Louis St Laurent. Newfoundland holds two plebiscites on its future, choosing to join Canada. Canada becomes part of the Marshall Plan.

1949 Asbestos strike in Quebec. Newfoundland joins Confederation. Royal Commission on National Development in the Arts, Letters, and Sciences (Massey Commission) is appointed. North Atlantic Treaty Organization is formed.

1950 Canada joins Korean "police action." Interprovincial oil pipeline is built from Edmonton to Superior, Ontario.

1951 Old Age Security Act passed by Ottawa. Eaton's department stores' employees strike. Aluminum Company of Canada begins the Kitimat project in British Columbia.

1952 First CBC television stations are opened.

1953 Quebec's Tremblay Commission on Constitutional Problems makes its report. Mackenzie Highway is completed to Northwest Territories. Transmountain oil pipeline is built from Edmonton to Vancouver.

1954 British Empire Games in Vancouver sees mile run for the first time in less than four minutes by both Roger Bannister and John Landy. St Lawrence Seaway opens. First iron ore leaves Ungava, Quebec. Canada joins a joint commission on Vietnam.

1955 Canso Causeway is opened in Nova Scotia, linking Cape Breton to the mainland.

1956 Canadian Labour Congress is formed from a merger of the Canadian Congress of Labour and the Trades and Labor Congress of Canada. The Unemployment Assistance Act is passed by Parliament. Trans-Canada Pipeline debate weakens the Liberal government. First transatlantic telephone cable is completed between Newfoundland and Scotland. Distant Early Warning (DEW) Line is established.

1957 Liberal government passes the Hospital Insurance Diagnostic Services Act. Diefenbaker's Tories win a minority government; St Laurent steps down. Lester B. Pearson wins the Nobel Peace Prize. Canada joins NORAD. The Canada Council is created.

1958 Inco strike. Lester B. Pearson is chosen Liberal leader. Diefenbaker Tories sweep the nation, including Quebec. Great Slave Railway is begun.

1959 Diefenbaker government decides to scrap the Avro Arrow. Maurice Duplessis dies.

1960 Royal Commission on Government Reorganization is appointed.

The post–World War II era, particularly before 1960, was a period of unparalleled economic growth and prosperity for Canada. Production and consumption moved steadily upward. Employment rose almost continuously. Canada substantially increased its workforce. Inflation was steady but almost never excessive. Interest rates were relatively low. The nation was in the midst of an uncharacteristic natural increase in its population growth rate that would become known as the baby boom. At the same time as many Canadians took advantage of the good times by conceiving children and moving to new homes in the suburbs, both the federal and provincial governments became active in providing new programs of social protection for their citizens. That network was not created without controversy, particularly of the constitutional variety, although the debate was still relatively muted until the 1960s. By that time, however, Canadian governments at all levels had become interventionist in a variety of areas, including culture.

Affluence

Economic prosperity and growth were at the root of all developments from 1946 to 1960 (and beyond). Almost all aspects of planning in both the public and private sectors were based on assumptions of constant growth, and such thinking seemed to work. Between 1946 and 1960, per capita income in Canada nearly doubled, thus increasing the Canadian standard of living. Canadians believed there were no limits to growth. Great Depressions were disasters of the past, and the standard of living could continue to rise. Politicians and their expert advisers argued that governments could now manage economies. They could correct for negative movements soon after they began. The operative economic wisdom was Keynesianism, named after the English economist John Maynard Keynes, whose writings provided much of the theoretical underpinning of the new affluence.

Quebec's Tremblay Commission on Constitutional Problems well described the prevailing wisdom in 1953:

The objective envisaged was the maintenance of economic stability and full employment. . . .

Both expenditures and investments, by individuals as well as by companies, should, therefore, be encouraged. Moreover, the government should take a part in this, and co-operate in stabilizing the economy and in ensuring full employment by its own expenditures and investments. This would demand from it an appropriate fiscal and monetary policy, as well as a programme of carefully planned public works. . . . The new policy necessarily entailed a considerable number of social security measures regarded as indispensable for the correction of variations in the economic cycle. (Kwavnick, 1973: 183–4)

In truth, the overall pattern of affluence was neither solely attributable to government management nor distinctive to Canada. It was general across the Western industrial world. It started, in part, with the rebuilding of the war-torn economies of Europe and Asia. It continued with heavy expenditures on military defence during the Cold War. Filling consumer wants after a generation's deferral of expectations helped. Then prosperity continued under its own momentum for a time, aided by the baby boom.

Foreign trade was an important component of Canadian affluence. The volume of imports and exports increased substantially. Canada became integrated into the American trading market as Great Britain decreased in importance as a trading partner. The government set the value of the Canadian dollar in relation to the American dollar, and attempted to control Canadian foreign exchange and Canadian domestic banking through the Bank of Canada. After 1954, banks were allowed to extend consumer credit and mortgage loans, although before 1967 they were limited in the interest they could charge. Canada's monetary policy was to increase the supply of money in circulation, producing inflation that eventually would run out of control.

The relative importance of various sectors of the domestic economy shifted in these years. Agriculture declined from 25 per cent of the total workforce in 1946 to 11 per cent in 1961. The real growth areas were in the public sector, particularly public administration and the services necessary to manage the new state. In 1946 just over 15 per cent of Canadians were employed in the public sector, but by 1961 that figure had increased to just over 25 per cent. Many of the public service employees were highly educated white-collar workers, and by 1960 over half of Canadians held white-collar jobs. Women in 1960 made up about 30 per cent of the workforce, with their pay about two-thirds that of males. Regional disparities in manufacturing continued and even grew. Central Canada, especially Ontario, experienced most of the gains in manufacturing. Ontario produced over 50 per cent of total manufacturing value added in the nation and dominated the manufacture of durable goods and big-ticket consumer items in many industries. In 1957, for example, Ontario turned out 98.8 per cent of Canada's motor vehicles, 90.7 per cent of its heavy industrial goods, 90 per cent of its agricultural implements, and 80.7 per cent of its major household appliances. Canadian manufacturing served two principal markets. One was the domestic consumer market, which exploded after 15 years of "doing without." The other was a huge market for military hardware to equip Canada's armed forces, which greatly increased in number after 1950. Canada was ambitious to produce homegrown equipment, but had to settle for subcontracting parts of Canadian orders through American branch plants. The Diefenbaker government's decision to scrap the Avro Arrow in 1959 ended the last serious Canadian venture in the independent development of military hardware.

Much of the employment growth in Canada from 1946 to 1966 was in the public sector. The size of the public service, federally, provincially, and municipally, grew from 222,000 to 909,000 in these years, a more than fourfold increase. © McCord Museum.

The resource economy did reasonably well. Beginning in 1947, when Imperial Oil brought in the major oil field at Leduc, in southern Alberta, there was significant expansion in western Canadian oil and gas. Most of the risk was assumed by Americans, and the Alberta oil industry was quickly taken over by multinational firms. Oil and gas began to be transported by pipeline from the West into the major centres of population and industry. Potash provided a major new resource for Saskatchewan, and uranium was a short-lived bonanza for northern Ontario. The burning of fossil fuels and the development of nuclear power were the growth areas in the energy industry. Hydroelectric generation, which accounted for almost 95 per cent of Canada's electrical capacity in 1946, had dropped to just over 75 per cent by 1960 and would be down to only half that by the 1970s, despite massive hydroelectric projects in many provinces, especially Quebec and British Columbia.

In this period of growth, nobody paid much attention to environmental issues. "Affluence," not "effluence," was the watchword. Prior to 1960, Canadians were only dimly aware of the dangers of "pollution," a word that had only just come into common use. Nuclear experts insisted that nuclear accidents were extremely unlikely and did not worry about the disposal of half-life radio-active nuclear wastes. Petrochemical plants dumped waste into surrounding waters and paper-processing plants dumped poisonous mercury and other effluents into rivers and lakes. Solid industrial waste was usually buried, often used as landfill to create new housing estates near large urban centres, such as the Love Canal area in New York near Niagara Falls. Many inland rivers and lakes deteriorated into cesspools of industrial waste and human sewage. Acid rain spread, unrecognized as an international problem. Farmers dumped chemical fertilizers and weed killers into the soil, where they eventually ended up in underground aquifers. Economic growth and development were the measures of all things, and the few Canadians preaching caution were often regarded as a lunatic fringe of troublemakers.

The boom of the post-war years encouraged the growth of American direct investment in Canada and the rise of the multinational corporation, which usually had headquarters in the United States and a branch-plant operation in Canada. By 1950 more than three-quarters of total foreign investment in the country was American, chiefly in mining, manufacturing, and petroleum. In 1959 foreign-owned companies controlled nearly 60 per cent of assets in Canadian mining, over 60 per cent of the oil and gas industry, and over 50 per cent of Canadian manufacturing. The extent of foreign ownership of all major Canadian industries in 1959 was 34 per cent, of which 26 per cent was owned by United States residents. American ownership was especially prevalent in the highly profitable consumer area, where production flourished on the backs of American technology and American promotion of goods and brand names. American advertising and cultural values created consumer demand on a continental basis, and Canadian subsidiaries fulfilled this demand for the Canadian segment of their market. Not until 1957, however, did American investment and the growth of multinationals become important public issues. As late as 1956, one of the leading textbooks in Canadian economic history referred to foreign investment as "one of the mainsprings of progress" without mentioning its less desirable aspects (Easterbrook and Aitken, 1956: 402). The foreign investment issue was brought to the public's attention by the Royal Commission on Canada's Economic Prospects, chaired by Walter Gordon. The report of the Commission, released after the Liberal government that had appointed it was defeated in 1957, observed that "No other nation as highly industrialized as Canada has such a large proportion of industry controlled by non-resident concerns" (*Royal Commission on Canada's Economic Prospects*, 1958: 384). The Commission's concern was not immediately shared by the public, however.

Part of the critique of American multinationalism was related to Canada's scientific research and development policy. Critics noted that Canada spent a far smaller proportion of its science dollar on the development side of research and development. They added that industry in Canada contributed a far smaller share of scientific activity than in any other highly industrialized nation. The reasons for these lags, many insisted, were to be found in Canada's ability as a branch-plant economy to import technology developed elsewhere. In 1959, for example, industry was responsible for only 39 per cent of scientific research in Canada, as opposed to 58 per cent in Britain and 78 per cent in the United States. By this time, the federal government's outlays in scientific activity were in excess of $200 million per year, while in 1959 Canadian industry spent only $96.7 million on research and development at home. Research money for the Avro Arrow was supplied not by A.V. Roe, but by the Canadian federal government. Moreover, 95 per cent of all Canadian patents between 1957 and 1961 involved foreign applicants, nearly 70 per cent of them American. Clearly, Canada spent large sums of public money on scientific research, but the nation was not getting much industrial advantage from the expenditures. Canadian scientists had co-operated with American counterparts to produce the IBM 101 electronic statistical machine in time for it to analyze the 1951 Canadian census data. But before long, the new technology became American, and Canadians were never in the front lines of the microchip revolution of later years. In 1962, expenditure on research and development as a proportion of sales averaged 0.7 per cent by all Canadian manufacturers, as opposed to 2 per cent by American manufacturers and even larger proportions in Germany and Japan.

An increased role for organized labour accompanied other economic trends of the affluent society. Union membership increased and unions were organized in a number of new industries. World War II had marked a major turning point for Canadian labour, which had fought any number of bitter strikes during the Depression in search of an unfettered right to bargain collectively with employers. It received precious little support from government in this effort. The percentage of union members in the total civilian labour force had actually declined slightly between 1929 and 1939. During the war, however, the federal government had decided to co-opt labour into the war effort. Both Ottawa and the provinces began the slow process of altering labour legislation to recognize and protect the rights to organization and collective bargaining. The key breakthrough came in 1944 when the federal government, by wartime Order-in-Council, introduced PCO 1003. This order introduced recently adopted American principles of compulsory recognition and collective bargaining, creating the machinery necessary to protect both management and labour in contested

cases. By 1946, 17.1 per cent of all workers and 27.9 per cent of non-agricultural workers belonged to unions.

With bargaining rights achieved, labour unions went on to hammer out working relationships with most of Canada's traditional industries. Improved working conditions and higher wages were the result. The process of coming to terms with employers was hardly a painless one. Throughout the 1950s there were never fewer than 159 strikes per year across Canada, involving between 49,000 and 112,000 workers annually. Important strikes that achieved national prominence included the Asbestos strike of 1949 in Quebec, the Eaton's strike of 1951, and the Inco strike of 1958 in Sudbury. A major breakthrough for public-sector unionism came at the very end of the 1950s when the postal employees organized and began demanding the right of collective bargaining. In 1956 the two largest Canadian umbrella organizations for labour—the Trades and Labor Congress of Canada and the Canadian Congress of Labour—merged as one consolidated body called the Canadian Labour Congress (CLC). This merger reduced jurisdictional disputes at the top of Canada's table of labour organization, although it did not deal with the question of the domination of so-called "international" unions by their American members.

The Cold War

By 1945, Canada was probably already too deeply enmeshed in its linkages with the United States ever to cast them aside. Great Britain, financially strapped, was not likely to provide much of a counterweight. Canadian involvement in the Cold War was almost inescapable. There were numerous signs in the last years of World War II that the Russians and the Americans were the emergent world superpowers, eager to carve up the world into respective spheres of influence. Countries like Canada were virtually excluded from the process of peacemaking with the defeated enemies, as well as from most of the significant diplomatic manoeuvring of the post-war period. The nation found itself unable to translate its wartime manpower and resource commitments into any post-war place in the decision-making corridors of power that would remake the world. Canada protested privately about being left out of the surrender agreement with Germany, being left out of the drafting of a unilateral statement ending the war, and being left out of the Italian surrender. The final straw may have been the Allied decision to admit France (a nation that had allowed itself to be occupied by the Nazis and had fought Germany with only an army in exile) to the ranks of the "Occupying Powers" of Berlin. As a result of the war, Canada did substantially increase its overseas diplomatic contacts, with 25 posts abroad in 1944 and 36 by 1947, but it hardly improved its international position. Towards the close of the war Canada tried to create some diplomatic distance from the Americans in their continual arm-wrestling with the Russians, but the notorious Gouzenko affair made it difficult for Ottawa to remain on sympathetic terms with the Russians.

Igor Gouzenko (1919–82) was an obscure cipher clerk in the Russian embassy in Ottawa. In September 1945 he brought material to the RCMP that demonstrated how the Russians had organized a spy ring in Canada during the war. Nowadays spying is taken for granted, but at the time Gouzenko's information and the subsequent arrests of Canadian citizens (including one member of Parliament) were absolutely shocking. Canada did not exchange ambassadors again with the Russians until after 1953. In public opinion polls in 1946, Canadians proved far more willing than people in other nations to believe that Russia sought to dominate the world. The Gouzenko incident would also send shock waves across the Western world, for loose ends from the files made it apparent that the Russians had suborned not only Canadians but their allies. Moreover, it became evident that the tight security connected with research on atomic energy carried on in Montreal had been breached. The Russians had received secret information that may have aided them in developing their own atomic bomb in 1949. With the two superpowers both possessing nuclear capability, the standoff that characterized the Cold War began in earnest. Unlike the British and French, the Canadian government declared its refusal to use nuclear power for military purposes.

Economic considerations impelled Canada in an inevitable direction as the international situation unfolded and the nation became America's docile jun-

ior partner. Prime Minister King was leery of a complete economic integration proposed by the Americans late in the war—and supported by many of his own civil servants—but Canada and the United States became closer trading partners than ever before. Moreover, when the American Congress approved the Marshall Plan early in 1948—by which the United States proposed to rebuild war-torn Europe with unrestricted gifts of money and goods—Canada was forced to do something. If European reconstruction was limited solely to American goods, Canadian trade would shrink to nothing. Canada needed market access into the American program, that is, permission for Europe to use American money to buy Canadian goods. The US readily agreed. King used North Atlantic security as a way out of continental free trade. A security treaty would not only deflect reciprocity but, as a multilateral arrangement, might provide a much-needed international counterbalance against American military domination. The Americans were not enthusiastic about a multilateral arrangement for North Atlantic security, but the Canadians pressed hard. Some Canadian diplomats even wanted non-Atlantic Commonwealth countries admitted, and Escott Reid, the deputy undersecretary of state for external affairs, sought a treaty that encompassed social and economic issues as well. The Americans ultimately accepted the North Atlantic Treaty's military and security provisions, particularly the centralization of command under what would inevitably be an American general. They quietly scuttled other aspects of the alliance.

The Search for Middle-Power Status

By the time NATO was established in 1949, the Cold War had extended beyond Europe into Asia, where a Communist government headed by Chou En-lai had taken over China. Communism made gains in other places like Indochina and Korea, which had been partitioned after the war. The United States always saw these Communist governments as mere extensions of international Communism rather than as movements of legitimate national liberation. In 1950 North Korea invaded American-supported South Korea. The Americans took

BACKGROUNDER

Canada and Cold War Espionage

Igor Gouzenko with a copy of his novel, The Fall of a Titan, *about life in Stalinist Russia, 15 October 1954. Gouzenko's novel won the Governor General's Award in 1954. Canadian authorities gave Gouzenko a new identity, but the former spy wore a hood over his face whenever he made a public appearance. CP LASERPHOTO.*

On 5 September 1945, a cipher clerk in the Russian embassy in Ottawa named Igor Gouzenko returned to his office and removed a collection of 109 documents that he had previously extracted from the files. Arranging the documents around his body, he managed to leave the embassy without detection. He took the documents to the night editor at the *Ottawa Journal*, who suggested that he take them to the RCMP. Gouzenko had great difficulty in finding anyone to take him seriously. At one point he was told, "Nobody wants to hear anything but nice things about Stalin these days." Eventually he found an audience in the RCMP for his story that a Soviet spy ring was operating inside Canada, and five Canadians were named as Russian agents, although none of them had access to highly sensitive material. Gouzenko's disclosures are often taken as the beginning of the so-called "Cold War," a period in which a good many individuals were accused of serving as Russian agents; some of them actually were. Part of the problem was that during the Depression years, Communism had been popular, especially with university students, because it was virtually alone in opposing fascism and in offering a concrete program for dealing with the economic hard times. Then, after the war began, Stalin's Russia became an important ally of the Western alliance. Assistance to Russia for the duration of the war was a patriotic duty. After the war, the Gouzenko affair and the disclosures of the ex-Communist Elizabeth Bentley in the United States, as well as the emergence of the Soviet Union as a military threat and the later revelations that the British intelligence services had been seriously compromised by internal Soviet agents, led to frantic efforts to root out Communists at home. Most of those exposed were so-called "fellow travellers" who were attracted by the Communist ideology but were not Russian agents. Nonetheless, sufficient evidence existed of the passing to the Russians of military secrets, especially involving nuclear weapons, to fuel continual American paranoia.

Continued...

One Canadian later caught up in the web of suspicion was the diplomat E. Herbert Norman (1909–57). Norman had grown up in Japan, the son of Methodist missionaries, before joining the Canadian Foreign Service in 1939. During his university years he had flirted with Communism, and as a Canadian official during the occupation of Japan he had shown some sympathy for the Japanese Communist Party. He was exonerated after an investigation in 1950. Although Norman was a close friend of Lester Pearson, the American government never trusted him, especially after his name came up in testimony before the US Senate Subcommittee on Internal Security in 1957. Norman committed suicide in Cairo in April 1957 while serving as Canadian ambassador to Egypt. Many contemporaries viewed Norman as a victim of witch-hunting. Two books about his career published in 1986 came to diametrically opposed conclusions about his involvement with Communism. The last gasp of Cold War spies came to Canada in 1965, when a former East German prostitute/call girl and possible Soviet agent named Gerda Munsinger was associated by the media in a sex scandal involving several members of the government of John Diefenbaker.

advantage of a temporary Soviet boycott of the Security Council of the United Nations to invoke universal collective security in regard to the Korean situation. The Canadian government was in a quandary. It had no peacetime military of its own to send, nor was it enthusiastic about participating in collective security under the American aegis.

The Korean War increased the pressure for a military buildup. By 1953 the defence budget stood at nearly $2 billion, up tenfold since 1947. Public opinion in the 1950s consistently supported rearmament. The policy-makers at the Department of External Affairs did their best to give Canada an autonomous international presence, developing a Canadian reputation for sending small numbers of soldiers to trouble spots to supervise international agencies and monitor local conditions. Peacekeeping operations were carried out in Indochina and the Middle East, especially Cyprus. The nation's standing reached its high point in 1957 when Lester B. Pearson won the Nobel Peace Prize for his efforts to end the 1956 hostilities in Suez. Pearson, with American support, found a way for Britain and France to back out of an impossible situation created by their ill-conceived invasion of Egypt to protect the Suez Canal. Canada had earned its place among the "middle powers," a characterization that became popular with Canada's international relations specialists at the same time as it flattered the nation's pretensions. But the world changed rapidly after Suez, and middle-power status altered with events.

The Retreat from Internationalism

Part of the gradual change in Canada's place in the world was a result of technology. When, in 1953, the USSR added a hydrogen bomb to its nuclear arsenal, Canadians became even more conscious that their nation sat uneasily between the two nuclear giants. Everyone's attention turned to air defence. Canada expanded the RCAF and began development of the famed CF-105 (the Avro Arrow). The United States pushed for increased electronic surveillance in the Arctic. In 1955 Canada agreed to allow the Americans to construct at their own expense a series of northern radar posts called the Distant Early Warning (or DEW) Line. The Americans also pressed for an integrated bilateral air defence system, the North American Air Defense Command (NORAD), which was agreed to by the Diefenbaker government soon after it took office in 1957. The Canadian government made a half-hearted attempt to educate its citizens on the dangers of nuclear war, but they were so horrible and unthinkable that most Canadians resolutely refused to pay much attention.

The Baby Boom and the Suburban Society

Canadians emerged from World War II with 15 years of disruption behind them. Normal expectations for family life had been interrupted in various ways. During the Depression, marriage and birth rates had decreased and the average age at marriage had risen. Between 1939 and 1952 the marriage rate jumped substantially, especially among the young. More family units were formed each year, while the birth rate and the annual immigration intake rose. Birth rates climbed because women who had married early tended to begin bearing children early as well—and to continue expanding their families while remaining at home. The result was a substantial increase in the total numbers of children in Canada between 1941 and 1961—the baby boom—a demographic phenomenon that occurred in the United States during the same period. As these children arrived at each stage of life in waves, their sheer numbers put heavy pressure on the facilities that had to accommodate them. The phenomenon hit primary education in the 1940s and then rolled progressively through the Canadian educational system and other aspects of society as the baby boomers got older. Secondary schools were affected in the 1950s, universities in the 1960s, employment in the later 1960s, and so on.

We do not entirely understand why this demographic blip occurred. Pent-up deferral of expectations during the Depression before the early 1940s is part of the answer, as is the absence of so many young men during the war. The fulfillment of deferred expectations, however, does not explain why an entire nation should suddenly decide to marry earlier and raise larger families. A better explanation is probably to be found in the fantasy package of a better life for Canadians, fuelled by post-war affluence. The urge affected Quebecers as well as anglophone Canadians. Pierre Vallières described his father's post-war dream: "We'll be at peace. The children will have all the room they need to play. We'll be masters in our own house. There will be no more stairs to go up and down. . . . Pierre won't hang around the alleys and sheds any more. . . . The owner was prepared to stretch the payments out over many years. . . . Life would become easier. . . . He would enlarge the house. A few years from now, Madeline and the 'little ones' would have peace and comfort" (Vallières, 1971: 98). In 1945 the Vallières family moved to Longueuil-Annexe, one of the "mushroom cities" that grew up around Montreal.

What Canadians thought they wanted—and what the media told them was desirable—was a detached bungalow, preferably in a nice suburban neighbourhood, surrounded by green grass and inhabited by a traditional nuclear family. This fantasy included a wife who was a homemaker and a houseful of perfect children. "Suburbia" was always less a geographical reality than a mental and emotional space. It is a convenient term that can be used to describe the idealized social world of the post-war period. After the war, a popular domestication of values extended into the ranks of the lower-middle and traditional working classes. Post-war suburbia was not only highly traditional in its gender roles but tended to be retrogressive in its emphasis on the role of the female as child-bearer and nurturer. In its consumer orientation, as well as in its child-centredness, it was a powerful force.

Houses became homes, easily the most expensive physical object possessed by their owners. So much time and emotional energy could be devoted to the edifice that it often seemed to possess its owners. The house focused the life of the nuclear family, and at the same time permitted individual members to have their own private spaces. Ideally, each child had a bedroom, for example, and a large recreation room in the basement provided a place for the children to play and gather. The kitchen was often too small for gathering, and the living room, increasingly after 1950, was the home of the television set. Advertising and articles in the media exalted the roles of housewife and mother as the epicentre of this world. Radio, television, and the record player all made it possible for popular culture to be consumed without ever leaving the house.

Central to any post-war middle-class household were its children, around whose upbringing the parents' lives increasingly revolved. The baby-boom generation grew up in a child-centred atmosphere in both home and school. Older standards of discipline and toughness in the parent–child relationship were replaced by permissiveness. New child-rearing attitudes found their popular expression in *The Pocket Book of Baby and Child Care* by the American pediatrician Benjamin Spock, which outsold the Bible in Canada after the war. Spock replaced more austere Canadian manuals. The book was one of the earliest mass-market paperbacks, sold over the counter at drugstores and supermarkets for less than 50 cents.

The North Atlantic Treaty, 1949

The North Atlantic Treaty was signed at Washington on 4 April 1949. The preamble and the first five articles are reprinted below.

The Parties to this Treaty reaffirm their faith in the purposes and principles of the Charter of the United Nations and their desire to live in peace with all peoples and all governments.

They are determined to safeguard the freedom, common heritage and civilization of their peoples, founded on the principles of democracy, individual liberty and the rule of law.

They work to promote stability and well-being in the North Atlantic area.

They are resolved to unite their efforts for collective defense and for the preservation of peace and security.

They therefore agree to this North Atlantic Treaty:

ARTICLE 1. The Parties undertake, as set forth in the Charter of the United Nations, to settle any international disputes in which they may be involved by peaceful means in such a manner that international peace and security, and justice, are not endangered, and to refrain in their international relations from the threat or use of force in any manner inconsistent with the purposes of the United Nations.

ARTICLE 2. The Parties will contribute toward the further development of peaceful and friendly international relations by strengthening their free institutions, by bringing about a better understanding of the principles upon which these institutions are founded, and by promoting conditions of stability and well-being. They will seek to eliminate conflict in their international economic policies and will encourage economic collaboration between any or all of them.

ARTICLE 3. In order more effectively to achieve the objectives of this Treaty, the Parties, separately and jointly, by means of continuous and effective self-help and mutual aid, will maintain and develop their individual and collective capacity to resist armed attack.

ARTICLE 4. The Parties will consult together whenever, in the opinion of any of them, the territorial integrity, political independence or security of any of the Parties is threatened.

ARTICLE 5. The Parties agree that an armed attack against one or more of them in Europe or North America shall be considered an attack against them all; and consequently they agree that, if such an armed attack occurs, each of them, in exercise of the right of individual or collective self-defense recognized by Article 51 of the Charter of the United Nations, will assist the Party or Parties so attacked by taking forthwith, individually and in concert with the other Parties, such action as it deems necessary, including the use of armed force, to restore and maintain the security of the North Atlantic area.

Any such armed attack and all measures taken as a result thereof shall immediately be reported to the Security Council. Such measures shall be terminated when the Security Council has taken the measures necessary to restore and maintain international peace and security.

Source: National Defence Headquarters, Department of National Defence, *The North Atlantic Treaty* (Ottawa: Queen's Printer, 1995) [includes a facsimile of the original treaty signed at Washington]. Reprinted by permission of the publisher.

In its pages the reader could find continual reassurance. Use your common sense, said Spock; almost anything reasonable is okay. "Trust Yourself" was his first injunc-

tion. The good doctor came down hard against the use of coercion of any sort. In toilet training, for example, he insisted that "Practically all those children who regu-

Say "We Want Margarine"

The following article appeared in the April 1948 issue *Chatelaine*, the leading Canadian magazine for women at the time. Margarine was banned in Canada from 1886 to 1948, although from 1917 to 1923 the ban was lifted because of dairy shortages. During the ban margarine was smuggled to Canada from Newfoundland. After this prohibition was ended in 1948, the sale of coloured or uncoloured margarine remained an issue in many provinces for many years. The magazine had a Consumer Council that it polled on critical issues.

From coast to coast, in the cities and in the country four fifths of Canadian housewives say, "We want margarine." The attitude of many was summed up by one woman who said, "We have a prairie family near us with six young children who never see butter because of its price. Everyone should be able to have it as a substitute, because of its nutritional value."

A very high percentage of the rural women—more than three-fifths—many of them wives of dairy farmers selling cream in the dairy market were fair-minded enough to say that large families in moderate circumstances could not afford butter at its present prices and should therefore have the opportunity of buying a cheaper substitute.

A few Councillors who were in favor of margarine "on principle" were not sure whether they would use it because they had never tasted it. One Councillor asked, "What is margarine—do you use it in your tea?"

Margarine went under a ban in Canada 25 years ago. It has been hushed so much that a whole generation has grown up without ever having seen it. On the other hand, many housewives know that margarine is a good nourishing, cheap food and that Canada is the only country in the world in which it is banned. As for price, margarine sells in the United States today as low as .39¢ a pound, compared to butter which has gone as high as $1 a pound.

The Canadian Medical Journal last August stated quite bluntly that "from economic and nutritional aspects, good margarine is superior to butter."

Both margarine and butter contain 80% fat. Margarine is made from vegetable oils—cotton-seed, soybean, corn and peanut. These fats are usually churned with pure skim milk to give them the dairy taste. Units of vitamin A are added, bringing the product up to and frequently beyond, the vitamin standard for butter.

In its natural form, margarine has a yellowish color not unlike butter. Manufacturers in the United States, however, are compelled by law to remove this natural color by bleaching, so that it will not be mistaken for butter, and to enclose with each pound a small envelope of yellow coloring matter for the housewife to knead into the margarine. . . .

Last year a bill favoring the lifting of the ban on margarine was defeated in the Senate. Two more bills will be brought up during the present session, one in the Senate and one in the House of Commons.

Source: Sylvia Fraser, ed., *Chatelaine: A Woman's Place: Seventy Years in the Lives of Canadian Women* (Toronto: KeyPorter Books, 1997) 121.

larly go on soiling after 2 are those whose mothers have made a big issue of it and those who have become frightened by painful movements." Spock explained that children passed through stages. Once parents recognized what stage of development their child had reached, they could understand otherwise incomprehensible behaviour and recognize that seemingly exceptional problems were really quite common.

The baby boom combined with the attitudes of the permissively raised Spock generation and the new affluence to produce a category of adolescence segmented from and sandwiched between childhood and adult society. More and more young people were encouraged to remain in school longer. Progressive-minded educators treated them as a distinct social phenomenon. The authors of *Crestwood Heights* (1956), a study of a wealthy Toronto suburb, found a central theme in the "difficulties experienced by the child in living up to the expectations of both parents and the school for 'responsibility' and 'independence'." They labelled the 16–19 age group as one of "Dependent Independence." The loss of community through urbanization and suburbanization provided a real challenge for social control. Kept out of the workforce, teenagers did not become full adults. Law and custom combined to prevent them from enjoying full adult privileges. These kids had considerable spending power. Encouraged to live at home, the youngsters were not often required to contribute their earnings (if any) to family maintenance. Instead, their parents gave them pocket money or allowances. Canadian teenagers rapidly became avid consumers, providing a market for fast food, clothing fads, acne medicine, cosmetics, and popular music. Melinda McCracken has explained that "to be a real teenager you had to drink Cokes, eat hamburgers [known as nips in Winnipeg because the local Salisbury House chain sold them as such], French fries [known in Winnipeg as chips, in the English fashion], go to the Dairy Queen, listen to the Top Forty and neck" (McCracken, 1975: 72).

Between 1946 and 1960 Canadian education, responding partly to the baby boom, partly to changing social expectations, transformed itself entirely. Canadians had long accepted the concept of universal education in the primary grades. In the 1940s and 1950s education for all was extended to secondary levels by raising the school-leaving age to 16. In 1945 there were 1,741,000 children in provincially controlled schools. By 1960–1 that figure had risen to 3,993,125. The expenditure per pupil in public schools nearly tripled between 1945 and 1958. Thousands of new schools had to be built to accommodate the increased student population. Teachers, who before 1946 had needed only a year or two of training in teachers' college, by the 1960s had to have a university

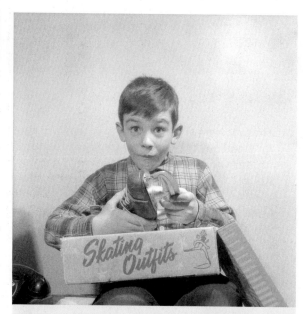

The baby-boom generation was child-centred, and Canadian youth rapidly became avid consumers. This photograph connects the new consumers with that Canadian passion, skating. The box holds what are probably a young man's first skates. Are there further details to be derived from this photo? Chris Lund/National Film Board of Canada. LAC, PA-111396.

degree. In 1956 the authors of *Crestwood Heights* observed that the flagship suburban community they had studied was, "literally, built around its schools." In "Crestwood Heights" (Toronto's Forest Hill), education was "aimed primarily at preparing pupils for a middle-class vocation in a highly-industrialized culture" (Seeley, Sim, and Loosley, 1972 [1956]: 224). Such was the goal of baby-boomer education all across Canada by the early 1960s.

Before the mid-1950s no one anticipated the arrival of a serious educational crisis, for in the decade after the war, classes in existing schools simply got larger while a few extra teachers were hired. But finally the problem of overcrowding became too obvious to ignore. Shortage of space was only partly a result of the baby boom. The new insistence on high school diplomas for everyone represented a profound social revolution and created a need for more room at the universities. Canadians saw more education as the key to dealing with modern industrial conditions. Curiously, however, Canada lagged badly behind other countries in terms of vocational and practical education, preferring instead to force the vast majority of its students into traditional academic endeavours. Much of the thinking that justified expanded education was imported from the United States, but these ideas increasingly were accepted by Canadian parents and taxpayers—particularly after 1957, when the Russians put Sputnik into orbit and inadvertently gave rise to a concerted campaign for educational reform throughout North America.

Immigration

Canada ended World War II with neither an immigration nor a refugee policy sufficient for the situations in which it would soon find itself, particularly internationally. The Canadian government and the Canadian people were, by and large, exclusionist, racist, and not very humane in their attitudes towards immigration. Over the next few years, this position would change, however. Circumstances, as well as slowly changing values, would literally force Canada to accept millions of immigrants, including both displaced persons and refugees (the distinction between the two was never entirely clear in the eyes of the public). Whether the people came from now non-existent countries or had been uprooted or fled from states in which they no longer had homes, by 1962 the government would overhaul its immigration procedures to bring at least a formal end to racist immigration policy.

All of Canada's resources in late 1945 and early 1946 were devoted to transporting its troops home. Some of them had been in Britain since 1939. Partly as a result of the length of the stay abroad, almost 50,000 Canadian soldiers had found wives in Europe, mainly in the United Kingdom, although some soldiers had married women on the continent, especially in Holland. There were over 20,000 children from these marriages. Obviously these dependants would have to be allowed to accompany their soldier husbands and fathers back to Canada, and the Canadian Department of National Defence facilitated matters as expeditiously as possible, not only admitting these women and children without question, but also providing them with transport, documentation, and the transfer of money and possessions as well. The brides were informed there would be only a single one-way journey provided at government expense. Being uprooted was not an easy experience for many of these women, but they were for the most part welcomed enthusiastically in their new homes.

By the end of 1945, perhaps two million refugees and other displaced persons remained in allied territory, mostly in Germany but also in Austria and Italy. The majority had been housed in refugee camps. Few of these people had proper documentation, and more than a few had been Nazi soldiers and collaborators—even war criminals—who now posed as innocent victims. Establishing the legitimacy of each refugee was virtually impossible; therefore, Canadian officials did not want to accept immigrants from these camps. An investigation into immigration policy was conducted in May of 1946 by the Canadian Senate's Standing Committee on Immigration and Labour, which, to the surprise of immigration officials, supported such immigration. This report emphasized that "Canada, as a humane and Christian nation, should do her share toward the relief of refugees and displaced persons" (Standing Committee of the Canadian Senate on Immigration and Labour, 1946: 628). The Committee also criticized the government for its failure to produce a proper immigration policy.

The same month as the Senate hearings, the Canadian cabinet amended PC 695—the 1931 Order-in-Council still in effect—with PC 2071, permitting the admission of refugees with close relations in Canada. This was not intended to open Canada to a flood of immigrants. All existing immigration regulations were to be observed, and the definition of a "first-degree" relative was narrowly limited. Canadian immigration officials used the absence of inspection facilities as a reason for not processing first-degree relatives more rapidly. A Gallup poll in April of 1946 had indicated that two-thirds of Canadians opposed immigration from Europe. A subsequent poll in October of that year asked: If there were to be immigration, what nationalities would the respondent most like to keep out of Canada? The Japanese ranked first, the Jews second. Meanwhile, international pressure was building on Canada to help out with the refugee situation, and External Affairs became concerned that the United Nations might impose an arbitrary quota on Canada.

In the middle of the prairie outside Calgary, a billboard announces the new "engineered" suburb of Glendale Meadows in August 1958. What is noteworthy about this photograph is the location of the billboard in a huge vacant field that soon will be filled with the new development. Photo Rosetti's Studio. Glenbow Archives, NA-5093-558.

After months of debate in the Canadian press and in the cabinet, Prime Minister Mackenzie King read a formal statement on immigration policy to the House of Commons on 1 May 1947. King insisted that Canada wanted to encourage immigration, but also that Canada's "absorptive capacity" must be taken into account. He did not further define "absorptive capacity," which many Canadians chose to see as an economic measure. Others thought it a coded term for racism, an interpretation that gained force from King's spirited defence of the nation's right to pursue a discriminatory immigration policy that would not appreciably alter the makeup of the Canadian population, which, of course, was essentially of European descent. King further declared that although Canada's membership in international organizations did not oblige it to accept specific numbers of refugees and displaced persons (a barb directed towards External Affairs), "We have, nevertheless, a moral obligation to assist in meeting the problem, and this obligation we are prepared to recognize" (quoted in Knowles, 1997: 132). In the wake of King's statement, five teams of immigration officials visited camps in Austria and Germany in the summer of 1947 to select potential immigrants. A new system of screening was put into effect, and an expansion of the term "close relative" was introduced. Those selected were mainly under the labour selection category. They were granted visas and transported to a port of embarkation where they signed labour contracts. On arrival in Canada, each immigrant got money for railway tickets and meals. Most of the security concerns were over potential Communists rather than ex-Nazis.

Contributing to the new influx of displaced persons were fresh pressures on the Canadian government in 1947. First, the rampaging economic prosperity being supervised by C.D. Howe (Minister of Reconstruction and Supply) required more labour. "The speeding up of the immigration movement," he insisted, had to be "treated as a matter of high priority" (quoted in Margolian, 2000: 77). Second, the nature of the refugee lobby changed substantially. Symptomatic of this shift was the establishment in June 1947 of the Canadian Christian Council for Resettlement of Refugees (CCCRR). This organization was composed of various German immigrant aid groups and concentrated on helping refugees from Germany and Austria, especially the *Volksdeutsche*, those Germans who had lived outside Germany's borders. With the assistance of the CCCRR, more than 120,000 refugees ultimately were admitted to Canada, placing the nation behind only the United States, Australia, and Israel in the number of refugees it received in the post-war period.

The influx of displaced persons to Canada from 1948 to 1952 was distinguished by several contradictory features. One was the inability of the Canadian authorities totally to prevent Jews from joining the flow, however hard they tried. Canada put Jews low on the list of desired immigrants, partly for cultural reasons but also because of what the authorities thought prospective employers expected of new immigrants, chiefly robust health and considerable strength. Most post-war Jews, it was argued, could not have coped with a regimen of hard physical labour. What clearly was needed was an alternate program. Jewish activists insisted that war criminals like Martin Bormann (Hitler's private secretary) could enter Canada more easily than Jews and, indeed, the immigrants of these years may well have included as many as 1,500 war criminals and Nazi collaborators. Another feature of these years was the arrival of the first "boat people," as several thousand people from the Baltic area made their way independently to Canada aboard small and often unseaworthy vessels. They were usually greeted sympathetically and often allowed to remain by special Order-in-Council.

The hard-labour aspect of Canadian criteria for immigrants caused many problems for immigration officials. Early in 1948, for example, the Communists took over Czechoslovakia, forcing thousands to flee the country, including many of its civil servants. But such people were not eligible under existing immigration policy to enter Canada. One Canadian immigration official commented of the Czech diplomats clamouring for admission to Canada, "As an ex-member of the profession, I may perhaps be forgiven if I suggest that the average diplomat is not likely to be very much use at anything else—particularly at the kind of initial jobs that are commonly available for immigrants" (quoted in Avery, 1995: 159). Highly trained professionals generally proved a major problem for nations receiving immigrants after the war; Canada was not exceptional in this regard. Local professional organizations and licensing authorities insisted on protecting the public from the unqualified, while the sorts of credentials offered by a displaced person from a European nation usually made little sense or seemed incomplete. Most receiving nations, including Canada, insisted that the professionals, especially the doctors, either take jobs where the receiving country's own nationals would not go—such as to the north, in Canada—or else requalify for their profession. Canada was not only unsympathetic to professionals but also to intellectuals and artists, such as those from Czechoslovakia.

By 1949 Canada was finally brought to the realization that its concentration on human brawn was biting off its nose to spite its face. A new sponsorship program allowed up to 500 highly trained displaced persons into Canada, although it emphasized that most admitted could not immediately practise their skills. On the other hand, some countries, particularly the United States, had always been quite willing to accept skilled enemy aliens—even those openly Nazi—if they were scientists working in such areas as weapons research. Few scientists, no more than 50, were admitted to Canada before 1950. In a well-received book published in 1951, economist Mabel Timlin actually studied the question of "absorptive capacity," concluding that Canada was capable of accepting larger numbers of immigrants from an economic standpoint and that such acceptance, by increasing the population, "should mean a higher physical product per capita and hence higher real incomes for Canadian citizens" (Timlin, 1951: 122).

The displaced persons who came to Canada in the years immediately after the war shared much in common with one another. Most had suffered years of emotional turmoil, both in Europe and then in Canada. The

New arrivals are examined in Immigration Examination Hall at Pier 21 in Halifax, Nova Scotia. Judging by their dress, these immigrants are arriving from Europe. The papers on the officer's desk suggest the amount of documentation required to enter Canada. By the expressions on their faces, these candidates are obviously anxious. Chris Lund/National Film Board of Canada. Photothèque collection, LAC, PA-111579.

sorts of jobs available to most immigrants, at the bottom of the occupational chain, tended to be in remote districts and subject to seasonal unemployment. The Canadian government provided little counselling or other assistance for the newcomers, leaving voluntary organizations to fill the gap as best they could. On the other hand, the post-war newcomers had the great psychological advantage of knowing that they could never return to a former life—thus providing a sense of finality and permanence to their new situation—and that almost any material conditions were better than those they had suffered in the refugee camps.

In June 1950, by Order-in-Council PC 2856, Canada expanded admissible categories of European immigrants to include any healthy individual of good character with needed skills and an ability to integrate. That same year saw the Department of Citizenship and Immigration established to replace a previous administrative structure in which immigration had been a branch of the Department of Mines and Resources. Canada now had an immigration policy of sorts, and a separate agency to administer it. In 1951 Canadian immigration policy reached out tentatively beyond Europe. The Canadian government agreed with the governments of India, Pakistan, and Ceylon to admit a few additional newcomers from each of these nations beyond the old quotas on Asians.

As many recognized by 1952, Canada desperately needed to overhaul and rethink its immigration policy. That goal was hardly achieved in the new Immigration Act of that year, produced after only four days of hearings by a House of Commons subcommittee that heard testimony mainly from the large transportation companies. Most of the other players involved in immigration, such as the trade unions and the ethnic organizations, were not heard at all. As a result the 1952 Act dealt mainly with administrative procedures rather than new initiatives. It expanded the discretionary powers of the cabinet and the Immigration Department to select immigrants, even on a case-by-case basis, but did not much alter the criteria used in the selection. Many found the Act concerned mainly with keeping people out. These included peculiar customs, unsuitability for Canadian conditions, and probable inability to become readily assimilated into full Canadian citizenship. The noisiest complaints about the 1952 Act came from the ethnic communities, who organized to lobby for their own particular agendas. The 1952 Act had little to say about refugees and nothing to say about the United Nations Refugee Convention of 1951, which provided a legal definition of a refugee as someone:

> owing to well-founded fear of being persecuted for reasons of race, religion, nationality, membership of a particular social group or political opinion, is outside the country of his nationality and is unable or, owing to such fear, is unwilling to avail himself of the protection of that country; or who, not having a nationality and being outside the country of his former habitual residence as a result of such events, is unable or, owing to such fear, is unwilling to return to it.

Critics saw several reasons for the silence on refugees. One was the common belief that refugees were looking for temporary asylum rather than permanent resettlement. Another was the concern that not all refugees were necessarily responsible citizens driven out of their countries for the wrong reasons. Finally, there was the racial factor. Canada took some characteristic steps in 1956 when it decided as a humanitarian gesture to admit some of the 900,000 refugees living in camps in the Middle East. A Canadian immigration team visited camps in Jordan and Lebanon, selecting 98 potential citizens from the 575 candidates presented to them by international refugee organizations. Eventually, 39 heads of families, primarily of Palestinian origin, were admitted to Canada in 1956. The tokenism manifest here is evident when the selection process is compared with that employed during and after the Hungarian uprising of November 1956.

Canadians had seen the events in Hungary unfold on their television screens, with young student "freedom fighters" armed with nothing but stones facing Soviet tanks in the streets. Occurring as it did in the midst of the Cold War, the plight of the more than 200,000 refugees who fled to Austria quickly gained public sympathy. Immigration Minister Jack Pickersgill moved quickly, and before the end of November he announced the government's plan to provide free passage to Canada for every refugee who met Canadian admissions standards. By the spring of 1957, Canada had brought nearly 20,000 Hungarians to North America on board more than 200 chartered airplane flights, and by the end of the year another 10,000 Hungarians had arrived in Canada. These refugees were mainly young male students with urban backgrounds; many were Jewish. The new arrivals were, of course, fervently anti-Communist, which simultaneously made them popular with Cold Warriors—the House of Commons welcomed them enthusiastically almost to a person—and to some extent unpopular with some of the older generation of Hungarians in Canada, whose politics leaned further left. The enthusiasm of their welcome may have led some of the newcomers to assume that life in Canada would be easier than it turned out to be, particularly as many suffered from severe trauma because of their experiences.

Not all the immigrants who came to Canada in the years after World War II remained in the country. One student of that immigration calculated that about 23 per cent of all post-war immigrants had left the country by 1961, and further estimated "that Canada succeeded in retaining approximately 60 per cent of the immigrants who entered the country from the United States, about 70 per cent of those from Britain, and 80 per cent of those from other countries" (Richmond, 1967: 228). For most post-war European immigrants to Canada, their commitment to their new nation was fairly strong. In many cases, immigrants had few family members and sometimes no country to which to return. In other cases, a return to a much less prosperous lifestyle at home was possible but hardly desirable. For the British, the years immediately after the war were

In 1957, nearly 20,000 Hungarian emigrants received free passage to Canada following the Hungarian uprising in 1956. Photo by Keystone/Getty Images.

ones of deprivation, but economic conditions gradually returned to normal in the United Kingdom, and social conditions under the "welfare state" may even have improved, particularly for the working classes. In any case, upward of 100,000 British immigrants to Canada returned to their homeland during the 1950s. Most had been reasonably successful economically but had not substantially improved their social or occupational standing. Those who had married (and/or had children) in Canada were far more likely to remain, and single people, especially females, were far more likely to return home. The presence of close relatives in Canada was also important in the decision to remain.

In 1958 Prime Minister John Diefenbaker appointed a woman as Minister of Immigration. Ellen Fairclough (1905–2004) was a Hamilton businesswoman and was the first female appointed to a federal cabinet post. Immigration was not expected by Diefenbaker to be a heavy responsibility, and Fairclough was given Indian Affairs as well. But a number of general problems related

to immigration had surfaced by the later 1950s. Three were of critical importance. First and foremost were the ongoing difficulties with the sponsorship program, by which those already in the country could sponsor close relatives as immigrants. Second, there was the need for an expanded and liberalized selection policy, particularly in terms of attracting non-Europeans. Third, there was a need for administrative reform.

Fairclough first tackled the sponsorship program. With the virtual end of the European refugee influx in the early 1950s (except for the Hungarians), the basic way in which immigrants got to Canada was through being sponsored by close relatives already in the country. The sponsorship system, begun in 1946, had some advantages, as it authorized chain migration (by which one immigrant sponsored another) and provided a means of integrating the newcomers quickly into the Canadian community, as well as of preventing them from becoming public charges. The national group that took greatest advantage of sponsorship was the Italians. More than 240,000 Italian immigrants arrived in Canada between 1946 and 1961, over 90 per cent of them sponsored by relatives, by far the heaviest proportion of sponsored arrivals among any immigrant group. Critics complained that many of these newcomers would not have qualified for admission had they not been sponsored.

Most family-sponsored Italians were either dependants (women, children, the elderly) not likely to enter the Canadian labour force, or unskilled males able to work only as labourers on heavy construction sites and thus likely to flood the unskilled job market. More than one-half (60 per cent) of these newcomers were from southern Italy, with the regions of Abruzzi, Molise, and Calabria providing the vast bulk of the immigrants. Most sponsors were male, and especially before 1956, males predominated in the immigration. But the chains gradually expanded, and by the later 1950s whole families and entire villages were coming to Canada. By the end of the decade, Immigration Department studies indicated that fewer than 10 per cent of these new arrivals would have been admitted to Canada under other circumstances. Because of the volume of Italian immigration, the Italian agents for immigrants to Canada committed fraudulent practices, chiefly the misrepresentation of facts on immigration applications. The Immigration Department began a deliberate bureaucratic slowdown of Italian immigration, as well as introducing an informal quota of 25,000 immigrants per year. The result was a huge backlog of cases, well in excess of 50,000.

Fairclough managed to get cabinet approval for an Order-in-Council in 1959 (PC 59/310) that limited the entry of non-dependant relatives into Canada. This limitation immediately affected the Italian flow but also the flow from other Mediterranean countries—such as Portugal and Greece—that featured large extended families and chain migration. The ethnic communities of these nations raised a wave of protest, claiming the new policy discriminated against them. "Fairclough tried to defend her policy by pointing out that the sponsorship system was itself discriminatory since 'well qualified Italians who wished to migrate to this country had little or no chance of having their applications considered unless they were in the sponsored categories'" (Avery, 1995: 176). She insisted that over the long

term the limitation on sponsorship would produce a more diversified immigration. But she was forced to back down, stating that she was asking the cabinet to withdraw the Order-in-Council in favour of new regulations to be introduced later. This initiative failed partly because the issues were not clearly understood and partly because the government had not taken sufficient account of the vociferousness of the ethnic community; when push came to shove, the government did not want to alienate ethnic voters.

Post-war immigration greatly changed the face of Canada, especially in Ontario. Most of the new immigrants settled in the larger cities of the province, or in urban concentrations in other provinces. The Canadian city became honeycombed with ethnic neighbourhoods, featuring churches, markets, bakeries, restaurants, and clubs to cater to particular local tastes.

Aboriginal People

As in earlier periods, one group that did not fully benefit from affluence and growth was the Aboriginal population. Improvements in First Nations medical care began in 1945 when responsibility for it was transferred from Indian Affairs to the Department of National Health and Welfare. This shift helped close gaps but did not eliminate them, chiefly because improved health care was not a panacea; it treated only the symptoms, not the causes of First Nations problems. At this time, infant mortality rates among Native peoples were greatly reduced for the first 28 days of life, but these rates continued to run four to five times the national average for the remainder of infants' first year. A change in major causes of death from infectious to chronic diseases occurred, but overall Indian and Inuit mortality rates still ran at more than twice the national average, and the incidence of death from accidental causes and suicide increased. Accidental and violent death was third on the list of killers for all Canadians, but first for First Nations—and this although automobile accidents were not common in most Native communities.

Alcohol was probably the major health hazard, less from long-term effects than from accidents and violence, neither of which could be dealt with effectively by

The Honourable Ellen Fairclough. Photo by FPG/Archive Photos/Getty Images.

improvements in medical service. Native people drank for the same reasons that other socio-culturally dislocated and economically disadvantaged people around the world did: out of frustration and a desire to escape. The First Nations were slow to organize to improve their conditions. A number of Saskatchewan groups merged into the Federation of Saskatchewan Indians at the end of the 1950s, however, and in 1961 the National Indian Council was formed "to promote unity among Indian people, the betterment of people of Indian ancestry in Canada, and to create a better understanding of Indian and non-Indian relationships" (quoted in Patterson, 1972: 177).

The Growth of the State

Government at all levels—federal, provincial, and municipal—grew extremely rapidly after the war. For the Dominion government, the extension of its power and authority represented a continuation of wartime momentum. For provincial governments, extensions of power were necessary to counter federal incursions in areas traditionally reserved for the provinces. All levels of government found the Canadian public responsive

Doctors and nurses of Indian and Northern Health Services check the health of Aboriginal people at a clinic at a Hudson's Bay Company post, 1945. Only at the close of the war did the Canadian government begin to show concern about the serious discrepancies between Aboriginal health and that of most Canadians. LAC, 1983-120 NPC.

to the introduction of new social services, even if it was piecemeal. The emergence of a much more powerful and costly public sector was fuelled partly by increased social programs, partly by the growth of a Canadian public enterprise system after the war.

While the Canadian public enterprise system went back to the nineteenth century, the development of Crown corporations greatly accelerated during and especially after World War II. Both federal and provincial governments created Crown corporations, publicly owned and operated. They modelled management structures on private enterprise and usually administered these corporations on a hands-off basis. Many Crown corporations came into existence to provide important services that could not be profitably offered by private enterprise. There was a tendency for public enterprise, almost by definition, to risk unprofitability. The CCF government of Saskatchewan created many Crown corporations from the time of its election in 1944. One of the largest public enterprises of the 1950s, the St Lawrence Seaway, was a Crown corporation. For many rural Canadians the extension of electricity into all but the most remote corners of the country was a great development of the post-war period. Many provinces consolidated electric utilities in Crown corporations after the war to extend services. The federal government had hoped to expand Canada's social services after the war, at least partly to justify continuing control of the major tax fields it had acquired under wartime emergency conditions. At the Dominion–Provincial Conference on Reconstruction, which began on 6 August 1945 (the day the first atomic bomb was dropped on Japan), Ottawa discovered that not all the provinces were willing to withdraw permanently from the fields of personal and corporate income tax. Quebec and Ontario, particularly, were equally unenthusiastic about surrendering their constitutional rights to social services. The provincial rebuff to Ottawa in 1945 did not mean that the Dominion gave up on social security measures. Both funding and constitutional haggling, however, would be continuing problems.

While we often talk about the Canadian welfare state, there is little evidence that many people in Canada, much less in the federal government, had any notion of a truly comprehensive and integrated national

social security system that would include full employment, housing, and education as social rights of all Canadians. Social protection in Canada would instead grow a step at a time through the activities of all levels of government. Sometimes new programs responded to overt public demand, sometimes they met obvious public need. Frequently job creation was the immediate rationale for a social program. Often a particular program of social protection was intended to provide a platform on which a government or political party could campaign. Political proponents of such programs hoped that the opposition would demur, thus providing a convenient election issue. Oppositions frequently failed to take the bait, accepting the programs and avoiding electoral battles. A patchwork of social programs thus emerged in fits and starts.

Canada ended the war with a limited federal pension program, a universal family allowance scheme, and housing legislation designed chiefly to provide employment. In 1945 Ottawa had also proposed to the provinces a national universal pension scheme for Canadians over 70 (with a means test provincially administered for those 65 to 69), a national public assistance scheme for the unemployed, and a health insurance scheme to be shared by the provinces and the federal government. The almost inevitable failure of the Dominion–Provincial Conference on Reconstruction to achieve these objectives meant that federal progress on social protection moved ahead extremely slowly. Apart from the creation of the Central Mortgage and Housing Corporation to assist in providing low-cost mortgage loans to Canadian families and a limited home-building program (10,000 houses per year), little happened on the housing front in the 15 years after 1945. On the health-care front, the government in 1948 established a fund for health research and hospital construction, but did little else on health until 1957 when it passed the Hospital Insurance and Diagnostic Services Act. This legislation allowed the federal government to provide 50 per cent of the cost of provincial hospital insurance plans. A new Old Age Security Act of 1951 provided a $40-per-month pension to all Canadians over the age of 70, but still insisted on a means test for those between 65 and 69. In 1956 a limited federal Unemployment Assistance Act with a means test passed

Parliament. Education remained almost entirely a provincial matter before 1960.

In 1945, the last year of the war, federal expenditure was just over $5 billion, with another $451 million spent by the provinces and $250 million by municipalities. In 1960 the Dominion still spent $5 billion, although far less on the military, but provincial governments now spent $2.5 billion and municipalities another $1.7 billion. Much of the increase went to social services. The result was a vast expansion in the numbers of government employees. In 1945, the last year of the war, the Dominion had 30,240 permanent civil servants and 85,668 temporary ones. At the beginning of 1961, it employed 337,416 Canadians, most of them "permanent" and many of them female. Both provincial and municipal employment grew even faster. The provinces employed 50,000 in 1946 and 257,000 in 1966, while the municipalities increased from 56,000 in 1946 to 224,000 two decades later. By 1960 there was a sense (at least on the federal level) that matters could get out of hand. The Diefenbaker government in that year created the Royal Commission on Government Organization to improve efficiency and economy. It was chaired by J. Grant Glassco (1905–68).

The Shape of Politics

At the federal level there were two major parties, the Liberals and the Progressive Conservatives. In this period there were other federal parties as well, chiefly the CCF and Social Credit. The nature of the Canadian electoral system—particularly the "first past the post" method of determining victorious candidates in single-member constituencies—combined with the continued presence of a multiplicity of parties to reduce to inconsequence the relationship between the popular vote and the number of seats in the House of Commons. True political mandates were difficult to find in such electoral results. The Liberals never won more than 50 per cent of the popular vote in any election in the period 1945–60, although they came close in 1949 and 1954. Only the Diefenbaker government of 1958 was elected by more than half of actual votes cast. The correlation between popular vote and number of seats could be quite low for both major

and minor parties. The system tended to translate any edge in the popular vote for a major party into considerably larger numbers of seats and to dissipate votes for other parties. Third parties were much better off if their support was concentrated in a few ridings (as was true for Social Credit) and not spread widely across the country (as was the case for the CCF). In 1953, for example, the Liberals had 48.8 per cent of the popular vote to 31 per cent for the PCs, 11.3 per cent for the CCF, and 5.4 per cent for the Social Credit Party. These percentages translated into 171 Liberal seats, 51 PC, 23 CCF, and 15 Social Credit.

The Liberals had a number of advantages in the pursuit of continued federal power, of which two were absolutely critical. Above all they had the ongoing support of Quebec, which elected one of the largest blocks of seats in the House of Commons. Support from francophone Quebec had come to the Liberals in the 1890s following the ascension of Laurier to the Liberal leadership and the recent memory of the execution of Louis Riel, was solidified during the Conscription Crisis of the Great War, and was further confirmed by Mackenzie King's management of that same issue during World War II. The Liberals did not lose a federal election in Quebec between 1896 and 1958, usually winning more than three-quarters of the available seats. To triumph nationally without Quebec's support, an opposition party needed to win the vast majority of seats in the remainder of the country, including Ontario (in which the two major parties were always fairly evenly matched). The Tories did win anglophone Canada in 1957. Such a victory could produce only a minority government, however. The Diefenbaker sweep of 1958 was the exception that proved the rule. In other elections the Liberals were able to persuade Quebec's francophone voters that the competing parties were unsympathetic to French Canada.

The apparent Liberal stranglehold on Quebec had its impact on the other parties, particularly in terms of choice of leaders and electoral strategies. During this period, neither the Progressive Conservatives nor the CCF ever seriously considered selecting a leader from Quebec—not even a unilingual English-speaker, let alone a French Canadian. Nor did the other parties make much of an effort to campaign in French

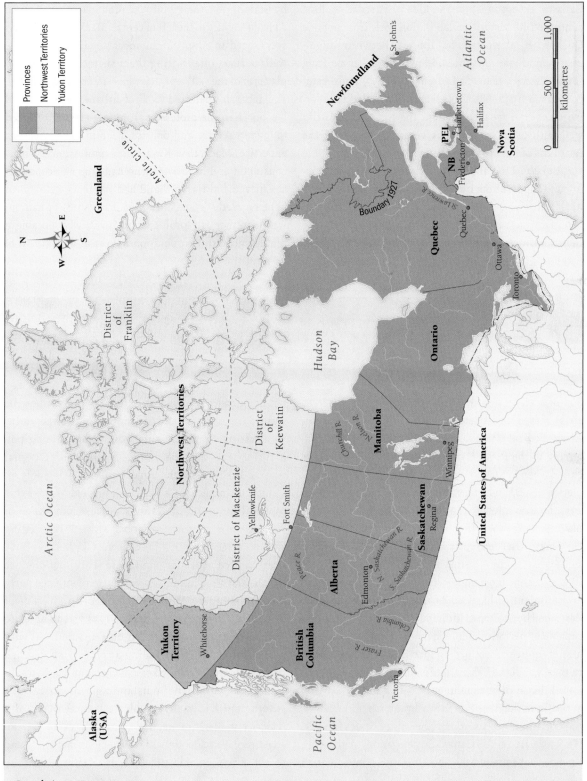

Canada in 1949.

Canada, except in 1958. The Liberal Party, therefore, continued its historic collaboration with francophone Quebec. It alternated its leaders between anglophones and francophones, following Mackenzie King (1919–48) with Louis St Laurent (1948–57) and Lester B. Pearson (1958–68). This association tended to polarize Canadian federal politics. The Liberals also did well with other francophone voters, particularly the Acadians of New Brunswick.

But the Liberal political advantage was not confined to support from francophones. While national political parties needed to appeal to a broad spectrum of voters across the nation in order to gain power, only the Liberals consistently succeeded in this appeal, chiefly by staking out their political ground outside French Canada slightly to the left of centre. Mackenzie King had specialized in adopting the most popular goals of the welfare state, often lifting them shamelessly from the platform of the CCF, a practice his successors continued. The Liberals preferred to find urbane, well-educated leaders from the professional middle classes, oriented to federal service and politics. Each man had his own expertise. Mackenzie King was a professional labour consultant and negotiator who had studied economics at Chicago and Harvard and had written a well-known book entitled *Industry and Humanity* (1918). St Laurent was a former law professor at Laval, who became a highly successful corporation lawyer and president of

Biography

Lester Bowles (Mike) Pearson

Son of a Methodist clergyman, Lester Pearson (1897–1972) served as a stretcher bearer with the Canadian Army Medical Corps during World War I before transferring to the Royal Flying Corps. His military career ended when he was hit by a London bus. Following completion of a BA in history at the University of Toronto in 1919, he won a fellowship at the University of Oxford, playing hockey for Britain in the 1920 Winter Olympics. He remained a keen sports fan throughout his life. After some years teaching history at the University of Toronto, he became the most important of O.D. Skelton's "young men of talent" at External Affairs. This group was once described by Skelton as individuals of "all-round ability, capable of performing in widely different assignments at short notice." From 1935 to 1940 he was first secretary in the Canadian High Commission in London, and followed this appointment in 1942 with a similar posting at the Canadian Legation in Washington before becoming Canadian Ambassador to the United States in 1945. He was part of the Canadian delegation to the conference that founded the United Nations, and in 1946 became deputy minister at External Affairs, where he worked tirelessly to fit Canada into the post-war world.

Pearson continued this work after entering politics in 1949 and becoming Minister of External Affairs. Disliked by the Americans for being soft on Communism and not a very ardent Cold Warrior, his proposal for a United Nations peacekeeping force in Suez in 1956 won him a Nobel Peace Prize, setting Canada on its way as a peacekeeper. In January 1958 Pearson became leader of a Liberal Party out of office for the first time in over 20 years. He rebuilt the party and became Prime Minister of a minority government in April 1963. One of his first actions was to agree to arm American missiles based on Canadian soil with nuclear warheads, thus ending a controversy that had bedevilled the Diefenbaker government for years. In office, Pearson was not outstandingly successful. His government had many problems, and the lack of a majority in Parliament made virtually every day an adventure. Pearson himself was not good at the cut and thrust of parliamentary debate, especially when com-the Canadian Bar Association. Pearson had begun as a history professor at the University of Toronto before joining the Department of External Affairs as a mandarin and professional diplomat. None of these men had earned a doctorate, but all held civilian appointments that in our own time would probably require one.

The Progressive Conservative Party also had three leaders in this period: John Bracken (1942–8), George Drew (1948–56), and John Diefenbaker (1956–67). Bracken and Drew had been successful provincial premiers with little federal experience, while Diefenbaker had been an opposition spokesman in the House of Commons from 1940. Bracken had been a university professor (of field husbandry) and administrator before entering politics.

The other two had been small-town lawyers. All three were regarded as being to the left of their parties, and the PC party platforms of these years looked decidedly progressive. Diefenbaker was *sui generis*, a brilliant if old-fashioned public orator and genuine western populist. All the PC leaders had strong sympathies for the ordinary underprivileged Canadian, although only Diefenbaker managed to convince the public of his concerns. None of these men spoke French comfortably, and they left what campaigning was done in Quebec to others.

The Co-operative Commonwealth Federation had emerged from the war with high hopes, gaining 15.6 per cent of the popular vote and 28 members of Parliament in the 1945 federal election. Its popularity decreased

pared to the oratorical flourishes of Diefenbaker, his Conservative counterpart. Both at home and abroad times were changing. The world was no longer particularly sympathetic to Canada's self-proclaimed role as a middle power, and Canadians were very much of two minds about both the military and the nation's foreign obligations. The integration of Canada's armed forces, a major policy initiative of Pearson's government, was a tough sell. Moreover, the emergence of a new attitude of independence on the part of Quebec led to various efforts, often stumbling, to conciliate Quebec. Despite the problems, Pearson's governments had some triumphs, including the introduction of an enhanced pension plan, the start of a universal medicare system, and a largely triumphal Centennial Year (marred mainly by French President Charles de Gaulle's notorious "Vive le Québec" speech in Montreal in the summer of 1967). Pearson retired from office in 1968 and was replaced by Pierre Trudeau.

Lester B. Pearson. Duncan Cameron, LAC, e007150488.

regularly thereafter, however. By 1958 it was reduced to eight MPs and 9.5 per cent of the popular vote. This erosion of support came about partly because the CCF was mistakenly thought by some to be associated with international Communism, and partly because much of the Canadian electorate regarded it as both too radical and too doctrinaire. The CCF showed no strength east of Ontario and was not a credible national alternative to the two major parties. After its 1958 defeat, the CCF remobilized through an alliance with organized labour (the Canadian Labour Congress), which in 1961 would produce the New Democratic Party under the leadership of former Saskatchewan Premier T.C. (Tommy) Douglas. The Social Credit Party won some scattered seats in Alberta and Saskatchewan after the war, but would achieve prominence only after Robert Thompson (b. 1914) became president of the Social Credit Association of Canada in 1960 and party leader in 1961.

Liberal dominance before 1957 was moderated less by the opposition parties than by other factors. One was the increased size and scope of the apparatus of bureaucracy, including a "mandarinate" at the top of the civil service. Powerful senior civil servants stayed in their posts despite changes of minister or government. They provided most of the policy initiatives for the government. Another important limitation was the force of public opinion, which often restrained policy initiatives and provided a public sense of fair play. The Liberals under St Laurent lost the 1957 election for many reasons, but one of the most critical was a public sense that they had become too arrogant. Government closure of debate over the Trans-Canada Pipeline in 1956 served as a symbol for Liberal contempt of the democratic process. As the new leader in 1958, Lester Pearson blundered in, challenging the minority government of John Diefenbaker to resign in his favour without offering any compelling reasons for so doing.

At the provincial level, few provinces enjoyed genuine two-party politics. Long-governing parties with near monopolies were common, and even in Atlantic Canada, where there was a long tradition of trying to keep provincial and federal governments of the same party, the party in power was not necessarily Liberal. The Tories, under Robert Stanfield, took over Nova Scotia in 1956; Tories ran New Brunswick from 1951 to 1961. Quebec was controlled by Maurice Duplessis's Union Nationale. The Tory "Big Blue Machine" ran Ontario, while Alberta (1935–72) and British Columbia (beginning in 1952) were governed by Social Credit. In British Columbia, W.A.C. Bennett (1900–79) took advantage of an electoral change (the preferential ballot), designed by a warring coalition to keep the socialists out of power, to win enough seats to form a minority government in 1952. Continuing to exploit brilliantly the social polarities of a province divided into free enterprisers and socialists, Bennett never looked back. The CCF governed Saskatchewan. There was no provincial Liberal government west of Quebec between 1945 and 1960, although the coalition government of Manitoba was usually headed by a Liberal.

Liberal success in Newfoundland was a product chiefly of unusual local circumstances. Joseph R. Smallwood parlayed strong Liberal support for Confederation with Canada into an unbroken tenure as the province's first Premier from 1949 until early 1972. After a somewhat complicated journey, Newfoundland joined Canada in 1949. Effectively bankrupt, the province had surrendered its elective government to Great Britain in 1933. It was governed until 1949 by an appointed commission, which balanced the budget but was not very popular. After 1945 the British government sought to get rid of its colonial obligations and ordered a National Convention elected in 1946 to decide Newfoundland's future. In a preliminary referendum in 1948, 69,400 voters (44.5 per cent) voted for a return to the pre-1933 situation, 64,066 (41.1 per cent) voted for Confederation with Canada, and 22,311 (14.3 per cent) voted for the continuation of the Commission of Government. Seven weeks later, on 22 July 1948, a second referendum brought an 84.9 per cent turnout: 78,323 Newfoundlanders (52.3 per cent) voted for Canada and 71,344 (47.7 per cent) for the resumption of Crown colony status. Confederation did best outside the Avalon Peninsula and St John's. The Canadian cabinet accepted the decision on 27 July 1948, allowing Smallwood, now leader of the Liberal Party, to head an interim government that easily won the province's first election in many years.

Joseph Roberts (Joey) Smallwood

Joseph Roberts Smallwood. Alamy Image ID: B65N9A, copyright © Bert Hoferichter/Alamy.

Born near Gambo, Newfoundland, the son of a boot-maker, "Joey" Smallwood (1900–91) became a journal-ist and spent some years in New York City as a "pro-gressive" reporter. He returned to Newfoundland to become involved in politics, but became better known as an amateur historian and radio broadcaster; his radio program, *The Barrelman*, was extremely popular during the late 1930s. During World War II he operat-ed a pig farm near the American air base at Gander, feeding the animals with garbage from the base. When Britain decided in 1945 that Newfoundland would be given a chance through referendum to de-cide on the form of government that might replace the appointed Commission of Government installed by Britain in 1933, Smallwood resumed his political activity. A supporter of Confederation with Canada, Smallwood was elected to the Newfoundland National Convention established in 1946 to determine the col-ony's constitutional future, and then was chosen to advise on the options to be placed on the referendum ballot. At the National Convention, he spoke often and effectively against a return to independent government and spent the next two years campaigning for Canada, much assisted by the promise of family allowances for every Newfoundland family. He led the pro-Canada forces to a narrow victory in the second of two referen-dums in 1948, and helped convince the Canadian gov-ernment to agree to Confederation despite the relatively small margin of the referendum vote in favour of joining Canada. As a reward, he was appointed by Canada as the new province's first premier, and he rode this advan-tage to a Liberal Party electoral victory in May 1949. He would remain in office until 1972.

In power, Smallwood's government began by attempting a variety of modernizations, including the establishment of industrial plants, educational reform (especially the replacement of denominational schools with a public system and the establishment of Memorial University of Newfoundland in 1949), and efforts to move the inhabitants of remote outports into larger "resettle-ment centres." Most of the reforms were controversial and heavily criticized, and Premier Smallwood in later years became increasingly involved with corporate million-aires (who got concessions of raw resources) while fend-ing off in the legislature attacks on his family's behaviour as a St John's landlord. Smallwood ran the Newfoundland government as a personal fiefdom, remaining in power largely because of the introduction of new spending by Ottawa. His party was finally beaten in the 1971 election, and he resigned from office in early 1972. He made sev-eral comeback efforts before finally leaving public life in 1977. In retirement he edited a four-volume Encyclopedia of Newfoundland, which may well prove to be his most lasting contribution to his province.

French Canada after World War II

The scope of social and economic change in French Canada, especially after 1939, went largely unheralded in the remainder of the nation until the 1960s. Pierre Elliott Trudeau began his editorial introduction to his book on the Asbestos strike of 1949—entitled "The Province of Quebec at the Time of the Strike"—with the words, "I surely do not have to belabour the point that in the half century preceding the asbestos strike, the material basis of Canadian society in general, and of Quebec society in particular, was radically altered" (Trudeau, 1974: 1). But in English Canada before 1960, the popular press was fascinated by Maurice Duplessis and his conservative Union Nationale; by ignoring the changes that were actually occurring, journalists presented a distorted picture of Quebec society. Duplessis mixed heavy-handed attacks on civil liberties and trade unions with traditional nationalism and laissez-faire economic policy, while ignoring the underlying social changes and debates within Quebec. For many English-speaking Canadians, Quebec remained stereotyped as a priest-ridden rural society inhabited by a simple people. Because Quebec had been lagging in the socio-economic aspects of modern industrialism, its rapid catch-up became more internally unsettling and externally bewildering. As Trudeau pointed out, by the 1950s Quebec was no longer behind the remainder of Canada in most social and economic indicators. Many Canadian commentators outside Quebec who were aware of the province's transformation assumed that the continued electoral success of Duplessis and the Union Nationale represented confusion on the part of many French Canadians. Since social and economic modernization, in the long run, should lead to French-Canadian assimilation into the majority society of North America, said external observers, in the short run it must be causing internal chaos.

The standard post-war assumptions about Quebec's modernization—that it meant short-term confusion and long-term loss of distinctiveness—were not particularly valid. The socio-economic transformation was accompanied by a series of profound ideological shifts within Quebec society that shook its very foundations. The patterns of that development ought to have been comprehensible to anyone familiar with what was happening elsewhere in developing societies. The power and authority of defenders of traditional Quebec nationalism, including the Roman Catholic Church, were being swept away by a new secular nationalism that had become fully articulated under Duplessis. The main opposition to the new nationalism came less from the old nationalism than from a renewed current of nineteenth-century liberalism adapted to twentieth-century Quebec conditions. In the 1960s these two competing ideologies would find popular labels as "separatism" and "federalism."

The new nationalism was profoundly different from the old in its intellectual assumptions, however similar the two versions could sound in rhetorical manifestos. In the first place, while often espousing Catholic values, the new nationalism was profoundly anticlerical. It opposed the entrenched role of the Church in Quebec

Quebec Premier Maurice Duplessis giving a speech, 1950. Duplessis (1890–1959) dominated Quebec politics as Premier from 1936 to 1939 and from 1944 until his death in 1959. Le Soleil/The Canadian Press.

society. In the second place, the new nationalism had no desire to return to a golden age of agricultural ruralism, but instead celebrated the new industrial and urban realities of modern Quebec. It insisted that Quebec nationalism had to be based on the aspirations of the newly emerging French-Canadian working class, which meant that nationalists had to lead in the battle for socio-economic change. While scorning international socialism because it would not pay sufficient attention to the particular cultural dimensions of French Canada, the new nationalists pre-empted much of the vocabulary and economic analysis of Marxism, including the essential concept of proletarian class solidarity. In their insistence on nationalism, they were hardly traditional Marxists. The post-war world, however, saw many examples of similar movements that combined Marxist analysis with national aspirations. The new nationalists—particularly the younger, more militant ones—were able to find intellectual allies and models everywhere. The external neo-Marxism most commonly cited came from the French ex-colonial world or from Latin America. The new nationalists had long insisted that the key to their program was an active and modern state. The homogeneous secular state represented the highest articulation of the nation and was the best means of liberating humanity. Traditionalist forces in Quebec had historically collaborated with forces in Canada to keep French Canadians in their place. The active state envisioned by the nationalists was Quebec, not Canada.

Opposition to the new nationalism came from a tiny but influential group of small-l liberal intellectuals centred on the journal *Cité libre*. This publication was founded by Pierre Elliott Trudeau (1919–2000) and Gérard Pelletier (1919–1997), among others, at the height of the Duplessis regime, to which it was a reaction. These liberals were as revisionist in spirit as the new nationalists, but they were simultaneously suspicious of what they regarded as simplistic doctrinaire thinking. They were committed to the new rationalism of the new social sciences. As Trudeau wrote in an oft-quoted manifesto:

We must systematically question all political categories bequeathed to us by the intervening generation. . . . The time has arrived for us to borrow from architecture the discipline called "functional," to cast aside the thousands of past prejudices which encumber the present, and to build for the new man. Overthrow all totems, transgress all taboos. Better still, consider them as dead ends. Without passion, let us be intelligent. (Quoted in Behiels, 1985: 69)

Trudeau's small group was even more fiercely anti-clerical than the new nationalists, perhaps because its members still believed in the need for a revitalized Catholic humanism and criticized the Church from within. It was equally critical of traditional French-Canadian nationalism, which it regarded as outdated, inadequate, and oppressive. *Cité libre* preferred to locate French Canada within an open multicultural and multinational state and society. Not only traditional nationalism but all nationalism was unprogressive and undemocratic.

At the end of the 1950s most Quebec intellectuals had arrived at some similar conclusions, however different the routes. The traditional nationalism in Quebec—of Catholicism, of the Union Nationale—led nowhere. The dead hand of the Church had to be removed. A modern state, secular and interventionist, was needed to complete Quebec's modernization.

There was some disagreement over the nature of this modern state. The new nationalists were inclined to see it as a liberating embodiment of French-Canadian collectivities, while the *Cité libre* people saw it more as a regulating mechanism. It only remained to persuade the general populace of the province of the need for change.

Signs of the profound changes that had occurred and were still occurring in Quebec could be seen in the province's intellectual and artistic communities. In 1948 Paul-Émile Borduas released his famous manifesto, written originally in 1947. *Refus global* was a rambling series of passionate, almost poetic utterances attacking virtually everything in Quebec society at the time. Some young painters were not satisfied with the combination of spontaneity and traditional spatial perspectives advocated by Borduas. Led by Fernand Leduc, they produced a manifesto in 1955—signed "Les Plasticiens"—that was less inflammatory than *Refus global*, but that also insisted on artistic

Refus Global

In 1948, in Montreal, the painter Paul-Émile Borduas (1905–60) released a manifesto signed by himself and a number of other Quebec artists and intellectuals. An excerpt follows.

The magical harvest magically reaped from the field of the Unknown lies ready for use. All the true poets have worked at gathering it in. Its powers of transformation are as great as the violent reactions it originally provoked, and as remarkable as its later unavailability (after more than two centuries, there is not a single copy of Sade to be found in our bookshops; Isidore Ducasse, dead for over a century, a century of revolution and slaughter, is still, despite our having become inured to filth and corruption, too powerful for the queasy contemporary conscience).

All the elements of this treasure as yet remain inaccessible to our present-day society. Every precious part of it will be preserved intact for future use. It was built up with spontaneous enthusiasm, in spite of, and outside, the framework of civilization. And its social effects will only be felt once society's present needs are recognized.

Meanwhile our duty is plain.

The ways of society must be abandoned once and for all; we must free ourselves from its utilitarian spirit. We must not tolerate our mental or physical faculties' being wittingly left undeveloped. We must refuse to close our eyes to vice, to deceit perpetuated under the cloak of imparted knowledge, of services rendered, of payment due. We must refuse to be trapped within the walls of the common mould—a strong citadel, but easy enough to escape. We must avoid silence (do with us what you will, but hear us you must), avoid fame, avoid privileges (except that of being heeded)—avoid them all as the stigma of evil, indifference, servility. We must refuse to serve, or to be used for, such despicable ends. We must avoid deliberate design as the harmful weapon of reason. Down with them both! Back they go!

MAKE WAY FOR MAGIC! MAKE WAY FOR OBJECTIVE MYSTERY!

MAKE WAY FOR LOVE!

MAKE WAY FOR WHAT IS NEEDED!

We accept full responsibility for the consequences of our refusal.

Self-interested plans are nothing but the stillborn product of their author.

While passionate action is animated with a life of its own.

We shall gladly take full responsibility for the future. Deliberate, rational effect can only fashion the present from the ashes of the past.

Our passions must necessarily, spontaneously, unpredictably forge the future. . . .

We need not worry about the future until we come to it.

Source: Ramsay Cook, ed., *French-Canadian Nationalism: An Anthology* (Toronto: Macmillan of Canada, 1969), 280–1. Reprinted with permission of the author.

freedom. It said that its subscribers were drawn to "plastic qualities: tone, texture, forms, lines, and the final unity between elements" (quoted in Davis, 1979: 18). Abstractionism quickly ceased to be regarded as particularly avant-garde in Quebec. In the theatre, some attempt was made to break out of the constraints imposed by realism. One particularly striking example was *Le Marcheur* (The Walker) by Yves Thériault, which was presented in 1950. It featured a dominant father (never seen on stage), who controlled the lives of everyone around him at the same time that he united them in their hatred for him. The father could be seen as the traditional French-Canadian paternal tyrant, or Premier Duplessis, or the Church.

Federal–Provincial Relations

The 1945–6 Dominion–Provincial Conference on Reconstruction had served as the arena for the renewal after the war of constitutional conflict between the Dominion and its provinces. In August 1945 the federal government tabled a comprehensive program for an extended welfare state based on the tax collection and economic policy of a strong central government. It sought the co-operation of the provinces to implement its plans. Ottawa wanted agreement that it could keep the emergency powers it had acquired to fight the war, especially the power to collect all major taxes. The Conference adjourned for study, finally meeting again in April 1946. At this point Quebec and Ontario in tandem simultaneously denounced centralization while insisting on a return to provincial autonomy. Ontario had some social programs of its own in the planning stages. Quebec, led by Duplessis, wanted to keep control of social powers in order not to have them implemented. In the wake of this meeting, the federal government offered a "tax rental" scheme to the provinces, whereby it would collect certain taxes (on incomes, corporations, and inheritances) and distribute payment to the provinces. Ontario and Quebec went their own ways, but the remaining provinces (and Newfoundland after 1949) accepted tax rental, which (along with suitable constitutional amendment) had been recommended by the Rowell-Sirois Commission in 1940.

Constitutional revision was no easy matter to contemplate. As we have seen, conflict had been literally built into Confederation by the British North America Act. The Dominion of Canada was a federal state, with a central government in Ottawa and local governments in the provinces. While the intention of the Fathers of Confederation had been to produce a strong central government, they had been forced by the provinces (especially what would become Quebec) to guarantee them separate identities. These identities were protected through an explicit division of powers between federal and provincial governments in sections 91 and 92 of the British North America Act of 1867. The division thus created reflected the state of political thinking in the 1860s.

It gave the federal arm the authority to create a viable national economy. It gave the provinces the power to protect what at the time were regarded as local and cultural matters. Some of the provincial powers, such as those over education, were acquired because the provinces demanded them. Others, such as the powers over the health and welfare of provincial inhabitants, were not regarded by the Fathers as critical for a national government. Lighthouses and post offices were more important than public medical care in the 1860s.

Over time the division of powers gave the provinces the responsibility, in whole or in part, for many of the expensive aspects of government, including health, education, and welfare. Provincial ability to raise the revenue needed to meet these obligations was limited, however. Many important aspects of welfare came to be shared among governments. The BNA Act's division of powers was clearly dated, ambiguous, and contentious. Despite the miracle of Canada's survival, the Constitution was constantly strained. Then, as now, critics of the existing system stressed its tensions, while its defenders lauded its capacity for survival.

One of the key problems was the settling of disputes over interpretation of the BNA Act itself. The Act provided for a judicature modelled on British arrangements, with a Supreme Court at the top. This Court, established in 1875, was not always the court of final recourse on constitutional matters. Until 1949 constitutional questions could be finally appealed to a British imperial court, the Judicial Committee of the Privy Council of the United Kingdom. In the years after Confederation, the JCPC had interpreted the Constitution in ways highly favourable to the provinces. Even with the successful elimination, after the war, of this example of continued colonialism, amendment of the Constitution was extremely difficult. Amending procedures were not spelled out in the Act itself. The convention had grown up that amendment required the consent of all provinces, which was not easy to obtain. Moreover, such amendment could ultimately be achieved only by an Act of the British Parliament.

By the mid-twentieth century, Canadian political leaders had worked out a variety of informal means for dealing with matters of constitutional disagreement. One of the most important was the federal–provincial conference, which was employed regularly after 1945 to deal with financial business and gradually came to address constitutional matters as well. So long as the Union Nationale government of Maurice Duplessis represented Quebec at these gatherings, Quebec stood by a traditional view of the 1867 arrangement. The province protected its existing powers fiercely, but did not particularly seek to expand them. Another dimension was added to the post-war constitutional situation through John Diefenbaker's insistence on the introduction of a Canadian Bill of Rights, however.

The Americans had produced their Bill of Rights (the first 10 amendments to their 1787 Constitution) as part of the process of ratifying the Constitution. In Canada, the British constitutional tradition insisted that Parliament was supreme, while the courts automatically protected against the abuse of power. The BNA Act had protected some minority rights, but had displayed little interest in the rights of the individual, which were crucial to the American approach. This notion of spelling out rights—for individuals or collective groups—was a potentially profound change in the Canadian Constitution. Diefenbaker's Bill for the Recognition and Protection of Human Rights and Fundamental Freedoms, fulfilling campaign promises of 1957 and 1958, passed the federal Parliament in 1960. As it was limited to the federal level, and the rights it protected could be overridden by national emergencies, it had little immediate impact. A full 10 years would go by before the Canadian Supreme Court would hear a case based on the Bill of Rights, but its implications for constitutional reform—particularly when combined with the growth of new and politically conscious minorities in the 1960s—were substantial.

At the end of the 1950s the Canadian Constitution stood on the cusp of great change. Canadians ought to have recognized that neither constitutional nor federal–provincial problems were solely the product of the presence of Quebec in Confederation. Nevertheless, the issue of Quebec became inextricably bound up with increasing federal–provincial tensions. Constitutional reform would become the panacea for the nation's divisions.

The Rise of Canadian Culture

Culture in Canada and Canadian Culture (the two were never quite synonymous) after World War II emerged as major public issues. This was a major development of the post-war period. Culture had not been entirely ignored before 1945, but it had always taken a back seat to political and economic matters. Canada's cultural performance (or lack of it) was explained chiefly in terms of priorities. Culture was a luxury that would come only with political and economic maturity. Such maturity was now at hand. A number of parallel developments affecting culture occurred after 1945. One of the most obvious saw both federal and provincial governments attempt to articulate and implement public cultural policy. The policy initiatives were driven chiefly by concerns to protect homegrown culture from being overwhelmed by external influences. They helped create a variety of new cultural institutions in the post-war period. On the creative level, many contemporary artists began deliberately cultivating a naive or native style, with considerable public success, thus helping to breach the older boundaries of art and culture. Other artists enthusiastically joined international movements.

Canada was hardly alone in discovering that culture in its various forms was an important matter in the post-war world. Few nations, however, had a greater need for conscious cultural policy than Canada. It was a nation without a single unifying language and with at least two of what many after 1945 began to call "founding cultures." At the same time, francophones and anglophones often meant something quite different when they talked about culture. While nobody doubted that French Canada's culture was distinctive, defining the culture of the rest of the nation was more problematic. More than most nations, Canada was exposed to external cultural influences, particularly from its behemoth neighbour to the south, the United States. The Americans purveyed to Canada and then to the world a profoundly American cultural style, anchored in popular culture.

In 1945 (or at any point earlier), Canada had considerably more cultural activity than most Canadians would have recognized at the time. One of the problems was that cultural commentators relied on highly restrictive critical canons and categories. Much of Canada's cultural life went on outside the boundaries of what critics and experts usually regarded as Culture with a capital C. Canadians became involved in culture on a non-professional basis for their own pleasure. The resultant culture came from

BACKGROUNDER

Distant Early Warning (DEW) Line

From the beginning of World War II on, Canadian control of the Arctic faced a serious challenge from the United States, and especially from American military scientists, who sought a key role for the region in security arrangements and were able to take advantage of the Russian threat during the Cold War to achieve it. Canada, of course, was situated between the two superpowers and directly in the path of the probable line of air attack across the Arctic. Although in early 1945 a Canadian working committee had recommended joint co-operation with the Americans, provided that all military installations in Canada and Newfoundland remained under Canadian control, that principle quickly became difficult to maintain. The Americans began in 1946 by proposing a line of weather stations across the North, assuming that since Canada had limited financial resources, the Canadians would be pleased to allow Uncle Sam to build and run them. In early 1947 the Canadian cabinet approved the Joint Arctic Weather Station program. In 1950 three new radar lines were proposed, and the Pinetree Line, running across the fiftieth parallel, was begun in 1951 with the Americans providing two-thirds of the necessary men and money. This line was too close to population centres—and too far south—to be useful, and it was soon followed by the Mid-Canada Line—90 unmanned stations and eight large control stations along the fifty-fifth parallel employing Doppler radar—built and manned by Canada between 1954 and 1957. In November 1954 the US and Canada agreed to a third radar line along the Arctic coast from Alaska to Baffin Island at the sixty-ninth parallel. This DEW Line of 22 stations was funded by the Americans using Canadian construction firms and some Aboriginal labour. The early warning systems would be useless without interceptor aircraft at the ready, and the result was NORAD, another joint command system dominated by the Americans. At the same time, the Avro Arrow, a Canadian aircraft designed as an interceptor, had to be scrapped. The introduction of intercontinental ballistic missiles (ICBMs) soon rendered the radar lines militarily useless, and they were shut down in the 1960s. What the various manoeuvrings over the DEW Line clearly demonstrated was that Canada could not afford to defend its vast territories from Soviet attack, and would have to sacrifice some sovereignty (officially described as joint co-operation with the Americans) in order to survive.

The Dew Line and Mid-Canada Line. From Shelagh Grant, Polar Imperative: A History of Arctic Sovereignty in North America *(Vancouver: Douglas & McIntyre, 2010), 325. Reprinted with permission from the publisher.*

Vincent Massey (left), chairman of the Royal Commission of Arts, Letters, and Sciences, presents Prime Minister Louis St Laurent with a copy of the Commission's official report. Chris Lund/National Film Board of Canada. LAC, PA-116801.

folk traditions more than from high art. Moreover, it was not necessarily distinctly Canadian. By 1945, Canadian government—particularly at the federal level with the Public Archives, the National Gallery, the National Film Board, and the Canadian Broadcasting Corporation— already had a substantial if largely unrecognized role in culture. Prime Minister St Laurent was told during the 1949 elections that the Liberals might lose votes to the CCF from "those Canadians who have a distinct national consciousness and feel that more should be done to encourage national culture and strengthen national feeling." As a result, St Laurent appointed the Royal Commission on

National Development in the Arts, Letters and Sciences, usually known as the Massey Commission after its chairman, Vincent Massey.

The Massey Commission existed because its time had come. It did not invent a cultural policy but merely publicized one. While its recommendations were crucial in increasing government involvement in the arts, they were precisely the ones envisioned in the Commission's terms of reference, which were in turn a product of considerable lobbying by well-established arts groups. The Commission held extensive public meetings, receiving 462 briefs and listening to 1,200 witnesses. The witnesses, reported its

BACKGROUNDER

Asbestos Strike of 1949

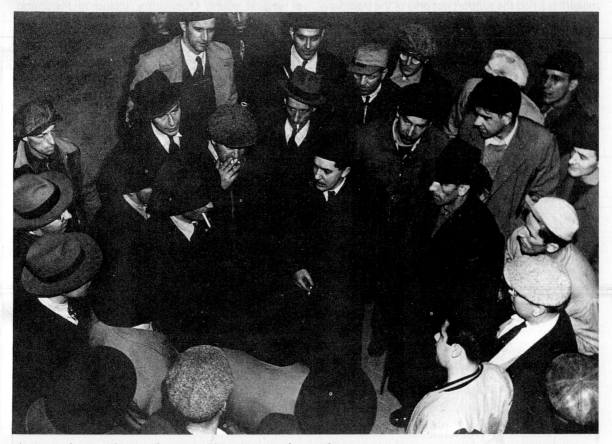

The 1949 Asbestos strike in Quebec. Metropolitan Toronto Reference Library.

The strike against the owners of asbestos mines around Sherbrooke, Quebec, that broke out in February 1949 was arguably the most important and influential labour dispute in the province during the years of Maurice Duplessis from 1935 to 1959. The strike polarized the province and closed most of the asbestos mines for four months. It marked the beginning of the end for Duplessis's Union Nationale, which had supported the anglophone owners (both Americans and Canadians) in their refusal to grant a first contract to the unions of the Confédération des Travailleurs Catholiques du Canada (CTCC), which had organized the industry under secretary-general Jean Marchand (1918–88). Union demands included the removal of the dangerous dust from the mill, an automatic check-off of union dues (the so-called Rand Formula), and a series of wage increases.

A number of key points characterized this strike. The first was that working conditions in the mines—particularly the constant exposure to asbestos dust and its danger to health—were truly appalling and caught the attention of the public in and outside

Continued...

An indoor photo of the Diefenbunker, the controversial shelter built between 1959 and 1961. It was intended to house the Canadian government in the event of a nuclear attack. Now a museum, its existence, and its original purpose, stand as a reminder of the fears of the period. Iouri Goussev/flickr.

Timeline

1960 Introduction of Enovid. Royal Commission on Government Organization is created. Jean Lesage and the Liberals defeat the Union Nationale in Quebec. Bill of Rights passes federal Parliament.

1961 National Indian Council is founded. Canadian content regulations are introduced for television. CTV is formed. New Democratic Party is organized.

1962 Federal election returns a Diefenbaker minority government. Hydro-Québec is formed. Lesage government wins again with the slogan "Maîtres chez nous."

1963 Lester Pearson becomes Prime Minister at the head of a Liberal minority government. Parent Commission reports on education in Quebec. Royal Commission on Bilingualism and Biculturalism is formed.

1964 Family allowances are expanded. Brock University is founded. New Canadian flag is adopted.

1965 Student Union for Peace Action is founded. National Pension Plan is introduced, with a separate plan for Quebec. War on Poverty begins. Simon Fraser University and York University are opened.

1966 Federal Medical Act of 1966 is passed. Union Nationale defeats Liberals in Quebec.

1967 Canadian Centennial Year celebrations (including Expo 67). Official national anthem is adopted. Royal Commission on the Status of Women is appointed. National Hockey League is expanded, with no new Canadian teams. René Lévesque resigns from the Quebec Liberal Party.

1968 Michel Tremblay's play *Les Belles-Soeurs* is produced. Federal divorce reform is introduced. Canadian Métis Society and the National Indian Brotherhood are formed. Special Senate Committee on Poverty is established.

1969 Criminal Code amendments dealing with abortion and homosexuality are introduced. Sir George Williams University Computer Centre is occupied by protesting students. Montreal Expos begin play. White Paper on Indian policy is published. Pierre Trudeau's Liberals are elected with large majority. Official Languages Act is passed.

1970 Commission of Inquiry into the Non-Medical Use of Drugs (Le Dain Commission) delivers its interim report. Robert Bourassa's Liberals win over the Union Nationale in Quebec. October Crisis of 1970.

1971 New federal Unemployment Insurance Plan.

1972 "Waffle" purged from NDP. Bobby Hull signs with Winnipeg Jets of the World Hockey Association.

Periods in history are seldom neat and tidy. Decades and centuries have a nasty tendency to spill over their technical dates. The era from 1958 to 1972 in Canada will always be labelled "the sixties." Life in those years was a bit like riding on a roller coaster. Revolution was in the air, but it never quite arrived. Everything seemed to be happening at roller-coaster speed. Although the ride was frequently quite exhilarating, the view from the front seemed to open into a bottomless abyss. Almost every positive development had its downside. The Canadian economy continued to grow, but the unpleasant side effects became more evident. Government sought to reform the legal system regarding divorce while the rates of marital breakdown reached epidemic proportions. The Roman Catholic Church internationally introduced a series of unprecedented reforms, but Canadians stopped attending all churches in record numbers. An increasing number of students at Canadian universities became concerned about American influence in Canada, only to be influenced themselves by American student reaction to the war in Vietnam. A variety of collective minorities began insisting on their rights, the acceptance of which would require the complete remaking of social justice—and, indeed, society—in Canada. The nation celebrated its Centennial in 1967, the most memorable event of which was probably an off-the-cuff public exclamation by French President Charles de Gaulle.

The usual picture of Canada after World War II shows a naive and complacent society that, with the aid of imported American ideas, suddenly questioned virtually all its values. There are a number of important qualifications to make to such a view. There was more ferment under the surface in post-war Canada than was recognized at the time. In many respects, ideas and behaviour that had previously been underground suddenly shifted into the public arena. Discontent was a product of the rising expectations caused by economic affluence. As is so often the case, much confrontation occurred because institutions did not change rapidly enough. Canadians were able to take over much of the American critical vocabulary because of their profound suspicions of the American system. Social critics in the United States struck a chord with Canadians who had similar feelings about the contradictions of American society and culture.

The "Radical Sixties"

The era 1958–72 involved complex currents and countercurrents. Discussion of even the most major movements can only scratch the surface. Nonetheless, any account of the sixties must begin by considering three of the period's most striking developments: a broad societal shift towards liberalization; the appearance of a youth-centred counterculture; and the emergence of newly energized collective minorities in Canadian society. Sixties rhetoric was able to find a venue on radio and television. The reformers were the first radicals ever to have access to colour television. Only a few contemporaries ever managed to get beneath the rhetoric to understand the substance of the critique.

The Emancipation of Manners

The sixties have been credited with (or blamed for) a revolution in morality in which the traditional values of our Victorian ancestors were overturned virtually overnight. Firmly held moral beliefs do not collapse quite so rapidly or easily, of course. Rather, a belief system that was already in a state of decay and profoundly out of step with how people actually behaved in their daily lives was finally questioned and found wanting. A previous Canadian reluctance to examine morality ended. The brief upsurge of formal Christianity that had characterized the post-war era suddenly terminated. Canadians ceased attending church in droves. The phenomenon was especially evident in Catholic Quebec. The shifts involved were international ones that went much further elsewhere in the industrialized world than in Canada. By comparison with Sweden or California, for example, Canadian manners appear in retrospect to have remained quite old-fashioned.

The liberation of manners occurred simultaneously on several visible levels. The old media taboos against sexual explicitness, obscenity, and graphic depiction of violence virtually disappeared. Television attempted to maintain the traditional standards, but TV news itself constantly undermined that self-restraint with its coverage of what was happening in the world. The sixties were probably no more violent than any other period in

BACKGROUNDER

Africville

A historic, impoverished black community on the south shore of Bedford Basin in Halifax, Nova Scotia, Africville was cleared in the later 1960s by the city for highway construction and port development. Unfortunately, the city had failed to consult adequately with the residents of Africville, who did not regard their community as a slum to be razed, but as a living entity worthy of continuation. Africville had been settled after the War of 1812, initially as a place to put blacks who had supported the British during the hostilities. Few of these blacks actually came directly from Africa, despite the name. During the nineteenth century two railway lines—the Nova Scotia Railway (to become the Intercolonial) and the Halifax and Southwestern Railway (to become Canadian National Railways)—joined up in Africville. Not surprisingly, many of the community's residents were employed by the railroads as cleaners and Pullman porters. The community did not share equally in the developing infrastructure of Halifax. It was particularly deficient in schools, roads, water, and sewerage. About the only city services it enjoyed were undesirable ones, such as an infectious disease hospital, a slaughterhouse, and, in 1958, a garbage dump.

After World War II, the relocation of Africville became an agenda item for city politicians and city planners. Relocation proposals were adopted by the city without a hitch, often unanimously in city council, inevitably operating on the assumption that moving the community was in its best interests. Most of the demolition of Africville occurred between 1964 and 1967, although not until 1970 was the last house destroyed. The move was seen by many in the city as part of the relocation of the city dump, a conjunction not lost upon its inhabitants. Because so few residents held clear title to their land there was little initial resistance to relocation, particularly when most residents were paid $500 and given promises of social assistance and access to public housing. Not surprisingly, many of those promises were never fully kept, and public housing was no substitute for the earlier sense of ownership of dwelling units, however ramshackle. Whenever the city had asked for the views of residents, they responded by opposing removal, but no organized movement of protest ever congealed except for the establishment of the Halifax Human Rights Advisory Committee (HHRAC), an organization that sought to assist the residents of Africville with their removal and to help them get a decent deal from the city, rather than to oppose removal per se. Only since 1970 has Africville emerged as a powerful symbol of racist oppression in Canada; the Africville site was declared a national historic site in 2002, and in 2010 the Halifax city council formally apologized for the removal.

Source: Jennifer T. Nelson, *Razing Africville: A Geography of Racism* (Toronto: University of Toronto Press, 2008).

human history. However, constant television coverage of the decade's more brutal events, increasingly in "living" colour, brought them into everyone's living room. The memories of any Canadian who lived through the period include a veritable kaleidoscope of violent images: the assassinations of John F. Kennedy, his brother Robert, and Martin Luther King Jr; the Paris and Chicago student riots of 1968; scenes in Vietnam (including the My Lai murders of innocent civilians and the defoliation of an entire ecosystem). Closer to home, there was the October Crisis of 1970. Canadians liked to believe that violence happened outside Canada, especially in the United States. Canadians somehow were nicer. On the eve of the October Crisis, the Guess Who, a Canadian rock group, had a monster hit, the lyrics of which pursued some of the most common metaphors of the time. "American Woman" identified the United States with violence and Canada's relationship with its southern neighbour in sexual terms, a common conceit of the time.

As for sexuality, it became more explicit. Canadians began to talk and write openly about sexual intercourse, contraception, abortion, premarital sex, and homosexual behaviour. In place of the winks and nudges that had always accompanied certain "unmentionable" topics, a refreshing frankness appeared. Many of the issues of sexuality revolved around women's ambition (hardly new) to gain control of their own bodies and reproductive functions. Part of the new development was the rapid spread of the use of Enovid, the oral contraceptive widely known as "the pill" after its introduction in 1960. The pill seemed to offer an easier and more secure method of controlling conception. Its use became quite general before some of its unpleasant side effects came to light. One of the pill's advantages was that the woman herself was responsible for its proper administration. The birth rate had already begun declining in 1959, and probably would have continued to decline without the pill. Enovid symbolized a new sexual freedom—some said promiscuity—for women that gradually made its way into the media. By the mid-1960s, popular magazines that had previously preached marriage, fidelity, and domesticity were now featuring lead articles on premarital sex, marital affairs, and cohabitation before marriage.

Language, at least as the media used it, was equally rapidly liberated. Canadian writers—whether in fiction, poetry, drama, film, or history—had usually employed a sanitized and almost unrecognizable version of spoken French or English. Earle Birney's comic war novel *Turvey* (1949) suggested the use of profanities by Canada's soldiers by means of dashes in the text. But *Turvey* only hinted at the larger reality. In everyday life many ordinary Canadians used not only profanities but a rich vocabulary of vulgar slang that could be found in few dictionaries of the day. In French Canada, that everyday language was called *joual*. While earlier writers like Gabrielle Roy and Roger Lemelin had suggested its use, later writers such as Michel Tremblay (b. 1942) actually began to employ it. Tremblay's play *Les Belles-Soeurs*, written in 1965 but not produced until 1968 because of

concerns about its language, cast its dialogue in *joual*. His later plays added sexually explicit themes, including transvestism and homosexuality. By 1970 both language and themes previously considered unsuitable became public across the country.

The state played its own part in the reformation of manners. Pierre Elliott Trudeau achieved a reputation that helped make him Prime Minister by presiding over a reformist Department of Justice from 1967 to 1968. He became associated with the federal reform of divorce in 1968, as well as with amendments (in 1969) to Canada's Criminal Code dealing with abortion and homosexuality. Trudeau's remark that the state had no place in the bedrooms of the nation struck a responsive chord. He was Prime Minister in 1969 when a commission was appointed to investigate the non-medical use of drugs. While its interim report, published in 1970, did not openly advocate the legalization of soft drugs, such as marijuana, its general arguments about the relationship of law and morality were symptomatic of the age. The commission maintained that the state had the right to limit the availability of potentially harmful substances through the Criminal Code. At the same time it added that it was not necessarily "appropriate to use the criminal law to enforce morality, regardless of the potential for harm to the individual or society" (Addiction Research Foundation, 1970: 503–26).

Justice Minister Pierre Elliott Trudeau with Prime Minister Lester B. Pearson at the federal–provincial conference of February 1968. Cameron, D., LAC, C-25001.

Earle Birney, winner of the 1950 Leacock Medal. His comical war novel Turvey *(1949) had relied on dashes to suggest the profanities used by Canadian soldiers. By the 1960s, such self-censorship had disappeared from literature. Stephen Leacock, LAC, C-31956.*

The concept that it was not the state's function to enforce morality flew in the face of the Canadian tradition, which had always embodied morality in the Criminal Code. The new liberalism informed many of the legal reforms of the later 1960s. A number of Roman Catholic bishops, in a brief to a special joint committee of the legislature on divorce in 1967, stated that the legislator's goal should not be "primarily the good of any religious group but the good of all society" (*Proceedings of the Special Joint Committee of the Senate and House of Commons on Divorce*, 1967: 1515–16). Such liberated thinking paved the way not only for a thorough reform of federal divorce legislation, making divorce easier and quicker to obtain, but also for amendments to the Criminal Code in 1969 regarding

abortion. Termination of pregnancy became legal if carried out by physicians in proper facilities, and following a certification by a special panel of doctors that "the continuation of the pregnancy of such female person would or would be likely to endanger her life or health." The Criminal Code was also amended in 1969 to exempt from prosecution "indecent actions" by consenting couples over the age of 21 who performed such acts in private.

The reformation of manners, if not morals, based on the twin concepts that the state had no place in enforcing morality and that individuals were entitled to decide on the ways in which they harmed themselves, was largely in place by 1969. There were clear limits to liberalization, however. Since 1969 Canada has witnessed a resurgence of demands for state intervention in areas where liberalization was held to produce adverse consequences. Thus many women's groups have come to advocate stricter legislation on obscenity and indecency, particularly in the media, in order to protect women and children from sexual abuse.

The Counterculture

One of the most obvious manifestations of the ferment of the sixties was the rebellious reaction of young baby boomers against the values of their elders, a movement that came to be known as the counterculture. Many Canadian rebels of the period took much of the style and content of their protest from the Americans, although they had their own homegrown concerns, especially in Quebec. As in the United States, youthful rebellion in Canada had two wings, never mutually exclusive: a highly politicized movement of active revolution, often centred in the universities and occasionally tending to violence; and a less overtly political one of personal self-reformation and self-realization, centred in the "hippies." Student activists and hippies were often the same people. Even when different personnel were involved, the culture was usually much the same, anchored by sex, dope, and rock music. The participants in the two Canadian branches of youthful protest also had in common distinctly middle-class backgrounds, for these were movements of affluence, not marginality.

BACKGROUNDER

Sir George Williams University Student Protests

A wave of university student protests swept across Europe and North America in the late 1960s, touched off by the failure of universities to react swiftly enough to changing student sensibilities in manners, morals, politics, and internal governance. Canada's protests were, on the whole, restrained and non-violent. The most extreme incidents occurred in Montreal in February 1969 at Sir George Williams University, an institution that had come into existence in 1934 when the Montreal Young Men's Christian Association (YMCA) reorganized its adult education programs by creating Sir George Williams College, named after the founder of the London YMCA. It became a university in 1948, and moved into a new high-rise building in the city's downtown in 1966. Given its origins in adult education, it was not surprising that Sir George Williams University had an open admissions policy, a full-scale evening program, and many part-time students, largely made up of immigrants who had come to Montreal in the 1960s. In many ways the university was innovative, but its administrators were traditionalist when it came to dealing with students.

The student problems at the university were at least partly rooted in the Montreal immigrant experience of the decade, particularly for blacks from the Caribbean, who had greatly increased in number after 1960 and had suffered from a good deal of racism. The trigger was a student complaint against a biology professor, who was accused of failing students for racist reasons. As often happened, the university administration failed to understand the real issues and handled the case badly. At one point, a number of students abandoned a university committee hearing into the case, and occupied a computer lab on the ninth floor of the main campus building, where they instituted a sit-in, ultimately barricading themselves in and closing down phones and elevators. Unfortunately, the university made matters worse at this point by calling in the police to deal with the protestors. The result was a confrontation between riot police and students ending in an orgy of violence and destruction, with computers tossed out windows, fires set, student records destroyed, and 97 protestors, many of them black, being arrested. The student ringleaders included several individuals who became subsequently prominent, such as Roosevelt "Rosie" Douglas. He was imprisoned for several years for his role in the affair, was deported to his home island of Dominica, and ultimately became its prime minister.

Five years later, in 1974, Sir George Williams merged with a Jesuit school in Montreal, Loyola College, to become Concordia University.

Source: Dennis Forsythe, ed., *Let the Niggers Burn! The Sir George Williams Affair and Its Caribbean Aftermath* (Montreal: Black Rose Books, 1971).

The United States was the spiritual home of the sixties counterculture in English Canada. Americans had gone further than anyone else both in suburbanizing their culture and in universalizing education. The rapidly expanding university campus provided an ideal spawning ground for youthful rebellion. The campus had helped generate, in the civil rights movement, a protest crusade that served as a model for subsequent agitation. Civil rights as a public concern focused attention on the rhetorical contradictions of mainstream American society, which preached equality for all while denying it to blacks. It also mobilized youthful idealism and demonstrated the techniques of the protest march and civil disobedience, as well as the symbolic values of popular song. When some American blacks left the civil rights movement, convinced that only violence

Contemporary Views   LE CANADIEN.

The Use of Drugs

In 1969 the newly elected Trudeau government appointed a Commission of Inquiry into the Non-Medical Use of Drugs (the Le Dain Commission, after its chairman, Gerald Le Dain). That commission made its interim report in 1970, recommending that the government move towards decriminalization of "soft" drugs such as cannabis. Its recommendations were largely unheeded. The interim report included a number of transcriptions from testimony before it, and those who gave testimony included the British rock musician John Lennon. The following testimony is from a university professor in eastern Canada.

I have enjoyed smoking marijuana and hashish several times, and I feel that if they are made legal, we have far more to gain than lose. I think they can be easily incorporated with our way of life in Canada without eroding any but purely materialistic or exploitative values. Marijuana does not provide an escape from reality any more than alcohol, sex or a drive in the country: we know we cannot be high all the time; we enjoy taking a trip (in both senses of the word) and we remember it with pleasure, but we know that we have to come back home again and go to work, and continue our everyday life. I have so often heard the argument that pot or hashish lead to hard drugs. For the vast majority of pot smokers, this is rubbish. It is the argument that temperance societies use against alcohol: social drinking leads to alcoholism. I have never had the slightest desire to shoot anything into my arm, nor do I want to try speed in any of its forms. There will always be a few disturbed people in our world, and I don't think that laws should be made for that tiny minority. . . .

I wrote to John Turner last winter deploring the persecution of young long-hairs by the police and the RCMP As many people have observed, this leads not to a lessening of pot and hash smoking, but to a disrespect for the police. I would like to see the force more respected, because, as we all know, police need public support and sympathy in order to perform efficiently. What sympathy can they expect when they disguise themselves as hippies in order to infiltrate and arrest them? Hippies are not communists circa 1947, and this police tactic only degrades the officer who undertakes it, as well as the force in general. The hippies feel that the RCMP is acting out of ignorance and fear; they believe that pot-smoking is good, and there is no reason why they should change their minds: they are working from experience, and RCMP actions, no matter how "legal," spring from institutionalized paranoia.

I am not underestimating the temporary upheaval which legalizing marijuana and hashish might cause in certain sectors—police, puritans, all those who wish to force their own limits of freedom and pleasure on the country as a whole. I think we should have the right to choose for ourselves whether we want to smoke or not. I think we have far more to gain than to lose by legalizing pot . . . .

Source: *Interim Report of the Commission of Inquiry into the Non-Medical Use of Drugs* (Ottawa: Queen's Printer, 1970), 292–3. Reproduced courtesy of The Privy Council Office, with the permission of the Minister of Public Works and Government Services, 2007.

could truly alter the status quo, they provided models for urban guerrilla activity, including the growing terrorist campaign in Quebec that was associated with separatism. (French-Canadian youths could identify with Pierre Vallières's *White Niggers of America*.)

In English Canada, what really ignited the revolt of youth was the war in Vietnam. In retrospect, the extent to which Vietnam dominated the period becomes even clearer to us than it was to people at the time. The war became the perfect symbol for the sixties generation of everything that was wrong with mainstream American society. It was equally exportable as an emblem of American Evil, representing everything that the rest of the world hated about the United States, including its arrogant assumption that it was always morally superior. For these reasons, Vietnam was central to the Canadian counterculture in a variety of ways. Hostility to American policy in Vietnam fuelled Canadian anti-Americanism, as a paperback book about the United States entitled *The New Romans: Candid Canadian Opinions of the U.S.* demonstrated in 1967. This hostility also connected young Canadians with the burgeoning American protest movements. Many Canadian university faculty members recruited during the decade were Americans, most of them recent graduate students critical of American policy. They were joined in their sympathies by an uncounted number of American war resisters (some said as many as 100,000 at the height of the war), the majority of whom sought refuge in communities of university students or hippies in large Canadian cities.

The youthful reaction advocated an eclectic kind of socialism—Marxist-influenced, democratically oriented, and idealistically verging on romanticism—that is usually referred to as the New Left. The movement was much better at explaining what was wrong with the present system than at proposing workable alternatives. It had no example of a large-scale society that operated on its principles. Nevertheless, Canadian student activists rose to positions of power in their universities, establishing several national organizations, such as the Student Union for Peace Action (1965). Student radicalism flourished at a few universities, such as Simon Fraser, York, and the Université de Montréal. Many of the less extreme student activists joined the Waffle wing of the NDP, which attempted to radicalize that party in the direction of economic nationalism and social reform. Perhaps the most publicized student protest in Canada occurred in February 1969 when the computer centre at Sir George Williams University in Montreal was occupied for two weeks to protest racial intolerance and the "military, imperialistic ambitions of Canada in the West Indies" (quoted in Forsythe, 1971: 9).

Despite the incident at Sir George Williams, youthful protest was not quite the same in Quebec as in Anglo-Canada. While Quebec's young were no less alienated than their anglophone compatriots, their anger found an outlet in opposition to Canadian federalism's colonial oppression of their own province. Young people of university age (although seldom at university) formed most of the active cells of the Front de libération du Québec (FLQ), including the one that provoked the October Crisis of 1970. The FLQ's rhetoric and tactics during the crisis were clearly modelled on extreme movements of protest in the United States and Europe. English-speaking Canadian students talked of the "student as nigger," but French Canadians saw their entire society as comparable with that of the blacks in the US or an oppressed Third World nation (Kostash, 1980: 250). Radical young Quebecers were able to become part of a larger movement of protest and reform that cut across the age structure of Quebec society. Unlike their counterparts in English Canada, young protestors in Quebec were not cut off from the mainstream of adult society.

"The bureaucratic forms of organization shared by communism and capitalism," wrote one American activist, "were embodiments of insult to the ideals of individualism, spontaneity, mutual trust and generosity that are the dominant themes of the new sensibility" (quoted in Kostash, 1980: 250). Such ideals motivated the hippies, who accordingly dropped out of mainstream society. Earlier generations of middle-class Canadians had dutifully struggled up the ladder of success. Many of the sixties generation lacked such ambition or direction. They were their parents' children, searching for personal self-fulfillment through any possible means. For some, the quest led to vulgarized versions of Eastern mystical religions. For others, it led to communes close to nature, often on remote islands. For the vast majority, it certainly meant experimenting with hallucinogenic drugs, particularly cannabis, and a sexual freedom bordering on promiscuity in an age when sexually transmitted diseases seemed easily treatable with antibiotics. Such experiments, together with a revolution in popular music, were the core of the sixties for participants and onlookers alike. Rock music was almost impossible to define, incorporating as it did so many musical styles ranging from black rhythm and blues to traditional folk music to Indian ragas to medieval Gregorian chant. Nevertheless, rock served as the symbol that both united the young and separated them from their parents.

Anti-Vietnam War protestors make their way to the US Consulate in Montreal, 19 February 1966. Opposition to the Vietnam War became a principal issue for many Canadian students during this period. Montreal Star, LAC, PA-173623.

It is impossible to define a precise moment at which the bubble of the sixties' youth energy burst. Many of the characteristics and tendencies of the period continued in fragmented fashion into the succeeding decades. But at the end of the sixties the naive beliefs of the young received a series of shocks when American student activists were ruthlessly suppressed at Chicago (1968) and Kent State (1970). At the same time, the central rallying point—American involvement in Vietnam—was gradually removed. In Canada, the founding of the Parti Québécois in 1968 provided a place within the system for many Quebec student activists. Two years later the October Crisis demonstrated how far some activists were prepared to go in the use of violence, and how far the Canadian state was prepared to go in suppressing it. The purging of the NDP's Waffle movement in 1972 perhaps completed the process of neutralizing activism, at least in English-speaking Canada. Some

observers explained the collapse of the sixties youth movements in terms of demography. Young people got older and acquired jobs. Perhaps. In any event, by 1973 only memories of the "good old days," often in the form of the lyrics of rock songs, were left for most of the sixties generation.

The Rise of Militant Collectivities

While much youthful protest disappeared at the end of the decade, the baby boomers had joined in some movements that outlasted the era. The sixties saw a number of previously disadvantaged groups in Canadian society emerge with articulated positions and demands. These included, among others, Aboriginal peoples, blacks, women, and homosexuals. To some extent, all these groups shared a common

Canadian Writers View the United States

In 1968 the Canadian poet Al Purdy asked a number of his fellow writers in Canada to contribute their views of the United States to a collection he intended to publish. The following two poems came from George Jonas and Robin Mathews, respectively.

American Girl: A Canadian View

It is reassuring
To spend part of a night
With an American girl.

Chances are she will not resemble
The leaders of her nation
In speech, figure, or stance:

If she has imperialistic designs
She may draw you without a struggle
Into her sphere of influence.

Then you'll find her battledress
Fit for her private battles,
See not her battleships but hear her battlecries,
And melt (perhaps with a wistful smile)
Before the native napalm of her eyes.

But she'll seem to be prepared
To give as well as to accept
Some foreign aid

And by midnight or so
While the fires of her manifest destiny smoulder
You'll be all ready to slip across
The world's longest undefended border.

—*George Jonas*

Centennial Song

Canada, my beauty,
everybody's love,

white flower of diamond-studded North,
let me tell you that
a tired prostitute beyond her prime,
dejected, hungry,
full of malice and uncertain fear
would throw her charms away less openly,
would exercise more choice
than you have ever done,
would charge at least a reasonable rate,
would try to be
(within the perils of the trade)
a self-respecting whore;
And What Is More
even in her wildest state
of drunken self-delusion,
howling at a corner
where the newsies thrive,
she wouldn't let you see her
stopping people —
friends and neighbours,
even relatives,
shouting with paranoid insistence
upon decency and moral strength,
that she is living better now than ever,
friends with everyone, and that
despite all rumour, not a shred
of proof has ever been produced
to show that she
(as gossips say)
is being regularly screwed.

—*Robin Mathews*

Source: Al Purdy, ed., *The New Romans: Candid Canadian Opinions of the U.S.* (Edmonton: Hurtig, 1968), 53, 74. "American Girl" reprinted by permission of the author.

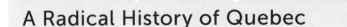

Contemporary Views

A Radical History of Quebec

In 1970 a small book of polemical history by the Manitoba-born author Léandre Bergeron, entitled *Petit Manuel d'Histoire du Québec*, became an unexpected runaway bestseller in Quebec. It was translated into English in 1971 as *The History of Quebec: A Patriot's Handbook*. The following excerpt from the book's Foreword gives some idea of its approach.

Our elite has told us stories about our past but has not set our past in the context of History. The stories they told us were conceived to keep us, the Québécois, outside History.

The elite who collaborated with the English colonizer after the defeat of the Rebellion of 1837–38 behaved like the elites of all colonized peoples. Instead of fighting to rid Quebec of the colonizer, they turned back to a "heroic" past to avoid facing the present. They went about glorifying the exploits of figures like Champlain, Madeleine de Verchères and martyred missionaries to make us believe that at a certain epoch we too were great colonizers and nation builders. Since we were colonized by the English we could find compensation in the fact that we had colonized the Red man. Our elite had us dreaming about the great French Empire of America of Frontenac's time to save us from the real humiliation of being a conquered people imprisoned in Confederation. . . . With the American capitalist industrialization of Quebec, a more "enlightened" and secular elite undertook to revise our past. Under the guide of "objectivity" and of scientific research of "historical facts," historians in our universities accumulated many facts and documents.

But there the work ended. This kind of historian places himself outside history. He is like an angel of knowledge rummaging through humanity's garbage dumps to extract material for neat obituary notices. In these terms our history is a long disinterment confirming without admitting it, our defeat and subjection. In borrowing the Americans' research methods, these historians also borrowed their point of view: according to which American capitalism sets the supreme order, and the small nations, relics of another era, are marginal.

Recently, a few of our historians have been daring to interpret the facts, daring to orient their historical work within the context of Québécois life, and daring to set themselves within the framework of the evolution of the people of Québec toward their liberation.

The latter orientation characterizes this handbook of Quebec history. We Québécois are an imprisoned people subjected to colonization. To change our situation we must first understand the historical forces that brought it about. Once we have defined the forces that reduced us to colonial status, and those that keep us there today, we can identify our enemies correctly, study the relationship of forces carefully and engage in struggle more effectively.

Source: Léandre Bergeron, *The History of Quebec: A Patriot's Handbook* (Toronto: NC Press, 1971), [vii–viii].

sense of liberation and heightened consciousness during the heady days of the sixties, as well as some common models and rhetoric. The several black movements in the United States, especially civil rights and black power, were generally influential. It was no accident that almost every group, including French Canadians, compared itself with American blacks.

While on one level other emerging collectivities could hardly avoid sympathizing with French Canada, on another level the arguments and aspirations of Quebec often seriously conflicted with those of other groups. Many collectivities sought to mobilize federal power to achieve their goals, often seeing the provinces and provincial rights as part of their problem.

As with so many other long-standing Canadian problems, that of the Aboriginal peoples moved into a new activist phase. Earlier, in the 1920s, the League of Indians, formed in 1919, had struggled for attention and against internal divisions. The state and the Canadian polity were not ready for a pan-Indian organization (Dickason and Newbigging, 2015: 232). In the 1960s Native leaders built partly on their own traditions of constructing organizations to speak for First Nations and Inuit concerns. In 1961 the National Indian Council (NIC) was founded. This organization was formed by Native people—many of whom had recently moved to the city—who hoped to combine the concerns of status and non-status Indians. Métis were also involved in the NIC. In 1968 political incompatibility led to the dissolution of the National Indian Council and the formation of two new groups: the Canadian Métis Society (which in 1970 renamed itself the Native Council of Canada) representing Métis and non-status Indians, and the National Indian Brotherhood (which would become the Assembly of First Nations) representing status Indians. Activists were also able to take advantage of American models and Canadian federal policy, particularly the 1960 Bill of Rights. The search for new sources of raw materials for exploitation in the Canadian North threatened Aboriginal ways of life, forcing them into the political mainstream. By the end of the decade, an emerging Native militancy was able to marshal its forces to confront the federal government when it tried to rethink the Aboriginal problem.

In 1969 the Department of Indian Affairs, under Jean Chrétien (b. 1934), published a White Paper on federal Indian policy. All-encompassing in its reassessment,

In this photo, from left to right, are George Manuel, President of the National Indian Brotherhood from 1970 to 1976, Aurilien Gill, 3rd Vice President of the Association of Indians, and Chief Max Louis, 2nd Vice President of the Association of Indians, at a news conference. The twentieth century saw a rise in Aboriginal activist groups that sought to bring Native issues to the political forefront. © Bettmann/Corbis.

the document had three controversial recommendations: the abolition of the Indian Act (and the Department of Indian Affairs), which would eliminate status Indians; the transfer of First Nations lands from Crown trust into the hands of the First Nations; and the devolution of responsibility for Aboriginal people to the provinces. The White Paper touched off bitter criticism in all quarters, not least because it had been generated with little prior consultation with Native groups. It produced the first popular manifesto for Canadian Aboriginals in Harold Cardinal's *The Unjust Society: The Tragedy of Canada's Indians* (1969), which argued for the re-establishment of special rights within the strengthened contexts of treaties and the Indian Act.

The White Paper was consistent with federal policy towards all minorities, including French Canadians, at the end of the 1960s. It called for the advancement of the individual rather than the collective rights of Native peoples:

> The Government believes that its policies must lead to the full, free, and non-discriminatory participation of the Aboriginal people in Canadian society. Such a goal requires a break with the past. It requires that the Aboriginal people's role of dependence be replaced by a role of equal status, opportunity, and responsibility, a role they can share with all other Canadians. (*Statement of the Government of Canada on Indian Policy*, 1969: 5)

An assimilationist document, the White Paper insisted that treaties between the Crown and Aboriginals had involved only "limited and minimal promises" that had been greatly exceeded in terms of the "economic, educational, health, and welfare needs of the Indian people" by subsequent government performance (*Statement of the Government of Canada on Indian Policy*, 1969: 5). Allowing Aboriginal people full access to Canadian social services (many of which were administered provincially) would mark an advance over existing paternalism.

Ottawa seemed surprised that Native people responded so negatively to the White Paper, conveniently ignoring its implications for the concepts of treaty and Aboriginal rights. Prime Minister Trudeau defended the policy as an enlightened one, noting that "the time is now to decide whether the Indians will be a race apart in Canada or whether they will be Canadians

BACKGROUNDER

White Paper on Indian Policy

The White Paper on Indian policy was a federal government publication of 1969 released under Indian Affairs Minister Jean Chrétien. Intended to stir up public debate on the subject, it served mainly as a major catalyst for the rise of Aboriginal consciousness at the end of the 1960s. As one First Nations leader observed at the time, "No single action by any Government since Confederation has aroused such a violent reaction from Indian people." The White Paper dealt with all aspects of native policy, but its principal recommendations were threefold: the abolition of the Indian Act (and the Department of Indian Affairs) within five years, which would mean an end to special status for Indians; the transfer of Indian lands out of Crown trust directly into the hands of the Indian people themselves; and the devolution for responsibility for aboriginals from the federal government to the provinces. The White Paper touched off an unexpected hostile reaction in Aboriginal quarters, producing the first popular manifesto for Canadian First Peoples in Harold Cardinal's *The Unjust Society: The Tragedy of Canada's Indians* (1969), which argued for the re-establishment and reinvigoration of special rights within the strengthened contexts of treaties

Continued...

and the Indian Act. Cardinal labelled the White Paper as a "thinly disguised programme of extermination through assimilation."

The White Paper, in broad outline, was consistent with federal policy of the time towards all minorities, including French Canadians. It called for the advancement of the individual rights of Indians rather than the collective rights of Native peoples as a special ethnic/racial minority: "The Government believes that its policies must lead to the full, free and non-discriminatory participation of the Indian people in Canadian society. Such a goal requires a break with the past. It requires that the Indian people's role of dependence be replaced by a role of equal status, opportunity and responsibility, a role they can share with all other Canadians." The White Paper insisted that treaties between the Crown and Aboriginal peoples only produced limited and minimal promises" that had been greatly exceeded in terms of the "economic, educational, health and welfare needs of the Indian people" by subsequent government policies. Allowing Indians full access to Canadian social services (most of which were provincial responsibilities) would mark an advance over existing paternalism, although it conveniently ignored outstanding issues of dispute such as treaty rights and Aboriginal rights.

Prime Minister Trudeau defended the new policy as an enlightened one, insisting that "the time is now to decide whether the Indians will be a race apart in Canada or whether they will be Canadians of full status." He added, "It's inconceivable, I think, that in a given society one section of the society have a treaty with the other section of the society. We must all be equal under the law." But as many Aboriginal leaders pointed out, Indians did not want to be abandoned to the provinces, but rather enabled to take their place "with the other cultural identities of Canada."

of full status." He added, "It's inconceivable, I think, that in a given society one section of the society have a treaty with the other section of the society. We must all be equal under the law" (Indian–Eskimo Association of Canada, 1970: Appendix 8).

Like other collectivities that discovered a new voice in the 1960s, Canadian women had been quietly preparing for their emergence (or re-emergence) for many years. Whether or not one took a patient view of the lengthy period of quiescence from the enfranchisement of women to the blossoming of the women's liberation movement—and most modern feminists understandably did not—some things had changed, and some political experience had been acquired. The Committee on Equality for Women, which organized in 1966 to lobby for a Royal Commission on the status of women, consisted of experienced leaders from 32 existing women's organizations united by their feminism. Their first delegation to Ottawa was ignored. Laura Sabia (1916–96), president of the Canadian Federation of University Women and leader of the call for a national evaluation of women's status, responded with a classic sixties threat: she would lead a women's protest march on the capital. The Pearson government behaved characteristically. Although not convinced that women had many legitimate grievances, it dodged trouble by agreeing to an investigation "to inquire and report upon the status of women in Canada, and to recommend what steps might be taken by the federal government to ensure for women equal opportunities with men in all aspects of Canadian society" (*Report of the Royal Commission on the Status of Women in Canada*, 1970: vii). The Royal Commission on the Status of Women, established in 1967, examined areas under provincial as well as federal jurisdiction and made its recommendations based on four operating assumptions: the right of women to choose to be employed outside the home; the obligation of parents and society to care for children; the special responsibilities of society to women because of maternity; and, perhaps most controversially, the need for positive action to overcome entrenched patterns of discrimination. The Commission's report provided a program that would occupy mainstream feminism for decades to come.

Virtually simultaneous with the Royal Commission was the emergence of the movement usually known as women's liberation. This articulate and militant branch of feminism had begun in the United States as an off-shoot of the student movement, partly a product of the failure of male student leaders to take women seriously. Women's liberation shared much of its rhetoric with other leftist movements of decolonization. "[Woman] realizes in her subconscious what [Herbert] Marcuse says," went one manifesto: "Free election of masters does not abolish the masters or the slaves" (quoted in Kostash, 1980: 169). Not surprisingly, the liberationists found their organizing principles in issues of sexuality, particularly in the concept that "woman's body is used as a commodity or medium of exchange" (quoted in Kostash, 1980: 196). True liberation would come only when women could control their own bodies, especially in sexual terms. Thus birth control and abortion became two central political questions, along with more mundane matters, such as daycare and equal pay for equal work. Such concerns brought feminists into conflict with what became known as male chauvinism at all levels of society. At the beginning of the 1970s, the women's movement stood poised at the edge of what appeared to be yet another New Day.

The minority perhaps most closely linked to the women's liberationists was composed of homosexuals and lesbians. Like the libbers, the gays (a term they much preferred to other more pejorative ones) focused their political attention on sexuality, particularly the offences enshrined in the Canadian Criminal Code. By the late 1950s more advanced legal and medical thinking had come to recognize the value of decriminalizing homosexual activity, at least between consenting adults. The sixties would see the expansion of this view, partly because of public lobbying by a number of gay organizations, such as the Association for Social Knowledge (1964), that emerged in the period. An increasing number of gay newspapers and journals also made their appearance. Like other minority groups, gays and lesbians began to concentrate on constructing a positive rather than a destructive self-identity. The 1969 revisions to the Criminal Code did not legalize

homosexuality, but they did have a considerable effect on the gay community. It was now possible, if still courageous, to acknowledge one's homosexuality (the usual term was "coming out of the closet"). The ranks of openly practising gays greatly expanded. It was also possible to become more aggressive in support of more homosexual rights, and the first gay liberation organizations were formed in Vancouver, Montreal, Toronto, and Ottawa in 1970 and 1971. These groups led the way in advocating the protection of sexual orientation in any human rights legislation adopted by the government.

By the early 1970s a number of collectivities were making new demands for constitutional reform and political change. The political and constitutional agenda of Canada was no longer confined to such matters as extending the welfare state, satisfying Quebec, or redefining the federal–provincial relationship. It now had to take into account a variety of organized and articulate subgroups of Canadian society—of which Aboriginal peoples, blacks, women, and gays were only the most vocal—insisting that their needs also deserved attention.

A Still Buoyant Economy

Behind all the reform sentiment of the sixties was a persistently prosperous economy. Inflation (which ran at an annual average rate of 2.1 per cent between 1959 and 1968) and interest rates remained manageable. The nation continued to provide jobs for most of its expanding population, with unemployment rates under 6 per cent for most of the period. Critics might note that these rates were substantially higher than in other highly industrialized nations, where unemployment was under 2 per cent. But for the vast majority of Canadians, the performance of the economy seemed more than satisfactory, particularly after 1963, when a veritable explosion of construction projects began and foreign trade blossomed. Everywhere there were the visible signs of prosperity in the form of cranes and hard hats. Montreal and Toronto built subway systems. Large and small shopping malls sprouted up everywhere. Cultural

BACKGROUNDER

Royal Commission on Bilingualism and Biculturalism

The federal government attempted in the 1960s to deal with the growing separatist sentiment in Quebec in a variety of ways, one of which was the creation of a Royal Commission on Bilingualism and Biculturalism. The Commission was set up in 1963, to recommend steps to be taken to develop an "equal partnership between the two founding races, taking into account the contribution made by the other ethnic groups to the cultural enrichment of Canada." The Commission stuck firmly to its mandate, despite the very real limitation of its terms of reference. The major problem, of course, was that a cultural dualism based on the concept of two founding peoples flew in the face of much of the nation's historical realities. In its final report the Commission skirted around the fact that the "two founding races" did not include Canada's Native peoples, arguing that "Our terms of reference contain no allusion" to them. When the Commission invited public testimony, it discovered that many Canadians did not believe in two founding peoples. It was forced to deny that other ethnics represented a "third force" in Canadian society, insisting that "those of other languages and cultures are more or less integrated with the Francophone and Anglophone communities" and were to be seen as cultural groups rather than structural building blocks.

In the end—as the Commission recognized in both its opening remarks and its recommendations—its principal concern had to be with language and bilingualism. Most Canadians were prepared to accept that the nation should implement equality for the two languages it declared "official," and it was probably unfortunate that the Commission strayed into other more contentious ground, such as the definition and implications of culture, and failed to challenge more directly some of the assumptions behind its terms of reference. Its principal recommendation was implemented by the Official Languages Act of 1969, which declared French and English to be official languages with equal status in all jurisdictions under federal jurisdiction. As discussed later in this chapter, Book IV of the Commission's report, titled *The Cultural Contribution of the Other Ethnic Groups*, led to Canada's first Multiculturalism Act in 1971, the establishment of a federal cabinet position dealing with multiculturalism, and the recognition of Canada as a multicultural society. Most other recommendations required provincial co-operation and were more difficult to implement.

---

facilities proliferated. Each province put up new university buildings. Equally important were a number of projects in the North, usually associated with hydroelectric expansion. The bellwether of the Canadian economy continued to be Ontario, still the only province with a mixed economy balanced between manufacturing and primary production. Ontario contained such a large proportion of the nation's people that its successes consistently raised national averages.

The averages disguised marked discrepancies and disparities. Some of them were regional. Overall, the most seriously disadvantaged area was the Atlantic region—the Maritime provinces plus Newfoundland. Per capita average income in this region was persistently more than 30 per cent below the figures for the other provinces, and a much larger proportion of the population than elsewhere worked in marginal primary resource extraction, which was often seasonal in nature. Even after taxes, Ontario's per capita income in 1970 was 70 per cent higher than Newfoundland's. Many commentators insisted, however, that the real regional disparity was between the industrial heartland of central Canada and the resource hinterland that constituted most of the remainder of the country. Canadians were

Judy LaMarsh

Judy LaMarsh. CP PHOTO.

Julia Verlyn "Judy" LaMarsh (1924–80) was born in Chatham, Ontario, and educated in Niagara Falls. After graduation from Hamilton Normal School, she served in the Canadian Women's Army Corps from 1943 to 1946, translating Japanese documents. After the war she attended Victoria College and Osgoode Hall. In 1950 she joined her father's law firm. LaMarsh first ran for Parliament in 1960, winning a by-election in Niagara Falls. In 1962 she became part of the "Truth Squad" that shadowed Prime Minister John Diefenbaker on his campaigns across the country, offering "corrections" and "constructive criticisms" to the Prime Minister's

comments and speeches. This participation drew her to the attention of the media. A short, overweight woman, she took to wearing obvious wigs and knee-high leather boots. She was an extremely easy target for cartoonists to caricature, with increasing cruelty; and she was by her own account "publicity prone," a situation hardly aided by her tendency to shoot from the lip. In 1963 she made a famous appearance at a benefit impersonating a gold-rush prostitute.

Upon re-election in 1963, LaMarsh was made a member of the Pearson cabinet and became Minister of Health and Welfare, a key portfolio that enabled her to capture many headlines. She personally helped draft the legislation for the Canada Pension Plan that was passed under her ministership. She was probably better known for having given up smoking while Minister of Health and Welfare, however. LaMarsh subsequently became Secretary of State, in charge of Canada's Centennial festivities, travelling thousands of miles to participate in celebrations and helping to entertain visiting dignitaries, including the royal couple. She also was partly responsible for the creation of the Royal Commission on the Status of Women. Not a fan of Pierre Elliott Trudeau, she made a negative comment about him that was caught on tape at the 1968 leadership convention. She subsequently retired from politics, leaving the incoming Parliament extremely short of women members. In retirement LaMarsh wrote a notorious memoir of her years in politics, *Bird in a Gilded Cage*, which received a huge advance and sold many thousands of copies.

naturally drawn to the more prosperous regions, while the Atlantic region and Saskatchewan and Manitoba lost population in the 1960s through out-migration. A perception of disparity underlay much of the nation's political discontent. Some disparities were not regional at all, although they often had geographical overtones. Low

wages, high unemployment, low labour force participation, and a limited tax base (constraining the financing of public services) together created higher incidences of inequality in some provinces. Young people under 25 were twice as likely to be unemployed as Canadians over that age, for example, and youth unemployment

TABLE 10.1 Unemployment Rates by Region, 1961–1970

Year	Atlantic	Quebec	Ontario	Prairies	BC	Canada
1961	11.3	9.3	5.5	4.6	8.5	7.2
1962	10.8	7.5	4.3	3.9	6.6	5.9
1963	9.6	7.4	3.8	3.7	6.4	5.5
1964	8.2	6.3	3.3	3.1	5.3	4.7
1965	7.4	5.4	2.5	2.6	4.2	3.9
1966	6.4	4.7	2.5	2.1	4.6	3.6
1967	6.6	5.3	3.1	2.3	5.2	4.1
1968	7.3	6.5	3.6	2.9	6.0	4.8
1969	7.5	6.9	3.1	2.9	5.0	4.7
1970	7.6	6.9	4.3	4.4	7.7	5.9

Source: Department of Regional Economic Expansion/Industry Canada, Major Economic Indicators, Provinces and Regions (Ottawa: Queen's Printer, 1971), Table 2.4.

skyrocketed in marginal areas. Substantial evidence was advanced in this period showing that an individual's ethnic group, racial origin, and gender also affected economic success. And then there were the poor. What constituted real poverty in Canada remained a matter of continual debate. What was indisputable, however, was the inequality of national personal income in Canada. The wealthiest 20 per cent of Canadians earned over 40 per cent of the income, and the poorest 20 per cent earned less than 6 per cent. Most of those in the poorest 20 per cent, it should be added, were employed.

Some of Canada's endemic economic problems were better publicized (if not better resolved) in the 1960s. There were a number of obvious weak points. One was in the food-producing sector. Canadian farmers continued to find that increased mechanization and use of fertilizers meant that fewer hands were needed to produce larger crops. Canadian farms became ever more capital-intensive, marginal lands less attractive, yet returns to the farmer remained sluggish. Most increases in food costs to the consumer were caused by non-agricultural factors, such as transportation and processing, rather than by increased returns to the farmer. The farm population in Canada had been declining absolutely for decades, and this era was no exception. Between the 1961 and 1971 censuses, the number of farm residents fell from 2,072,785 to 1,419,795. Drops were especially marked in Prince Edward Island and Manitoba. As for the fishery, the admission of Newfoundland to Confederation in 1949 only increased the numbers of fishers in serious difficulty. Experts' warnings about overfishing were ignored by governments eager to create programs to aid fishers and fishing communities.

By the end of the period, a handful of environmentalists had begun pointing out the damage being done by those reaping resources without concern for conservation practices and the consequences of pollution. American author Rachel Carson's *Silent Spring* (1962) first called the attention of many Canadians to the evils of toxic chemicals in the environment, and the infamous story of Grassy Narrows in 1970 reinforced the message. At Grassy Narrows, in northwestern Ontario, a pulp mill upstream from the Grassy Narrows Reserve pumped lethal mercury into the waters from which the Aboriginals took their fish. Many inhabitants were systematically poisoned in the process.

Moreover, the issue of foreign ownership, first introduced by the Gordon Commission in 1958, took on a new life in the later 1960s when it became associated with American multinational corporations. Radical younger scholars such as Mel Watkins (b. 1932) called for the repatriation of the Canadian economy. Watkins headed the Task Force on the Structure of Canadian Industry, which in February 1968 released a report entitled *Foreign Ownership and the Structure of Canadian Industry* (the Watkins Report). Such critiques of American multinationalism merged with a widespread Canadian hostility to the policies of the United States, especially in Vietnam, as well as with the concerns of those worried about maintaining a distinctive Canadian identity. Public opinion shifted considerably between 1964 and 1972 over the question of further investment of US capital in Canada. According to a 1964 Gallup poll, only 46 per cent of Canadians thought there was already enough American investment, and 33 per cent wanted more. By 1972, 67 per cent said that was enough, and only 22 per cent wanted further amounts.

TABLE 10.2 Percentage of Employment in Manufacturing by Region, 1961 and 1969, and Average Wage in Manufacturing, 1969

Region	Employment (000s)	1961 Share (%)	1969 Share (%)	Average Wage ($)
Atlantic	76.8	4.6	4.5	4,995
Quebec	527.0	33.6	31.2	5,542
Ontario	836.9	47.8	49.5	6,228
Prairies	119.8	6.9	7.1	5,888
BC	130.7	7.7	7.7	6,591

Source: Department of Regional Economic Expansion/Industry Canada, Major Economic Indicators, Provinces and Regions *(Ottawa: Queen's Printer, 1971), Tables 3.3, 3.1.*

TABLE 10.3 Average Income of Salaried Males in Fourteen Ethnic Groups, Quebec, 1961

Ethnic Group	Income ($)	Index
General Average	3,469	100.0
British	4,940	142.4
Scandinavians	4,939	142.4
Dutch	4,891	140.9
Jewish	4,851	139.8
Russians	4,828	139.1
Germans	4,245	122.6
Poles	3,984	114.8
Asians	3,734	107.6
Ukrainians	3,733	107.6
Other Europeans	3,547	102.4
Hungarians	3,537	101.9
French Canadians	3,185	91.8
Italians	2,938	84.6
Native Indians	2,112	60.8

Source: Canadian Dimension *5, 8 (Feb. 1969): 17.*

Canadian nationalism emerged in the labour movement as well in the 1960s. This issue combined with others, particularly discontent among younger workers with the traditional nature of union leadership and organization. The older union leaders were not much interested in broad reform issues. They tried to dampen the reactions against local branches of international (i.e., American-dominated) unions that were seen as collaborators with American multinationals in both the "sellout" of Canada and the maintenance of the "military-industrial complex." By the later 1960s many rank-and-file union members expressed discontent with American domination. The Americans took more money out of the country in dues than they returned in assistance; they failed to organize outside traditional industrial sectors; they often supported American military adventurism abroad; and, finally, they did not understand Canada and treated Canadian members with contempt. At least so went the complaints. Withdrawal from international unionism began seriously around 1970, and would increase over the next few years as wholly

Canadian unions grew in numbers and membership. One of the major factors in the homegrown union movement was the success of public-sector unionism in the 1960s. In 1963 the Canadian Union of Public Employees organized, and in 1967 thousands of civil servants repudiated staff associations and formed the Public Service Alliance of Canada. Outside the civil service, but within the public sector, unionization was particularly marked in the teaching and health-care professions. Strikes by postal workers, teachers, and even policemen irritated large sectors of the Canadian public. Anger at the interruption of what many Canadians saw as essential services would eventually help make the unions easy targets in the 1970s as scapegoats for Canada's newly emergent economic problems.

Political Leadership

For much of the period, the Liberal hegemony of the King–St Laurent years appeared to be broken or at least bending. Not until the arrival of Pierre Trudeau did the Liberals get back on track, and that was at least partly because Trudeau represented a new style of political leadership, consonant with the age of television. John Diefenbaker, who became Prime Minister in 1957 and swept to a great victory in 1958, had a very old-fashioned political style. His bombastic speeches sounded as if they had been rhetorically crafted in the nineteenth century, and he revelled in being a House of Commons man, good in the specialized cut and thrust of debate in that legislative body. Diefenbaker inspired tremendous loyalty from some members of his party, but he seldom created confidence in his capacity to master public affairs. He was better at being the Leader of the Opposition than Prime Minister. Diefenbaker held a variety of contradictory positions; his latest biographer calls him a "Rogue Tory." He was a populist reformer at the head of a party that contained many genuine conservatives. He was simultaneously a Cold Warrior and a Canadian nationalist, holding both positions equally fervently. Despite his electoral successes in Quebec in 1957 and especially 1958, Diefenbaker was always associated (and associated himself) with English Canada. Diefenbaker's administration gave way to the Americans

on the big principles while balking over the unpleasant consequences and details. Diefenbaker, moreover, was thoroughly detested by American President John F. Kennedy, who referred to "the Chief" as one of the few men he had ever totally despised. Three related issues—the decision to scrap the Avro Arrow, the acceptance of American Bomarc-B missiles on Canadian soil, and the government's reaction to the Cuban Missile Crisis of 1962—illustrate the government's problems.

When Diefenbaker terminated the Avro Arrow project early in 1959, he did so for sound fiscal reasons. The plane had no prospective international market and would be inordinately expensive to build only for Canadian needs. The Prime Minister justified his decision in terms of changing military technology and strategy. An aircraft to intercept bombers would soon be obsolete, said Dief, and what Canada needed were missiles obtainable from the Friendly Giant. It turned out that Canada still needed fighters, however, and the country had to buy some very old F-101 Voodoos from the Americans. By cancelling Canada's principal technological breakthrough into the world of big military hardware in return for an agreement whereby parts of equipment purchased by Canada from the American defence industry would be assembled in Canada, Diefenbaker probably accepted reality. But the Bomarc-B missile was armed with a nuclear warhead, and Canada had a non-nuclear policy. Diefenbaker thus refused to allow the Bomarcs to be properly armed, erroneously insisting that they could be effective with non-nuclear warheads. The question took on new urgency in 1962 after President Kennedy confronted the USSR over the installation of Russian missile bases in Cuba. As Soviet ships carrying the missiles cruised westward towards Cuba and Kennedy threatened war if they did not turn back, NORAD automatically ordered DEFCON3, the state of readiness just short of war. Neither Diefenbaker nor his ministers were consulted—much less informed—about this decision. The Prime Minister was furious that a megalomaniac American President could, in effect, push the button that would destroy Canada.

In the end Nikita Khrushchev backed down in the fearsome game of nuclear chicken, but Cuba changed Canadian public opinion, which had tended to be against nuclear armament. The crisis provoked con-

The revolutionary Avro Arrow, seen here in 1957, was scrapped by the Diefenbaker cabinet in 1959. This decision was the start of a heated debate regarding nuclear arms, which would eventually lead to the collapse of Diefenbaker government. CP PHOTO.

siderable media discussion of the government's prevarications and inconsistencies over nuclear and defence policy. NATO made it quite clear that Canada was part of the nuclear system. Liberal leader Lester Pearson announced that the Liberals would stand by the nation's nuclear commitments even if the government that had made them would not. There was no point in housing nuclear weapons on Canadian soil if they could not be instantly deployed in the event of a crisis. Such defence blunders did Diefenbaker no good in the 1962 election. By January 1963 defence issues had reduced his cabinet to conflicting factions. The minority government fell shortly afterwards. Traditional Canadian nationalism as practised by John Diefenbaker was simply not compatible with the missile age.

During much of Diefenbaker's leadership of the Progressive Conservative Party from 1956 to 1967, his chief political opponent was Lester B. (Mike) Pearson.

The contrast between the two men was instantly apparent, and the "Dief and Mike" show (in the Commons and outside) was the joy of political cartoonists and satirists for that entire decade. Pearson was a soft-spoken former diplomat who had won a Nobel Peace Prize for conciliation in the Suez Crisis of 1956. Quietly ambitious, he had little House of Commons or domestic political experience. Apart from the 1958 election, the nation never gave either Pearson or Diefenbaker a mandate to govern, thus perhaps reflecting its suspicion of their qualifications. The voters preferred Diefenbaker in 1957, 1958, and 1962 (the first and the third elections producing minority governments), and Pearson in 1963 and 1965 (both times in a minority situation). Pearson was better able to govern with a minority, since his party could arrive at unofficial understandings with the CCF-NDP, something not possible for the Diefenbaker Tories. Pearson was no more able than Diefenbaker to rein in ambitious colleagues or provinces, however. The decade 1957–67 was one of constant federal political turmoil and federal–provincial hassles.

The returning Liberals, who regained power in 1963 under Pearson, spent most of the 1960s attempting to implement the integration of Canada's armed forces, mainly on the grounds that duplication of resources and command structures was an expensive luxury the nation could not afford. A unified Canadian military would be both leaner and meaner, capable of remaining within acceptable budget figures. A White Paper to this effect was released in March of 1964, and Bill C-90, which amended the National Defence Act by creating a single Chief of Defence Staff, was introduced into the House of Commons on 10 April 1964. The amendments producing a fully integrated military headquarters with a single chain of command received royal assent on 16 July 1964. The country and its politicians, however,

John Diefenbaker and Lester Pearson, 30 January 1958. This photograph was taken two weeks after Pearson became Leader of the Liberal Opposition. Duncan Cameron, LAC, PA-117093.

continued to hold schizophrenic attitudes towards the Canadian military, its foreign obligations, and Canada's overseas role. Canada wanted to control its own destiny, which probably required a neutral stance internationally. Neutrality in international affairs would cost even more than the American and NATO alliances, however, so everyone pretended that Canada could hold the line on military spending and still honour its commitments through administrative reform. At the same time, Canada began a long, slow, gradual process of reducing its armed forces, a process that was still underway in the twenty-first century.

Despite Prime Minister Pearson's high profile as a successful world diplomat, his governments were not distinguished for their triumphs in the international arena. In fairness to Pearson, the world was changing in other ways not sympathetic to Canada's self-proclaimed role as a middle power. After 1960 the United Nations General Assembly opened its doors to dozens of Third World countries, most of them recently emerged from colonial status and quite hostile to the Western democracies. The new complexities of politics and expectations within the General Assembly, and in the various collateral UN organizations, worked against a highly developed and industrialized nation such as Canada—populated chiefly by the descendants of white Europeans—which also happened to be a junior partner of the United States. In UN bodies Canadian diplomats found themselves in the embarrassing position of defending the country's internal policy, particularly towards Aboriginal peoples, in the face of criticisms of racism and insensitivity to human rights. Canada was not in the same league as South Africa, perhaps, but its record on human rights was a hard one to explain internationally. At the same time, the success of the European Economic Community (first established in 1958) made Western European nations more important international players, while Japan had succeeded in restoring its industrial position. As a result, Canada became less important among the industrial nations at the same time that it became less credible in the Third World.

It was not only the configuration of world politics that had altered by the 1960s. So had the policy of the United States. President Kennedy and his successor,

Lyndon B. Johnson, were actually more hard-bitten and confrontational Cold Warriors than their predecessors, Truman and Eisenhower. The latter had been extremely embarrassed in 1960 when the Russians shot down an American U-2 spy plane and captured its pilot, Francis Gary Powers. Kennedy, on the other hand, authorized dirty tricks by the CIA in foreign countries, and he made no apology when they were exposed. His only regret about the abortive 1961 Bay of Pigs invasion of Cuba by US-backed Cuban exiles, for example, was that it had failed. Most important, however, both Kennedy and Johnson permitted their governments to become ever more deeply involved in the quagmire of Southeast Asia. In 1945, Ho Chi Minh declared the Democratic Republic of Vietnam, with Hanoi as its capital, to be independent of French colonial control. When the French government proved incapable of defeating the armed "insurgents," Canada in 1954 became involved in attempts at international control. It served as one of three members, with Poland and India, of a joint commission. Canada was actually eager to participate to bolster its middle-power pretensions in the world. The 1954 commission set the pattern for the next 20 years: one Iron Curtain nation, one Western ally of the United States, one neutral power, with votes often going against Canada as the American supporter. From the outset Canada had deceived itself into believing that it had a free hand to carry out its work without either upsetting the Americans or appearing to act merely as a lackey of the United States.

When the American administration gradually escalated both US involvement and the shooting war in Vietnam after 1963, Canada's position became increasingly anomalous, both on the commission and outside it. Lester Pearson was still hoping to mediate in April 1965 when he used the occasion of a speech in Philadelphia to suggest that the American government might pause in its bombing of North Vietnam to see if a negotiated settlement was possible. He was soon shown the error of his ways in no uncertain terms. In a private meeting with Lyndon Johnson shortly thereafter, the American President shook Pearson by his lapels and criticized Canadian presumptuousness with Texas profanity. Vietnam certainly contributed to a new Canadian mood in the later 1960s, both in Ottawa and on the main streets of the nation. Canadians

now sought to distance themselves from the policies of the "Ugly Americans," although never by open withdrawal from the American defence umbrella.

The victory of Pierre Trudeau in 1968 marked a new era, which by the early 1970s saw a return to Liberal hegemony. The Tories had chosen Robert Stanfield (1914–2003) to succeed Diefenbaker. The soft-spoken Stanfield seemed a good match for Lester Pearson, but could not compete with the trendy and articulate Trudeau. Like the pop stars he seemed to emulate, Trudeau was capable of repackaging his image (and his policies) to suit conditions changing so fast they seemed to be "blowin' in the wind." Not only was Trudeau a thoroughly bilingual French Canadian who was likely to appeal to Quebec, but he was continually able to convince the electorate that he was far more of a reformer than his subsequent policies would indicate. After years of apparently irresolute national leadership, Trudeau also seemed to be a strong figure. In some respects he was, as his behaviour in the October Crisis of 1970 demonstrated. The Prime Minister did not hesitate for a moment to invoke the War Measures Act and employ the military against the FLQ. Most of the nation appreciated his decisiveness.

The era was also characterized by a number of long-serving and highly visible provincial premiers, who provided considerable stability for the provincial cause in the regularly held federal–provincial conferences. While federal leadership had been ineffective for the 10 years before Trudeau, almost all the provinces had seemingly strong leaders. There continued to be little genuine two-party politics anywhere in Canada. Instead, dominant parties were usually in control. In Newfoundland Joey Smallwood still governed virtually unopposed. In New Brunswick Louis Robichaud was in control from 1960 to 1970. Ontario had John Robarts, Manitoba had Duff Roblin, Saskatchewan had Ross Thatcher, while Alberta still had Ernest Manning and British Columbia was led by W.A.C. Bennett. Few of these governments were Liberal. Ross Thatcher (1917–71) headed the only provincial Liberal government west of Quebec between 1945 and 1972, and he was a vociferous critic of the federal Liberals. By the early 1970s the only provincial governments controlled by the Liberals were in Prince Edward Island and Quebec. Pierre Trudeau's conception of liberalism and federalism certainly did not accord with that of Quebec's Liberal Premier, Robert Bourassa (1933–96).

No matter who was in charge and at what level, the size and scope of the apparatus of bureaucracy continually expanded. The scope of bureaucracy had political as well as economic implications. The larger it got, the harder it was to manage. A host of journalists and popular commentators attacked governments at all levels for mismanagement and waste, but as one commentator astutely pointed out, "It is true that the initial motive for reforms may be the outsider's simple-minded belief that gigantic savings can be effected. But once set an investigation afoot and the economy motive gets quickly overlaid with the more subtle and difficult problems of improved service and efficiency" (Hodgetts, 1968: 7–8). The Royal Commission on Government Organization, appointed by Diefenbaker in 1960, found itself unable to effect major changes in the bureaucracy, particularly in downsizing the scope of operations. All governments, including federal Liberal ones, increasingly found themselves entrapped by the actions of their predecessors and by the difficulties of dismantling systems once created. Government was becoming more difficult and the nation increasingly impossible to lead.

Immigration Reform

The conversion, within the space of a single generation, from a very insular and parochial nation to one that was relatively sophisticated and cosmopolitan, much more capable of toleration of ethnic differences, has been one of the most remarkable and underrated public changes in Canadian history. One factor in the change of attitude was World War II, a war in which over a million Canadians served in the military, more than half of them overseas. Unlike the Great War, which most Canadian soldiers spent in disgusting trenches on the continent of Europe, World War II actually gave Canadians some foreign experience. Over a quarter of a million troops spent up to four years in Great Britain, waiting for the Big Show of D-Day to begin and at least sometimes playing at being tourists. Canadian soldiers fought in Italy and through France, the Low Countries, and Germany. Such fighting was not nice but it was considerably more

broadening than life in a muddy trench. That over 50,000 Canadians met foreign girls and got to know them well enough to propose marriage suggests some of the possibilities. The American popular song of World War I had queried, "How you gonna keep 'em, down on the farm, after they've seen Paree?" That question was really much more relevant for Canada in 1945 than in 1918.

A second factor was the post-war immigration itself. Between 1946 and 1972 more than 3.5 million "new Canadians" entered the country, an average of about 135,000 per year. Even after emigration to other nations from Canada is subtracted (since people, especially recent arrivals, also *left* the country in substantial numbers), the net gain was well in excess of two million. By 1971, one in every four Canadians claimed an ethnic origin other than British, French, or Aboriginal. The changes are detailed in Table 10.4.

Proportionate to the total population, the post-World War II figures for immigration were not as significant as the earlier influxes of immigration to Canada before Confederation and before the Great War, but the post-war immigration was different. Unlike earlier arrivals, many of whom ended up on isolated farmsteads on the frontier, this population settled almost exclusively in the cities, especially those in Ontario and Quebec, transforming them enormously in the process. Before 1945, for example, Toronto had been a predominantly Anglo-Saxon city, where only in certain areas could any language other than English be heard. By 1961 it was a city of ethnic neighbourhoods. Although Montreal had always been bilingual rather than unilingual, the sense of it as a polyglot city was present by the 1960s, as was the case in almost all of the larger cities of Canada west of the Atlantic region. The urban concentration of the post-war immigration made for the emergence of multi-ethnic cities.

A third factor in the new acceptance of cultural diversity was the rapid transformation into modern times of the rural communities of Canada between 1945 and 1960. In 1945 most rural Canadians lived in virtual isolation in a world of unpaved roads, horse-powered vehicles, cash shortages, and an absence of telephones and electricity. By 1960 the roads had been paved. The horse had been replaced by the tractor and the automobile. Farm families now had cash, from the monthly

BACKGROUNDER

Expo 67

The Canadian Pavilion at Expo 67, dominated by a huge inverted pyramid. The dome beside it was clad with enlarged photos of Canadian scenes.

The Centennial Year bash of 1967 was a bipartisan extravaganza. Plans for the 100th anniversary of Confederation had begun under John Diefenbaker and continued under Lester Pearson. Canada had initially lost its bid for an international world's fair in 1967 to the Soviet Union, but the Russians had backed out and Canada replaced them at virtually the last minute (at least in terms of preparing for such a complex event). Substantial amounts of money were spent by Ottawa (some of it naturally filtered through the provinces and municipalities) on public buildings to serve as Centennial monuments, such as the National Arts Centre in Ottawa (which opened in June 1969) and Confederation Centre in Charlottetown. A national train loaded with exhibits toured the country, and various other manifestations of celebration

Continued...

included a catchy birthday song by Bobby Gimby ("Can-a-da, We Love You"). Canadians were slow to warm to the hoopla, at least before the opening of the Canadian Universal and International Exhibition at Montreal, familiarly known as Expo 67, which had as its theme Man and His World (Terre des Hommes) and the participation of some 120 governments from around the globe. Canadians surprised themselves—and the world—by surmounting a host of organizational obstacles to create what many acknowledged to be the greatest world's fair ever. Much credit was given to Montreal mayor Jean Drapeau for his persistent leadership. The magnificent displays in many buildings of architectural distinction and innovation (Buckminster Fuller's geodesic dome for the American Pavilion and Moshe Safdie's Habitat '67, a Canadian experimental modular housing project, were among the most talked about), a World Arts Festival, and excellent services and staff attracted 50 million paid admissions. The Canadian Pavilion was dominated by a huge inverted pyramid (the Katimavik, an Inuit word for "meeting place"). The dome alongside was clad with rows of enlarged photographs of Canada and the show-space in the foreground featured continuous entertainment by choirs, dancers, folksingers, and other performers and musicians from across the country.

As well as performing, Canadians themselves attended in great numbers to enjoy the exposition's 90 pavilions, riding on the mini-rail that connected the entire site. Though financial overruns and construction problems were the stuff of legend, tourist revenues generated by the exhibition were almost double the official $283 million cost; much of the money was spent in Quebec. All difficulties were easily dismissed in the euphoria and pride of having produced an undisputed world-scale triumph. Although it is always impossible to measure the impact on the national psyche of events like Expo 67, most commentators felt that the fair had made a significant positive contribution to Canadian self-confidence.

mothers' allowance cheque from the federal government, if from no other source. Virtually every family had a telephone, and the world of electricity meant milking machines, electric stoves, and refrigerators, as well as radios, television sets, and stereos. Rural and farm families had become plugged into the larger industrial economy rather than isolated from it, and there would be no going back.

Both the preference for urban life of post-war immigrants and the rural transformation helped contribute to a fourth factor in the change, which was the overall extent to which Canada became an urban nation in the years after 1945, especially in the provinces of Ontario and Quebec. This new wave of urbanization was based on a transportation shift to automobiles and trucks, the change from industrial to service production, and suburban development, as well as on the influx of immigrants and rural Canadians into the urban centres. In 1941 only 55 per cent of Canada's people lived in cities. That figure grew to 62.9 per cent in 1951 and 69.7 per cent in 1961. By 1971 over three-quarters of the Canadian population lived in an urban environment. Cities have usually been responsible for breaking down the old traditionalism of a society, and for long-resident Canadians in the post-war period, they did their job. It must be added that for many new arrivals, large cities and the resultant concentration of ethnic groups in complete communities meant that Canadian cities could actually slow acculturation rather than speed it up.

A fifth factor, related in part to rural transformation but involving the entire society, was the rapid modernization of Quebec. Between 1939 and 1960 Quebec caught up socially and economically with English-speaking Canada. The process involved substantial industrialization and urbanization. Quebec ceased to be a traditional society with its values based upon Catholicism. Symptomatically, the birth rate in Quebec in these years dropped from one of the highest in Canada to one of the

TABLE 10.4 Population by Ethnic Origin,1951–1971

Ethnic Group	1951	1961	1971
British Isles	6,709,685	7,996,669	9,624,115*
English	3,630,344	4,195,175	
Irish	1,439,635	1,753,351	
Scots	1,547,470	1,902,302	
Welsh, etc.	92,236	145,841	
French	4,319,167	5,540,346	6,180,120
Other European	2,553,722	4,116,849	4,959,680
Asiatic	72,827	121,753	285,540
Other**	354,028	462,630	518,850***

*By 1971 Statistics Canada had decided no longer to separate the British into national groups.
**Including Eskimo, Native Indian, Negro, West Indian, and not stated.
***Americans are included nowhere in this table because Statistics Canada did not regard the people of the United States as an ethnic group; Americans were listed under their "national origins."

lowest. The socio-economic transformation was accompanied by a series of profound ideological shifts within Quebec society that shook its foundations to the very core. The patterns of that development were relatively comprehensible to anyone familiar with what was happening elsewhere in developing societies. Traditional forms of defensive nationalism, including the power and authority of the Church, were eventually swept away by a new powerful and secular form of nationalism that had already become fully articulated in the years before 1960. The main opposition to the new nationalism came less from the old nationalism than from a renewed current of nineteenth-century liberalism adapted to twentieth-century Quebec conditions. In the 1960s, these two competing ideological currents would find popular labels in Quebec as "separatism" and "federalism." Quebec's new internal nationalism meant that the province no longer served as a brake on federal policies of liberalization and that, instead, the province's demands helped contribute to change. The "Quiet Revolution" of the 1960s would be a major impetus to a number of new Canadian policies. Most Quebecers were quite happy to accept ethnic minorities so long as they were prepared to speak French and associate themselves with the aspirations of Quebec. In the process of dealing with the new Quebec, a succession of Canadian govern-

ments would remake policy towards immigration and ethnic culture.

Finally, as discussed in Chapter 9, the new communications media, particularly the general expansion of television right across the Canadian population after 1950, increasingly plugged Canadians into the world. While television put Canadians back into their homes, clustered around the TV set to watch their favourite shows, it also helped force them out of their narrow insularity, not so much into their local communities as into the international world previously beyond their ken. It was not lost on Canadians that Richard Nixon was defeated in the 1960 American election by John F. Kennedy in no small part because Nixon sweated profusely and appeared to have a five-o'clock shadow during the first-ever televised presidential debate—in less than a decade Canadians would choose their own charismatic, media-savvy politician, Pierre Trudeau, to lead the country. And during the tense days of the Cuban Missile Crisis, the ongoing developments became "must-see" television in Canada just as they were in the United States.

Just as immigration in the post-war period changed Canada's view of itself, so did immigration policy change the character of immigrants to Canada. As we saw in Chapter 9, Ellen Fairclough, the Minister of

Immigration, sought unsuccessfully in 1959 to limit family immigration sponsorship to immediate family members, but she persisted with immigration reform. In 1962 she tabled in the House of Commons new immigration regulations that removed racial discrimination and introduced skill as the major criterion for unsponsored immigration. Such a policy was consistent with Prime Minister Diefenbaker's 1960 Bill of Rights, which rejected discrimination based on race, colour, national origin, religion, or gender. With this change to immigration policy, sponsored immigration—which was continued— almost immediately became by definition part of the old discriminatory system favouring European over non-European immigrants, since there were many more Canadians of European descent to sponsor new arrivals. According to the deputy minister of immigration:

> Our prime objective in the proposed revision is to eliminate all discrimination based on colour, race or creed. This means that, if we continue to allow Greeks, Poles, Italians, Portuguese and other Europeans to bring in the wide range of relatives presently admissible, we will have to do the same for Japanese, Chinese, Indians, Pakistanis, Africans, persons from the Arab world, the West Indies and so forth. The only possible result of this would be a substantially larger number of unskilled close relatives from these parts of the world to add to the influx of unskilled close relatives from Europe. (Quoted in Hawkins, 1972: 112)

To avoid this result, he added that it was going to be necessary to open the door to close relatives from all parts of the world and to reduce somehow the flow of European close relatives. However, section 31(d) of the regulations did not open the sponsorship door to non-Europeans.

The new regulations also provided for an Immigration Board semi-independent of the Immigration Department to hear appeals, except in sponsorship cases. On the front of illegal Chinese immigration, the government decided to declare an "amnesty" to all Chinese who had arrived illegally in Canada before 1 July 1960. This was the first of a long series of amnesties that would be declared to deal with illegal immigration to Canada. The Liberals complained in Parliament that this cosmic shift in Canadian policy had occurred without any public debate, which was of course true. Whether Canadian public opinion would have sustained such a non-racial policy in 1962 is, of course, quite doubtful. The new non-racial policy did not have an immediate impact on Canada because of the low level of immigration in the early 1960s. The low levels were a result of budget cutbacks to the Department of Immigration under the Diefenbaker government caused by financial rather than policy considerations. At the same time, it must be admitted that the Diefenbaker cabinet saw immigration as an unpleasant and necessary evil upon which as little money as possible should be spent.

Although there had been some shift in country of birth of immigrants after 1945, in 1965 Britain still provided nearly 30 per cent of the newcomers, continental Europe nearly half, and the United States 10 per cent, leaving only a little over 10 per cent of immigration originating in the remainder of the world. At this time, all of the top 10 "nations of origin" except the United States were still European. In 1966 the Liberal government of Lester B. Pearson epitomized much of the official Canadian philosophy of immigration when it put immigration under the same minister as manpower in the Department of Manpower and Immigration. The opposition in Parliament criticized the melding of immigration policy into the labour portfolio, preferring instead a department of citizenship and immigration. The deputy minister of the new Department of Manpower and Immigration found his task no easy one, reporting in his memoirs:

> Politicians were understandably chary of defining immigration policy at all precisely. On one hand, there was a broad public sentiment in favour of easy immigration; so many Canadians, if not immigrants themselves, had known parents or grandparents who were. There was also strong humanitarian sentiment on behalf of the oppressed and the deprived. And behind these general attitudes were powerful special interests: business wanting

both skilled professionals and cheap labour; expanding universities wanting professors with doctorates not available in Canada; richer people wanting domestic servants. And, of course, recent immigrants wanted their relatives and friends to join them, and ethnic organizations had strong interests in the growth of their particular communities. (Kent, 1988: 407)

The new ministry sounded out public opinion in 1966 through the publication of a White Paper on Immigration Policy. This document argued for the recruitment of workers with high degrees of skills, regardless "of race, colour or religion." It also insisted that the government should not hesitate to keep out misfits and criminals. Public hearings on the White Paper by the Special Joint Committee of the Senate and House of Commons on Immigration began in November of 1966.

The Joint Committee heard a full spectrum of opinion from what Tom Kent has called the "special interests." The Confederation of National Trade Unions (CNTU) in Quebec opposed an emphasis on skills, insisting that such a policy would represent an international brain drain in which Canada would weaken Third World nations by taking their professionals. The Canadian Labour Congress agreed, adding that unskilled immigrant workers were needed to carry out "tasks which native born or already established immigrants refuse to perform because of their better training." The Mining Association of Canada definitely wanted at least 4,000 semi-skilled workers admitted per year, noting, "The type of immigrant we have in mind has been the backbone of the labour force of the mining industry in the past. . . . a man has to be physically fit; but his education is not too important, so long as he can read or write." Canadians would not work in mines, reported one witness from the mining interests, because "there are no roads, no TVs, no cars, few girls, little or no liquor and most people recoil from the idea of working underground" (quoted in Avery, 1995: 181). No mention was made by this witness of the danger or relatively low pay experienced by miners. Most Canadian industrialists advocated the admission of the unskilled,

although the Canadian Manufacturers' Association and the Canadian Medical Association both stressed the need for those who were technologically prepared. The Canadian Jewish Congress emphasized humanitarian concerns, "the need for people to find asylum." Many ethnic organizations applauded the new emphasis on skills, but most also insisted on the maintenance of the sponsorship category.

Having listened to the interest groups, the ministry moved quickly to major reform of immigration policy, instituting in 1968 a major new mechanism for immigration selection, the "points system." According to Tom Kent (1988: 410), "If we could identify and define the various factors affecting a person's ability to settle in Canada, and attach relative weights to them, then immigration officers would have a consistent basis on which to assess potential immigrants." Thus, education, employment opportunities, skills, age, and the immigration officer's assessment of potential were all to be awarded points adding up to a maximum total of 100. The points system—skills had only limited support from the hearing—was put in place apart from sponsorship, which was continued (although with reduced categories) because of its support from corporate Canada, trade unions, and ethnic groups.

A new procedure allowing for the application for immigration status from within the country was also introduced and would ultimately become one of the most controversial parts of the new immigration law. This last policy was prompted chiefly by the appearance as visitors in Canada of American draft evaders and was intended to regularize requests for landed immigrant status from this particular group of refugees. In the late 1960s as many as 100,000 Americans seeking to avoid service in the Vietnam War had come to Canada and were sheltered by Canadians and the Canadian government. The points system officially eliminated discrimination on the grounds of race or class but managed to perpetuate several traditional features of Canadian policy. By awarding large numbers of the points required for acceptance as an immigrant to Canada on the basis of occupation, education, language skills, and age, it continued both the economic rationale for immigration and the selectivity of the process.

The Beginning of International Drift

After Pierre Trudeau succeeded Pearson in April 1968, an undeclared and never co-ordinated policy of retreat from middle-power pretensions was accelerated. Trudeau had long been critical of Canada's foreign and defence policies. Soon after his accession to office, he initiated formal reviews, which the Departments of National Defence and External Affairs found most threatening. The Prime Minister was particularly eager to raise "fundamental questions," such as whether there was really a Russian threat to world order, or whether the US "[would] sacrifice Europe and NATO before blowing up the world" (quoted in Granatstein and Bothwell, 1990: 17). The bureaucrats were not comfortable with such questions, nor were several of Trudeau's cabinet colleagues. Trudeau had a reputation as an internationalist, but he disliked the military, and ultimately proved much more comfortable with domestic matters than external ones. For Trudeau, protecting the sovereignty of Canadian territory was far more important than international peacekeeping. Defence budgets continued to be cut and active Canadian involvement in NATO was pared to the lowest limits of allied acceptability. The best-known armed action by the Canadian military was its occupation of Quebec during the October Crisis of 1970. In 1973 Canada sent a large military mission to Vietnam to serve on a revised International Commission for Control and Supervision. Its purpose was to allow the Americans to withdraw from that troubled corner of the world, but the Commission was not able to act effectively. The Trudeau government called it home in mid-1973. Canada was no longer a self-defined middle power. It had no clear conception of its place or role in world affairs.

Canada's problem in the world was basically simple. Its economic indicators entitled it to major-league status, but its population was small and its close relationship with the United States inevitably consigned it to being a minor-league subsidiary player. The Canadian image abroad was as perplexing as its policies. On the one hand, the country continued its irritating habit of preaching from on high to nations that did not regard themselves as morally inferior. Catching Canada in hypocritical moral contradictions became a favourite international game. Canada's multilateral involvements limited its abilities to provide practical support for human rights issues, despite some internal pressures to adopt a more interventionist human rights position. On the other hand, Canada continued to be one of the most favoured destinations for immigrants from around the world. Ordinary people accepted that life was better in Canada. Indeed, surveys regularly listed Canada at the top of the international standard-of-living table.

Whatever the Department of External Affairs was or was not doing, Canadians themselves became citizens of the world in a way that would have been incomprehensible to earlier generations. By the early 1970s, relatively cheap airplane tickets to go anywhere in the world had become an accepted part of life. In the 1960s the kids had travelled the world, carrying backpacks festooned with the Canadian flag and sleeping in youth hostels. Now their parents followed them, staying in hotels that were just like those at home. Almost every Canadian family had at least one member with photographs of a major overseas expedition. Cheap airfares also brought relatives from abroad to visit Canada. All this travel combined with new immigration to make Canada an increasingly cosmopolitan place to live. Canadians drank less beer and more wine, much of it imported. They ate in restaurants with exotic cuisines, learned to cook similar food at home, and insisted that this type of food be available at their local supermarkets.

Pierre Trudeau's attempt to reorient Canadian foreign policy met with limited success. He managed to reduce Canada's military commitment to NATO and to reduce the size of Canada's armed forces. In 1972 the government produced a policy document that recommended a "Third Option": less dependence upon the Americans. But if Canada moved away from the Americans, where would it go? The obvious answer was to Europe. Canada had waited too long and had become too closely identified with (not to mention integrated in) the American economy. The fizzle of the European initiative was followed by a similar effort in Asia, with perhaps slightly better success.

The Expansion of the Welfare State

Part of the reason for the continual expansion of government bureaucracy was regular (if unco-ordinated) expansion of the Canadian welfare state. Politicians viewed expanded social services as popular vote-getters, and no political party strenuously opposed the principles of welfare democracy. Although the Diefenbaker government was not associated with any major program, it had initiated a number of reviews and Royal Commissions, the recommendations of which would pass into legislation under the Liberals. The minority Pearson government was pushed towards improved social insurance by the NDP, its own reforming wing, and competitive pressures from an ambitious Quebec and other provinces. Were Ottawa not to introduce new national programs, the federal government could well lose control of them to the wealthier and more aggressive provinces. The expansion in 1964 of family allowances to include children up to the age of 18 who were still in school merely imitated something introduced by the Lesage government in 1961. In 1965 the federal government attempted to introduce a national contributory pension scheme, but settled for one that allowed Quebec its own plan.

The changing demography of Canada guaranteed that there would be continual pressures on the government to improve the pension system. Those who wanted improved benefits were able to make common ground with those who sought to control costs. Both could agree on the superiority of a contributory scheme. The Medical Care Act of 1966 built on provincial initiatives with a cost-sharing arrangement. By 1968 all provinces and territories had agreed on cost-sharing arrangements with Ottawa that produced a social minimum in health care. For most Canadians, access to medical service (doctors and hospitalization) would thereafter be without charge. Occasionally cynicism triumphed. Early in 1965 Prime Minister Pearson wrote his cabinet ministers asking for suggestions of policy initiatives that would shift attention from political harassment by the opposition over mistakes and difficulties. The result was a Canadian variation of Lyndon Johnson's War on Poverty. Canada proposed a full utilization of human resources and an end to poverty. Actual reforms were not very significant.

The first Trudeau government, responding to the reform euphoria of the era, actually contemplated shifting the grounds of social protectionism in "the Just Society." To bureaucrats and political leaders in the late 1960s the emphasis of mainstream reform had been to carry out the agenda of the 1940s for the establishment of a "social minimum" providing basic economic security for all Canadians. Now, at least briefly, they debated the possibility of expanding the welfare state to include some measure of income distribution. Poverty came to be seen as a serious problem worthy of public focus. The Economic Council of Canada in 1968 described the persistence of poverty in Canada as "a disgrace." Later that same year a Special Senate Committee on Poverty was established under Senator David Croll's chairmanship. In 1971 this committee produced a report, *Poverty in Canada*, which insisted that nearly two million people in Canada lived below the poverty line. More radical critics, in *The Real Poverty Report* that same year, put the figure much higher.

Poverty not only characterized the lives of millions of Canadians, but it was structural, regional, and related to racial and gender discrimination. A number of schemes were suggested, including a guaranteed income for low-income families as part of the family allowance package. The year 1970 had already seen the publication of a federal White Paper called "Income Security for Canadians," which pointed out the escalating costs of social insurance and criticized the principle of universality that had previously governed Canadian policy. The ultimate result was the new Unemployment Insurance Plan of 1971, which extended and increased coverage without actually addressing the concept of a guaranteed minimum income for all Canadians. At about the same time, Ottawa eliminated a separate fund for Canada pension contributions and began considering them as part of the general revenue of the government.

Reformers had long insisted that access to education was one of the social rights to which all Canadians were entitled. Increasing access meant creating new facilities. The presence of the baby-boom generation

TABLE 10.5 Expenditures on Personal Health Care as a Percentage of Gross Provincial Product and Personal Income, Ontario, 1960–1975

Year	GPP	Personal Income
1960	3.76	4.62
1961	3.95	4.98
1962	4.04	5.04
1963	4.14	5.17
1964	4.15	5.40
1965	4.18	5.47
1966	4.08	5.35
1967	4.43	5.67
1968	4.69	5.99
1969	4.76	6.04
1970	5.06	6.32
1971	5.32	6.57
1972	5.17	6.18
1973	6.56	6.05
1974	6.38	8.23
1975	6.94	8.57

Source: K.J. Rea, The Prosperous Years: The Economic History of Ontario 1939–75 (Toronto: University of Toronto Press, 1985), 119.

of university expansion in Canada. Not only were new facilities constructed, but 20,000 new faculty members were recruited, most of them from the United States. By 1970 public spending on education had risen to 9 per cent of the gross national product, and represented nearly 20 per cent of all taxes levied by all three levels of government.

Before 1970 the disagreement between the universalists and the means testers had been relatively muted. Both sides could agree that there had been an absence of overall integrated planning in the growth of the welfare state. Little attention had been paid to the long-range implications of any policy. Bureaucracies and programs had been allowed to expand with no thought for tomorrow. The later 1960s had introduced a new ingredient into the mix, however. Governments began routinely spending more money than they were receiving.

Quebec

In the 1960s the average Anglo-Canadian discovered that Quebec was unhappy with Confederation. That discovery was part of the completion of Quebec's transformation into a secularized, urbanized, and industrialized region that differed little in many respects from its central Canadian neighbour, Ontario. The transformation was often associated with the Quiet Revolution in the first half of the decade, a term used by the media to describe the modernization of Quebec. The structural changes to French-Canadian society had already taken place before 1960, even though at the close of the 1950s traditional French-Canadian nationalism in Church and state, symbolized by the Union Nationale, still seemed to prevail. The critique of tradition had already been elaborated and the program of reform for Quebec was well articulated. All that remained was to fit the government of Quebec and popular aspirations together. That task was begun by the provincial Liberal Party, led by Jean Lesage (1912–80), which defeated the Union Nationale and came to power in 1960. The leading Liberal strategists did not realize at the time just how ready Quebec was for change, or how easily the traditional institutions and ways would crumble once they were confronted by

gave urgency to that implication. Parents were much attracted to the practical benefits of education in providing future employment and a better life for their children. The results in the 1960s were enormous pressures on education budgets and increasing demand for the production of more and better teachers. School authorities attempted to ease some of their problems by consolidating rural education through use of the ubiquitous yellow school bus, a process that continued into the early 1970s. Teachers acquired more formal credentials, became better paid, and organized themselves into a powerful professional lobby that was sometimes even unionized. By the late 1950s virtually everyone could agree on the need for universal high school education, and by 1970 over 90 per cent of Canadian children of high school age were in school. Increasing numbers of high school graduates were entitled to a university education, and the decade of the 1960s was the golden age an activist government composed of politicians drawn from Quebec's new middle and professional classes.

The first major step had to do with hydroelectricity. The tradition that had to be overcome was the long-standing Quebec fear, nurtured for decades by the Union Nationale, of anything resembling economic statism (or socialism or communism). *Anti-étatisme* in Quebec was not the same thing as a do-nothing government. Under Duplessis, the provincial government had spent a lot of money on public services, including many hydroelectric projects to assist rural electrification. What the Minister of Natural Resources, René Lévesque (1922–87), proposed on 12 February 1962, without consulting his colleagues, was the enforced government consolidation of all existing private hydroelectric companies into one massive Hydro-Québec. Hydroelectricity was an ideal place to fight the battle of nationalization, partly because electrical generation and supply was a public enterprise right across North America, partly because it directly touched the pocketbook of the rural Quebecer, who was most likely to oppose state action. Despite a famous 'Jamais!' from Premier Lesage, nationalization was quickly accepted by the Liberal cabinet as a winning campaign issue, and the Liberals took it to the province in 1962 with the slogan "Maîtres chez nous." Led by Lesage and a compelling Lévesque, the Liberals managed to turn Hydro-Québec into a symbol of the economic liberation of Quebec from its colonial status, thus co-opting the new nationalism with a vengeance. Liberal expenditures on welfare state reform and public enterprise tripled the provincial budget in the early 1960s, which saw provincial government involvement in almost every economic, industrial, and social activity in Quebec.

The other great symbolic reform of Lesage's Quiet Revolution was the secularization and modernization of Quebec's educational system. Since before Confederation, education had been in the hands of the Catholic Church, which staffed its schools chiefly with priests and nuns teaching a curriculum slow to change from the nineteenth-century classical one. By 1960 the Church itself was in trouble, not just in Quebec but around the world. Criticism of Quebec education was led by a Catholic clergyman, Brother Jean-Paul Desbiens (1927–2006), who published the best-selling

Les Insolences de Frère Untel (translated in 1962 as *The Impertinences of Brother Anonymous*), based on a series of letters he had written to *Le Devoir* in 1959. The spate of responses to Frère Untel, many of them in the form of letters to editors of newspapers, demonstrated that he had struck a chord in the province. Lesage responded with a provincial commission of inquiry into education, chaired by the vice-rector of Laval University, Monseigneur Alphonse-Marie Parent. The Parent Commission's hearings produced a battery of complaints and indictments of the Quebec system, most of which the Commission endorsed in its 1963 report. The Parent Commission called not only for modernization along North American lines but for administration by a unitary secular authority. Armed with this endorsement, in 1964 the Lesage government passed Bill 60, which for the first time placed education in Quebec under provincial administration. Quebec education was thereafter rapidly brought up to national standards.

The Lesage government also sensed the importance of Frère Untel's call for the preservation and extension of French-Canadian culture and the French language. It had already created the Ministry of Cultural Affairs in 1961, which presided happily—with grants and other forms of support—over a veritable explosion of French-Canadian art and writing in the 1960s. The Ministry of Cultural Affairs in many ways typified the Quiet Revolution. The Lesage government was not so much the agent of change in Quebec as its *animateur*. As such it was the beneficiary of years of preparation by others. What the Liberals did was to identify some of the key problems, thus liberating the new-found aspirations of Quebec. Nevertheless, Lesage's government was defeated in 1966 by a rejuvenated Union Nationale under Daniel Johnson (1915–68), chiefly because it had failed to follow to its nationalist conclusion the logic of the revolution over which it had presided. The Union Nationale continued the Lesage program with louder nationalist rhetoric. In 1970 the party in turn was defeated by the Liberals under the new party leader, Robert Bourassa, partly because it was squeezed between the Liberals and the newly formed Parti Québécois (PQ), partly because too many of its leaders had suffered fatal heart attacks (as had similarly happened to the Union Nationale a decade earlier when first Duplessis and then his successor, Paul Sauvé, died).

Quebec's attitude towards Confederation changed perceptibly during the 1960s. Under Duplessis, Quebec supported provincial rights to prevent Ottawa from taking control of them. Under Lesage and his successors, provincial powers were something to be exercised positively as Quebec built its own welfare state and accompanying bureaucracy. Quebec's newly empowered middle class became increasingly conscious of the powers beyond their reach. A substantial separatist movement developed in the province, its most visible example the FLQ. This organization, founded in March 1963, soon began a terrorist campaign to publicize its views. In November 1967, René Lévesque took a more traditional path towards political change when he resigned from the Quebec Liberal Party and began organizing the Parti Québécois, which was devoted to some form of independence. Along with increased constitutional militancy came increased fears for the future of the French language, with many French Canadians turning a suspicious eye on the immigrant groups in Quebec who were still educating their children in English. By 1970 no Quebec politician wanted to be publicly associated with anything less than provincial autonomy. The first round of separatist agitation came to a climax in October 1970 when two cells of the FLQ kidnapped a British diplomat, Trade Commissioner James Cross, and a Quebec cabinet minister, Pierre Laporte, murdering the latter.

The Nation and Quebec

Although John Diefenbaker had come to power with the assistance of Quebec voters, neither "the Chief" nor his English-Canadian supporters ever really attempted to understand Quebec's aspirations. It was left to the Liberal minority governments of Lester Pearson to respond to what was obviously a feistier Quebec. To some extent, most Canadians were prepared to be sympathetic with Quebec, since few could conceive of a nation

Contemporary Views

A Critique of Education in Quebec

In 1960 a book published in Quebec quickly sold over 100,000 copies. *Les Insolences de Frère Untel* was a savage critique of the Church-controlled system of education in the province. Its anonymous author was a Marist brother named Jean-Paul Desbiens (1927–2006). Its chief target was the spreading street French of the working classes of Quebec, called *joual*, which the author labelled "The Language of Defeat." The following excerpt is from the 1962 English version, *The Impertinences of Brother Anonymous*.

In October, 1959, André Laurendeau published a short column in *Le Devoir* in which he qualified the speech of French Canadian students as "joual talk." He, not I, invented the name. It was well chosen. The thing and the name are alike, both hateful. The word joual is a summary description of what it is like to talk joual, to say joual instead of *cheval*, horse. It is to talk as horses would talk if they had not long since plumped for the silence and the smile of Fernandel.

Our pupils talk joual, write joual, and don't want to talk or write in any other way. Joual is their language. Things have gone so far that they can't even tell a mistake when it is shown them at pencil point. "The man what I talk to," "We are going to undress themselves," and the like do not bother them. In fact, such expressions seem elegant to them. It is a little different when it comes to mistakes in spelling, and if a lack of agreement between noun and adjective or the omission of an s is pointed out, they can identify the error. But the vice is deeply rooted at the grammatical level, and on the level of pronunciation. Out of twenty pupils whose names you ask at the opening of school, not more than two or three will be comprehensible the first time. The others will have to repeat themselves. They say their names as if they were confessing a sin.

Joual is a boneless language. The consonants are all slurred, a little like the speech of Hawaiian dancers, according to the records I have heard, Oula-oula-oula-alao-alao-alao. . . . Joual, this absence of language, is a symptom of our non-existence as French Canadians. No one can ever study language enough, for it is the home of all meanings. Our inability to assert ourselves, our obsession with the past, are all reflected in joual, our real language. Witness the abundance of negative turns of speech in our talk. Instead of saying that a woman is beautiful, we say she's not bad-looking, instead of saying that a pupil is intelligent, we say he's not stupid; instead of saying that we feel well, we say we're not too bad. . . . Now we approach the heart of the problem, which is a problem of civilization. . . . . All our civilization is joual. . . . We live joual because our souls are impoverished, and so we speak it.

Source: *The Impertinences of Brother Anonymous* (Montreal: Harvest House, 1962), 27–8.

without its francophone province. Pearson adopted three strategies. One was co-operative federalism, a concept exemplified in a series of agreements (1963–5) between Ottawa and the provinces, which accepted the need for consultation and flexibility, chiefly by having Ottawa give up many of the constitutional pretensions it had been insisting upon since the 1940s. This strategy ran aground because, as one political scientist put it, "Quebec's demands for autonomy appeared to be insatiable" (Smiley, 1970: 48–66). Later critics would regard Ottawa's concessions as the beginning of the end for a strong federal state.

A second strategy dealt with the symbols of sovereignty, with the government looking towards reform before 1967 and the Centennial Year of Confederation. A new Canadian flag was adopted by Parliament in 1964 after the Liberals ended the debate through closure; a new national anthem was approved in 1967. Centennial Year gave everyone a chance to display the new flag and sing the new anthem. Substantial amounts of money were spent on the celebration, with its centrepiece the Canadian Universal and International Exhibition at Montreal, familiarly known as Expo 67. The show was attended by millions of Canadians.

That summer an event occurred that shares an almost equal place in the history of the period. The occasion was the visit of French President Charles de Gaulle.

From the outset, Ottawa and Quebec had jostled over protocol for the visit. On 24 July de Gaulle stood on the balcony of a Montreal hotel with open arms, receiving the tumultuous applause of half a million Quebecers. It was an emotional moment. He spoke of cherished memories such as the liberation of France in 1944. Then, before the huge crowd and a television audience of millions, he concluded: "Vive Montréal! Vive le Québec! Vive le Québec libre!" Whether de Gaulle had deliberately insulted the Canadian government and people (the official Pearson position) or had merely referred to Quebec's efforts to affirm its identity (the position of Quebec Premier Daniel Johnson) was irrelevant. The exclamation had been vociferously cheered, and the nation had been given yet another reminder of its deep division.

The final policy initiative of the Pearson Liberals was the concept of equal partnership, including the notions of cultural dualism and "two founding cultures." The Royal Commission on Bilingualism and Biculturalism was set up in 1963 to implement equal partnership. The Commission discovered, to its surprise, that not all Canadians believed in cultural dualism. It ended up recommending official bilingualism, which was implemented by the Official Languages Act of 1969. By the time bilingualism was formally adopted, Quebec had passed well beyond the stage of accepting its implications. Many political leaders were calling for a policy of unilingualism

Prime Minister Pierre Trudeau arriving at the Notre-Dame Basilica in Montreal for the funeral of Pierre Laporte, 20 October 1970. An FLQ cell had seized Laporte on 10 October, and his body was found a week later in the trunk of a car at the St-Hubert airport. His murder helped to justify the federal government in its imposition of the War Measures Act. LAC, PA-113490. Montreal Gazette. Reprinted by permission.

within the province. After the earlier entrance of Quebec's "Three Wise Men" (Jean Marchand, Gérard Pelletier, and Pierre Trudeau) into Parliament and the cabinet in 1965, Pearson's resistance to Quebec had stiffened, however.

Quebec was not the home of all French Canadians, for there were hundreds of thousands of francophones living outside that province. The need to provide continuing protection for this outlying population was a principal argument of the federalists within Quebec. Francophones outside Quebec were understandably ardent federalists, and they were the chief beneficiaries of bilingualism and biculturalism. Only in New Brunswick were the francophones (the Acadians) sufficiently concentrated geographically and sufficiently numerous to regard themselves as a distinct people. The 1960s saw a renaissance of Acadian culture and

a new political awareness that Acadian interests had to be served. Thus both major New Brunswick parties supported bilingualism, French-language education (including a university at Moncton), and the entrenchment of Acadian culture in the province. Bilingualism and biculturalism helped rejuvenate francophones elsewhere in Canada, most of whom were fluently bilingual. Not only did they gain advantages in obtaining federal employment in their regions, but their educational and cultural facilities received a good deal of financial assistance from the federal government as well, as did numerous other organized ethnic groups once multiculturalism became official policy in 1971.

"Non-charter" ethnic groups had vociferously informed the Royal Commission on Bilingualism and Biculturalism of their unhappiness with the con-

The Ideology of the FLQ

On 5 October 1970 two armed men kidnapped British Trade Commissioner James Cross from his home in Montreal. A few hours later a communiqué from the abductors, a cell of the Front de libération du Québec, was received. It was later broadcast as demanded by the abductors. Sandwiched in the middle of the document, between specific demands, the FLQ summarized its ideology.

. . . Through this move, the Front de libération du Québec wants to draw the attention of the world to the fate of French-speaking Québécois, a majority of which is jeered at and crushed on its own territory by a faulty political system (Canadian federalism) and by an economy dominated by the interests of American high finance, the racist and imperialist "big bosses." When you examine the origins of Confederation you are in a better position to understand what were the true interests ($$$) which inspired those who were called the Fathers of Confederation. Besides, in 1867, the Quebec people (Lower Canada) were not consulted as to the possibility of creating a Confederation of existing provinces. It was a question of big money and these questions are only sorted out by interested parties, the capitalists, those who possess and amass capital and the means of production and who, according to their sole needs and requirements decide on our whole lives as well as those of a race of people.

Thousand of Québécois have understood, as did our ancestors of 1837–38, that the only way to ensure our national as well as economic survival is total independence.

The Front de libération du Québec supports unconditionally the American blacks and those of Africa, the liberation movements of Latin America, of Palestine, and of Asia, the revolutionary Catholics of Northern Ireland and all those who fight for their freedom, their independence, and their dignity.

The Front de libération du Québec wants to salute the Cuban and Algerian people who are heroically fighting against imperialism and colonialism in all its forms, for a just society where man's exploitation by man is banished. However, we believe that the only true support we can give these people moving towards their liberations is to liberate ourselves first. During and after our struggle we shall offer much more than the usual sympathy of shocked intellectuals confronted with pictures showing aggression in a peaceful and blissful setting. . . .

WE SHALL OVERCOME. . . .

Source: J. Saywell, "The Ideology of the FLQ," from *Quebec '70: A Documentary Narrative*, 37–8. © University of Toronto Press, 1971.

cept of two languages and two cultures, insisting that such a policy offended those not part of the "charter" community. The Commission had devoted a separate book of its final report to the "other ethnic groups," and seemed to be suggesting that there was more to Canada than simply two cultures. Indeed, in 1971, as we have seen, more than one in every four Canadians was not a member of the charter communities. On 8 October

1971, Prime Minister Pierre Trudeau declared in the House of Commons a federal government policy of "multiculturalism within a bilingual framework." The policy would involve, he said, assistance to all Canadian cultural groups to continue to grow, to "overcome cultural barriers to full participation in Canadian society," to interact with other cultural groups, and to become conversant in one of Canada's two official languages

Louis Joseph Robichaud

Born in the village of Saint-Antoine-de-Kent, about 20 miles north of Moncton, his father was the village's only storekeeper, the local organizer for the Liberal Party, and a community leader. Louis Robichaud (1925–2005) remembered an extremely happy childhood, although most of it was spent in the midst of the Great Depression. In 1940 he enrolled in the Collège du Sacré-Coeur in Bathurst, New Brunswick, intending to become a priest. By 1943, however, he decided that he was not suited for the priesthood. He also determined that he was not interested in the military. In 1947 he left Saint-Antoine for Quebec City to enrol in the Faculty of Social Sciences at Laval University, where he was much influenced by Father Georges-Henri Lévesque, an outspoken opponent of Maurice Duplessis and the Union Nationale. He spent his student years with Acadian friends and in attendance at the sessions of the Quebec Legislative Assembly, and soon determined to enter politics as early as possible.

Robichaud returned from Laval to Bathurst to article in the law office of Albany Robichaud, then settled in Richibucto, the county seat of Kent County, in early 1952 to establish his practice. A few months later, he was chosen as the provincial Liberal candidate for Kent County, thus following in the Liberal tradition of his father and of most Acadians in the province. He was elected by a margin of four votes, although the provincial party went down to a resounding defeat. By the time of the 1956 election, Robichaud was one of the leading spokesmen for his party, although he was young and not very well known around the province. Nonetheless, he declared himself a candidate for the Liberal leadership when it became available in 1958. He won on the third ballot. An extremely energetic campaigner, he led the Liberals to an unexpected victory in the 1960 provincial election, and followed this campaign with two more electoral successes. He was one of the youngest provincial premiers ever elected, and was also the first Acadian premier actually to win an election. Robichaud modernized both the health-care system and the educational system, but he was proudest of his Equal Opportunity program, which attempted to guarantee that all provincial services were the same right across the province. In 1963 he established the Université de Moncton, the first French-language university in the province, and in 1969 his government passed legislation making the province officially bilingual. After the Liberals were defeated in 1970, he served for several years as Canadian chairman of the International Joint Commission before joining the Senate in late 1973, serving until retirement in 2000.

Source: Michel Cormier, *Louis J. Robichaud: A Not So Quiet Revolution* (Moncton, NB: Faye Editions, 2004).

(quoted in Hansard, *Debates in the House of Commons*, 8 Oct. 1971). The reaction from Quebec was immediate and negative. French Canadians, probably quite accurately, saw the emphasis on multiculturalism as a way to deflect the aspirations of Quebec by demonstrating that its linguistic and cultural aspirations were not unique and could not be considered apart from the needs of other communities in Canada. René Lévesque described multiculturalism as a "red herring" designed "to give the impression that we are all ethnics and do not have to worry about special status for Quebec." Many French Canadians were incensed that Trudeau had chosen to link multiculturalism with language as well as culture. According to more than one commentator in Quebec, multiculturalism had reduced the Quebec fact to an ethnic phenomenon.

The government embodied multiculturalism in a Canadian Consultative Council on Multiculturalism, created in 1973, and in a separate section of the Department of the Secretary of State (the Multiculturalism Directorate), which was given funds to support multicultural activities of various sorts. Much of the funding was devoted to the support of ethnic research and scholarship, contributing to an explosion of ethnic studies, although money was also made available to ethnic organizations for various purposes and was subject to considerable criticism. The ethnic community was not united in its response to the funding for multiculturalism. Some members of the ethnic community complained that the funds were "minuscule," while others pointed to the waste of money on meaningless projects. In the wake of the federal policy, various provincial governments also proclaimed policies of multiculturalism and began funding ethnic organizations and ethnic studies. The concept of multiculturalism was introduced into most provincial educational curricula to socialize schoolchildren to the new complexities of Canadian society, although not much was done about providing education in ethnic languages.

While multiculturalism was introduced as a highly politicized policy by a Prime Minister who did not really take minority ethnic causes very seriously, it struck a responsive chord with many Canadians. For Pierre Trudeau, multiculturalism was probably mainly part of a Quebec strategy that also may have been important as part of a conscious elimination of ethnic and racial discrimination. For many Canadians, however, it would become part of a new definition of national identity, a statement of the Canadian "mosaic" in contradistinction to the American "melting pot." The mythology of the mosaic would become even more powerful after the introduction of the Canadian Charter of Rights (again by Trudeau) in 1982. Before long, many Canadians had quite forgotten the Prime Minister's contextualization of multiculturalism as being "within a bilingual framework." It would eventually become such a potent metaphor that many Canadians felt that their behaviour had to live up to its ideal.

Canadian Culture

In some senses, Canadian culture—quite apart from its multicultural aspects—came of age in the 1960s. Years of development of cultural infrastructure within the private sector, combined with a new government recognition of the need for conscious cultural policy and an enormous expansion of the Canadian university system, brought at least elite culture to a flowering. A national cultural policy, first articulated by the Massey Commission, was actually implemented under Diefenbaker and Pearson. Intended to foster a distinctive Canadian identity in the face of the ubiquitous Americans, it employed all possible cultural strategies, ranging from subsidies (the Canada Council) and protectionism (policy regarding Canadian magazines and Canadian content regulations for television introduced in 1961) to regulated competition (the Board of Broadcast Governors, established in 1958, licensed new television stations, which came together as a new television network in 1961 called CTV). Within the realm of "serious" culture, Canadian governments at all levels were prepared to spend large amounts of money to produce works that would meet international standards. To a considerable extent they succeeded. Whether the culture that resulted was Canadian Culture was, of course, another matter entirely.

Perhaps the greatest success story was in Canadian literature. Before the 1960s the market for, and interest in, works of literature by Canadian writers was not strong. There was no tradition of indigenous literary criticism, only a handful of literary periodicals existed, and almost nothing approximating a literary community could be found anywhere outside Quebec. In 1976 critic Northrop Frye noted "the colossal verbal explosion that has taken place in Canada since 1960" (Frye, 1976: 849). That explosion saw a number of Canadian writers achieve international critical recognition. *The Apprenticeship of Duddy Kravitz* by Mordecai Richler (1931–2001), published in 1959, met with great popular success and established Richler as a major writer. Duddy Kravitz entered Canadian popular culture as an ethnic wheeler-dealer desperate for the security of land. Richler was not the first novelist to mine the rich vein of ethnicity in Canada, but he was the first to mythologize the urban ghetto, its inhabitants, and way of life. In 1966 he confessed: "No matter how long I continue to live abroad, I do feel forever rooted in Montreal's St Urbain Street. This was my time, my place, and I have elected to get it exactly right" (quoted in Woodcock, 1979: 27).

Margaret Laurence (1926–89) was another Canadian novelist who created a mythologized Canadian space.

Having lived with her husband in Somalia and Ghana from 1950 to 1957, she was residing in Jordan when her African novel, *This Side of Jordan* (1960), appeared. Soon afterwards, she completed the first of her four "Manawaka" novels, which brought her international acclaim. *The Stone Angel* (1961), *A Jest of God* (1966), *The Fire-Dwellers* (1969), and *The Diviners* (1974) could be read on many levels and are arguably the most richly textured fiction ever produced by a Canadian writer. Laurence's setting may have been as far removed from urban Montreal as it was possible to get, but like Richler, she created a place out of what she knew. The mythical town of Manawaka, set somewhere on the Canadian prairies, was a strongly conceived and living entity, linking some powerful female protagonists struggling against hypocritical Scots-Canadian constrictions and their own pasts. Noting that she was not much aware that her "so-called Canadian writing" was Canadian, Laurence once commented that "this seems a good thing to me, for it suggests that one has been writing out of a background so closely known that no explanatory tags are necessary" (quoted in Woodcock, 1969: 9).

With a smaller readership than fiction commanded, poetry not only held its own but acquired a substantial audience. Irving Layton (1912–2006), Earle Birney (1904–95), and Al Purdy (1918–2001) were sent on reading tours by their publisher and became almost as adept in performance as in writing. Performance of a different kind marked the career of Leonard Cohen (b. 1934), who straddled the worlds of high and popular culture when he set some of his poems to music, wrote new songs, and sang them to his own guitar accompaniment. Cohen had played in a band in his teens and published his first book of poetry, *Let Us Compare Mythologies*, in 1956 at the age of 22. It was followed in the sixties by two novels, including his haunting classic *Beautiful Losers* (1966), and by several poetry collections that were exceptionally appealing to the younger generation in their imagery and themes. In 1968, he refused a Governor General's Award for his *Selected Poems*. In the same year his first record album, *Songs of Leonard Cohen*, appeared, soon to be followed by *Songs from a Room* (1969). A few of his songs had already been performed by Joan Baez and Judy Collins, but Cohen's own liturgical baritone was the perfect vehicle for popularizing them. By 1970

Margaret Laurence, c. 1960. Dave Buchan, Vancouver Sun.

he was widely recognized as part of the pantheon of poet-singers that included Bob Dylan, Donovan Leitch, and Paul McCartney. Such songs as "Suzanne," "Bird on a Wire," "It Seems so Long Ago, Nancy," and "The Story of Isaac" entered the consciousness of the counterculture. Cohen captured perfectly youth's scorn for hypocrisy. His songs counselled survival by withdrawal from the contests of life into a private world of the spirit, not in triumph or failure but in endurance through ceremony and self-understanding. These were powerful messages for the Woodstock generation. Ironically, while Cohen's songs contained almost no specific Canadian references, his sense of self-deprecation and self-abnegation was generally accepted as quintessentially Canadian.

The sixties also saw the creation of a number of small presses across the nation and the emergence of "Can Lit" as an acceptable field of study. By 1970 virtually every Canadian university offered an undergraduate course in Canadian literature, and a critical canon had more or less been established, which naturally emphasized the distinctly Canadian qualities of Canadian writing. Without a new breed of scholarly critics who were prepared to take Canadian writing seriously—and without the subsidies that helped sustain author, critic, teacher, and journals—that writing would have developed more slowly. McClelland & Stewart's enduring New Canadian Library series began in 1958, offering during the sixties mainly reprints of classic and long out-of-print novels. *Canadian Literature,* "the first review devoted only to the study of Canadian writers and writing," was founded in 1959 by George Woodcock (1912–95). The collectively written *Literary History of Canada* was published by the University of Toronto Press in 1965. At the beginning of his "Conclusion" to the first edition of this work, Northrop Frye (1912–91) wrote:

> This book is a tribute to the maturity of Canadian literary scholarship and criticism, whatever one thinks of the literature. Its authors have completely outgrown the view that evaluation is the end of criticism, instead of its incidental by-product. Had evaluation been their guiding principle, this book would, if written at all, have been only a huge debunking project, leaving Canadian literature a poor naked *alouette* plucked of every feather of decency and dignity. True, the book gives evidence on practically every one of its eight hundred odd pages, that what is really remarkable is not how little but how much good writing has been produced in Canada. (Klinck, 1965: 821)

For many critics, the challenge was to reveal quintessential Canadian qualities in the imaginative elements of the literature. Québécois fiction shared in the cultural flowering, with the anger and violence of language and subject matter, and with radical changes in syntax and formal structure, not only mirroring but fostering the spirit of liberation and the new goals of Quebec society.

The coming of age of Canadian writing was not matched by a similar maturation in Canadian book publishing, which found itself subject to several disturbing market trends, most notably an inability to make money in a retail climate dominated by foreign publishers. Ryerson Press, the oldest major publisher in Canada and supported by the United Church of Canada, was so much in debt that it was sold in 1970 to the American firm McGraw-Hill. In the same year, the Ontario government appointed a Royal Commission on Book Publishing (1970) and had to rescue McClelland & Stewart from an American takeover. Even though the federal government established a policy of giving support to Canadian-controlled publishing firms through such agencies as the Canadian Book Publishing Development Program and the Canada Council—as did provincial governments in various ways, including through the Ontario Arts Council—Canadian publishing had entered an era of chronic precariousness that the quality of the writing available to be published only served to emphasize. The relatively small market for English-language books in Canada, the enormous volume of foreign books available, the dominance of foreign-owned publishers, and the self-defeating policy of allowing full return of unsold books—all of these factors put Canadian-owned publishers at a competitive disadvantage. For authors even to be successfully published in the United States had its disadvantages, since the American publishers would sell their leftover books (known as "remainders") in Canada at a fraction of the price the Canadian publisher was still asking for the same book. Publishers in Quebec experienced less difficulty than those in the rest of Canada, despite the small market. Apparently the people of Quebec were more willing to buy books about themselves and their culture from local publishers, and there was less American competition.

The effect of the socio-economic changes in Quebec on writing in that province was considerable. The influence was reciprocal: one fuelled the other. The literary transformation began in the late 1950s with *La Belle Bête* (1959) by the 20-year-old Marie-Claire Blais (b. 1939). This novel astonished the reading public (no less in its English translation, *Mad Shadows*) and scandalized the clergy with its portrayal of characters representing various kinds of moral and physical ugliness, and for its powerful impressionistic scenes of betrayal, disfigurement, pyromania, murder, and suicide. Blais was discovered outside Quebec by the American critic Edmund Wilson, who observed that she showed herself

CANADA   Material Culture

Habitat 67

Built for Expo 67, the intention of Habitat 67, designed by Moshe Safdie, was to mix natural elements and open space into dense urban space. Now a widely recognized Montreal landmark, each of the original 158 multi-level apartment units provided vistas and even space for a small garden. Image by Jerry Spearman.

A housing complex near the St Lawrence River in Montreal, Habitat 67 was originally designed as a thesis project by Moshe Safdie, an Israeli-born architecture student at McGill University. Safdie's design received the highest mark at McGill and the gold medal. Several years later his thesis supervisor suggested that it be incorporated into the plans for Expo 67, where its construction was financed by the federal government.

A huge complex, it consists of 354 prefabricated reinforced concrete forms, arranged to produce 158 apartments (now reduced to 146 by redevelopment) on a multi-level configuration connected by sky-ways. Each unit has its own private terrace, and the complex was intended to serve as a model for future urban planning, combining as it did suburban living in an inexpensive downtown apartment structure. The system turned out to be much more expensive to build than the architect had intended, however, and its prefabricated modularity has not produced large numbers of imitators in the realm of housing. In the area of commercial development, particularly with corporate restaurants and retail chains, prefabrication has continued to be popular.

Stylistically, Habitat 67 has been called the classic Canadian example of "brutalist" architecture, a very popular architectural movement especially influential in the 1960s. Brutalist architects revelled in the ugliness and lack of finish of their buildings, which often were large and fortress-like, typically announcing their structural makeup on their exteriors. Brutalism has become in many quarters a synonym for ugly, although the term actually has its origin in Corbusier's "béton brut," or "raw concrete." It has also become associated with badly built and decaying housing developments in many countries, but especially behind the Iron Curtain. As well, it has been linked with European philosophical totalitarianism.

Considered a fantastic experiment, materially, Habitat 67 was a unique way of looking at the growing mass-produced nature of the latter twentieth century. By using only eight concrete forms, Safdie proved that uniform objects could be used to make innovative concepts. Lego building blocks were actually employed in the early stages of design, and the interconnectedness of the construction evokes a sort of childish creativity. The pre-stressed, reinforced concrete that such structures are made of does not age well. Instead, it crumbles and stains as it gets older, further complicating the survivability of similar structures.

"incapable of allowing life in French Canada to appear in a genial light or to seem to embody any sort of ideal" (Wilson, 1964: 147). The literary transformation that began in the late 1950s continued throughout the next decades. The anger and violence of language and subject matter, radical changes in syntax and formal structure, the freeing of style and content from the constraints of tradition, not only mirrored but fostered the spirit of liberation and the new goals of Quebec society. This work was no longer called French-Canadian but "Québécois" fiction. The journal *Parti pris* (1963–8), founded just after the first wave of FLQ bombings with an *indépendantiste* and Marxist perspective, published in January 1965 a special issue entitled *Pour une littérature québécoise*—giving a name, quickly adopted, to the current and future works of francophone writers in Quebec. That issue also promoted the use of *joual* in creative writing. The poet Paul Chamberland (b. 1939), one of the founding editors, wrote that "any language must be shaken to its very foundations through the disfigurement inherent in our common speech, and in the lives of all of us." Most of this literary explosion went unheeded in English-speaking Canada, partly because of the scarcity (and difficulty) of translations, but also, one suspects, because of the uncongenial spirit behind it.

Canadian scholarship, like other areas of elite culture, expanded and was strengthened in the 1960s. A combination of grants from the Canada Council, the Social Sciences and Humanities Research Council of Canada (SSHRC), and the National Research Council, together with an increase in the number of Canadian universities, vastly added to the numbers of academics and research students. Canadian scholarship grew not only in volume but in reputation, achieving international recognition in many disciplines.

One field that had great difficulty coming to terms with the rapidly changing world of scholarship was Canadian history. Canadian historians almost by definition could not aspire to international repute, since in the broader scheme of things the history of Canada was of little interest to anyone outside the country. For most historians of Canada working within the English-speaking tradition, Canadian history was National History. The focus was unremittingly progressive. The country was settled, adopted representative government, turned responsible government into the union of the provinces, and with union moved gradually but inexorably towards full nationhood. Quebec, of course, had its own paradigm, equally nationalistic and political in nature. This comfortable mindset was overturned when younger historians began asking new questions about race, class, ethnicity, and gender that emerged out of the political turmoil of the late 1960s. These younger scholars also questioned the glaring

Northrop Frye, c. 1967. Frye was a Canadian literary critic who had an international reputation for various works of literary theory. His theories integrated Canadian literature into the international canon. Brigdens Limited.

neglect in the traditional approach towards Aboriginal peoples, women, the working classes, and racial minorities. To these changes, Quebec historians added their own, often influenced by new European schools of analysis. Research and writing in Canadian economic and social history began to ask implicitly whether the old paradigm of nation-building was flexible and capacious enough to integrate the new methodologies and theories. By 1970 it was increasingly clear that the old fabric would not hold, although neither mainstream Canadian historians nor the revisionists had any idea of how to reweave it. Although the traditional synthesis had broken down, a new history had not yet appeared.

A new maturity and international acceptance of culture produced in Canada was to be found everywhere. We can see one major shift in the performing arts, where an amateur tradition of the 1950s was transformed quite swiftly into a full-fledged professional system operating from coast to coast. For example, Winnipeg—a

middle-sized, geographically isolated urban centre with no particular tradition of cultural patronage—by 1970 was supporting a fully professional symphony orchestra; the Royal Winnipeg Ballet and other dance companies; an opera association mounting several works each year; the Manitoba Theatre Centre, an acclaimed model for regional theatre, whose impressive Mainstage opened in 1970; an active art gallery; and a major concert hall. Thanks to various centennials, similar facilities and institutions soon existed in every major urban centre across Canada. By 1970 no important Canadian city or region was without its own professional theatre company, art gallery, and symphony orchestra.

Created with substantial public monies in the form of block grants from all levels of government, new arts institutions initially relied heavily on recent immigrants to Canada for professional expertise. Many of these professionals became teachers and sponsors of spinoff activities. It was not long before highly qualified younger Canadians were ready to step into these companies and organizations, and a substantial local audience had been developed. One of the secrets of public success in music and theatre was the introduction of annual subscription campaigns. Unlike audiences in New York, London, Paris, or Berlin, where tickets were sold for individual events, patrons of Canada's performing arts were asked to buy blocks of tickets in advance to guarantee an audience. If by 1970 the personnel in the performing and exhibitory arts were mainly Canadian, the repertoire on display tended to be largely an international one, both in origin and in style. Canadian artists, playwrights, composers, and choreographers still had trouble finding their own place and audience within the standard repertoire regardless of their style. How their art could be distinctly Canadian was an open question that ate away at the hearts of many Canadian creative people throughout the period.

The 1960s were also a critical decade for popular culture, particularly that valiant effort to keep the Canadian identity from being totally submerged by American influences. The record was mixed, as developments in Canadian sports well demonstrate. Nothing could be more quintessentially Canadian, for example, than hockey. But that sport entered the post-war period in the hands of the American entertainment industry,

Marie-Claire Blais

Marie-Claire Blais.

Marie-Claire Blais was born in Quebec City in 1939. She received her early education from Catholic nuns, but soon became disillusioned with academic subjects, leaving school at age 15 to work in a factory. She subsequently attended Laval University and began writing. Her earliest novels, *La Belle Bête* and *Tête Blanche*, brought her to the attention of the distinguished literary critic Edmund Wilson, who described her in a *New Yorker* article on Canadian literature as the most promising young author in the country. As a result, she was able to study in Paris on a Guggenheim Fellowship. From the beginning, Blais's fiction had been experimental in language, form, and thematic content. She was one of the first Quebec novelists to break with realism, in favour of a surreal world of street dialogue and menacing sexuality.

In her work, Blais reflected major tensions in Quebec society. She was extremely conscious of the ways in which Quebec had oppressed its women. *Une saison dans la vie d'Emmanuel,* published in 1965, explores the life of a farm family during the months following the birth of the sixteenth child, Emmanuel, and emphasizes the brutality with which society responded to the older children's yearnings for something better. It won the Prix France-Canada and the Prix Médicis, and became a favourite topic for literary critics. Three semi-autobiographical novels with Pauline Archange as the central character, published between 1968 and 1970, echoed the critique of their parents by the younger generation in the 1960s.

In the 1970s Blais wrote about homosexuality. *Les nuits d'underground* (1978) was an evocative study of the everyday life of a lesbian frequenter of gay bars in Montreal. The later novels became increasingly characterized by stream-of-consciousness third-person narrative. Blais also published poetry and drama. For many readers, Blais became the epitome of the alienated artist and intellectual in modern Quebec society. Like the books of Gabrielle Roy, Blais's novels have all been translated into English, and she is one of a handful of Quebec novelists fully accessible to anglophones in Canada and beyond.

and the situation never really altered. By the 1960s only at the NHL level did Canadian teams have any real representation (two of six teams, in Toronto and Montreal). At the minor-league level only Vancouver had a profes-sional team. The NHL finally expanded in 1967, adding six new American franchises in what was hoped were hockey hotbeds like St Louis and Philadelphia. Not even Vancouver, to its chagrin, could get a look-in. The chief argument against new Canadian teams was related to television. American TV viewers would not watch professional sports played by "foreign" teams, said the experts, and the secret of expansion's success was a US national television contract. In 1969, on the other hand, Major League Baseball granted a National League franchise to a Montreal team to be called the Expos, demonstrating that if the local markets were big enough, the moguls could be won over, at least temporarily. As for the Canadian Football League, it entered its most successful decade to date. Teams became totally professional and drew considerable crowds. The fans appeared quite satisfied with the Canadian game and its differences from the American one—the size of the field, the number of downs, the "rouge"—and with the large number of Canadians who, thanks to a quota system on imports, played it.

In September 1961 the federal government finally took some initiative on the problem of sports in Canada. Bill C-131, intended to "encourage, promote and develop fitness and amateur sport in Canada," passed both Houses of Parliament unanimously. Much of the bill's bipartisan political support was a result of public outcry over Canada's poor performance in international competitions, including hockey, and was part of the country's Cold War posturing. Speaking about amateur sports at that time, Opposition leader Lester Pearson (who had played lacrosse and hockey while at Oxford) said: "all the publicity attached to international sport and the fact that certain societies use international sport, as they use everything else, for the advancement of prestige and political purposes, it is a matter of some consequence that we in Canada should do what we can to develop and regain the prestige we once had, to a greater extent than we now have in international competition" (quoted in Morrow, 1989: 328). Although the legislation was deliberately vague, it allowed the government to subsidize amateur coaches and teams, particularly in national and international competitions. In 1968 the National Advisory Council, set up under the Act to recommend policy and oversee its implementation, was shunted to one side in favour of professional bureaucrats within the Ministry of National Health and Welfare. Amateur sports in Canada had been taken under the wing of the welfare state. In that same year Pierre Trudeau promised in the election campaign a new study of sports in Canada. The *Report of the Task Force on Sports for Canadians* was published in 1969. Despite the increased government involvement in and subsidization of amateur sports, in 1976 Canada acquired the dubious distinction of becoming the first (and so far only) nation to host the Olympic Summer Games (in Montreal) without winning a gold medal.

Conclusion

On the whole, the developments in sports were remarkably similar to those in other cultural sectors, and indeed the nation in general. By the early 1970s sport had been thoroughly drawn into the net of federal and provincial government policy, turned over to the bureaucrats and bean-counters. It had not yet answered the question of whether excellence and Canadian-ness were truly compatible, although the sense was that a sufficient expenditure of money would in the end resolve all problems. Unbeknownst to its participants, however, sport in Canada was about to share with other aspects of the Canadian experience a new sense of existing on the edge of some kind of precipice, about to free-fall into new and unknown territory. What consequences the fall would have were anybody's guess, although there were increasingly loud mutterings about the limits of growth. After 1972 Canadians would have to explore together the implications of a world in which not all things were possible. They would discover, as money and resources became more limited, that the infighting could be extremely fierce.

Joseph Jean Béliveau

Jean Béliveau. AP Photo/File/CP.

Born in Trois-Rivières, the eldest of eight children, Jean Béliveau (1931–2014) moved in 1937 with his family to Victoriaville, a town in central Quebec, halfway between Montreal and Quebec City. He was educated in Victoriaville schools, and played his first game of hockey on a backyard rink, remaining apart from the organized version of the sport until the age of 12. By age 15 he was playing amateur hockey and was highly prized by the Montreal Canadiens, with which he signed a contract stating that if he decided to play professionally he would join that team. He resisted turning professional until the Canadiens, in a ploy to get him to play for them, bought the entire Quebec Senior Hockey League in which he was playing and changed it from an amateur league to a minor pro

hockey league. The result was that Béliveau, de facto, became a professional, and hence he began playing professionally for Montreal in 1953, the start of an illustrious career that ended in 1971 after 18 seasons in the National Hockey League.

Although not enormously large for a hockey player by twenty-first-century standards, Béliveau was regarded as huge for his time, at six-foot-three (1.9 cm) and 205 pounds (93 kg). This size led to his being nicknamed "Le Gros Bill," after the very large and genial title character in a 1949 Québécois film. His career saw one long series of triumphs, playing for the dominant team of his era. Over his years with the Canadiens, they won 10 Stanley Cup titles, and he scored 503 goals and added 712 assists, making him one of the league's top point-scorers of all time. His scoring abilities were not the feature for which he was most renowned, however. He was always most praised for his gravitas, polish, and quiet leadership qualities, and he served as an executive for the hockey club for many years after his retirement as a player, gaining another seven Stanley Cup titles. Twice he refused offers from Prime Minister Brian Mulroney of a Senate seat, and later, when Jean Chrétien was Prime Minister, he declined to have his name put forward as a candidate for Governor General. Béliveau's number was retired in 1971 and he was elected to the Hockey Hall of Fame in 1972 without having to wait the usual three years after retirement. Although the Canadiens have had many great stars over the years, Jean Béliveau, among the team's fans, was probably the most beloved player of all time. He died in December 2014.

Historiography

How "Revolutionary" Was Quebec's 1960s Quiet Revolution?

Matthew Hayday, University of Guelph

The 1960s in Quebec are usually referred to as the Quiet Revolution. The period witnessed bureaucratic modernization, government intervention in the private sector, and secularization of the province's key institutions. It stood in stark opposition to the *Grande Noirceur* (or Great Darkness) era of the Maurice Duplessis administration, when the Catholic Church controlled social services, English-Canadian and American businesses dominated the private sector, and the government repressed unions. Quebec society changed dramatically, with a tumbling birth rate and adherence to Catholic teachings declining precipitously. A transformed and confident culture, proud of Quebec's distinctive language, was emerging.

Much of the early scholarly literature about the Quiet Revolution contended that these were "revolutionary" shifts in the province, and debated where these changes originated. Early class-based explanations were posited during the 1960s by sociologist Hubert Guindon, and were more fully elaborated in the mid-1970s by political scientists Kenneth McRoberts and Dale Posgate in *Quebec: Social Change and Political Crisis* (1976). They argued that a new francophone middle class, educated in the 1940s and 1950s, and frustrated at the lack of opportunities in a job market dominated by the clergy and anglophone corporate leaders, was responsible for the changes that occurred during the Quiet Revolution. In the late 1970s and early 1980s, Marxist-inspired analyses from authors including Dorval Brunelle, Gilles Bourque, and Anne Legaré argued that, in fact, a Quebec-based francophone bourgeois class (of various forms) was the motor of the Quiet Revolution. The new middle class, from this perspective, was the product, not the agent, of these changes. William Coleman's *The Independence Movement in Quebec, 1945–1980* (1984), developed a synthesis approach, arguing for a "coalition of classes" explanation of the Quiet Revolution, coupled with ideological shifts in the province.

In the mid-1980s, scholarship on the Quiet Revolution moved into broad political overviews, including Dale Thomson's landmark biography/history, *Jean Lesage and the Quiet Revolution* (1984), which probed the internal workings of the Quebec government during these crucial years. Michael Behiels's *Prelude to Quebec's Quiet Revolution: Liberalism versus Neo-Nationalism, 1945–1960* (1985) traced the development of the two main intellectual schools of thought that shaped the Quiet Revolution's reforms, with supporters of each group playing a major role in bringing down the Union Nationale and then shaping both provincial and federal policy agendas in the 1960s.

The revolutionary nature of the 1960s reforms was emphasized by politicians, intellectuals, and groups who were wedded to this agenda. And yet, the existence of a *Grande Noirceur* or a Quiet Revolution suggested that Quebec had an exceptional history, and not in a good way—that it had lagged behind other parts of North America and been stultified by its unique Catholic, French culture. A revisionist school of historians, led by Paul-André Linteau, René Durocher, Jean-Claude Robert, and François Ricard, published major new syntheses of Quebec history in the mid-1980s. Their *Quebec since 1930* (1991) emphasized issues such as urbanization, labour mobilization, and economic and technological development. They argued that in most sectors, Quebec had been a "normal" society following a standard North American developmental trajectory, and the impact of the Quiet Revolution was more limited than others suggested.

In the early 2000s, scholars reassessed the role of Quebec's Catholic Church. Louise Bienvenue, E.-Martin Meunier, and Jean-Philippe Warren considered how lay Catholic organizations and Catholic action groups contested the conservative Church hierarchy's positions during the Duplessis era. This approach informs

Michael Gauvreau's *The Catholic Origins of Quebec's Quiet Revolution, 1931–1970* (2008), which argues that the origins of Quebec's Quiet Revolution may be found within the prior three decades of a transforming Quebec Catholicism.

More recently, conservative Quebec historians have sought to rehabilitate the Duplessis years on the basis of their free-market liberalism, and recast Quebec's right-wing intellectuals as participants, rather than opponents, of the Quiet Revolution's modernization projects. This argument is promoted in work by scholars such as Xavier Gélinas (*La droite intellectuelle québécoise et la Révolution tranquille* [2007]) and Lucia Ferretti.

A transnational turn has also informed recent scholarship on the Quiet Revolution, including how Quebecers responded to the global collapse of empires and decolonization. Sean Mills's *The Empire Within: Postcolonial Thought and Political Activism in Sixties Montreal* (2010) demonstrates how international decolonization shaped the way that Montrealers thought about the role of their French-speaking province within English-speaking Canada and North America. These global trends shaped social movement activism during the era of the Quiet Revolution, as well as broader discourses of liberation and independence. In this regard, Quebecers were one of many national groups worldwide that responded to the new spirit of decolonization and self-determination.

Short Bibliography

Axelrod, Paul. *Scholars and Dollars: Politics, Economics and the Universities of Ontario 1945–80*. Toronto, 1982. An excellent study of the post-war universities in Ontario, emphasizing the expansion of existing universities and the creation of new ones, as well as distinct shifts in the justifications for higher education.

Behiels, Michael, ed. *Quebec since 1945*. Toronto, 1987. An admirable and comprehensive collection of articles on post-war Quebec.

Bergeron, Léandre. *The History of Quebec: A Patriot's Handbook*. Toronto, 1971. A translation of a radical "people's" history of Quebec, strongly separatist in tone.

Cardinal, Harold. *The Unjust Society: The Tragedy of Canada's Indians*. Edmonton, 1969. The first attempt to tell the First Nations' story from the Native standpoint.

Clairmont, Donald, and Dennis Magill. *Africville: The Life and Death of a Canadian Black Community*, rev. edn. Toronto, 1987. A work documenting the destruction of Africville, a black community on the outskirts of Halifax, which insists it was improper and unnecessary.

Desbiens, Jean-Paul. *The Impertinences of Brother Anonymous*. Toronto, 1962. The famous critique of Quebec politics and culture that caused a furor when first published.

Forsyth, Dennis, ed. *Let the Niggers Burn: The Sir George Williams University Affair and Its Caribbean Aftermath*. Montreal, 1971. An account of the most famous Canadian incident of student protest.

Handler, Richard. *Nationalism and the Politics of Culture in Quebec*. Madison, Wis., 1981. A detailed analysis of the manifold ways in which Quebec nationalism has influenced Quebec culture and cultural policy.

Kenneally, R.R., and J. Sloan. *Expo 67: Not Just a Souvenir*. Toronto, 2010. An interdisciplinary look at the most successful World's Fair of the twentieth century.

Kinsman, Gary. *The Regulation of Desire: Sexuality in Canada*. Montreal, 1987. A pioneering study of sexuality and its treatment by the state.

Levitt, Kari. *Silent Surrender: The Multinational Corporation in Canada*. Toronto, 1970. The most notorious statement of the nationalist critique of foreign investment and the multicultural corporation in Canada.

Morton, W.L. *The Canadian Identity*. Toronto, 1961. An effort to discover the essence of Canada by one of its leading historians.

Royal Commission on Bilingualism and Biculturalism. 1969. *Report*, 6 vols. Ottawa: Queen's Printer. The key document in the struggle for bilingualism and biculturalism.

Saywell, John. *Quebec 70: A Documentary Narrative*. Toronto, 1971. A useful account of the FLQ crisis of 1970.

Simeon, Richard. *Federal–Provincial Diplomacy: The Making of Recent Policy in Canada*. Toronto, 1972. A fascinating study of the international implications of Canadian federalism.

Vallières, Pierre. *White Niggers of America*. Toronto, 1971. A brilliant polemical memoir about living as a French Canadian.

Weaver, Sally M. *Making Canada's Indian Policy: The Hidden Agenda 1968–1970*. Toronto, 1981. A sober account of Canadian Aboriginal policy in a crucial period of re-evaluation.

Study Questions

1. Identify at least one way in which Canadian manners were emancipated during the 1960s in each of the following areas: religion, the media, literature, sexuality, and the law.

2. Explain why the "counterculture" was mainly a youthful phenomenon.

3. Canada was never directly involved in the Vietnam War. Why did this war have such a strong impact on Canadian society?

4. Identify four militant collectivities that arose in the 1960s. For each, summarize briefly their goals.

5. What do Tables 10.1 and 10.2 tell us about unemployment in the 1960s?

6. In what ways did the Quiet Revolution change Quebec society?

7. Of the factors listed in the text as changing Canada's immigration policy, which in your view was most important?

8. What three policies did the Pearson government develop to deal with Quebec's aspirations? Comment on the effectiveness of these policies.

9. Was Expo 67 successful?

Visit the companion website for *A History of the Canadian Peoples*, fifth edition for further resources.

www.oupcanada.com/Bumsted5e

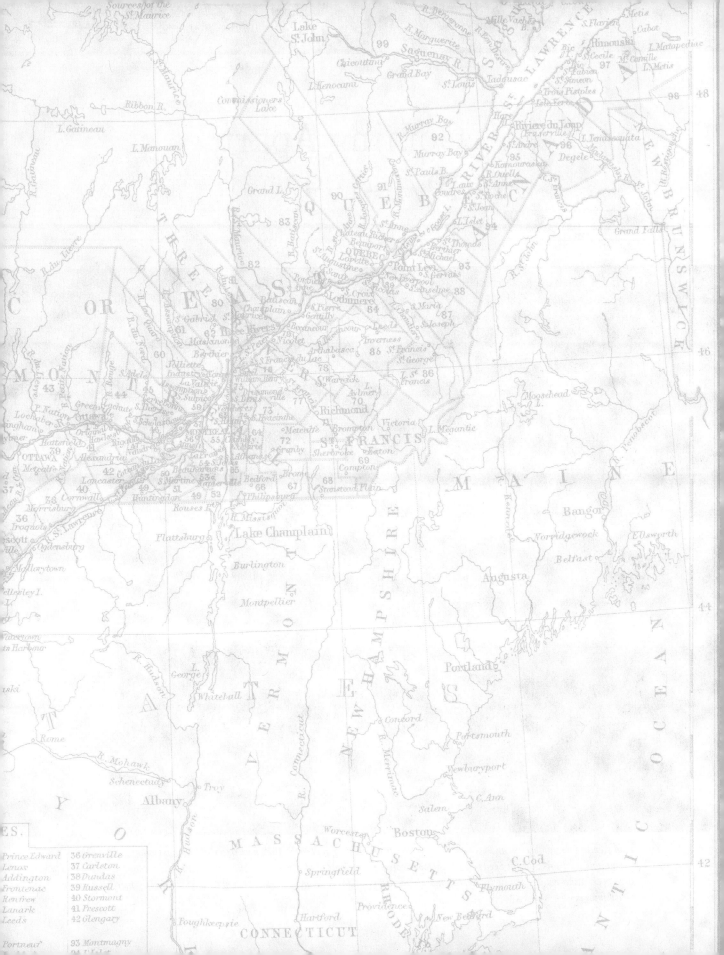

11 Coming Apart, 1972–1992

Paul Henderson (number 19) and his teammates celebrate the winning goal of the 1972 hockey series between Canada and the USSR. Canadians used this Summit Series–winning goal, scored on 26 September 1972 at the Luzhniki Ice Palace in Moscow, as proof of their hockey supremacy, despite the narrow margin of victory and their team's struggles on home ice. Photo by Melchior DiGiacomo/ Getty Images

Timeline

1972 Canada–Russia hockey series. Trudeau Liberals win in close election. NDP defeats W.A.C. Bennett in British Columbia.

1973 OPEC raises price of oil. Robert Bourassa's Liberals are elected in Quebec, but the Parti Québécois finishes strong.

1974 Trudeau Liberals win another close election. Trudeau imposes wage and price controls.

1976 Canadian Airline Pilots Association strikes. Montreal Olympics are held. Parti Québécois wins power in Quebec. Joe Clark is chosen leader of the Tories.

1977 Quebec government passes Bill 101.

1978 Task Force on National Unity tours Canada.

1979 Joe Clark's Tories win minority government but the government falls in December.

1980 Trudeau's Liberals are swept back to power. Quebec referendum results in 60 per cent "Non" and 40 per cent "Oui" on question of sovereignty-association. Trudeau proposes constitutional reform.

1981 Supreme Court rules on federal constitutional initiative. The PQ is re-elected in Quebec. The "Gang of Nine" cuts a deal on the Constitution. Revised constitutional package passes Parliament.

1982 A revised Constitution is approved by the British Parliament.

1983 Brian Mulroney replaces Joe Clark as Tory leader.

1984 Trudeau retires and is succeeded by John Turner. Brian Mulroney leads Progressive Conservatives to a federal sweep. The Cirque du Soleil is formed.

1985 PQ defeated by Robert Bourassa's Liberals. 22 June 1985: Air India bombing disaster.

1986 Mulroney government negotiates Free Trade Agreement with the US.

1987 Meech Lake agreement is reached between the federal and provincial governments.

1988 Mulroney's Tories win again. Mulroney signs redress agreement with National Association of Japanese Canadians. Ben Johnson wins a gold medal at Seoul Olympics, which is later revoked because of a positive steroid test.

1989 Fourteen female engineering students are gunned down in Montreal.

1990 Meech Lake Accord fails to be ratified by all provinces within required three years. Lucien Bouchard forms the Bloc Québécois. Mohawks confront Quebec government at Oka. Audrey McLaughlin is chosen as first female party leader in Canada. Jean Chrétien becomes Liberal leader.

1991 Goods and services tax officially introduced.

1992 Charlottetown Accord is reached. Toronto Blue Jays win World Series. National referendum rejects the Charlottetown Accord.

After a quarter-century of optimism, the years following 1972 presented Canadians with a different picture. Everything, from the economy to the very nation itself, suddenly seemed to be in a state of confusion bordering on disintegration.

The Problems of Liberal Federalist Nationalism

Until the early 1970s the post-war era, for most Canadians, had been a time of affluence and optimism. It was characterized by a nationalism anchored by strong central federal government. This relatively positive climate had been achieved by policies dominated by twentieth-century small-l liberalism, a delicate balancing act that accepted an economic system based on private enterprise and corporate capitalism while also attempting to provide a social welfare safety net for the nation's citizens. Not all the resulting policies were influenced by Keynesian economics, but many of them were. Such policies were the operative ones for governments throughout the Western industrialized world. They were non-partisan. All major Canadian political parties at all levels of government—ranging provincially from the Socreds of the West to the separatists of Quebec—were essentially exponents of variants of liberalism with a small "l."

If the political consensus sought by all democratic governments in this period was formally dominated by liberal economics, the constitutional framework in which the liberalism was to operate increasingly produced conflict. For much of the period before 1970, the Liberal Party had combined liberal economics with a constitutionally centralized federalism. Although the Progressive Conservatives, in their six years of power between 1957 and 1963, had demonstrated different emphases, even they had not seriously contemplated overturning the broad framework. As we have seen, the Liberal consensus had come under attack in the 1960s, mainly from the left. It began seriously unravelling in the 1970s, and was in tatters by the beginning of the 1990s.

The Canadian political arena seemed incapable of dealing with both economic problems and constitutional problems simultaneously, at least at the same level of intensity. The period after 1972 saw an alternation of focus between the Constitution and the economy. The two questions were not entirely divorced, of course. One of the major arguments of the federalists was that only strong national policies could deal with the problems of the economy and with the demands of minorities not geographically embodied into provinces and regions. Moreover, while constitutional matters were largely under the control of Canadians, economic ones were chiefly international. After the election of a Tory government under Brian Mulroney in 1984, both nationalism and federalism were jettisoned for free trade and Meech Lake, while the principles of liberal economics were replaced by privatization, clawbacks, and deregulation.

No single factor or event can possibly be isolated as responsible for the collapse of the liberal federalist-nationalist consensus in Canada. Instead, an accumulation of what Marxist analysts would call "contradictions"—matters that simply could not be resolved within the consensus—would eventually defy attempts at management, compromise, or hopeful neglect. The contradictions would come together at centre stage to produce a series of what the media liked to label "crises." Many of the pressures were not really of Canada's own making but were part of international trends over which no Canadian government had very much control. Increasingly, politicians and the public came to feel that all political responses were defensive reactions to unmanageable situations, and that all policies were merely band-aids placed over festering wounds. Public trust in the nation's political leaders declined as the consensus disintegrated and was not replaced by a new paradigm. Cynicism became entrenched at the core of the Canadian national psyche. To some imponderable extent, the increase in cynicism and the gradual emergence of ever more unalloyed self-interest as the mainspring of human action contributed to the further deterioration of the old consensus. World War II had been fought on the basic principles of the deferral of expectations and the need for national sacrifice for the greatest good of the greatest number—a classic liberal utilitarianism. Canadians, whether as private individuals or as voting citizens, became increasingly less willing to buy such arguments. They became ever more prepared to accept the calls of leaders who, by implication or open assertion, opposed either waiting or sharing.

In 1973 a ceasefire agreement allowed the United States to withdraw from Vietnam, and the American process of national disillusionment continued with the Watergate affair, in which an apparently successful President was eventually forced to resign on 9 August 1974 rather than risk removal from office by impeachment for years of lying to the public. In Canada, Vietnam seemed less important than the October Crisis, bringing to the fore the Parti Québécois, which succeeded in electing seven candidates in the 1970 Quebec election. Then on 6 October 1973—the Jewish holy day of Yom Kippur—the Arabs and Israelis went to war, as they had done periodically for many years. On this occasion, however, events in the Middle East had an immediate impact on the world and on Canada. The Arab oil exporters (who dominated the world market) embargoed shipments of oil to nations supporting Israel. Shortly thereafter, the Organization of Petroleum Exporting Countries (OPEC), which for 13 years had been a toothless cartel, managed to agree on another price increase, more substantial than the modest one announced before the Yom Kippur War. The price of oil more than tripled in 1973, and all Western industrialized nations suddenly realized how much their economies had depended on a constant supply of cheap oil.

Perhaps more than any other single commodity of the post-war era, oil symbolized the economics of the age of affluence as well as its North American problems. Cheap oil made possible the development of large, powerful, and comfortable automobiles—the "Yank Tanks" as they were called in Canada before they briefly became the "Detroit Dinosaurs"—that sat in every suburban driveway and clogged every freeway. Those freeways, of course, had been paved with materials conjured out of petroleum derivatives. The manufacture and sale of instantly obsolescent, gas-guzzling automobiles, as well as the construction of roads that connected thousands of new suburban developments and shopping malls, were major components of post-

war economic prosperity in both the United States and Canada. Some saw the car as a symbol of post-war progress, while others saw it as a sex symbol. Either way, a 20-horsepower electric engine could hardly provide the same effect. The typical Detroit automobile not only consumed gas and oil as if there were no tomorrow, but discharged harmful hydrocarbons—serious contributors to the air pollution that increasingly affected everyone's health. Detroit engineering—never renowned for its flexibility—was slow to respond to the need for fuel efficiency brought about by significantly higher oil prices. By the time it had moved to smaller vehicles, the Japanese had taken command of the North American automobile market, a fact that strongly suggested a new world trading order.

If petroleum—literally as well as symbolically—fuelled the contradictions of the North American economy, it also exposed Canadians to a number of distinctly homegrown problems. Many of these matters had already been newsworthy before OPEC pulled the plug, but they seemed more urgent and apparent as the nation searched for a viable energy policy to respond to the "crisis." The Canadian petroleum industry, located chiefly in Alberta, was almost entirely owned and operated by multinational corporations, most (though not all) of them American-based. Oil, indeed, was one of those resources that most obviously epitomized the problems of foreign ownership that were addressed by a series of governments and task forces in the early 1970s. Moreover, although the petroleum still in the ground was a Crown resource, the Crown involved was the province and not the federal state. When the problems of jurisdiction over offshore oil were added to provincial control of oil as an internal natural resource, the result was a key item of potential dispute in federal–provincial relations. Most oil consumption in Canada occurred in the industrialized East, while most of the raw material was in the resource-rich West, a discrepancy that exacerbated regional tensions. Finally, increased petroleum prices had a ripple effect throughout both the Canadian and world economies. Prices rose overnight, and an already steady inflation soared to new highs at a time when Canadian labour unions had only recently succeeded in establishing themselves in many key industries, especially in the public sector. Having achieved full recognition of collective bargaining, union organizers next moved for improved working conditions and higher wages to match the cost of living. OPEC's price increases, with promises of more to come, thus affected Canada in several vulnerable areas: foreign ownership, federal–provincial relations, regional conflicts, and labour relations.

Virtually the only long-standing problem that oil did not seem to affect directly was Quebec. On 29 October 1973, only three weeks after the start of the Yom Kippur War, Quebecers went to the polls to elect a new provincial government. From the outset of the contest between the Liberals of Robert Bourassa and the Parti Québécois headed by René Lévesque, the chief issue had been the desirability of a separate Quebec. Both parties had worked to polarize the electorate on this simple issue. The result, on the surface, was a resounding victory for the Liberals: 1,600,000 votes (54.8 per cent of the total votes cast) to 897,000 for the PQ, and 102 seats in the legislature to six for the PQ. Nonetheless, the Péquistes had improved their performance over the 1970 election in almost every riding, and did exceptionally well among younger voters in Montreal. Post-election studies suggested that the majority of Liberal supporters had favoured federalism and a majority of PQ supporters wanted independence for Quebec. The anglophone voters were much more staunchly federalist than the francophones. In any event, separatism had suddenly become respectable. While no other province was prepared to join the PQ in the front lines of the quest for a new constitutional arrangement for Canada, resource-rich provinces like Alberta certainly favoured new guarantees of constitutional autonomy for the provinces.

The relationship between Quebec separatism and Canada's economic problems after 1973 was difficult to determine. In 1976 the PQ won a somewhat surprising victory, not necessarily to be interpreted as a mandate for separatism or sovereignty-association, although one of its pre-election platform planks was the promise of a referendum on sovereignty-association. When the referendum was held in May 1980, the "Nons"—those opposed to sovereignty-association—won 60 per cent to 40 per cent. The PQ, however, were re-elected the next year. Especially after the referendum, the federal government under Pierre Trudeau turned its attention from the economy to the Constitution. Trudeau himself was not only a federalist Quebecer but a constitutional lawyer far more comfortable with the intricacies of the British North America Act than with oil-price equalization or economic planning. Oil and the Constitution were scarcely the only issues after 1973, but they were certainly front and centre for many years. The various attempts to resolve the problems they helped to create (as well as the ones they obscured) precipitated the deterioration of the post-war consensus.

Pressure for continual expansion of the welfare state came from many directions before 1980, because income security became essential to the federal government's power, representing as it did the main link between Ottawa and the people. After 1980, however, contrary tendencies became evident and eventually dominant. Canada's economic and social problems would continue to produce demands for expansion of social insurance, but with the erosion of revenue and intense international competition, the federal government increasingly focused on restraint and privatization. Before 1992, no major element of the existing welfare net had actually been eliminated, however. Pension benefits for the elderly even improved. But the government cumulatively reduced the universality of the system of family benefits through the income tax system. In unemployment compensation, revised regulations increased the waiting period, making it more difficult to use unemployment funds as income supplements. The notorious goods and services tax (GST) was a thoroughly regressive tax that hit hardest at the poor. Still, the greatest irony of government policy towards social welfare remained unchanged from the earlier part of the century. The government of Brian Mulroney was continually concerned about spending and the deficit, but had no trouble finding funds to support its military co-operation in the Gulf War of 1991. The unsolved riddle of social justice was still a challenge.

The Shape of Federal Politics

The Ottawa scene from 1972 to 1992 divides into two periods, with the break coming in 1984. During most of the first period the Liberals under Trudeau clung

John Edward (Ed) Broadbent

Ed Broadbent (left). CP Images. THE CANADIAN PRESS/UPC/Rod MacIver

Born in Oshawa in 1936 into a family of auto workers, Broadbent attended Trinity College, Toronto (graduating in 1959) and went on to earn a Ph.D. from the University of Toronto in political science in 1966. His thesis was on the political ideology of John Stuart Mill. In 1965 he was appointed a faculty member in the political science department at York University in Toronto, but in 1968 he ran for Parliament as an NDP candidate from his home riding, and squeaked through to victory. While entering political life directly from a career in academia was not a unique occurrence, it was fairly unusual, probably more possible in the NDP than in any other Canadian political party. In Ottawa, Broadbent developed a reputation as an articulate member of the NDP's left wing, and his popularity in his home riding increased considerably over the years. In 1975 he was

elected leader of the NDP to succeed Stephen Lewis, who had suffered a disastrous defeat in the 1974 parliamentary election, in which the NDP had lost little in the popular vote but was substantially decimated in terms of number of seats. The problem to a large extent was that the NDP had kept the Trudeau Liberal minority in office from 1972 to 1974, but got little credit from the electorate for its efforts and instead was squeezed between the major parties.

Broadbent rebuilt the party after the 1974 debacle, focusing on hard-core economic issues. He ran into some trouble in 1981 over his support of the patriation of Canada's Constitution, but his leadership in 1984 produced 30 seats. For a time in the mid-1980s he consistently scored higher in the public opinion polls than any other party leader, particularly as the leader most trusted by Canadian voters. This vote of confidence did not translate into additional votes for the NDP, which continued to have trouble with electorates east of Ontario. In the 1988 election he was again criticized by many in the party, this time for not making the recently negotiated Free Trade Agreement with the United States a major campaign issue and for his support of the Meech Lake Accord. Broadbent stepped down as NDP leader in 1989, but returned briefly to parliamentary politics in 2004 at the behest of Jack Layton. Since his second retirement in 2006 he has been a fellow at Queen's University and has more recently chaired the Broadbent Institute, a think-tank that bills itself as a non-partisan champion of progressive change.

tenaciously to power in a series of very close elections (1972, 1974, and 1980), although they were replaced in office briefly, in 1979, by a minority Tory administration headed by Joe Clark. This period was one of a gradual Liberal Party deterioration paralleling the unravelling of the small-l liberal consensus of the post-war era. In

1984 the Tories under Brian Mulroney swept to power in the most decisive election since 1945, exceeding even the Diefenbaker sweep of 1958 in percentage of popular votes and number of seats. As with most decisive electoral shifts in Canada, the one in 1984 involved a massive reorientation of votes in Quebec and

Ontario. The change in Quebec was particularly critical, although it was not clear whether Quebec's party shift was a long-term one, or precisely what it meant. At the end of their tenures of office, both Trudeau and Mulroney engendered enormous currents of fierce voter hostility in a general atmosphere of public mistrust of politicians. This mistrust would continue for decades.

Whether Mulroney's Tories actually represented a different political vision that could serve as the basis for a new consensus was always an open question. Certainly they sought to move to the consensual centre, which public opinion polls and voting behaviour suggested had become dubious about many of the old assumptions, but there was no clear evidence that a new political paradigm was emerging from the shards of the old liberal one. Instead, the events of his second administration suggested that Mulroney, like Diefenbaker a generation earlier, was simply perplexed and confounded by the chaos of the disintegration of federalism. The problem of Quebec, which came to dominate public attention across Canada in the late 1980s and early 1990s, contributed to further confusion.

The Liberals

The fortunes of the federal Liberal Party between 1968 and 1984 became increasingly associated with Pierre Elliott Trudeau, its leader for most of that period. The identification was partly due to television's relentless search for visual images and Trudeau's brilliant mastery of the medium. But it was also a result of Trudeau's operating as a loner, not encouraging strong colleagues to emerge around him. Trudeau's "arrogance," the term most often used to describe his behaviour, was personal, not political. As a French Canadian who had always firmly opposed Quebec separatism, he had little scope for manoeuvre when public opinion polarized in that province. As an equally strong federalist, he had no more time for western expressions of provincial or regional autonomy than he did for Quebec's. A central Canadian urban intellectual, he could not empathize with the problems of either the Atlantic region or western Canada. The East never deserted him, but by 1980 "western alienation" had reduced the number of Liberal MPs west of Ontario to two (both from Manitoba).

Never a fervent party man, Trudeau did not cultivate the grassroots. The powerful Liberal political organizations that had flourished before 1970 were allowed to wither away in most provinces, surfacing when federal patronage was to be dispensed but not at federal election time. Trudeau distressed many Canadians with forthrightness ("Just watch me" in regard to soldiers in the streets of Montreal during the October Crisis), vulgarity bordering on obscenity (one four-letter word in the House of Commons was transcribed as "fuddle duddle," a raised-finger gesture to a western crowd appeared in newspapers across the nation), and personal unconventionality. Perhaps most damaging of all was an increasing tendency to treat almost everyone (members of his own caucus, the opposition, reporters, the voters) as ill-informed and irrational. Trudeau's public persona oscillated between that of a genial swinger (who could date Barbra Streisand) and that of a university professor facing a particularly stupid class.

Trudeau had announced his intention of retiring in 1979 following the Liberals' unexpected electoral defeat. But the Clark minority government fell before his replacement could be chosen. The Liberal caucus persuaded him to lead the party into the unanticipated election of 1980, and he remained in power for four more years. In 1984 Trudeau made his retirement stick. He was succeeded by John Turner (b. 1929), who had waited in the wings for years. Chosen on 16 June 1984 as Liberal leader and becoming Prime Minister two weeks later, Turner dissolved Parliament on 9 July for the fateful 1984 election. Turner was born in England but was thoroughly bilingual. His decision regarding the election was a difficult one. He chose to run as a fresh face, on the momentum of his selection as leader, rather than to remain in office to attempt to improve the government's image. He had no new policies. Instead he was encumbered by the twin albatrosses of Trudeau's mounting unpopularity and the growing collapse of the liberal consensus. To everyone's surprise, he also proved utterly inept on television. The weak Liberal showing of 1984 (40 seats in the House of Commons) was hardly unexpected. Something better was hoped for by the party in 1988, however. In that election the Liberals did even worse in Quebec than in 1984, and Turner was a lame duck on election night. He was finally replaced in the summer of 1990 by Jean Chrétien (b. 1934), another veteran of earlier Liberal governments. Chrétien was a loyal party man and a proven campaigner. His leadership opponents had labelled him "Yesterday's Man" with some justification, but lacked sufficient credibility or charisma to beat him.

The Progressive Conservatives

Robert Stanfield led the Tories to three successive defeats at the hands of the Trudeau Liberals. He was too low-key and not compelling. Stanfield spoke French badly and his party did poorly in Quebec during his leadership (four seats in 1968, two in 1972, and three in 1974). He was followed as Tory leader by Alberta MP Joe (Charles Joseph) Clark (b. 1939), who emerged from nowhere as the compromise "progressive" candidate at the 1976 leadership convention. "Joe Who?" never did establish a distinct personality with the voters, except as a man who was accident-prone. In 1979 his Tories received 136 seats to 114 for the Liberals. Clark formed a minority government despite having won only two seats in Quebec (to 67 for the Liberals). He tried to govern as if he had a majority, mistakenly assuming either that other parties would support him in Parliament rather than face another election or that the nation would rally to his banner in a new election. Neither assumption was true. The NDP refused to support Clark, especially over the privatization of Petro-Canada. His government fell on a motion of non-confidence about the budget, involving gasoline pricing. Clark remained party leader

Prime Minister Trudeau and the newly elected Premier of Quebec, Robert Bourassa, at the federal–provincial conference of September 1970, in Ottawa. The two men co-operated closely during the early 1970s. Duncan Cameron/LAC, PA-117468.

after the disastrous election of 1980, but in June 1983 he was replaced by "the Boy from Baie Comeau," Brian Mulroney (b. 1939).

Brian Mulroney entered Canadian politics at the highest level without ever having held public or elected office, although he had been active in the political backrooms for years. Unlike Clark, whose public utterances were unpolished and delivered in a boyish tenor (he reportedly took elocution lessons to lower his voice), Mulroney was a fluent speaker, perfectly bilingual, and possessed of one of the richest and most mellifluous voices ever heard in Canadian politics. He was an experienced labour lawyer and corporation executive, at his best in behind-the-scenes conciliation. Mulroney understood the need for Tory success in Quebec, and he brought a number of new faces into the campaign, some of whom were refugees from the old Union Nationale. In 1984 he successfully captured the centre of the new Canadian political spectrum. Although Mulroney's Tories promised they would not dismantle the existing welfare state, they put an ominous emphasis on "fiscal responsibility." They were equally committed to better relations between Canada and the United States, which meant less economic nationalism, as well as improved relations between Ottawa and the provinces (especially Quebec), which meant surrendering federalist pretensions.

Once in office with an enormous majority, including 58 seats from Quebec, Mulroney succeeded in 1986 in negotiating a free trade agreement with the United States and the Meech Lake constitutional accord with the provinces. On the coattails of these successes the Tories won again in 1988, with 63 of their 169 seats coming from Quebec. Mulroney's second term was an unmitigated disaster. Given the amount of public support he had enjoyed in 1984 and 1988, the rapid growth of hostility to Mulroney in the early 1990s was quite remarkable. A variety of things went wrong. Government spending got quite out of hand. What was supposed to be a progressive tax reform, the GST, proved to be the most unpopular tax ever introduced in Canadian history, doubly resented for the way the Tories stacked the Senate to ensure its passage. The GST replaced previously hidden levies with an all-too-visible tax computed at the cash register. Unlike

Brian Mulroney in 1983, the year before he became leader of the Progressive Conservative Party, MP for Central Nova, and leader of the Opposition. He was elected Prime Minister the following year. Ed McGibbon/LAC, PA-146485.

provincial sales taxes, it was applied to everything without exception. With the provincial taxes, the GST meant a surcharge of nearly 20 per cent in several provinces on most consumer spending. Meech Lake failed, and in a national referendum in October 1992 the nation rejected its successor, the Charlottetown Accord. Much of Canada came to believe that the Tory constitutional deals, especially with Quebec, not only made too many concessions but had actually stirred up unnecessary trouble.

Other National Parties

Throughout this period the New Democratic Party remained the constant third party. Its continuity was exemplified by the steadiness of its popular vote in federal elections, which ran between 15 and 20 per cent, and by the steadiness of its policies, which were indisputably federalist, nationalist, and liberal. Some complained that the party was not sufficiently socialist. It had certainly purged its socialist wing, the Waffle, in the early 1970s. But it was still unable to make inroads east of Ontario, and was consistently the big loser when the popular vote was translated into parliamentary seats. From 1971 to 1975 the NDP was led by David Lewis (1909–81), the son of Russian immigrants to Canada and a Rhodes scholar who had spent a lifetime associated with the CCF-NDP. His selection as leader followed a bitter fight with the radical caucus within the party. From 1972 to 1974 the Lewis-led NDP propped up the minority Liberal government, arguably turning it to the left, but paying for the collaboration at the polls in 1974.

In 1975 Ed Broadbent (b. 1936), a former political science professor at York University, succeeded Lewis. Broadbent's national position in Canada in the 1980s was a peculiar one. He consistently headed the polls as the most popular and trustworthy national leader, but his party was never able to increase its public support. In 1990 Broadbent was replaced by Audrey McLaughlin (b. 1936), a former social worker from the Yukon Territory who spoke halting French and had no appeal in Quebec. Her selection as the first female party leader in Canada, however, marked the NDP as yet again in advance of the other parties, for feminist issues were part of the unresolved agenda of Canadian politics in the 1990s.

The Provinces, the Constitution, and the Charter of Rights

The Shape of Provincial Politics

The provinces continued to have difficulty generating truly viable two-party or multi-party systems. Instead, most provinces operated through a single dominant party (often outside the two major federal ones) that remained in office in election after election, producing what C.B. Macpherson described for Alberta as a "quasi-party" system. A single dominant party, Macpherson argued, satisfied voters and mediated local conflict by insisting that the important battle was against external forces symbolized by the Canadian federal government. Conflict with Ottawa had been an endemic feature of provincial politics and government since Confederation. Offers to out-bash the opposition regarding Ottawa were standard fare in provincial elections, particularly highly contested ones. Party identification with government in Ottawa was always extremely dangerous when provincial rights issues were on the table.

In some ways the 1970s were hard on dominant parties in the provinces. Four long-dominant provincial parties went down to defeat: the Liberals in Newfoundland and Quebec, and the Socreds in Alberta and British Columbia. It was never clear whether the coincidence of these defeats was part of a much larger political shift, the product of changing economic circumstances, or mere accident. In any event, political veterans like Joey Smallwood, Ernest Manning, and W.A.C. Bennett were replaced by younger leaders such as Peter Lougheed (b. 1928) in Alberta, Brian Peckford (b. 1942) in Newfoundland, and Bill Bennett (1932–2015) in British Columbia. For the younger men, federal–provincial relations were not conditioned by depression, war, or post-war prosperity so much as by provincial self-interest ruthlessly pursued.

Federal–Provincial Relations

The 1970s

Throughout the 1970s federal–provincial relations were dominated by oil, Quebec, and abortive constitutional reform. In June 1971, at the federal–provincial conference held in Victoria, the Trudeau administration made another effort to agree on a formula for constitutional repatriation that would satisfy Quebec's aspirations. Three points are worth noting about the 1971 discussions: first, entrenching rights in a charter was regarded as one way to reassure those who feared losing British constitutional protection; second, Quebec did not achieve a sufficiently distinctive place in Confederation to suit its demands; and finally, only Quebec and Ontario were given perpetual vetoes (other provinces could together mount a veto only using complicated co-operative formulas). The question of constitutional reform was not picked up again until 1980, by which time much had changed for both Canada and its provinces. Oil and the whole question of resource management had become subjects of continual tension between some of the provinces (led by Alberta) and the federal government after 1973. Before OPEC pulled the plug, Alberta had often single-handedly opposed Ottawa over resource management. With non-renewable resources now hot commodities, more provinces recognized the advantages of provincial autonomy. Only PEI, Manitoba, and New Brunswick were left to visualize their provincial self-interest as best served by a strong federal government. By 1980 the rich provinces, usually led by hard-headed businessmen who insisted that they put balance sheets ahead of sentiment, were ready to help dismantle Ottawa's centralized arrangements, especially in the area of social insurance programs.

The Parti Québécois and the Constitution

The occasion for a new round of constitutional discussions was provided by the Parti Québécois, not through its electoral victory of 1976 but through its referendum on sovereignty-association of 1980. The PQ victory came as a shock to English-speaking Canada, although it was really quite predictable. The Bourassa government in Quebec had been badly shaken by charges of scandal and corruption on top of its seeming inability to deal expeditiously with either the separatists or Pierre Trudeau. It had lost considerable face when the Canadian Airline Pilots Association went on strike in June 1976, ostensibly over safety but really over bilingualism, an issue that only the federal government could resolve. Rumours of cost overruns and construction disasters in the preparations for the 1976 Summer Olympics in Montreal had been rife for years. Bourassa's government was not directly involved in the problems, which were primarily the responsibility of Mayor Jean Drapeau's Montreal government, but Drapeau was a Liberal ally and Bourassa had waffled

over intervening. The province took over the Olympics construction only at the last minute. There were similar concerns over the control of the James Bay hydroelectric development, but in the summer of 1976 these were not so immediately visible in Montreal as the Olympics fiasco. A resurgent Parti Québécois won over many voters who did not normally support it, as the electorate simultaneously rejected Bourassa's Liberals and embraced Lévesque's party.

Issues are never tidy in any election. No evidence suggested that the PQ, despite its resounding victory, had received any mandate for its well-publicized sovereignty-association. The Parti Québécois had insisted that it would not act unilaterally on separation without a provincial referendum. Voters could thus support the reformist social democratic zeal of the PQ without signing on to its extremist constitutional position. English-speaking Canada, however, responded to the Quebec election by assuming that separatism had triumphed in Quebec. The nation had to be saved at any cost. Had Lévesque sought to renegotiate the constitutional issues in the immediate wake of the victory, he might have been offered some sort of two-nations formula; but the PQ was committed both to internal Quebec reform and to a democratic approach to separation.

In office Lévesque's PQ successfully pursued policies of economic and linguistic nationalism. Its most controversial legislation was Bill 101, which went well beyond an earlier piece of Bourassa legislation (known as Bill 22) in its effort to turn Quebec into a unilingual francophone province. Bill 101 made it necessary for most Quebecers, regardless of their background or preference, to be educated in French-language schools. Only those temporarily resident in Quebec or whose parents had been educated in English-speaking schools in the province were exempted. The bill also insisted that French was the only legal medium in business and government, requiring the elimination of virtually all English-language signs in the province. In 1979 the Quebec government produced a White Paper detailing what it meant by sovereignty-association. It wanted "a free, proud and adult national existence" within the context of a series of joint Quebec–Canada institutions, including a court of justice and a monetary authority

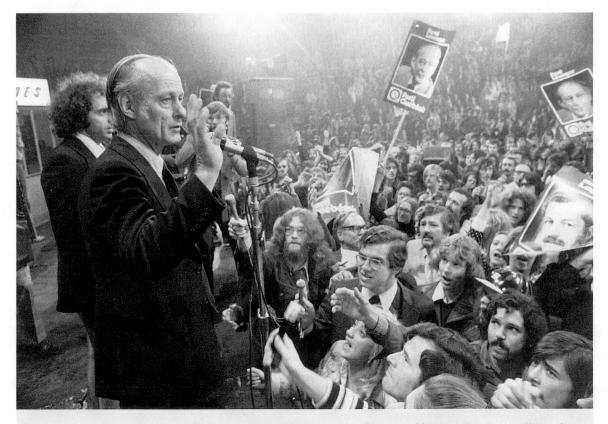

René Lévesque on provincial election night, 29 October 1973. Lévesque lost his seat and his party lost one as well. But the PQ increased its percentage of the popular vote from 23 per cent to 30 per cent, and became the official opposition. Duncan Cameron/ LAC, PA-115039.

(Québec conseil exécutif, 1979). A totally independent Quebec, it insisted, would still have access to Canada and its economy. Outside the ranks of the converted, the scheme seemed far too lopsided in Quebec's favour. The proposal was a unilateral Quebec initiative.

As had been promised, there was a referendum, eventually scheduled for 20 May 1980. Referendums are notoriously tricky political instruments. They often encourage "No" votes. Certainly the non-francophone population of Quebec (less than 20 per cent of the whole), although vehemently opposed to a "*Oui*" vote, were not by themselves numerous enough to reject sovereignty-association, but in the end almost 60 per cent of the province's voters and even a bare majority (52 per cent) of its francophones voted "*Non*." This fairly decisive result left 40.5 per cent of the Quebec population, and just under half of its francophones,

in favour of sovereignty-association. Nevertheless, Quebec had publicly rejected separation from Canada. The nation responded by breathing a collective sigh of relief and calling for a new federalism. Forgotten for the moment was the simple truth that pressure for change of the fundamental sort represented by separatism does not go away because of one setback at the ballot box.

The First Round of Constitutional Revisions

Canadians had discussed and debated both national unity and constitutional change since the PQ victory in 1976. More than enough proposals for reform floated about the country. Many surfaced in the travelling road show (known as the Task Force on National Unity) sent across Canada in 1978. Out of the flurry of activity and the myriad suggestions, several points were clear. One was that many Canadians—including a fair proportion of academics and lawyers, if not historians—were prepared to make relatively major alterations in the British North America Act, the document that served as the nation's Constitution. A second was that the vast majority of anglophone Canadians were prepared to make substantial concessions to keep Quebec within Confederation. A third point, perhaps less well understood by the public, was that the anglophone provinces of Canada—led by the western provinces of Alberta, British Columbia, and Saskatchewan and strongly supported by Nova Scotia and Newfoundland—had developed their own agenda for constitutional reform. These provinces saw Ottawa's federalism as operating almost exclusively in the interests of central Canada. They were quite prepared to take advantage of Quebec's moves towards greater autonomy, particularly if these pressures reduced Quebec's influence within Confederation and allowed for constitutional change in the best interests of other provinces. What the other provinces wanted most was unrestricted control over their own natural resources and reform of some of Ottawa's governing institutions, notably the Senate and the Supreme Court, to reflect regional interests. The Trudeau government had seemed on the verge of conceding much of the provincial program when it was defeated in 1979. The Clark government had not dealt with the issue when it, too, failed at the polls.

BACKGROUNDER

Chronology of Quebec Separatism

March 1963	Front de libération du Québec is founded.	26 Aug. 1977	Bill 101 makes French the official language of Quebec.
November 1967	René Lévesque resigns from the Quebec Liberal Party and begins organizing the Parti Québécois.	15 April 1980	Sovereignty referendum campaign begins.
		14 May 1980	Trudeau promises constitutional reform.
25 June 1968	Pierre Trudeau is elected with a large Liberal majority.	20 May 1980	Sovereignty-association is defeated, 60 per cent to 40 per cent.
7 July 1969	Canada becomes officially bilingual through the Official Languages Act.	2 Oct. 1980	Trudeau announces that the Constitution will be repatriated.
October 1970	Kidnapping of James Cross and Pierre Laporte. War Measures Act is invoked.	13 April 1981	PQ wins a majority in the Quebec election.
29 Oct. 1973	PQ wins six seats in the Quebec election and becomes the official opposition.	2–5 Nov. 1981	Ottawa and nine anglophone provinces reach a deal on the Constitution. Lévesque claims he has been stabbed in the back.
15 Nov. 1976	PQ wins majority in Quebec election and takes over government.	1 July 1982	Queen gives royal consent to a new Constitution.

21 July 1985	René Lévesque retires.
3 October 1985	Pierre-Marc Johnson, new leader of the PQ, becomes Quebec Premier.
2 Dec. 1985	Liberals under Bourassa defeat Johnson's PQ and form a new government.
3 June 1987	Meech Lake Accord is negotiated.
1 Nov. 1987	Death of René Lévesque.
17 March 1988	Jacques Parizeau is elected new leader of the PQ.
2 June 1990	Meech Lake Accord fails when Manitoba and Newfoundland fail to ratify within deadline. Quebec says it will not take part in further constitutional deals.
25 June 1990	Seven independent Quebec MPs, led by Lucien Bouchard, form the Bloc Québécois.
28 Jan. 1991	Quebec Liberal Party calls for a decentralized Canada.
27 March 1991	Bélanger-Campeau Commission recommends a referendum on sovereignty by November 1992 if there is no deal with Canada.
24 Sept. 1991	Ottawa proposes recognition of Quebec as a distinct society, Senate reform, Aboriginal self-government, economic union, and adjustments to federal–provincial powers to give provinces more control.
12 March 1992	First formal federal–provincial meeting since the failure of Meech Lake.
7 July 1992	Federal government, nine provincial premiers (all but Quebec's), and Aboriginal leaders agree on a new formula for reform.
4 August 1992	Bourassa meets with other premiers and PM Mulroney.
19–23 Aug. 1992	Charlottetown Accord is negotiated, including Senate reform, Aboriginal self-government, an expanded House of Commons, some new power arrangements, and a provincial veto over future change to federal institutions.
18 Sept. 1992	National referendum campaign on Charlottetown begins.
26 Oct. 1992	Canadian voters reject Charlottetown, 54 per cent to 45 per cent.
25 Oct. 1993	Federal Liberals under Chrétien demolish the Tories and NDP; Bouchard's BQ forms the official opposition in Commons with 55 seats.
11 Jan. 1994	Bourassa resigns and is succeeded by Daniel Johnson.
12 Sept. 1994	PQ elected in Quebec and promises referendum on sovereignty.
12 June 1995	Parizeau, Bouchard, and Action Démocratique (ADQ) leader Mario Dumont form a coalition to fight for *"Oui"* on referendum.
30 Oct. 1995	Sovereignty rejected, 50.7 per cent to 49.3 per cent; turnout for the referendum is an astonishing 93.5 per cent of eligible voters.
31 Oct. 1995	Parizeau resigns as PQ leader.

Continued...

11 Jan. 1996	Lucien Bouchard is chosen PQ leader and Quebec Premier.	20 Aug. 1998	Canadian Supreme Court rules that Quebec cannot unilaterally separate from Canada. After a clear majority vote in favour of sovereignty, Quebec would have to negotiate with Canada to "address the interests" of various parties, including the linguistic and cultural minorities.
18 Jan. 1996	Bouchard resigns as BQ leader.		
17 Feb. 1996	Michel Gauthier is chosen as head of BQ.		
Sept. 1996	Quebec nationalist Guy Bertrand wins right in Quebec Superior Court to seek a court injunction against a new sovereignty referendum.		
28 Feb. 1997	Federal Justice Minister Allan Rock insists Quebec has no right to declare independence from Canada unilaterally, even in the event of a pro-secession referendum.	21 Sept. 1998	Parti Québécois National Council agrees not to hold another referendum until there is a good chance of winning it.
		30 Nov 1998	Parti Québécois wins 77 seats of 125 in Quebec provincial election.
March 1997	Gilles Duceppe elected Bloc leader.		
2 June 1997	Bloc Québécois wins 44 Quebec seats in federal election to 26 for Liberals and 5 for Conservatives.	8 March 2001	Lucien Bouchard resigns from office and is replaced by Bernard Landry.
		14 April 2003	Liberals under Jean Charest win Quebec election.
15 Sept. 1997	At a meeting of the anglophone premiers of Canada, seven principles are adopted to promote the distinctive character of Quebec, but the declaration is rejected by Premier Bouchard since it is not part of the Constitution.	June 2005	Bernard Landry steps down as PQ leader.
		Nov. 2005	André Boisclair, an acknowledged gay politician, is chosen as PQ leader.
		23 Jan. 2006	Federal election sees Bloc win only 42 per cent of popular vote and 61 Quebec seats. This is regarded as a setback to the sovereignist movement.

The opportunity presented to Prime Minister Trudeau by the Quebec referendum, when he called a first ministers' conference for early June 1980, was real, if dangerous. Once the box of constitutional revision was opened, it might never be closed. From the federalist perspective, it was necessary to deal with Quebec's aspirations without conceding too much to the other provinces, none of which was controlled by a Liberal government and all of which had their own visions of change. Ottawa's most consistent ally was Ontario, confirming regional charges that it had been the chief beneficiary of the old federalism. Quebec did not participate in the new discussions, but it could not be churlish about them. Its best strategy was to allow the anglophone provinces to initiate the dismantling of Confederation. Indeed,

Canadian Charter of Rights and Freedoms

The following clauses of the Charter of Rights and Freedoms are of most relevance to the present discussion. The Charter includes 34 clauses and can be accessed online at: www.efc.ca/pages/law/charter/charter.text.html.

RIGHTS AND FREEDOMS IN CANADA.

1. The Canadian Charter of Rights and Freedoms guarantees the rights and freedoms set out in it subject only to such reasonable limits prescribed by law as can be demonstrably justified in a free and democratic society.

FUNDAMENTAL FREEDOMS.

2. Everyone has the following fundamental freedoms:
    (a) freedom of conscience and religion;
    (b) freedom of thought, belief, opinion and expression, including freedom of the press and other media of communication;
    (c) freedom of peaceful assembly; and
    (d) freedom of association.

DEMOCRATIC RIGHTS OF CITIZENS.

3. Every citizen of Canada has the right to vote in an election of members of the House of Commons or of a legislative assembly and to be qualified for membership therein.

MAXIMUM DURATION OF LEGISLATIVE BODIES/
CONTINUATION IN SPECIAL CIRCUMSTANCES.

4. (1) No House of Commons and no legislative assembly shall continue for longer than five years from the date fixed for the return of the writs at a general election of its members.
    (2) In time of real or apprehended war, invasion or insurrection, a House of Commons may be continued by Parliament and a legislative assembly may be continued by the legislature beyond five years if such continuation is not opposed by the votes of more than one-third of the members of the House of Commons or the legislative assembly, as the case may be.

ANNUAL SITTING OF LEGISLATIVE BODIES.

5. There shall be a sitting of Parliament and of each legislature at least once every twelve months.

MOBILITY RIGHTS OF CITIZENS/RIGHT TO MOVE AND GAIN LIVELIHOOD/AFFIRMATIVE ACTION PROGRAMS.

6. (1) Every citizen of Canada has the right to enter, remain in and leave Canada.
    (2) Every citizen of Canada and every person who has the status of a permanent resident of Canada has the right
        (a) to move to and take up residence in any province; and
        (b) to pursue the gaining of a livelihood in any province.
    (3) The rights specified in subsection (2) are subject to
        (a) any laws or practices of general application in force in a province other than those that discriminate among persons primarily on the basis of province of present or previous residence; and
        (b) any laws providing for reasonable residency requirements as a qualification for the receipt of publicly provided social services.
    (4) Subsections (2) and (3) do not preclude any law, program or activity that has as its object the amelioration in a province of conditions of individuals in that province who were socially or economically disadvantaged if the rate of employment in

Continued...

that province is below the rate of employment in Canada. . . .

LIFE, LIBERTY AND SECURITY OF PERSON.

7. Everyone has the right to life, liberty and security of the person and the right not to be deprived thereof except in accordance with the principles of fundamental justice. . . .

TREATMENT OF PUNISHMENT.

12. Everyone has the right not to be subjected to any cruel and unusual treatment or punishment.

SELF-INCRIMINATION.

13. A witness who testifies in any proceedings has the right not to have any incriminating evidence so given used to incriminate that witness in any other proceedings, except in a prosecution for perjury or for the giving of contradictory evidence.

INTERPRETER.

14. A party or witness in any proceedings who does not understand or speak the language in which the proceedings are conducted or who is deaf has the right to the assistance of an interpreter.

EQUALITY BEFORE AND UNDER LAW AND EQUAL PROTECTION AND BENEFIT OF LAW/AFFIRMATIVE ACTION PROGRAMS.

15. (1) Every individual is equal before and under the law and has the right to the equal protection and equal benefit of the law without discrimination and, in particular, without discrimination based on race, national or ethnic origin, colour, religion, sex, age or mental or physical disability.

(2) Subsection (1) does not preclude any law, program or activity that has as its object the amelioration of conditions of disadvantaged individuals or groups including those that are disadvantaged because of race, national or ethnic origin, colour, religion, sex, age or mental or physical disability.

OFFICIAL LANGUAGES OF CANADA/OFFICIAL LANGUAGES OF NEW BRUNSWICK. ADVANCEMENT OF STATUS AND USE.

16. (1) English and French are the official languages of Canada and have equality of status and equal rights and privileges as to their use in all institutions of the Parliament and government of Canada.

(2) English and French are the official languages of New Brunswick and have equality of status and equal rights and privileges as to their use in all institutions of the legislature and government of New Brunswick.

(3) Nothing in this Charter limits the authority of Parliament or a legislature to advance the equality of status or use of English and French. . . .

one of the principal characteristics of this round of constitutional discussion was that Quebec's concerns were not front and centre. General consensus was developed on economic issues, balancing provincial resource control against federal economic planning. But other questions remained difficult to resolve. Ottawa wanted to entrench a Charter of Rights in any new constitutional document, chiefly to guarantee francophone linguistic rights across the nation, but the majority of the provinces (including Quebec) objected to such a Charter as threatening their own rights. The provinces, for their part, wanted an amending formula that would allow all provinces the right of veto and the right to opt out of any amendments that they regarded as threatening their powers. This round of discussions broke down in September 1980. As Prime Minister Trudeau had been threatening for months, Ottawa prepared to take unilateral action.

Politically, the federal constitutional package developed in Ottawa was carefully calculated. As an ardent federalist, a trained constitutional lawyer, and an exponent of *realpolitik*, Pierre Trudeau was clearly in his element. The new proposal called for the elimination of recourse to the British Parliament for amendment of the British North America Act ("repatriation"). It also contained a Charter of Rights, which by establishing the rights of other collective minorities was intended to prevent the French Canadians from being treated as an exceptional case. The package also provided for a new method of amendment—through national referendum initiated in Ottawa—to be used in the event of provincial obstructionism. The Trudeau government was prepared to pass the package through the federal Parliament and send it to Britain for approval without recourse to either the Supreme Court of Canada or the provinces, although it clearly infringed on the informal "right" of the provinces to consent to constitutional change. Not surprisingly, the federal NDP supported this position, leaving the Progressive Conservative minority in Parliament to oppose it and voice the objections of nearly all the provinces except (again not surprisingly) Ontario.

Parliamentary amendments eliminated some of the least saleable features of the original proposal and introduced some new wrinkles, including the specific affirmation of "aboriginal and treaty rights of the aboriginal peoples of Canada" (McWhinney, 1982: 176). The Liberal government had neatly set against each other two sets of rights, one the human rights protected in the entrenched Charter and the other the provincial rights ignored in both the amending process and the Charter itself. Eight of the provinces (excluding Ontario and New Brunswick), often unsympathetically referred to in the media as "the Gang of Eight," organized as the leading opponents of unilateral repatriation, although Quebec and the English-speaking premiers had quite different views on positive reform.

The first major hurdle for the federal initiative was the Supreme Court of Canada, to which constitutional opinions from several provincial courts had gone on appeal. If the federal government won support from the Supreme Court, it would render untenable the provincial claim that the package was unconstitutional. While the Supreme Court deliberated, René Lévesque and the PQ won a resounding electoral victory in Quebec. The win did not, of course, resolve the deep contradiction that the PQ represented as a separatist party committed to non-separatist action, but it did reactivate Quebec on constitutional matters. Although the British government had refused to deal officially with the provincial premiers (much as it had in 1867 when Nova Scotia sent Joseph Howe to London), Canada's Native peoples set up their own lobbying office in London. They had some claim to direct treaty connections with the British Crown and a decent legal case. The Supreme Court of Canada handed down its ruling on 28 September 1981. Many Canadians had trouble comprehending both the process and the decision, since neither the constitutional nor the political role of the Canadian Court was as well understood as that of its American equivalent.

As one constitutional expert commented, the decision was, in legal terms, "complex and baffling and technically unsatisfactory." In political terms, such complexity was doubtless exactly what the Supreme Court intended. Essentially, by a 7–2 decision, it declared the federal patriation process legal, since custom could not be enforced in courts. It then opined, by a 6–3 decision, that federal patriation was unconventional. Since most of the legal arguments against the process revolved around violations of constitutional "convention" (or custom), these two opinions were mutually contradictory, although in law Ottawa had won. What the politicians could make of a result that said, in effect, that the federal package of repatriation was, strictly speaking, legal but at the same time improper was another matter.

In the end the nine English-speaking premiers, including seven of the original Gang of Eight, worked out a deal with Prime Minister Trudeau on 5 November 1981. Trudeau made substantial concessions—for example, abandoning the provision for a referendum. Ontario joined Quebec in agreeing to drop its right of veto in favour of a complex formula that ensured that either one or the other (but not both) would have to agree to any amendment. This represented less of a loss for Ottawa than for the central provinces, especially Quebec. At the same time, provinces that had refused to concur with constitutional change had the right to remain outside its provisions until they chose to opt in, a considerable move from Trudeau's earlier positions. Trudeau's greatest concessions were in the Charter of Rights, particularly the so-called "notwithstanding" clause, which allowed any province to opt out of clauses in the Charter covering fundamental freedoms and legal and equality rights, although not other categories of rights, including language rights. There was disagreement over the intention of the negotiations regarding Native peoples, resulting in a temporary omission of the clause guaranteeing Aboriginal treaty rights, which subsequently had to be restored by Parliament. As for a definition of those rights themselves, there was to be a constitutional conference to identify them.

The final compromise satisfied the nine anglophone premiers. It certainly strengthened in theory the rights of the provinces to opt out of the Charter on critical issues, including both Native rights and women's rights, through use of the "notwithstanding" clause. Perhaps understandably, both Native groups and women's groups vowed to fight on in opposition to the package as revised. As for Quebec, all it had lost was some of its self-perceived distinctive status in Confederation. That loss would prove fairly crucial, however, for Quebec would consistently refuse to accept the constitutional reforms on the grounds that one of Canada's two "national wills" had not been consulted. That position would lead to another attempt at provincial unanimity at Meech Lake in 1987.

The revised constitutional package passed the Canadian Parliament in December 1981 and the British Parliament early in 1982. The latter had resolutely refused to become involved in the various protests against the new agreement, thus surrendering its role as court of last resort against unconstitutional actions within Canada. Canadians at the time did not fully appreciate what had happened constitutionally or what the changes would mean. The principle of patriation had been purchased at considerable expense by the Trudeau government. The Charter of Rights did reflect the principle that collective and individual rights transcending the British North America Act (and its conception of relevant players) had to be carefully guarded. But in place of the earlier British constitutional position that the legislature (federal and provincial) was the source of protection, the Charter

established the American constitutional notion that the court system would enforce fundamental rights over the legislature and the government responsible to it. In place of the earlier concept that Parliament was supreme, it introduced a whole new series of formal checks and balances limiting parliamentary supremacy.

A good example of the Charter principles in action would come in 1988, when Prime Minister Brian Mulroney signed a Redress Agreement between the National Association of Japanese Canadians and the Canadian government regarding the handling of Japanese Canadians during and after World War II. In letters to 20,000 Japanese Canadians in 1990, the Prime Minister acknowledged that the wartime treatment "was unjust and violated principles of human rights as they are understood today."

The new Constitution not only gave new powers to the provinces, it also recognized new and rather amorphous political collectivities in the Charter of Rights, which was somewhat less concerned than the American Bill of Rights with defining the rights of individuals and somewhat more concerned with delineating collective rights. Thus, in addition to providing equality before the law for individuals facing discrimination "based on race, national or ethnic origin, colour, religion, sex, age or mental or physical disability" (section 15.1), the Charter also specifically permitted in section 15.2 "any law, program, or activity that has as its object the amelioration of conditions of disadvantaged individuals or groups," including (but not limited to) those disadvantaged by discrimination as in section 15.1. Moreover, Aboriginal and treaty rights of the Aboriginal peoples, although deliberately not defined, were entrenched, as were sexual equality and multiculturalism. Although at first glance these Charter provisions seemed to represent the ultimate triumph of liberalism, in several respects they did not. In the first place, the liberal Charter provisions were balanced by the increased power given to the provinces to control their own resources and to call their own shots about the applicability of the Charter and any constitutional amendments. In the second place, the constitutional introduction of a whole series of new collectivities created further complications for an already overloaded political process. In the end this would help stifle the

Prime Minister Trudeau looks on as Queen Elizabeth II signs Canada's constitutional proclamation in Ottawa, 17 April 1982. The Canadian Press/Ron Poling.

liberal impulse itself. Finally, the well-publicized antics of the politicians over the Constitution contributed to a further reduction in the esteem with which those politicians were held by an increasingly cynical Canadian public.

Constitutional Revision: Rounds Two and Three

The 1982 Charter, with its explicit and implicit recognition of both collective and individual rights, was hardly the last word on the subject. A body of case law would have to be developed by the courts, especially the Supreme Court of Canada, which became the ultimate arbiter charged with interpreting the vague terminology of the document. Governments offered no clarification. The Charter simply became a wild card

exercised by the Supreme Court of Canada on behalf of Canadians, arguably more amenable to change than the parliamentary system.

In 1987 the Mulroney government fastened on one of the loose ends of the 1982 constitutional process, Quebec's refusal to accept the 1982 Constitution. By this time RenéLévesque had retired (in June 1985) and the PQ had been defeated in December 1985 by the Liberals under a rehabilitated Robert Bourassa. Once again in power, Bourassa offered to compromise. Mulroney summoned a new "Gang of 10" to a closed-door session on 30 April 1987 at Meech Lake, where a revised constitutional arrangement acceptable to Quebec was worked out. While Quebec was to be constitutionally recognized as a "distinct society" and given further concessions, including a veto over most amendments to the Constitution, there were also inducements to the other provinces, which would also enjoy some gains in autonomy. The federal government would compensate all provinces for programs they refused to join. Each province was given a veto over further amendments. There was to be regular discussion of Senate reform, although no particular formula was agreed upon. Nevertheless, there was a consensus among participants that the federal Parliament, and the legislatures of all 10 provinces, would have to approve the agreement by early June 1990—the lengthy time frame allowed for public hearings and feedback—or the arrangement was dead.

The three years permitted between the Meech Lake meeting and the deadline for approval created many difficulties. While the Mulroney government understandably insisted that no changes could be made in the agreement until it had been formally approved, not every provincial government felt bound by the particular terms accepted by whoever happened to be premier in April 1987. The subsequent public debate made clear that not all Canadians agreed with what was perceived as a further dismantling of central authority in favour not merely of Quebec but of all the provinces. The poorer have-not provinces—led by Manitoba, New Brunswick, and eventually Newfoundland—were concerned that few new federal programs would be mounted if the richer provinces had the option of receiving federal funds for their own programs. Other collectivities, such as Aboriginal peoples and women, worried that their rights were being bartered away to the provinces. Across the country, suggested revisions sprang up like grass, many of them offering structural panaceas, such as a reformed and more effective Senate.

As the deadline for acceptance loomed, only Manitoba and Newfoundland held out, the latter having rescinded an earlier legislative endorsement after Brian Peckford's Tories were defeated by the Liberals under Clyde Wells (b. 1937). Prime Minister Mulroney, drawing on his experience as a private-sector negotiator, called the premiers and other provincial political leaders into closed-door sessions designed to shame them into support on the eve of the deadline.

This tactic appeared to work, but in Manitoba, Cree leader and NDP MLA Elijah Harper (b. 1949) objected to the Accord on the grounds that it neglected Aboriginal people. Harper delayed debate on the Accord, preventing the legislature from voting to ratify it before the deadline. Since Manitoba was not going to approve, Newfoundland's Wells backed off from a previous commitment to gain his province's legislative endorsement. In the end, the two provinces refused endorsement and Meech Lake failed. Ominously, in the last days before the deadline, several Conservative MPs from Quebec, led by Minister of the Environment, Lucien Bouchard (b. 1938), left the government to form a pro-separatist Bloc Québécois. In the post-mortems on Meech Lake, a number of points stood out. One was that after 1987 the popular support for Brian Mulroney (and the federal PCs) and Meech Lake had declined together. Quebec understandably interpreted the mounting hostility to Meech Lake in English-speaking Canada as directed specifically against the "distinct society," but the fact was that most Canadians appeared to be prepared to allow Quebec its autonomy. What people objected to was the extension of that autonomy to the other provinces, a process that would balkanize the nation. Moreover, Elijah Harper's action called attention to Meech Lake's incompatibility with the collective rights recognized by the Canadian Charter. During the summer of 1990 the failure of Meech Lake was followed by an extremely nasty confrontation between Aboriginal peoples in Quebec, led by the Mohawks of Oka, and the Bourassa government. Bourassa called in the federal armed forces, as he had done in the October Crisis of 1970.

The crushing defeat in early September 1990 of one of the main supporters of Meech Lake, Premier David Peterson of Ontario, by the NDP led by Bob Rae (b. 1948) was perhaps another straw in the wind. Certainly the NDP's achievement of power (for the first time) in Ontario suggested that there might be a resurgence of the left. The NDP's victory proved illusory, as it was based chiefly on hostility to Peterson's government. Subsequent 1991 NDP victories in British Columbia and Saskatchewan only demonstrated the electorate's discontent and the NDP's inability to establish a new political paradigm.

The federal government spent most of 1991 attempting to figure out how to allow for "democratic

BACKGROUNDER

The Growth of Government Spending

The traditional Keynesian system—in which spending deficits were not by themselves a significant problem—had become conventional wisdom because it offered alternative economic approaches to those of the Great Depression that had so obviously not worked. Though political leaders in the thirties had balanced budgets and even cut spending to suit reduced revenues, a great many people suffered in the process. According to Keynes, balancing budgets was exactly the wrong thing to do in times of depression. Instead, governments needed to spend money in order to stimulate the economy, correcting the deficits of bad times by creating higher revenues and, by extension, good times. Some liberal economists even held that deficits need never be retired, although the age-old problem with public deficits is that they really represent government debt that has to be maintained through the payment of interest to those from whom the money is borrowed. By the 1970s a number of automatic mechanisms were built into the burgeoning welfare state's safety net that greatly increased public expenditures. When new programs were added to existing automatic spending, the result was such a rapid increase in deficits that they became a public issue.

Two competing explanations existed to explain the growth of government spending. One saw increased spending as natural, inevitable, and incremental, the product of a modern society that had new demands and expectations. The Canadian decisions to support universal public education and universal health care both involved the funding of systems that were labour-intensive and not very susceptible to savings through technology (indeed, new technology only increased the costs). The other explanation was rooted in the self-interest of collective decision-making and has usually been called the "public choice" view. It argued that the self-interest of politicians for electoral popularity, of civil servants for larger budgets, and of the populace for new entitlements all combined to produce constant pressure on budgets. Public choice is far more cynical an explanation than incrementalism, and tended to substantiate the suspicion harboured by many Canadians that their political leaders were selfish and corrupt, a view unfortunately too often substantiated by the behaviour of the politicians.

input" into the process of constitutional revision. The Mulroney administration was far too unpopular simply to force through legislation. Public hearings were followed by weekend conferences, none of which provided much direction. Canada had no tradition of consultative reform. In the end, another series of closed-door meetings between Ottawa and the anglophone provinces, subsequently joined by Quebec in August 1992 at Charlottetown, produced a revised package. This one offered Quebec a distinct society, the provinces a veto, the Aboriginal peoples self-government, and the country reform of both the Supreme Court and the Senate. The nation voted on the package in a referendum on 26 October 1992, the day after the Toronto Blue Jays won the World Series. (The World Series was named after the New York newspaper the *World* and had no international implications.) To the simultaneous amusement and consternation of Canadians, in the opening ceremonies, the United States Marine Corps had inadvertently carried the Canadian flag upside down. The eventual victory sparked an outpouring of Canadian nationalism across the country. Some commentators openly feared for a country that could find togetherness only by celebrating the success of a

NDP MLA Elijah Harper sits in the Manitoba legislature holding an eagle feather for spiritual strength as he continues to delay debate on the Meech Lake Accord, 19 June 1990. Harper's refusal to support a unanimous declaration by the legislature made it impossible for Manitoba to meet the deadline. The Meech Lake Agreement was dead. The Canadian Press/Wayne Glowacki.

TABLE 11.1 Results by Province of the 26 October 1992 Referendum on the Charlottetown Accord

Province/ Territory	Percentage Yes	Percentage No
Newfoundland	62.9	36.5
Nova Scotia	48.5	51.1
Prince Edward Island	73.6	25.9
New Brunswick	61.3	38.0
Quebec	42.4	55.4
Ontario	49.8	49.6
Manitoba	37.9	61.7
Saskatchewan	45.5	55.1
Alberta	39.6	60.2
British Columbia	31.9	67.8
Northwest Territories	60.2	39.0
Yukon	43.4	56.1
National	44.8	54.2

The Rise of Aboriginal Rights

collection of highly paid foreign athletes. How the win factored into the referendum is not known.

Six provinces (including Quebec) voted "No." The national totals were 44.8 per cent in favour of the agreement and 54.2 against (see Table 11.1). Polls indicated that Charlottetown failed because the majority of Canadians regarded the agreement as a bad one. Poorer provinces favoured Charlottetown, while poorer, younger, and less well-educated Canadians opposed it. According to one poll, household income of $60,000 per year was the economic cutoff between "Yes" and "No," while a university degree was the educational one. Most of those who voted "No" believed that their vote would have no negative consequences for the nation. Perhaps.

The various debates over the Constitution and the Charter became more complex with the addition of new players and new issues in the constitutional mix. One of the most important new issues involved the Aboriginal peoples of the nation, who counted for over a million Canadians by 1991 (Table 11.2) and, with a very high birth rate, represented the most rapidly growing sector of the Canadian population.

Since Confederation, most First Nations have been paternally governed under the Indian Act. Beginning in the 1970s, the First Nations have increasingly widened the meaning of "Aboriginal rights." These rights fall into several categories. The first are those rights that Aboriginal peoples have as a result of having been the first inhabitants of North America, and are usually called "Aboriginal rights." These include rights to land that the First Nations have occupied since before European intrusion, and a right to self-government. There are also "treaty rights," which result from specific written arrangements between European governments, especially the British government and its Canadian successor, and First Nations peoples. Since the first arrival of the Europeans, treaties have been negotiated, chiefly to extinguish Native title to much of the land of North America. Aboriginal and treaty rights were entrenched without specifics in the Constitution Act of 1982 and in its Charter of Rights and Freedoms. This entrenchment has led the Canadian courts to become much more aggressive in defining and defending Aboriginal rights, especially in comparison with the American courts. The Canadian public has had great difficulty in understanding the concept of Aboriginal rights, although the ongoing saga is regularly reported in the media.

TABLE 11.2 Aboriginal and Métis People in Canada, by Province, 1991 Census

Province/ Territory	Aboriginals	Métis
Newfoundland	5,846	1,600
Prince Edward Island	1,665	185
Nova Scotia	19,950	1,590
New Brunswick	11,835	980
Quebec	112,590	19,475
Ontario	220,140	26,905
Manitoba	76,375	45,580
Saskatchewan	69,390	32,840
Alberta	99,655	56,305
British Columbia	140,570	22,290
Northwest Territories	5,875	565
Yukon	11,095	4,320
Total	783,980	212,650*

This official figure probably under-represents the total by as much as 200,000.
Source: Statistics Canada.

Aboriginal Title

In some parts of Canada, notably Labrador, northern Quebec, the Far North, and most of main- land British Columbia, historic land cession treaties were never negotiated, and consequently the Native peoples of these areas had no ascribed treaty rights and were in effect squatters on their own land. In 1969 Frank Calder of the Nisga'a people brought a court action before the British Columbia court, claiming Aboriginal title to 1,000 square miles in northwestern British Columbia. The case eventually reached the Supreme Court of Canada, which upheld a BC finding against Calder on a technicality. But despite the seeming defeat, the Supreme Court had agreed with Calder that there were such things as Aboriginal rights and title. As one of the judges wrote in his decision, "The fact is that when the settlers came the Indians were there, organized in societies and occupying the land as their forefathers had done for centuries. This is what Indian title means." Aboriginal title came up again in *Guerin v. the Queen* (1985), where the Supreme Court insisted that Aboriginal title predated European occupation and thus served as a check on the Crown's right to deal with lands. The recognition of Aboriginal title was temporarily set back by a decision of the BC Supreme Court in 1991 in the Gitksan–Wet'suwet'en case. Here Justice Allan McEachern rejected the claim to title, partly on the grounds of the absence of proper evidence. The judge did not regard Native oral history as sufficient, although he ruled that the plaintiffs had unextinguished non-exclusive Aboriginal rights, other than right of ownership. This ruling left major questions unresolved for several years.

The Economy

One of the many reasons for the failure of Keynesian economics was that after 1972 the system no longer worked according to its rules. Government management, even wage and price controls, could not prevent runaway inflation, high interest rates, high levels of unemployment, and substantial poverty. With the manufacturing economies of the industrialized world fully recovered and new competition from the industrializing world emerging daily, Canadian manufacturing was in serious structural trouble. So, too, were the farmers and the fishers. Symptomatically, the government's complex attempt, after 1973, to create a new national energy policy—based on a federally owned petroleum company to be called Petro-Canada—created only controversy.

As usual, Canadians had trouble understanding the intersection of international and domestic economic problems. They sought a reassuring way of comprehending their difficulties, for the notion that the country was internationally uncompetitive could not be seriously entertained. There were several potential scapegoats at hand. The bankers could have been blamed for the interest rates, or the businessmen for the unemployment. Instead, the country chose to fasten on the most visible and immediate of the trinity of troublesome indicators—inflation—and on a single factor to explain it. Polls taken in 1975 indicated that Canadians were willing to believe that the chief culprits on the inflation front were too-powerful labour unions demanding unreasonable wage settlements. Labour unions were understandably attempting to protect their members in the context of the new economic situation. They wanted wage increases to keep pace with inflation and opposed management efforts to rationalize or modernize their workforces through layoffs or by getting rid of redundancies. Strikes in many industries, including a much-publicized postal strike in the summer of 1975, made the demands of labour appear unreasonable. When police, firefighters, nurses, and teachers began taking similar steps, Canadians became alarmed. Not only were key public services threatened with interruption, but wage settlements in the public sector would have to be financed either with higher taxes or with deficit spending.

Although the extent of government deficits would not become a major public issue until later, by the early 1970s all levels of Canadian government were well into deficit financing. High interest rates made the government debt much more expensive to service. The economic problems of the period set into motion a series of automatic mechanisms, built into the social services safety net, that greatly increased public expenditures. Even without those economic problems, spending on social services constantly escalated according to some mysterious law of increased demand and expectation. The propensity to expand the civil service had its own logic. A variety of conservative economists now appeared to criticize the government's spending principles. Like the public, Pierre Trudeau's federal Liberals talked about the need for structural reform of the economy, but they were unable to confront the problems before the dangers posed by the PQ victory led to a renewed concern with the Constitution. Like all other governments around the world, Ottawa continued to spend more than it collected in taxes and revenue. In 1970 the per capita debt figure of the Canadian government was $795. By 1990 it was $14,317. (Table 11.3 shows how the total federal debt had grown since Confederation.) Between 1981 and 1990, the total debt of the federal government soared from $100 billion to $380 billion. The last budget surplus had been in fiscal 1972–3.

Not surprisingly, the deficit was used as a weapon by conservatives opposed to the continued expansion of social assistance. These critics—headed by spokesmen for the business community—insisted that increases in social assistance programs were largely responsible for the problem, and they maintained that a balanced budget could be achieved only by making deep cuts in such programs. In reality, the deficit was caused mainly by the same people who worried most about it. Concern about deficits was accompanied by fear of runaway inflation, and the war against inflation was waged chiefly by the Bank of Canada through its control of interest rates. High interest rates created substantial unemployment, which in turn meant reductions in income tax revenues and increased expenditures on unemployment insurance and welfare. According to one economist, almost two-thirds of the 1992 deficit was caused by lost tax revenues from unemployment and increased costs of social assistance; the remainder was the result of high interest payments to creditors. A team of economists at the University of Toronto examined the reasons for the 1989–92 recession in Canada. They concluded that the chief factor was the Bank of Canada's consistent anti-inflationary/high interest policies. Many Canadians had been convinced by neo-liberal politicians and pundits, however, that dismantling the welfare state was the only way to deal with huge budgetary deficits. At the same time, most public opinion polls indicated

TABLE 11.3 Federal Government Debt (millions of dollars)

| Dates | Net Federal Debt | Gross Federal Debt | Marketable Bonds | Treasury Bills | Components of the Gross Debt | | | |
					Savings Bonds	Other Securities	Pension Plans	Other Liabilities
1866–7	76	93	69	-	-	-	-	24
1917–18	11,192	1,863	1,428	75	-	-	5	355
1949–50	11,645	16,723	12,882	450	891	850	175	1,475
1974–5	23,958	55,289	14,490	5,360	12,915	51	12,978	9,825
1983–4	162,250	210,841	58,994	41,700	38,204	3,228	37,988	30,727
1990–1	385,047	443,278	147,104	139,150	34,444	4,514	74,807	43,259

Source: Adapted from Statistics Canada, Canada Year Book 1994 (Ottawa: Statistics Canada Catalogue no. 11-402, 1994), 304.

that the vast majority of the electorate was not eager to surrender their social benefits.

Like the government, the Canadian consumer lived increasingly in Tomorrowland. Canadian consumer debt more than doubled in the 1980s, increasing in small but steady stages from 18.7 per cent of personal income to over 20 per cent. Much of that debt was incurred through the medium of plastic credit cards. In the last year of the decade alone, the number of bank credit-card transactions increased from just over 100 billion to 150 billion. Residential mortgage debt nearly tripled. Over 10 years Canadian personal consumer debt (including mortgages) increased from 54.1 per cent of disposable personal income to 71.7 per cent, despite heavier taxes and truly debilitating interest rates.

Despite its talk of privatization, such as selling the assets of the Canada Development Investment Corporation, the Mulroney government backed away from an open confrontation with the welfare system. Instead, it took back benefits (such as the family allowance) from those with higher incomes and concentrated on increasing revenue through improving economic prosperity. The main vehicle for this increased prosperity was to be a new economic relationship with Canada's largest trading partner, the United States.

The eventual Free Trade Agreement, characteristically negotiated in secret during 1986 and 1987, ran to 3,000 pages of legal technicalities. Tariffs would gradually be removed, leaving Canadians astonished to discover that tariffs were not much responsible for the disparity between what goods cost in American and Canadian stores. Canadians were equally surprised to find that "free trade" did *not* apply to ordinary people shopping in the United States and returning to Canada with their purchases. The national debate over the deal generated little useful information. Not even the economic experts could safely predict the ultimate effects of the treaty, although most orthodox economists favoured it in principle. Some critics complained that the Canadian negotiators had gained less than useful access to the American market in return for continental economic integration. This was a futile argument, since most of that integration had already occurred. Only a fraction of total Canadian–American trade was actually affected by the treaty.

The most telling criticism was that the Free Trade Agreement did *not* revolutionize Canadian–American economic relations. Instead, the FTA was merely a cosmetic overhaul of the existing continental arrangement. Including the Mexicans in the North

American Free Trade Agreement, which took effect in 1994, was potentially more significant, but many observers could see few advantages to Canada in an economic partnership with a nation possessing a lower standard of living and cheaper labour.

After 1975 the Canadian economy more or less settled down to rates of unemployment, inflation, interest charges, housing costs, and taxation that would have previously been regarded as disastrous. Only food costs remained unaffected, which was not good news for the farmer. Indeed, agriculture re-emerged as a major economic problem for the nation. Despite quotas and marketing boards, the Canadian farmer continued to produce more than the market could consume, especially when that market was also being supplied by American farmers. No Canadian doubted that farmers were part of the backbone of Canadian society, but it was also obvious that farmers were leaving their farms in droves, both because they could not make a decent living and because of the continued attractions of the city's amenities. The government preferred financial assistance for farmers to higher food prices. The problem was that not all farmers would be supported. In 1986 Agriculture Canada admitted that its solution to the "farm problem" was to encourage thousands of marginal farmers—perhaps up to 20 per cent of the total—to leave the business. To state openly that there were too many farmers was to play with political dynamite. That the government did so was a graphic illustration of how much the nation had changed since Confederation, which had been conceived in part to allow Canada to open a new agricultural frontier.

Although the opposition in Parliament wanted to know how the "one-in-five" farmer would be chosen for elimination, there was no mystery about who was most at risk: younger entrant farmers, any farmer heavily in debt, and any "inefficient" farmer. These categories were often mutually reinforcing. Young farmers often had to buy their land at inflated prices. To be efficient they needed to borrow money at high rates of interest in order to buy expensive equipment and machinery. When farm commodity prices turned downward, many farmers were in serious trouble, although it must be added that the costs of modern farming increasingly made it an uneconomic proposition for most farmers.

The solution—significantly higher prices for farm crops—was simply not popular. Canadians were willing to pay increasing sums for more convenient packaging and marketing of the food they ate but were not prepared to put more money into the pocket of the farmer.

There were economic slowdowns in the early 1980s and early 1990s. From the standpoint of its conservative intentions, the welfare state worked. In both slowdowns the social protection apparatus clicked in, and while more families fell below the poverty line, there were few demonstrations in the streets. Canadians became conscious that jobs were harder to get and harder to keep. The young responded to the lack of jobs by seeking further education in courses that promised some immediate economic payoff, but they did not become radicalized. Perhaps they were too busy working to keep up the payments on their credit cards.

Canadian Society

A number of social trends characterized Canadian society in the 1970s and 1980s. One was a constant increase in the traditional indicators of "instability"— divorce, suicide, rape, crime, and sexually transmitted diseases. Canada seemed to be coming apart socially as well as constitutionally and economically. Another trend was an increase in abuse (often violent) of others and extreme self-indulgence, both products of alienation. These trends were also linked to the power of the media, which on the one hand publicized what had long been occurring beneath the surface, and on the other hand produced new consumer fads, fashions, and even needs. A third trend involved the baby-boom generation, which was coming up to early retirement in the 1990s, at which point they would aggravate a fourth trend, the increasingly rapid growth in numbers of elderly Canadians. A final development of the era was the increased visibility of racial minorities, resulting in new social problems.

In 1974 a study found that suicide had become Canada's fifth-ranked cause of "early death" (i.e., death between the ages of one and 70). Suicide rates continued to rise, and were especially serious among young males in general and young Aboriginal males in particular, reaching epidemic proportions in some communities. A 1984 National Task Force on Suicide in Canada indicated that the causes were "complex and multifactorial," adding that "inter-provincial studies appear to show that there has been a change in the contemporary fabric of society with lessened self-restraints and lowered morals (anomie). This coincides with a period of expanding economy, greater affluence as a whole, high-technology industrialization, and increased unemployment" (National Task Force on Suicide in Canada, 1984: 9). A similar explanation could have been advanced for many of Canada's "morbidities."

Another set of rising statistics related to crimes of violence against the person. From 1982 to 1987 crimes against property increased 0.1 per cent, while crimes of violence increased 30.1 per cent. On 23 June 1985, an Air India jet carrying mainly Canadian passengers exploded in mid-air over Ireland, victims of a bomb. Despite the suspicions, charges were not actually laid against Sikh extremists until 15 years later. From 1987 to 1991 violent offences increased another 29.8 per cent, while total criminal offences increased by only 11.5 per cent (see Table 11.4). On 6 December 1989 a lone gunman, apparently a misogynist, killed 14 female engineering students at the École Polytechnique in Montreal. This horrifying event occurred near the close of a year in which, according to one estimate, over 32,000 Canadian women had been raped. The number of divorces had been 32,389 in 1972, rising to 90,985 in 1987 before beginning to decline slightly in numbers. By the late 1980s it was estimated that well over half of all Canadian children born after 1980 would at some point experience life in a broken home. As divorce increased, marriage declined. Moreover, the number of common-law relationships more than doubled between 1981 and 1991.

The incidence of racial and sexual abuses of various kinds appeared to increase dramatically. The general professional consensus was that abuse had not become more common but that it was now more likely to be reported. Racial and sexual abuses that might have gone unrecorded in previous generations were now openly publicized. Wife-beating—for decades the most common domestic crime on the police blotter—became a matter of public concern. Not surprisingly, much of the abuse was directed against the less powerful—children, women, Aboriginal peoples, and visible minorities—by traditional authority figures ranging from fathers to pastors to teachers to policemen and judges. On one level it was possible to take solace in the fact that such improper behaviour was now being addressed. On another it was possible to argue that what had changed was not so much the behaviour of people in authority as society's willingness to tolerate the excesses of this type of behaviour. Both the extent of the abuse and the undermining of authority to which it contributed were distressing. Canadians could no longer believe that they were all good guys living in the Peaceable Kingdom, nor could they continue to believe in the inherent beneficence of authority figures or in the fairness of the Canadian judicial system.

The revelations of the post-1972 period, particularly in the 1980s, could only contribute to a growing national

TABLE 11.4 Offences by Type, 1987–1991

Type	Percentage change rate/100,000					
	1987	1988	1989	1990	1991	1987–91
Violent offences	219,381	232,606	248,579	269,381	296,680	+29.8%
Property offences	1,468,591	1,457,361	1,443,048	1,551,278	1,726,226	+12.8%
Other offences	1,276,036	1,265,861	1,300,005	1,343,397	1,470,454	+10%
Total	2,960,908	2,955,828	2,992,632	3,164,056	3,440,671	+11.5%

Source: Adapted from Canada Year Book 1994 *(Ottawa: Statistics Canada Catalogue no. 11-402, 1994), 222.*

mood of sullen cynicism with regard to authority, which was hardly appeased by the unimaginative and self-seeking behaviour of the politicians. No institution proved itself above reproach, and all institutions demonstrated their willingness to cover up their inadequacies and failures. Some of the most shocking revelations came from Newfoundland, where a provincial inquiry in 1989 brought to light evidence of the sexual abuse of children by priests and brothers of the Roman Catholic Church at the Mount Cashel Orphanage. Such evidence was soon augmented by material indicating that the clergy of all the major denominations had been abusing Aboriginal children for years in residential schools and orphanages. The situation was not improved by the discovery that the Canadian system of justice was hardly very just, at least not when it came to Aboriginal people or accused murderers. The ways in which the system failed Donald Marshall, who served 11 years in prison for a murder he did not commit, were particularly instructive in this regard.

Even the Red Cross, previously a model of institutional altruism, proved susceptible to incompetence and cover-up. The Canadian Red Cross had managed Canada's blood supply service since 1947, but the relationship between the government and the Red Cross had never been clearly defined. It remained unclear what government agency was responsible for assuring the safety of the blood supply, and for this reason it was difficult for the government to respond to problems when they emerged. In the late 1970s and early 1980s there were blood shortages in some parts of Canada, and this made the Red Cross reluctant to introduce screening measures that might further reduce the supply. As a consequence, the Canadian blood transfusion service in the early 1980s was sometimes (if infrequently) using blood infected both with the human immunodeficiency virus (HIV) and with infectious hepatitis C. Much of the infected blood was given to hemophiliacs, who because of their medical condition require a constant series of transfusions. Approximately 1,200 people were infected with HIV and 12,000 with hepatitis C through blood transfusions before the Red Cross introduced security measures to test for these viruses in 1985. Even after bringing the system back under control, it would take another dozen years to establish why the problem had occurred in the first place, as both government and Red Cross officials attempted to avoid the possible imputations of responsibility.

Other forms of abuse were self-inflicted, often related to short-term gratification without regard for long-term consequences. The availability of drugs continued to increase steadily. Alcohol abuse continued unabated, along with substance abuse of many descriptions, including gasoline sniffing; and the use of steroids by athletes became common. Canada's most notorious substance abuser was the Olympic sprinter Ben Johnson (b. 1961), whose gold medal at Seoul in 1988 was ignominiously stripped from him for using steroids. Johnson initially denied the charge but eventually had to acknowledge his guilt at a well-publicized public inquiry. The most dangerous drug of all was tobacco. Canadian adults, reflecting the health consciousness of the baby boomers, led the way internationally in quitting smoking during the late 1980s. The young, however, remained undeterred by cigarette prices, which were often in excess of $6 per pack. One calculation revealed that tobacco would ultimately kill eight times as many 15-year-olds as automobile accidents, suicide, murder, AIDS, and drug abuse combined. Self-inflicted abuse was part of the new world of self-indulgence. Those who made their way to the top could reward themselves with luxuries and expensive toys. Sniffing cocaine became an indulgence of choice among the affluent. As for the poor, they had access to little pleasure that was not addictive and physically harmful.

Because AIDS is mainly a sexually transmitted disease, with a high incidence among homosexuals and the sexually adventurous, it became a favourite target for moralists in the 1980s. Many concerns were expressed that AIDS would encourage a judgmental response from Canadians with regard to both homosexuality and sexual freedom, but these concerns were not borne out in the available survey literature. While surveys indicated that relatively few Canadians were morally judgmental, they also demonstrated much ignorance about AIDS and its prevention. Moreover, Canadians responded far less vigorously to the fear of infection than one might have expected, given the media attention AIDS received. In one Canadian study in 1989, for example, 63 per cent of those questioned knew that sexual intercourse was the most common way of becoming infected with AIDS,

BACKGROUNDER

The Montreal Massacre of 1989

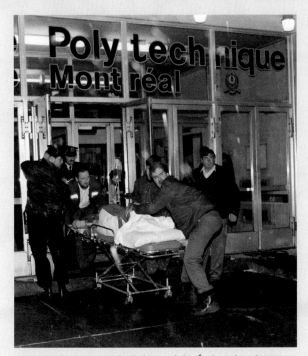

An injured person is wheeled out of the École Polytechnique in Montreal after a lone gunman, Marc Lépine, opened fire on 6 December 1989, killing 14 female students. The Canadian Press/ Shaney Komulainen.

In the late afternoon of 6 December 1989, a young man named Marc Lépine entered the building of the École Polytechnique, the engineering school of the Université de Montréal. He carried a semi-automatic rifle (which he had purchased at a Montreal sporting goods store a few weeks before) and a hunting knife, and had a lengthy suicide note in his inside jacket pocket. Although considerable controversy ensued over the reasons that motivated him, there is little dispute over his subsequent actions. Lépine wandered about the building aimlessly before entering a lecture theatre about 5:10 p.m. There he interrupted a student presentation, ordering the class to opposite ends of the room, separated by sex. They obeyed only after he fired a shot into the ceiling. He then ordered the men to leave, and interrogated the women, announcing, "I am fighting feminism." One student protested that she was only a student, and was told, "You're all a bunch of feminists. I hate feminists." Lépine then opened fire against the women, killing six and wounding three others. He next proceeded further within the building, still shooting at women. He ended up in a first-floor cafeteria, where he shot more students, mainly women, then walked up an escalator, wounding two men and a woman in the process. Entering another classroom, he shot and killed more women, stabbing one wounded victim with his knife. He then ended his rampage by exclaiming, "Ah, shit," and shooting himself fatally in the head. The killer left 14 dead, and another 14 people (including four males) wounded.

If there was little disagreement about what Lépine had done, there was considerable controversy over what his rampage meant. The majority view—shared by the media, the government, and leading feminist organizations—was that Lépine's actions were symptomatic of a broad undercurrent of hostility and violence against women endemic in Canadian society. A vocal minority, however, saw the incident as the product of a madman, perhaps related to childhood trauma, perhaps to increasing social problems facing Canadians of both genders. For some, the killer's misogyny was more a product of *his* illness than that of society's. No public inquiry into the incident was held, the authorities regarding such a process as being too painful for the families of the victims. The perpetrator's suicide note and the results of an extensive police investigation were withheld from the public for similar reasons, although the contents of the note were ultimately leaked to the media. The killings sealed Quebec's support for gun-control legislation, and certainly produced an improved emergency response procedure—by police in Montreal and elsewhere—to similar incidents in the future. Commemorations of this incident, on its date, still are held across Canada.

and about half identified homosexuals as the people most likely to become infected. Virtually everybody (90 per cent) believed that the best prevention was safe sex. Eighty-one per cent of those surveyed regarded having sex with one partner in a long-term relationship as a "very effective" means of prevention, while 78 per cent considered complete sexual abstinence "very effective." Only 41 per cent rated condoms a "very effective" method of protection against AIDS. At the same time, however, only 54 per cent of male and 41 per cent of female respondents said they had changed their sexual behaviour because of the risk of AIDS infection; truly safe sex was far from the Canadian norm. Not only did large numbers of respondents take no precautions, but the study suggested a tendency, particularly among males, for people with more knowledge of AIDS to take greater risks. Other studies suggested that only about half of Canadians between 15 and 19 years of age thought they were at risk from sexually transmitted disease, and thus about half of this age group presumably took no precautions. Chlamydia became far more common than AIDS among the young.

In many ways the post-1970 era was dominated by the baby-boom generation. Before 1970 the boomers had their chief impact on the educational system. Now they put pressure on the employment system not only by their sheer numbers but by their educational qualifications. Not all were able to get the jobs for which they had prepared. The tightness of the job market, combined with the increased consumer requirements of the boom generation, produced more childless working couples and further lowered fertility rates. By the 1980s the baby boomers' demand for detached housing drove up housing prices in most of the nation's larger cities. Even after the inevitable bust, prices could never return to previous levels. In cities of premium-priced housing (such as Toronto and Vancouver), it was estimated that less than a quarter of those seeking to purchase their first house could qualify for a mortgage. Many boomers had money to spend on nice things: "My Tastes Are Simple," read one popular bumper sticker, "I Like the Best." Marketing strategies to reach these consumers included slick magazines distributed free to homes in neighbourhoods with the appropriate demographics. Articles featured various aspects of

affluent lifestyles—home (re)decorating, gourmet foods eaten at home or in restaurants, and luxury travel. The boomers continued their fascination with the 1950s and 1960s pop and rock music of their youth. The music nostalgia industry thrived. Radio stations that for decades had tried to appeal to the kids suddenly shifted their programming to the "Golden Oldies" in a blatant attempt to capture the largest single audience segment: middle-aged baby boomers.

The progressive aging of the Canadian population was neither a new development of the post-1970 period nor a distinctly Canadian one. By 1991 life expectancy for Canadian men had reached 74 years and over 80 years for women. The leading causes of death in Canada all were diseases of the old (Table 11.5). The emerging conception of a "crisis" was primarily connected with what seemed to be the increased costs associated with the elderly—pensions and health care—in the welfare states of the advanced world. Part of the problem was that the proportion of the population who were productive members of the workforce able to finance the care of the aging was constantly declining. In 1983 in Canada there were 18 people over 65 years old for every 100 aged 18–64. One prediction suggested that there would be 52 people over 65 for every 100 between 18 and 64 by 2031.

Pensions had always been based on the notion that the working generation would support the retired one. One study in the mid-1980s argued that by the year 2021 the funds required for public pensions would be three and one-half times greater than in 1976, given the continuation of the 1976 level of payments. Without a high level of pension support, the elderly would become an even greater proportion of Canadians below the poverty line. In 1986, 46.1 per cent of unattached females over the age of 65 were below that level. Longer life obviously meant more demands on the health-care system, culminating in the potential need for expensive nursing home facilities. In 1986, only 9 per cent of Canada's elderly could be accommodated in nursing homes. Studies demonstrated that the cost of medical care for the last year of life was substantially greater than for the entire earlier lifespan. The problem was to decide when the last year had come and what medical strategy to adopt.

The increased visibility of racial minorities was especially evident in the nation's larger cities, where

BACKGROUNDER

The Oka Crisis

The Oka crisis was a localized confrontation between the Mohawks of Kanesatake and the town of Oka, Quebec, that lasted for nearly three months over the summer of 1990. It drew substantial national attention as a result of widespread media coverage. The origins of the dispute dated to the early eighteenth century and the grant by Louis XV of a seigneury to the Sulpicians for a seminary and mission to the Iroquois, which set in train disputes over this contested territory that never had been resolved. The town of Oka planned to extend a golf course and build a condominium complex, but the Mohawks claimed the land in question as a burial ground. The land had not only been claimed by the Mohawks, but had been the subject of a federal legal case, the result of which was the rejection of the Mohawk claim on legal grounds in 1986. Because of that decision, the town had not bothered with Mohawk claims when it announced in 1989 that it was expanding the golf course and erecting condominiums. The Mohawks had protested the town's actions, even raising a barricade preventing access to the land in question, and were supported by Quebec's Minister of Native Affairs.

On 11 July 1990 the mayor of Oka asked the Sureté du Quebec to clear away the protestors, alleging criminal activity around the barricades. The police used tear gas and percussive grenades against the protestors, and the scene turned into a running gun battle. The police retreated, leaving behind cruisers and a bulldozer. One Sureté corporal was killed by a bullet that penetrated a part of his body not protected by his bulletproof vest. The Mohawks were subsequently joined by Aboriginals from across Canada. A portion of the Mercier Bridge, a major route into Montreal, was blockaded by protestors from Kahnawake, a reserve community on the St Lawrence just south of Montreal, and automobile traffic in the area was severely disrupted. The federal government agreed to buy the disputed land, a solution disapproved of by the Mohawks. The RCMP were called in, but were unable to open the roads, and so on 8 August Quebec Premier Robert Bourassa called for military "aid to the civil power," a move opposed by Canadian Prime Minister Brian Mulroney. The army was called in, however, and the Mohawks eventually threw down their arms. The controversy, which had spontaneously grown out of control and involved a number of issues operating well beneath the surface of events not well understood by Canadians, sparked a number of books and films. It was an example of heightened tensions between First Nations and Canadian governments at the time, and of conflict among the various levels of government in the country.

they tended to congregate. This concentration only encouraged racism. Despite higher levels of media attention, government expenditure, and Aboriginal self-consciousness, the demographic realities of Native life, while improving, continued to recall conditions in nations generally regarded as the most backward on the planet. Infant mortality and overall death rates ran high. Conditions on many remote reserves continued to be absolutely deplorable. It was not surprising that many Aboriginals migrated to cities like Winnipeg, where they met considerable social disapproval.

One of the most significant developments for Aboriginal peoples was the Mackenzie Valley Pipeline Inquiry, which played out in the years 1974–7. Inquiry chairman Justice Thomas Berger completely rewrote the rules for such inquiries by taking his hearings to

Document

A Launch into Space

The space shuttle *Discovery* was launched on 22 January 1992. The first Canadian female astronaut, Roberta Bondar (b. 1945), recalls the launch.

Dr Roberta Bondar. © Canadian Space Agency, 2005.

We're going to do it! I wonder briefly whether I'll have to use any of my bail-out training. Even in this modest amount of light, the bail-out cue is visible, stuck on a mid-deck locker. It is awe-inspiring to be sitting here, looking at a checklist in this green glow. Just beyond my black boots that will protect my feet if things get out of hand, the cue card details two bail-out sequences. The only thing left to think about now is keeping the differences in the two scenarios, or modes, clear in my mind. In the first one—that's before the liftoff—I need to take off the chute before rolling out of the chair. If I have to use the "Mode 1 pad egress" to get out in any emergency situation on the launch pad, it will be unassisted and will take place in the next three minutes. One more time through the checklist:

Visor down and locked.

Pull the green apple.

Pull the quick-disconnect/lap belts.

Release chute.

Evacuate.

Slide wire.

In the second bail-out sequence, after the launch, I keep the parachute on. It's so automatic now. One glance at the cue card, and I'll plug into the right escape mode.

As we leave the Earth, I sing to myself:

O Canada,

Our home and native land!

True patriot love . . .

Source: Roberta Bondar, *Touching the Earth* (Toronto: Key Porter Books, 1994), 20–1. Reprinted with permission by Key Porter Books Ltd. Copyright © Roberta Bondar, 1994.

the people in remote communities who would be most affected by the proposed pipeline and by paying close attention to what they said, but he stamped on the public (and political) consciousness that development had to take into account the needs of Native peoples in a more thoroughgoing manner than had previously been the case. His report even became a best-seller (Berger, 1977). This was, arguably, the watershed event that brought Aboriginal issues into broad public awareness. It certainly made it impossible for the politicians to

TABLE 11.5 Leading Causes of Death, Canada, 1990

	Male		Female	
	No.	Rate	No.	Rate
Disease of the circulatory system	38,823	296.3	36,266	269.0
Cancer	28,865	220.3	23,560	174.8
Respiratory disease	9,351	71.4	6,921	51.3
Accidents and adverse effects	9,064	69.2	3,993	29.6
Diseases of the digestive system	3,961	28.2	3,303	24.5
Endocrine disease, etc.	2,533	19.3	2,939	21.8
Diseases of the nervous system	2,275	17.14	2,580	19.1
All other causes	9,358	71.2	8,434	62.7
Total, causes	104,230	793.3	87,996	652.8

ignore Aboriginal peoples just a few years later when it came to crafting the Charter.

Immigration

While the Canadian population continued to migrate from rural areas to cities and the surrounding suburbs, because of declining birth rates it also became increasingly dependent for its growth on immigration. That inflow increased its shift from the highly industrialized and earlier preferred nations of Western Europe and North America that had once represented Canada's sources of newcomers. Canada was no longer a special land of opportunity for citizens of the European Community, who lived in economies as prosperous. The new immigrants were largely from Third World countries in Africa, the Caribbean, Latin America, and Asia. The shift was facilitated by the changes in Canadian immigration policy and procedures. In 1973, Hong Kong, the Philippines, Jamaica, Trinidad, and India appeared among the top 10 countries of origin for Canadian immigrants.

In 1975 Immigration Minister Robert Andras tabled another government discussion document in the House of Commons, the so-called "Green Paper." A special joint committee of the House of Commons and Senate held almost 50 public hearings across Canada on the Green Paper. The hearings seemed to confirm that Canadians wanted to continue accepting relatively large numbers of new immigrants but not to open the nation's doors to unrestricted admissions. The result of the national discussion was another major Immigration Act, that of 1976, which stated Canadian goals regarding immigration and insisted on the need to plan for the future. The Act recognized three classes of immigrants: the family class (relatives of Canadian residents), the humanitarian class (refugees and displaced persons), and an independent class.

Immigration regulations were revised in 1978 to alter the points system by placing greater importance on practical experience and to change the refugee situation by creating a new program of refugee sponsorship. Most of the Vietnamese boat people, about 50,000, entered Canada under this plan between 1979 and 1984. Quebec was the only province to take full advantage of federal opportunities built into the legislation of 1976 and 1978 to assume new provincial powers in immigration matters. As a result, Quebec could now in practice select its own immigrants. Ontario and Nova Scotia also signed more limited immigration agreements with Ottawa. Whether or not Quebec could attract and hold its share of the immigration total was another matter entirely. Many immigrants were not enthusiastic about education in French for their children. Tough language legislation led to considerable out-migration. Fewer francophones came to Quebec.

By the mid-1980s the traditional sources for Canadian immigrants were producing only about 30 per cent of the total and their share continued to drop. Moreover, the pattern was shifting simultaneously in other ways as well. Asia continued to be the principal supplier of immigrants. But the number of people from the Caribbean area increased and those from Central and South America continued to come, as did those coming from the Middle East and Africa. The 1980s also witnessed the rise again of the refugee question, both internationally and in Canada. Between the end of World War II and the new Immigration Act of 1978, more than 300,000 refugees—mainly European but including 7,000 Ugandan Asians in 1971 and 7,000 Chileans in 1973—had been admitted to Canada under the relaxation of formal regulations. Those fleeing strife and disasters came to Canada in increasing numbers, occasionally by unusual means, such as the lifeboat loads of Tamils who were picked up off the coast of Atlantic Canada in 1986. Debate over Canada's refugee admission policy after 1978 revolved around both overseas selection by visa and the issue of individuals already in Canada claiming refugee status without any previous processing or documentation (Dirks, 1995).

The visa question was an old one. The Canadian government has long tried to insist on proper visas for those entering the country. This policy forms a preliminary screen for identifying arrivals (immigrants or not) undesirable on medical or security grounds. When people applying for entry into Canada have visas issued by Canadian officials at foreign posts, the immigration officers know they have been pre-screened. Demand for visas for all visitors grew after the increased number of terrorist activities around the world beginning in the 1960s. The crash of an Air India airliner in 1985, in which Canadian authorities suspected that a bomb had been planted in Vancouver airport, reminded Canada of the problem. Despite its obvious advantages, however, insistence on visas has always been contentious in Canada for several reasons. First, political refugees may

not have proper documentation and may be unable to get it. Humanitarian organizations in Canada vehemently opposed insisting on proper documentation for all visitors and immigrants. Second, visas may be hard to obtain in countries in which the Canadian presence is fairly limited. To get a visa may require lengthy travel to a national capital, for example, or even outside the country. As was well known, Canada used an absence of official presence as one way to reduce applications for immigration from some places. This was certainly the case for a country like Guyana. As a result, Canada in the 1980s did not insist on a strictly enforced visa policy. One of the most serious problems was caused by visitors who outstayed their permitted period for visits. Some

By the mid-1980s, the majority of immigrants arriving in Canada came from countries in Asia. In this photo, a young Vietnamese boy waits with his family to be processed at an immigration centre in Montreal. © Owen Franken/Corbis.

suspected that these overstays were a way for people to get around the screening mechanisms. Nationals from some countries for which Canada did not require visas, chiefly India, Portugal, and Guyana, were particularly likely to overstay. It should be emphasized that potential immigrants who were able to afford to come to Canada as visitors and then remain in the country claiming refugee status were not usually impoverished peasants, but rather highly skilled professionals. Their entrance into their professions in Canada was hampered both by their use of the refugee route and by the typical reluctance of Canadian professional organizations to recognize foreign education and experience.

A related question was whether people would be allowed to apply for permanent residence (i.e., formally become "landed immigrants") from inside the country. This issue again criss-crossed the problem of controlling immigration and the related problem of determining refugee status. By the early 1970s there was a substantial backlog of appeals from rejected applicants for landed status from those within and without the country, and in 1972 the regulation permitting application from within Canada was rescinded. But it continued to be possible to remain in the country by special minister's permit, a procedure employed mainly for family members of residents for compassionate reasons. Moreover, the practice of allowing a determination of refugee status from within, made possible by the 1976 and 1978 Immigration Acts, became increasingly common. The machinery of refugee status determination had not been intended as a way for avoiding routine admission procedures, but this was what it became in the later 1970s and early 1980s. The number of refugee claimants totally clogged the immigration system. Altered American regulations in 1986, which granted amnesty to illegal immigrants who arrived in the US before 1982, subjected those after 1982 to threat of deportation. Many of those threatened hoped to come to Canada, posing an additional burden on the system. An "amnesty" was declared in 1986, allowing almost all refugees resident in Canada—some 63,000—to remain in the country as residents. In 1987 the Mulroney government introduced new legislation to deal with the refugee situation, but by the time the revised system went into operation there was already another major backlog, with over 122,000

residents claiming refugee status. Many of these claims were regarded by the authorities as patently improper. However, those whose cases had not been heard could not work and their families often went on provincial and municipal welfare. Ultimately, clearing the backlog took over three years.

While it was claimed that Canada's record with refugees was one of the best in the world—the nation allowed more refugees relative to its own population to immigrate than any other nation—many critics insisted that it needed to do far more. Canada's behaviour towards refugees was increasingly contrasted with its policy towards rich business people. Beginning in 1986 individuals with substantial amounts of capital (initially $250,000, later reduced to $150,000) could invest this money in projects approved by provincial governments and thereby gain admission to Canada. This scheme was heavily criticized in many quarters on a variety of grounds, including the charge that the imported capital helped drive up the real estate markets in a few Canadian cities, such as Vancouver and Toronto.

By the 1990s many Canadians had become concerned about the new patterns of immigration, as indicated by places of birth of immigrants during the 1980s (Table 11.6). These changes in source countries for immigrants to Canada could be seen as finally confirming popular fears and paranoia expressed over many years. By 1991, the European share of Canadian immigration was down to 20.2 per cent. Even with the addition of those coming from the United States, newcomers of European origin represented less than one-quarter of the total of 230,781. In 1991, Africa sent 7.2 per cent of the total, Asia 53 per cent, the Caribbean area 8.2 per cent, and South America 4.5 per cent. The top 10 sources for immigrants to Canada between 1981 and 1991 had been, in order, Hong Kong, Poland, the People's Republic of China, India, the United Kingdom, Vietnam, the Philippines, the United States, Portugal, and Lebanon. As these statistics indicate, the number of people in the underdeveloped nations of the world seeking admission to Canada had increased, and doubtless would continue to increase.

Most people from the underdeveloped nations were visibly different from the majority of the host population

TABLE 11.6 Immigrants Arriving by Place of Birth, 1981–1990

Place	Number	Percentage
Europe	351,511	26.4
Great Britain	81,460	6.1
Portugal	38,630	2.9
France	15,256	1.1
Greece	6,884	0.5
Italy	11,196	0.8
Poland	81,361	6.1
Other	116,724	8.8
Africa	72,941	5.5
Asia	619,089	45.5
Philippines	67,682	5.1
India	90,050	6.8
Hong Kong	96,982	7.3
China	74,235	5.6
Middle East	90,965	6.8
Other	199,175	15.0
North & Central America	114,073	8.6
US	63,106	4.7
Other	50,967	3.8
Caribbean & Bermuda	89,908	6.7
Australasia	5,877	0.4
South America	67,936	5.1
Oceania	10,040	0.8
Other	375	
Total	2,416,423	

Source: *Adapted from* Canada Year Book 1994 *(Ottawa: Statistics Canada Catalogue no. 11-402, 1994), 116.*

in Canada. Many of the newcomers represented racial, religious, and cultural backgrounds considerably unlike those of the traditional Canadian population, producing considerable potential strains on Canadian society. People of Third World origin, who had represented less than 1 per cent of the Canadian population in 1967, by 1986 represented 4.6 per cent, and those from the Third World totalled 30 per cent of all foreign-born in Canada. Between 1981 and 1991, the number of followers of Islam in Canada grew from 98,165 to 253,260, the number of Buddhists from 51,955 to 163,415, and the number of Sikhs from 67,715 to 147,440. In a Canada of high structural unemployment (close to 10 per cent even in times of "prosperity") the newcomers might take jobs away from Canadians, a continued public fear however often researchers and immigration experts insisted that it was a myth. Moreover, for better or worse, in terms of locating themselves geographically, the new immigrants behaved in many ways little different from earlier ones. They flocked to a few large Canadian cities, mainly in English-speaking Canada, eschewing rural areas, Atlantic Canada, and Quebec. In the 1993 federal election, at least one political party, the Reform Party, began to talk openly of closing the door to immigration. Few Canadians were prepared to go that far, but many were worried about how a fair and just immigration policy could be developed.

In 1993 the Liberal government of Jean Chrétien announced that it would maintain a Canadian immigration intake at about 1 per cent of the total Canadian population. The resulting annual immigration figures since that date have been more than 200,000, up from the figures of the 1970s and 1980s. Such an intake did not begin to satisfy the demands of people from around the world who wanted to immigrate to Canada. It did mean that Canadian society would never be suddenly overwhelmed by people of different backgrounds. Nevertheless, over a protracted period, these sorts of numbers—especially if they continued to come from the Third World—would have a profound cumulative effect on the makeup of the Canadian population, including the languages spoken in this officially "bilingual" country, as shown in Table 11.7.

Canadian Culture

After 1972 Canadians discovered that culture had not only moral, intellectual, and aesthetic dimensions but powerful economic implications as well. Canadian

TABLE 11.7 Canadian Population by Mother Tongue, 1996 Census

Total Population	28,528,125
Single Response	28,125,560
English	16,890,615
French	6,636,660
Non-official Languages	4,598,290
Chinese	715,640
Italian	484,500
German	450,140
Polish	213,410
Spanish	212,890
Portuguese	211,290
Punjabi	201,785
Ukrainian	162,695
Arabic	148,555
Dutch	133,805
Tagalog	133,215
Greek	121,180
Vietnamese	106,515
Cree	78,840
Inuktitut	26,960
Other non-official languages	1,198,870
Multiple Responses	402,560
English and French	107,945
English and non-official language	249,545
French and non-official language	35,845
English, French, and non-official language	9,225

Source: Adapted from Statistics Canada, 1996 Census, nation tables.

bureaucrats began to talk about "cultural industries" instead of just culture, about "measuring jobs and spinoffs" as well as enlightenment. At about the same time, governments began to discover how much money they had been putting into various aspects of culture since the halcyon days of the 1950s and 1960s. An additional debate over cultural policy focused on how to limit and to supplement the vast public expenditures on activities ranging from university research to art events. To the extent that it was regarded as a non-essential, culture was extremely vulnerable to budget-cutting. Canadian cultural policy was hotly debated, particularly since the politicians sought to use cultural policy to other ends, notably in the area of multiculturalism. The always artificial distinction between commercial and non-commercial culture had now been partially overcome by the inclusion of cultural enterprise in the economy. Thus, popular culture (including sports) came to be more frequently recognized as a legitimate part of culture.

One of the defining events of a lifetime for many Canadians was the Canada–Russia hockey series of 1972. The largest television audience ever assembled in Canada was glued to the TV, mesmerized. Paul Henderson of the Toronto Maple Leafs scored the game- and series-winning goal in the closing seconds of the final game of the eight-game series. Despite this moment of national togetherness, the schism between francophone and anglophone cultures was constantly widening, and all levels of government continued to jostle for advantage. The result was a strong sense of diffusion and decentralization—some would say regionalization (although not merely geography was involved)—of what had once been perceived as a monolithic cultural establishment. Such developments paralleled and reinforced the retreat of centralism in the political and constitutional area, while contributing to the sense that Canadian society was unravelling.

By 1990 the *Canada Year Book* could call the cultural sector "the fourth largest employer in Canada." A few years earlier, a 1985 Statistics Canada compendium entitled *Arts and Culture: A Statistical Profile* had estimated that in 1982 culture's share of the gross domestic product was $8 billion, calculated that there were 280,000 Canadian arts-related jobs in the 1981 census, and insisted that arts jobs were growing more quickly than the total labour force in all provinces. The 1986 Task Force on Funding in the Arts revised the economic dimensions of the cultural sector upward to $12 billion and the job numbers to 415,000. Despite the billions of dollars of public support, however, government spending on arts-related culture represented only about 2 per cent of the total of government expenditure at all levels. Moreover, little of the vast sum spent on culture trickled down to the primary producers—the writers, painters, actors, and composers. Government surveys of artists from 1978 to 1984 indicated that very few Canadians could make a living from the sale of their work or talents. Most held other employment, often in teaching. At the same time, the fact that even a few thousand Canadians could

conceive of making a living as professional producers of culture certainly distinguished the post-1970 period from earlier times.

Little enough changed in terms of the distinctive Canadian content of culture in Canada, still seen by many observers as a major problem. The statistics were revealing. In book publishing, for example, titles published in Canada in 1984 (most written by Canadian

BACKGROUNDER

The Canada–Russia Hockey Series, 1972

By the early 1970s it was clear that the total dominance Canada had enjoyed in hockey—the game it had invented and nurtured—was a thing of the past. Canada had withdrawn from international competition because its best players were regarded as professionals in a world where national sports teams whose players were supported by the state (such as the team of the Soviet Union) were considered to be amateurs. Canadians took solace in the thought that the so-called amateur teams had never played Canada's best players, who were employed by the National Hockey League. Alan Eagleson (b. 1933), the director of the NHL Players Association, was instrumental in brokering an exhibition series of eight games between Canada and the USSR played in September 1972—four in each country, before the start of the NHL season—which, although unofficial and played for no trophy or recognized title, was commonly accepted in both countries as settling the question of world supremacy.

The Canadians were so confident of victory that they paid little attention to the disadvantages under which they would operate in the series. The Russians trained year-round, while the Canadian players would be out of shape, coming off a summer of off-ice relaxation. The last game of the series, played in Moscow on 28 September 1972, was one of those rare

occasions where virtually every Canadian, with bated breath, watched on television or listened on the radio to a single sporting event. The first seven games had been played to a virtual standoff. Canada had won one and drawn one of the first four games, played on Canadian soil. Initial Canadian complacency had turned to desperate urgency, with Boston Bruins star Phil Esposito offering much-needed emotional leadership. Team Canada played better in Russia, winning two of the first three games played. The players were rounding into better shape, and were relieved of the pressure of performing before home crowds. The final game was both a seat-squirmer and a barnburner. The Russians took an early lead, the Canadians stormed back, and Paul Henderson of the Toronto Maple Leafs scored the winning goal (of both the game and the series) with 34 seconds remaining in regulation time.

The series was fascinating on several levels. It pitted a Russian team that featured fast skating and skilful puck movement against a Canadian contingent that took a more physical approach to the game. For many, the series was seen as a struggle between Western capitalism/democracy and Russian communism/totalitarianism, as well as between two very different styles of hockey. It certainly was a landmark for Canadian nationalism.

Paul Henderson holds up the hockey jersey he wore when he scored the game-winning goal in game eight of the Canada–Russia Summit Series. The jersey was sold at auction for a record-breaking US$1,067,538 on 22 June 2010. Canadian Press/Nathan Denette.

authors) accounted for only 25 per cent of books sold. Nearly half the books sold to Canadians came directly from foreign sources. Twelve foreign-controlled firms in 1984 had 89 per cent of the sound-recording market in Canada, most for recordings made outside Canada. In one week in 1986 the top seven TV shows in English-speaking Canada all were American. The situation was quite different in French Canada, where all seven top shows were locally produced (see Table 11.8). In the 1980s there was great hope for satellite and cable technology, but while these improved access for many Canadian viewers, they did little for actual Canadian content.

Government support for High Culture further aided a respectable Canadian showing in areas of traditional activity, such as painting and literature. But at the very time Canadian High Culture was achieving international recognition, the idea of High Culture was breaking down. In addition, tensions were developing between what came to be labelled "national" and "regional" cultures, not to mention between French and English Canada. Before the late 1960s, a major problem for Canadian creators was receiving public exposure outside Toronto and Montreal.

The small presses and galleries that cropped up in the country, especially after 1970, became possible for

several reasons. One was the allocation of new provincial funding for the arts, often from the revenues of publicly authorized gambling activities. In Quebec, cultural subsidies were a matter of high politics. Another was the emergence of local cultural entrepreneurs in what was now a large enough market for culture in second-tier cities such as Quebec, Halifax, and Winnipeg. Almost inevitably the new publishers and galleries tended to stress local themes and settings. Cultural regionalism grew to match political regionalism.

It began to appear that the very concept of a Canadian National Culture was an artificial one, impossible for most Canadian artists to realize in a fragmented nation. Precious few books published in Quebec were ever translated into English, for example. The success of multiculturalism and the changing face of immigration only complicated the situation further. One exception to all generalizations about culture in Canada began in 1984, when a group of young street performers in Montreal organized a festival that toured Quebec in celebration of the 450th anniversary of the landing of Jacques Cartier. The organizers built on a long tradition of the burlesque in Quebec and incorporated the more recent expression of avant-garde theatre in the province. The show toured in a large blue-and-yellow tent. It was a circus without animals or freaks, featuring acrobatic performances, brilliant costumes, and imaginative choreography with rock music accompaniment. This "Cirque du Soleil," as it came to be called, was a huge success at Expo 86 in Vancouver. It took California by storm in 1987. The company toured the United States in 1988, went to Europe in 1990, and Japan in 1992. It established permanent circus shows in Las Vegas in 1992 and later at Walt Disney World in Florida. By the late 1980s it was recruiting performers around the world and began touring a number of different productions, with accompanying music composed by René Dupéré. Over the 1990s, the Cirque du Soleil became Canada's (or Quebec's) best-known cultural export, providing further evidence that Canada could take the lead in the imaginative creation of culture that crossed all sorts of boundaries.

In early 1991, when the Quebec government of Robert Bourassa finally responded to the collapse of Meech Lake, it listed immigration, health, manpower, and cultural matters as the key areas in which it would demand increased constitutional powers. "As far as

TABLE 11.8 Percentage of Television Viewing Time Devoted to Canadian and Foreign Programming in Prime Time (7 p.m.–11 p.m.), 1984–5 and 1992–3

	1984-5		1992-3	
	English			
	Canadian	Foreign	Canadian	Foreign
CBC	62.0	38.0	81.7	18.3
CTV	20.8	79.2	17.3	82.7
Global	7.9	92.1	17.4	82.6
Independent	16.4	83.6	17.9	82.1
	French			
SRC (Radio-Canada)	72.1	27.9	90.9	9.1
TVA	46.2	53.8	66.3	33.7
TQS	54.8	45.2	47.6	52.4

Source: Reprinted by permission of CBC.

culture is concerned, yes we should be in charge," announced Liberal Minister of Cultural Affairs Liza Frulla-Hébert in January 1991. "We have to work toward being the one and only one giving the pulse of Quebec culture. Listen, culture belongs to Quebec" (*Winnipeg Free Press*, 25 Jan. 1991). No Canadian could doubt that in Quebec, culture was lively and distinctive, certainly better able to withstand American influence than elsewhere in Canada. Whether Quebec Culture was a National Culture became, in the end, a question more susceptible to political than intellectual answers.

International Affairs

After 1975, Canada returned to closer ties with the United States. Aside from perennial concern over trade figures and the occasional international confer-

Material Culture

The Pearson Cup

By the late 1970s, professional baseball was well established in Canada. Minor and independent league baseball was found throughout the country except in Atlantic Canada. The Expos had arrived in Montreal as a National League team in 1969, and the Toronto Blue Jays followed, added to the American League in 1977. With the founding of a second Canadian team, an unofficial championship named after Lester B. Pearson was inaugurated in 1978. The metal Cup has the bilingual engraving "La Coupe Pearson Cup" over a portrait of Pearson. The Cup, which has a scalloped lip with matching, opposing handles, stands on a small wooden plinth making the prize 40 cm high. The front panel features the team logos in front of crossed bats. The right side of the base features circular baseball panels with the name of each year's winner. Damage to the base on the left side is likely ascribed to the disuse the Cup fell into following the 1986 season, when interest had waned and the two teams found it inconvenient to play an exhibition during the regular season, which meant the risk of player injury and the loss of a precious off-day in the long schedule. At this

Manager Jim Fanning of the Montreal Expos holds the Pearson Cup after his Expos defeated the Toronto Blue Jays, 7–3, at Exhibition Stadium in Toronto, 2 September 1982. The Pearson Cup was named after former Prime Minister Lester B. Pearson, who had been president of the Montreal Expos from 1969 to 1972. The Cup was awarded after exhibition games between Montreal of the National League and the newly minted Toronto Blue Jays of the American League between 1978 and 1986. It returned briefly when interleague play was introduced, but after the Expos franchise moved and became the Washington Nationals following the 2004 season, the Cup was no longer contested. Photo by Jeff Goode/Toronto Star via Getty Images.

time, the National and American Leagues played each other only in the World Series, so the games were exhibitions that did not count towards the standings. The game alternated between Olympic Stadium in Montreal and Exhibition Stadium in Toronto. Gate revenue was used to support Canadian amateur baseball.

The first game, hosted and won 5–4 by Montreal, had the further Canadian connection of Chatham, Ontario, pitcher Bill Atkinson earning the win in relief in front of 20,221 fans. The 1979 game ended in a tie, with the Expos winning twice more before Toronto earned its first victory in 1983. (In 1981 no game was played because of a players' strike.) The Blue Jays would then win twice more, in 1984 and 1986, with 1985 ending in another tie. Competition for the Cup was resuscitated briefly in 2003 and 2004, when the Expos and Blue Jays met in interleague play. Fittingly, in both seasons each team won three games so the Cup went nowhere.

Following the 1986 season, the game, and the competition for the Cup, was disbanded for nearly 20 years. While the game sold 11,075 tickets in Montreal in 1985, only about 6,000 fans actually appeared, and that was the most tickets sold for an Expos-hosted year since the first. In Toronto, conversely, the game had never failed to draw less than 20,000 fans. Even so, the games managed to raise over half a million dollars for Canadian amateur baseball, split 35–35–30 between Baseball Quebec, the Ontario Baseball Association, and the remainder to other national programs.

Although the exhibition game was no longer played after 1986, baseball went on to new heights in Canada well into the early 1990s. The Blue Jays replaced the Pearson Cup games with games against the team of the National Baseball Institute, which drew remarkably well, including over 100,000 to a pair of games in Winnipeg. Both the Expos and Blue Jays became highly competitive, with the Blue Jays winning the World Series in both 1992 and 1993. A players' strike in 1994 cancelled the World Series, although the Expos were a lock for the playoffs, and an all-Canadian World Series appeared quite possible.

With an increased number of graduates of Canadian amateur baseball that came with the increases of exposure and funding, more and more Canadians were playing professionally during the late 1990s and 2000s, including major award winners. Larry Walker (Maple Ridge, BC), who began his big league career with the Expos, won the National League Most Valuable Player award in 1997 while playing for the Colorado Rockies, and Eric Gagne (Montreal), who played for the Los Angeles Dodgers, garnered the Cy Young award, given to each league's top pitcher, in 2003.

The Pearson Cup, that object of material culture representing the period when Canada had two teams in Major League Baseball, was donated to the Canadian Baseball Hall of Fame in St Mary's, Ontario, after the demise of the Expos. Over the years of the on-and-off competition, each team had won nine games, with two ties.

ence attended by the Prime Minister, Canada's relations outside North America assumed a very low profile during the 1980s. Canadians expected precious little from foreign policy initiatives. The Free Trade Agreement with the Americans merely confirmed what everyone knew.

The key international developments of the 1980s were totally beyond Canada's control. The first was *glasnost*, the process of liberation from the repression of communism in the Soviet Union. The Soviet regime had been opening up for decades, but no one was prepared for the rapid changes of the later 1980s when the Russians made it clear that they were no longer prepared to prop up unpopular governments in Eastern Europe and wanted to shift their own internal priorities in what appeared to be capitalistic and democratic directions. The most obvious symbol of collapse was the razing of the Berlin Wall, which was demolished, along with the government of East Germany, in November 1989, clearing the way for German reunification in late

1990. This event ultimately permitted Canada to close its last two military bases on German soil in 1993.

Conclusion

For many Canadians, especially those in English-speaking Canada, the years after 1972 were characterized by considerably less optimism and buoyancy than the previous quarter-century had been. In historical development, disparate events often come together in surprising ways to weave a complex web. This was the case with such seemingly unrelated trends as the rise of Quebec separatism; the growing power of the provinces; the international oil crisis; the shift away from trade protectionism and a managed economy; the weakening of Christian belief; and the passage through life of the baby boomers. The result was a Canadian society concerned mainly with hedonism and anxiety, displaying all the morbid symptoms that might have been expected.

Historiography

Revision and Agency in the Telling of Aboriginal History

Lianne Leddy, Wilfrid Laurier University

In June of 1990, Elijah Harper, an Oji-Cree chief from Red Sucker Lake and an NDP MLA, filibustered in the Manitoba legislature with an eagle feather in his hand, delaying long enough to help bring about the end of the Meech Lake Accord. Harper was not alone in his discontent with the lack of Indigenous voices in the nation's political discourse. The summer of 1990 brought more discord when the Mohawk people of Kanesatake took a stand at Oka, Quebec, for 78 days against the expansion of a golf course on their traditional lands. Of course, Indigenous activism had been on the rise since the 1970s, but in the late 1980s and throughout the 1990s radical action became a common tactic across

the country, from Gustafsen Lake, British Columbia, to Esgenoopetitj (Burnt Church), New Brunswick. Radical Indigenous action captured national attention, and in response to the Oka crisis in particular the Mulroney government in 1991 created the Royal Commission on Aboriginal Peoples (RCAP), which reported in 1996 with more than 400 recommendations to improve Indigenous–settler relations in Canada. Indigenous peoples were also taking action in the court system: the *Delgamuukw* decision in 1997 recognized the importance of Indigenous oral traditions as legal evidence, and the 1999 *Marshall* decision recognized Mi'kmaq fishing rights. It was the dawn of a new, more confrontational era in the relationship between Indigenous peoples and the Canadian state as Indigenous people asserted their rights.

Historians do not write in isolation and their work is framed by their own times. It is not a coincidence that there was an explosion of revisionist literature in Indigenous history in Canada in the 1990s as Indigenous peoples across the country demanded sovereignty, social and environmental justice, and the recognition of land and fishing rights. Indigenous history is interdisciplinary, meaning that while many of the scholars working in the field are and were historians, important historical work also is produced by scholars trained in archaeology, anthropology, and geography.

Before the mid-twentieth century, Indigenous peoples often appeared in history books (if they did at all) as silent figures without agency—that is, the power to shape their own destinies. They were depicted as existing only as dependants of the fur trade and as fighting in wars only as pawns of European powers. Sometimes, they were viewed as noble in their lack of civility, but they vanished altogether from Canada's national history after the North West Rebellion, which they were (wrongly) accused of helping to incite. Their own stories were not the focus of historical inquiry, and their actions were not evaluated in the context of their own perspectives.

The first wave of revisionist history began in the 1970s and 1980s with the work of Bruce Trigger (e.g., *The Children of Aataentsic: A History of the Huron People to 1660*, 1976), A.J. Ray (*Indians in the Fur Trade*, 1974), Robin Fisher (*Contact and Conflict: Indian–European Relations in British Columbia 1774–1890*, 1977), Jennifer S.H. Brown (*Strangers in Blood: Fur Trade Company Families in Indian Country*, 1980), and Sylvia Van Kirk (*Many Tender Ties: Women in Fur-Trade Society*, 1980). These scholars tended to focus on fur-trade relationships, contact with Europeans, and, in some cases, the effect of missionary activities. J.R. Miller's *Skyscrapers Hide the Heavens*, first published in 1989, was one of the first accessible syntheses of Indigenous history in this country. These scholars tended to focus on events before Confederation, and they were revising what had been written by previous historians.

With calls for Indigenous land rights and greater social justice ringing through the Canadian media, in the early 1990s historians turned to more recent events, specifically the development of Indian Affairs policies and the Indian Act, to challenge Canada's identity as a peaceful, post-colonial country. People suddenly wanted to understand the colonial forces that had created contemporary conflicts, as Indigenous peoples had not vanished after Confederation, but rather, they had been ignored. The first institutional history of the Department of Indian Affairs was E. Brian Titley's 1986 biographical study, *A Narrow Vision: Duncan Campbell Scott and the Administration of Indian Affairs in Canada*, which examined the celebrated Confederation poet's long-lasting and damaging impact as deputy superintendent general of Indian Affairs. Sarah Carter showed that Indian Affairs policies were to blame, not Indigenous peoples, when she challenged the pervasive myth that Indigenous people made poor farmers in *Lost Harvests: Prairie Indian Reserve Famers and Government Policy* (1990). Of course, the cornerstone of the federal government's policy of assimilation and cultural destruction was the residential school system, which was the subject of J.R. Miller's *Shingwauk's Vision: A History of Residential Schools* (1996) and John S. Milloy's *A National Crime: The Canadian Government and the Residential School System, 1879–1986* (1999). It is telling that the last residential school only closed in 1996 as these books were going to print. Collectively, these scholars emphasized the victimization of Indigenous peoples at the hands of the state but also their capacity to resist these incursions.

More recently, scholars have examined the gendered experiences of colonialism, building on the earlier work of Brown and Van Kirk. These historians highlight both Indigenous and settler women's views, and the ways in which they create and transgress boundaries long defined by patterns of colonialism. While Olive P. Dickason (the Métis author of the landmark work, *Canada's First Nations: A History of Founding Peoples from Earliest Times*, first published in 1992) was one of the first Indigenous historians publishing in Canada, more Indigenous people are writing their own histories (e.g., Basil Johnston, *Indian School Days*, 1988; Daniel

Paul, *We Were Not the Savages: Collision between European and Native American Civilizations*, 3rd edn, 2007 [1993]). There has also been an increased awareness among non-Indigenous scholars of the need to include Indigenous perspectives and voices. To that end, more historians are using oral history methods to balance the perspectives contained in official documents, as church and government records were typically written by non-Indigenous men. In an effort to ensure that the research being done is relevant and that the findings assist in community development, some scholars have embarked on community-based research projects.

Short Bibliography

Bashevkin, Sylvia. *True Patriot Love: The Politics of Canadian Nationalism*. Toronto, 1991. An important study of the way politicians have bent Canadian nationalism to their own purposes.

Berger, Thomas R. *Northern Frontier, Northern Homeland* (Report of the Mackenzie Valley Pipeline Inquiry), 2 vols. Ottawa, 1977. A key document in the history of social justice in Canada.

Bibby, Reginald. *Fragmented Gods: The Poverty and Potential of Religion in Canada*. Toronto, 1987. A perceptive account of the state of religion in Canada as of the mid-1980s, based on specially conducted national surveys and standard public opinion polls.

Cairns, Alan. *Disruptions: Constitutional Struggles, from the Charter to Meech Lake*. Toronto, 1991. An analysis of the constitutional problems of the 1980s by one of Canada's leading constitutional specialists.

Corse, Sarah. *Nationalism and Literature: The Politics of Culture in Canada and the United States*. Cambridge, 1997. A stimulating comparative study of recent cultural policy in the field of literature in the United States and Canada.

English, John. *Just Watch Me: The Life of Pierre Elliott Trudeau 1968–2000*. Toronto, 2009. A compelling account of Trudeau's years in power and beyond.

Frazer, William. *The Legacy of Keynes and Friedman: Economic Analysis, Money, and Ideology*. Westport, Conn., 1994. An intellectual history of one of the major ideological disagreements in North America in the late twentieth century.

Giangrande, Carole. *Down to Earth: The Crisis in Canadian Farming*. Toronto, 1985. A discussion of the reasons Canadian farmers were in serious financial trouble in the 1980s.

Gwyn, Richard. *The Northern Magus*. Toronto, 1980. A solid early biography of that complex Canadian, Pierre Elliott Trudeau.

Harris, Michael. *Unholy Orders: Tragedy at Mount Cashel*. Markham, Ont., 1990. An exposé of one of the first of Canada's sexual abuse scandals within a major religious denomination.

Jenish, D'Arcy. *Money to Burn: Trudeau, Mulroney, and the Bankruptcy of Canada*. Toronto, 1996. A partisan analysis of the "crisis" of the deficit, presenting it as the major challenge to the present generation of Canadians.

McDonald, Neil, and Trevor McDonald. *Aboriginal Peoples: Past and Present: Summary of the History, Rights and Issues Relating to Aboriginal Peoples in Canada*. n.p., 2000. A good introduction to a complex question.

McQuaig, Linda. *Shooting the Hippo: Death by Deficit and Other Canadian Myths*. Toronto, 1995. A study by a leading radical economic and social analyst who insists that the deficit was an invented crisis, easily soluble.

McWhinney, Edward. *Canada and the Constitution, 1979–82*. Toronto, 1982. A well-balanced contemporary narrative.

Morgan, Nicole. *Implosion: An Analysis of the Growth of the Federal Public Service in Canada, 1945–1985*. Montreal, 1986. An explanation of the growth of Canada's federal bureaucracy.

Parsons, Vic. *Bad Blood: The Tragedy of the Canadian Tainted Blood Scandal*. Toronto, 1995. An angry look at one of the worst examples of the failure of public policy in the arena of public health.

Savoie, Donald. *The Politics of Public Spending in Canada*. Toronto, 1990. A dispassionate discussion of the financial crisis in Canada as of 1990.

Study Questions

1. What roles did the economy and the Constitution play in the disintegration of the liberal federalist nationalist consensus during the 1970s?

2. In what ways did oil illustrate the excesses and weaknesses of the age of affluence?

3. After winning a second enormous majority for the Progressive Conservative Party in 1988, Brian Mulroney quickly became one of the most unpopular prime ministers in Canadian history. Identify and explain three reasons for his fall from grace.

4. If you think of the attempts at constitutional reform from 1980 to 1992 as a battle between the federal government and the provinces, who would you say won? Explain your answer.

5. What provisions did the Meech Lake Accord make regarding immigrants to Quebec? Why do you think Quebec wanted these provisions?

6. What did the Donald Marshall case reveal about the status of Aboriginal people in the Canadian justice system?

7. How did immigration remake Canadian society between 1980 and 1990?

8. What does the table on television-viewing in 1996 tell us about Canadian viewing habits in that year?

9. In about 10 years, the Cirque du Soleil grew from a ragtag band of street performers to an international cultural institution. What factors led to the Cirque's success?

Visit the companion website for *A History of the Canadian Peoples*, fifth edition for further resources.

www.oupcanada.com/Bumsted5e

12 Freefalling into the Twenty-First Century, 1992–2001

Paul Okalik, the first premier of Nunavut, signs the official documents proclaiming the territory separate from the Northwest Territories on 1 April 1999. Although geographically large, the territory itself was, and remains, sparsely populated, predominantly by Inuit. Territorial status was granted in order to give these people more control over their government and their future. Nick Didlick/AFP/Getty Images.

Timeline

1990 Japanese Canadians who lost property and were interned during World War II receive payment and written apology from Canadian government. Lucien Bouchard leaves PC Party, forms Bloc Québécois.

1991 Royal Commission on Aboriginal Peoples formed.

1992 Referendum on Charlottetown Accord.

1993 Kim Campbell is chosen leader of the Progressive Conservative Party and becomes Prime Minister of Canada in June. In October the Liberals win a great victory. Jean Charest becomes PC leader.

1994 NAFTA proclaimed. PQ victory in Quebec.

1995 Mike Harris's Tories demolish the NDP in Ontario. Separatism defeated in Quebec in close referendum vote. Quebec Nordiques leave for new home in Colorado.

1996 Sheldon Kennedy accuses his former hockey coach of sexual abuse.

1997 Liberals win another federal victory, PQ a victory in Quebec. Asia–Pacific Economic Co-operation (APEC) meeting held in Vancouver. Canada agrees to Kyoto Accord on greenhouse gases. Supreme Court hands down judgment in *Delgamuukw* case.

1998 Jean Charest steps down as federal PC leader to lead Quebec's provincial Liberal Party. Joe Clark becomes PC leader. United Church apologizes to Aboriginal people for residential school abuse.

1999 United Alternative convention held. Adrienne Clarkson becomes Governor General of Canada.

2000 Molson's "I Am Canadian" advertising campaign begins. In July, Stockwell Day is chosen over Preston Manning to lead the Canadian Alliance. In November the Liberals win their third term in office.

If one listened to the journalists and the media pundits, Canada and Canadians lived in a constant state of crisis and turmoil in the 1990s, lurching from one emergency to the next without any road map to the future. While such may well have been the case, in this view there is little perspective. The "news" almost by definition has no sense of history. Certainly Canada was not unique in its problems, which almost without exception were occurring in other places around the world. Even the potential disintegration of the Canadian Confederation was hardly unique. Movements of national liberation were everywhere, and contrary to the situations in Bosnia, the USSR, and Sri Lanka—to name but a few troubled nations—at least in Canada the conflicting sides were not yet armed camps. Moreover, despite the nation's well-publicized problems, most of the population of the remainder of the world would have probably traded their situation for that of the average Canadian. Canada continued to rank at or near the top of everyone's world standard-of-living table. As for the claim that Canada lacked direction, this statement could have been equally true at any time in the past. With hindsight, historians can offer some notion of what the direction was and what the ultimate outcome would be. We can see an inexorable line from the Great Depression through World War II to the social service state, for example. Those who live in the midst of the maelstrom, however, can have little sense of how the issues and paradoxes of the moment will eventually be resolved. Nor can the participants in the chaos of the moment tell whether the resolution will be progressive or retrogressive, apocalyptic or gradual. About all we can say with assurance is that the future is—as it always has been—uncertain. That fact is not in itself a crisis. Moreover, all things are relative. By comparison with what happened in 2001 and after, the period of the 1990s seemed quite humdrum.

Politics

At the federal level, the most important political development was probably the triumph of the Liberal Party in the 1993 election, combined with the absolute collapse of the Progressive Conservative Party and its replacement by two openly antagonistic regional parties. National political parties had failed abysmally at the polls before (the Liberals in 1918, the Tories in 1940). Regional parties (such as the Progressive Party) had temporarily risen to prominence. What was new about the election of 1993, of course, was the emergence in the House of Commons of two regional parties of equal strength, the Reform Party and the Bloc Québécois, each committed to irreconcilable policies and their combined seats unequal to the large Liberal majority. These two regional parties both tended to draw their strength from voters who had previously supported the Tories. At the same time, the Liberals did win a major victory, but without any evidence of new policies.

By the close of 1992 it was clear that Prime Minister Brian Mulroney's popularity ratings, consistently lower

Prime Minister designate Kim Campbell with Brian Mulroney outside the official residence at 24 Sussex Drive, Ottawa, 14 June 1993. Although her time as Prime Minister was short-lived, she is the only female Prime Minister that Canada has ever had. What, if anything, does this say about women's political equality today? The Canadian Press/Tom Hanson.

than any other Canadian Prime Minister had previously experienced, were not likely to improve with time.

At the leadership convention that ensued in June 1993, Kim Campbell (b. 1947) was chosen on the second ballot to lead the party. Campbell, a British Columbian who had originally been associated with the Social Credit party in that province, thus became Canada's first female Prime Minister. Although a relative newcomer to federal politics, she had more experience than Brian Mulroney did at the time of his election as Prime Minister in 1984. She had held two major cabinet portfolios beginning in 1989. The Tories apparently hoped that her gender and her refreshing "candour" would lead the country to see Campbell as a fresh face, although her credentials in French Canada were hardly up to those of the man she had beaten out (Jean Charest of Quebec). Some observers, particularly among feminists, argued that Campbell had been chosen as a "sacrificial lamb" to bear the brunt of the inevitable election defeat about to occur. In any case, like John Turner a decade earlier, Campbell inherited the enormous unpopularity of her predecessor. She had little time to establish a new government image before having to call an election.

Jean Chrétien's Liberals were in some ways well prepared for the contest, certainly financially, although the party platform was somewhat of two minds, committed to carrying on the welfare state while balancing the budget and reducing the deficit. Chrétien was hardly a brilliant campaigner, but he proved adequate to the task, much aided by a series of blunders by Campbell and her advisers. The worst occurred shortly before the end of the campaign, when Campbell was unable to distance herself quickly enough from a negative political ad campaign suggesting that Chrétien was handicapped. (He had contracted Bell's palsy when he was young, and consequently the left side of his face was partially paralyzed.) Negative campaigning in the media had become common in the United States, but this one backfired by generating popular sympathy for the Liberal leader. Submerged under the national media attention given to Campbell and Chrétien were a series of fascinating local races featuring a variety of third parties, of which the Reform Party and the Bloc Québécois proved on election day to be the most attractive to the voters. The Liberals did not so much receive a mandate as triumph over an otherwise badly divided field headed by the singularly inept Tories.

Biography

Jean Chrétien

Jean Chrétien, c. 1999. The Canadian Press/Tom Hanson.

Born in Shawinigan, Quebec, on 11 January 1934, Jean Chrétien was the eighteenth of 19 children (not all of whom lived beyond infancy) born to a relatively poor family in the midst of the Depression. He attended Laval University, studying law, and practised in Trois-Rivières from his call to the bar in 1958 to his election to the House of Commons in 1963. A childhood illness left him deaf in one ear and partially paralyzed the left side of his face. After serving as parliamentary secretary to Prime Minister Pearson and then to Finance Minister Mitchell Sharp, Chrétien was appointed by Pearson as Minister without Portfolio in 1967 and over the next 17 years held virtually every important portfolio in a series of Liberal governments, culminating as Secretary of

Continued...

State for External Affairs and Deputy Prime Minister in 1984 under John Turner.

Chrétien resigned his seat in 1986 and left public life for a few years, but was chosen head of the Liberal Party in 1990. He was the most prominent contender for the leadership, and many argued that he deserved it for long and loyal service to the party. He had many strengths. He was a proven campaigner, particularly in French Canada, and he cultivated the image of a guileless small-town French Canadian—"the little guy from Shawinigan"— more shrewd than clever. Never flashy, he had strong support within local Liberal organizations. His opponents tried to label him "Yesterday's Man," and he offered no new visions, which may have been an advantage against his principal rivals, Sheila Copps and Paul Martin Jr.

Chrétien came to power in the Liberal sweep of 1993, and most of his 10 years as Prime Minister were spent without any serious opposition, either in the Commons or at the hustings. This lack of opposition made it possible for him to survive his own mistakes in judgment and the corruption of his Quebec associates. He was in constant hot water—over "Peppergate" (the use by police of pepper spray on demonstrators during the 1997 APEC meeting in Vancouver), over his association with real estate promoters in his riding, over his physical response to an anti-poverty activist when, as Prime Minister in 1996, he wrestled to the ground the protestor blocking his path with what he later termed a "Shawinigan Handshake."

The Reform Party had been organized in October of 1987 by (Ernest) Preston Manning, son of the long-time Alberta Social Credit leader, Ernest Manning. Its backbone was in traditional Alberta and British Columbia Socred constituencies, but it had some appeal as far east as Ontario among retired Canadians and young first-time voters. Preston Manning was a professional management consultant. He was a colourless speaker, but his lack of charisma was somewhat redeemed by a self-deprecating humour seldom seen among major political leaders. The Reform Party stood four-square for the traditional, often populist, values of the Anglo-Canadian West. It wanted to cut federal spending, to reform Parliament to make it more responsive to the popular will, and to provide for the equal treatment of provinces and citizens alike. The party had no time for the sovereignist pretensions of Quebec or for French-Canadian culture. Reform liked multiculturalism little better than biculturalism. Manning indicated his willingness to contemplate new limitations on immigration to Canada, although he was not pressed hard on the issue.

As for the Bloc Québécois, it was associated both within and without Quebec with its major campaign issue, the separation of that province from the Canadian Confederation, and with its leader, Lucien Bouchard. Born in St-Coeur-de-Marie in 1938, Bouchard had been a lawyer in Chicoutimi before his appointment as

Canadian ambassador to France in 1985 by the Mulroney government. In the election of 1988 he had run as a successful PC candidate, but he had left the party before the 1992 referendum on the Charlottetown Accord to sit as an independent committed to a sovereign Quebec. The responses to Bouchard pointed to some interesting cultural differences between francophone Québécois and other Canadians. While many of the former found Bouchard compelling and charismatic in the traditional pattern of *le chef* (the best example of which had been Maurice Duplessis), anglophones inside and outside the province were not attracted to him in the slightest.

Not only were the PCs—soon after the election led by Jean Charest (b. 1958)—reduced to a mere two seats on 25 October 1993, but both they and the NDP (with nine seats) lost official standing in the House of Commons. This loss of standing was particularly serious for the NDP, which had relied heavily on Commons financial support for its Ottawa infrastructure. With 54 seats to Reform's 53, the Bloc Québécois became the official opposition, offering the somewhat anomalous spectacle of "Her Majesty's Loyal Opposition" committed to the destruction of the institution in which it was participating. The Liberals had a pretty easy time in most respects, since the opposition was unable to agree on very much and lacked numerical strength anyway. In power, the Chrétien government continued to exhibit the ambiguities of its

Opposition leader Preston Manning at a post-election news conference in Calgary, 3 June 1997. Manning's Reform Party was limited as a national party by its lack of support in Quebec and the Maritimes. The Canadian Press/Frank Gunn.

campaign platform, trying to reduce federal expenditure and the deficit without doing serious damage to any of the major social programs—or its image. A major review of the entire welfare and unemployment system, headed by Lloyd Axworthy (b. 1939), ended up making essentially cosmetic changes to the system designed to make it more difficult to remain for long periods on social assistance or to use welfare to subsidize seasonal employment. The government predictably sought to save money by cutting deeply into cultural programs and the military, and by reducing the amount of transfer payments to the provinces for health and higher education. As the time for another election approached, the Liberals had precious little in positive accomplishment to take to the nation, however.

Despite the many weaknesses of Chrétien's government, the Liberals won easily in 1997. This victory was less the result of Liberal success than of opposition failure. The opposition forces were still divided regionally, with Bouchard's Bloc Québécois dominating in Quebec and Manning's Reform and Charest's Progressive Conservatives dividing the vote outside Quebec. While the PCs did best outside the West, Reform got all of its 60 seats from the four western provinces, especially Alberta and British Columbia, where western alienation continued to be strong. The NDP still could not mount an eastern breakthrough and was hampered by its lack of a strong or imaginative platform; the party was badly divided between those who wanted to make it the radical alternative and those who thought such a stance would be the kiss of death. The Liberals collected 155 seats to 145 for the combined opposition, despite gathering only 38.4 per cent of the total vote.

The most obvious need of the political right was for a unified conservative opposition. This was far more difficult to obtain than might have been expected, given the potential prize of national political power were it accomplished. In April 1998, Jean Charest stepped down as leader of the national PCs to become leader of the Quebec Liberal Party. This shift of allegiance probably bothered the voters outside Quebec less than those within the province. Into the national gap stepped Joe Clark, the leader and ex-Prime Minister earlier dismissed from the leadership in favour of Brian Mulroney. Clark was popular with backroom Tories in eastern Canada, but hardly anybody else.

In early 1999, 1,500 delegates assembled in Ottawa at a United Alternative convention, which hoped to lay the framework for a new political party of the right. Most of these delegates were members of the Reform Party, and there was little enthusiasm for this initiative from either the BQ (who were not invited) or the Tories (who were). The United Alternative turned into the Alliance Party. Most Reform members shifted their allegiance, but Joe Clark resolutely remained outside the new umbrella. Preston Manning attempted unsuccessfully to become the Alliance's new leader, but was thwarted by a relative newcomer named Stockwell Day. Day was selected, in July 2000, probably because he seemed the only viable alternative to Manning, who graciously stepped aside as leader of the opposition in Day's favour. Manning had been rejected because he was perceived to be unacceptable outside western Canada. Unfortunately, Day proved to be less than compelling as a political leader. His first appearance in the role saw him don a wetsuit and ride a jet ski to meet the media. There was also the lingering problem of a lawsuit filed against him by a lawyer whom Day had criticized for defending a pedophile; the legal costs were assumed by the province of Alberta. Day was forced to lead the Alliance (officially the Canadian Reform Conservative Alliance) into an election within a few months of his selection and before he was able either to put his mark on the party platform or to develop any popular new initiatives.

In the 2000 federal election, the Liberals actually gained both in seats and in percentage of the popular vote. The number of Liberal seats increased to 172 and the party's percentage of the popular vote grew to 40.8 per cent. Some of the increase was at the expense of the Bloc Québécois, which dropped from 44 to 38 seats, although a number of seats were also taken from both the Progressive Conservatives and the NDP. The Alliance gained in seats over the Reform total in 1997, winning in 66 ridings, although still exclusively in western Canada. As leader of the opposition, Stockwell Day proved ineffective. Before long, leading members of his caucus, including Deborah Grey and house leader Chuck Strahl, were publicly criticizing Day's leadership. By April 2001, most of the caucus had turned against him and 13 walked out; six of the 13 subsequently returned.

Meanwhile, Prime Minister Chrétien came under attack in the House of Commons, in the media, and in his own caucus over his involvement with developers in his riding for whom he solicited government support. As well, there were a number of other ethically dubious interventions. The government's newly appointed ethics adviser ruled in all cases brought before him that Chrétien had broken no guidelines, but neither the opposition nor the public was entirely convinced. One of the chief issues in the Liberal caucus involved succession politics. Chrétien was widely expected to step down soon after his 2000 victory, and every potential leadership candidate tried to build up a financial war chest and support against the day the Prime Minister either announced his departure or authorized open campaigning for his successor.

Developments at the provincial level confirmed the split personality of the electorate. The public was concerned about the size of the deficits and was generally opposed to higher taxes, but at the same time was not at all enthusiastic about deep cuts in social programs. Whether these sentiments were held by the same people or by different groups of voters was not entirely clear. In Alberta, the Tory government of Ralph Klein (1942–2013) won a big election victory in 1993 on a platform of realistic government budgeting. Klein carried through with major budget cuts, although because of Alberta's relative wealth, these probably hurt less than they would have in a province like Nova Scotia. In Ontario, the NDP government of Bob Rae (b. 1948), which had not succeeded in controlling finances and had run afoul of the province's trade union movement in its attempts to cut the costs of its civil service, was demolished in 1995 by the Tories led by Mike Harris (b. 1945). The chief campaign issue was government spending. When Harris actually began to cut spending, however, the cries of wounded outrage were deafening. In Ontario, as elsewhere, there was some evidence from the polls that Canadians were actually prepared to pay higher taxes to preserve some of their social benefits, particularly in the health-care sector.

The reasons for the 1994 electoral victory of the Parti Québécois—or the mood of the electorate in that province—were, as usual, clouded by the sovereignty issue. The Bourassa government had not controlled spending,

but the PQ did not present itself in the campaign as the party of fiscal restraint. In 1997 Bouchard's PQ easily won re-election over Jean Charest's Liberals by campaigning chiefly on a platform of preserving a "zero deficit," which obviously meant deep cuts to education, social services, and health care. The party kept a low profile on separatism, and this probably only confused the electorate. The big winner in the 1997 election was the Action Démocratique du Quebec, led by an articulate young former Liberal named Mario Dumont (b. 1970) who advocated sovereignty-association. The ADQ presented a right-wing alternative to the two major parties and picked up much support from those who in earlier days would have supported the Union Nationale. Although the NDP was wiped out in 1995 in Ontario and in 2001 in British Columbia, in both cases standing accused of fiscal irresponsibility, it

Biography

Jacques Parizeau

Born in Montreal, Jacques Parizeau (1930–2015) was educated at Montreal's College Stanislas, a subsidiary of College Stanislas de Paris, and subsequently earned a doctorate in economics from the London School of Economics. Returning to Quebec, in the 1960s he advised the Quebec government on a variety of fronts, including the nationalizations of Hydro-Québec and of the Asbestos Corporation. He also worked on the establishment of the Quebec Pension Plan. In 1969 he joined the Parti Québécois as a committed sovereignist, and in 1976 he became René Lévesque's Minister of Finance, serving until 1984, when he resigned because he felt Lévesque was no longer sufficiently committed to Quebec sovereignty. In 1987 he rejected an offer to become appointed to the Senate of Canada, and a year later he was elected leader of the PQ to succeed Pierre-Marc Johnson, who had lost the election of 1985.

Parizeau fought his first election campaign not long after becoming leader, and the PQ did not do very well. The party performed much better in 1994, winning a

majority in the legislature. One of his campaign promises was a referendum on sovereignty within a year of the election, and he honoured his promise. In the referendum campaign itself, Parizeau was forced to surrender the spokesman role to Lucien Bouchard (the leader of the federal Bloc Québécois), who was regarded by many as a more charismatic figure and a better campaigner more likely to sway the voters in favour of a "yes" vote. The result of the hard-fought campaign was a defeat for sovereignty by a small margin, although 60 per cent of francophones voted in favour of separation. In conceding defeat on national television, Parizeau attributed the loss to "money and ethnic votes," an accusation he subsequently repudiated. Soon after the referendum loss, he resigned as Premier, probably less because of his faux pas—if it was such—than because of the defeat itself and his failure to bring Quebec to his cherished goal. In the years after retirement he kept a low profile, although he did emerge to oppose the Quebec Charter of Values proposed by the PQ in 2013. Two years later, on 1 June 2015, he died in Montreal.

came to power in Manitoba in 1999 to replace a Tory government that had come to grief over mismanagement of health care. What was evident everywhere in Canada was that no politician or political party had any fresh ideas for resolving the fiscal dilemma.

The Constitution

Any hope that the referendum defeat of the Charlottetown Accord had put a lid on constitutional matters was ended by the 1994 PQ victory in Quebec. Led by Jacques Parizeau (b. 1930), the PQ moved inexorably towards another Quebec referendum on sovereignty. Parizeau had initially opposed sovereignty-association but gradually came to see it as a way to satisfy some soft nationalists. Realizing that one of the major problems with the 1980 referendum had been the uncertainty regarding both the question and any consequent action, Parizeau sought to tie down the new question. He had legislation passed defining the terms. In June 1995 he and the two other separatist leaders, the BQ's Bouchard and the ADQ's Dumont, agreed on a plan. Quebecers would be asked to authorize the Quebec government to open negotiations with Ottawa on sovereignty-association. If the province gave a mandate and if an agreement with Canada was not reached within a year, Quebec would unilaterally declare sovereignty. By joining forces, the three leaders hoped to allay fears that the Quebec government would, in Parizeau's words, "jump the gun" on a declaration of sovereignty. The vote was soon set for 30 October 1995. The official question was "Do you agree that Quebec should become sovereign, after having made a formal offer to Canada for a new Economic and Political Partnership, within the scope of the Bill respecting the future of Quebec and of the agreement signed on June 12, 1995?"

In the beginning the federalist ("Non") forces seemed to be well in control of the situation. Experts expected the usual ballot bonus for the federalists, who would turn out a higher proportion of their supporters. They also anticipated the usual conservative response to uncertainty. For the most part, Ottawa kept its distance from the campaign, allowing Liberal leader Daniel Johnson to carry the "Non" message to the electorate. The federal strategy was to do as little as possible to fuel the sovereignist position.

Then, with polls showing a marked advantage for the "Non" side, Lucien Bouchard actively entered the fray. Bouchard had only recently recovered from a rare bacterial infection that cost him a leg and nearly his life. He had not been originally expected to be an important campaigner, but the province was clearly not excited by Parizeau and Dumont. Bouchard introduced a new level of emotion into the campaign, simplifying the issues considerably. For many Quebecers, the need to move forward on the constitutional front became the key question in the referendum. When the need for constitutional change rather than the need for sovereignty became the real referendum question, the situation rapidly deteriorated for the federalist forces. What had earlier been a ho-hum campaign suddenly turned into a real barnburner. At the last minute, Prime Minister Chrétien revealed the panic in Ottawa by offering Quebec concessions, including yet another "distinct society" constitutional proposal.

The vote turned into a cliff-hanger as virtually every eligible resident of Quebec cast his or her ballot. The final turnout—over 94 per cent of the total electorate—has seldom been matched except in police states with compulsory voting. Millions of Canadians remained tuned to their television sets until late in the evening, waiting for the decisive result. Finally, it became clear that the "Non" forces had won a narrow victory. In the end, 2,362,355 Quebecers (or 50.6 per cent) of the total voted "Non," while 2,308,054 (or 49.4 per cent) voted "Oui." The young, the francophone, and the Quebecer outside Montreal led the way in voting "Oui." There were many informal complaints about voting irregularities, but the vote was allowed to stand. Premier Parizeau had prepared a gracious speech of conciliation to accompany a sovereignist victory. In his bitter acknowledgement of failure on national radio and television, he was less gracious, blaming anglophones and ethnics for thwarting the aspirations of francophone Quebec. As Parizeau spoke, the cameras panned around the crowd of people gathered at "Oui" headquarters. Many were in tears. Parizeau's impulsive attack turned much public opinion against him, even within his own party. Within hours he announced his resignation. In February 1996 he would be officially replaced by Lucien Bouchard.

Mario Dumont, Jacques Parizeau, and Lucien Bouchard at a rally for "Oui" supporters in Longueuil, Quebec, 29 October 1995. The referendum vote was held the following day. After Parizeau, the PQ would not gain enough power to force another referendum. The Canadian Press/Paul Chiasson.

In the wake of the referendum, the Chrétien government passed a unilateral declaration in the Canadian Parliament that recognized Quebec as a distinct society, but as virtually everyone had come to appreciate, this gesture was too little too late. French Canadians in Quebec had made clear their desire for a new constitutional relationship with Canada. Virtually the only question remaining was whether or not a sovereign Quebec would remain within some sort of Canadian Confederation. Post-referendum polls continued to emphasize that Quebecers wanted to remain within Canada, but not under its present Constitution. Canadians turned to debate the next step in the ongoing constitutional process. One of the most difficult parts of this debate was trying to figure out a process for generating a new constitutional arrangement, since most of the previous approaches appeared discredited.

Any new constitutional arrangement would have to deal with more than merely the aspirations of Quebec. One of the most important additional items on the agenda for constitutional reform was the First Nations, who wanted the constitutional entrenchment of their conception of Aboriginal self-government. Although in many ways this position parallels Quebec's own position with respect to Canada, that province rejects Aboriginal claims to sovereignty within its jurisdiction. This refusal helps explain the insistence of the Quebec government in early 1996 that "Quebec is indivisible." The Constitution Act of 1982, while entrenching the existing Aboriginal and treaty rights of the First Nations, had not really come to terms with Aboriginal self-government, chiefly because the First Nations and Ottawa were so far apart on the subject, as was shown in the ensuing few years by three unproductive constitutional meetings of first ministers and Native leaders, which had been mandated in the new Constitution Act. The Aboriginal peoples have insisted that their governments should be based on inherent jurisdiction as a historic right. For many Aboriginals this involves sovereign jurisdiction and the independent right to make laws and institutions for their people and their territory, since these rights were not surrendered with treaties. The militants object to the concept of Aboriginal self-government as an equivalent of municipal government, delegated to the First Nations by those jurisdictions (Ottawa and the provinces) that claim the sovereignty under the Crown and Constitution of Canada. As sovereign governments, First Nations would deal only as equals with Ottawa, which the Native people insist still owes them a heavy debt of financial responsibility. As municipal governments, they would become the agents of the senior governments, with only those powers allowed them by those governments. To recognize the First Nations (more than 500 bands) as sovereign would certainly be more possible in a Constitution that so accepted Quebec. For many Canadians, however, such recognition would not only further balkanize the country but would create independent jurisdictions within Canada that benefited from their Canadian affiliation but held no concurrent responsibilities under it. As the new millennium began, Quebec became more concerned with economic problems than with sovereignty issues, but all observers recognized that separatism could very easily slip back into the spotlight.

The Economy

The Canadian economy had now been running for a long time without correcting itself. In the 1990s some of the traditional indicators were positive for economic growth. Inflation was low, interest rates were low and constantly falling, and the Canadian dollar was lower against other world currencies. The resulting economic growth rate was slow, but constantly upward. Foreign trade continued to be buoyant, although mainly in the resource sector and associated industries. On the other hand, construction starts were stagnant and sales of new cars were lower than had been the case since the early 1980s. The Americans chipped ominously away at the Free Trade Agreement whenever doing so worked to their advantage. The buoyant real estate market of the 1980s was no more, even in the still overheated British Columbia economy. Household debt was up to 89 per cent of disposable income. Most important, official unemployment rates were over 10 per cent nationally, while some of the regional figures were alarming, with rates above the national average east of Ontario and below it from Ontario westward. Official unemployment in Newfoundland in 1994 was 20.4 per cent, and in Quebec 12.2 per cent. These figures, of course, included only the people still looking for work. Many of those previously employed in dead industries like the Atlantic fishery had simply given up, as had quite a few of the young.

Finding a job was not easy. Keeping one was equally difficult. Downsizing continued to be the order of the day. Governments at all levels were attempting to reduce their workforces, and almost every private enterprise was trying (with some success) to make do with less. Even those who still had their jobs lived in constant fear of the next round of rationalization. As for the rationalizers, there was growing evidence that downsizing was no more self-correcting than other economic strategies. According to hopeful economic theory, once business profits went up substantially, excess profits would be reinvested in expansion. This was at least partly the thinking behind the practice of keeping business taxes low in what came to be known as "Reaganomics," after the American President who had campaigned on this view. What often seemed to be happening in the 1990s, however, was that the increasing profits were simply distributed to the shareholders. Nonetheless, governments hesitated to increase the tax rates.

Perhaps as disturbing as the nagging fear of the chop for those who still had jobs was the absence of recognizable new career growth areas for those seeking to prepare themselves for employment. The education counsellors had virtually run out of suggestions for viable careers. There were still plenty of jobs in the part-time, semi-skilled (and low-paid) end of the workforce. "Working at McDonald's" became the catchphrase. "McJobs" became the term encompassing all such employment, which had no attractive future whatsoever

The Collapse of the Cod Fishery

From the first European sightings of the Newfoundland coastal waters, their most impressive feature was the huge number of codfish (*Gadus morhua*) available to be harvested. It would appear that the northern cod fishery was reasonably self-sustaining until the 1950s, when new technology introduced into the fishery began to put strains on the natural resource. The first chief culprit was the international fleet of "factory trawlers" that appeared on the Grand Banks after World War II. The trawlers came from a variety of nations, and not only netted large numbers of fish, but processed them on shipboard before transporting the catch back home to feed a hungry populace. The annual total catch began slowly to decline, and in 1976 the United States and Canada finally responded to the situation by declaring their marine jurisdiction extended to 200 miles offshore and closing their fisheries within this limit to foreign interests. Unfortunately, the Canadian government then proceeded to allow Canadian fishing trawlers, chiefly those of large corporations, to replace the foreign ones. The Canadian vessels employed additional new technology, dragging ever larger nets along the ocean bottom, scooping up anything and everything. The result was the virtual destruction of a fragile ecosystem poorly understood by the Canadian government and its fisheries managers, who too often failed to listen to the local inshore fishers. The government did not close the fishery until 1992, by which time the damage had been done and the possibility of rejuvenation was problematic. By 1995 the amount of cod in existence had declined to only about 1,700 tonnes and whether the fishery could ever recover was in considerable doubt. One of the few bright spots in the picture was that the decline of predatory groundfish meant that other marine species—such as snow crab and northern shrimp—could now flourish, and by 2014 the economic value of these invertebrates was roughly equal to that of the previous cod fishery, although the proceeds were going into different pockets. Many of the displaced cod fishers proved unable to take advantage of the new opportunities, and an entire way of life in Newfoundland was lost along with the codfish. The story of the cod fishery served as a prime example of "the tragedy of the commons" for environmentalists concerned with the over-exploitation of natural resources.

and provided few or no fringe benefits. The younger generation faced with such employment prospects came to label itself Generation X. The post-baby boomers who, through no fault of their own, had arrived at adulthood after all the decent jobs were taken had little to look forward to. Generation X was both hedonistic and bitter, a volatile combination. The creation of new jobs was high on the wish list for most Canadians, but particularly for the young.

One economic growth area continued in household appliances and equipment. What had once been luxury items now became necessities, and new gadgets were being introduced every day. As had been the case for over a century with household equipment, constant reductions in price through technological innovation made mass marketing possible. In 1980 few homes had microwave ovens. By the mid-1990s over 80 per cent of households owned them. By 1994 more than half of Canadian households possessed a gas barbecue, and over 25 per cent of Canadian homes had some kind of air conditioning. Compact-disc players and home computers had exploded from a standing start in the late 1980s, and by 1995 were in over 50 per cent of households. Much of the electronic household gadgetry was assembled abroad, providing jobs only on the retail sales and highly technical service ends. At the same time, there was obviously room for employment in computers. Canadians established some reputation for software development.

Connected to the enormous expansion of the home computer were the growth of e-mail and the use of computer networks for both business and personal communication. By 1996 the Internet—another communications medium in which Canadians had taken the lead, especially in terms of usage—had become so popular and overloaded that it no longer worked very well. Never designed for mass participation, the Internet had grown without any regulation whatsoever, which was part of its attraction and would increasingly become part of its problem. While there was a future in the computer and the microchip, this was a highly technical business that required special skills and special aptitudes. Business publications were full of stories of successful Canadian initiatives involving the glitzy new technologies, but they never explained how this would translate into large-scale employment for average Canadians.

The high-tech industries collapsed into chaos on 11 September 2001, the day a group of terrorists succeeded in orchestrating an air attack on the United States involving four hijacked airliners. This "meltdown" might have occurred differently under other circumstances, but there was plenty of evidence that the technological sector had expanded far too rapidly and with far too little attention being paid to proper management and accounting practices. What was collapsing was a typical overheated boom. Osama bin Laden and his conspirators were allowed to take entirely too much credit for the economic chaos that followed "9/11."

The private enterprise philosophy associated with the growth of schools of management at the universities had, by the 1990s, been operative for nearly 20 years. There was precious little evidence, however, that the economic thinking of the free enterprisers had produced a more satisfactory economy for most Canadians than had Keynesianism. Unemployment remained high nationally and was even higher in certain regions and among certain age groups. Like earlier economic pundits, the private enterprisers insisted that their theories had not yet been given a fair chance, but few

Canadians wanted to take the gamble. As for the free trade agreements made with the Americans, the jury remained undecided, although there was increasing evidence that they were not unqualified successes. The North American Free Trade Agreement (NAFTA), which extended the earlier Free Trade Agreement (FTA) to include Mexico, took effect on 1 January 1994 with very little controversy and even less publicity. Subsequently, a number of well-publicized incidents suggested that there was little in NAFTA to protect Canadian business from American vested interests, if those interests sought to exercise their power. Thus the American softwood lumber industry, in the most highly publicized case, successfully argued that their Canadian counterparts were competing unfairly by pursuing policies that were perfectly acceptable under NAFTA. The result was the introduction of heavy surcharges on imports of Canadian lumber into the United States. As for Mexico, it became a haven for automobile manufacturers seeking to escape the high wages paid in Ontario. By the beginning of the new century, moreover, even the financial press in Canada—always sympathetic to free trade—began to run stories about the hollowing out of Canadian business. This process, by which management and executive power is taken out of the country and placed at head office, usually in the United States, had long been one of the major concerns of the opponents of free trade.

Globalization

Scholarly studies in the 1970s and 1980s had often called into question the market view of industrial development, but regional economic integration gave a new boost to convergence theories. These theories predicted the gradual spread across the globe of similar patterns of economic life once constraints were removed. While the academic economists were careful to confine their theories to the economic realm, the business press and other popularizers quickly applied such thinking to a variety of forces, such as new communications technologies and the mobility of capital, and identified something that came to be labelled "globalization." The term first appeared sometime in the late 1980s. Kenichi

Omae's *The Borderless World: Power and Strategy in the Interlinked Economy* (1990) was probably the key text. The globalizers argued that international flows of capital, services, goods, and people, in a world of instant communications and liberal trade policies, were not being controlled—indeed, could not be controlled—by traditional national agencies.

The proposed Multilateral Agreement on Investment (MAI) became the epitome of the new order in which a rampant international capitalism would sweep everything before it. This global treaty on investment aligned the capital-exporting nations of the industrial West against the less developed nations. The Organization for Economic Co-operation and Development (OECD), which consisted of the 29 most highly developed nations of the world (including Canada), set a target date of 1997 for the introduction of the new world order. The MAI generated an enormous amount of opposition, not just from the developing countries, but from the developed nations as well. Much of the consciousness-raising and organization behind this opposition was made possible by the Internet, which thus demonstrated that it could be a force of resistance as well as of liberalization. In this case, the Internet served as the principal medium for anti-globalization activists to organize and to publicize an international arrangement that the bankers and politicians had deliberately kept out of the public eye as much as possible. The critics argued that the MAI gave to multinational corporations a series of political powers that had for several centuries been regulated by the nation-state. Under the MAI, international corporations could be treated no differently from domestic ones, and the nation-state could impose no unusual performance requirements upon them. While the introduction of the MAI was quietly abandoned in the face of considerable opposition and criticism, the threat of some form of multilateral agreement by the rich nations of the West remained very much in place. The morphing of the General Agreement on Tariffs and Trade (GATT) in 1995 into the more highly institutionalized and powerful World Trade Organization (WTO) suggested the direction of the threat. Such a spectre fuelled many of the fierce public demonstrations at various economic summit meetings held by the leading industrial nations in the late twentieth and early twenty-first centuries.

Perhaps the most publicized Canadian reaction occurred at the Asia–Pacific Economic Co-operation (APEC) meeting in Vancouver in November 1997. APEC was a meeting of 18 nations proposing a free trade zone in the vast Pacific region of the globe. Demonstrators were alarmed by this example of globalization (one group of University of British Columbia opponents argued, "if you thought NAFTA was scary, wait until you hear about APEC"). But the APEC meetings provoked other concerns as well. Many demonstrators were upset that Canada was hosting several heads of state whose record on human rights was undistinguished, including Jiang Zemin of China and General Suharto of Indonesia. UBC students were unhappy that the meeting was being held on their campus (at the Museum of Anthropology) without their consent. Student demonstrators were doused by the RCMP with pepper spray when they did not move aside quickly enough, resulting in what came to be called "Peppergate." The RCMP insisted that it was only responding to orders from the Canadian government, while Prime Minister Chrétien's response was: "Pepper? I put that on my plate." A formal investigation was held to get to the bottom of the matter. It did not really resolve the question of who was responsible for the pepper spray, although in the process the reputation of the Prime Minister's Office was probably damaged by its failure to fully co-operate in releasing top-secret government files. The Canadian public became increasingly sensitized to the dangers of secrecy and stonewalling.

The MAI and its various offshoots posed a somewhat different problem for Canada than did North American free trade. Both were held by their critics to threaten the Canadian nation-state, but free trade encouraged mainly a North American economic integration, while globalization went much further. A number of pundits saw continental economic integration as leading inevitably to political and social integration (or "convergence," as it came to be called), although most theories dealt with the economic arena. In the late 1990s, Conrad Black's new newspaper, the *National Post*, became a vocal advocate of total North American integration, although the paper softened its stance after being purchased by the Asper family early in the new millennium. Convergence theory is not monolithic. Instead, a number of alternative scenarios have been advanced by various convergence theorists. One scenario emphasizes strong market forces and weakened governments. Another talks about imitation of the best way to operate—the mimicking of "best practices"—as a consequence of institutional competition. A third scenario speaks of convergence through enforced international agreement, as in the European Economic Community or in NAFTA. A minority of theorists would insist that not just external forces but concomitant internal ones are necessary to bring about convergence. And not all economists agree that convergence is necessarily the way of the future. Most of those who disagree emphasize the continued ability of the nation-state to resist and adjust to new pressures. In the jargon of the economist, the "border effect" continues to be a silent but powerful retardant to convergence. Moreover, there is now an explicit backlash within many nations to integration and globalization, and this is producing new political alliances and new ways of preserving the power of the nation-state.

A related economic problem for Canada involved the extent to which the nation could afford to be pressured by the international community on environmental concerns. In 1997 an international summit meeting at Kyoto, Japan, had agreed on a world protocol

Prime Minister Jean Chrétien and Environment Minister David Anderson shake hands following the House of Commons vote on ratification of the Kyoto Accord, 10 December 2002. The Canadian Press/Tom Hanson.

BACKGROUNDER

The Internet

Trailing slightly behind the home computer, but obviously connected to it, was the Internet, involving the growth of e-mail and the use of information stored on the Web for both business and personal communication. Canada played an important role in the Internet's development and in its growing popularity. The Internet had its origins in the need of the American military to communicate quickly and easily with its forces around the world. Research began on such a system in 1967, and e-mail was developed in 1971. The term "Internet" was first used in 1982, and the same year Canadian speculative science fiction author William Gibson coined the term "cyberspace," which he popularized in his 1984 novel, *Neuromancer*. In 1984, as well, the domain name system was first introduced. In 1985 Canadian universities were given access to a network—NETWORTH—on which digital computer messages could be transmitted. This was the outgrowth of NETNORTH, a network of eight universities headed by the University of Waterloo in 1983. The University of Waterloo would take the lead in computer/Internet development over the next decades, which helps to explain why Waterloo became the centre of the Canadian cyberspace industry. The year 1985 also saw the appearance of the first American commercial online system, which four years later as Quantum Computer Services, introduced the famous online greeting, "You've Got Mail." The World Wide Web was formed in 1989 to link thousands of network sites, and about the same time a computer language called HTTP was developed to create websites. The first search engine was developed at McGill University in 1990. Search engines made possible the use of the Internet as a retriever of information. Innovation escalated after 1990. In 1991 Quantum became America Online (AOL), and in 1992 AOL went public on NASDAQ. AOL was joined by other commercial services such as CompuServe, which pioneered in 1994 by offering new interface software linking up with Microsoft Windows operating systems. In December 1994 Microsoft offered a web browser for Windows 95. Mailings and searches from 1995 were done by connecting a computer with a telephone line via a modem. This arrangement was slow, cumbersome,

and expensive. Both downloading and uploading took much time and could tie up a telephone line for hours. Broadband appeared early in the new millennium, enabling users to split phone lines between Internet and telephone, simplifying the connections.

As Clifford Stoll had demonstrated in 1989 in his *The Cuckoo's Egg: Tracking a Spy through the Maze of Computer Espionage*, the Internet had developed without any regulation whatsoever, and users were slow to catch on to the dangers of hacking, an activity that was as old as the computer itself. The Internet was also slow to appreciate the danger of malware and the introduction of computer viruses, which could be easily introduced into computers via the Internet connection. A series of well-publicized virus attacks in the late 1990s virtually laid the system low, and both the potential for spying and for malicious hacking led, at the end of the century, to a new focus on security. By 2000 Canadians were among the most ardent users in the world of e-mail and the Internet, which in the next millennium would completely revolutionize the way in which books and music were distributed and enjoyed.

for environmental improvement, most notably through reducing the emission of hydrocarbon gases that many scientists blamed for the so-called "greenhouse effect" and other pollution. The extent of the greenhouse effect was still being debated, in the public press if not by the scientific community. But the larger question involved the economic costs of complying with Kyoto. The lead in the creation of the Kyoto Accord had been taken by the nations of industrialized Europe, which for a variety of reasons had managed to go much further in reducing industrial pollution than had North America. Europe was supported by a developing world community that either had little polluting industry or did not intend to observe the protocol. The Americans bowed out of the Kyoto Accord, calling it too expensive to implement. As one of the few nations in the world seriously affected, Canada continued to debate the question, although in

typically Canadian fashion Kyoto got tied up in constitutional hassles between the federal and provincial governments over jurisdiction.

External Affairs

The demise of Communism did not occur without difficulty. In many of the Iron Curtain nations, it turned out that the Communist regime had been the only force supporting unity and stability, whatever the price. Movements of national liberation tore apart the USSR itself, as well as other ethnically complex constructions, such as Yugoslavia. Civil war among Serbs, Croats, and Muslims in Bosnia became an international concern. The transition to a capitalistic economy was so painful that many citizens of the old Soviet bloc began voting in free elections for their former Communist masters. By the mid-1990s it was clear that the Cold War was indeed dead. What would replace it as a principal of international dynamics was not so clear.

The elimination of Communist repression did not necessarily save the world for democracy. As if to demonstrate the fragility of international peace, in the summer of 1990 the Iraqi army invaded Kuwait, one of the small independent oil-rich principalities on the Persian Gulf. The world witnessed the unusual spectacle of American–Russian co-operation at the United Nations, and elsewhere, in opposition to Saddam Hussein's move. With Russian approval, President George H.W. Bush sent American forces to the Persian Gulf. Canada contributed three ancient destroyers to the international force. For the first time, Canada's military involvement abroad did not feature the army but regular naval and air force units. Paradoxically, despite earlier military unification, the Canadian services did not act jointly as a national force in this conflict, at least partly because the forces of other nations (especially the United States) were still organized more conventionally. The Canadians did co-operate very successfully with their allies. The Canadian navy considered its work in the Gulf War highly successful, particularly given the equipment with which it had to operate. The Canadian government got just what it wanted: an active, limited, and relatively inexpensive (about $1 billion) operation within a coalition in which Canadians served apart from direct American control.

In some ways the collapse of the Cold War temporarily opened up new ways for Canadians to offer their services to the world. Canadian peacekeepers were in constant demand around the world, ultimately serving in such trouble spots as Somalia and Bosnia with a singular lack of effectiveness. Canada also flirted with the dangers of diplomatic isolation in 1995, as its attempts to enforce limits on offshore fishing led to an open confrontation with the Spaniards. Fortunately, there was enough support for the Canadian position behind the scenes to discourage Spanish militancy. The crisis was resolved peacefully.

Canadian involvement in the United Nations' Balkan peacekeeping was suggested by the Mulroney government as early as 1990 and reiterated in 1991, but the Mulroney initiative was not popular with Canada's

allies. The British foreign secretary told Mulroney, "Trouble with you Canadians is you think there is a solution to every problem" (quoted in Gammer, 2001: 81). Nevertheless, Canada persisted in driving the United Nations and NATO forward on the Balkan peacekeeping front, and it could hardly avoid contributing to a peacekeeping force for Bosnia in 1993 despite recognition of the difficulties of the situation. To a considerable extent, Canadian commanders on the scene were, if anything, more aggressive than the government had intended, and the military did its best to adapt to Canada's doctrines of interventionism in the early 1990s.

Lack of success, lack of funding, and some nasty scandals reduced the credibility of Canada's military to the point that by 1997 the nation could fully anticipate that Canada's armed forces would no longer be

Peacekeeping in Cambodia: Corporal Corena Letandre of the Canadian Forces' 2 Service Battalion comforts a hospitalized child. © *All rights reserved. Reproduced with the permission of DND/CAF, 2015.*

serving anywhere in the world but at home. The Somalia Commission of Inquiry concluded:

> Many of the leaders called before us to discuss their roles in the various phases of the deployment refused to acknowledge error. When pressed, they blamed their subordinates who, in turn, cast responsibility upon those below them. They assumed this posture reluctantly—but there is no honour to be found here—only after their initial claims, that the root of many of the most serious problems resided with "a few bad apples," proved hollow.

We can only hope that Somalia represents the nadir of the fortunes of the Canadian Forces. There seems to be little room to slide lower. One thing is certain, however: left uncorrected, the problems that surfaced in the desert in Somalia and in the boardrooms at National Defence Headquarters will continue to spawn military ignominy. The victim will be Canada and its international reputation.

A total withdrawal from Europe had been delayed by peacekeeping in Yugoslavia, but in early 1996 Canada announced it was acting unilaterally to bring its forces

The Somalia Affair

In 1997 a Commission of Inquiry made its final report on the behaviour of Canadian troops in Somalia in 1993. The following extract explains the background to the inquiry.

In the spring, summer, and fall of 1992, the United Nations, concerned about the breakdown of national government in Somalia and the spectre of famine there, sought international help to restore some semblance of law and order in Somalia and feed its starving citizens. Canada, among other nations, was asked to help. After months of planning and training, and after a change in the nature of the United Nations mission from a peacekeeping mission to a peace enforcement mission, Canadian Forces personnel, as part of a coalition of forces led by the United States, were deployed for service to Somalia, mainly in December 1992. Many of the Canadian personnel involved in the deployment belonged to the Canadian Airborne Regiment Battle Group (CARBG), itself made up largely of soldiers from the Canadian Airborne Regiment (a paratroop battalion), with other army personnel added to it, including A Squadron, an armoured car squadron from

the Royal Canadian Dragoons, a mortar platoon from 1st Battalion, the Royal Canadian Regiment, and an engineer squadron from 2 Combat Engineer Regiment.

On the night of March 16–17, 1993, near the city of Belet Huen, Somalia, soldiers of the Canadian Airborne Regiment beat to death a bound 16-year-old Somali youth, Shidane Arone. Canadians were shocked, and they began to ask hard questions. How could Canadian soldiers beat to death a young man held in their custody? Was the Canadian Airborne Regiment suitable or operationally ready to go to Somalia? Was racism a factor in improper conduct within the Regiment? Before long, Canadian media began to publicize accounts of other incidents involving questionable conduct by Canadian soldiers in Somalia. Major Barry Armstrong, surgeon to the Canadian Airborne Regiment, acting in fulfilment of his military duties, alleged that an earlier incident on March 4, 1993, where an intruder was shot dead and

Continued...

another was wounded by Canadian Airborne soldiers, appeared to have been an execution-style killing. And so, other questions arose: Were incidents in Somalia covered up, and, if so, how far up the chain of command did the cover-up extend? Did the Canadian Forces and the Department of National Defence respond appropriately to the allegations of cover-up? And perhaps most problematic of all, were the mistreatment of Shidane Arone and other incidents of misconduct caused by a few "bad apples," or were they symptomatic of deeper institutional problems in the Canadian military at the time—problems relating to command and control, accountability, leadership, or training? If so, did these problems still exist?

The Canadian Forces responded in many ways to the death of Shidane Arone and other incidents that occurred in Somalia. Several courts martial, arising mostly though not exclusively from misconduct relating to the death of Shidane Arone, were launched and concluded. . . .

But perhaps more important, the Canadian Forces recognized the need for additional measures to respond to public concern about what happened in Somalia. Accordingly, the Chief of the Defence Staff of the Canadian Forces appointed an internal board of inquiry under section 45 of the National Defence Act to look into issues arising from the Somalia operation. The board conducted the first phase of its work from April to July 1993. The board's final report made several recommendations for change. However, its terms of reference were restricted in two ways. First, to avoid challenges to its jurisdiction under the Canadian Charter of Rights and Freedoms, it was essentially precluded from looking into incidents that could give rise to court martial proceedings. . . . Second, its focus was on issues such as leadership and discipline relating to the CARBG, which included the antecedents of the CARBG in Canada and higher headquarters in Somalia before and during its deployment there. Thus, it had no authority to look into the actions or omissions of persons at the highest levels of the chain of command within the Canadian Forces. As well, the hearings were not open to the public. It was intended that there would be a second phase of the inquiry to address issues not addressed in its first phase.

Critics argued that an open inquiry was needed to get to the truth of what happened and why. Representatives of the Liberal Party of Canada, the official opposition at the time the board of inquiry was established, argued for an open public inquiry under the National Defence Act. When the Liberals gained power after the 1993 federal election, they continued to express this view. However, as more revelations suggesting possible cover-up and other disclosures were made, the Government eventually decided to establish a public inquiry independent of the military that would have the power to subpoena witnesses not belonging to the military. As a result, on March 20, 1995, this Commission of Inquiry, governed by the federal Inquiries Act, was created. This act sets out the statutory powers and responsibilities of inquiries, generally giving us broad powers to summon and enforce the attendance of witnesses and to require the production of documents.

Source: *Dishonoured Legacy: The Lessons of the Somalia Affair: Report of the Commission of Inquiry into the Deployment of Canadian Forces to Somalia: Executive Summary* (Ottawa: Minister of Public Works and Government Services, 1997), I, 1–3; notes omitted. Reproduced courtesy of the Privy Council Office, with the permission of the Minister of Public Works and Government Services, 2006.

home. Somalia and Bosnia were both public relations disasters that marked an end to a new Canadian willingness to intervene in local disputes. In the former, supposedly highly disciplined Canadian soldiers brutalized the locals. In the latter, Canadian peacekeepers seemed unable to accomplish anything positive and were often held as impotent hostages by the warring factions.

In the end, the Chrétien government chose to return to a more traditional interpretation of peacekeeping, in which Canada served as a neutral arbitrator rather than an interventionist peacekeeper. To a considerable extent the withdrawal to neutral peacekeeping was a product of the failure of the military to be successful, complicated by the military insistence that success required better hardware and increased expenditures. Chrétien cancelled several large orders for new hardware the military commanders deemed necessary to keep the forces competitive. Public exposure of Canadian soldiers' racism and brutality towards one another did little for either image or morale. One battalion of paratroopers, the Canadian Airborne, was totally disbanded. Canadian troops did yeoman duty in two domestic emergencies, a major flood in Manitoba in May 1997 and a devastating ice storm in Quebec in January 1998. Both actions served to refurbish the military's public image and self-confidence.

At the same time, for a few brief years in the late 1990s, many Canadians were heartened by the "soft power" initiatives of Lloyd Axworthy (b. 1939), the Foreign Affairs Minister. Axworthy was instrumental in working with a coalition of international non-governmental organizations to achieve in 1997 the Ottawa Convention to Ban Landmines, which won for the NGO coalition the Nobel Peace Prize. Then, in 1998, he worked with the Norwegians to create the bilateral Lysøen Declaration to promote a human security agenda and, that same year, was a leader in establishing the International Criminal Court. His retirement from politics in 2000 to accept an academic position and the 9/11 attacks on the United States less than a year later (not to mention the American refusal to sign on to the Ottawa Convention or the International Criminal Court) have meant that these important initiatives are perhaps less widely recognized than they might be.

In a related manner, Canadian General Roméo Dallaire (b. 1946) brought attention to the need (and failure) of the international community to respond to the impact of conflict on civilian populations. In late 1993 Dallaire became force commander of UNAMIR, the United Nations military mission in Rwanda established in October 1993 during the Rwandan Civil War. The UN mission included a handful of Canadian peacekeepers along with others from Belgium, Bangladesh, and several African countries. Not long after he took command, Dallaire discovered the likelihood that a massacre of moderate Hutus and Tutsis in Rwanda was in the works, but he was unable to prevent the ensuing genocide of an estimated one million people because the UN and individual countries were slow to respond. His personal mental anguish upon returning to Canada and the publication in 2004 of *Shake Hands with the Devil: The Failure of Humanity in Rwanda*, his account of his experiences, led to a greater public awareness of post-traumatic stress disorder and of the shortcomings of the peacekeeping paradigm.

The disarray of the military and the withdrawal from an active peacekeeping role in Africa seemed symptomatic of Canada's international posture. The idealism of earlier days was now replaced by incompetence and impotence. Public opinion polls by the end of the century routinely reported that Canadians no longer expected to be defended from foreign aggression by their own military.

Canadian Society

The Immigrants

Straddling the gap between international concerns and domestic policy was immigration, one of the "hot button" issues of the decade. The fundamental questions were the same as always. How many immigrants should Canada admit, particularly given the shortage of employment opportunities for members of Generation X and the fragility of the nation's urban infrastructure? By the 1990s, many of the immigrants to Canada came from the Third World.

The new Canadian immigrants came from six vastly different regions: Africa, the Caribbean, the Middle East, and three regions of Asia—South Asia, Southeast Asia, and East Asia, especially China (see Table 12.1). Most were members of visible minorities. A substantial number were Muslims. The 1991 census indicated 253,265 Muslims. Ten years later the census counted 579,740 adherents of Islam. Many of the new arrivals were political refugees from highly repressive regimes, and their situation in Canada was dominated by that previous experience. There were bad memories, and guilt about loved ones left behind. Many newcomers to Canada suffered from depression and required extensive psychological assistance to manage from day to day. Those who became caught in the refugee backlog of the 1980s—which meant they were unable legally to work until their status had been formally determined—were obviously often seriously disadvantaged. The Canadian government in July 1994 finally made it possible for failed refugees to become legitimate permanent residents. The visible minorities from the Third World settled almost exclusively in the large cities of Ontario and Quebec, as well as in Vancouver. They were also most likely to be the targets of racial hostility, both from the general population and from law enforcement agencies. Most immigrants were not refugees, but those who were often experienced poor service from public assistance programs. As usual, the newcomers clustered in poorer urban sections, where they often became associated in the public mind with the problem of ethnic gangs.

Multiculturalism contributed to the positive reception of the immigrants, although many commentators complained that Canada failed to state adequate limits

TABLE 12.1 Top 10 Source Countries of Immigrants to Canada, 1991–2001

China, People's Republic	197,355
India	158,170
Philippines	122,075
Yugoslavia	67,750
Sri Lanka	67,585
Pakistan	57,940
Taiwan	53,750
US	51,440
Iran	47,075
Poland	43,370
Total top 10 countries	859,450 (46.9%)
All other countries	922,300 (53.1%)

Contemporary Views

Practising Islam in Toronto and Edmonton

We are Muslims, we believe in the Islamic religion, and we practised it in our country. People from all over the world, every continent, every country maybe, come to Canada, so all the religions are here. We go to mosque on Fridays instead of Sunday like the Christians. On Saturday and Sunday, there are certain religious classes, but sometimes it is difficult to get transportation. The nearest mosque is on Dundas [Street, in Toronto]. It's too far away, so sometimes it is difficult to get there. I'm Muslim, but I'm not a very religious person. We have our own clothes and our own culture. We like and are very proud to wear our traditional dresses in the summertime. Whether you are very religious or not, winter is your master because you have to wear what the other people wear. But in the summertime, we are very comfortable wearing our dresses, our style. If you are married, you have to cover your hair. That's for religious purposes. We have different sheekh (religious leaders). Those are in the top ranks of the religion. In some circles, if you are a woman, whether you are married or not, you have to cover your body except for maybe your eyes, your face. Our tradition is the Somali tradition. We cover our hair and our body. We are all Muslim, but some wear short dresses the way that they like. They pray five times a day, but they wear whatever they like, and others have some restrictions, but it depends, just like Catholicism.

We pray five times a day. Sometimes we pray as a family, but it is not compulsory to do it together. Amina prays on her own and the others do so as well, but on the weekend, if we are all together, we pray together in the morning (Subah), at noon (Duhur), evening (Asar), [night (Maghrib)] and the final prayers (Isha). That's five prayers. We pray before sunrise, after two o'clock, at six, at nine, and at ten we pray the last one before we go to bed. If it is not possible for them to pray during the day, when they come home, they have a late prayer.

Source: Elizabeth McLuhan, ed., *Safe Haven: The Refugee Experience of Five Families* (Toronto: Multicultural History Society of Ontario, 1995), 192–4.

One of the Five Pillars of Islam that we used to always follow before we came to Canada was to pray five times daily and to attend the mosque on Fridays. Generally speaking, the places from which we came and their style of life was organized in such a way that neither of these posed any real difficulties. What are we to do here, when the work day is so closely regulated by the clock? Some people bring prayer rugs to work and then use their breaks and part of their lunch time for their prayers. Others have had to give up some of their daily prayers. Almost no one has been able to get time off from work on Fridays, so working people generally attend mosque very early in the morning or after work. Ramadan also poses some difficulties, but of a different kind. During the month of Ramadan [the ninth month of the Islamic year] we are supposed to refrain from all food and drink from dawn to dusk. Again, where we come from the days and nights are about equal, so that with practice this fast goes smoothly. But try it in Edmonton, where the late summer days are almost eighteen hours long!

Source: Norman Buchignani and Doreen M. Indra, with Ram Srivastava, *Continuous Journey: A Social History of South Asians in Canada* (Toronto: McClelland & Stewart, 1985), 188–9. Reprinted by permission of the author.

on what the larger society would accept, encouraging the newcomers to believe that they could continue traditions that were not generally approved in their new home while carrying on battles inherited from the old country. Further complicating immigrant reception in Canada was what became known as "deskilling." According to one study, "the landed immigrant cohort of 2000 was dominated by one single occupational group: professional occupations in natural and applied sciences" (Couton, 2002). Canadian employers and professional bodies (usually governed under provincial jurisdiction) have long insisted that their employees and members have Canadian work experience and have looked with suspicion on foreign credentials, which are held to be non-transferable because of the problem of guaranteeing quality. This problem would be recognized after 2000 and addressed by several governments.

The Aged

While all symptoms of social morbidity continued their alarming progress, perhaps the most disturbing trends occurred at the opposite ends of the life cycle, particularly among the aging. The first of the baby boomers were coming up to (early) retirement, soon to be followed by the deluge. That the system was really not ready for this event became increasingly clear. In 1995 the Canadian Institute of Actuaries (CIA) reported that in 1992 retired Canadians (numbering 19 per cent of the working-age population) had paid $9 billion in taxes and received $54.4 billion in public funds in a variety of forms, including medical treatment. By 2030 the percentage of retired Canadians would be up to 39 per cent of those eligible to work. The payout at 1992 rates would be well beyond the capacity of the system to absorb. The present system worked only because the demand upon it had not yet grown sufficiently. The CIA concluded that the present system of social insurance payments was not "sustainable in [its] current form. Contributions will rise. Benefits will be cut; retirement ages deferred; universality curtailed." Surveys suggested that many Canadians had begun to appreciate the difficulties, although most were still confused and few had any solutions. According to one survey, most Canadians feared that the Canada Pension Plan would be unable to look after their retirement, but fewer than 15 per cent had more than $10,000 put away somewhere apart from their CPP pensions. The age at which most Canadians still expected to retire was 59, although the experts and the politicians were now suggesting that such an age was simply a pipe dream for most people.

Retirement pensions were only part of the problem. The other major concern was health care, the cost of which continued to spiral upward despite desperate efforts by provincial governments to bring it under control through cost-cutting and privatization. Per capita health-care expenditure (in constant 1986 dollars) had progressively and annually increased from $1,257.25 in 1975 to $1,896.27 in 1993. The proportion of gross domestic product devoted to health care had gone up from 7.1 per cent in 1975 to 10.1 per cent in 1993. Although these Canadian figures were not as alarming as the corresponding American ones—the proportion of GDP given to health care in the US had increased from 8.4 per cent in 1975 to 14.4 per cent in 1993—they pointed to a financial crisis if they were not capped somehow. Much of the increasing cost involved care for the elderly, and life expectancy continued to advance. The baby boom and increased life expectancy together produced the demographic prospect of ever larger numbers of elderly people making increasing demands on the health-care system.

While provincial governments closed hospitals and reduced the numbers of beds available within those remaining, Canadians began to debate hard questions, such as the extent to which the terminally ill should be offered the expensive treatment that medical science now had at its disposal. Even if the elderly were not given expensive treatment, their increasing numbers produced a housing problem. Only one out of every four Canadians expected to have to look after his or her parents in old age, which was far too low an estimate of future realities. But even if all Canadians took in their still functioning elderly, the numbers of those requiring extensive care beyond the home were bound to increase enormously. Dealing with seniors was clearly the most important problem facing the social insurance system, particularly given the national sense that deficit financing was already too high. One could only sympathize with the younger generation, unable to establish themselves in careers but still being asked to finance the post-retirement years of their elders. According to one study by the Research for Public Policy group, younger Canadians would have to pay increasingly more in taxes than they would ever receive in social benefits to maintain the present structure, which was not only "unsustainable" but "immoral." But this was not the only morality question surrounding health care. Much of the cost of the health-care system continued to be absorbed in looking after seniors in their last months of life. Few Canadians wished to do less, whatever the cost. Despite all the rhetoric, health care was still more of an ideological issue than a practical one for most Canadians. While some might want the opportunity to jump queues to get their needs looked after more quickly, not many Canadians really sought to cut into the basic principle of universal health care available to all. For many, access to free health care had become one of the major factors of the Canadian identity. According to one oft-quoted comedian, a Canadian was an unarmed American with free and universal health-care coverage.

Redress for Historic Abuse

Early in 1990, thousands of Canadians received from the Minister of State for Multiculturalism and Citizenship a letter enclosing a substantial cheque and an "acknowledgement signed by the Prime Minister." The recipients were Japanese Canadians who had been uprooted from their homes in 1942 by the Canadian government. The cheque was for "redress" (or compensation, as it was usually called) and the document from the Prime Minister acknowledged that "the treatment of Japanese Canadians during and after World War II was unjust and violated principles of human rights as they are understood today." Japanese Canadians had first organized to seek redress in 1977, at the time of the centennial of the first arrival of Japanese in Canada. The government of Pierre Trudeau had refused to consider action on this issue, but the Progressive Conservative opposition was more sympathetic. After Brian Mulroney's Tories swept to power in 1984, the Japanese renewed their efforts, which led finally on 22 September 1988 to an agreement between the National Association of Japanese Canadians and the Canadian government (Miki and Kobayashi, 1991). This agreement symbolized the changed attitudes towards both ethnicity and redress at the end of the twentieth century. The government's action with respect to the Japanese encouraged a variety of other groups to apply for redress, including the Ukrainian aliens interned by Canada during the Great War and the Acadians deported from Nova Scotia in the 1750s.

When the unsinkable ship the *Titanic* went down in the Atlantic Ocean in 1912, it took with it over 100 Canadian victims. The literature on the *Titanic* demonstrates quite clearly that the tragedy could have been prevented, and that responsibility for the disaster was systemic and widely distributed. But what is perhaps often forgotten is that most of the survivors and the families of the victims never seriously considered demanding a public inquiry or government compensation. Nor did they engage in class-action litigation in the courts to the same end. Disasters in Canada were traditionally regarded as acts of God. The federal government did supply compensation for victims of the Halifax Explosion of 1917, but that was because the disaster was regarded as a war matter. When the notion of public assistance for disaster losses began to take hold in Canada after World War II, compensation was not initially regarded as a matter of right or of reparation. Rather, it was one of

relief and generosity, which meant that it was not really compensation at all. Victims of the Manitoba Flood of 1950 received assistance from the federal and provincial governments, as well as from a privately raised relief fund. We do not understand just how disaster relief gradually became translated into a right of compensation, but by the 1990s that concept was clearly in place.

Part of the shift was doubtless associated with the rise of insurance to cover various sorts of damage, including malpractice and accidental injury to property and person, and the increasing insistence on dealing with such matters in the courts. Seeking damages for injury through the courts is, of course, something that has been with us as long as there have been civil courts. The practice was greatly escalated in the United States

David Suzuki (b. 1936), left foreground, marches at the Redress Rally on Parliament Hill on 14 April 1988. Suzuki, as a child, was uprooted with his family from their Vancouver home and sent to an internment camp during World War II. He became a Canadian academic scientist and a widely respected CBC program host and leading environmental advocate. The government signed a redress agreement on 22 September 1988, officially offering an apology to Japanese Canadians for their treatment during the war. Reprinted with permission from Gordon King Photography.

after World War II, with juries awarding ever larger damage amounts, often exceeding the defendant's ability to pay them. In the process, the concept of liability was transformed by the courts. In recent years, simple damage suits have grown into class actions, in which a large, amorphous body of victims engages in litigation. Prime examples of such actions, of course, are the cases that have been introduced against various tobacco companies for illnesses resulting from smoking. We may not understand the way this trend developed, but it is perfectly clear that one of the major social issues in Canada in the last third of the twentieth century was the appearance of the idea that someone must be held responsible for every negative consequence. (A related concept is that every victim is entitled to compensation for his or her injury.) In the context of Canada's Aboriginal peoples this clearly was the outstanding social issue in Canada at the end of the century.

Aboriginal Peoples

In 1996 there were some 554,000 status Indians in Canada. Two-thirds of them lived on about 2,600 reserves in over 600 registered bands, and the remainder resided

Document

Report of the Aboriginal Justice Inquiry of Manitoba, 1991

Manitoba's Aboriginal Justice Inquiry was appointed in 1988 and reported in 1991. It was composed of Manitoba Justices Alvin Hamilton and Murray Sinclair. Justice Sinclair later chaired the Truth and Reconciliation Commission (2009–15) that investigated the abuse and consequences of the Indian residential schools in Canada.

Manitoba's justice system is founded on laws written in the English and French languages. It is a complex system whose practitioners must undergo years of training. It has many specialized terms, so that even a person relatively well conversant in English or French likely will not understand the subtleties of the law and legal proceedings. . . .

It is a costly system. By our estimate, taking into account Manitoba's share of federal expenditures on justice, the Manitoba Department of Justice, municipal police forces, conservation officers, the child welfare system, and non-government agencies and expenditures, approximately half a billion dollars are spent each year on justice in Manitoba. With Manitoba's Aboriginal population representing 12 per cent of the total population of the province and more than 50 per cent of the jail population, it is clear an enormous amount of money is being spent dealing with Aboriginal people.

It is for many Manitobans an awe-inspiring and revered system, one which links them to a centuries-old struggle for the right of people to be ruled by laws. To Aboriginal people it appears in a very different light.

> One of the most powerful symbols of European-based cultures is the scales of justice. This portrays the goals and obligations of all who work within the Canadian justice system. It proclaims that each person's right, each point of view, is to be accorded fair and equitable weight. Justice respects, protects, and offers redress to restore that balance of fairness and equity. . . .

our democratic government   gouvernement démocratique

chiefly in larger southern cities such as Winnipeg. In addition, there were 41,000 Inuit. The numbers of non-status Indians and Métis are harder to estimate. The number accepted by the government is 210,000, but the total across Canada at that time was probably at least 500,000. Despite increased levels of media attention, government expenditures, and Aboriginal self-awareness, the realities of Native life—while improving—continue to recall conditions in the poorest underdeveloped countries of the world. In the 1990s, the First Nations for the first time were popularly perceived as an important Canadian political "problem," perhaps the most important and controversial one of the decade. The immediate crisis was not over the demographics of Native life, although particular cases of violence and abuse continued to make newspaper headlines. The problem was really three related issues that came to prominence in the nineties. The first was how to deal with the land rights of the Indigenous peoples. The second was how to deal with Native administration and the Aboriginal insistence on the right to self-government. The third was how to make reparations for earlier mistreatment of Aboriginals, particularly in the residential school system of Canada.

The police forces of Manitoba are the first point of contact with the justice system for most Aboriginal people. The relationship is clearly an uneasy one. We heard many complaints about insensitivity and abuse....

The courts also were accused of insensitivity. In particular, residents of remote Aboriginal communities complained about the circuit court system which administers justice on a periodic, fly-in basis. Many people who spoke to us felt that court personnel did not understand community problems and had no comprehension of cultural differences.

> We didn't make the laws, although we have to live with them. There is no understanding of the cultural differences, the value system of people, and the values of their families, the values of their children, the values of things in life. There's no understanding of that in a lot of the communities by the enforcers, by the law, by the judges that make sentences. The only thing they know is that the person is coming up on the docket and he has to be charged according to the letters or the figures or statistics, whatever they have. That's the only understanding they have.

> Ed Campbell
> The Pas

The related problems of unfamiliar language and unfamiliar concepts of justice pose serious problems to those who come before courts.

> Perhaps, no one has ever thought of this, but how terrifying it must be for the Aboriginal person not to speak the language of the court system. This is like the old educational system, where our children were forced to a school that is totally alienated from them.

> Rebecca Ross
> Cross Lake

Source: *Aboriginal Justice Implementation Commission Report*, vol. 1, ch. 1. http://www.ajic.mb.ca/volume1/chapter1.html; note omitted.

Land Rights

The Aboriginal peoples had long attempted to claim their land rights. Those claims came under three headings. First were the claims resulting from agreements or treaties made with the Crown, whether before Confederation, between 1871 and 1921 (the so-called numbered treaties, 1–11), or in modern times. Second were claims based on continuing Aboriginal title (established historically). Finally, there were specific claims, usually involving either improper seizure of land or government failure to pay proper compensation for lands seized legally. In 1969, the Trudeau government established the Indian Claims Commission to deal with land claims, but the slow pace of negotiations soon led the Aboriginal peoples to turn to the courts for redress. A series of landmark court decisions, many of them in the Supreme Court of Canada, gradually produced new policies from the federal and provincial governments. Over the ensuing years, a number of historic agreements would be reached with Aboriginal peoples, although the settlement of claims was a slow, labyrinthian process. Literally hundreds of land claims have been raised, and not all have been dealt with, either through negotiations or through the courts. By and large, the courts have not so much settled land claims as maintained the Aboriginal right to hold them and to negotiate them with the government.

In 1973, the Supreme Court of Canada ruled in the *Calder* case that the Nisga'a of British Columbia had Aboriginal title to their land that had never been extinguished. Mr Justice Wilfred Judson concluded: "The fact is that when the settlers came the Indians were there, organized in societies and occupying the land as their forefathers had done for centuries. This is what Indian title means. What they are asserting in this action is that they had a right to continue to live on their lands as their forefathers had lived and that this right has never been lawfully extinguished." Mr Justice Emmett Hall added, "What emerges from the . . . evidence is that the Nishgas in fact are and were from time immemorial a distinctive cultural entity with concepts of ownership indigenous to their culture and capable of articulation under the common law." In August 1973, Minister of Indian Affairs Jean Chrétien stated publicly that the federal government was committed to settling Aboriginal land claims.

A Supreme Court ruling in 1973 that the Quebec government could not continue with its James Bay hydroelectric project until it had resolved Aboriginal claims led to the historic James Bay and Northern Quebec Agreement in 1975 between the province and the James Bay Cree and Inuit, which is generally considered to be the first modern land claim agreement. It provided for $225 million in financial compensation, as well as establishing landownership and usage in the region of northern Quebec. Aboriginal rights and treaty rights were recognized in the 1982 Constitution Act, although individual cases would have to be decided by the courts. In 1984, in a final ruling in *Guerin v. The Queen* (a case brought in 1975 by the Musqueam Indian band in Vancouver), the Supreme Court of Canada recognized that Aboriginal rights in Canada predated Confederation.

In 1984 a suit filed in the Supreme Court of British Columbia by 35 Gitksan and 13 Wet'suwet'en chiefs contested 58,000 square kilometres of land in the province. The case (known as the *Delgamuukw* case) was heard from 1987 to 1990, and a decision was brought down on 8 March 1991. Before this decision, the Supreme Court of Canada had ruled in 1990 in *Sparrow v. The Queen* that section 35 of the Constitution Act protected Aboriginal rights, which it insisted must be dealt with by the courts in a generous manner. In his decision in the *Delgamuukw* case, Chief Justice Allan McEachern of the BC court denied the plaintiffs the right to exclusive landownership and self-government, in large measure because he rejected the oral history on which the claims had been based. As a result of this case, the government of British Columbia and the First Nations agreed to a treaty-making process. In the meantime, however, the plaintiffs in *Delgamuukw* appealed, and were rejected again on their major points in 1993. Another appeal was heard by the Supreme Court of Canada, with a decision handed down on 11 December 1997. The Supreme Court did not rule on title, indicating that the case would be better resolved through negotiations. But it did indicate that oral histories are "a repository of historical knowledge for a culture" (quoted in Dickason with McNab, 2009: 330–1), and that the courts must "come to terms with the oral histories of Aboriginal societies, which for many Aboriginal Nations, are the only record of their past" (Chief Justice Lamer, in *Delgamuukw v. British Columbia*, 3 S.C.R., 1997). On 16 July 1998, the federal and British Columbia governments signed a final agreement with the Nisga'a people, which granted them 1,930 square kilometres of land, self-government, and a large amount of cash; as part of the agreement, the Nisga'a gave up their tax-free status under the Indian Act.

Aboriginal Self-Government

Aboriginal self-government was another long-standing question in Canada (Engelstad and Bird, 1992). The First Nations insisted that the assertion of ultimate sovereignty over the land by the Crown interfered with both Aboriginal land rights and the rights of Aboriginals to govern themselves according to their own laws in their traditional territories. Considerable historical evidence exists to indicate that historically the Crown did not usually attempt to assert its direct political authority over Aboriginal land. Exactly how the government or the courts viewed the legal relationship between the Crown and the First Nations was and is another matter entirely. In most instances, Aboriginal self-government follows the municipal model, with local councils ultimately responsible to the Crown, although several First Nations organizations insist that it must become something more (Royal Commission on Aboriginal Peoples, 1993).

In May 1993, the federal government agreed not only to settle the Inuit land claims to the eastern Arctic, but to establish a new territory (to be called Nunavut) with a new form of Aboriginal self-government—that is, an inclusive public government not run exclusively by or for the Aboriginal people. In fact, however, because the Inuit comprise close to 85 per cent of the Nunavut population, it will remain a self-governing Aboriginal territory for the foreseeable future. This arrangement came after agreement in principle had been reached in 1990. The demand for self-government originated with the Inuit, who had refused to surrender it in the years of discussion over land rights. The new territory, which was hived off from the Northwest Territories, came into existence on 1 April 1999. In Nunavut's legislative assembly, Inuktitut and English are the two official languages. Some observers have argued that Nunavut is not really run by the Inuit, since the federal govern-

ment continues to have a strong presence through its agencies, co-management boards, and financial dealings with the territory. Instead, they say, Nunavut has something more like a highly traditional colonial government (Wall, 2000: 143–67).

Residential Schools

The beginnings of the residential school system long predated Confederation. In the seventeenth century, schools were usually part of the missionary work of the churches, designed both to educate Aboriginal people and to assimilate them into European society. Residential schools came in a variety of forms, although in the nineteenth and early twentieth centuries the most common were the so-called industrial schools. The government of Canada shared in the administration of these schools from at least 1874. By the end of the nineteenth century, the schools had shifted from being church institutions partly funded by the government to being government institutions operated by the churches. Their purpose also shifted, from assimilating students into European society by teaching them a trade to preparing them for life on controlled reserves. From an early date, there was an undercurrent of abuse and intimidation connected with the schools, for their rationale was based on the (often forcible) removal of children from their families in order to "civilize" them and convert them to Christianity. Most of the schools had rules against speaking Native languages and practising Native religious beliefs; these rules were typically enforced through corporal punishment and their effect was to denigrate Aboriginal cultures.

In 1922, Dr Peter Bryan published the story of a national crime: *Being a Record of the Health Conditions of the Indians of Canada from 1904–1921*, which charged that the schools had experienced extremely high mortality rates during the period covered by his book. His allegations were sustained by Dr A. Corvette, although nothing was done at the time about the problem. In 1884, school attendance became compulsory for all status Indians until age 16 and in many places residential schools were the only available option for obeying the law.

In 1969, the government of Canada took over the administration of the schools and they gradually

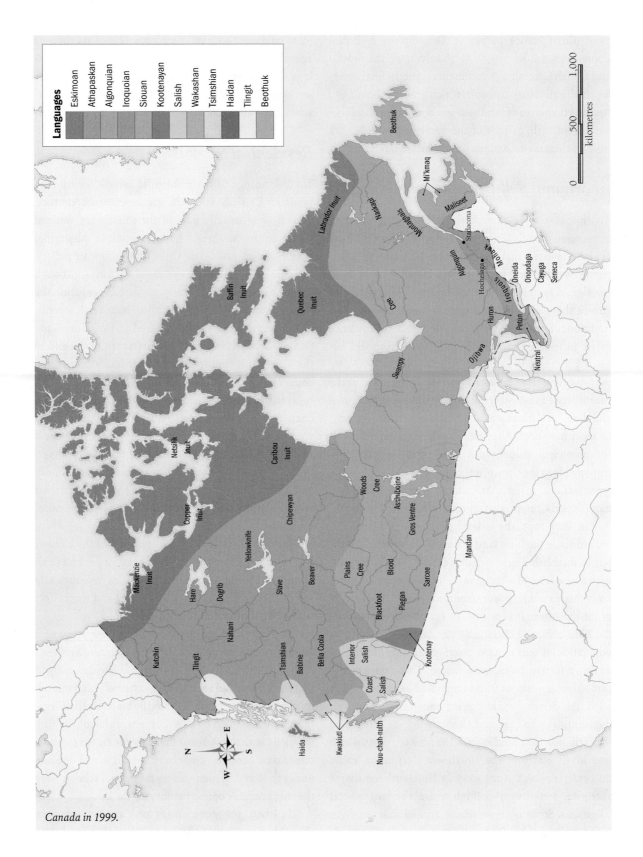

Languages

Eskimoan
Athapaskan
Algonquian
Iroquoian
Siouan
Kootenayan
Salish
Wakashan
Tsimshian
Haidan
Tlingit
Beothuk

1,000
500
0
kilometres

Beothuk

Mi'kmaq

Maliseet

Labrador Inuit

Naskapi

Montagnais

Stadacona

Algonquin

Hochelaga

Mohawk

Iroquois

Oneida

Onondaga

Cayuga

Seneca

Huron

Petun

Neutral

Baffin Inuit

Quebec Inuit

Cree

Swampy

Ojibwa

Netsilik Inuit

Caribou Inuit

Copper Inuit

Woods Cree

Assiniboine

Gros Ventre

Mandan

Mackenzie Inuit

Hare

Dogrib

Yellowknife

Slave

Beaver

Plains Cree

Blood

Piegan

Blackfoot

Sarcee

Chipewyan

Nahani

Kutchin

Tlingit

Tsimshian

Babine

Bella Coola

Interior Salish

Kootenay

Coast Salish

Haida

Kwakiutl

Nuu-chah-nulth

N E S W

Canada in 1999.

Delgamuukw v. British Columbia

Late in 1997 the Supreme Court of Canada handed down a judgment on appeal from the Court of Appeal of British Columbia. The case had been brought to the Supreme Court by Delgamuukw (a.k.a. Earl Muldoe) on behalf of a number of Gitksan and Wet'suwet'en "houses" following the earlier rejection of their Aboriginal claims by the British Columbia court. A portion of the judgment follows, specifically some of the dissenting opinion of Justices La Forest and L'Heureux-Dubé. This excerpt suggests the complexity of the reasoning involved.

The reasons of La Forest and L'Heureux-Dubé JJ. were delivered by

187   LA FOREST J.—I have read the reasons of the Chief Justice, and while I agree with his conclusion, I disagree with various aspects of his reasons and in particular, with the methodology he uses to prove that aboriginal peoples have a general right of occupation of certain lands (often referred to as "aboriginal title").

188   I begin by considering why a new trial is necessary in this case. It is true, as the Chief Justice points out, that the amalgamation of the appellants' individual claims represents a defect in the pleadings and, technically speaking, this prevents us from considering the merits of the case. However, in my view, there is a more substantive problem with the pleadings in this case. Before this Court, the appellants sought a declaration of "aboriginal title" but attempted, in essence, to prove that they had complete control over the territory in question. The appellants effectively argued on appeal, as they did at trial, that by virtue of their social and land tenure systems—consisting of Chief authority, Houses, feasts, crests, and totem poles—they acquired an absolute interest in the claimed territory, including ownership of and jurisdiction over the land. The problem with this approach is that it requires proof of governance and control as opposed to proof of general occupation of the affected land. Only the latter is the sine qua non of "aboriginal title." It follows that what the appellants sought by way of declaration from this Court and what they set out to prove by way of the evidence were two different matters. In light of this substantive defect in the pleadings, a new trial should be ordered to permit a reassessment of the matter on the basis of these reasons.

189   In my view, the foundation of "aboriginal title" was succinctly described by Judson J. in *Calder v. Attorney-General of British Columbia*, [1973] S.C.R. 313, where, at p. 328, he stated: "the fact is that when the settlers came, the Indians were there, organized in societies and occupying the land as their forefathers had done for centuries. This is what Indian title means . . . ." Relying in part on Judson J.'s remarks, Dickson J. (as he then was) wrote in *Guerin v. The Queen*, [1984] 2 S.C.R. 335, at p. 382, that aboriginal peoples have a "legal right to occupy and possess certain lands, the ultimate title to which is in the Crown." As well, in *Canadian Pacific Ltd. v. Paul*, [1988] 2 S.C.R. 654, this Court stated, at p. 678: "The inescapable conclusion from the Court's analysis of Indian title up to this point is that the Indian interest in land is truly *sui generic*. It is more than the right to enjoyment and occupancy although . . . it is difficult to describe what more in traditional property law terminology." More recently, Judson J.'s views were reiterated

Continued...

in *R. v. Van der Peet*, [1996] 2 S.C.R. 507. There Lamer C.J. wrote for the majority, at para. 30, that the doctrine of aboriginal rights (one aspect of which is "aboriginal title") arises from "one simple fact: when Europeans arrived in North America, aboriginal peoples *were already here*, living in communities on the land, and participating in distinctive cultures, as they had done for centuries" (emphasis in original).

190   It follows from these cases that the aboriginal right of possession is derived from the historic occupation and use of ancestral lands by aboriginal peoples. Put another way, "aboriginal title" is based on the continued occupation and use of the land as part of the aboriginal peoples' traditional way of life. This *sui generis* interest is not equated with fee simple ownership; nor can it be described with reference to traditional property law concepts. The best description of "aboriginal title," as set out above, is a broad and general one derived from Judson J.'s pronouncements in *Calder, supra*. Adopting the same approach, Dickson J. wrote in *Guerin, supra*, that the aboriginal right of occupancy is further characterized by two principal features. First, this *sui generic* interest in the land is personal in that it is generally inalienable except to the Crown. Second, in dealing with this interest, the Crown is subject to a fiduciary obligation to treat aboriginal peoples fairly. Dickson J. went on to conclude, at p. 382, that "[a]ny description of Indian title which goes beyond these two features is both unnecessary and potentially misleading." I share his views and am therefore reluctant to define more precisely the "right [of aboriginal peoples] to continue to live on their lands as their forefathers had lived"; see *Calder*, at p. 328.

191   The approach I adopt, in defining the aboriginal right of occupancy, is also a highly contextual one. More specifically, I find it necessary to make a distinction between: (1) the recognition of a general right to occupy and possess ancestral lands; and (2) the recognition of a discrete right to engage in an aboriginal activity in a particular area. I defined the latter in *R. v. Côté*, [1996] 3 S.C.R. 139, at para. 97, as "the traditional use, by a tribe of Indians, that has continued from pre-contact times of a particular area for a particular purpose." The issue in *Côté*, as in *Van der Peet*, was whether the use of a particular fishing spot was really an aspect of the aboriginal peoples' way of life in pre-contact times; see also in the *Van der Peet* trilogy *R. v. Gladstone*, [1996] 2 S.C.R. 723, and *R. v. N.T.C. Smokehouse Ltd.*, [1996] 2 S.C.R. 672. In all those cases, the fishing rights asserted by the aboriginal claimants were not associated with a more general occupancy of the affected land. By contrast, the present case deals with a general claim to occupy and possess vast tracts of territory (58,000 square kilometres). This type of generalized land claim is not merely a bundle of discrete aboriginal rights to engage in specific activities. Rather, it is, as the Chief Justice states, at para. 111, the "right to use land for a variety of activities, not all of which need be aspects of practices, customs and traditions which are integral to the distinctive cultures of aboriginal societies." These land-based activities are, of course, related to the aboriginal society's habits and mode of life.

192   I note, as well, that in defining the nature of "aboriginal title," one should generally not be concerned with statutory provisions and regulations dealing with reserve lands. In *Guerin, supra*, this Court held that the interest of an Indian band in a reserve is derived from, and is of the same nature as, the interest of an aboriginal society in its traditional tribal lands. Accordingly, the Court treated the aboriginal interest in reserve lands as one of occupation and possession while recognizing that the underlying title to those lands was in the Crown. It was not decided in *Guerin, supra*, and it by no means follows, that specific statutory

provisions governing reserve lands should automatically apply to traditional tribal lands. For this reason, I am unable to assume that specific "reserve" provisions of the Indian Act, R.S.C., 1985, c. I-5, and the Indian Oil and Gas Act, R.S.C., 1985, c. I-7, apply to huge tracts of land which are subject to an aboriginal right of occupancy.

Source: *Delgamuukw v. British Columbia*, [1997] 3 S.C.R. 1010.

disappeared, the last closing in 1996. Both churches and government were slow to respond formally to the tide of complaints from the Aboriginal community about the treatment of their children in the residential schools, although stories of physical and sexual abuse were recounted before every commission that investigated the treatment of Aboriginal people in Canada, including the Royal Commission on Aboriginal Peoples (1991–6). The Anglican Church formally apologized to the Aboriginal community for its part in the schools in 1993, and the federal government and the United Church followed in 1998.

In the 1990s, Aboriginal victims of the residential schools began to take the federal government to court over their treatment. The government in its turn insisted on involving the various churches as co-defendants, in the process virtually bankrupting at least the Anglican Church of Canada and a number of its dioceses. By the end of the decade there were more than 8,000 such cases pending. Early in January 1998, the government of Canada announced a program (*Gathering Strength: Canada's Aboriginal Action Plan*) to deal with past injustices, based on reconciliation and concrete action for the future. The government issued a statement of reconciliation acknowledging its part in the residential schools and apologizing for its actions. It offered $350 million to help heal the injuries, but was not able to come to terms with the litigants. In 2007, a $1.9 billion settlement to survivors was agreed upon. Finally, on 11 June 2008, Prime Minister Harper, on behalf of the Canadian government, made a formal apology in the House of Commons, attended by the leaders of five national Aboriginal organizations and by many residential school survivors, for the damage caused by the schools to individuals, families, and communities. A month ear-

lier, in May 2008, an Indian Residential Schools Truth and Reconciliation Commission was established, but this symbolically significant body got off to a rocky start, with its head, an Ontario judge of Aboriginal descent, resigning within months and the other two commissioners stepping down a few months later. A reconstituted Commission began its work in June 2009 under the leadership of Justice Murray Sinclair, the first Aboriginal judge in the Manitoba court system.

Contemporary Abuse

Charges of sexual abuse were not confined to incidents far in Canada's past. In September 1996, the National Hockey League's Sheldon Kennedy (b. 1969) told the Calgary police that between the ages of 14 and 19 he had been sexually abused more than 350 times by his nationally known hockey coach. The coach admitted the offences and was sentenced to prison early in 1997. After the sentencing, Kennedy's interviews with the press created a considerable controversy. One question that was asked repeatedly was whether the whistle should have been blown much earlier on the abusive coach. The main question, however, centred on the extent to which Kennedy's experience was an aberration. Kennedy did his best to help others, particularly in a campaign to raise funds for a home for sexual abuse victims. Despite his well-publicized in-line skate across Canada in 1998, this venture foundered under the burden of bad management.

Other cases of abuse continued to surface in the media, usually involving authority figures who took advantage of their positions. Understandably, such cases always involved a concern that the good reputation of the vast majority of authority figures would be sullied

Material Culture

The VQA Wine Label

VQA wine label. THE CANADIAN PRESS/Kenneth Armstrong.

Until the late twentieth century, Canada's wine industry was underdeveloped and largely overlooked, even by local consumers. While beer and whiskey both became synonymous with Canadian alcohol production during Prohibition and in the years that followed, Canadian wines were considered inferior, mostly due to grapes that were best suited to fortified wines like sherry or port. Following World War II, new wine-making technologies, access to different varieties of grape, and increased consumer interest in wine from non-traditional markets led to the development and success of a number of Canadian wineries.

Most of Canada's wine comes from two regions, the Okanagan Valley in British Columbia and the Niagara Peninsula in Ontario. The Vintners Quality Alliance (VQA) was founded in Ontario in 1988, followed by a BC VQA the following year. Originally intended as an industry group to support and regulate the Niagara region's wine, the Vintners Quality Alliance Act became Ontario provincial law in 1999, and was intended to "establish and maintain an appellation of origin system for Vintners Quality Alliance wine that will allow consumers to identify such wines on the basis of the areas where the grapes

are grown and the methods used in making the wine" (http://www.e-laws.gov.on.ca/html/statutes/english/elaws_statutes_99v03_e.htm). Similar legislation was passed in BC in 2005. Appellations are legally defined geographic regions, in which specific kinds of wine grapes can be grown. Ontario and BC both have four DVAs (Designated Viticultural Areas), which give appellations formal status, while Nova Scotia has one.

As an identifier, the VQA label is distinctive, if simple and understated. In Ontario, the three letters are found in the centre of an octagonal shield, typically in a metallic colour. Emblazoned either on the neck of the bottle, on top of the cork, or on a wrapper covering both the neck and mouth of the bottle, the shield signifies that the wine in the bottle is from Ontario. As well as acting as an advocate for Ontario wines, the VQA includes verification of grape origins and compliance with production and quality standards. All wines are analyzed, tasted, and reviewed before being released as VQA-designated wines, to confirm that they are made with Canadian grapes from the designated appellation. The regulations are strictly enforced, and by earning the VQA label a vineyard is proving not only its affiliation but its Canadian identity. The BC VQA does not have an equivalent shield, and British Columbia wines typically list their affiliation on the labels found on the body of the bottle. The identity provided by VQA labelling is increasing in importance. Although not dominant, Canadian wine has a growing share in a Canadian alcohol market that is drinking more wine now than it ever has. By conferring the shield onto a bottle, the VQA is giving consumers a quick and easy shorthand to identify which wines come from Canada, and a better opportunity to buy Canadian wine. It is also a sign of quality, and assures the consumers that the wine they are buying meets a certain standard in its origins, preparation, and potability.

by the behaviour of a few bad actors. Much evidence suggested that abusive behaviour was not common, but attempts on the part of higher authorities to deny it or sweep it under the carpet were all too frequent. The problem was not confined to Canada. In 2002, the international furor over abusive behaviour by priests of the Roman Catholic Church forced the Vatican for the first time to deal publicly with the issue.

Canadian Culture

Economic restraint in the 1990s hit hard at Canada's cultural industries, almost all of which had relied heavily on public subsidies. Cutbacks were inevitably accompanied by exhortations to financial responsibility and efforts to seek assistance from the private rather than the public sector. Much of the slack was taken up by cost-cutting and private fundraising. Ways of raising money became increasingly imaginative and required far more attention from cultural administrators. Too much of the increased revenue, said some critics, came from state-run gambling and privately run lotteries. Public involvement in fundraising was not necessarily a bad thing, for those in the community who helped raise money developed close ties with the enterprise. Few of the mainline establishment organizations in dance, classical music, and the theatre were actually forced out

Document

The United Church Apology to First Nations Peoples regarding Residential Schools, 26 October 1998

At the conclusion of a four-day meeting of the United Church's General Council Executive, the moderator of the United Church, the Right Reverend Bill Phipps, read the following announcement.

I am here today as Moderator of the United Church of Canada to speak the words that many people have wanted to hear for a very long time. On behalf of the United Church of Canada I apologize for the pain and suffering that our church's involvement in the Indian Residential School system has caused. We are aware of some of the damage that this cruel and ill-conceived system of assimilation has perpetrated on Canada's First Nations people. For this we are truly and most humbly sorry.

To those individuals who were physically, sexually and mentally abused as students of the Indian Residential Schools in which the United Church of Canada was involved, I offer you our most sincere apology. You did nothing wrong. You were and are the victims of evil acts that cannot under any circumstances be justified or excused. We pray that you will hear the sincerity of our words today and that you will witness the living out of this apology in our actions in the future.

We know that many within our church will still not understand why each of us must bear the scar, the blame for this horrendous period in Canadian history. But the truth is we are the bearers of many blessings from our ancestors, and therefore we must also bear their burdens. We must now seek ways of healing ourselves, as well as our relationships with First Nations peoples. This apology is not an end in itself. We are in the midst of a long and painful journey. A journey that began with the United Church's Apology of 1986, to our Statement of Repentance in 1997 and now moving with this apology with regard to Indian Residential Schools. As Moderator of the United Church of Canada I urge each and every member of the church, to reflect on these issues and to join us as we travel this difficult road of repentance, reconciliation and healing.

Source: Excerpt, "Apology to Former Students of United Church Indian Residential Schools, and to Their Families and Communities" (1998) by The Right Reverend Bill Phipps, Moderator of the United Church of Canada. www.united-church.ca/beliefs/policies/1998/a623. Used with permission.

of existence, although everyone complained that there was no room for experimentation and risk-taking in the new financial climate. A few specialized operations bit the dust, and several symphony orchestras were threatened with extinction by militant musicians' unions. Nevertheless, despite the constant cries of crisis, the private sector did seem able to fill most of the gaps in the establishment world of haute culture.

Curiously enough, popular culture seemed more genuinely affected by fiscal restraint than did elite culture. The long decline of the Canadian Broadcasting Corporation continued unabated, and Parliament carried on with annual cuts to the corporation's operating budget. Across the corporation as a whole, regional production was the first to suffer. The CBC's problems were many. Not all services ought to have been in equal trouble, however. The radio services were generally acknowledged to be the best in the world. Radio-Canada's television operation in French consistently outdrew the opposition, producing almost all of the most-watched television programs in Quebec.

The sinkhole was English-language television, which had never been able to carve out a satisfactory niche for itself in an increasingly complex viewing world. The introduction of a variety of new Canadian-based cable networks in 1994 further eroded the CBC's position as a showcase for Canadian programming. Few seemed willing to scrap the television service, however. Another government commission, this one chaired by Pierre Juneau, recommended an increase in Canadian content, an end to commercial advertising, and additional revenue from taxes on the competing services. CBC-TV would no longer have to compete in the world of commercial television but would instead become a Canadian version of America's Public Broadcasting System, appealing to the higher instincts of the viewing public. There was no certainty that these recommendations would be accepted. What was definite was that the corporation would have to make do with less. Huge staff cuts were announced, with more to follow. Like employees of almost every other enterprise in Canada, those at the CBC could only look forward to further downsizing.

The prospects for Canadian content were improved to some extent by the expansion of specialty cable channels on television, although much of the new production came in the form of cooking shows and competitive sports channels. No shortage of Canadian talent existed in the field of comedy. *Saturday Night Live* and *SCTV* were both successful comedy programs of the late 1980s featuring a number of Canadian comedians who subsequently had major careers in the United States. *The Kids in the Hall*—with an all-Canadian cast—flourished in the early 1990s. Most of the humour on these shows was generically North American in content, but the McKenzie brothers from *SCTV*, portrayed by Rick Moranis and Dave Thomas, were an exception: two small-town Canadians—"hosers"—who swilled beer, sported toques, talked incessantly about hockey, and struck a chord in their considerable audience. *The Red Green Show* satirized the same kind of rural Canada. It was particularly subtle in its approach, superficially accepting the masculine values of the hunting-and-fishing set while constantly poking fun at them as well. Curiously enough, Red Green achieved considerable popularity in the United States. Several of the show's catchphrases, including "Keep your stick on the ice," passed into the larger national vocabulary. More directly political—and thus strictly Canadian in its appeal—was the *Royal Canadian Air Farce*, a very popular CBC program aired on television from 1980 to 2007. Its "chicken cannon" regularly blasted a Canadian prominent in the current news.

One of the most powerful examples of Canadian content came in television commercials produced by the Molson Brewing Company, the makers of the beer labelled "Canadian." Molson released a number of ads with subtly anti-American themes, and in March 2000 produced a nationalist "rant" entitled "I Am Canadian," which was the talk of the nation for many months. The rant was very simple. An ordinary Joe stands before a slide display of Canadian backgrounds while he recites his litany, which included such lines as: "I believe in peace keeping, not policing, diversity, not assimilation, and that the beaver is a truly proud and noble animal." According to one account, high school students chanted the rant spontaneously in the corridors of their schools (*Calgary Herald*, 30 Apr. 2000). Many commentators wondered why it was a beer company and not the government that was involved in promoting Canadian pride. Characteristically, the Americans did not seem to notice the commercial at all.

Royal Canadian Air Farce *cast members Luba Goy, Don Ferguson, John Morgan, and Roger Abbott with politician Preston Manning (seated left). Air Farce Productions Inc.*

It was not clear whether the problems of professional sports in Canada were caused by budgetary restraint in the public sector, although it *was* clear that sports teams in Canada could no longer be sustained by massive infusions of indirect aid from the public purse, often in the form of arena facilities. This changing attitude combined with other factors to cause a number of disasters. One was an international market in player salaries with which Canadian teams could not successfully compete. The Canadian Football League, faced with escalating costs and declining attendance in the later 1980s and early 1990s, responded aggressively to its problems by expanding directly into the United States. This strategy proved absolutely disastrous. The new American franchises all folded after a season or two, leaving behind nothing but confusion and a trail

of debt. The CFL regrouped and actually achieved some success as an acknowledged minor league protected by the National Football League. As for hockey, American integration finally caught up with it. The Quebec Nordiques left Canada for Colorado in 1995 and the Winnipeg Jets announced their departure for Phoenix, Arizona, early in 1996. Many experts in the 1990s calculated that the Edmonton Oilers, Calgary Flames, and Ottawa Senators could not be far behind, although all three teams continued to hang on and even prosper in the new century. The National Hockey League, now run by high-powered American business executives, decided that Canadian franchises in smaller cities were not sufficiently profitable. The NHL refused to share television revenue equally and made impossible demands in terms of the facilities and financing of arenas, thus literally forcing the franchises to move to greener pastures.

A similar situation prevailed in baseball. The Montreal Expos had responded to years of money-losing seasons in 1994 by dismantling a team that might have won the World Series had not a players' strike led to cancellation of the post-season. Eventually, the American executives decided to eliminate the team altogether, and Major League Baseball took over control of the team for a few years, with some home games being played in Puerto Rico, until it finally found a new home in Washington, DC, in 2005. In professional basketball, the Vancouver Grizzlies of the National Basketball Association moved to Memphis in 2001, the team's unsuccessful financial record since the establishment of the franchise in 1994 aggravated by a series of bad management decisions.

For many years Canadians have insisted that hockey must be maintained as Canada's national sport. In recent years the federal government has indicated its willingness to add NHL hockey to the list of cultural items that it is committed to protecting. Exactly where hockey fits into the overall cultural picture is as difficult to assess as the nature of its problems. The very extent of the integration of hockey into the American entertainment industry is one of the difficulties—as the agonized discussion over the transfer of hockey icon Wayne Gretzky from Edmonton to Los Angeles demonstrated in August 1988. But globalization is just as serious a problem. Since the 1980s the number of Canadian-born hockey players in the NHL has steadily declined, and the number of Canadian-born superstars has declined even more precipitously.

Since the professionals now stock the teams in international hockey, Canadian teams had not been

Members of the Canadian women's hockey team pose with their coach, Danielle Sauvageau, and their gold medals after defeating the US team 3–2 at the Salt Lake City Winter Olympics, 21 February 2002. Having failed to reach the gold medal game in 1998, the team has since won four consecutive Olympic finals. PHOTO PC/AOC/Mike Ridewood.

able to dominate the annual world championships or the Winter Olympics (with the exception of the 2002 and 2010 Games). Indeed, they had not been dominant in international competition for the previous half-century because Canadian amateurs were competing against essentially professional teams from the Soviet bloc countries. Many critics have suggested that the Canadian system has failed to produce large numbers of highly skilled players because it is not sufficiently committed to elite development, although Canada's success in the men's junior world ice hockey championships would seem to challenge this analysis: during the 1990s the Canadian junior team won seven International Ice Hockey Federation Under-20 world championships, including five in a row, and then won five more consecutive world titles from 2005 to 2009. The Canadian national women's hockey team won seven consecutive world titles without consoling many Canadians about the situation in men's hockey.

Canadian women's hockey at the international level was one of the great sports success stories of the 1990s—not to mention the 2002 and 2006 Olympics—but the women's team was still unable to make many inroads into a sport dominated by the ethos of the male professionals.

Conclusion

While in the larger scheme of things one pattern of historical development has always been cyclical, few analysts believed that Canada could ever return to the optimistic prosperity of the 1950s. Instead, the road ahead seemed at best to consist of a series of hard choices. How Canadians and their political leaders would come to terms with such decisions was an open question, even before the attack on the World Trade Center on 11 September 2001 changed the world.

Historiography

Canadian Peacekeeping in the Tumultuous 1990s

W.A. Dorn, Canadian Forces College

Canada earned an enviable reputation as one of the world's foremost peacekeepers during the Cold War. It was the only country to have contributed soldiers to every United Nations mission during that period. When the Nobel Prize was awarded to UN Peacekeepers in 1988 about 10 per cent of the UN total were Canadians. With the end of the Cold War and the rise of protracted ethnic conflicts in hot spots around the world, Canadian peacekeepers continued to be in demand, especially as the number of UN operations doubled within two years. Canada retained its rank as the number-one contributor to UN operations, in part because of its reputation for military professionalism, multiculturalism, bilingualism, efficiency, and fairness, as well as a history free from being a colonizing power abroad. Canadian politicians from all parts of the political spectrum supported internationalism and UN missions. In 1992–3, Canada

helped bring an end to the civil war in Cambodia and supported the first free election in that country after years of genocide and fighting. Canadian peacekeepers, now including police and civilians as well as soldiers, also helped bring peace and democracy to Central America by supporting and verifying peace accords.

But the peacekeeping experience soon turned sour and the Canadian reputation was marred when several Canadian soldiers shot and tortured Somali youths while on a US-led mission in that country (see "The Somalia Affair" box in this chapter). In Rwanda, Canadian General Roméo Dallaire was serving as the UN force commander when genocide was unleashed. While the general won praise for his effort to save lives—and some 20,000 were saved—he suffered post-traumatic stress disorder after being unable to acquire additional UN troops and witnessing the slaughter first-hand. To

Continued...

its credit, Canada was the only country to reinforce the mission during the genocide, but that small contingent was hardly the international intervention that was needed to stop the massacre. An end to the genocide only came with the defeat of government forces by rebel forces in July 1994, which was followed by a more strongly mandated peacekeeping force led by another Canadian general. Meanwhile, in Bosnia, Canadian soldiers struggled against ruthless and racist forces, sometimes having to cede ground to aggressors. Only after NATO dropped bombs to enforce international demands did the conflicting parties come to the negotiating table and sign the 1995 Dayton Peace Accords. A NATO-led force under US leadership was given a robust peacekeeping role—something Canadian soldiers preferred to the UN's weaker rules of engagement.

In the second half of the 1990s, the number of UN peacekeeping forces around the world declined from a previous high of 80,000 to only 10,000. Canada followed suit, going from 3,300 military personnel to only 300. Although Canada did support UN peace operations in Haiti, and supplied a force commander in 1997, it sent most of its peacekeepers under NATO to the Kosovo Force after contributing to NATO's bombing campaign to stop Serbian aggression. In the new century, UN peacekeeping came back into demand and the numbers of peacekeepers surged. However, Canada did not re-engage. The memories of Somalia, Bosnia, and Rwanda weighed heavily on the minds of Canadian soldiers and politicians. It was only after the signing of the peace accord between Ethiopia and Eritrea in 2000 that Canada sent several hundred soldiers under the United Nations flag. These operated under the Standby High-Readiness Brigade for UN Operations (SHIRBRIG), whose headquarters was based in Copenhagen. The creation of SHIRBRIG had been promoted by Canada after the Rwandan genocide as a necessary means to respond rapidly with peacekeeping forces in times of urgency. Canada was instrumental in SHIRBRIG's first deployment in 2000, but for only a half-year. When the 11 September 2001 attacks shocked the nation and the world, with the loss of almost 3,000 lives, including 24 Canadians, the country and its military quickly turned its attention away from peacekeeping to war-fighting and counter-insurgency operations in Afghanistan. Canadian Special Forces seized alleged Al Qaeda and Taliban members, often turning them over to US forces for imprisonment in places like Guantanamo Bay. Thus began a decade of involvement in Afghanistan, in which the Canadian polls showed far from unanimous support. While peacekeeping remained popular with Canadians, the war-fighting and counter-insurgency in Afghanistan was much less popular. Canada contributed few troops to UN missions, although it continued to pay its assessments to the UN peacekeeping budget "in full and on time," ranking seventh among financial contributors. Despite the decline in the number of Canadian soldiers deployed in peacekeeping, the activity remained popular among Canada's population, with the majority ranking it as "Canada's most positive contribution to the world."

Short Bibliography

Bibby, Reginald. *The Bibby Report: Social Trends Canadian Style*. Toronto, 1995. A useful survey of material about Canadian society in the 1990s.

Clarke, Tony. MAI: *The Multilateral Agreement on Investment and the Threat to Canadian Sovereignty*. Toronto, 1997. An impassioned defence of Canadian sovereignty in the age of globalization.

Driedger, Leo. *Multi-Ethnic Canada: Identities & Inequalities*. Toronto, 1996. A careful scholarly study of ethnicity in modern Canada.

Engelstad, Diane, and John Bird, eds. *Nation to Nation: Aboriginal Sovereignty and the Future of Canada*. Toronto, 1992. A collection of essays on Aboriginal governance.

Long, David, and Olive Patricia Dickason, eds. *Visions of the Heart: Canadian Aboriginal Issues*, 2nd edn. Toronto, 2000. An important collection of essays that serves as an introduction to the First Nations and their problems at century's end.

Mackey, Eva. *The House of Difference: Cultural Politics and National Identity in Canada*. Toronto, 2002. A provocative analysis of the new cultural agendas of the political parties in the 1990s.

Magder, Ted. *Canada's Hollywood: The Canadian State and Feature Films*. Toronto, 1993. An important analysis of the failures of Canadian cultural policy, particularly in the area of film.

Magosci, Paul Robert, ed. *Encyclopedia of Canada's Peoples*. Toronto, 1999. A monument to the scholarship of the 1990s in Canada.

Miki, Roy, and Cassandra Kobayashi. *Justice in Our Time: The Japanese Canadian Redress Settlement*. Vancouver, 1991. An account of the redress process involving the Japanese, written by one of the participants.

Randall, Stephen, and Herman W. Konrad, eds. NAFTA *in Transition*. Calgary, 1995. A collection of essays on NAFTA that includes an important study by John Thompson on Canadian cultural policy.

Report of the Sub-Committee on the Study of Sport in Canada. Ottawa, 1998. The first attempt by Parliament to study sport in Canada, chaired by David Mills. The report begins with the premise that professional sport is an important part of the fabric of sport in the nation.

Silver, Jim. *Thin Ice: Money, Politics, and the Demise of an NHL Franchise*. Halifax, 1995. A case study of the problems of professional sport in contemporary Canada.

Watson, William. *Globalization and the Meaning of Canadian Life*. Toronto, 1998. A relatively sanguine account of globalization and its Canadian impact.

Windshuttle, Keith. *The Killing of History: How Literary Critics and Social Theorists Are Murdering Our Past*. New York, 1997. Despite its sensationalist title, this book is a responsible and intelligent critique of the relationship between historical study and new postmodern theories, written by an Australian historian.

Study Questions

1. List and explain three factors that contributed to the collapse of the Progressive Conservative Party in the federal election of 1993.

2. What was the main reason for the opposition's failure to mount a successful challenge to the Liberal domination of Parliament after 1993?

3. Define in your own words the term "globalization."

4. Explain why Canada's aging population created a crisis in health care.

5. Why did sexual abuse become an important social issue in the 1990s?

6. What significant gains did Canada's Aboriginal peoples make in regard to land rights in the 1990s?

7. In one sense the "I Am Canadian" rant was just another beer commercial. Why did it become such a popular phenomenon?

8. Was the collapse of the cod fishery preventable?

Visit the companion website for *A History of the Canadian Peoples*, fifth edition for further resources.

13 Into the New Millennium

A military cortège transports the body of Corporal Nathan Cirillo from Ottawa to Hamilton, Ontario. Cirillo was on honour guard at the National War Memorial in Ottawa when he was shot and killed by Michael Zehaf-Bibeau, who was subsequently killed during his failed raid on Parliament Hill's Centre Block. Cirillo's death, along with the murder of Warrant Officer Patrice Vincent in a parking lot days earlier, outraged many Canadians, and both attacks were identified as terrorism by the Prime Minister. The Canadian Press/Patrick Doyle.

The twenty-first century opened with an apprehended crisis: international fears that millions of computers worldwide would not click over into the new century (as 1999 had to alter to 2000) proved largely illusory. At the same time, the panic suggested the extent to which the world was now dependent on the computer and digital technology. That dependence would only increase in the ensuing years. Canadians would be subjected to an unbelievable array of daily events, most of which would turn out to be true, and to a series of disasters proclaimed by the media, many of which turned out either to be false or, at worst, grossly exaggerated. The term "crisis" became the most overused word in many people's vocabularies, its incidence enhanced by 24-hour news channels on the television and the instant accessibility of information on the Internet.

For most North Americans, the new millennium probably did not begin immediately, but actually took effect on 11 September 2001, the day a group of terrorists hijacked a number of passenger airplanes and deliberately flew them into selected targets in the United States. Horrific as the events of that day were to Americans and Canadians alike, their true significance became apparent only as the shock waves settled. The United States government and its citizens understandably treated the attacks as a national disaster of unprecedented proportions, responding with a host of extreme measures, in which Canada became inescapably entwined, even as the nation tried to stand apart from them. As a consequence, Canadian–American relations moved to centre stage and would remain there for a number of years.

While Canada's immediate response to 9/11—as it came to be called—was enormous sympathy for the United States, combined with a spontaneous welcoming and sheltering of thousands of American air passengers inadvertently forced out of the sky into Canadian airports, Canada would have much difficulty with the George W. Bush administration's "with us or against us" response to its self-declared "war on terrorism," especially as the war widened to focus on Iraq. A willingness to join a military invasion of Iraq became the litmus test of any nation's standing with the United States. Most countries failed the test, particularly when the Americans couched the reasons for invasion in terms of the "weapons of mass destruction" the Iraqis were

alleged to have stockpiled. Public opinion polls indicated that two-thirds of Canadians opposed Canadian involvement in Iraq except as part of a United Nations force, and the UN was clearly not willing to intervene. As a gesture of goodwill, Canada in early 2002 agreed to contribute troops to a military task force in Afghanistan, and thus began the opening of Canadian involvement in Afghanistan that would bedevil the nation for nearly a decade. It was the first deployment of Canadian ground troops in combat since Korea. In the end, American President George W. Bush, with the support of Congress, acted unilaterally to begin the war. It was quickly over. No weapons of mass destruction were ever found. The resulting problem was that the Americans had begun a war with no concept of how to end it. The United States committed thousands of troops to occupation, pacification, and supposed rebuilding of democracy, and Iraq came increasingly to look like a modern iteration of Vietnam.

As for Canadian–American relations, Washington was clearly disappointed that a nation prospering under the American defence umbrella should adopt such an independent military posture, while Canada became increasingly convinced that the Americans had made a mistake in Iraq. The worsening of relations with the United States in the early years of the new millennium, however, was not a simply a consequence of the war on terrorism and military action (or lack of it) in Iraq. The real problems were created by the complexities of two thoroughly integrated economies and societies in which the power relationships were unequal.

Homeland Security

The immediate and understandable response of the Americans to 9/11 was to insist on improved security and safety, especially within the borders of the United States. They began with airports but soon were tightening border crossings. The ambition was the complete elimination of terrorism, an impossible goal given the democratization of technology and the willingness of the new breed of terrorists to sacrifice their own lives to the cause. The North American public proved to have a very low pain threshold. Worse still, each terrorist incident led to more desperate measures of prevention, often at the sacrifice of basic human rights. The chief threats to Canadians were not the terrorists themselves, but the American security responses, which greatly compromised the open border between the two neighbouring and friendly nations. For several hundred years, Canadians and Americans had enjoyed a special relationship along their border. The relationship was greatly altered in the first years of the new millennium. The American goal was that every foreign visitor—including Canadians—would need indisputable proof of identity, preferably a passport. In 2000 less than 30 per cent of Canadians held passports, but by 2014 the figure had climbed to over 70 per cent. At the same time, many recent immigrants to Canada now hailed from countries that feel threatened by aggressive American security. Moreover, the Canadian border is not the same as the one the US shares with Mexico, which has continuing problems with substantial illegal immigrants.

BACKGROUNDER

Omar Khadr

Courtroom sketch of Omar Khadr during his hearing in April 2010. Photo © REUTERS/Janet Hamlin/Pool.

Omar Khadr (b. 1986) is a Canadian citizen born in Toronto whose treatment by the United States and his own government has not only been very controversial but, for many, symptomatic of the abuse of human rights involved in the battle against terrorism. Khadr's father was a member of Al Qaeda and a personal friend of Osama bin Laden. He took his son to Pakistan, and then to Afghanistan, where the boy became involved in the fighting, accused of throwing a grenade that killed an American soldier. Although doubts remain that he would have been able to have thrown the grenade, given his condition and his location in the building where he was found, the 15-year-old—by definition, a child soldier—was captured by the Americans on 27 July 2002 and taken to their detention centre at Guantanamo Bay, Cuba, in October of that year. He was treated as an adult, constantly interrogated, and subjected to long periods of solitary confinement. He made several confessions, which he subsequently repudiated.

The Canadian government was never very supportive of Khadr during his confinement, and resolutely refused to ask for his repatriation despite the pleas of many Canadian and international organizations. A series of Canadian courts have ruled that Khadr was being treated improperly by the Canadian government. The Supreme Court of Canada in January 2010 ruled 9–0 that Canada had violated Khadr's rights under the Charter of Rights, but stopped short of ordering his return to Canada. By this time a large majority of the Canadian people believed that Khadr had been victimized. In July of 2010, the Federal Court of Canada issued an ultimatum that the Conservative government must act on the Khadr file within a week by providing "a list of remedies for its breach of Omar Khadr's constitutional rights," as the earlier ruling had instructed,

Continued...

or the Court could be compelled to act for the government (*Toronto Star*, 6 July 2010, 6). After several military tribunals failed to get off the ground, with military-appointed lawyers for Khadr resigning, being let go by Khadr, or being summarily replaced by the American military, a new trial was scheduled to begin in July 2010, then delayed until mid-August, just over eight years after Khadr's capture. It appeared to be a case that both the Canadian Harper government and the US administration of Barack Obama, who had promised to close down the Guantanamo detention centre, wished would just go away.

In the end a deal was made. Khadr pleaded guilty to murder in violation of the rules of war, and apologized to the widow of his "victim." The Americans were prepared to repatriate him to Canada after one more year in prison. Khadr was returned to Canada in September 2012, first to maximum security in

Ontario, and then, in February 2014, he was transferred to the medium-security Bowden Institution in Innisfail, Alberta. In July 2014 the Alberta Court of Appeal ordered that he be transferred from the federal facility to a provincial prison because of his status as a child when he was apprehended, but the federal government, with its tough-on-crime-and-terrorism agenda, appealed to the Supreme Court of Canada, which was to hear arguments in 2015. This will be the third time his case has gone before Canada's highest court. In the meantime, Khadr's eyesight was reported to be failing, a result of shrapnel wounds from the 2002 firefight when he was captured. On 7 May 2015 Khadr was released on bail to live with his Canadian lawyer, Dennis Edney, and his family in Edmonton, and in his first interviews he showed himself to be an articulate and thoughtful young man who merely wanted to be given a chance.

The Tale of Two Mad Cows

Bovine spongiform encephalopathy (BSE), more commonly known as "Mad Cow Disease," is a neurological disorder found in cattle but transmittable to humans, where it manifests itself with rapid mental deterioration. A serious outbreak of the disease occurred in Europe in 1992–3. Ten years later, Canada announced the discovery of its first case, in Alberta. A few months later a case in the United States was traced back to Canada. The Americans responded immediately by closing their border to Canadian cattle. The embargo lasted until well into 2005. Many Canadian farmers in the 1990s had shifted their efforts to the production of cattle, partly for an American market served by its own cattle producers, who embraced the new policy. Establishing mutually acceptable standards of infection proved difficult. The situation was exacerbated by

several factors. One was the extent of inequality in a highly interdependent trade relationship. The Canadian farm industry was much more dependent on cattle than were the Americans, especially after it restructured to leave more slaughterhouse and meatpacking functions to those south of the border, concentrating instead on the export of live cattle. Another was the difficulty of finding satisfactory mechanisms for dispute resolution, a general problem in the new era of more open trade.

The disagreement over live cattle gradually altered by widening into a struggle over the labelling of meat products exported from Canada to the United States. Since 2008, Canadian meat exports—of beef, pork, and chicken—have been seriously affected by an American policy of requiring detailed labelling, regarded as expensive and unnecessarily onerous by Canadian producers. Free trade in meat is also hampered by health regulations, reflected in labelling, that control the extent and kind of hormones that can be used to raise the animals.

Softwood Lumber

The dispute over softwood lumber—the easy-to-saw lumber used in most building construction—has been going on far longer than the disagreement over live animals and meat products. At issue here has been the American charge that the Canadian lumber industry receives unfair subsidies. Most Canadian timber is owned by the Crown and the fee for harvesting on public lands (stumpage rights) is set by administrative practice rather than by open auction, as it is in the United States. The American Coalition for Fair Lumber Imports (CFLI), a lobbying group heavily subsidized by the American lumber producers, has long urged the American Department of Commerce to apply countervailing duties on Canadian lumber imported into the United States because of unfair subsidization. After 9/11 the CFLI was able to get the United States Department of Commerce to levy a tariff of 18 per cent and a combined levy of 27.22 per cent on Canadian lumber. Canada appealed to a NAFTA panel, which ruled in August 2003 that, while the Canadian industry might be subsidized, the American tariff was much too high. Subsequently, a World Trade Organization panel agreed that the tariffs were too extreme: while the Canadian stumpage rights clearly benefited Canadian companies, the advantage was not sufficient to be labelled a subsidy. The Americans appealed and yet another panel confirmed the earlier decision. In the end, the dispute was settled politically in 2006 by negotiations between the Bush government and the Harper minority government. The softwood lumber business was influenced mainly by power considerations. The Americans refused to accept rulings under the conflict resolution mechanisms of various free trade treaties; Canada could not enforce the favourable decisions it had received and, therefore, was ultimately forced to bilateral negotiations for a solution.

Energy

The interdependence of the Canadian–American energy relationship—in oil, natural gas, electricity generation and transmission, and even in water management (for water supplies much of Canada's electricity)—continued to grow into the new millennium. It was shaped in the early years of the twenty-first century by a number of factors. First, Canada within its own boundaries has had a surplus of energy in all three major energy sectors, while the United States saw demand exceed supply in both petroleum and natural gas. Canada's energy resources lie in less densely populated parts of the country, creating disagreement between energy-consuming provinces such as Ontario and energy producing provinces, as well as between developers and residents (often Aboriginal peoples) in the resource-rich regions. Moreover, oil and gas have to be moved from source to market via various means susceptible to environmental disaster, leading to extensive lobbying by environmental groups. This means that Canadian energy policy is a hotly contested political issue, both at home and abroad. The proposed Northern Gateway pipeline to transport Alberta crude to the Pacific coast has been halted, probably permanently, by a combination of environmental opposition and objections from various Native groups.

Second, American energy demands and energy policy are continual and extensive, thus encouraging Canada to develop its energy resources, possibly more rapidly than in the nation's best interests. At the same time, through fracking (hydraulic fracturing)—the deliberate breakup of rock layers under liquid pressure to extract oil and natural gas—the United States in recent years has greatly increased its own production of those resources significantly. US oil production in 2014 reached 8.5 million barrels per day (bpd), up from a low of 5 million bpd in 2008, while natural gas output is up 32 per cent over the same period. The fracking technique is of unknown long-term environmental damage, but this consideration will not stop its short-term exploitation. Nor will disasters such as the catastrophic train derailment in Lac-Mégantic, Quebec, interfere with its continuation (although this disaster involved the transport of highly combustible light crude from the Bakken shale deposits in North Dakota). As a result, the Americans are considerably less dependent on Canadian production than they were a few years ago, which translates into an increased reluctance to authorize the construction of extensive pipelines from Alberta across American territory into American refineries. An American decision on the Keystone XL pipeline, pro-

BACKGROUNDER

The Lac-Mégantic Derailment

Lac-Mégantic is a small town in the Eastern Townships of Quebec, the site of one of the worst train disasters in Canadian history. On the night of 6 July 2013, a train of 74 cars full of crude oil being transported from North Dakota to a refinery in New Brunswick careened into the downtown section of the town, producing an explosion and fire that caused 42 known deaths and left five persons missing. The train was running on a railway line owned by the Montreal, Maine and Atlantic Railway (MMA), an American company that had acquired it—a former part of the Canadian Pacific system—in 2003. The MMA had been operated for years on an extremely cost-conscious basis, with maintenance deferrals and staff reductions bringing crews to an absolute minimum. It had a most unsatis-factory safety record, but was still allowed by the Canadian regulatory agency to operate its trains with only single-person supervision. Most of its tank cars were old and of an obsolete design and construction liable to accident. The lead locomotive in use on the night of the disaster was both old and inadequately repaired. The engineer—the only crew member on board the train—parked it unattended atop a hill on the main line outside Lac-Mégantic, setting its brakes and leaving the lead engine running with its cab unlocked and unsecured. While the exact reasons for the failure of the braking systems have been in dispute, there is no doubt that the braking systems failed, allowing the train to roll downhill as a runaway into the centre of Lac-Mégantic, where it derailed at 1:14 a.m. Sixty-three of the 74 tank cars were dam-aged, spilling six million litres of highly volatile crude oil and igniting an almost immediate explosion and series of fires. Environmental damage was substan-tial. As well as killing many residents, particularly at a late-night spot in the town core, the accident led to the evacuation of several thousand. The centre of the fire and explosion were still inaccessible to firefighters almost a day later; at least 30 buildings and dozens of businesses were destroyed. The American CEO of the railroad made a subsequent belated and highly criticized visit to the town, and soon took the MMA into bankruptcy.

Public investigations by the Transportation Safety Board (TSB) of Canada found many violations of existing safety regulations, as well as evidence of bad practice that was not properly regulated. Criticism emerged that the oil being carried was unusually inflammable, perhaps because it was pro-duced by fracking, and its volatility had not been properly identified. The TSB would not address the first of these issues. In August 2014 the TSB did iden-tify 18 interconnected causes for the accident, most involving MMA inadequacies but some involving the TSB's failure of supervision. Many municipalities in Canada after the disaster expressed concern that railways carrying dangerous goods were shipping on rail lines too close to populated areas. For most Canadians, the disaster was the first sign of the dan-gers of the cross-country transportation of crude oil by rail, a practice that had increased substantially (and gone unnoticed) over the previous few years. Suddenly, pipelines seemed less menacing than they had been.

jected to cross mid-America, was deferred several times until President Obama on 24 February 2015 vetoed a bill to approve the project. Finally, various trade agree-ments and other integrations—as well as an increased American supply of oil and gas—have considerably reduced Canadian options.

Global Issues

The Environment

Many of the questions facing Canadians and their governments in the new millennium had both continental and global implications. What was once called "global warming," for example, and is now perhaps best labelled "climate change" is a hot-button topic that is clearly with us to stay, however much both Canadian and American governments would like it to go away. By 2014, two absolutely contradictory and irreconcilable conclusions had been reached about climate change. One, articulated by virtually all scientists and experts, agreed that climate change was real and had to be addressed. The evidence was overwhelming, they insisted. The greenhouse gases emitted mainly by the industrialized nations were indeed increasing the amounts of heat-trapping gases in the atmosphere. This in turn was not only gradually raising the world temperature, but causing a variety of other results, including more extreme weather conditions and loss of biodiversity. On the other hand, the governments of both the United States and Canada have concluded that little could be done practically to reduce significantly carbon dioxide pollution, at least not by mechanisms such as the Kyoto Protocol. The chief problems were that too many nations did not buy into Kyoto and refused, as well, to cut emissions, insisting that the cost—a shift away from the capitalist paradigm of ever-increasing economic growth—was too high for the gains. Distressingly, substantial publicity about Kyoto and the greenhouse effect failed to penetrate very far into the Canadian public consciousness, partly because most climate change activists are doomsayers typically overstating their case to get public attention. Moreover, many of these doomsayers are really moral reformers, seeking to return the world to some past state of Arcadian and pre-technological simplicity. Nevertheless, while far more Canadians (60 per cent) than Americans or Britons believe that climate change is a fact and has been caused by human agency, it remains uncertain how much of their way of life they are willing to sacrifice to improve the situation.

In 2014, a report was released by the international Intergovernmental Panel on Climate Change (IPCC), an agency established by the United Nations Environment Programme and the World Meteorological Organization in 1988 to provide, under UN auspices, reliable information on climate change. While it emphasized that climate change was accelerating and influencing every ecosystem, mainly in a negative manner, it also made the point that global warming should not be seen as the only international problem and that other factors must be addressed in order to understand and come to terms with the ongoing situation. This fifth assessment report of the IPCC dealt with three kinds of problems: (1) those in which climate is clearly the major influence, such as rising sea levels, ocean acidification, and arctic melting; (2) those where climate's impact is more manageable, such as its effect on health; and (3) those where climate is affecting the range of plant and animal species, including agricultural yields. The first set of problems can best be dealt with only by a drastic reduction in carbon emissions, it maintained. The second set can be addressed by improving basic public health, and the third can be addressed, at least partially, by improved agricultural strategies and techniques. The report makes clear that adaptation to change might in many cases work better than the total prevention of change.

Canada helped deal the final blow to the Kyoto Accord in May of 2006, when the Canadian government called for the gradual elimination of Kyoto with no alternative offered to replace it. Part of Canada's concern was to be in step with the United States, which was highly critical of the protocol, and part was because of concern over Canada's global economic competitiveness. Since that time, the Conservative government has increasingly distanced itself from specific measures to counter climate change, and has not been active at international gatherings such as the United Nations Climate Change Conference held in Copenhagen in 2009 or the international summit meeting on climate change held in New York in 2014.

Pandemic Disease

While international co-operation on greenhouse gases has seemed impossible to achieve, a much higher degree of agreement has proved possible on other global fronts, including pandemic disease. Quick action by Canadian and international authorities in 2003 kept well under control a potentially serious outbreak of severe acute respiratory syndrome (SARS) apparently brought from Hong Kong to Greater Toronto, although the advisory of the World Health Organization (WHO) against unnecessary travel to Toronto had serious implications for the city's tourist industry. In 2009 an apprehended international epidemic of swine flu of the H1N1 variety proved that the Canadian public was skeptical of the efficacy of a massive inoculation program well publicized by the government to prevent a potential disaster. Canadian medical researchers have been in the forefront of virus research, including the development of an experimental vaccine that has shown some promise of proving effective in the treatment of Ebola, a deadly virus ravaging West Africa. Canada as a nation has contributed money for protective equipment for the WHO in West Africa, as well as over $5 million in aid to relief organizations working in the region. A number of cases of Ebola were treated in the United States in 2014 but the disease was slow to arrive in Canada. Still, much evidence existed that were it to appear, Canadians would be slow to take it seriously.

International Conflict and the Canadian Military

As we have seen in earlier chapters, a series of Canadian governments dating back to the 1960s have engaged in efforts to convince the Canadian public that a continually decreasing proportion of the federal budget devoted to the military was compatible with both national security and Canadian international obligations. As a proportion of gross domestic product, Canadian military spending has consistently decreased since the early days of the Cold War, and during the twenty-first century Canada's defence expenditures have been regularly less than those of most NATO allies. In 2012, Canada ranked fourteenth in the world in total military expenditures, but of those nations above Canada in total military expenditures only Japan spent a lower proportion of its GDP. In 2013, Canada's military spending, at 1 per cent of GDP, was lower than that of all but seven of 28 NATO member countries.

In 2002 Canada committed military forces in Afghanistan as a necessary gesture to its overall alliance with the United States. Those military forces were increased in number and their combat role grew after the new Conservative government came to power in 2006. The Canadian role in Afghanistan was quietly shifted from peacekeeper to combatant in a new kind of war in which peacekeeping and humanitarian activities were combined with actual fighting. The result of the shift was a raised level of casualties, including in mid-May 2006 the death of Nichola Goddard, the first female Canadian soldier ever killed in combat. The Canadian public began to complain that soldiers were being killed without a clear rationale, and in 2008, Prime Minister Harper pledged that Canada would leave Afghanistan by 2011. That pledge was kept, although some Canadian troops did remain in the country in so-called training roles. Although most of Canada's combat troops were eventually brought home, they have had much trouble with post-combat stress disorders and suicides. News reports have circulated that some soldiers have hidden their problems, fearful of losing full pensions if they are prematurely demobilized. Despite these problems, the Canadian government has been willing to become involved, albeit in mainly peripheral ways, in various foreign conflicts. Most notably, it contributed fighter-bombers, surveillance aircraft, tankers, and a warship to a coalition effort in Libya in 2011, commanded by a Canadian general. This coalition declared success after a few months and withdrew from combat involvement. In 2014 Canada agreed to join another coalition, this time to counter the rapidly spreading success of the Islamic State in the Middle East. Here the stakes are higher and the end game, as in Afghanistan, much less clear. In March 2015, the Harper government extended its original commitment of six months for another year and broadened its share of the bombing campaign to include Syria as well as Iraq.

One of the casualties of the Afghan involvement was the virtual end to Canadian peacekeeping operations around the world. For half a century, Canadians had prided themselves on the use of their military for peaceful rather than warlike purposes. But the nature of the world had changed, and as Canadian experiences in Kosovo and Somalia had demonstrated, maintaining a stance above and beyond the conflict had become increasingly difficult. Moreover, Canada

The casket of Captain Nichola Goddard is carried by members of the Royal Canadian Horse Artillery into St Barnabas Church in Calgary, 26 May 2006. Goddard was the first female Canadian soldier ever killed in combat. © TODD KOROL/X00147/Reuters/ Corbis.

could not provide 2,000 soldiers for Afghanistan and elsewhere at the same time. At the end of March 2006, the Canadian Forces made a final withdrawal of 190 troops from the Golan Heights, where a Canadian presence had been maintained since shortly after the Yom Kippur (October) War of 1973. After this withdrawal, Canada would have fewer than 60 peacekeepers serving under the United Nations flag, and most of these were police officers rather than soldiers. Few Canadians seemed aware—or concerned—with what had happened.

Lebanon

One of Canada's most curious international involvements occurred in Lebanon in 2006. For many years Lebanon was an overall part of a simmering Middle Eastern crisis that flared up from time to time. A sporadic civil war was fought in the country between 1975 and 1990. During the war, thousands of Lebanese left the country and immigrated abroad, many to Canada, where they became Canadian citizens. This movement was encouraged by the Canadian government, which made special concessions to allow Lebanese with Canadian relatives—Lebanese had immigrated to Canada in small but persistent numbers since the 1880s—into Canada. By the 2001 census, there were officially 142,635 people of Lebanese origin in Canada, although unofficial estimates put the total at closer to 250,000. Most were francophones who settled in Quebec, although there were also communities in Ottawa, Edmonton, and Toronto. In 1982, Israel invaded Lebanon to uproot a Palestinian government that had grown up there. The invasion was successful in reducing Palestinian raids on Israel, but led to the growth of the Shiite Hezbollah movement unalterably opposed to Israel and to an Israeli presence in Lebanon. Hezbollah came to control most of southern Lebanon and especially the city of Beirut, claiming that the withdrawal of Israeli troops from the country represented its victory. Beginning in 1990 and especially after the Israelis left in 2000, Lebanon had been rebuilt and returned to something resembling normalcy. As many as 40,000 Canadians, part of the earlier Lebanese diaspora, returned to Lebanon after 1990 and especially after 2000, either for extended visits with families or as permanent residents. By 2006, few people in Canada, and certainly few in the Canadian government, recognized that a large Canadian population had become entrapped in the rising conflict between Israel and Hezbollah that erupted in that year.

Canada, along with other Western nations, ultimately offered to evacuate its citizens if they could travel successfully to the Mediterranean coast. The journey was a difficult one, and undoubtedly kept down the numbers who managed to take advantage of the offer. In the end, about 10,000 Canadian citizens resident in Lebanon were extracted from the country by sea and air. The remainder, except for the eight members of a Lebanese-Canadian family killed by an Israeli attack, waited for the ceasefire finally brokered by the United Nations in mid-April.

The Arctic

One belief that most Canadians share is in the Arctic, both as an integral part of the nation and as the repository of great riches, once they can be unlocked from a hostile environment. The recent evidence of global warming, which has hit the polar regions with far greater and more immediate force than anywhere else, has raised the possibility that Arctic resources might be available sooner than anyone could have expected when Canada first agreed to assume British claims to Arctic sovereignty. Now, the Conservative government has tried to validate these claims with the 2014 discovery at the bottom of Queen Maud Gulf of the HMS *Erebus*, Sir John Franklin's ship from his ill-fated 1840s expedition to find a Northwest Passage. One recent book by an environmental scientist has predicted that climate change will turn Canada (along with other northern nations) into economic superpowers by 2050. This prediction certainly supports the vision of the Harper government for the Arctic since 2006. The melting of sea ice does pose a challenge to Canada's stewardship of the northern polar region, for as the northern seas become increasingly navigable it will become ever more necessary for Canada to be able to demonstrate its ability to enforce its laws and regulations in a region previously protected by year-round ice.

But the greatest threats to the Arctic probably come not from foreign interlopers but from Canadians themselves: from those who refuse to recognize the reality of climate change, from those who allow the need for government budget stringency to take precedence over the strategic needs of the region, and from those eager to exploit its rich resources as rapidly as possible and without thought for tomorrow. Any one of these three constitutes sufficient danger, but it is possible we will see all three converge. At the same time, the future for the traditional—or current—way of life of the Aboriginal peoples of the Arctic and of the Subarctic is not terribly promising. Climate change in the North may make mineral resource exploitation possible, but at the expense of the animal population of the region and of infrastructure, from ice roads to building foundations, that depends on permanently frozen ground. Canada's record in the past of enabling its Aboriginal people to adapt to changing economic and social conditions has hardly been very encouraging.

Canadian Politics

The Meltdown of the Liberal Party

While relations with the United States (and with other nations as well) were perceptibly shifting, so too was domestic politics. The two shifts were not much connected. International events seldom had much impact within the nation, except perhaps for the groundswell of public approval for Prime Minister Chrétien when he refused to support the United States in Iraq. Chrétien's huge majority in the House of Commons after the 2000 election was largely illusory, caused by the increased number of political parties with some popular support combined with the biases of the Canadian electoral system. A true Liberal sweep would not have seen the opposition Reform/Alliance increase its popular vote by 6 per cent. From the very beginning of the new Parliament, too many Liberals spent too much time positioning themselves to succeed Chretien, who was perceived to be on his way out. The frontrunner was Finance Minister Paul Martin, who in 2002 retired from the cabinet and ran a double campaign, both to force the Prime Minister out and to position himself as replacement. By 2003 there were, in effect, two Liberal Parties in Canada, one led by Chrétien and the other led by Martin. The government was greatly embarrassed by the gun control fiasco, in which a program supposed to be virtually self-supporting turned out to be costing more than $1 billion, and at that was incomplete. This evidence of fiscal mismanagement was joined by further illustrations of incompetence and illegality at all levels, including countless examples of corruption in Quebec. A commission of inquiry headed by Mr Justice John Gomery of Quebec eventually exonerated Paul Martin, who had become Liberal leader and hence Prime Minister in November 2003, but several associates of Jean Chrétien were indicted for fraud in a sponsorship scandal where government contracts were paid to Quebec advertising firms for work that was never done.

The Resurgence of Conservatism

While the federal Liberal Party was reeling from a year of mudslinging that left everyone soiled and exhausted, closed-door meetings between the Canadian Alliance and the Progressive Conservatives in late 2003 had resulted in the formation of the Conservative Party of Canada (CPC). The 2000 election had emphasized that the Liberals could govern forever if they faced both a divided conservatism and a sovereignist party in Quebec. The two conservative parties represented different conservative traditions. The Progressive-Conservatives, based mainly in eastern Canada, were strong nationalists and supporters of state-operated social programs, while the Alliance, as heir to the western-dominated Reform

Party, was both socially and fiscally conservative, with strong roots in fundamentalist religion and populism; it was opposed to centralized federalism. The Alliance had toned down its doctrine, realizing that a genuinely right-wing message was unlikely to flourish nationally in Canada. The new federal Conservative Party, having dropped the "Progressive" moniker, was favourably disposed to the international use of military force and believed in balanced budgets and free enterprise. On 20 March 2004 it chose Stephen Harper as its leader. Harper had helped engineer the merger. He was young, articulate, able, and extremely self-assured. His French was decent and constantly improving.

In the 2004 election, the Tories behaved responsibly and with considerable party discipline. Extreme statements were held to a minimum. Prime Minister Martin was forced to argue that the Conservatives had a "hidden agenda" (presumably on health care and hot-button social issues), a charge echoed by the new leader of the NDP, Jack Layton. Electorate concern about a "phantom platform" may have led some voters to pull back at the last minute from what the polls had predicted would be a Conservative victory. Instead the Liberals formed a minority government facing an opposition divided into Tories and 54 Bloc Québécois members, all from Quebec, who were much hampered by their party's sovereignist position.

Minority Governments, 2004–2011

The Liberal minority government of 2004 was a quite shaky one, and when the NDP tried to gain more concessions on social programs as the price of its continued support, Martin refused. The government fell on 28 November, 2005, 171–133, on a motion of confidence. In the ensuing election, the buzz in hundreds of Tim Hortons restaurants (now owned by an American firm but still the place where most Canadians bought and drank their morning coffee and "r-r-r-rolled up the rim to win") was simple: it's time for a change. The threat of a hidden agenda seemed less convincing, Stephen Harper kept the right-wing rhetoric to a minimum, and all other parties lost seats to the CPC. Paul Martin immediately resigned as party leader as soon as the results were announced. Stephen Harper now led a minority government that would have to avoid major mistakes. He did so partly by insisting on tight control over the relations between his government and the media. The national press was soon chafing about "managed news" and lack of transparency, charges that would continue to plague Harper and the Tories throughout their lengthy tenure in office. One of the few early political decisions Harper took was to abandon the Kelowna Accord for Aboriginal peoples, which had been negotiated between the Liberal government, provincial governments, and Native leaders, in 2005. The decision caused little public outcry. The Harper government was clearly aided for some time by the disarray within the Liberal Party, which had no natural leader to replace Paul Martin. The result was an unseemly scramble among as many as a dozen lesser figures. And when, at an exciting convention on 2 December 2006,

the Liberals selected Stéphane Dion as their new leader, he was a weak compromise chosen because supporters of the two leading candidates—Bob Rae and Michael Ignatieff—would not accept the other. Both carried excess baggage into the convention, Rae as former NDP Premier of Ontario, Ignatieff as an academic who spent most of his career outside of Canada. Dion lasted only long enough to lead the party to a disastrous defeat in the 2008 election. Despite the Liberal debacle, Stephen Harper in 2008 did not gain a majority. The electorate, visibly cynical about politics and politicians, seemed content to be governed by a parliamentary minority that was extremely cautious about big steps. A further blow to the credibility of Canada's political leaders came when a German businessman accused former Prime Minister Brian Mulroney of improper behaviour in his lobbying dealings regarding the European Airbus.

Contemporary Views

The Rules of the Game

Graham Steele was a long time NDP MLA from Nova Scotia. This excerpt is from his memoirs.

Here's what I learned about politics from eight years in opposition.

Being in politics makes you dumber, because the longer you're in politics the dumber you get. That's because you learn habits of behaviour and speech that serve political purposes but are at odds with the way normal people think and talk. As the habits become engrained, you no longer even notice that you're thinking and acting like a politician. You do it because it works.

These are the rules of the game:

- Get yourself re-elected. Like the sex drive among primates, the drive to be re-elected drives everything a politician does.

- Spend as little time as possible at the legislature. There are no voters there, so any time spent there is wasted. Go where the voters are. Go home.

- Perception is reality. Since people vote based on what they believe to be true, it doesn't matter what is actually true. This is at the root of all the dark political arts.

- Keep it simple. Policy debates are for losers. Focus on what is most likely to sink in with a distracted electorate: slogans, scandals, personalities, pictures, images. Find whatever works, then repeat it relentlessly.

- Put yourself in the spotlight. People are more likely to vote for someone they've met or feel they know or at least have heard of. If it's not in the news, it didn't happen.

- Politics is a team sport, part 1: Loyalty. You can't accomplish anything as an individual. No matter what, stick with your team.

- Politics is a team sport, part 2: Always be attacking. There are other teams that want to take away

Continued...

your job at the next election. You have to beat them, and if you can, destroy them.

- Don't leave a paper trail. You don't want to leave any evidence that runs against your own story. If you're explaining, you're losing.

- Fight hard to take credit, fight harder to avoid blame.

Deny that these are the rules of the game.

Source: Graham Steele, *What I Learned about Politics: Inside the Rise—and Collapse—of Nova Scotia's NDP Government* (Halifax: Nimbus Publishing, 2014).

Biography

Stephen Harper: The Early Years

Prime Minister Stephen Harper speaks during a press conference at the end of the G8 summit in Lough Erne, Northern Ireland, 18 June 2013. © BEN STANSALL/POOL/epa/Corbis.

Born in Toronto in 1959, Stephen Harper was educated at Richview Collegiate Institute in Etobicoke before moving to Alberta, where he worked as a computer programmer before attending the University of Calgary. He received a BA in 1985 and an MA (Economics) in 1991 from Calgary. A supporter of the Liberal Party in high school, he opposed the Trudeau government's energy policy and became chief aide to Tory MP Jim Hawkes in 1985 before leaving the PC Party in 1986.

Harper was quickly recruited by Preston Manning for the incipient Reform Party, made a speech at its founding convention in 1987, and served as chief policy officer in 1988 at the time of the drafting of the 1988 election platform. He ran for Parliament in the 1988 federal election but was defeated by Jim Hawkes. Harper subsequently became executive assistant to Reform MP Deborah Grey in 1989 and wrote speeches for her until 1993. As Reform's policy officer to 1992, Harper argued that Reform needed to expand its regional base and criticized radical extremism. He broke with Manning in 1992 over the Charlottetown Accord, which Harper wholeheartedly opposed, and defeated Hawkes in the 1993 election. In the Reform Party caucus, Harper quickly developed a reputation as a bright newcomer, opposed to centralizing federalism and socially conservative; he opposed same-sex marriage and gun control legislation, for example.

But Harper was never comfortable in the Reform Party or with Preston Manning's leadership, seeing both as too populist, and he resigned his parliamentary seat in early 1997 to become an officer of the National Citizens' Coalition. He opposed appeasement of Quebec forced from his leadership by his own party and his interim replacement, Michael Ignatieff, agreed to support a Conservative budget. In the 2011 election campaign, Layton performed well in the leaders' debates, using his colloquial French to great advantage, and NDP candidates in Quebec began to move ahead of Bloc candidates in many ridings. The party won 59 seats in Quebec to become the official opposition. Layton had health problems during the campaign, and he took a leave from his post as leader on 25 July 2011. He died of cancer less than a month later, on 22 August. He was given a state funeral.

TABLE 13.1 2011 Canadian Election Results: National Totals and by Province/Territory

	Bloc Québécois	Conservative	Green Party	Liberal	NDP	Other	Total
2008							
Seats	49	143	–	77	37	2	
% Votes	10.0	37.6	6.8	26.2	18.2	1.2	
2011							
Seats	4	166	1	34	103	0	
% Votes	6.0	39.6	3.7	18.9	30.6	0.9	
Newfoundland		1	–	4	2	–	7
52.6		28.3	0.9	37.9	32.6	0.3	
Prince Edward Island		1	–	3	–	–	4
73.3		41.2	2.4	41.0	15.4	0.1	
Nova Scotia		4	–	4	3	–	11
62.0		36.7	3.9	28.9	30.3	0.1	
New Brunswick		8	–	1	1	–	10
66.2		43.8	3.2	22.6	29.8	0.6	
Quebec	4	5	–	7	59	0	75
62.9	23.4	16.5	2.1	14.2	42.9	0.9	
Ontario		73	–	11	22	–	106
61.5		44.4	3.8	25.3	25.6	0.9	
Manitoba		11	–	1	2	–	14
59.4		53.5	2.6	16.6	25.8	0.6	
Saskatchewan		13	–	1	–	–	14
63.1		56.3	2.6	8.5	32.3	0.2	
Alberta		27	–	–	1	–	28
55.8		66.8	5.2	9.3	16.8	1.9	
British Columbia		21	1	2	12	–	36
60.4		45.6	7.7	13.4	32.5	0.8	
Northwest Territories			–	–	1	–	1
53.9		32.1	3.1	18.4	45.8	0.6	
Nunavut		1	–	–	–	–	1
45.7		49.9	2.0	28.7	19.4	–	
Yukon		1	–	–	–	–	1
66.2		33.8	18.9	32.9	14.4	–	

Note: Official voter turnout in 2011 was 61.1 per cent. Detailed official election results on a riding-by riding basis are available at the Elections Canada website: http://www.elections.ca/scripts/resval/ovr_41ge.asp?prov=&lang=e.

Source: http://www.sfu.ca/~abeard/elections/results.html.

separatism, arguing that "Quebec separatists are the problem and they need to be fixed." After the Canadian Alliance was formed in 2000 and chose Stockwell Day as leader, Harper co-authored with a number of prominent Alberta politicians, including 2006 Alberta Conservative leadership candidate Ted Morton, the "Alberta Agenda," which called for the provincial government to "build firewalls around Alberta" to prevent continued redistribution of Alberta's wealth to less affluent provinces. He also insisted that Canada "appears content to become a second-tier socialist country." Harper ran for the Alliance leadership against Stockwell Day in March 2002 and won on the first ballot. He became leader of the opposition two months later, resigning the post early in 2004 to run for the leadership of the newly united Conservative Party of Canada. He won easily.

Document

Airbus Scandal

The extent to which politics and business have shared a symbiotic and sometimes shady relationship has a long history in Canada, dating back to the 1873 Pacific Scandal that saw Canada's first Prime Minister, John A. Macdonald, and his government resign. Well over a century later, ex-Prime Minister Brian Mulroney was called to account by the Oliphant Commission for some of his business dealings after he left office, but was still an MP, in what became known as the Airbus Scandal. The scandal originally related to the awarding of Air Canada contracts to purchase new planes from the European manufacturer Airbus, and the possibility of cash kickbacks to those in government, while Mulroney was Prime Minister. The following is from the report of the inquiry into some of Mulroney's dealings with Karlheinz Schreiber, a German businessman who paid him large cash amounts for unknown services.

Question 11   Were these business and financial dealings appropriate considering the position of Mr. Mulroney as a current or former prime minister and Member of Parliament?

Question 12   Was there appropriate disclosure and reporting of the dealings and payments?

FINDINGS

Question 11 of the Terms of Reference directed me to determine whether the business and financial dealings between Mr. Schreiber and Mr. Mulroney were appropriate considering the position of Mr. Mulroney as a current or former prime minister and member of parliament.

In answer to this question, I find that Mr. Mulroney's conduct in his business dealings with Mr. Schreiber was not appropriate; and that Mr. Mulroney's conduct in his financial dealings with Mr. Schreiber was not appropriate.

With respect to Question 12, disclosure and reporting, I find that Mr. Mulroney failed to take any steps to document the dealings and payments when he entered into his agreement with Mr. Schreiber on August 27, 1993, or when he received the two subsequent payments on December 18, 1993, and December 8, 1994. What he could have done was simple. First, he could have arranged for the agreement with Mr. Schreiber to be in writing. Second, he could have issued receipts for

Continued...

the cash he received and entered the fact of the receipt of cash on the books of his company, Cansult—a company incorporated for the very purpose of operating Mr. Mulroney's consulting business. Third, he could have deposited the cash he received from Mr. Schreiber into an account at a bank or other financial institution—an action that would, I suggest, have been in accord with business acumen and with standard business practice.

I find that Mr. Mulroney did not declare a reserve under the *Income Tax Act* regarding the cash he received on any of the seven occasions when he could have done so. I am not saying he was legally obligated to do so. However, I rely on his decision not to do so to support my finding that there was not appropriate disclosure and reporting of the payments.

I find that Mr. Mulroney acted inappropriately in failing to disclose his dealings with Mr. Schreiber and the payments he received when he gave evidence at his examination before plea in 1996.

I find that Mr. Mulroney failed to heed the advice of Luc Lavoie, his spokesperson, when Mr. Lavoie advised him to go public regarding his relationship with Mr. Schreiber. In doing so, Mr. Mulroney failed to take advantage of an opportunity to disclose appropriately his dealings with Mr. Schreiber and the payments he received.

I find that Mr. Mulroney acted inappropriately in misleading William Kaplan when he (Mr. Kaplan) was preparing to write *Presumed Guilty: Brian Mulroney, the Airbus Affair and the Government of Canada* (1998), a book in which he intended to defend Mr. Mulroney's reputation.

I also find that, when Mr. Kaplan was in the process of writing his series of articles for the *Globe and Mail* in November 2003, Mr. Mulroney acted inappropriately in the manner in which he attempted to persuade Mr. Kaplan not to publish the articles. I find that the foregoing actions of Mr. Mulroney were clearly a calculated attempt on his part to prevent Mr. Kaplan from publicly disclosing Mr. Mulroney's dealings with Mr. Schreiber and the cash payments he had received from him.

In summary, I find that Mr. Mulroney's conduct in failing to disclose and report on his dealings with and payments from Mr. Schreiber was not appropriate.

Source: Commission of Inquiry into Certain Allegations Respecting Business and Financial Dealings between Karlheinz Schreiber and the Right Honourable Brian Mulroney (the Oliphant Commission, chaired by Jeffrey J. Oliphant), *Report: Volume 1, Executive Summary* (Ottawa: Minister of Public Works and Government Services Canada, 2010), 58–9.

Majority Government, 2011–2015

Stéphane Dion was replaced as Liberal leader by Michael Ignatieff, whose family background was impeccable, but who had spent most of his adult life outside Canada as a university academic. His career path opened him to charges that he had returned to Canada only to begin politics at the top, and Tory attack ads on television in 2009 made much of the situation. Perhaps more to the point, Ignatieff came across to voters as entirely too cerebral, and Canadians never warmed to him the way they did to NDP leader Jack Layton, a thoroughly bilingual native of Quebec based in Ontario. The results of the 2011 federal election were in some ways a shocker. Many observers were surprised that the poor administration of the G20 summit by the Conservative government—incredibly expensive and marred with considerable violence made possible by its location in downtown Toronto—seemed to have little impact on the electorate. In the end, few pundits doubted that Harper's Tories would win, but few expected the Liberals to do quite so badly, especially in Quebec, or the NDP to perform quite so well, mainly making their gains in Quebec. Bloc Québécois voters abandoned the party federally in droves, mostly leaving for Layton's NDP.

In the wake of the election, Ignatieff resigned and was replaced by Justin Trudeau as Liberal leader, while Layton tragically died of cancer and was replaced by Thomas Mulcair. As for Stephen Harper, he proved with

John Gilbert (Jack) Layton

Jack Layton speaks during Question Period in the House of Commons in Ottawa. © CHRIS WATTIE/Reuters/Corbis.

Son of a prominent Progressive Conservative politician, Jack Layton (1950–2011) was born in Montreal and grew up in nearby suburban Hudson, Quebec. He was active in politics from his high school days, subsequently attending McGill University to earn an Honours BA in political science. As an undergraduate, he was greatly influenced by the Canadian political philosopher Charles Taylor, who introduced him to the work of C.B. Macpherson. From Macpherson, Layton inherited a strand of political idealism—"Idealists imagine a positive liberty that enables us to build together toward common objectives that fulfill and even surpass our individual goals," Macpherson once wrote—that remained with him throughout his life. He received an MA in 1971 at York University and his Ph.D. from York in 1983, and over a decade from 1974 to the mid-1980s taught at Ryerson Polytechnical Institute, York University, and the University of Toronto.

In 1982 Layton entered politics, unexpectedly winning a seat on the Toronto city council and becoming a voice for the left. He opposed SkyDome and later the Toronto attempt to host the 1996 Summer Olympics. After the 1988 municipal elections, Layton led a coalition of New Democrats and independents that controlled the city council. That same year he married Olivia Chow. This was his second marriage, the first having been to his childhood sweetheart in 1970. Layton deliberately cleaned up his previously scruffy appearance to run for mayor of Toronto in 1991, but he was hurt by his earlier opposition to the Olympics and by the current unpopularity of the provincial NDP government, losing badly. In 1993 he ran unsuccessfully for the House of Commons in the Rosedale riding, but a year later he was again elected to the Toronto city council. Throughout the remainder of the decade he stayed in the public eye as leader of the Federation of Canadian Municipalities.

In 2003, Layton was elected leader of the NDP, which he led from outside the House of Commons until his election as MP for Toronto-Danforth in 2004. During the campaign Layton demonstrated his ability to cause controversy and gain headlines, as well as showing an appeal in Quebec, but the party ended up with only 19 seats, far fewer than Layton had predicted. Nevertheless, he manoeuvred his handful of MPs into a position of power in a divided House of Commons and entered the 2006 election as an appealing party leader who succeeded in raising the party's number of MPs to 29. The party responded with a resounding vote of confidence. The NDP gained more seats (up to 37) in 2008, and Layton joined Liberal leader Stéphane Dion and Gilles Duceppe of the Bloc Québécois in successful negotiations to form a coalition to govern instead of the Tories, calling another election after an assured defeat of the minority Harper government in the Commons. As it turned out, Governor General Michaëlle Jean allowed the Prime Minister to prorogue Parliament instead and the coalition attempt failed, in part because Dion was

Continued...

a majority to be more of what Canadians had earlier seen. His government cut taxes, moved towards a balanced budget, held the line on new social programs, and worked hard to increase employment, often by further encouragement to resource development. Many of his budget cuts were in the areas of culture and science policy, provoking outraged responses from a highly articulate segment of the population. In foreign policy the Tories were pro-Israeli and pro-Ukrainian, clearly more interventionist than earlier Liberal governments. In style, Harper proved aggressively partisan—particularly fond of the television attack ad—and continued his bad relationship with the media, especially the parliamentary press gallery. He had several well-publicized disasters, the first involving the purchase of fighter planes from the United States, and another involving high-profile appointments to the Senate of individuals accused by the Auditor General of making improper expense claims. The latter provided days of reality television on Canadian news channels in which Harper came suspiciously close to telling untruths in Parliament. Aboriginal policy continued to be a problem,

particularly as the number of cases of disappearances and murders of Aboriginal and Métis women continued to accumulate and remain unsolved into 2015. Harper met demands for a national inquiry with an insistence that the cases represented a criminal problem rather than a broader social one, a position belied by virtually every television newscast (see Table 13.2).

In Quebec, Premier Pauline Marois called a new election in late February 2014, years before the expiration of her mandate, in the hopes of converting into a legislative majority the favourable publicity over her handling of the 2013 Lac-Mégantic disaster and her Parti Québécois's proposed secular charter that would prohibit civil servants from wearing overt religious/ethnic symbols such as hijabs or turbans. Marois very pointedly distanced the PQ from its earlier sovereignist aspirations, but for some reason failed to recognize the dangers in the well-publicized candidacy for her party of Pierre Karl Péladeau. Péladeau, a very wealthy and influential media figure in Quebec who owned or controlled nearly half the media in the province, was far to the right of the PQ on most social issues, as well as

TABLE 13.2 Canadian Female Homicides, 1980–2012

Province/Territory	Aboriginal	Non-Aboriginal	Unknown Ethnicity	Aboriginal Victim Proportion (%)
Newfoundland	10	57	1	15
Prince Edward Island	0	10	0	0
Nova Scotia	5	163	4	3
New Brunswick	5	125	0	4
Quebec	46	1,445	11	3
Ontario	114	1,901	48	6
Manitoba	196	188	13	49
Saskatchewan	153	116	7	55
Alberta	206	533	2	28
British Columbia	205	890	8	19
Yukon	10	8	0	56
Northwest Territories	42	3	1	92
Nunavut	20	0	0	100
Total Canada	**1,017**	**5,439**	**95**	**16**

Source: Reprinted with the permission of the RCMP.

a known sovereignist. When he announced on 9 March 2014 that he was running because he wanted Quebec to become an independent country, the opposition Liberals, who had been floundering under the leadership of Philippe Couillard, suddenly had their campaign issue, and they rode it hard. It quickly became clear that most Quebecers did not want another referendum on sovereignty, which certainly implied that most people in the province were not eager for an independent Quebec. The problem, many analysts emphasized, was that independence was no longer something particularly sought by the younger generation, as had been the case in the 1970s and 1980s, when the baby boomers of Quebec had been hot for sovereignty. The years since 1970 had seen support for sovereignty eroded by increasing Quebec autonomy in economic and immigration terms, as well as by more protection for the French language in the schools, the workplace, and in everyday life. If sovereignty was no longer a hot-button issue, the so-called "charter of values" certainly was, and it proved to be unpopular with voters. The result was a stunning and somewhat unexpected defeat for the PQ, with Marois not just failing to retain the premiership but also her seat. The Liberals, under Couillard, found themselves back in power in *la belle province*.

The Canadian Economy

On the whole, the Canadian economy has performed reasonably well in the new millennium, especially in comparison with other Western nations. In the earlier years of the twenty-first century, Canada converted a protracted period of high commodity prices and high domestic construction demand into general employment growth that seemed to have no end. By 2006 the nation had seen 13 years of employment gains, with unemployment rates at a 30-year low. Over this period employment growth had averaged 2 per cent per year. To some extent, Canada shared in an international boom, but the Canadian government ran high surpluses as the international balance sheet was continually in Canada's favour. One problem was a weakening American dollar, which meant that a more highly valued Canadian one was reducing the nation's international competitiveness. Another was the high price of gasoline at the pump, which proved more an aggravation than a deterrent to Canadian fondness for gas-guzzling sports utility vehicles and pickup trucks. Other weak spots in a generally prosperous picture included tough times for farmers, pummelled by mad cows and bad weather. Tourism, especially travel to Canada from the United States, was down substantially, as Americans tended to travel at home. Canada's clean air and clean beaches were no longer a sufficient attraction to cross the border. The Atlantic provinces, highly dependent on tourism, suffered the most. Curiously, despite the well-publicized problems of the farmers, the three western provinces posted the greatest gains in job creation and economic development, mostly in primary resources and the support services for those industries.

Then came the financial disaster of 2008–9, which struck hardest in the United States and radiated outward to the rest of the world. The American meltdown was triggered in the first instance by the collapse of an overheated real estate market that had led Americans to believe that they could trade up endlessly. Low mortgage rates encouraged many homebuyers to purchase houses beyond their means, and when the bubble burst, defaults and foreclosures spiralled. Many American financial institutions had tied securities to mortgages in mysterious ways, and as the housing market collapsed, these securities and the credit based on them proved worthless. Government regulation, moreover, had fallen well behind the innovative nature of the credit expansion; there was much chicanery at work as well. Both financial institutions and individuals were overleveraged—i.e., in debt beyond their capacity to pay. Canadian banking was both better regulated and more conservative, and so it was not much involved in either the bubble or the ensuing crisis. Canada was adversely affected by the international fallout, however. The Canadian government was forced to intervene to save several corporations from collapse, especially in the automotive industry, and to create employment through public spending. After 2008, Canadian economic growth and job creation rates flattened out, although Canada did not experience anywhere near the extent of the economic meltdown of the United States and some other European countries.

The general performance of the Canadian economy after 2008—it bent but did not break—had several important consequences. One was that the Canadian housing market did not collapse, and continued to be buoyant through 2014. Housing prices, adjusted for inflation, grew 49 per cent from 2001 to 2009 and another 19 per cent from 2009 to 2012. Experts and bankers worried continually. According to *The Economist* magazine in September 2014, Canada's housing was among the most overinflated in the world, with many signs of an American-style meltdown in prospect. One of those signs was a level of household debt of $1.64 for every dollar of annual disposable income, the same sort of level experienced in the United States and Britain at the time of the meltdown. Some argued that most of the inflation was in a few key markets, such as Toronto, Montreal, Calgary, and Vancouver, and mainly in a few segments of those markets, especially condominiums. Others pointed out that no continual increase in price of anything, much less housing, lasted forever.

Another result of relative Canadian economic stability after 2009 was that the Canadian market became much more attractive as an area for expansion to American and other retailers, and a number of high-profile companies such as Target and Marshalls opened in Canada in recent years. Target Canada, for one, found the going much harder than it expected, and less than two years after opening the first of over 100 stores Target's Canadian offshoot filed for bankruptcy in January 2015 and moved to liquidate all of its inventory and close the stores. But the introduction of large American retailers inevitably hollows out the retail sector of less competitive Canadians, especially those running small businesses. On a separate but related front, the iconic Canadian restaurant chain, Tim Hortons, which freed itself from American ownership in 2006, was purchased by another American competitor, Burger King, in the summer of 2014, announcing it would move its corporate headquarters from Canada for tax reasons. For how long the chain could continue to present itself credibly as Canadian in the face of the corporate record was another question entirely.

Contemporary Views

Adrienne Clarkson

Adrienne Clarkson was born in Hong Kong in 1939 and immigrated to Canada with her family in 1942 as refugees from the Japanese occupation. She was the first visible minority person to be Governor General (1999–2005), as well as the second woman. This is an excerpt from her memoirs.

We don't admire our politicians because they are nice people, no matter what we say. I think we want them to do the job for us, and we grudgingly admire a certain level of ruthlessness that is just this side of manslaughter. It was said about the avuncular Prime Minister Harold Macmillan of Great Britain that he proved in his dealings with his cabinet that "greater love hath no man than that he should lay down his friends' lives to save his own."

My personal view is that that the world of politics is like this because it is a male world with male values—the worship of triumphalism, contempt for weakness, and distrust of compassion. All of these are male feelings and attributes and, even though women are now part of the political world, I suspect that many of them feel discomfort and a certain hollowness because that world is so masculine. The late Judy LaMarsh's amusing observation that there was no female lavatory on Parliament Hill when she was elected is a funny aside to real life. Sometimes the most trivial things tell us a great deal, and the lack of female lavatories is one of them. Does it

Continued...

mean that women are not supposed to have the same basic needs and that they are not thought of in the same way that men are? I still think our political system is absorbing the shock of having women in it. After all, things don't integrate that quickly, and it has only been eighty years since women were declared persons.

Many students of the psyche tell us that the best-developed personality contains elements of the masculine and feminine, but Jung talks about the soul in each of us, the *anima* in the man and the *animus* in the woman. It is only when you are aware of where your soul is located, and how to properly express it, that you are able to become fully developed.

What I have seen in political life has made me realize that the anima in male politicians may be there but is quite often described as a killer *anima*—that is, a monstrous feminine streak that attempts to kill their humanity, strangle it at birth as it were. The same thing can happen to a woman with a killer *animus*. But politics is the place where you see men behaving this way with the most blatant freedom. The system of competition, of winning, of annihilating, encourages this behaviour.

When this is all there is, the direction of a country is lost. We know that people develop disgust or distaste for what they can see is a dehumanizing attempt to use power, which, after all, is given only temporarily to those who are elected.

Source: Adrienne Clarkson, *Heart Matters* (Toronto: Penguin Canada, 2007), 215–16.

Canadian Society and Culture in the Meltdown Era

Given the volatility and complexity of developments in the new millennium, it was hardly surprising that social and cultural signals in Canada often were difficult to interpret. Only a few examples of the difficulties can be explored here.

Boomers, Sandwiches, and Boomerangs

The constraints of a static economy in the twenty-first century have led to an increased visibility of certain social phenomena relating to households and families: sandwiched parents and boomerang kids. Sandwiched parents, all members of the baby-boom generation, are those caring simultaneously for aging parents on the one hand and adult children on the other. According to the 2011 census, 42.3 per cent of young adults aged 20–29 were still living with their parents, a figure up

TABLE 13.3 Public Approval Rates (%) on Hot-Button Social Issues in Canada, the United States, and United Kingdom, 2013

Issue	Canada	United States	United Kingdom
Contraception	91	79	91
Sexual relations between unmarried partners	83	59	82
Divorce	80	65	70
Having children outside of marriage	78	53	74
Gambling	70	63	60
Stem cell research	65	52	56
Doctor assisted suicide	65	35	61
Same-sex sexual relations	64	40	55
Abortion	60	36	54
Death penalty	53	58	50

Source: The Economist, 13 September 2004, 42.

substantially from 26.9 per cent in 1981. More males (46.7 per cent) than females (37.9 per cent) were among the adult children still at home, and about a quarter of those children had once left the nest and returned to it. In 2014, over eight million Canadians provided care-giving for old or disabled friends and relations, and more than two million dealt with both adult children and the elderly at the same time. The reason for having to look after the old and disabled is plain enough, but the chil-dren (and especially the boomerang kids) are a more complex business. Their numbers have increased sub-stantially enough from earlier eras to represent a recog-nizable trend. Most adult children living at home do so because of high housing costs, high university costs, high debts accumulated to attend university, and low wages after graduation. The probability of having adult chil-dren at home was substantially increased if parents lived in a single-family dwelling in one of the larger cities of Ontario, or in Vancouver. A much smaller percentage of parents in rural areas or small towns were likely to have adult children living at home.

Related to the new realities of living arrange-ments for adult children was a substantial shift in the utility of a university education, especially in the arts disciplines, and a considerable increase in the amount of debt accumulated by university students pursuing their degrees. In 2014, the average Canadian student was carrying a debt load in excess of $20,000. That debt load included, collectively, $15 billion worth of federal- and provincial-sponsored debt, on both of which the default rates are high. In addition, students have borrowed from their parents and from banks, which have been quite willing to open and extend credit card balances to students. When these debt loads are combined with high unemployment rates among students leaving university, the result is a real social problem. It may also become a real problem for Canadian universities, which are finding increasing difficulty in finding employment for many of their graduates. The truth of the matter may be that the days of riding a university education to prosperity and upward mobility are over, and Canadian students may have to reconceptualize their career plans to suit the new economic conditions.

Religion and Church Attendance

Most of the mixed messages regarding religious faith and organized religion in Canada were singularly con-fusing. Polls and detailed studies have persistently revealed that most Canadians believed in God and that many had enjoyed spiritual experiences, but regular church attendance in Canada, especially in the main-line churches, continued to fall precipitously, especially among the young. A survey by the *Huffington Post* in 2012 showed that over half of young Canadians never attended a religious institution, and only 12 per cent said they went weekly. Christians were slightly more regular than were Jews or Muslims. Attendance was low-est in Quebec. Another poll, taken in April 2006, found that regular church attendance had decreased 4 per cent since 1996 and that less than half of Canadians polled went to church more than once a year.

Many reasons have been advanced for this state of affairs, with one common explanation being that the young feel that they have better things to do with their time. This analysis, of course, begs the question, which ultimately revolves around the extent of ongoing belief in the teachings of organized religion. Whether the prominence of the churches in sexual abuse and Aboriginal residential schools played any part in the situation is not known. More likely, the disconnect between the teachings of the churches and modern mor-ality have been influential. Curiously enough, the atti-tude towards church attendance in Canada was quite different from that in the United States, where almost 40 per cent of Americans went to church at least once a week, a figure that has remained unchanged since 1900. The difference between the United States and Canada, many observers have suggested, is that the Americans have many more evangelical congregations. In any event, statistics on churchgoing indicate a substantial difference in values between the United States and Canada in an important aspect of daily life, and provide a challenge to those who claim that the basic values of Americans and Canadians have converged.

That both Americans and Canadians were quest-ing for something spiritual they were not currently getting in their churches has been well demonstrated by the plethora of books dealing with spirituality outside the confines of organized religion, including books on spiritualism, witchcraft, and demonology. Among Christians, we have seen an increased interest in the Gnostic writings of early Christianity. These writings offer a more human Jesus and a far less dogmatic approach to belief. Indeed, dogmatism has clearly been part of the problem, as churches not affiliated with larger, traditional denominations have been more successful at finding and retaining members. How the mainline churches would respond to this continued evidence of interest in matters of the spirit—but not in their organizations—is another matter. So far the record is not encouraging.

An Alternate Religion: Hockey

Professional hockey recovered nicely from a National Hockey League lockout that lasted from 15 September 2004 to mid-June of 2005. Attendance has been buoyant at all levels of the game, although it remains the case that, particularly at the professional level, most Canadian hockey players play for teams based in the United States. The return of NHL hockey to Winnipeg in 2011, when the floundering Atlanta Thrashers relocated and became the new Jets, has led to an increase in speculation that other struggling US franchises would move north into both previously failed markets such as Quebec City, but also to Saskatoon and to Markham and other locations in the Ontario megalopolis.

No Canadian team has won the Stanley Cup since Montreal in 1993. As a result, for many Canadians, the test of the well-being of Canadian hockey has resided at the international level. Here Canada has done well. The Canadian teams of both genders have won at the Winter Olympics in 2002, 2010, and 2014. Other Canadian teams, notably the Juniors, have done equally well, with the IIHF World Under-20 championship becoming a major annual event over the Christmas holiday. It appears unlikely, at this point, that the National Hockey League will continue to allow its athletes to participate in the Olympics beyond 2014, much preferring a World Cup of hockey (as in soccer) in place of the

badly tarnished Olympic brand and the manipulation of the season schedule that participation requires.

Perhaps the most serious problem for hockey—in Canada and around the world—has been the increasing evidence that the violence of the sport has serious implications for both the short-term and long-term health of its players. Concussions are held to be the major culprit, and much publicized evidence has been presented involving both hockey and North American football showing that protracted concussions lead to dementia and related health issues in later life. The traditional hockey enforcer, and the fighting associated with that role, has come particularly under scrutiny, with a number of high-profile deaths of both active and recently retired players. Some defenders of the game insist that it would cease to have much meaning if all violence were removed from it, while hockey administrators everywhere are desperately seeking ways of reducing the number of concussions without changing the overall shape of the game. In the meantime, polls in Canada have indicated that large numbers of parents have lost enthusiasm for seeing their sons and daughters play the game, particularly because its demands for equipment and facilities make it one of the most expensive sports played anywhere in the world. One well-publicized media report in 2014 noted that hockey was significantly more expensive than horseback riding, and cheaper only than waterskiing. The average cost for a child to play hockey was $1,666 per year, which did not include the almost inevitable travel costs of out-of-town league games and tournaments.

Many observers have insisted that hockey will inevitably lose ground to less expensive sports, notably soccer and basketball. Canada hosted the 2015 women's World Cup in soccer, and continued success of the women's team, which won bronze at the 2012 Olympics, may continue to draw fans and athletes to "the beautiful game," as does the introduction of Major League Soccer franchises in Toronto, Montreal, and Vancouver. In basketball, in both 2013 and 2014, Canadians—Anthony Bennett and Andrew Wiggins, respectively—were chosen number-one overall in the NBA draft. The increased number and success of Canadian players, as well the success of Canada's lone franchise, the Toronto Raptors, may also be drawing eyes and interest to

Canadian James Naismith's invention. Such changes would doubtless strike a blow to the Canadian psyche rooted in ice and snow, shifting the country away from being simply hockey-mad and instead having a more diverse sports landscape.

Material Culture

The Newfoundland Moose Sign

Although all provinces have signs warning about moose on highways, the ones in Newfoundland are particularly important for road safety. Tom Clausen/Shutterstock.

The moose is the largest member of the deer family. A full-grown male stands over six feet tall and can weigh from 800 to 1,800 pounds. Moose are a traffic hazard in practically all Canadian provinces, where they roam fairly freely, and nearly every province has its version of a moose warning road sign.

Nowhere, however, are moose more of a problem than in Newfoundland, the home of somewhere between 170,000 and 230,000 of the animals. According to the RCMP and Royal Newfoundland Constabulary, the number of vehicle accidents involving moose is on the increase in the twenty-first century, increasing from an annual average of 452 in the years 2000–8 to 800 (with two fatalities) in 2012. There is even an organization devoted to lobbying for a reduction in their numbers.

Ironically, the moose is not native to the island of Newfoundland but was introduced from New Brunswick in 1904, being turned loose not far from Gros Morne National Park. The moose was brought to Newfoundland to replace a declining caribou population that had been decimated by sport hunting. Introducing moose was part of an effort to turn the island into a "paradise for sportsmen," attracting wealthy Americans to hunt and fish on the island and to spend money at sports camps and tourist lodges along the newly constructed railroad—and perhaps ultimately to invest in the exploitation of Newfoundland's natural resources. The moose flourished because, aside from hunters, it had no natural predators on the island, although why moose succeeded when the caribou did not is unclear, although the relative lack of grazing space for caribou herds may be a possible explanation.

Later in the twentieth century, hunting for moose had become firmly embedded as an annual traditional among residents, especially in the rural areas, and moose meat was not only a staple on island tables but a key ingredient in many traditional island dishes. Moose, therefore, have become an important part of Newfoundland's cultural heritage. They are also ecologically troublesome. Moose are top-heavy creatures that do not like to lower their heads to graze. As a result, they prefer to feed among young balsamic firs and hardwoods after reforestation. Moose grazing, say biologists, could have a serious negative impact on the sustainable growth of island timber.

The diamond-shaped, yellow moose sign is a material reflection of human tampering in the natural environment. While it has been adapted into the daily

Continued...

life of the province, the moose has also become a major danger for motorists, and continues to increase in population, largely unchecked. In comparison to the moose signs of other provinces, the signs found in Newfoundland reflect this, depicting the crashed car in the face of an unscathed moose. Compared to other such signs, the inclusion of the human impact is significant.

Source: Allan Byrne, "The Introduction of Moose to the Island of Newfoundland," 15 Sept. 2012, http://www.seethesites.ca/media/48059/introduction%20of%20moose.pdf.

Health, Health Care, and the Elderly

The efficacy of the Canadian health-care system and its cost have been the subjects of continual controversy during the new millennium. Canadians heard much about their system, most of it singularly ill-informed, in the course of the American debate over health-care coverage in 2009 and 2010. Questions have been raised about affordability, particularly in light of the aging of the Canadian population discussed in Chapters 11 and 12. One report, for example, by the Parliamentary Budget Officer, issued on 19 February 2010, asked whether the fiscal structure of the federal government was sustainable, given the increasing number of Canadians out of the workforce and making greater demands on both health care and other elderly benefits (see Table 13.4).

It concluded that sustainability was impossible without significant changes to the system. Other think-tank reports have suggested similar dire consequences over the ensuing years. Most of the conflicting arguments involve ideology, and not all experts are agreed. A substantial minority insisted that health-care costs have been stable for years and would not necessarily increase as the population aged, since the next generation of senior citizens would be healthier and require less medical attention for much of their extended life expectancy. Others have insisted that higher health-care costs were chiefly in the private sector, and need not become more draining on the public purse.

Also debatable were the statistics on infant mortality. International statistics showed that while the number of deaths of infants under one year of age per 1,000 live births was declining in Canada, it was falling less than

TABLE 13.4 The Private Cost of Long-Term Care in Canada

Province	Retirement homes/residences $ Yearly Cost		Nursing homes $ Yearly Cost	
	Minimum	Maximum	Minimum	Maximum
Alberta	12,000	65,000	18,100	22,100
British Columbia	13,000	70,000	11,650	37,100
Manitoba	15,000	42,000	12,400	28,900
New Brunswick	9,600	54,000	N/A	41,250
Newfoundland	20,100	50,000		33,600
Nova Scotia	23,000	72,000	22,500	38,000
Ontario	14,000	132,000	20,800	29,300
PEI	7,200	63,000	N/A	28,300
Quebec	6,000	42,000	13,100	21,100
Saskatchewan	16,600	60,000	12,600	23,900

Source: Bank of Montreal, Living to 100: The Four Keys to Longevity, July 2014. Senioropolis Inc, 2014.

in many other developed and industrialized countries. The media kept reporting the low ranking of Canada on this sensitive indicator of the general health of the population. One problem is that it is hard to compare statistics from one country to another (or in Canada, from one province to another). Variations in recording techniques could well account for a large proportion of the difference between nations, as could the relative success of Canada in delivering infants well before term.

The Internet and Popular Culture

Canadians continued to demonstrate an extraordinary willingness to try and use new technologies. In the process, digital technology became inextricably intertwined with Canadian popular culture. The nation began the millennium well advanced in its use of the Internet, and this continued to be the case. In 2014, 86 per cent of Canadians used the Internet, placing Canada behind only the United Kingdom (at 87 per cent) for world supremacy. Eighty-two per cent of Canadians used social media, compared to 75 per cent of Americans, although Canada ranks twelfth in the world in the number of hours spent using social media each day, clocking in at 2 hours and 19 minutes per day. In 2013, more than half of all Canadians shopped on the Internet. Our Internet usage has penetrated more deeply into the population than elsewhere, especially among middle-aged and elderly people. Canadian use of technology, particularly smart phones, has become increasingly problematic. Among young people, texting has become the most important single cause of automobile fatalities in that segment of the population.

The use of the Internet, which is totally unregulated by the Canadian government, has had important consequences for the media in the country. Radio listening via the Internet has increased greatly, cutting into the markets for local radio stations. Even more important has been video streaming, which makes it possible to receive video over the Internet instead of via cable television. By hooking the computer up with the television, Canadians can obtain 24-hour sports, including access to all major league and many minor league sporting events. Similarly, a number of services, mainly American, have sprung up to provide Canadian viewers via their computers, by sub-

scription, with enormous libraries of films and archived television programs. Netflix, the largest streaming service, has refused to disclose the number of its Canadian subscribers, although current polls suggest that up to 30 per cent of English-speaking Canadian households are customers. In September 2014, Netflix defied the Canadian Radio-television and Telecommunications Commission (CRTC) by refusing to provide data on its Canadian operations, including its number of subscribers. The company insisted that as an Internet operation it could not be regulated by the CRTC. If Netflix succeeds in this defiance, it will render the regulatory efforts of the CRTC, especially with regard to Canadian content regulations, much more problematic. Fortunately, wherever Canadian culture resides, it is probably not really on the television.

Conclusion

Ongoing Issues and Hope for the Future

By 2014 Canada had exposed itself to international scrutiny, first at the Vancouver Olympic Winter Games and then at the G8 and G20 international summits, held at Deerhurst Resort near Huntsville, Ontario, and in downtown Toronto over a single week in June 2010. On neither of these occasions did the image of the nation—of which Canadians are so protective and proud—remain unsullied. At the Winter Games, the death of a Georgian luger on a training run before the official opening marred the scene, amid charges that Canada was not allowing visiting athletes equal time to practice for competitive events. As for the hosting of the international summits, Canadians were treated in Toronto to the unedifying spectacle of thousands of Toronto policemen equipped with helmets, clubs, and riot shields beating up protestors in the heart of the city. In any case, both the Games and the summits reminded Canadians that their nation was but a small part of a larger world that was, said the alarmists, teetering on the brink of any number of catastrophes in the new millennium.

More recently, the emergence of the self-styled Islamic State caliphate (variously acronymed as ISIS,

Biography

Robert Bruce (Rob) Ford

Rob Ford participates in a mayoral debate hosted by the Canadian Tamil Congress in Scarborough, Ontario. © *FRED THORNHILL/ Reuters/Corbis.*

A member of a prominent suburban Toronto family active in politics and business, Rob Ford, born in 1969, attended Carleton University and was elected to the Toronto city council in 2000, serving there until his election as Toronto's sixty-fourth mayor in 2010. He ran on a platform of cutting expenses and taxes, and was strongly supported in the northern suburbs of the city, which recently had been amalgamated into the city and were aggrieved about their neglect in favour of the older central core. From the start of his political career, if not before, Ford was embroiled in controversy, both personal and political. There was a history of domestic disputes and even violence, beginning in 2008,

as well as a series of incidents involving his coaching of various high school football teams. From the beginning of his council membership, Ford was well known for passionate speeches, for his earthy vocabulary, and for his parsimoniousness, as well as for his attentiveness to his constituents. In the 2010 mayoral election Ford captured the suburban vote, and once in office he criticized the city's watchdog officials as unnecessary. He balanced the city's budget in 2011 and continued to argue for reduced services and higher user fees. His rapid transit policy was highly controversial.

From the beginning, Ford's relationship with Toronto's media was a troubled one, with continued reports of public drunkenness and erratic behaviour. In May of 2013, an American website reported that it had viewed a video in which Ford had appeared to smoke crack cocaine, and two *Toronto Star* journalists wrote that they, too, had seen the video, although no one was able to produce a physical copy. The Toronto police department had Ford under constant investigation for drug use and for his friendship with known criminals, although no charges were ever filed. Ford nevertheless had a running feud with Toronto's chief of police. Ford ultimately acknowledged that he had used marijuana and in November 2013 admitted that he had smoked crack. More videos surfaced and Ford again apologized for his behaviour, disarmingly stating, "I am not perfect." Also in November 2013, the Toronto city council stripped Ford of most of his mayoral powers, although it did not dismiss him because it lacked the power. Throughout the second half of 2013 and into early 2014, Ford's antics were a daily feature of Canadian news telecasts and often were reported by the American media with an air of amusement. After another round of admissions of bad behaviour and apologies, in May of 2014 he checked himself into a clinic for drug and alcohol addiction, and shortly after leaving it he was admitted to hospital with what proved to be a rare form of cancer, leading to his withdrawal from a mayoralty race where, despite his well-publicized problems, he was running a strong campaign. The Ford saga was an excellent example of Canadian-content reality television. Many viewers across the nation were unable to understand how he could continue to enjoy a high level of popular support in Toronto. Whether the city's public image was seriously damaged by the Ford spectacle was another matter.

ISIL, and DAESH), another militant Muslim terrorist organization in Iraq and Syria; the appearance of Ebola, a deadly pandemic disease in West Africa; and the shooting down of a civilian aircraft over war-torn Ukraine all suggested the uncertainties of the world in which Canadians lived. The killing of two Canadian soldiers on Canadian soil in October 2014—the vehicular homicide of Warrant Officer Patrice Vincent and the shooting death of Corporal Nathan Cirillo—brought these uncertainties closer to home than ever. That Michael Zehaf-Bibeau, Cirillo's killer, was killed in a shootout in the Centre Block of Parliament showed just how vulnerable even our most protected sites can be.

Domestically, Canada continues to come under fire for the treatment of Aboriginal peoples both past and present. A UN report, published in May 2014, emphasized the current challenges and determined that there is a crisis in Aboriginal communities even in terms of

Protestors confront riot police in downtown Toronto during G20 protests in June 2010. Some protestors vandalized storefronts and destroyed city property, resulting in widespread criticism of the Toronto Police Service. At the same time, the use by the police of "kettling"—surrounding large groups of people and confining them for lengthy periods in small areas—was attacked by many, as was the fact that many police removed their name badges to avoid identification for their overly zealous response to protestors. The Canadian Press/Christian Lapid.

basic needs. The Truth and Reconciliation Commission has exposed numerous failures by the Canadian government, and released the executive summary of its report on residential schools on 2 June 2015, which includes close to 100 recommendations for change and healing of the relationship between Aboriginal peoples and the rest of Canada. The federal government response was muted.

Canada is also continuing to see itself lag behind the rest of the world on issues regarding the environment. Recent shifts in provincial politics, including new initiatives in Ontario and Quebec, may begin to turn the tide on this issue. Federally, however, government policies regarding oil extraction and carbon emissions can be described as lax at best.

In the midst of the ongoing gloom and doom, however, most Canadians managed to carry on. The number of gardening centres and the sale of garden plants increased enormously in the twenty-first century, as did the sale of gourmet foods and fine wines. Ever larger numbers of Canadians in winter took chartered flights to semi-exotic destinations in warmer climates. Home renovation and cooking programs became extremely popular on television, and their success was reflected in the explosion of domestic construction and redecorating projects across the country.

Although Canadians are having trouble finding their way in the world, we should not conclude on a negative note. Today, most Canadians live longer, earn more, are better educated, travel more, and possess more stuff than ever before. A few might wish to return to simpler times, but most would not care to go back to an era in which there were no life-saving drugs, little family planning, and only a primitive welfare and health-care system, although that would take them back only to the 1930s. Fewer would care to go still further back in time, to a period when only men voted and unabashed sexism and racism were taken for granted, although such would have been the case in the days when the nation was founded. On nearly every indicator of quality of life—health care and standards, cultural accomplishment, social infrastructure, gross national product per capita, civil rights and liberties, and per capita purchasing power—Canada continues to be a world leader. Such statistics only confirm what Canadians instinctively know: Canada is a great country and a good place to live.

The 2015 Federal Election: Moving Forward

Canadians' vision for the future of their country and its place on the world stage came to the fore during the federal election of 2015. The election was held on 19 October, following the longest campaign (78 days) in modern times. Gradually the parties unveiled their campaign strategies. The Tories emphasized a stable economy and national security. The NDP, who started the campaign ahead in the polls, focused on fiscal responsibility. Over the course of the campaign, both parties failed to excite the electorate: Prime Minister Harper interacted only with carefully chosen supporters in structured campaign events, while NDP leader Thomas Mulcair seemed to have trouble engaging with Canadians, mostly presenting himself and his party as non-Conservative, but with unexpected forays into Conservative territory (e.g., promising a balanced budget).

Conversely, Liberal leader Justin Trudeau, who had been disparaged for months by Tory television attack ads, projected youthful energy and offered fresh ideas. These ideas included deliberate deficit spending on much-needed infrastructure and tax breaks for middle-class Canadians. The Liberals put together a package of over 300 items, promising action on most of the hot-button items of the day. As the Liberals rose in the polls, the Tories became aware of their own diminishing popularity, and the NDP came to realize—too late—that they should have put a greater effort toward running against the Liberals.

In the midst of the campaign, the Syrian refugee crisis in Europe intruded into the usually insular Canadian world. In early September, photos and video of a small child's drowned body on a Mediterranean beach brought the issue fully to the world stage. Faced with few safe alternatives, the boy's family had tragically chosen to embark on a dangerous sea voyage to Europe, where they planned to join thousands of other refugees pushing north in hopes of a better life. Reports that the boy's family had been aiming to eventually resettle in Canada evoked an emotional response among Canadians, and many started questioning what their country could do to help those fleeing troubles in Syria. The Liberals were the only party that responded seriously to the humanitarian crisis, promising to resettle 25,000 refugees in Canada by the end of 2015. At the same time, the Conservatives were widely criticized for their mismanagement of the crisis.

As the election got nearer, it was clear that the Liberals had captured the imaginations of Canadians, and the result was a stunning victory that gave the party an overwhelming majority: 184 seats to the Tory 99, with the NDP winning only 44. Whether the Liberals could deliver on all their promises was another matter. A terrorist attack in Paris in early November increased concerns about national security, and many Canadians called for enhanced vetting procedures for immigrants and refugees. By early December, despite firm plans to welcome several thousand Syrian refugees in the following weeks, it was clear that the Liberals' goal of resettling 25,000 in Canada by the end of the year had been overly optimistic. Moreover, despite Canada's loudly trumpeted attendance at the 2015 UN Climate Change Conference in Paris, many Canadians felt that Trudeau and his fellow Canadian delegates could have made a stronger commitment to curbing carbon emissions and promoting sustainable development. At the same time, most Canadians were encouraged by the new governments' commitment to openness and willingness to consider reform in Ottawa.

Justin Trudeau, Canada's twenty-third prime minister, leaving the podium after delivering a speech at Canada House in London, England, 25 November 2015. Underestimated by many at the beginning of his campaign, Trudeau presented a message of positivity and change that resonated with many Canadians, and he was elected with a majority Liberal government on 19 October 2015© THE CANADIAN PRESS/Adrian Wyld.

Short Bibliography

Adams, Michael. *Fire and Ice: The United States, Canada, and the Myth of Converging Values*. Toronto, 2003. A study arguing that the United States and Canada were not becoming socially more alike.

Clarkson, Adrienne. *Heart Matters*. Toronto, 2006.

Doern, Bruce, and Monica Gattinger. *Power Switch: Energy Regulatory Governance in the 21st Century*. Toronto, 2003 THE CANADIAN PRESS. A careful analysis of how energy was regulated.

Drache, Daniel. *Borders Matter: Homeland Security and the Search for North America*. Halifax, 2004. A Canadian nationalist looks at the homeland security issue.

Koh, Tommy, et al., eds. *The New Global Threat: Severe Acute Respiratory Syndrome and Its Impacts*. River Edge, NJ, 2003. A multi-authored and international account of SARS.

Kolbert, Elizabeth. *Field Notes for a Catastrophe: Man, Nature, and Climate Change*. New York, 2006. A powerful vision of world disaster.

McDougall, John N. *Drifting Together: The Political Economy of Canada–US Integration*. Toronto, 2006. Argues the case for convergence.

McKinney, Joseph. *Political Economy of the U.S.–Canada Softwood Lumber Trade*. Orono, Maine, 2004. An analysis of the softwood lumber business, sympathetic to the United States.

Smith, Lawrence. *The World in 2050: Four Forces Shaping Civilization's North*. New York, 2010. A leading climate scientist looks into the future.

Steele, Graham. *What I Learned about Politics: Inside the Rise—and Collapse—of Nova Scotia's NDP Government*. Halifax, 2014. A memoir that provides valuable insight into the inner workings of modern provincial politics.

Study Questions

1. Would Canadian–American relations in the early twenty-first century have been very much different without 9/11? Why or why not?

2. Why did the Liberal Party lose the 2006 election?

3. What was the "mad cow" kerfuffle really about?

4. How has the new millennium been harder for Canada than earlier periods?

5. In your view, which of the many threats to world peace in the twenty-first century is the most dangerous? What factor or factors are the most threatening to Canadian stability and prosperity?

6. How have social media changed Canada?

7. What does Table 13.3 tell us about Canadian attitudes and social values in 2013? How do you think they compare to 20 years ago? 50? 100?

Visit the companion website for *A History of the Canadian Peoples*, fifth edition for further resources.

 www.oupcanada.com/Bumsted5e

Epilogue: The Speed and Balance of Canadian History

Fugit inreparabile tempus.
("It escapes, irretrievable time.")
— Virgil, *Georgics*

The Speed of History

Virgil's comment on the irretrievability of time is more typically attributed as *Tempus Fugit* ("Time Flies").

And in the modern world, the flight of time is verging on supersonic.

Like everything else in the twenty-first century, the need to interpret what is happening in the present, and to contextualize it within the past, is virtually instant. This kind of contextualization is possible because of our constantly growing digital world. In the case of certain kinds of data, such as sports statistics, box office sales, and election results, this is fairly easy to do, if one can properly compensate for such matters as era, inflation, and voting rights limitations. For other information, contextualization is much more complicated.

Notable in particular are the 24-hour news cycle, the omnipresence of the Internet and social media, and the constant need for content those outlets have combined to create. This need for content has made quick interpretation necessary, even for the most important of issues. Take, for example, the way that we perceive the actions of Canadians participating in foreign wars. As many as 50,000 pre-Confederation "Canadians" are said to have participated in the US Civil War between 1861 and 1865.[1] Hundreds of Dominion of Canada volunteers participated in the Spanish Civil War, volunteering in large numbers for the international brigades starting in 1937,[2] even when other governments were actively trying to prevent their citizens' participation. Dozens, if not hundreds, of Canadian Jews have fought to create and to defend the state of Israel, in both the past and the present. One such Canadian volunteer was Ben Dunkelman, a World War II veteran who commanded the Israeli 7th Brigade and is credited as being largely responsible for the capture of northern Galilee in 1948.[3] As recently as July 2014, 145 Canadians were a part of the Israel Defence Force's lone soldier program,[4] actively serving in the IDF in combat capacities. However, many Canadians did not and do not know about these volunteer soldiers, then or now.

In comparison, news of the relatively small number of Canadians either enlisting or attempting to enlist to fight for the Islamic State (ISIS) in the Middle East—and of the actions being taken to prevent them from doing so— is extensively covered by every media outlet. Attempts by Muslim Canadians to join a foreign conflict are treated very differently from those of volunteers of the past. Many who lived in Canada in the mid-nineteenth century still had strong family connections in the United States. In the case of the Spanish Civil War, few of the volunteers, if any, had familial or religious connections to Spain. In large part, the differing treatment is due to the fear of extremism and international terrorism that has been thematic in the twenty-first century. However, it might be worth remembering that what today we call international terrorism was around at the time of Confederation in the form of the Fenians. That being said, the increased information that is easily available to anyone with an Internet connection, combined with the need to constantly generate content for both online and television news sources, has certainly been a factor in how frequently such news is brought to the public eye.

What is often being missed, of course, is the placement of such actions in the larger historical context. While Canadians going to fight foreign wars is topical, it is far from the only situation in which this contextualization is occurring.

History, like Time, is moving faster. In some cases, the contextualization of the events of the present is not necessarily the realm of historians at all. There is a very real danger for historians in interpreting events in the moments they occur. The importance of Rob Ford, his shenanigans, and his March 2014 *Jimmy Kimmel Live* appearance, for example, seemed enormous when the revisions to this textbook began. For the first time a Canadian municipal official was taking on international prominence, albeit for dubious reasons. Today, those events seem a lot less meaningful than they did at the time. Mr Ford has been through a great deal, both in private and in the public eye, and yet the city of Toronto has moved forward with its own scandals, successes, and the omnipresent futility of the Maple Leafs both with and without him as mayor. There will certainly be a time in the future when the actions of Rob Ford, as a man and as a politician, will make for entertaining and possibly enlightening reading. Whether that reading will be of historic significance, or simply an interesting footnote to the period, remains to be seen.

At the same time, there have always been problems in history in underestimating the impact of events in the middle distance. Louis Riel will always remain a prime example of this in a Canadian context. Hanged as a traitor in 1885 and treated as such at the time, today Riel is much more regularly seen as the father of Manitoba and a hero, both of the province and of the Métis.

Even worse—as the voluminous data and findings of the Truth and Reconciliation Commission (TRC) are released—is the discovery that the past has been covered up, or largely ignored. The results and revelations seem to be even beyond the imaginings of those who knew or who have always acknowledged that there was evil in the actions of some governments and some church representatives during the residential school period.

Looking at these events with the benefits of hindsight is what allows historians to fully unpack the meanings and impacts of the actions. Time is what allows the placing of these events in the larger context. It is for other fields of academia and the public record to discuss the present, and even the near present.

Moments exist, whether they are constructed or not, that most would acknowledge as being notable. The Women's World Cup took place in the summer of 2015. The Senate scandal audit was produced, finding over a million dollars in unnecessary spending, and costing $24 million to generate (and this scandal, like Rob Ford, was lampooned on American television). The Harper government continues to lock horns with the Supreme Court of Canada. While that in itself is not notable, the rate at which the government has "lost" is nothing short of prodigious—by having laws judged unconstitutional, such as the attempts at Senate reform, or by being opposed to what the Court itself determines to be allowed, such as Aboriginal title, assisted suicide, or the basic human rights of Omar Khadr.

Already, Justin Trudeau's Liberals have made small, but potentially significant, changes that may have lasting historical impact. The reinstatement of the long-form census and the unmuzzling of government scientists, for example, were quick, inexpensive responses to major concerns held by many Canadians. Also promising were the First Ministers' conference of November 2015 (the first since 2009) and the invitation to the leaders of other parties to attend the 2015 UN Climate Change Conference in Paris (although the conference itself may prove to be as ineffective as earlier summits like Kyoto).

Changes to marijuana legalization now seem inevitable, with a number of Canadians already making or preparing to make their fortunes openly. It is possible that the next edition of this textbook will discuss how the Harper Conservatives were on the wrong side of not one, but two "Green" revolutions.

It is easy to see that the actions undertaken to continue to promote primary resource acquisition and the transportation of oil and gas are fraught with unsustainable, short-term gains, not to mention actual and potential disasters. In a world trying to rid itself of fossil fuels, and given the Lac-Mégantic disaster and Barack Obama's presidential veto of the Keystone XL pipeline, not to mention the 2015 drop in oil revenues, Canada's reliance on oil to buoy and drive the economy seems doomed. Conversely, Harper's opposition to a potential boom crop in the form of cannabis seems more and more antiquated. The success of marijuana legalization in parts of the United States, the profitability of the illegal yet unprosecuted marijuana culture of British Columbia, the emergence of publicly traded marijuana producers such as "Tweed," based in Smiths Falls, Ontario, and the growing weight of potential tax revenues may finally alter the prohibition governments have supported and public opinion has opposed. Some 2014 polls showed as much as 68 per cent of Canadians supported decriminalization.[5]

Whether History is made on any of these issues, only Time will tell.

History in the Balance

We must address the call by Justice Murray Sinclair to reassess not only the way we teach history, but the way that we approach it. Sinclair, the chair of the TRC, has on multiple occasions pointed out the uneven and sometimes inaccurate portrayal of First Nations. He argues that if reconciliation is to be possible this view of First Nations needs to change, not only in a historical context, but in a modern one as well. The history that was taught to the current generation of politicians and business leaders, Sinclair argues, is one of the major barriers in making progress towards the equitable treatment of Aboriginal people across the entire spectrum of Canadian society.

It may be difficult to fully explore the role of Aboriginal actors in the historical record, for many of the same reasons that it is hard to detail the lives of women in the past. Most of what comprises the historical record was written by white men, who by and large came from the more privileged classes. Too often these writers discounted the contribution and value of those less privileged, and commentary tended to involve either surprise or disdain. This was by no means limited to Aboriginals, as it is for similar reasons that we have difficulty detecting women, children, the poor, and the disenfranchised in the historical record. There is simply much less information that has been preserved, studied, refined, or published on these groups. Often, we know more about the actions imposed upon people from these groups than about the actions they chose for themselves.

The existence of blanks in the historical record does not mean that we should not try to fill them. History in the twenty-first century has a growing amount of data to draw upon. In many cases, it is being driven by the same factors that are speeding it up. Archives that were nearly impossible to access are being digitized and made available to new populations of scholars, and communication between collections on opposite sides of the world has allowed for never-before-considered connections to be made in moments. Advances in archaeology, in both the laboratory and in the field, and the increased study of material culture are constantly pushing the boundaries of what we can learn outside of the written historical record, and are changing the ways that we approach the accepted narrative. The push for academic interdisciplinarity has made co-operation between the fields, and the ability to access those elements of research easier as well.

A more modern, but more importantly, a more balanced look at Canadian history is necessary. It is hoped that this book is the beginning stage of an effort to do just that, albeit one limited by both the knowledge of the authors and the information presently available. Scholarship, if not curriculum, has made great strides to move towards the exploration, and re-examination, of history in a way that looks at more than just the rich, white men in suits.

Fortunately, the opportunity for further strides is upon us. The new Liberal government has pledged "to make new" the federal government's relationship with Canada's Indigenous peoples. Along with more respectful discourse and a renewed focus on education, Trudeau has also pledged to lift the 2 per cent funding cap for on-reserve programs and to enact all of the close to 100 recommendations of the Truth and Reconciliation Commission. These changes could not only dramatically alter Canada's present, but also help to rectify mistakes made in Canada's past.

In the coming years, Canadians will experience the centennial commemoration of World War I, the celebration of Canada's 150th birthday, and the 350th anniversary of the founding of the Hudson's Bay Company; undoubtedly, these major observances will lead to the re-examination of key moments in Canada's past, and how those moments contributed to shaping the Canada of today. Government-supported and -endorsed initiatives to discuss the truths—both beautiful and ugly—that surrounded each of these historical developments could go a long way toward addressing imbalances in Canada's historical narrative.

As with all things, adjusting our view of the past and what it means for the present takes time. Efforts must start soon, however, or the knowledge, and the moment, could easily be lost. Because, as Virgil noted, *fugit inreparabile tempus*. Time does not just fly; it is irretrievable once it is gone.

—*Michael C. Bumsted*
December 2015

Notes

1. J. Boyko, *Blood and Daring* (Toronto: Knopf Canada, 2013).

2. Michael Petrou, *Renegades: Canadians in the Spanish Civil War* (Vancouver: University of British Columbia Press, 2008).

3. R. Lowenstein, "North American Volunteers in the Israeli Army." http://www.jewishvirtuallibrary.org/jsource/History/IsraelArmy.html.

4. K. Clarke, "Dozens of Canadians Have Gone to Israel to Take Up Arms for the Jewish State." *National Post*, 23 July 2014. http://news.nationalpost.com/news/dozens-of-canadians-have-gone-to-israel-to-take-up-arms-for-the-jewish-state#__federated=1.

5. Ekos Politics: http://www.ekospolitics.com/index.php/2014/01/two-thirds-of-canadians-support-de-criminalization-of-marijuana.

References

Abella, Irving, and Harold Troper. 1991. *None Is Too Many: Canada and the Jews of Europe, 1933–1948*, rev. edn. Toronto: Lester and Orpen Dennys.

Abraham, Thomas. 2005. *Twenty-First Century Plague: The Story of SARS*. Baltimore: Johns Hopkins University Press.

Adams, Michael. 2003. *Fire and Ice: The United States, Canada and the Myth of Converging Values*. Toronto: Penguin.

Addiction Research Foundation. 1970. *Summary with Comments on the Interim Report of the Commission of Inquiry into the Non-Medical Use of Drugs*. Toronto: Addiction Research Foundation.

Akins, T.B., ed. 1869. *Selections from the Public Documents of the Province of Nova Scotia*. Halifax: n.p.

Allen, Robert S. 1992. *His Majesty's Indian Allies: British Indian Policy in the Defence of Canada, 1774–1815*. Toronto: Dundurn Press.

Arthur, E. 1986. *Toronto: No Mean City*. Toronto: University of Toronto Press.

Avery, Donald. 1986. "The Radical Alien and the Winnipeg General Strike of 1919." In J.M. Bumsted, ed., *Interpreting Canada's Past*, vol. 2, 222–39. Toronto: Oxford University Press.

———. 1995. *Reluctant Host: Canada's Response to Immigrant Workers, 1896–1994*. Toronto: McClelland & Stewart.

Axtell, James. 2001. *Natives and Newcomers: The Cultural Origins of North America*. New York: Oxford University Press.

Bakker, Peter. 1989. "Two Basque Loanwords in Micmac." *International Journal of American Linguistics* 55, 2: 258–60.

Ballantyne, R. 1879. *Hudson's Bay: or, Everyday Life in the Wilds of North America*. London: T. Nelson and Sons.

Barnholden, Michael. 2009. *Circumstances Alter Photographs: Captain James Peters' Reports from the War of 1885*. Vancouver: Talonbooks.

Behiels, Michael D. 1985. *Prelude to Quebec's Quiet Revolution: Liberalism versus Neo-Nationalism, 1945–1960*. Montreal and Kingston: McGill-Queen's University Press.

Bell, W.P. 1990. The *'Foreign Protestants' and the Settlement of Nova Scotia: The History of a Piece of Arrested British Colonial Policy in the 18th Century*. Fredericton, NB: Acadiensis Press.

Benson, A.B., ed. 1937. *The America of 1750: Peter Kalm's Travel in North America*, 2 vols. New York: Dover.

Berger, Carl. 1986. "The True North Strong and Free." In J.M. Bumsted, ed., *Interpreting Canada's Past*, vol. 2, 154–60. Toronto: Oxford University Press.

Berger, Thomas R. 1977. *Northern Frontier, Northern Homeland*, 2 vols. Report of the Mackenzie Valley Pipeline Inquiry. Ottawa: Supply and Services Canada.

Binnie-Clark, G. 1914. *Wheat and Woman*. Toronto: Bell & Cockburn.

Bliss, Michael. 1972. "Canadianizing American Business: The Roots of the Branch Plant." In I. Lumsden, ed., *Close the 49th Parallel: The Americanization of Canada*. Toronto: University of Toronto Press.

Bourassa, Henri. 1912. *Canadian Club Addresses 1912*. Toronto: Warwick Bros & Rutter.

Bowker, A., ed. 1973. *The Social Criticism of Stephen Leacock: The Unsolved Riddle of Social Justice and Other Essays*. Toronto: University of Toronto Press.

Boycott, Owen. 2010. "Brown Apologises for Britain's 'Shameful' Child Migrant Policy." *The Guardian*, 24 Feb.

Brebner, J.B. 1927. *New England's Outpost: Acadia before the Conquest of Canada*. New York: Columbia University Press.

Brode, P. 1984. *Sir John Beverley Robinson*. Toronto: University of Toronto Press.

Bumsted, J.M., ed. 1969. *Documentary Problems in Canadian History*. Georgetown, Ont.: Irwin-Dorsey.

———. 1971. *Henry Alline, 1748–1784*. Toronto: University of Toronto Press.

———, ed. 1986. *Understanding the Loyalists*. Sackville, NB: Mount Allison University Press.

———. 1994. *The Winnipeg General Strike of 1919: An Illustrated History*. Winnipeg: Watson and Dwyer.

Calgary Herald, 1 March 2003.

Campbell, Patrick. 1937. *Travels in the Interior Inhabited Parts of North America in the Years 1791 and 1792*, ed. H.H. Langton. Toronto: Champlain Society.

Canada Year Book. 1959. Ottawa: Queen's Printer.

———. 1990. Ottawa: Queen's Printer.

———. 1994. Ottawa: Statistics Canada.

Carr, E.H. 1964. *What Is History?* Harmondsworth, UK: Penguin.

Carson, Rachel. 1962. *Silent Spring*. Boston: Houghton Mifflin.

Carter, Sarah. 1990. *Lost Harvests: Prairie Indian Reserve Farmers and Government Policy*. Montreal and Kingston: McGill-Queen's University Press.

Cell, Gillian, ed. 1982. *Newfoundland Discovered: English Attempts at Colonisation, 1610–1630*. London: Hakluyt Society.

Charlevoix, Pierre-François-Xavier de. 1866 [1744]. *History and General Description of New France*, 4 vols. Trans. John Gilmary Shea. New York.

Christensen, Deanna. 2000. *Ahtahkakoop: The Epic Account of a Plains Cree Head Chief, His People, and Their Struggle for Survival, 1816–1896*. Shell Lake, Sask.: Ahtahkakoop Publishing.

Clark, Arthur H. 1968. *Acadia: The Geography of Early Nova Scotia to 1760*. Madison: University of Wisconsin Press.

Clark, C.S. 1898. *Of Toronto the Good: A Social Study*. Montreal: Toronto Publishing Co.

Clark, E.A. 1988. "Cumberland Planters and the Aftermath of the Attack on Fort Cumberland." In M. Conrad, ed., *They Planted Well: New England Planters in Maritime Canada*. Fredericton, NB: Acadiensis Press.

Coles, Bryony. 2006. *Beavers in Britain's Past*. Oxford: Oxbow Books.

Commission of Inquiry into the Non-Medical Use of Drugs. 1970. *Interim Report*. Ottawa: Queen's Printer.

Conrad, Margaret, et al., eds. 1988. *No Place Like Home: Diaries and Letters of Nova Scotia Women 1771–1938*. Halifax: Formac.

Cook, Ramsay. 1969a. *Provincial Autonomy: Minority Rights and the Compact Theory, 1867–1921*. Ottawa: Queen's Printer.

——, ed. 1969b. *French-Canadian Nationalism: An Anthology*. Toronto: Macmillan.

Cook, Sharon Anne. 1995. *Through Sunshine and Shadow: The Woman's Christian Temperance Union, Evangelicalism, and Reform in Ontario, 1874–1930*. Montreal and Kingston: McGill-Queen's University Press.

Couton, Philippe. 2002. "Highly Skilled Immigrants: Recent Trends and Issues." *Isuma: Canadian Journal of Policy Research* 3, 2 (Fall).

Craig, G.M., ed. 1963. *Lord Durham's Report*. Toronto: McClelland & Stewart.

Crouse, Nellis. 1954. *La Moyne d'Iberville: Soldier of New France*. Ithaca, NY: Cornell University Press.

Cuff, R.D., and J.L. Granatstein. 1977. *The Ties That Bind: Canadian–American Relations in Wartime from the Great War to the Cold War*. Toronto: Samuel Stevens Hakkert & Co.

Cuthand, S. 1978. "The Native Peoples of the Prairie Provinces in the 1920s and 1930s." In I.A.L. Getty and D.B. Smith, eds, *One Century Later: Western Canadian Reserve Indians since Treaty 7*, 31–2. Vancouver: University of British Columbia Press.

Davis, Ann. 1979. *Frontiers of Our Dreams: Quebec Painting in the 1940's and 1950's*. Winnipeg: Winnipeg Art Gallery.

Department of Regional Economic Expansion. 1971. *Major Economic Indicators, Provinces and Regions*. Ottawa: Queen's Printer.

Dickason, Olive Patricia. 2002. *Canada's First Nations: A History of Founding Peoples from Earliest Times*, 3rd edn. Toronto: Oxford University Press.

—— with David T. McNab. 2009. *Canada's First Nations: A History of Founding Peoples from Earliest Times*, 4th edn. Toronto: Oxford University Press.

—— and William Newbigging. 2015. *A Concise History of Canada's First Nations*, 3rd edn. Toronto: Oxford University Press.

Dirks, Gerald E. 1995. *Controversy and Complexity: Canadian Immigration Policy during the 1980s*. Montreal and Kingston: McGill-Queen's University Press.

Doern, Bruce, and Monica Gattinger. 2003. *Power Switch: Energy Regulatory Governance in the 21st Century*. Toronto: University of Toronto Press.

Dollier de Casson, F. 1928 [1868]. *A History of Montreal 1640–1672*, ed. and trans. R. Flenley. London: J.M. Dent & Sons.

Drache, Daniel, 2004. *Borders Matter: Homeland Security and the Search for North America*. Halifax: Fernwood.

Duncan, Sara Jeannette. 1971 [1904]. *The Imperialist*. Toronto: McClelland & Stewart.

Durand, E. 1981. *Vignettes of Early Winnipeg*. Winnipeg: Frances McColl.

Dyer, G., and T. Viljoen. 1990. *The Defense of Canada: In the Arms of the Empire 1760–1939*. Toronto: McClelland & Stewart.

Easterbrook, W.T., and M.H. Watkins. 1962. *Approaches to Canadian Economic History*. Toronto: McClelland & Stewart.

—— and G.J. Aitken. 1956. *Canadian Economic History*. Toronto: Macmillan.

Eccles, W.J. 1983. *The Canadian Frontier 1534–1760*, rev. edn. Albuquerque: University of New Mexico Press.

——. 1987. *Essays on New France*. Toronto: Oxford University Press.

Ellis, John. 1975. *Eye Deep in Hell: Trench Warfare in World War I*. Baltimore: Johns Hopkins University Press, reprint 1989.

Engelstad, Diane, and John Bird, eds. 1992. *Nation to Nation: Aboriginal Sovereignty and the Future of Canada*. Toronto: Anansi.

Ewart, J.S. 1908. *The Kingdom of Canada: Imperial Federation, the Colonial Conferences, the Alaska Boundary and Other Essays*. Toronto: Morang.

Fairley, M., ed. 1960. *The Selected Writings of William Lyon Mackenzie*. Toronto: Oxford University Press.

Fingard, Judith. 1988. "The Relief of the Unemployed Poor in Saint John, Halifax, and St John's, 1815–1860." In P.A. Buckner and D. Frank, eds, *The Acadiensis Reader*, vol. 1. Fredericton, NB: Acadiensis Press.

Fisher, R. 1977. *Contact and Conflict: Indian–European Relations in British Columbia 1774–1890*. Vancouver: University of British Columbia Press.

Forsythe, D., ed. 1971. *Let the Niggers Burn: The Sir George Williams University Affair and Its Caribbean Aftermath*. Montreal: Black Rose.

Frégault, Guy. 1944. *Iberville le conquerant*. Montreal.

Frye, Northrop. 1976. "Conclusion." In C.F. Klinck, ed., *Literary History of Canada*, rev. edn, 849. Toronto: University of Toronto Press.

Gage, Thomas. Papers. William Clements Library, University of Michigan.

Gammer, Nicholas. 2001. *From Peacekeeping to Peacemaking: Canada's Response to the Yugoslav Crisis*. Montreal and Kingston: McGill-Queen's University Press.

Gattinger, Monica. 2005. "From Government to Governance in the Energy Sector: The State of the Canada–U.S. Energy Relationship." *American Review of Canadian Studies* 35, 2: 321–52.

Gérin-Lajoie, A. 1977 [1874]. *Jean Rivard*, trans. V. Bruce. Toronto: McClelland & Stewart.

Gerry, Thomas M.F. 1990–1. "'I Am Translated': Anna Jameson's Sketches and *Winter and Summer Rambles in Canada*," *Journal of Canadian Studies* 25, 4 (Winter).

Globe and Mail, 26 Mar. 2003, 20 May 2006.

Granatstein, J.L., and R. Bothwell. 1990. *Pirouette: Pierre Trudeau and Canadian Foreign Policy*. Toronto: University of Toronto Press.

Grant, George. 1965. *Lament for a Nation: The Defeat of Canadian Nationalism*. Toronto: Macmillan.

Grant, G.M., ed. 1876. *Picturesque Canada*. Toronto: Hunter, Rose & Co.

Gray, Charlotte. 1999. *Sisters in the Wilderness: The Lives of Susanna Moodie and Catharine Parr Traill*. Toronto: Viking.

Gray, J. 1966. *The Winter Years: The Depression on the Prairies*. Toronto: Macmillan.

Gunn, G.E. 1966. *The Political History of Newfoundland, 1832–1864*. Toronto: University of Toronto Press.

Haliburton, Thomas Chandler. 1838. *The Clockmaker: or The Sayings and Doings of Samuel Slick of Slickville*. London: Richard Bentley.

Halpenny, F.G., ed. 1976. *The Dictionary of Canadian Biography*, vol. 9. Toronto: University of Toronto Press.

Harper, J. Russell. 1966. *Painting in Canada: A History*, 2nd edn. Toronto.

Hatch, R. 1970. *Thrust for Canada*. Boston: Houghton Mifflin.

Hawkins, Freda. 1972. *Canada and Immigration: Public Policy and Public Concern*. Montreal and Kingston: McGill Queen's University Press.

Hind, H.Y. 1869. *The Dominion of Canada: Containing a Historical Sketch of the Preliminaries and Organization of Confederation*. Toronto: L. Stebbins.

Hodgetts, J.E. 1968. "The Changing Nature of the Public Service." In L.D. Musoff, ed., *The Changing Public Service*, 7–18. Berkeley: University of California Press.

Indian–Eskimo Association of Canada. 1970. *Native Rights in Canada*. Toronto: Indian–Eskimo Association of Canada.

Innis, H. 1948. *The Diary of Simeon Perkins, 1766–1780*, vol. 1. Toronto: Champlain Society.

Jackson, David J. 2005. "Peace, Order, and Good Songs: Popular Music and English-Canadian Culture." *American Review of Canadian Studies* 35, 2: 25–44.

Johnston, M. 1994. *Corvettes Canada: Convoy Veterans of WWII Tell Their True Stories*. Toronto: McGraw-Hill Ryerson.

Kahn, Agnan R. 2006. "Canada's Kandahar Balancing Act." *Maclean's*, 26 May.

Kealey, Greg, ed. 1973. *Canada Investigates Industrialism: The Royal Commission on the Relations of Labour and Capital, 1889*, abridged. Toronto: University of Toronto Press.

Keeble, Edna. 2005. "Defining Canadian Security Continuities and Discontinuities." *American Review of Canadian Studies* 35, 1: 1–23.

Keefer, T.C. 1853. *Philosophy of Railroads, Published by Order of the Directors of the St Lawrence and Ottawa Grand Junction Railway Company*, 4th edn. Montreal: J. Lovell.

Kent, Tom. 1988. *A Public Purpose: An Experience of Liberal Opposition and Canadian Government*. Montreal and Kingston: McGill-Queen's University Press.

Kert, Faye Margaret. 1997. *Prize and Prejudice: Privateering and Naval Prize in Atlantic Canada in the War of 1812*. St John's: International Maritime History Association.

Kinsman, Gary. 1987. *The Regulation of Desire: Sexuality in Canada*. Montreal: Black Rose.

Klinck, Carl, ed. 1976. *Literary History of Canada: Canadian Literature in English*, 2nd edn, 3 vols. Toronto: University of Toronto Press.

Knowles, Valerie. 1997. *Strangers at Our Gates: Canadian Immigration and Immigration Policy, 1540–1997*. Toronto: Dundurn Press.

Koh, Tommy, et al., eds. 2003. *The New Global Threat: Severe Acute Respiratory Syndrome and Its Impacts*. Singapore: World Scientific Publishing.

Kolbert, Elizabeth. 2006. *Field Notes for a Catastrophe: Man, Nature, and Climate Change*. New York: Bloomsbury.

Kostash, M. 1980. *Long Way from Home: The Story of the Sixties Generation in Canada*. Toronto: James Lorimer.

Kwavnick, David, ed. 1973. *The Tremblay Report*. Toronto: McClelland & Stewart.

Landry, Yves. 1993. *Orphelines en France pionèeres au Canada: les filles du roi au xviie siècle*. Montreal: Leméac.

Lévesque, René. 1986. *Memoirs*, trans. Philip Stratford. Toronto: McClelland & Stewart.

Library and Archives Canada. 1745. "Representation of the State of His Majesty's Province of Nova Scotia." 8 Nov.

Lower, A.R.M. 1973. *Great Britain's Woodyard: British North America and the Timber Trade, 1762–1870*. Montreal and Kingston: McGill-Queen's University Press.

Lucas, C.P., ed. 1912. *Lord Durham's Report*, 3 vols. Oxford: Clarendon Press.

McArthur, D.A. 1924. "The Teaching of Canadian History." *Ontario Historical Society Papers* 21.

MacBeath, G. 1966. "Charles de Saint-Étienne de La Tour." In G. Brown, ed., *Dictionary of Canadian Biography*, 592–6. Toronto: University of Toronto Press.

McCracken, M. 1975. *Memories Are Made of This: What It Was Like to Grow Up in the Fifties*. Toronto: James Lorimer.

MacDonell, Sister M. 1982. *The Emigrant Experience: Songs of Highland Emigrants in North America*. Toronto: University of Toronto Press.

McKinney, Joseph S. 2004. *Political Economy of the U.S.–Canada Softwood Lumber Trade*. Orono: University of Maine Press.

McLuhan, Marshall. 1951. *The Mechanical Bride: Folklore of Industrial Man*. New York: Vanguard Press.

Macphail, Andrew. 1915. Diary, vol. 1, 28 Dec. Macphail Papers, Library and Archives Canada.

McWhinney, E. 1982. *Canada and the Constitution 1979–1982*. Toronto: University of Toronto Press.

Magocsi, Paul Robert, ed. 1999. *Encyclopedia of Canada's Peoples*. Toronto: University of Toronto Press.

Marchilson, Gregory. 1996. *Profits and Politics: Beaverbrook and the Gilded Age of Canadian Finance*. Toronto: University of Toronto Press.

Margolian, John. 2000. *Unauthorized Entry: The Truth about Nazi War Criminals in Canada, 1946–1956*. Toronto: University of Toronto Press.

Marshall, J., ed. 1967. *Word from New France: The Selected Letters of Marie de l'Incarnation*. Toronto: Oxford University Press.

Marwick, Arthur. 1970. *The Nature of History*. London and Basingstoke: Macmillan.

Masters, D.C. 1936. *The Reciprocity Treaty of 1854*. London: Longmans Green & Company.

Michaels, Patrick J., ed. 2005. *Shattered Consensus: The True State of Global Warming*. Lanham, Md: Rowman & Littlefield.

Miki, Roy, and Cassandra Kobayashi. 1991. *Justice in Our Time: The Japanese Canadian Redress Settlement*. Vancouver: Talonbooks.

Mills, David. 1988. *The Idea of Loyalty in Upper Canada, 1784–1850*. Montreal and Kingston: McGill-Queen's University Press.

Monière, D. 1981. *Ideologies on Quebec: The Historical Development*. Toronto: University of Toronto Press.

Moodie, Susanna. 1852. *Roughing It in the Bush, or, Life in Canada*, vol. 1. London: Richard Bentley.

Moogk, Peter. 2000. *La Nouvelle France: The Making of French Canada, a Cultural History*. East Lansing: Michigan State University Press.

Morrow, Don. 1989. *A Concise History of Sport in Canada*. Toronto: Oxford University Press.

Morton, W.L., ed. 1970. *Monck Letters and Journals 1863–1868: Canada from Government House at Confederation*. Toronto: McClelland & Stewart.

National Task Force on Suicide in Canada. 1984. *Suicide in Canada*. Ottawa: Queen's Printer.

Naylor, R.T. 1975. *The History of Canadian Business, 1867–1914*, vol. 1. Toronto: James Lorimer.

Neatby, Hilda. 1972. *The Quebec Act: Protest and Policy*. Toronto: Prentice-Hall of Canada.

Nelles, H.V. 1974. *The Politics of Development: Forests, Mines & Hydro-Electric Power in Ontario, 1849–1941*. Toronto: Macmillan.

Nevitte, Neil. 1996. *The Decline of Deference: Canadian Value Change in Cross-National Perspective*. Peterborough, Ont.: Broadview Press.

Niagara Spectator, 11 Dec. 1817.

O'Neill, Kate. 2005. "How Two Cows Make a Crisis: U.S.–Canada Trade Relations and Mad Cow Disease." *American Review of Canadian Studies* 35, 2: 295–319.

Ormsby, Margaret. 1958. *British Columbia: A History*. Toronto: Macmillan of Canada.

Parker, Roy. 2009. *Uprooted: The Shipment of Poor Children to Canada, 1867–1917*. Vancouver: University of British Columbia Press.

Patterson, E.P. 1972. *The Canadian Indian: A History since 1500*. Toronto: Collier-Macmillan.

Perlin, George. 1997. "The Constraints of Public Opinion: Diverging or Converging Paths?" In Keith Banting, George Hoberg, and Richard Simeon, eds, *Degrees of Freedom: Canada and the United States in a Changing World*. Montreal and Kingston: McGill-Queen's University Press.

Petryshyn, Jaroslav. 1985. *Peasants in the Promised Land: Canada and the Ukrainians, 1891–1914*. Toronto: James Lorimer.

Pierson, Ruth Roach. 1990. "Gender and Unemployment Insurance Debates in Canada, 1934–1940." *Labour/Le Travail* 25 (Spring): 77–103.

Pope, Sir J. 1930. *Memoirs of the Rt. Hon. Sir John A. Macdonald*, vol. 1. Toronto: Oxford University Press.

Preston, R.A., ed. 1974. *For Friends at Home: A Scottish Emigrant's Letters from Canada, California and the Cariboo 1844–1864*. Montreal and Kingston: McGill-Queen's University Press.

Prince, Bryan. 2009. *A Shadow on the Household: One Enslaved Family's Incredible Struggle for Freedom*. Toronto: McClelland & Stewart.

Proceedings of the Special Joint Committee of the Senate and House of Commons on Divorce. 1967. Ottawa: Queen's Printer.

Province, The (Vancouver), 3 May 2006.

Pryke, K.G. 1979. *Nova Scotia and Confederation, 1864–1874*. Toronto: University of Toronto Press.

Quaife, M.M., ed. 1962. *The Western Country in the 17th Century: The Memoirs of Antoine Lamothe Cadillac and Pierre Liette*. New York: Citadel Press.

Québec conseil exécutif. 1979. *Québec–Canada, a New Deal: The Québec Government Proposal for a New Partnership between Equals, Sovereignty-Association*. Québec: Québec conseil exécutif.

Radforth, Ian, 2004. *Royal Spectacle: The 1860 Visit of the Prince of Wales to Canada and the United States*. Toronto: University of Toronto Press.

Rasporich, A.W. 1969. "National Awakening: Canada at Mid-Century." In J.M. Bumsted, ed., *Documentary Problems in Canadian History*, vol. 1, 225. Georgetown, Ont.: Irwin-Dorsey.

Rea, K.J. 1985. *The Prosperous Years: The Economic History of Ontario 1939–75*. Toronto: University of Toronto Press.

Reay, Dave. 2005. *Climate Change Begins at Home: Life on the Two-Way Street of Global Warming*. New York and London: Palgrave.

Recollections of the War of 1812. 1964. Toronto: Baxter Publishing Company.

Report of the Royal Commission on Broadcasting. 1957. Ottawa: Queen's Printer.

Report of the Royal Commission on National Development in the Arts, Letters and Sciences. 1951. Toronto: King's Printer.

Report of the Royal Commission on the Status of Women in Canada. 1970. Ottawa: Queen's Printer.

Rich, E.E., ed. 1949. "James Isham's Observations and Notes, 1743–9." *Hudson's Bay Record Society* 12: 85–7.

Richmond, Anthony. 1967. *Post-War Immigrants in Canada*. Toronto: University of Toronto Press.

Robertson, J.R. 1911. *The Diary of Mrs. John Graves Simcoe, Wife of the First Lieutenant-Governor of the Province of Upper Canada, 1792–1796*. Toronto: W. Briggs.

Rollings-Magnusson, Sandra. 2009. *Heavy Burdens on Small Shoulders: The Labour of Pioneer Children on the Canadian Prairies*. Edmonton: University of Alberta Press.

Romney, Paul, and Barry Wright. 2002. "Toronto Treason Trials, March–May 1838." In F. Murray Greenwood and Barry Wright, eds, *Canadian State Trials*, vol. 2, *Rebellion and Invasion in the Canadas, 1837–1839*, 62–99. Osgoode Society for Canadian Legal History. Toronto: University of Toronto Press.

Royal Commission on Aboriginal Peoples. 1993. *Partners in Confederation: Aboriginal Peoples, Self-government, and the Constitution*. Ottawa: Queen's Printer.

Royal Commission on Canada's Economic Prospects. 1958. *Final Report*. Ottawa: Queen's Printer.

Royal Commission on the Donald Marshall, Jr., Prosecution, vol. 1: Findings and Recommendations. 1989. Halifax: The Commission.

Royal Society of Canada. 1932. *Fifty Years' Retrospective 1882–1932*. Toronto: University of Toronto Press.

Rubio, M., and E. Waterston, eds. 1987. *The Selected Journals of L.M. Montgomery, vol. 2: 1910–1921*. Toronto: Oxford University Press.

Rutherford, Paul. 1982. *A Victorian Authority: The Daily Press in Late Nineteenth-Century Canada*. Toronto: University of Toronto Press.

Saywell, J. 1971. *Quebec 70: A Documentary Narrative*. Toronto: University of Toronto Press.

Seed, Patricia, 1995. *Ceremonies of Possession in Europe's Conquest of the New World, 1492–1640*. Cambridge: Cambridge University Press.

Seeley, J.R., R.A. Sim, and E. Loosley. 1972. *Crestwood Heights: A North American Suburb*. Toronto: University of Toronto Press.

Shkilnyk, Anastasia. 1985. *A Poison Stronger Than Love: The Destruction of an Ojibwa Community*. New Haven: Yale University Press.

Siegfried, André. 1907. *The Race Question in Canada*. London: E. Nash.

Sleeper-Smith, Susan, ed. 2009. *Rethinking the Fur Trade: Cultures of Exchange in an Atlantic World*. Lincoln: University of Nebraska Press.

Smiley, Donald V. 1970. "Canadian Federalism and the Resolution of Federal–Provincial Conflicts." In F. Vaughan et al., eds, *Contemporary Issues in Canadian Politics*, 48–66. Toronto: Prentice-Hall.

Smith, Laurence. 2010. *The World in 2050: Four Forces Shaping Civilization's Northern Future*. New York: Dutton.

Special Committee on Social Security. 1943. *Report on Social Security for Canada, Prepared by Dr. L.C. Marsh for the Advisory Committee on Reconstruction*. Ottawa: King's Printer.

Stacey, C.P. 1970. *Arms, Man and Governments: The War Policies of Canada 1939–1945*. Ottawa: Queen's Printer.

——. 1981. *Canada and the Age of Conflict: A History of Canadian External Policies, vol. 2: 1921–1948*. Toronto: Macmillan.

Standing Committee of the Canadian Senate on Immigration and Labour. 1946. *Senate Report no. 6*. Ottawa: King's Printer.

Stanley, G.F.G. 1977. *Canada Invaded, 1775–1776*. Toronto: Canadian War Museum.

Statement of the Government of Canada on Indian Policy. 1969. Ottawa: Queen's Printer.

Statistics Canada. 1957. *Manufacturing Industries of Canada 1957*. Ottawa: Queen's Printer.

——. 2010. "Study: Projections of the Diversity of the Canadian Population." *The Daily*, 9 Mar. www.statcan.gc.ca/daily-quotiden/100309/dq100309a-eng.htm.

Steele, S. 1915. *Forty Years in Canada: Reminiscences of the Great North-West . . . .* Toronto: McClelland, Goodchild & Stewart.

Stephens, H.F. 1890. *Jacques Cartier and His Four Voyages to Canada: An Essay with Historical, Explanatory and Philological Notes*. Montreal: W. Drysdale & Co.

Swainger, Jonathan. 2000. *The Canadian Department of Justice and the Completion of Confederation 1867–1878*. Vancouver: University of British Columbia Press.

Sykes, E.C. 1912. *A Home-Help in Canada*. London: G. Bell & Sons.

Tascona, Bruce, and Eric Wells. 1983. *Little Black Devils: A History of the Royal Winnipeg Rifles*. Winnipeg: Royal Winnipeg Rifles.

Thompson, John Herd, and Allan Seager. 1985. *Canada, 1922–1939: Decades of Discord*. Toronto: McClelland & Stewart.

Timlin, Mabel. 1951. *Does Canada Need More People?* Toronto: Oxford University Press.

Titley, Brian. 2009. *The Indian Commissioners: Agents of the State and Indian Policy in Canada's Prairie West, 1873–1932*. Edmonton: University of Alberta Press.

Toronto Star, 6 July 2010, 6.

Traill, Catharine Parr. 1846. *The Backwoods of Canada*. London: M.A. Nattali.

Troper, Harold Martin. 1972. *Only Farmers Need Apply: Official Canadian Government Encouragement of Immigration from the United States, 1896–1911*. Toronto: Griffin House.

Trudeau, Pierre Elliott, ed. 1974. *The Asbestos Strike*. Toronto: James Lewis and Samuel (translation of 1951 edition).

Trudel, Marcel. 1973. *The Beginnings of New France 1524–1663*. Toronto: McClelland & Stewart.

Turcotte, Martin. 2006. "Parents with Adult Children Living at Home." *Canadian Social Trends* (Spring): 2–9.

Vallières, Pierre. 1971. *White Niggers of America*. Toronto: McClelland & Stewart.

Verney, Jack. 1991. *The Good Regiment*. Montreal and Kingston: McGill-Queen's University Press.

Voisey, P. 1988. *Vulcan: The Making of a Prairie Community*. Toronto: University of Toronto Press.

Waite, Peter B. 1962. *The Life and Times of Confederation, 1864–1867: Politics, Newspapers, and the Union of British North America*. Toronto: University of Toronto Press.

——, ed. 1963. *Confederation Debates in the Province of Canada*. Toronto: McClelland & Stewart.

Wall, Denis. 2000. "Aboriginal Self-Government in Canada: The Cases of Nunavut and the Alberta Métis Settlements." In David Long and Olive Patricia Dickason, eds, *Visions of the Heart: Canadian Aboriginal Issues*, 2nd edn, 143–67. Toronto: Harcourt Brace.

Washington Post, 31 May 2006.

White, Richard. 1991. *The Middle Ground: Indians, Empires and Republics in the Great Lakes Region, 1650–1815*. New York: Cambridge University Press.

Williams, G., ed. 1969. "Andrew Graham's Observations on Hudson's Bay, 1767–1791." *Hudson's Bay Record Society* 27.

Williamson, J.A., ed. 1962. *The Cabot Voyages and British Discoveries under Henry VII*. Cambridge: Hakluyt Society of the University Press.

Williamson, M. 1970. *Robert Harris, 1849–1919: An Unconventional Biography*. Toronto: McClelland & Stewart.

Wilson, Edmund. 1964. *O Canada: An American's Notes on Canadian Culture*. New York: Farrar, Straus and Giroux.

Wingrove, Josh. 2010. "Stelmach Buys U.S. Ad Touting Oil Sands." *Globe and Mail*, 2 July. www.theglobeandmail.com/news/politics/stelmach-buys-us-ad-touting-oil-sands/article1627312.

Winnipeg Free Press, 13 Mar. 2006, 29 May 2006, 30 May 2006.

Woodcock, George, ed. 1969. *The Sixties: Writers and Writing of the Decade*. Vancouver: University of British Columbia Press.

——. 1979. *The Canadians*. Don Mills, Ont.: Fitzhenry & Whiteside.

Wright, E.C. 1955. *The Loyalists of New Brunswick*. Fredericton, NB: University of New Brunswick Press.

Wynn, G. 1980. *Timber Colony: A Historical Geography of Early 19th Century New Brunswick*. Toronto: University of Toronto Press.

Young, W. 1978. "Academics and Social Scientists versus the Press: The Policies of the Bureau of Public Information and the Wartime Information Board, 1939 to 1945." CHA *Historical Papers, a Selection from the Papers Presented at the Annual Meeting of the Canadian Historical Association*.

Index